In the Name of the Urban Poor

Access to Basic Amenities

AMITABH KUNDU

Sage Publications
New Delhi/Newbury Park/London

First published in 1993 by

Sage Publications India Pvt Ltd
M-32, Greater Kailash Market, Part I
New Delhi 110 048

Sage Publications Inc
2455 Teller Road
Newbury Park, California 91320

Sage Publications Ltd
6 Bonhill Street
London EC 2A 4PU

Published by Tejeshwar Singh for Sage Publications India Pvt Ltd, photo-typeset by Pagewell Photosetters, Pondicherry, and printed at Chaman Enterprises.

Library of Congress Cataloging-in-Publication Data

Kundu, Amitabh, 1948–
    In the name of the urban poor: access to basic amenities / Amitabh Kundu.
      p.   cm.
    Includes index.
      1. Basic needs—India. 2. Urban poor—India. I. Title.
HC440.B38K86   338.954′009173′2—dc20   1993   93–7507

ISBN 0–8039–9115–0 (US)
      81–7036–341–1 (India)

Contents

List of Abbreviations   6
List of Tables   9
Acknowledgements   15

1.   Introduction   17

2.   Assessing Urban Poverty and its Characteristics   23

3.   Management and Financing of Housing and
       Basic Amenities   46

4.   Programmes for Formal Housing, Shelter and
       Basic Amenities   113

5.   Levels of Housing and Basic Amenities—An
       Inter-State Analysis   185

6.   Levels and Quality of Housing and Basic
       Amenities Available to the Urban Poor   228

7.   Conclusions and Recommendations   279

Index   288

List of Abbreviations

ADB	Asian Development Bank
AIIMS	All India Institute of Medical Sciences
BHEL	Bharat Heavy Electricals Limited
BISR	Birla Institute of Scientific Research
BMRDA	Bombay Metropolitan Regional Development Authority
BSD	Box Surface Drain
BUDP	Bombay Urban Development Project
CGHS	Central Government Health Scheme
CIDCO	City Industrial Development Corporation
CIT	Calcutta Improvement Trust
CMA	Calcutta Metropolitan Area
CMC	Calcutta Municipal Corporation
CMDA	Calcutta Metropolitan Development Authority
CMPO	Calcutta Metropolitan Planning Organisation
CMWSA	Calcutta Metropolitan Water and Sanitation Authority
CPHEEO	Central Public Health and Environmental Engineering Organisation
CPIIW	Consumer Price Index for Industrial Workers
CPIMU	Consumer Price Index for Middle Income Urban Population
CPINM	Consumer Price Index for Non-Manual Employees
CPITU	Consumer Price Index for Total Urban Population
CPWD	Central Public Works Department
CSO	Central Statistical Organisation
CUDP	Calcutta Urban Development Project
DDA	Delhi Development Authority
DGHS	Director General of Health Services
EIUS	Environmental Improvement of Urban Slums
EPI	Expanded Programme on Immunisation
ESI	Employees' State Insurance
EWS	Economically Weaker Sections
FCI	Food Corporation of India
FICCI	Federation of Indian Chambers of Commerce and Industries
GHB	Gujarat Housing Board

GIC	General Insurance Corporation
HDFC	Housing Development Finance Corporation
HIG	High Income Group
HIT	Howrah Improvement Trust
HLA	Home Loan Account
HLS	Home Loan Scheme
HRA	House Rent Allowance
HSP	Home Savings Plan
HUDCO	Housing and Urban Development Corporation
ICDS	Integrated Child Development Services
IDSMT	Integrated Development of Small and Medium Towns
IIMA	Indian Institute of Management, Ahmedabad
ISHS	Integrated Subsidised Housing Scheme
KL	Kilolitre
KfW	Kreditanstalt fur Wiederaufbau (Germany)
LCS	Low-Cost Sanitation Programme
LIC	Life Insurance Corporation
LIG	Low Income Group
lpcd	Litres per Capita per Day
MCD	Municipal Corporation of Delhi
MHADA	Maharashtra Housing and Area Development Authority
MIG	Middle Income Group
MMDA	Madras Metropolitan Development Authority
MNP	Minimum Needs Programme
MOUD	Ministry of Urban Development
MUDP	Madras Urban Development Project
NAS	National Accounts Statistics
NBCC	National Building Construction Company
NBO	National Building Organisation
NCAER	National Council of Applied Economic Research
NCHSE	National Centre for Human Settlements and Environment
NCU	National Commission on Urbanisation
NDMC	New Delhi Municipal Corporation
NHB	National Housing Bank
NIUA	National Institute of Urban Affairs
NSS	National Sample Survey
NTPC	National Thermal Power Corporation
ODA	Overseas Development Administration
ORG	Operations Research Group
OSD	Open Surface Drain
PDS	Public Distribution System
PGIMER	Post-Graduate Institute of Medical Education and Research
PHC	Primary Health Centre

PHED	Public Health Engineering Department
PSP	Public Stand Post
PWD	Public Works Department
RGS	Revised Grant Structure
RBI	Reserve Bank of India
SAIL	Steel Authority of India Limited
S&S	Sites and Services (Scheme)
SBI	State Bank of India
SCB	Slum Clearance Board
SCS	Slum Clearance Scheme
SDO	Sub-Divisional Officer
SDS	Society for Development Studies
SFS	Self-Financing Scheme
SIHS	Subsidised Industrial Housing Scheme
SIP	Slum Improvement Programmes
SLR	Statutory Liquidity Ratio
SUP	Slum Upgradation Programme
TCPO	Town and Country Planning Organisation
TNHB	Tamil Nadu Housing Board
TNSCB	Tamil Nadu Slum Clearance Board
TUDP	Tamil Nadu Urban Development Project
UBS	Urban Basic Services
UCD	Urban Community Development
USAID	United States Agency for International Development
UTI	Unit Trust of India

List of Tables

2.1	Consumer Price Indices, 1970–71 to 1987–88	27
2.2	Number of Poor and Percentage of People below the Poverty Line in the 1970s and 1980s	29
2.3	Expenditure on Non-food Items in Urban Areas	36
2.4	Expenditure on Rent in Urban Areas—1983	39
2.5	Asset Structure of Households as on 30 June 1981 in Urban Areas	41
2.6	Pattern of Debt in Different Asset Categories as on 30 June 1981 in Urban Areas	41
3.1	Hospitals/Dispensaries Run by Local Bodies as on 1 January 1988	87
3.2	Administrative and Functional Structure of the PDS	100
3.3	Areas of Decision-Making at Various Levels	100
4.1	Financing of Formal Housing Schemes	114
4.2	Details of Schemes under the Hire-Purchase System in the Late 1980s	120
4.3	Terms and Conditions at which Public Housing Agencies get HUDCO Loans under the Hire-Purchase System, Revised up to September 1992	122
4.4	Details of Schemes under the Housing Loan System	126
4.5	Details of Savings-Linked Loan Schemes	130
4.6	Details of the Programmes for Shelter and Basic Services	136
4.7	Details of Shelter-cum-Services Schemes in the Late 1980s	152
4.8	Details of Sites and Services Schemes as in the Late 1980s	154
5.1	Percentage Distribution of Households over Types of Houses (All India)	186
5.2	Percentage of Households Residing in Rented and Non-Rented Houses over Monthly Rent Categories	188
5.3	Percentage Distribution of Households over Housing Types for each State/Union Territory in 1983	190
5.4	Percentage of Houseless Households, Households with no Exclusive Room, One Exclusive Room and Per Capita Floor Area by Size Class of Cities for Each State and Union Territory in 1981	192

5.5 Percentage of Households Residing in Rented Houses, Average Per Capita Monthly Rent Paid for Rented Houses, and Imputed Rent for Non-Rented Houses by States and Union Territories in 1983   195

5.6 Percentage Distribution of Households Residing in Rented Houses over Monthly Rent Classes by State/Union Territory in 1983   196

5.7 Percentage Distribution of Households Living in Non-Rented Houses over Monthly Imputed Rent Classes by State/Union Territory in 1983   197

5.8 Percentage of Urban Population Covered by a Water Supply System   199

5.9 Percentage of Towns without Protected Sources of Drinking Water in Selected States in 1981   200

5.10 Percentage Distribution of Persons over Major Sources of Drinking Water for Selected States in 1986–87   201

5.11 Percentage Distribution of Persons over Agencies of Construction and Major Sources of Drinking Water in Urban India in 1986–87   202

5.12 Percentage Distribution of Persons over Agencies of Construction of a Drinking Water System for Selected States in 1986–87   203

5.13 Percentage Distribution of Persons over Agencies and Sources of Drinking Water in 1986–87   205

5.14 Percentage of Urban Population Covered by Sanitation Facilities   207

5.15 Percentage Distribution of Households by Latrine Facilities in States and Union Territories in 1983   210

5.16 Percentage Distribution of Towns by Classes and Types of Sewerage/Drainage Facilities in Selected States, 1981   212

5.17 Percentage of Towns with Sewerage as a Method of Night Soil Disposal in 1981   214

5.18 Select Indices of Health Facilities for States in 1981   215

5.19 State-wise Indicators of In-Patient Hospital Facilities   218

5.20 State-wise Indicators of Out-Patient Medical Treatment in 1986–87   219

5.21 Indicators Concerning Fair Price Shops, 1990   221

5.22 Percentage of Urban Population Served (Fully or Partially) by the PDS to All Persons Buying the Items in 1986–87   223

5.23 Percentage of Quantity Purchased from the PDS to Total Purchase in 1986–87   225

5.24 Percentage of Persons not Fully Dependent on the PDS over Reasons for No Purchase and Partial Purchase in 1986–87   226

6.1   Percentage Distribution of Households by Monthly
      Per Capita Expenditure Class over Types of Houses
      in 1983   231
6.2   Percentage Distribution of Households by Nature of
      Structure and Housing Type over Monthly Per
      Capita Expenditure Classes in 1983   232
6.3   Per Capita Floor Area by Monthly Per Capita
      Expenditure Classes in 1986–87   233
6.4   Per Capita Rent, Percentage of Households
      in Rented Houses and Percentage of Expenditure on
      Rent by Monthly Per Capita Expenditure Class
      in 1983   234
6.5   Percentage Distribution of Households in Rented
      Houses over Monthly Rent Classes by Monthly
      Per Capita Expenditure Class in 1983   236
6.6   Percentage of Households Living in Non-Rented Houses
      among the Categories *katcha, pucca*, semi-*pucca*
      and All Houses in 1983   237
6.7   Actual and Imputed Rent per Unit Area for *katcha*,
      pucca and All Categories of Houses over Per
      Capita Expenditure Classes in 1983   238
6.8   Percentage of Households with Monthly Per Capita
      Expenditure of Rs. 125 or Less by House
      Category in 1983   239
6.9   Per Capita Floor Area and Actual and Imputed
      Monthly Rents and Rental Housing for Households with
      Per Capita Monthly Expenditure of Rs. 125 or Less by
      States/Union Territories in 1983   241
6.10 Percentage of Persons Using the Major Sources of
      Drinking Water to Total Persons over Consumption
      Fractiles in 1986–87   242
6.11 Specialisation Index for Major Sources of Drinking
      Water over Consumption Fractiles in 1986–87   244
6.12 Percentage of Persons by Major Sources of Drinking
      Water among Households belonging to the Bottom 40
      Per Cent Expenditure Fractile to All Persons in the
      Same Fractile in 1986–87   245
6.13 Percentage Distribution of Households over Types of
      Latrines by Per Capita Expenditure Classes in 1983   249
6.14 Percentage Distribution of Households over Latrine
      Facilities by Per Capita Expenditure Classes in 1983   250
6.15 Percentage of Households with Latrine Facilities among
      Households with Per Capita Consumption
      Expenditure up to Rs. 125 in 1983   251

6.16   Percentage Distribution of Hospitalised Cases over Per
Capita Consumption Fractiles, Social Groups and
Educational Categories in 1986–87   255

6.17   Percentage Distribution of Hospitalised Cases over Per
Capita Consumption Fractiles, Payment Categories
and Average Payment in 1986–87   257

6.18   Percentage Distribution of Treatment (other than
Hospitalisation) over Per Capita Consumption
Fractiles and Sources of Treatment in 1986–87   258

6.19   Percentage Distribution of Households by Reasons for
Using Private Doctors/Dispensaries in Delhi   259

6.20   Percentage Distribution of Households by Grievances
about Government Hospitals in Delhi   260

6.21   Percentage Distribution of Out-Patient Treatment over
Per Capita Consumption Fractiles, Payment
Categories and Average Payment in 1986–87   260

6.22   Specialisation Index for Different Systems of Medicine
by Per Capita Consumption Fractiles for
Hospitalisation Cases in 1986–87   262

6.23   Specialisation Index for Different Systems of Medicine
by Per Capita Consumption (Expenditure) Fractile for
Out-Patient Treatment   263

6.24   Percentage of Persons with Ailments Treated as
Out-Patients to All Persons with Ailments (Excluding
Hospitalisation Cases) in 1986–87   264

6.25   Specialisation Index for Reasons of Non-Treatment by
Consumption Fractiles, Social Groups and
Educational Categories in 1986–87   265

6.26   Percentage Share of Bottom 40 Per Cent Households in
the Total Hospitalisation Cases over Sources of
Treatment in Selected States   266

6.27   Percentage Share of Bottom 40 Per Cent Households in
Total Cases of Out-Patient Treatment over Sources
of Treatment in Selected States   267

6.28   Percentage of Persons Dependent Fully or Partially on
the PDS to All Persons over Consumption
Fractiles for Select Items in 1986–87   269

6.29   Percentage of Persons Dependent Fully on the PDS
to All Persons over Consumption Fractiles
for Select Items in 1986–87   270

6.30   Percentage of Quantity Purchased from the PDS
to Total Amount Purchased over Consumption
Fractiles for Select Items in 1986–87   273

6.31   Value of Purchase from the PDS as Percentage of
        Total Purchase over Consumption Fractiles for
        Select Items in 1986–87   274
6.32   Percentage of Persons belonging to the Bottom 40 Per
        Cent Expenditure Category Depending Solely on the
        PDS for Select Items in 1986–87   275
6.33   Percentage of Persons belonging to the Bottom
        40 Per Cent Expenditure Category Depending
        Partially on the PDS in 1986–87   276
6.34   Persons not Wholly Dependent on the PDS over
        Reasons for No Purchase or Partial Purchase of Select
        Items in 1986–87   277

Acknowledgements

This study is the result of team work. Ms. Darshini Mahadevia took the major responsibility for data collection and field survey on housing while Ms. Archana Ghosh did the same for water supply and sanitation. They helped in the writing of the concerned sections in the chapters on Management and Financing (Chapter 3) and on Programmes (Chapter 4). Ms. Mahadevia also helped in writing Chapter 2, entitled, 'Assessing Urban Poverty and its Characteristics'. Besides, both assisted in data analysis and the development of arguments at various stages of the study.

Dr. S.K. Thorat contributed to the analysis and writing of the sections on the Public Distribution System in Chapters 3 and 4. Dr. Saraswati Raju organised the slum survey in Delhi and assisted in the analysis of its results, incorporated in Chapter 6. Ms. Anita Nuna undertook the task of collection and analysis of data on health care.

I benefited a great deal from the comments of Professors D.T. Lakdawala, B.S. Minhas and M.K. Premi in the workshops organised to discuss the results of the study. The project was sponsored by the Ministry of Finance and the Planning Commission, Government of India.

Amitabh Kundu

1

Introduction

The Concern

The removal of poverty has been one of the basic objectives of development planning in India since its inception. This was, however, brought into the core of the planning exercise only during the Fifth Five-Year Plan. The consumption levels of different commodities were projected in this Plan by taking higher growth rates for people in lower consumption brackets. These levels were then used to determine the targeted production of different items through a multi-sectoral model. Extensive research has since been carried out by scholars working both within and outside the government on problems of poverty, its manifestations, temporal trends, spatial patterns, and so on. This resulted in the identification of theoretical solutions and the launching of programmes and schemes during the past few plan periods.

Despite this, and partly because of this, considerable confusion prevails not merely with regard to the strategy of poverty eradication but also on the basic issues relating to the process that generates poverty. Even the magnitude of the 'poverty population' remains under serious dispute. According to the Seventh Five-Year Plan, the number of persons living below the poverty line in rural areas was 253.1 million and 222.2 million for the years 1977–78 and 1984–85, respectively. For urban areas the poverty population was 53.7 million and 50.5 million for the two time periods. The figures indicate a decline in the percentage of the poverty population from 51.2 per cent to 39.9 per cent in rural areas, and from 38.2 per cent to 27.7 per cent in urban areas during this period (Planning Commission 1985). The estimates declined further in the year 1987–88 to 32.70 per cent and 19.40 per cent for the rural and urban areas, respectively. Questioning the methodology for balancing the consumption estimates from different sources at the macro level and the use of the Central Statistical Organisation's

(CSO) implicit consumer price index for updating the poverty line (cut-off level of consumption expenditure) adopted by the Planning Commission, Minhas and others (1987, 1991) have pleaded for alternate procedures. Their estimates do not show as sharp a fall in the percentage of the poverty population as noted by the Planning Commission. Researchers working with the consumer expenditure data obtained from the National Sample Surveys (NSS) placed the aggregative poverty estimate at around 45 per cent, the figure for urban areas being 38 per cent by the mid-1980s (Kansal 1988).

A few scholars working with micro-level data for one or a set of urban centres have arrived at totally different results, suggesting the poverty population to be much less than was estimated in the above studies. They demonstrate that the consumption expenditure on food and non-food items among the so-called economically weaker sections is much higher than is generally believed or is recorded in the secondary sources. They also argue that the poor have considerable potential for savings that can and should be mobilised through appropriate institutional systems and used for investment in housing, water supply, sewerage facilities and other public utilities. Studies conducted by several international development-cum-banking agencies have lent support to this assessment and policy perspective. Controversy prevails not merely on the macro dimensions of poverty but also with regard to the attributes of the poverty population and the factors responsible for it. Needless to say, the strategy proposed to tackle the problem of poverty, particularly the provision of basic amenities, depends to a large extent on the estimated size of the poverty population, assessment of the factors responsible for it, and its attributes, including the financial affordability of the poor.

During the past four decades of planned development, a complex and hierarchical organisational structure has been created through the initiative of the central, state and local governments to provide housing and other basic amenities to the urban population, particularly the poor. These organisations function fully or partially outside the market mechanism. It is, however, observed that despite the professed objectives and policy statements with regard to making these amenities accessible to people in the lower income brackets, large sections among them have to do without these. Several micro-level studies suggest that the percentage of population without these amenities has not diminished over the past ten years.

Bureaucratic delays, mismanagement, deficiencies in the distributional network are often noted as factors responsible for the benefits not reaching the targeted sections of the population. The demands for cost recovery, hikes in user charges, etc., being made on the concerned organisations in recent years, particularly because of the resource crunch in the economy, might lead to the adoption of solutions that will price the poor out of the delivery systems. It is against this background that the present study has been visualised. It analyses the existing organisational structure, the present schemes and those proposed, the amenities available to people in towns and cities in different size categories and different states, and the affordability of the people in the lower consumption categories, with the objective of proposing measures to improve the access of the poor to these amenities.

Scope and Objectives

The study has been restricted to five basic amenities: (*a*) shelter, (*b*) water supply, (*c*) sewerage and sanitation, (*d*) health care, and (*e*) public distribution of foodgrains. The analysis has been carried out in three stages. In the first stage, secondary information on the management system, the production and the distribution of urban amenities has been obtained from the organisations concerned. Quantitative and qualitative data on the programmes and schemes of the state and local bodies and procedures for thier formulation and implementation have been collected. These have been examined along with the various policy and evaluation reports/ documents to ascertain the extent to which the poor have benefited from them.

In the second stage, micro-level studies conducted by individual researchers, organisations and government departments on the access of the urban poor to basic amenities have been reviewed in an attempt to build up hypotheses and arrive at some tentative conclusions. NSS data have been used at this stage to determine the availability of some of these amenities to households in different fractiles of consumption expenditure. Field surveys have been conducted in select slums in different cities to cross-check some of the hypotheses and conclusions, particularly with regard to the factors hindering access of the poor to the amenities. At the final stage, the conclusions and recommendations of the study have been discussed with people's representatives, the concerned officials, researchers and experts in informal meetings and formal workshops organised for this purpose.

The study has the following objectives:

— To analyse the existing organisational structure at the state, city and town levels for providing basic amenities, and the vertical and horizontal interdependencies among them, and to identify the deficiencies in their functioning.

— To asses the capacity of the existing organisations to meet the needs and demands of the urban poor and the extent to which they have succeeded.

— To investigate the process of formulation, approval and implementation of programmes and projects by the central, state and local bodies to ascertain if the interests of the poor are indeed taken care of in their day-to-day system of decision-making.

— To analyse the consumption expenditure and saving potential of the urban poor in the context of the stipulations of increasing the user charges, recovering the current and capital costs, lowering the standards of the services to match affordability, etc., in many of the present and proposed schemes for urban/infrastructural development.

— To recommend specific measures through which the interests of the poor can be made the central focus of decision-making in the concerned organisations and their accountability to the people, particularly to the economically weaker sections, can be increased without compromising the efficiency of the production and delivery systems.

Scheme of Presentation

The second chapter reviews research studies, based on secondary data as well as primary surveys on income, consumption, saving, and saving potential of the economically weaker sections of the urban population. It examines the major areas of agreement and disagreement and highlights the possible reasons for the anomalies. Using the NSS data at the macro level, it analyses the expenditure pattern of households in lower expenditure categories on non-food items, specifically on housing and basic amenities, to assess their affordability for market solutions or some of the new government-sponsored schemes.

In the third chapter, the functioning of the public sector organisations managing five basic amenities—shelter, drinking water, sewerage/sanitation, health care, and distribution of foodgrains in the urban areas—has been discussed. The issues concerning separation of the responsibility for maintenance and capital expenditure, sources of financing these, provision of grants and loans from governmental and other institutions, collection of user charges, etc., have been considered in some detail.

The fourth chapter reviews the schemes and programmes implemented by the central and state governments during the past few years to strengthen the existing system or augment the facilities. An attempt is made both in the third and fourth chapters to assess the relevance or sensitivity of the organisations and schemes in different sectors towards the needs and problems of the urban poor.

In the fifth chapter, the level and quality of the amenities in cities and towns of different size categories have been analysed. The deficiencies and inadequacies identified at the state level have been viewed in relation to their organisational structure and schemes implemented in the recent past.

The sixth chapter examines the issue of access to the facilities of households in different expenditure categories based largely on the data from the 38th and 42nd rounds of the NSS. Information available through select micro-level studies and their results have also been used. Limited quantitative and qualitative data have been collected through field visits to a few cities and towns and the slums therein to assess the functioning of the public sector organisations and the access of the poor to the basic amenities. These have been used for the analysis in this as well as the previous chapters.

The seventh and final chapter proposes a set of recommendations to improve the access of the urban poor to the five amenities under consideration. Modifications in the existing organisational structure and urban development schemes have been suggested with this in view.

References

Kansal, S.M. (1988). 'Measurement of Poverty in India—An Evaluation', paper presented at the Second Seminar on Social Statistics, 4–6 February, Central Statistical Organisation, New Delhi.

Minhas, B.S., L.R. Jain, S.M. Kansal and M.R. Saluja (1987). 'On the Choice of Appropriate Consumer Price Indices and Data Sets for Estimating the Incidence of Poverty in India', *Indian Economic Review*, 22(1).

Minhas, B.S., L.R. Jain and S.D. Tendulkar (1991). 'Declining Incidence of Poverty in the 1980s: Evidence versus Artifacts', *Economic and Political Weekly*, 26(27 & 28).

2

Assessing Urban Poverty and its Characteristics

The Question of Affordability

It has been argued in recent years that the households below the poverty line in urban areas have considerable income and saving potential, both in real and financial terms. This proposition has often been supported by international development-cum-financing agencies such as the World Bank, Asian Development Bank (ADB), Ford Foundation, and the United States Agency for International Development (USAID), all of which advocate market-based solutions for the provision of basic amenities.[1] A few scholars have tried to demonstrate that the saving potential among the poor can be effectively mobilised through cooperatives, voluntary agencies and other institutional arrangements, and that many among the poor can afford public utilities at prices that can attract private investment into these sectors. Studies sponsored by USAID in South America attempt to show that the excessive concern regarding the question of 'ability to save' is misplaced and the thesis regarding economic marginality of the people in urban informal sectors, slum dwellers, pavement dwellers and others is an exaggeration (Lee 1986). The World Bank research study of sixteen cities in eight countries including India suggests that the 'normal housing expenditure among target groups typically identified for government sponsored housing projects varied from five per cent to over forty per cent of income' (Malpezzi, Mayo and Gross 1985).

A few micro-level studies in India too tend to favour this optimistic assessment of the income and saving potential of the urban poor, as also the market-based policy perspective. A study conducted by the Society for Development Studies (SDS), based on a sample drawn from six urban centres in Maharashtra, showed that the monthly income for an average household in the informal sector was over Rs. 800 in 1983. This is much higher than the average income for Maharashtra as per the CSO statistics. According to the study the informal sector households spent only 70 per cent of their income on food, clothing and shelter, while the corresponding estimate from the NSS for food alone (including fuel, lighting, *pan* and tobacco) for the years 1983 and 1986–87 was over 80 per cent for the bottom 40 per cent of the urban population in the country or the state of Maharashtra. The SDS study determines the savings rate for households with a monthly income below Rs. 350 as 15 per cent, which rises systematically with income, the figure being 22.5 per cent for the income group between Rs. 351 and Rs. 600, 27.9 per cent for the Rs. 601 to Rs. 1,000 category, 32.7 per cent for the group Rs. 1,001 to Rs. 1,500, and 42.5 per cent for the group above Rs. 1,500 (Lall 1986).

Another study by the SDS for the Ministry of Urban Development (MOUD) was based on a sample of households drawn from thirteen cities in India. The data were collected during October 1986 and June 1987. The study reveals that saving rates in the informal sector range between 7 per cent and 15 per cent and that the prospect of savings-linked loans to be provided by the National Housing Bank (NHB) would motivate these households to mobilise substantial additional savings at the same level of income. The study also predicts that a higher saving rate will be realised owing to the additional income generated through the investment in housing (Lall 1990).

A recent study by Mehta and Mehta (1992) of the city of Ahmedabad concludes that 'the housing expenditure appears to be independent of the household income (and) the poorest households are spending on an average 18 per cent of their income on housing . . . .' A few other scholars have argued, based on the experience of house loan-linked schemes launched by urban development authorities, that the urban poor can make substantial down payments and also pay monthly instalments of about 20 per cent of their income. Based on the fragmented evidence from projects funded by the Housing and Urban Development Corporation (HUDCO), Mulk Raj (1986) argues that housing and house improvement projects 'provide much better chance of saving mobilisation in the unorganised sectors.' He holds that the possession of a house tends to reduce (unnecessary) expenditure such as on entertainment, and increase the total family income by using the idle labour of the wife, children and other members. He, therefore, recommends putting 'tremendous pressure on the family to increase its income through such house loan schemes.'

Methodology for Estimating Urban Poverty

Estimates of population below the poverty line based on NSS data on consumer expenditure vary significantly, as mentioned earlier. In order to appreciate the poverty estimates at the macro level and the reasons for the variations therein, it will be worthwhile to briefly consider the methodology of computation. The differences occur basically because of three factors: (*a*) choice of the poverty line, (*b*) choice of the price index for updating the poverty line consumer expenditure, and (*c*) the methods for balancing the NSS and CSO estimates of consumption at the macro level.

Determining the Poverty Line (Critical Minimum Consumption Expenditure)

The first attempt to define the poverty line in India was made by a Working Group set up by the Planning Commission in 1962. It recommended a consumption expenditure of Rs. 20 per month at 1960–61 prices that would buy the minimum nutritional diet and possibly allow for certain essential non-food expenditure.[2] It suggested a higher figure of Rs. 25 for urban areas after taking into consideration the price differences between rural and urban areas. By implication the rural poverty line would be drawn at Rs. 19 only, further implying a rural-urban price differential of 32 per cent in 1960–61, which is definitely on the higher side since the NSS data reflect a rural-urban price differential of only 15 per cent. The only way to justify the higher figures for urban areas would be to assume larger essential non-food requirements such as transport, water supply and housing in these areas as compared to rural areas.

Dandekar and Rath (1971) based their calculations not on a normative diet specified exogenously, as done by the Planning

Commission, but on a minimum intake of 2,250 calories per capita per day. This minimum dietary requirement, when examined in the context of the NSS consumption pattern, determined the poverty line in 1960–61 at Rs. 14.2 and Rs. 22.6 for rural and urban areas, respectively. The urban-rural price differential thus works out to about 60 per cent which, most certainly, is on the high side. Dutta (1980), on the other hand, assumed the urban-rural price differential to be only 20 per cent, and estimated the poverty line urban consumption expenditure at Rs. 20. per month.[3]

The Seventh Five-Year Plan provided poverty estimates based on an approach similar to that of Dandekar and Rath. The Planning Commission methodology, however, marked an improvement as it took age, sex and activity-specific minimum calorie requirements into account. The minimum calorie requirement was assessed by the Nutrition Expert Group which recommended 2,100 and 2,400 calories for an average person in urban and rural areas, respectively. Based on the 28th round consumption data of the NSS for different income groups, the poverty lines for the year 1973–74 were drawn at Rs. 56.64 and Rs. 49.09 for urban and rural areas, respectively.

Updating the Poverty Line

To date, the figures of poverty line consumption expenditure have been worked out for only two years, viz., 1960–61 and 1973–74. To determine the poverty line for any other year, it is necessary to update the base year figures by applying a consumer price index. The CSO's implicit consumer price index, obtained by dividing the total consumer expenditure at current prices by that at constant prices for any year, is a convenient and popular index and, as mentioned earlier, was used by the Planning Commission to estimate poverty in the Seventh Plan period. This index, however, is available only for the country as a whole and not separately for rural and urban areas. The Consumer Price Index for Industrial Workers (CPIIW), on the other hand, is based on the consumption pattern of industrial workers that accounts for not more than 20 per cent of the population in urban areas. The Consumer Price Index for Non-Manual Employees (CPINM) is yet another sectional index based on the consumption pattern of only 16 per cent of the urban population. Finally, the Consumer Price Index for Total Urban Population (CPITU) would have limited use in measuring poverty as the consumption items for the higher fractiles would also be included in it.

In view of the inadequacy of the CSO's implicit index owing to its aggregative nature, and those of the CPIIW and CPINM because of their partial coverage, it may be useful to construct indices based on the consumption pattern of the middle income urban population (CPIMU) whose classification (into poor and non-poor categories) is likely to be affected by shifts in the poverty line. Minhas and others (1987a and 1987b) constructed such an index using the consumption pattern of the urban population belonging to the 23rd to 53rd percentiles. Based on the retail price data collected to build up the CPIIW and CPINM for the months covered by the respective NSS rounds, the CPIMU was constructed for the years 1970–71, 1972–73, 1973–74, 1977–78 and 1983–84, with 1970–71 as the base.

Table 2.1: *Consumer Price Indices, 1970–71 to 1987–88*

Years	CSO's Implicit Consumers Deflator	Urban			
		All Urban (CPITU)	Middle Urban (CPIMU)	Industrial Workers (CPIIW)	Non-Manual Employees (CPINM)
1	2	3	4	5	6
1970–71	100	100	100	100	100
1972–73	117	120	121	120	116
1973–74	139	142	145	147	135
1977–78	172	174	174	175	170
1983–84	288	283	285	285	274
1987–88	373	408	405	403	390

Source: Kansal (1988) and Minhas and others (1991).

It has been pointed out that the CSO's implicit index tends to understate the actual price rise which is captured more appropriately through the consumer price index for the middle range of population, as suggested by Minhas, Jain and Tendulkar (1991). This, however, is not clear from Table 2.1 which gives comparable figures up to 1987–88. It may be seen that the CSO's index was growing at a lower rate than the CPIMU or CPIIW during 1970–74, the trend reversing thereafter up to 1983–84. However, taking the figures for 1987–88, it is observed that the CSO's deflator understates the price rise to the extent of over 10 per cent for the urban population (CPITU) during 1983–88.

Adjusting Consumption Expenditure for Different Classes

One major difficulty in macro studies involving the measurement of poverty lies in the discrepancy between the aggregate consumption figures obtained from the CSO and the NSS, as the estimates from the former are larger than those from the latter. It is generally believed that the CSO figures are more reliable than the sample estimates of the NSS. One may, therefore, argue for an upward revision of the latter to correspond to the former. The Seventh Five-Year Plan document, however, estimates poverty by adjusting the NSS consumption series using a rather simplistic method. It revises the consumption level of every commodity and every income group upwards by a uniform percentage to balance the aggregate figures. The CSO's estimates may be more accurate than those of the NSS, but it is erroneous to assume uniform underestimation across the commodity groups. The NSS figure on food consumption, for example, is higher than that of the CSO by about 10 per cent, while for fuel it is higher by 30 to 40 per cent. It may be noted here that food and fuel together account for more than 80 per cent of the consumption expenditure of the poor. For non-food items, however, NSS figures are definite underestimations. Since different commodities are likely to have different weightages in the consumption basket of the people in the bottom or middle income categories, it will be necessary to have commodity-specific adjustments and not simple pro-rata adjustment, as is done by the Planning Commission. The resultant discrepancy is indeed very serious because the gap between the CSO and NSS estimates of total consumer expenditure, which was only 5 to 10 per cent in the 1970s, rose to over 21 per cent in 1983–84. The upward revision of the NSS consumption data by the Planning Commission is, therefore, the main reason for the underestimation of poverty in the year 1984–85. By correcting this flaw, one would place the urban poverty estimate somewhere between 35 and 40 per cent (see Table 2.2).

Table 2.2: *Number of Poor and Percentage of People below the Poverty Line in the 1970s and 1980s*

	Planning Commission Estimate	Direct All India Estimate		Aggregation of State Estimates	
	(Per cent)	*(No. in million)*	*(Per cent)*	*(No. in million)*	*(Per cent)*
	(1)	(2)	(3)	(4)	(5)
1970–71					
Urban	–	50.07	45.89	49.93	46.17
Total	–	301.76	55.05	305.90	56.25
1983					
Urban	28.10	65.96	38.33	68.39	39.74
Total	37.40	333.27	46.46	343.26	48.11
1987–88					
Urban	19.40	74.96	36.52	76.57	37.76
Total	29.20	336.42	42.70	357.83	45.85

Source: Minhas, Jain and Tendulkar (1991).

Note: All the estimates are computed taking the per capita consumption expenditure of Rs. 49.09 and Rs. 56.64 as the poverty lines at 1973–74 prices for the rural and urban areas, respectively.

It may be noted that the national level estimates of poverty population (columns 4 and 5) obtained by aggregating the state-level figures (computed by using state-specific poverty lines) are higher than those obtained by using the all-India poverty line on the distribution of per capita expenditure for the total or urban population (columns 2 and 3). The Planning Commission estimates (column 1) are, however, the lowest as these are computed by updating the poverty line on the basis of the CSO's implicit price index and pro-rata adjustment of consumption expenditure for all categories to make the NSS estimate equal to that of National Accounts Statistics (NAS).

It is important to note that Minhas and others (1987a and 1987b) have taken the poverty line for the base year as the standard and updated it through an appropriate price index, instead of working out the poverty line using the calorie norm and consumption pattern for the current year. Scholars often follow this approach as it is analytically more convenient than fresh estimation of the poverty line expenditure that would sustain the minimum calorie consumption. This is also because the calorie requirement for an average person is unlikely to change over a short period of a decade or so. However, there can be no theoretical reason to believe that updating the base year poverty line is a better method than computing it by using the consumption pattern and prices for the current year. Consumption pattern in the base year has no more validity than the least-cost bundle of goods prescribed by a dietician since neither has a bearing on the actual consumption habits of the population at a given point of time.

It is indeed true that over time the preference of the population in our country has shifted in favour of more expensive items of food. NSS data reveal that by the 1980s people were buying more expensive calories than they were in the 1970s; they were getting calories from milk, egg and meat rather than from cereals. This, to a very small extent, is true also for the people in lower consumption categories. This implies that some people are making a conscious choice for lower calorie consumption, sometimes even lower than the minimum normative requirement, by opting for more expensive sources of calories or by allocating a higher proportion of expenditure to non-food items. Can such people be considered non-poor? The question is important because they have the affordability to purchase, at the current prices, the same bundle of goods that provided the minimum calories in the base year, namely, 1973–74. They stand below the poverty line now only because of their changed consumption habits. It is interesting that while estimates based on the updated poverty line show a decline in the percentage of the poverty population, those obtained using the line computed for the current year by taking the changed consumption habits into consideration indicate a slight increase. Table 2.2 presents the percentage of poor in different years obtained by using different approaches, as discussed above.

It thus becomes clear that determining the exact percentage of population or households below the poverty line at the macro level for any year poses serious problems of a conceptual and empirical nature. Indeed, our inadequate knowledge on the question of nutritional requirements is responsible for some of the confusion.

However, the established norm of 2,100 calories per capita per day for urban areas should not be dismissed merely because certain groups of people in a year choose to buy fewer calories despite their ability to purchase an amount higher than this minimum requirement. Persons cannot be regarded as non-poor simply because they are now consuming a little milk or egg or meat at the cost of calories, remaining below the stipulated minimum level of (calorie) consumption. It is important that the entire poverty discussion in our country is based on the implicit assumption that the government has a role and responsibility in the provision of a certain minimum level of nutrition and basic amenities to the people. Therefore, the fact that people continue to remain below the normative level of calories, for whatever reason—including distortions of consumer preferences through advertisements, imperfect knowledge, etc.—is a cause for concern. It seems reasonable, therefore, to take the calorie norm determined by the Nutrition Expert Group as the basis until an alternate estimate is made available. Given this norm, the poverty population in urban areas works out to between 35 and 40 per cent, as noted earlier. In our analysis in the following sections, we have, therefore, focused attention on this segment of urban households and have analysed their pattern of consumption expenditure, ownership of durable assets and liabilities.

Studies at the Regional and Sub-regional Levels

Several studies at the regional and city levels, using data from the NSS and other sources including primary surveys, confirm the findings relating to low income, low consumption and very high proportion of consumption expenditure on food among the bottom 40 per cent of the urban households, as noted in the preceding section. The National Council of Applied Economic Research conducted a study (NCAER 1980) analysing the changing characteristics of a group of households at different points of time. The sample households in the year 1975–76 were drawn from 150 cities and towns and 237 villages, totalling 2,110 households from urban areas and 3,015 households from rural areas. The study reveals that 50 per cent of the urban households had annual incomes less than Rs. 4,562. Taking the average size of urban households as 5.8

persons (as obtained in the study), the per capita income figure could be computed at Rs. 65.55 per month. The urban poverty line (estimated by updating the 1973–74 base line) used by the Planning Commission for the year 1977–78 is Rs. 71.3 which, when adjusted by the Food Index of the Industrial Workers and the CPIMU, works out to Rs. 70.68 and Rs. 63.20, respectively, for 1975–76. It is thus obvious that the percentage of urban population below the poverty line was around or more than 50 per cent that year. It is important that the annual household income for all the agricultural and non-agricultural wage earners was Rs. 2,118 and Rs. 3,072, respectively, or Rs. 30.43 and Rs. 44.13 per capita per month. Both figures are below the consumption expenditure at the poverty line. It was noted in the study that the bottom 5 per cent of the households had negative savings while 5 to 20 per cent of the households had no positive savings. Amongst the bottom 50 per cent of the urban households, 54 per cent were wage earners and, although they claimed 22.08 per cent of the total income, had a modest share of 3.25 per cent in the total wealth and 1.50 per cent in total savings. The NCAER study also casts serious doubts on the postulate that the urban poor have a high saving/investment potential for housing. The bottom 50 per cent of the households had a share of only 4 per cent in the total physical investment, of which 37 per cent went in consumer durables, 34 per cent in agriculture, 13 per cent in livestock, 12 per cent each in business and housing and −7 per cent in gold. The average savings figure for them worked out to only Rs. 278 per household at 1975–76 prices. The bottom 40 per cent, however, had neither savings in terms of gold nor any housing investment.

The study by Radhakrishna and others (1988), based on the data collected by the Bureau of Economics and Statistics of Andhra Pradesh as part of the 38th round of the NSS, showed that the percentage of population below the poverty line in the urban areas of the state was well above 40 per cent. The figure declined from 70 per cent in the backward districts of Anantpur, Kurnool and Mahabubnagar to 50 per cent in the developed districts of East Godavari, West Godavari and Krishna. The most developed and fully urbanised district of Hyderabad showed the lowest poverty population of 20 per cent.

From a study conducted by the National Institute of Urban Affairs (NIUA 1988), based on data from twenty sample towns of various sizes, it can be inferred that about 50 per cent of the slum population lives below the poverty line.[4] The study further shows that about 80 per cent of the per capita expenditure of slum households below the poverty line is on food alone, excluding fuel, lighting, *pan* and tobacco. The figure corresponds well with that of the 38th round of the NSS for the bottom 40 per cent of the urban population which is reported as 70 per cent.

A survey of the three cities of Bangalore, Calcutta and Indore, conducted by the National Centre for Human Settlements and Environment (NCHSE 1987), indicates a higher incidence of poverty in the slums than noted in the NIUA study: the figures exceed 73 per cent, 89 per cent and 68 per cent for the three cites, respectively, and for all the three put together, the figure is above 80 per cent.[5]

Studies on individual metropolitan cities suggest that the incidence of poverty is high but less than that of an average urban centre. Based on survey data for the year 1986, the Operations Research Group found the poverty population to be about 62 per cent among the slum dwellers in Madras Metropolitan Area (Vaidya and Mukundan 1987). The study took Rs. 122 per capita per month as the poverty line and household size as 6.6 persons. The income distribution study undertaken by the Madras Metropolitan Development Authority for the year 1975 (MMDA 1980) reveals that 72.2 per cent of households had incomes below Rs. 350. Assuming an average household size of 5.5 persons and no savings, the *poverty line* household income at 1977–78 prices can be taken as Rs. 350 per month (ORG 1980). Since the price of food did not change significantly during 1975–77, the poverty line income for the survey year (1975) may not be significantly below Rs. 350 and, consequently, the poverty percentage would be about 60 per cent. Based on the data generated by this study, it can be shown that about 90 per cent of the slum population in Madras lives below the poverty line.

Prakasa Rao and Tewari (1979) analysed the income distribution, expenditure and savings pattern of the population in the city of Bangalore for the year 1973. Using the Planning Commission estimate of the poverty line and income/expenditure data obtained from their study, about 38 per cent of the households in the city could be identified as poor. Four important points emerge from this survey:

i. eighty per cent of the expenditure of poor households is on food and fuel;

ii. households with a monthly income up to Rs. 150 have almost no savings, in fact they have certain dissavings;

iii. about 75 per cent of the households in the above category have zero savings while 15 per cent report negative savings;

iv. fifty-four per cent of the households in the next higher category with an income between Rs. 150 and Rs. 299 per month also report no savings.

All this certainly casts serious doubts on the findings of the studies reviewed in the first section.

Statistics for Bombay from different sources do not place poverty estimates at a very high level. They are much below the figures noted for other metropolises. The slum census conducted in Greater Bombay in 1976 indicates that only 40 per cent of the slum households lived below the poverty line, the figure being 19 per cent for all households. Interestingly, NSS data from the 32nd round reveal that only 63 per cent of the total expenditure of all households in this city is on food and fuel, which is lower than the figure for other metropolises. A study on poverty in Bombay by the Tata Institute of Social Studies (Acharya and Trikha 1978) in 1977–78 shows that the average per capita income for the slum and pavement populations was above the poverty line. However, 80 per cent among the housed and 92 per cent among the homeless population in the sample did not report any savings. A study by the Bombay Metropolitan Region Development Authority (BMRDA 1981) similarly concludes that for 'industrial labour' expenditure exceeds income leading to perpetual indebtedness.

A study in the Union Territory of Delhi (undertaken during March-May 1980) reveals the staggering fact that households earning Rs. 1,400 per month are negative savers while those earning between Rs. 1,400 to 2,428 are non-savers (Ahmad 1982). The percentages of people belonging to these two categories were estimated as 33 and 25 per cent, respectively. Yet another study on the income-shelter linkage of the pavement dwellers in Calcutta (Jagannath and Haldar 1988) shows that they have a very low affordability for shelter. Despite significant variations in the percentage of earnings that can be spared for shelter across occupational categories, the figure does not rise even to 10 per cent. The statistically insignificant relationship between income, duration of stay, etc., with the willingness to pay for shelter, questions the theory regarding the possibility of generating substantial savings from among the poor households for investment in housing by designing appropriate schemes and institutions.

Expenditure on Housing and Other Non-Food Items by the Urban Poor

Using the information from the 38th and 42nd rounds of the NSS for the years 1983 and 1986–87, the percentage distribution of urban households in the bottom six expenditure categories[6] along with their rental and total non-food expenditure has been arrived at (see Table 2.3). Updating the base year (1973–74) poverty line of Rs. 56.64 for the urban population by the implicit price index of the CSO, the Planning Commission placed the line at Rs. 111.23 for the year 1983–84 and at Rs. 122.00 for 1984–85. For the year 1986–87, which is included in our analysis, the updated poverty line would be around Rs. 150. Keeping this in view, the characteristics of all households below the per capita expenditure of Rs. 150 have been analysed in Table 2.3. It may be mentioned that the decline in the share of households for the selected categories over time is primarily because of the inflationary increase in the consumption expenditure of the households and, as such, does not reflect a decline in the incidence of poverty.

Table 2.3 also reveals that the share of expenditure on *non-food items, excluding pan, tobacco, intoxicants, fuel and lighting*, has risen over the years.[7] The percentage share was 27.11 in 1972–73 (27th round), which increased to 32.45 in 1986–87 (42nd round). For the bottom 30 per cent of the households (approximately), the corresponding figure, computed by considering all categories up to an expenditure of Rs. 150, works out to less than 20 per cent in 1986–87. In 1983, the bottom 30 per cent of the households were covered by including a part of those people falling in the expenditure category of Rs. 100 to Rs. 125, along with those below it. Here again, the share of non-food expenditure was less than 20 per cent. It is important to note that there has been a marginal increase in this share over the years even for these households. For 1986–87,

Table 2.3: *Expenditure on Non-food Items in Urban Areas*

	Monthly Per Capita Expenditure Classes (Rs.)						
	0–60	60–70	70–85	85–100	100–125	125–150	All Classes
38th Round (1983)							
Per cent households to all households	3.8	3.4	7.2	8.6	14.7	12.7	100.0
Expenditure (%) on							
Non-food items (excluding							
(a) *Pan*, tobacco, etc., and							
(b) Fuel, etc)	12.22	14.21	15.37	17.65	20.11	23.29	27.11
Pan, tobacco and Intoxicants	2.98	2.65	2.61	2.84	2.80	2.61	2.44
Rent*	2.04	1.40	1.80	2.10	2.30	2.83	3.60
42nd Round (1986–87)							
Per cent households to all households	1.2	1.1	3.1	4.4	9.0	9.8	100.0
Expenditure (%) on							
Non-food items (excluding							
(a) *Pan*, tobacco, etc., and							
(b) Fuel, etc.)	16.53	11.72	10.37	13.81	15.55	19.06	32.45
Pan, tobacco and Intoxicants	2.63	3.18	3.34	3.21	3.04	3.34	2.77
Rent*	1.38	1.70	0.70	1.50	1.80	2.85	4.30

Source: Based on National Sample Survey Organisation data (1986, 1989).

* The figures are obtained using the actual rents paid and do not include the imputed rental value of owner-occupied houses.

the bottom 30 per cent of the households were covered by including the next higher expenditure category of Rs. 150 to Rs. 200 (along with the lower categories), which reported non-food expenditure of 21 per cent. It is thus clear that the households between the 30th and 40th percentiles spend, on an average, no more than 21 per cent on non-food items including utensils, clothing, footwear, other household durables, health care, shelter, water supply, sanitation and transport. For households in the lower percentiles the figure is lower.

It may be seen in Table 2.3 that the expenditure on *pan*, tobacco and intoxicants, described sometimes as 'minor vices' was significantly higher than rents for these categories both in 1983 and in 1986–87. It may also be noted that the former were definite underestimations because of non-reporting owing to individual and family inhibitions and social taboos. It is not possible to get any reliable estimate of the consumption of *pan*, tobacco, intoxicants and such items through production data by making adjustments for exports, imports, trade and transport margins as the relevant National Accounts Statistics (NAS) also have serious flaws. Minhas (1988) has, therefore, pleaded for dropping it altogether from the consumption calculations. Non-food expenditure, the way we have defined it, would, however, not increase even if we found that the actual expenditure on 'minor vices' is several times the present reported value. Any increase in the latter would only further depress the share of non-food expenditure.

The percentage of expenditure on rent was 3.6 in 1983 which rose marginally to 4.3 in 1986–87. The corresponding figures for the six lowest consumption categories were significantly below the national average (see Table 2.3). It is indeed true that the rents, as reported by the NSS, do not include imputed rental value of owner-occupied houses as it is not a part of household expenditure. The corresponding figures in Table 2.3 have been obtained by simply dividing the actual rents (paid) by the total consumption expenditure (of both rent-paying and non-rent paying households) in each category. Minhas (1988) has shown that the NAS estimate of gross rent, including the imputed value (for owner-occupied houses) and water charges, was 2.73 times the NSS figure in the year 1972–73. The ratio worked out to be 1.99 in 1977–78. One may therefore infer that the gross rental value in the 1980s was twice the actual rent repeated by the

NSS. Interestingly, information has been collected in the 38th round of the NSS which enables us to determine the gap between the actual rent and the total rental value (including the imputed value) more realistically. This alleviates the necessity of taking the NAS estimate on rent, which may be objected to on several conceptual grounds for temporal comparisons in the study.

The first row in Table 2.4 shows per capita rental expenditure obtained by dividing the rent (paid) by all persons in each category. Thus, while the numerator pertains to only the rent-paying households, the denominator includes persons in owner-occupied houses as well. The second row in the table is obtained by dividing the actual rent by people living in rented tenements. The third row gives the per capita imputed value of rent for owner-occupied houses only. The figures in the fourth row are the total rental values computed by aggregating the corresponding figures in the second and third rows, taking the number of households as weights. The last row gives the share of total rental value to total expenditure.[8]

Tables 2.3 and 2.4 give no definite idea of how much the urban poor are *prepared to pay* for housing or other basic amenities such as water, sanitation and health. It would be wrong *to put pressure on them* to reduce their food expenditure for this purpose because they are already deficient in nutrition. It is arguable whether the expenditure on these amenities or their savings can be increased by persuading them to give up or control their 'minor vices'. The habits of the poor are tied up with their physical, social and economic existence and can be altered only through a total development strategy. Moral lessons canvassed through posters or the media and campaigns by 'barefoot bankers' are unlikely to make a major impact.

The imputed expenditure on housing works out to be higher than the actual rentals for all categories (Table 2.4). This implies that among the urban poor, those who have formal or informal ownership of their plots, largely because of their arrival at the urban centres a few years earlier, are better off with regard to housing than those living in rental houses, comprising mostly the new migrants. The former would not, however, be able to pay as much rent as the imputed rental value out of their current earnings if they happen to lose the ownership or the present non-rental arrangements. Their actual rent-paying capacity would be less than the imputed rent as shown in Table 2.4.

Table 2.4: Expenditure on Rent in Urban Areas—1983

Per Capita Monthly Rent	Monthly Per Capita Expenditure Classes (Rs.)							All Classes
	0–60	60–70	70–85	85–100	100–125	125–150		
Actual rent for all households	0.68	0.93	1.37	1.97	2.60	3.88		5.93
Actual rent for households in rented houses	4.04	4.81	6.16	6.90	8.81	10.82		17.28
Imputed rental value for households in owner-occupied houses	7.38	8.67	9.99	22.10	16.36	19.67		23.98
Total (actual + imputed) rental value for all households	6.87	7.92	9.08	10.67	14.02	23.98		21.46
Per cent rental value (actual + imputed) to expenditure for all households	–	10.96	10.67	10.54	11.30	11.00		11.95

Source: National Sample Survey Organisation (1986, 1987).
Note: The Table presents the details for the bottom six classes and for all classes.

The analysis of the current expenditure pattern reveals that the NHB or even HUDCO-sponsored schemes for housing the urban poor, stipulating that a minimum of 20 per cent of their income be paid as instalment, are overtly optimistic. It may be argued that the possibility of owning a house through home-linked loans or any other scheme would increase the expenditure or savings for the purpose. However, the extent to which resources can be augmented at the household level by reducing unnecessary and unhealthy consumption is anyone's guess. Our analysis shows that the projects requiring the urban poor to spend significantly above 11 per cent of their expenditure or income (as savings are negligible) on housing cannot be sustained, given their present expenditure pattern. By their very design, these projects would miss the target groups and the benefits would flow to households in higher consumption brackets, as indeed has been recorded in several micro-level studies.

Bankability of the Urban Poor—Their Assets and Liabilities

The All India Debt and Investment Survey conducted by the NSSO as part of its 37th round, at the instance of the Reserve Bank of India, provides useful information on the assets and debts of households in different asset categories as on 30 June 1981. Some of the important characteristics of the urban households belonging to the bottom two (asset) categories are presented in Tables 2.5 and 2.6. The poorest 14.4 per cent of the households (with assets up to Rs. 1,000) own, on an average, assets worth only Rs. 373 while the figure for the next higher category (with assets between Rs. 1,000 and Rs. 5,000), comprising 17.5 per cent of the households, in Rs. 2,746. About 75 per cent and 50 per cent of the assets in these two categories are in the form of household durables that have very little value as collateral. The percentage of households owning land or buildings works out to be very small. The value of land and buildings together comes to roughly Rs. 40 and Rs. 700, respectively, for these two categories, against the national average of over Rs. 27,000.

Table 2.5: *Asset Structure of Households as on 30 June 1981 in Urban Areas*

Item	Asset Groups (Rs.)		Total
	Up to 1000	1000–5000	
Per cent households (HH)	14.4	17.5	100.0
Average value of assets (Rs.)	373	2746	40573
HH reporting land assets (%)	2.31	23.97	52.87
HH reporting building assets (%)	9.51	31.22	54.95
Land assets per HH (Rs.)	7	286	13133
	(1.9)	(10.4)	(32.4)
Building assets per HH (Rs.)	32	417	14459
	(8.6)	(15.2)	(35.6)
Durable household assets per HH (Rs.)	277	1362	6142
	(74.3)	(49.6)	(15.1)

Source: Based on data obtained from the Reserve Bank of India (1987).
Note: Figures in brackets are percentages to total value of the assets.

Table 2.6: *Pattern of Debt in Different Asset Categories as on 30 June 1981 in Urban Areas*

Item	Asset Group (Rs.)		Total
	Up to 1000	1000–5000	
Amount of cash dues (Rs.)	92	292	1024
Debts incurred (%) for household expenditure	81.3	66.0	35.0
From non-institutional sources	94.5	75.1	40.1
With personal and third party security	72.3	61.2	45.3
Without security	20.0	24.7	12.1
At zero interest rate	37.1	24.1	14.1
At more than 20 per cent interest rate	42.9	43.5	31.6

Source: Based on data from the Reserve Bank of India (1987).

The cash dues (debts) for the households in the bottom-most asset category is Rs. 92, while for the next higher category it is Rs. 292. Out of this paltry sum, much is spent for household purposes. It is important that about 95 per cent and 75 per cent of the debts in these two categories arise from non-institutional sources such as private money-lenders, shop-keepers, friends and relatives.

More than 40 per cent of the households in both categories obtain loans at an interest rate of more than 20 per cent per annum while the corresponding figure for all urban households is only 30 per cent. Paradoxically, a very high percentage of households in both the asset categories borrow without security or with merely personal/third party security and make no interest payments. Such loans are often obtained from shop-keepers and employers. Here the implicit rate of interest often works out to be very high because of the higher prices or other contractual obligations for the borrowers, including provision of free labour. Thus, the ownership pattern of assets and the nature of borrowings for the two bottom-most asset categories, comprising largely the urban poor, make it clear that bringing them into the fold of the formal banking system will call for enormous efforts on the part of public agencies.

Notes

1. See Asian Development Bank (1983), Foundation for Co-operative Housing (1972), Kanhert (1986), Mayo and Gross (1985), Struyk and Turner (1986), and United Nations (1978).
2. The Working Group perhaps considered the balanced diet prescribed by the Indian Council of Medical Research but did not explicitly indicate the statistical base for arriving at the figure of Rs. 20.
3. Several other scholars have also tried to determine the poverty line consumption expenditure for the base year 1960–61. Minhas (1970) and Bardhan (1970) took much lower figures for the rural poverty line, Rs. 17 and Rs. 15, respectively. Subsequently, Bardhan (1973) considered a minimum normative diet (as reported by the Central Government Employee's Pay Commission 1955–59) and arrived at a figure of Rs. 14 per month for the rural areas that would ensure the minimum food and non-food requirements at 1960–61 prices. Accordingly, after allowing a 15 per cent margin for higher urban prices, one would draw the urban poverty line at Rs. 16.2. Following similar methods and keeping a 10 per cent margin for urban over rural prices, Rudra (1974) worked out three alternate poverty lines based on three different specifications of minimum normative diets at Rs. 19.0, Rs. 27.3 and Rs. 33.7.
4. At 1987-88 prices, the poverty line income works out to be Rs. 154 per capita per month, or Rs. 9,224 per household per annum, when the food index for industrial workers is used to update the line and the average family size is taken as five members, in the NIUA study.
5. The percentage has been worked out by taking per capita consumption of Rs. 154 per month as the poverty line but considering only the households with per capita consumption below Rs. 150. The figure therefore is an underestimation of poverty.

6. Table 2.3 has been prepared by using the consumption expenditure data for nine categories from the bottom as per the NSS classification. The expenditure categories of Rs. 0–30, 30–40, 40–50 and 50–60 have been combined into one, i.e., Rs. 0–60, as these have very few observations.
7. Expenditure on fuel, light and such items used largely for the purpose of cooking, and on *pan*, tobacco and intoxicants, that are part of daily necessities for the poor, have been treated at par with food consumption which seems more appropriate than combining it with non-food expenditure as in the NSS.
8. The figures for total expenditure have also been revised by adding the incremental rental value.

References

Acharya, Sarathi and S.K. Trikha. (1978). *The City and its Poor—A Study of Bombay*. Tata Institute of Social Sciences, Bombay.

Asian Development Bank. (1983). *Regional Seminar on Financing of Low Income Housing, A Summary Report*, 7–12 February 1983, Manila.

Ahmad, A. (1982). *Saving Behaviour in a Metropolitan Economy*. Atlantic, New Delhi.

Bardhan, P.K. (1970). 'Green Revolution and Agricultural Labourers', *Economic and Political Weekly*, Special Number, July.

———. (1973). 'On the Incidence of Poverty in Rural India in the Sixties'. *Economic and Political Weekly*, Annual Number, February.

Bombay Metropolitan Regional Development Authority (1981). 'Non-Conventional and Alternative Approaches to Shelter for the Urban Poor-Experience in Bombay', theme paper presented at the MHADA Seminar, 7 January, Maharashtra Housing and Area Development Authority, Bombay.

Dandekar, V.M. and N. Rath. (1971). *Poverty in India*. Indian School of Political Economy, Bombay.

Dutta, B. (1980). 'Inter-Sectoral Disparities and Income Distribution in India, 1960–61 to 1973–74', *Indian Economic Review*, 15(2).

Foundation for Co-operative Housing. (1972). *Co-operative Housing and the Minimum Shelter Approach in Latin America*. United States Agency for International Development.

Jagannath, Vijay N. and Animesh Halder. (1988). 'Income-Housing Linkages: A Case Study of Pavement Dwellers in Calcutta', *Economic and Political Weekly*, 23(23).

Kanhert, Fredrich. (1986). 'Re-examining Urban Poverty and Employment', *Finance and Development*, 23(1).

Kansal, S.M. (1988). 'Measurement of Poverty in India—An Evaluation', paper presented at the Second Seminar on Social Statistics, 4–6 February, Central Statistical Organisation, New Delhi.

Lall, Vinay. (1986). 'Family Budgets and Savings of Informal Sector Households', paper presented at the International Workshop on Mobilisation of Informal Sector Savings, 8–12 December, Society for Development Studies, New Delhi.

Lall, Vinay. (1990). *Saving Mobilisation—Methods, Norms and Policies.* Society for Development Studies, New Delhi.

Lee, Michael. (1986). 'The Mobilisation of Informal Sector Savings: The USAID Experience', paper presented at the International Workshop on Mobilisation of Informal Sector Savings, 8–12 December, Society for Development Studies, New Delhi.

Madras Metropolitan Development Authority. (1980). *Structure Plan for Madras Metropolitan Area.* Vol. 1. Madras Metropolitan Development Authority, Madras.

Malpezzi, Sephan, Stephen Mayo and **David Gross.** (1985). *Housing Demand in Developing Countries,* World Bank Staff Working Papers No. 733. World Bank, Washington.

Mehta, Meera and **Dinesh Mehta.** (1992). *Metropolitan Housing Market: A Study of Ahmedabad.* Sage Publications, New Delhi.

Minhas, B.S. (1970). 'Rural Poverty, Land Redistribution and Development Strategy'. *Indian Economic Review,* 5 (New Series).

Minhas, B.S. (1988). 'Validation of Large Scale Sample Survey Data—Case of NSS Estimates of Household Consumption Expenditure', *Sankhya,* Series of Volume 50, Part 3 Supplement.

Minhas, B.S., L.R. Jain, S.M. Kansal and **M.R. Saluja.** (1987a). 'On the Choice of Appropriate Consumer Price Indices and Data Sets for Estimating the Incidence of Poverty in India', *Indian Economic Review,* 22(1).

———. (1987b). 'Measurement of General Cost of Living for Urban India: All India and Different States', paper presented at the General Conference of the Indian Association for Research in National Income and Wealth, Madras, November.

Minhas, B.S., L.R. Jain, and **S.D. Tendulkar.** (1991). 'Declining Incidence of Poverty in the 1980s: Evidence versus Artifacts', *Economic and Political Weekly,* 26(27 & 28).

Mulk Raj. (1986). 'Unorganised Sector Savings and the Role of Motivation through Housing', paper presented at the International Workshop on Motivation of Informal Sector Savings, 8–12 December, Society for Development Studies, New Delhi.

National Centre for Human Settlements and Environment. (1987). *A Study for the Formulation of Poverty Alleviation Programme for Urban Slums.* National Centre for Human Settlements and Environment, Bhopal.

National Council of Applied Economic Research. (1980). *Household Income and its Disposition.* National Council of Applied Economic Research, New Delhi.

National Institute of Urban Affairs. (1988). *Who the Poor Are? What they Do? Where they Live?* National Institute of Urban Affairs, New Delhi.

National Sample Survey Organisation. (1986). *Sarvekshana,* 9(4). Ministry of Planning, Government of India, New Delhi.

———. (1987). *Tables with Notes on Particulars of Dwelling Units* (38th Round). Department of Statistics, Government of India, New Delhi.

———. (1989). *Sarvekshana,* 38(1). Ministry of Planning, Government of India, New Delhi.

Operations Research Group. (1980). *Economic Profile of Madras, Metropolitan Area.* Vol. 1. Operations Research Group, New Delhi.

Planning Commission. (1985). *The Seventh Five Year Plan*, Vol. 1. Planning Commission, Government of India, New Delhi.

Prakasa Rao, V.L. and **V.K. Tewari.** (1979). *The Structure of an Indian Metropolis—A Study of Bangalore.* Allied, New Delhi.

Radhakrishna, R., S. Sudhakar Reddy and **Gautam Kumar Mitra.** (1988). *Determinants of Labour Force Participation and Living Standards.* Centre for Economic and Social Studies, Hyderabad.

Reserve Bank of India. (1987). *All India Debt and Investment Survey, 1981–82—Assets and Liabilities of Households as on 30th June, 1981.* Reserve Bank of India, New Delhi.

Rudra, A. (1974). 'Minimum Level of Living: A Statistical Examination', *Sankhya*, Series C, 36 (2 & 4).

Struyk, Raymond J. and **Margery Austin Turner.** (1986). *Finance and Housing Quality in Two Developing Countries—Korea and Philippines.* The Urban Institute Press and University Press of America.

United Nations. (1978). *Non-Conventional Financing of Housing for Low Income Households.* Department of International Economic and Social Affairs, New York.

Vaidya, Chetan and **K. Mukundan.** (1987). *Study on Home Improvement Loan Scheme—Madras Slum Improvement Programme.* Operations Research Group, Madras.

3

Management and Financing of Housing and Basic Amenities

Overview of the Macro-Level Scenario

The provision of housing and basic amenities to the growing population in towns and cities, especially to the poor, poses a major problem of urbanisation in the developing countries. In India, which figures in the middle rung of the hierarchy of low income countries,[1] the problem is quite serious. This is because the urban population has grown at a much faster rate than that of workers in the manufacturing sector or the national income. Even during the 1980s, when the growth rate of the urban population declined significantly, it was less than that of the economy in real terms.

The National Building Organisation (NBO 1984) had estimated the housing shortage in the country to be about 21.3 million dwelling units[2] in 1981, 16.5 million in rural and 4.8 million in urban areas. The seventh Five-Year Plan (1985–90) projected the shortage to be about 24.7 million (18.8 million in rural and 5.9 million in urban areas) at the beginning of the Plan period. Using specific normative standards, certain research organisations have placed the housing shortage much higher than the NBO estimate. The Birla Institute of Scientific Research (BISR), New Delhi, computed the total housing shortage in 1981 at 126.4 million,[3] 104.3 million in rural and 22.1 million in urban areas. The Indian Institute of Management, Ahmedabad (IIMA), also estimated the housing shortage to be significantly higher than that of NBO. The first estimate was a shortage of 39.4 million, 32.8 million in rural and 6.6 million in urban areas. According to an alternate set of assumptions by the IIMA, the shortage works out to be still higher—75.3 million dwelling units, 60 million in the rural and

15.3 million in the urban areas.[4] Some Western scholars have, however, questioned these normative approaches for estimating housing shortage. They have advocated the inclusion of all types of constructions for residential purposes as part of the national housing stock and work out housing deficits based on demand and afford- ability (Lee 1986). This change, from a supply-based to a demand- based approach towards estimating housing deficit, is likely to affect the organisational structure catering to housing activities in urban areas, especially for the urban poor.

Different estimates are available with regard to the population not covered by the water supply and sewerage system in the country. The National Institute of Urban Affairs (NIUA) had estimated the population without potable water and sewerage facilities in the year 1977–78 to be 25 per cent and 31 per cent, respectively. At the time the decadal programme for water supply and sanitation was launched in 1981, the Central Public Health and Environmental Engineering Organisation (CPHEEO 1983) had estimated those not covered by a safe drinking water system in the country at 395 million, or 57.1 per cent of the total population. The figure was 33 million in urban areas, i.e., about 20 per cent of the urban population. For sanitation facilities, the population not adequately covered in urban centres was much higher than the figure for water supply namely, 108 million or 73 per cent of the urban population. The Report of the National Commission on Urbanisation (NCU 1988) noted that the total supply of water in the urban areas was 9,500 million cubic metres per day. Taking the urban population estimate of 1988 to be 200 million and using the size class distribution of 1981, the NCU had computed the average consumption of water to be 145 litres per capita per day (lpcd) in Class I cities and 100 lpcd in other urban centres. These figures compare poorly with the per capita norm of 300 litres per day as recommended by planners.

Based on the conservative estimates of uncovered population given by the NIUA study, the Task Forces on Urban Development set up by the Planning Commission (1983) had worked out an investment figure of Rs. 8,000 crores at 1980–81 prices for the Seventh Plan period to provide the basic minimum services to the incremental urban population and clear a part of the backlog of uncovered population. The provision of affordability was, in a way, built into the cost estimates as no improvement was visualised in the plight of the 'people already covered', irrespective of the level and quality of services. The NCU had proposed doubling the proportion of plan expenditure for urban development and recommended a figure between Rs. 3,000 to Rs. 3,500 crores per year (the base year for the calculated amount is not known). Considering the inflation rate during the period 1980 to 1987 (NCU figures are assumed to be at 1986 or 1987 prices), the figure given by the NCU may not be very much higher than the estimate of the Task Forces. The Commission, however, feels that the amount is not adequate to provide basic urban services at a reasonable level, particularly to the urban poor. Based on the existing level of per capita consumption of water and the growth of urban population by .70 per cent by the year 2001, the NCU had worked out the total investment required for water supply to be around Rs. 15,000 crores per annum. Although this estimate was on the lower side, the Seventh Plan outlay for both water supply and sewerage in urban areas was only Rs. 2,935.64 crores. Thus, it is unlikely that the investment required to cover the total urban population with a reasonable level of services will be available in the near future.

In view of the inadequacy of resources available for urban development in the Five-Year Plans, the Task Forces on Urban Development, the NCU and several high-level committees have proposed strengthening the local bodies and augmenting their internal resources so that they themselves can meet a substantial portion of the required current and capital expenditures. The need for decentralisation is being emphasised by planners, policy-makers and administrators in the country. Further, several legislative and constitutional amendments are being proposed to allow the local bodies to function more effectively and generate more resources by augmenting their tax base or tapping sources other than taxation. However, the weak economic base of the cities and towns, particularly of the small and medium towns, difficulties in reforming the legal structure within a short time, and the lack of political will are likely to come in the way of generating resources at the local level. The possibility of the municipal bodies obtaining funds from commercial banks does not seem to be very promising in view of the cost of borrowing and various administrative and legal barriers. All this makes the provision of housing and basic services to the growing urban population a complex and challenging problem.

During the preceding decades of planned development, a complex, hierarchical organisational structure has been created through the initiative of the central, state and local governments to provide housing and other basic amenities to the urban population, partially outside the market mechanism. It has, however, been observed that despite the professed objectives and policy statements with regard to the accessibility of those in the lower income brackets to these amenities, large sections amongst them have to do without. Several micro-level studies suggest that the percentage of population denied these amenities has not declined over the past ten years. Bureaucratic delays, mismanagement, deficiencies in the distributional network are often noted as factors responsible for the benefits not reaching the targeted sections of the population. The demands for cost recovery, hikes in user charges, and so forth, being made on the concerned organisations in recent years, particularly because of the resource crunch in the economy, might lead to the adoption of solutions that could price the poor out of the delivery systems. It is against this background that an attempt has been made here to provide an overview of the organisational structure created for the provision of basic urban services, focusing on public sector institutions. The main purpose is to assess the accessibility of the poor in urban areas to the existing organisational system.

This chapter is divided into five sections. The next section, appearing after this introductory one, considers the role of different agencies responsible for housing activities in the urban areas and the interdependence between them. Keeping the focus on public sector agencies, the discussion also covers the institutions providing finance to the housing sector. The third section relates to the functioning of the agencies involved in the investment, maintenance and financing of water supply, sewerage and sanitation facilities. The fourth section looks at the role of central and state government agencies in the health delivery system in urban areas. The system of medical reimbursement, specifically for the employees of central and state governments and public sector undertakings, has also been discussed. The public distribution system, specifically for foodgrains, is presented in the fifth section.

Housing Scenario

Housing in urban areas is primarily the responsibility of individual residents, about 90 per cent of the investment and 70 per cent of the supply of housing units being in the private sector (USAID 1989). Small-scale private development is the dominant mode of house construction in the formal residential colonies, particularly in small and medium towns. Here, the responsibility for land development, planning, designing and house construction is that of the individual concerned, who usually undertakes this by employing the services of an engineer, architect or contractor. The responsibility of arranging finance[5] and purchasing land rests with the individual. Besides this formal sector housing, various informal (and sometimes illegal) methods of land acquisition and house building are resorted to, particularly in the slums and squatter settlements, in order to acquire a shelter. An estimated 30 to 40 million, that is, 20 to 26 per cent of the urban population lived in such settlements in 1981.[6] These shelter units are generally sub-standard, unhygienic and uninhabitable. One-third of the units added to the housing stock every year belong to this category and together they account for more than 50 per cent of the dwelling units in urban areas. This phenomenon is quite common in large cities. Apart from this, private developers undertake group housing schemes, generally in large cities. They take upon themselves the responsibility of land acquisition, development and house construction, besides helping the clients obtain long-term loans. There are also primary housing cooperative societies that take up similar housing projects for their members. These societies obtain assistance from various public agencies, specifically for land acquisition and finance, unlike the private developers. Finally, there are public sector organisations such as the housing boards, development authorities and city improvement trusts which are responsible for acquisition and development of land, planning and house construction, and the arrangement of long-term finance. The functioning of these public organisations has been analysed in some detail in the following pages.

Central Government Agencies

The Ministry of Urban Development (MOUD) at the centre is the apex policy-making body for urban development, including housing activities. It oversees the state-level programmes, lays down policy perspectives and builds up data systems for the country, besides launching projects for the benefit of certain targeted sections of the population.

The central government has a small share of direct responsibility in the housing sector. Through its Public Works Department, it undertakes housing schemes for its employees in all the union territories. Other central ministries and establishments, for instance, the Railways, Post and Telegraph Services, Port Trust Authorities, Radio and Telecommunications, Defence Services, the Reserve Bank of India, and public sector undertakings such as commercial banks and the Life Insurance Corporation (LIC), also construct houses and create housing estates for their employees in different cities.

Agencies at the State Level

Public sector housing is basically the responsibility of the state governments, which they undertake primarily through their housing boards. In Maharashtra, the Maharashtra Housing and Area Development Authority (MHADA) functions like a state-level housing board and has five Regional Housing and Area Development Boards. However, unlike in other states, there is another state-level agency, the City Industrial Development Corporation (CIDCO), which is the development authority for new towns and industrial estates, and which takes up housing projects as one of its major activities (Verma 1985). In Orissa, besides the state housing board, there are six Regional Improvement Trusts that undertake this responsibility. In the smaller states of north east India, housing activity is the responsibility of the government departments. The Works and Housing Department of the Government of Nagaland, the Local Administration Department in Mizoram, the Planning and Development Authority in Manipur and the Housing and Urban Development Unit of the Public Works Department in Arunachal Pradesh are the departments connected with this activity in the respective states. Apart from the housing boards, the Estate Department in Punjab undertakes housing projects. Special agencies, namely, Slum Clearance Boards, have been set up in several states such as Gujarat, Karnataka, Madhya Pradesh and Tamil Nadu for the purpose of rehabilitating slum dwellers. In some large cities, the slum wings of development authorities undertake this responsibility, for instance, the Slum Wing of the Delhi Development Authority (DDA), (currently with the DMC), and the *Bustee*

Unnayan wing of the Calcutta Metropolitan Development Authority (CMDA). In many other cities such as Bombay, Calcutta, Ahmedabad and Hyderabad, the municipal corporations have slum wings that take up housing schemes for the poor. However, with the shift in emphasis during the mid-1960s from slum clearance to slum upgradation, these boards and slum wings are only taking up schemes to improve the living environment or the quality of basic services in slums and other low income colonies. In addition to these, some states have created special organisations to provide housing to the economically and socially weaker sections of the population. In Andhra Pradesh, for example, the State Housing Corporation undertakes housing schemes for the weaker sections. In Kerala, there are several state-level housing agencies for various economically vulnerable sections of the population. These are the Kerala State Development Corporation for Scheduled Castes and Tribes, Kerala School Teachers and Non-teaching Staff Welfare Corporation Limited, and the Kerala State Development Corporation for Christian Converts from Scheduled Castes and Recommended Communities Limited.

A few other state-level agencies have been created to take up housing schemes for specific occupational groups. For example, housing corporations have been established for the employees of the Police Department in the states of Andhra Pradesh, Madhya Pradesh, Tamil Nadu, Punjab, Gujarat and Maharashtra. The Andhra Pradesh Health and Medical Housing Infrastructure Development Corporation and the Tamil Nadu Handloom Weavers' Cooperative Society Limited are examples. Besides these, the state governments themselves take up housing schemes for their employees through their Public Works Departments (PWDs). Some of the state public sector undertakings such as the State Electricity Boards and the State Transport Corporation construct houses for their employees. Finally, the state-level Industrial Development Corporations undertake housing projects for industrial workers, both in the public sector and for private companies.

City-Level Agencies

At the city level, apart from the State Housing Boards, development authorities take the major responsibility of designing and executing housing programmes. In some cities, for instance in

Rajasthan and Punjab, improvement trusts undertake this responsibility more or less like a development authority. In states such as Gujarat and Madhya Pradesh, a few large Municipal Corporations also undertake housing projects. In new towns and townships, various agencies have been created to take up housing programmes, for example, the Notified Area Committee (Rourkela) and the Special Area Development Authority (Korba). Union territories comprising one city only, like Chandigarh and Pondicherry, have housing boards whereas in Dadra and Nagar Haveli and Andaman and Nicobar Islands, housing has been left to cooperative housing societies. In towns and townships attached to large public sector projects like those of the Steel Authority of India Limited (SAIL), Bharat Heavy Electricals Limited (BHEL) and similar other organisations, residential colonies for employees are created by these public sector authorities themselves. Similar provision for housing has also been made by a few large private companies such as the Tatas, Birlas and Modis.

Primary Cooperative Societies

The role of primary cooperative societies in providing housing has been increasing over the years, particularly in large cities. Although public agencies at the central, state and city levels have been undertaking housing schemes, they have at the same time been encouraging cooperative housing activities. In recent years, it has become difficult to acquire land or finance through individual effort. Cooperatives get preferential treatment in obtaining land and finance from public sector agencies, particularly in cities where the development authority enjoys considerable control over land (as in Delhi). A certain minimum number of persons, as stipulated in the cooperative Housing Society Act of the state or union territories,[7] can form a cooperative and register it at the office of the Registrar of Cooperative Societies. Of late, these societies have been obliged to procure land on their own.

There are mainly two types of cooperative housing societies. The first is the individual ownership type where each member becomes the owner of the plot and the dwelling unit once the loan is repaid. The purpose of forming such a cooperative is to avail of housing loans, and building materials at concessional rates. However, such cooperative societies are no longer being registered. The second type, the co-ownership or tenant co-partnership societies are quite common today. Here, the members are joint owners of the land as well as the buildings. The members reside as tenants of the society and consequently no member can sell his or her plot individually. Initially, 25 to 40 per cent of the total cost is collected from the members as share capital while the remaining amount is raised through loans.

Construction Agencies

The above organisations and government departments with their overlapping jurisdictions are responsible for planning, procuring funds and designing housing projects in the urban areas. It is important to note that they usually do not undertake actual construction activities. In most instances, this work is contracted out to private firms, although there are a few housing boards that take up construction work through their own engineering wings. The Central Public Works Department (CPWD), which is a government department, undertakes construction activity for the central government and other central establishments. The National Building Construction Company (NBCC) is the only public sector company at the central level that takes up construction jobs for housing boards, cooperative societies, and so on. Finally, there are state-level construction corporations, such as the Uttar Pradesh Construction Corporation, which also take up housing projects, besides other construction work.

Housing Finance

Housing was an important governmental activity in the 1950s, claiming about 4 per cent of the total planned investment in the public sector and about 30 per cent of the total investment in housing. Massive projects were launched, both in the central and the state sectors, to rehabilitate the refugee population and provide shelter to the growing industrial labour force in the urban areas.[8] The schemes were funded largely through central funds, although these were implemented through state government departments and improvement trusts that were then in existence. As government funds were inadequate to meet the housing shortage in the country and various competing demands were made by other 'productive' sectors, the need to promote house construction in the private sector was recognised, particularly in the large urban centres. This led to the setting up of special financial institutions to support projects in housing and urban development in both public and private sectors during the 1960s and 1970s. The activities of the government relating to housing finance gained momentum in the 1980s, resulting in the multiplication of such institutions.

The Ministry of Finance, Government of India, through its policy of directed credit, has tried to increase the funds available to the housing sector. Public sector financial institutions have been instructed by the Ministry to allocate a part of their resources for housing. For example, the Life Insurance Corporation (LIC), the prime and the single largest lending institution for housing activity, has been directed to allocate 25 per cent of its annual accretions to housing, water supply, sewerage and other social sectors through loans to the Housing and Urban Development Corporation (HUDCO), National Housing Bank, housing finance institutions and others.[9]

These are three types of formal organisations which provide finance for housing activities: (*a*) institutions set up specifically for housing finance such as HUDCO and the National Housing Bank (NHB) which support group housing and plotted development programmes by giving loans to such agencies as housing boards, development authorities, as also the apex cooperative housing finance societies, which, in turn, lend to primary cooperative societies; (*b*) public sector financial institutions catering to housing as also other sectors, such as the nationalised commercial banks and the LIC; and (*c*) private sector institutions (supported by public agencies) like the Housing Development Finance Corporation (HDFC) that provide funds to individuals as well as to groups of individuals.

HUDCO, NHB and State-Level Housing Finance Agencies

Housing and Urban Development Corporation (HUDCO)

HUDCO, which was set up in 1970, provides loans for housing and other urban development projects such as land acquisition, basic sanitation and infrastructure development. Apart from an initial grant from the central government, it has been receiving funds at concessional rates from various public sector financial institutions such as the General Insurance Corporation (GIC), the National

Housing Bank (NHB), LIC (currently discontinued), the Unit Trust of India (UTI) and commercial banks, as also from certain international financial institutions such as the ODA (UK), KfW (Germany) and World Bank. HUDCO initially concentrated its efforts on the house construction programmes of public housing agencies but subsequently shifted its thrust to the provision of serviced plots and environmental improvement of slums in large cities. It has also initiated programmes to finance land and infrastructural development by local authorities, and at the same time provided funds to the primary cooperative housing societies through their apex bodies at the state level. It also had a scheme of financing private developers which was recently discontinued. At present, HUDCO's thrust is on (a) self-financing schemes in which the funds of public agencies are not tied up for long; and (b) cooperative housing schemes for which individual savings can be mobilised.

The rate of interest, period of repayment and amount of loan advanced by HUDCO vary from scheme to scheme, depending on the income levels of the beneficiaries. While for low income schemes, loans are given at an interest rate of 8 per cent to be repaid in twenty-two years, for commercial schemes the interest rate is 16 per cent with loan repayment in ten years.

In order to avail itself of a HUDCO loan, a housing agency must submit its scheme along with cost break-ups of land acquisition, development, construction and administration. Loans are sanctioned by HUDCO after a scrutiny of the architectural, engineering and legal aspects of the scheme, along with its cost details. The percentage of project cost sanctioned as loan by HUDCO varies from scheme to scheme and the balance must be raised by the housing agency.

A person can, on payment of a fee, register with a housing agency under a scheme that suits his/her income. Housing plots/units are allotted to beneficiaries either on a draw system or on a first-cum-first-served basis. Housing agencies initially went in for hire-purchase housing schemes under which the beneficiary pays only a fraction of the total price at the time of occupation. The balance is paid in instalments over a specified time period during which the beneficiary mortgages the plot or dwelling unit to the housing agency. After full repayment of the loan, the title deed of the plot or/and unit is transferred to the beneficiary, usually on a leasehold basis. This system was conceived to provide economically weaker sections access to housing as they could start living in their houses without making the full payment and thereby saving on rent. Recently, the thrust of housing agencies has shifted to self-financing schemes where the beneficiaries are required to pay the full price of the units before or at the time of occupation. This change has come about because the hire-purchase system was blocking the resources for a long time and the recovery rate under it was poor. These have become the major bottlenecks in the expansion of housing activities. It is, however, observed that such self-financing schemes have largely benefited people in higher income groups.

National Housing Bank

The establishment of the National Housing Bank (NHB) as an apex institution in 1988 with developmental, financial and regulatory functions is a reflection of the changing policy perspective in the housing scene. It is being argued that the government departments or the public agencies in housing (or in several other development sectors) should be reoriented to work as promoters and facilitators rather than as builders of housing units (see Ministry of Urban Development 1988; NHB 1989). Thus, the NHB is expected to facilitate housing activities by providing short-term loans to housing agencies for 'development and supply of land' and long-term loans to individuals for 'buying a developed plot and undertaking house construction'. It also provides equity support and refinancing facility to public and private housing companies.

As envisaged by the NHB, an individual is required to open a savings account, the home loan account (HLA), with any designated scheduled bank which would take the responsibility of dealing with him or her on its behalf. This would make the person eligible for a housing loan after three years. Savings, thus mobilised, are transferred to the NHB, which the latter would use for advancing loans to public housing agencies, to industries manufacturing building materials and, indirectly, to individuals. Consequently, such individuals can purchase a house or a developed plot from the public housing agencies on cash-down payment. This would enable the agencies to repay the loans to the NHB once the scheme is completed and housing units/plots handed over to the beneficiaries. Over and above advancing loans to individuals and the public housing agencies, the scheduled banks would be free to give short-term loans to industries associated with housing, particularly those engaged in the production of building materials, during the first three years

Individual loans are given by the commercial banks under the NHB's stipulations for a maximum period of fifteen years at rates of interest depending on the loan amounts. The rates vary from a minimum of 10.5 per cent to a maximum of 14.5 per cent. The rate of interest to the public agencies would vary from 13 per cent to 15 per cent with a higher rate for time and cost overruns.

The NHB would give preference to agencies undertaking housing projects in rural areas and small and medium towns. The public agencies would be required to formulate projects by earmarking at least 50 per cent of the land to be developed and 75 per cent of the plots, for smaller plots, viz., less than or equal to 60 sq.m. They are also required to reserve at least 75 per cent of the built-up accommodation for housing units with an area of less than or equal to 40 sq.m. The maximum plot size and built-up accommodation permitted are 200 sq.m. and 120 sq.m., respectively. The housing agencies would give preference to the home loan account holders in the allotment of units/plots. Account holders can borrow from the NHB even when they are not registered with any public agency under a housing scheme.

The NHB is raising its resources from already existing financial institutions such as Life Insurance Corporation(LIC), commercial banks (through SLR bonds), from international agencies such as the World Bank, US capital market, apart from the seed capital of Rs. 150 crores contributed by the Reserve Bank of India. The one time scheme of attracting deposits from non-resident Indians and people with black money has also contributed modestly to its resources.

Apex Cooperative Housing Finance Society

Most of the states and union territories have an apex cooperative housing finance society: for example, the Bihar State Housing Cooperative Federation Limited, the Madhya Pradesh State Cooperative Housing Federation Limited, the Maharashtra State Cooperative Housing Finance Corporation Limited, the Gujarat

State Cooperative Housing Finance Limited, and the Delhi Co-operative Housing Finance Society Limited. These institutions finance the primary cooperative societies within their jurisdiction against the first mortgage document of land and the constructed unit. The prerequisite for obtaining loans from any apex cooperative housing finance society is, therefore, the possession of land. It is, however, not mandatory for the primary cooperative society to approach any apex cooperative housing finance society for funds. The former can also approach private sector financial institutions such as the HDFC, the concerned employing organisation, or HUDCO for housing loans. When a primary cooperative society borrows from a public sector institution such as HUDCO, the loan amount is channelised through the apex cooperative housing finance society, which stands as a guarantor. The first mortgage documents in that case also lie with the apex cooperative society.

Other Public Sector Agencies Providing Housing Loans

Nationalised Commercial Banks

Nationalised commercial banks and cooperative banks give housing loans to individuals on terms fixed by the Reserve Bank of India (RBI). Prior to nationalisation, a negligible amount was disbursed by these banks to the housing sector, although they were not prohibited from doing so. After nationalisation, a savings-linked housing loan scheme was introduced but did not make much impact on the aggregate disbursement to the housing sector. This scheme remained basically a deposit scheme owing to the difficulties in advancing loans against the mortgage of immovable property. It was extremely difficult for banks to realise the loan amounts in case of default. In 1978, an attempt was made by the RBI to increase the housing loan disbursed through commercial banks by acting upon the recommendations of a Working Group set up for this purpose.[10] However, the allocation of finance to the housing sector did not exceed 0.26 per cent in 1985, 0.28 per cent in 1986 and 0.26 per cent in 1987 (of their total allocation) against the Working Group's projection of 0.50 per cent.

The role of commercial banks in housing finance is expected to increase with the adoption of the policy of establishing housing subsidiaries by several banks. Some of the banks have already been permitted by the government to establish their subsidiaries. The Housing Promotion Finance Corporation Private Ltd., a subsidiary of the State Bank of India (SBI), has equity participation of SBI, HDFC and other institutions such as the LIC and GIC. Their operations are in east and north-east India. Can-Fin Homes Ltd. is a subsidiary of the Canara Bank and has equity participation from Can Bank Financial Services, HDFC and UTI, besides its parent bank. This would contribute to housing finance in the union territory of Delhi and in south India. Finally, the Punjab National Bank is expected to confine its operations to north India. It may be mentioned that with the establishment of the NHB, the participation of other commercial banks in the field of housing finance is likely to increase.

Life Insurance Corporation

The Life Insurance Corporation, apart from providing finance to the housing boards, NHB, HUDCO and housing subsidiaries of the banks, also provides loans to individuals under its Own Your Home Scheme. While its interest rate for housing agencies varies between 7.5 per cent and 12.0 per cent, individuals get loans at a rate of 12 per cent and above. A new scheme, *Bima Niwas Yojana*, has recently been introduced for purchasing houses in the four largest metropolitan cities of Delhi, Bombay, Calcutta and Madras.

Private Housing Finance Institutions

The Housing Development Finance Corporation (HDFC) was set up in 1976 to channelise household savings as well as funds from the capital market into the housing sector. The HDFC has spread its activities through its eighteen branches in the states of Gujarat, Maharashtra, Tamil Nadu, Andhra Pradesh, Rajasthan and Uttar Pradesh and the union territories of Delhi and Chandigarh. It is expected to promote ownership housing in the urban areas through retail lending. Of late, the HDFC has been actively involved in promoting new institutions for housing finance, namely, the Gujarat Rural Housing Finance Corporation Limited (with support from the International Finance Corporation, Washington, the Aga Khan Fund for Economic Development, Geneva, and the Government of Gujarat), Housing Promotion and Finance Corporation

Limited (with the help of the State Bank of India and capital markets), Infrastructure Leasing and Financial Services Limited (with the Central Bank of India and UTI) and Can-Fin Homes Limited (with Canara Bank and UTI). In the case of the latter three institutions, the HDFC holds 20 per cent of their shares.

It is important to note that 57 per cent of HDFC funds on 30 June 1988 came from the deposits made by households. The figure was 60 per cent on 30 June 1987. These savings are mobilised through different deposit schemes, namely, the Loan Linked Deposit Scheme, Certificate of Deposit Scheme, Cumulative Interest Scheme and Home Savings Plan. The HDFC, like HUDCO, borrows from other financial institutions as well. However, unlike HUDCO, a part of its resources comes from the capital market through the issue of bonds and shares.

The HDFC has disbursed loans of about Rs. 1,000 crores for the construction of 2.5 lakh dwelling units (HDFC 1988). The average loan sanctioned per unit thus works out to a mere Rs. 40,000. Keeping in view the average income and the repayment capacity of the HDFC borrowers, it can be argued that the loan amount covers only a part of the total cost of land and construction.

The HDFC gives loans under various schemes to the individuals, associations of individuals, groups of individuals and individual members of cooperative societies. The rate of interest charged is related to the loan amount, which in turn is determined by the repayment capacity of the borrower. In determining this capacity, factors such as age, income, qualification, number of dependents, spouse's income, assets, liabilities, and the history of the stability and continuity of income and savings of the borrower are taken into consideration. The principle generally adopted is that the instalment should not exceed 30 per cent of the monthly income of the household. The borrower can choose the repayment period in the range of five to twenty years, not exceeding the time of his/her retirement. Besides, the HDFC operates the home loan account of the NHB.

It is important to note that HDFC finances the construction of new residential units by individuals whose immediate family members do not own any dwelling unit. The security, which is the first mortgage of the property to be financed, executed normally by way of deposit of the title deeds, is essential for the loan. In the case of property under construction, collateral or interim security is required which could be in terms of a bank guarantee, surrender of a Life Insurance Policy—the value of which is at least equal to the loan amount—guarantee from a sound and solvent guarantor, pledge of shares and such other investments acceptable to the HDFC. The title of the property should be clear, marketable and free from any encumbrance. The insistence on security for the loan has been the major hurdle in the way of low income households benefiting from the schemes.

Sensitivity of the System to the Poor

An overview of the organisational structure in the housing sector suggests that the primary concern has been augmentation of the total supply of land and dwelling units. It is true that the success of all the agencies in achieving even this limited objective has been extremely poor. However, a more important criticism would be that they have not taken into consideration the demand pattern and affordability of different sections of the population, particularly those in the lower income strata, in designing the housing projects. On the other hand, several of these agencies, by their very mandate and the financial and administrative stipulations guiding their activities, have explicitly excluded the poor. Although the central and state government departments and large public and private companies/corporations undertake housing for their employees, not many amongst them would figure below the poverty line. Similarly, the urban poor are unlikely to organise themselves into housing cooperatives and partake of the benefits extended to the cooperative sector. Further, the schemes launched by private entrepreneurs remain outside the reach of the urban poor. Hence, the only agencies that can be approached by the bottom 30 to 40 per cent of the population are those that belong to the public sector.

In the metropolitan and other large cities, municipal corporations and development authorities have slum wings as part of their organisations. Some states have Slum Clearance Boards at the state level which undertake shelter upgradation, environment improvement and house construction programmes exclusively for the urban poor. However, the funds available to these agencies have been meagre and their share in total investment in the housing sector has declined over the years. While no separate system of assessing the social benefits of the schemes for the poor has been designed so far, the demands of cost recovery and financial accountability have nevertheless been placed on them. Owing to the scarcity of funds and the incapacity of these agencies to build up revolving funds through financially feasible projects, the activities for the urban poor have been severely constrained in recent years.

The other public sector agencies such as the housing boards and development authorities have also been reorganising their modes of functioning to meet the criterion of financial efficiency. They are, thus, attempting to reduce their dependence on government grants (earlier available at nominal or no interest) and increase their shares of banking loans and internal savings. Still, they enjoy certain privileges, as a result of which they can provide subsidised plots or houses to their beneficiaries. All of them were established with lump-sum grants from the respective state governments. Grants were given also during the initial years and for some these are available even today. These are given primarily through ways-and-means loans (which are for meeting normal administrative expenses) that are often not repaid. In some instances, land has been made available to these agencies at prices below the market through the efforts of the state governments. But the motto of self-dependence is forcing many of them to either totally abandon or drastically reduce the schemes for the weaker sections in favour of more commercially viable schemes.

It can be observed that the dependence of all these public agencies on state funds has declined over the years. However, they obtain concessional finance from agencies such as the LIC, GIC, HUDCO, and now, commercial banks, according to government stipulations. The GIC provides housing loans at a 14 per cent rate of interest while the LIC rate varies between 7.5 and 12 per cent, depending on the purpose of the loan. The cheapest funds for housing the economically weaker sections come from HUDCO at an interest rate between 5 and 7 per cent. These three agencies also finance the apex cooperative housing finance societies which, in turn, pass on the funds to the primary cooperatives by charging 1 to 2 per cent more than their borrowing rate. The apex cooperatives are also allowed to raise their capital from the market through bonds at 11.5 per cent to 14 per cent rate of interest with government support. Their lending rates are, therefore, more than those of the LIC, GIC or HUDCO but less than the rates in the open market.

The most important reason why these agencies are able to supply land and housing at less than the prevailing market price is the increase in land value owing to massive government investment in infrastructure and basic services in the cities. The benefits thereof are reaped by the housing agencies and only a small fraction is claimed back by the government. In cases where they have been able to buy land at low prices under the Urban Land Ceiling Act or other acts, the benefits accrued work out to be much higher. This, however, has become increasingly difficult in recent years because of vested interests, interventions by the courts and indifference or lack of motivation among the concerned officials in public sector housing agencies.

It is, thus, evident that large subsidies have flowed into the housing sector over the past few decades. The most important question then is: What percentage of it has gone to households below the poverty line? It is difficult to answer this question because of non-availability of data on the real income of the beneficiaries, direct and indirect subsidy per dwelling unit and illegal transfer of properties. Nevertheless, a careful analysis of the functioning of these agencies and of the financial and administrative requirements to be met by the beneficiaries make it clear that in no way could these agencies reach a large number of the urban poor.

The most essential requirements—that of a permanent address and the necessity of a guarantor—become the major impediments in the way of the urban poor taking advantage of the formal housing schemes. The same is true for securing loans for housing as well. Besides the requirements of a permanent address and a guarantor, apex cooperative housing finance societies and the HDFC generally require (a) a clear and marketable title of land, (b) approval of building plans by the concerned local authority, and (c) contribution of a minimum of 25 per cent of the dwelling unit cost by the beneficiary before considering the loan application. However, for EWS (economically weaker sections) schemes financed by HUDCO, the requirements are less stringent and only 10 per cent of the total cost is required as initial contribution. It is well-known that the urban poor in general neither have legal ownership of land nor is it possible for them to get the approval of the local authority to build on the land occupied by them illegally. The poor can have access to shelter only if the land titles are given

to them at nominal rates through government intervention or if
dwelling units or plots are made available to them through public
agencies.

According to the revised ceiling cost of Rs. 22,000 prescribed by
HUDCO for the EWS units, the initial contribution amounts to
Rs. 2,500 only. But the monthly instalments, payable over a period
of twenty years,[11] work out to about Rs. 200. This amount is about
20 per cent of the income of households at the poverty line and
obviously more for those below the line. It is evident that both the
initial contribution and the monthly instalments are unaffordable
to the poor households because the assets owned by the bottom 32
per cent of the population, on average, are worth less than Rs. 1,000
and their monthly rents do not exceed Rs. 70 per month (RBI
1987). The cost of the dwelling units (and hence the initial contribution and monthly instalment) normally works out higher than that
mentioned because of the time taken in completing the elaborate
administrative procedures and the delays in construction. As a result,
the poor get priced out of even the most generous schemes, supposedly designed for them. It is observed that at the time of registration itself, households from the next higher income group apply for
the scheme. Even when the households from the targeted income
groups apply for it, they are pushed out of it through legal or
illegal transfers. The down payment and monthly instalment work
out to be much higher for schemes other than those of HUDCO.
Consequently, they are even more inaccessible to the poor.

Pattas or land rights have been given to slum dwellers by local
authorities and some state governments, often for political reasons.
Nonetheless, these have helped a small number of poor in getting
plots and housing loans. The benefits have mostly accrued to the
slum dwellers living on government and unobjectionable land only.
For the pavement dwellers, encroachers in parks and shopping complexes, and the slum dwellers occupying private lands and living in
highly dense shanties, finding land in the nearby areas has been
the major problem. The efforts at providing serviced land at great
distances from the city centre, as is the case under sites and
services schemes, have a low success rate. Physical proximity to
the sources of livelihood is essential for the economic survival of
the poor in the city. It is thus evident that the public sector housing
agencies have been able to reach only a small segment of the urban

poor owing to their very organisational set-up and methods of functioning. The liberalisation in the urban sector, including relaxations in administrative and legislative controls, will further weaken public control over land and restrict the capacity of government agencies to find land and shelter for the poor.

The recent attempts by the NHB to strengthen the capital market for housing, transform the public sector housing agencies into efficient production units while restricting their long-term lending activities, need to be reviewed in the context of the affordability of the poor. The NHB has abolished the income criterion for determining the loan size and the rate of interest and has linked them to the size of the plot. There is no *a priori* reason to assume that only people in lower income brackets would opt for smaller plots or smaller loans. Furthermore, under liberal market conditions, as envisaged by the NHB, it would be difficult to ensure that one household does not own more than one plot or house. The monthly instalments for a loan of say Rs. 18,000 (sanctioned by banks authorised by the NHB) would work out to be much higher than those for HUDCO loans owing to a higher interest rate of 13.5 per cent and a shorter recovery period. Also, the stipulation of a saving period of three years (of at least Rs. 30 a month) before the loan can be sanctioned does not reflect a recognition of the urgency of the housing needs of the poor.

Housing agencies, instead of borrowing from HUDCO, LIC or GIC, would be borrowing from the NHB at 13 to 15 per cent rate of interest. The period of their repayment has been drastically shortened. It would now generally be three to five years as compared to the long-term loans offered by HUDCO, LIC and GIC for a period of ten to fifteen years. Both these would increase the cost of the dwelling unit, taking it much beyond the affordability limit of the urban poor.

The NHB loan would be available for the purchase of a plot or a house from a private individual/company or a public agency. A clear title to the land is essential in the case of the former. In the case of the latter, it is proposed to do away with the lengthy land acquisition procedures so as to increase the supply of serviced plots. Both would imply the purchase of land from the market by the individual or the housing agency. Given the market price of a minimum plot size of 20 sq.m., ranging from Rs. 5,000 to 20,000 in the peripheries of the metropolitan and large cities[12] (the prices in the core area being much higher), the purchase of land by the urban poor would be out of the question. It is the public housing agency alone that can provide land to the poor, if it follows the policy of cross-subsidisation.

Sewerage and Sanitation Facilities

The responsibility of providing basic services such as water, sewerage, sanitation and solid waste disposal lies with the state governments which they fulfil through (a) their own departments, (b) state-level boards and corporations, (c) statutory and non-statutory bodies at the city level, and (d) local bodies. The central government, through its Ministry of Urban Development (until recently the Ministry of Works and Housing), overviews the developments in this sector, lays down policy perspectives for the country, builds up data systems, promotes research and initiates actions in key areas through centrally sponsored schemes. The Town and Country Planning Organisation (TCPO) and the Central Public Health and Environmental Engineering Organisation (CPHEEO) are the two technical wings of the Ministry. While the TCPO monitors and coordinates the implementation of some of the central government schemes such as Urban Basic Services (UBS), Environmental Improvement of Urban Slums (EIUS), Integrated Development of Small and Medium Towns (IDSMT), besides providing technical guidance to state-level planning and implementing agencies, the activities of the CPHEEO are restricted mainly to the provision of technical guidance.

Investments in Capital Works

Developmental and maintenance responsibilities for the provision of drinking water, sewerage, sanitation and solid waste disposal facilities have been separated and assigned to different agencies. Capital works in these sectors in most of the states are undertaken by the concerned state government departments such as the Public Health Engineering Department (PHED), the Public Works Department (PWD), the Urban Development Department, and the Department of Local Self-Government, through their divisional and district offices. Alternatively, some states (about eleven) have set up Water Supply and Sewerage Boards and much of the responsibility for building up capital assets has been transferred to them. This holds true for the states of Karnataka, Maharashtra, Kerala, Punjab and Uttar Pradesh, among others. These boards sometimes take up development projects on their own but mostly on behalf of the state governments, the local bodies, slum boards, universities, and, at times, private organisations. In states such as Tamil Nadu, the Directorate of Municipal Administration also takes up certain water supply projects, although the basic responsibility lies with the state-level board. Besides these, housing boards as well as some large municipal bodies make investments in these services within their project area or jurisdiction. Finally, several large public as well as private sector undertakings and agencies (including the Railways) build water supply and drainage systems within their townships or localities as in Rourkela, Bhilai, Jamshedpur and Modinagar. As a rule, they also maintain the facilities.

This organisational structure takes care of the capital works in the concerned sectors in most of the towns and cities, barring a few metropolitan cities. In the metropolises of Delhi, Bombay and Ahmedabad, the local bodies are financially strong and the capital projects are often designed and implemented by the local bodies or their subsidiaries with the approval of their state governments.[13] Bangalore and Madras have separate Metropolitan Water Supply Boards, with a structure and functions similar to those of the state-level boards discussed earlier. The only difference here is that these boards construct as well as maintain the facilities and thus serve the consumers directly, a role which is generally played by the municipal bodies in other cities.

Besides the municipal corporations and metro-level water boards, urban development authorities also invest in water supply, sewerage and sanitation facilities. In several cities both local bodies and development authorities undertake capital projects. Within the Calcutta Metropolitan Area (CMA), the Calcutta Metropolitan Development Authority (CMDA), Calcutta Metropolitan Water and Sanitation Authority (CMWSA), Calcutta Improvement Trust (CIT), etc., take up capital projects besides the concerned municipal bodies, the housing board and state government departments such as the PWD, the Irrigation Department and the Waterways Department. Thus, unlike the city-level boards of Bangalore and

Madras, the CMWSA is not the only agency responsible for capital projects. Under the Calcutta Urban Development Project—III (CUDP—III), a two-tier organisational structure has emerged wherein the CMDA acts as the coordinating, evaluating and monitoring agency, while the CMWSA, CIT, Howrah Improvement Trust (HIT), Calcutta Municipal Corporation (CMC), Howrah Municipal Corporation and other local bodies take up the responsibility of executing the projects. Most of the local bodies, because of the inadequacy of managerial and technical staff, are assisted by the CMDA and other state government departments in discharging their functions.

In the metropolitan cities of Kanpur, Lucknow, Pune and Nagpur, state-level water boards are responsible for capital works. In the city of Hyderabad the responsibility lies with the Hyderabad Metro Water Works whereas in Jaipur it rests with the PHED. In most of the states, the PHED is responsible for capital expenditure only in smaller cities and towns.

In the states where capital investment in water supply, sewerage and sanitation is the direct responsibility of the state government, funds are made available in the state plans and budgets. In others, where there are state-level boards, state projects and central-level projects are executed through the boards.[14] Provision of funds is made in the central and/or state budget for the loans and grants for the project.

In projects undertaken by the boards on behalf of municipal bodies, the responsibility of arranging funds is that of the latter and these are normally financed through a combination of loans and grants. The loans are generally obtained from the LIC while the grants come from the state governments.[15] It is important to note that the local bodies do not have direct access to LIC funds. The boards draw the loans on a state government guarantee, although the responsibility of repayment lies with the local bodies. The loans from the state government to the local bodies are also routed through the board but here the repayment of the principal amount takes places via the boards while the interest is often paid directly to the state government. HUDCO also provides funds for infrastructural schemes, such as water supply and sanitation projects, to municipalities, corporations and other government bodies in towns with a population not exceeding 10 lakhs as per the 1981 Census. HUDCO finances up to 50 per cent of the project cost while the balance is to be met by the state government or the borrowing agency. The loan is to be repaid within twelve years with an interest of 10.25 per cent per year. For several municipalities, public contribution constitutes a portion of the total funds.[16] The loan/grant combination varies with the status of the local body, the grant amount being higher in the case of a smaller municipality. In some states like Gujarat, for instance, these grants-in-aid are made available to the local bodies on an 'as and when' basis depending upon the availability of funds under the state plan. In many states, however, water supply projects for towns with a population less than 20,000 are financed entirely through state government grants-in-aid.

The boards are also called upon to take on the responsibility of construction and maintenance by private companies or universities, but the latter arrange for funds mostly on their own without borrowing from either the government or other agencies. Sometimes slum boards or municipalities meet the entire project cost out of their own resources and ask the boards to undertake the projects on their behalf. In such cases, the former deposit the required funds with the water boards. The latter in turn construct, operate and maintain the projects for the former on payment of specific charges. These are generally known as deposit contribution projects.

In addition, the boards take up capital projects on their own, using their internal resources supplemented by borrowings from state governments, the LIC and other agencies. Besides, the boards can also raise open market loans and borrow from the nationalised banks to lend to the municipal corporations. Finally, international agencies such as the United States Agency for International Development (USAID) and the World Bank occasionally finance water supply and sanitation projects. The existing integrated urban development projects supported by the World Bank in some states also include water supply and sanitation as major components.[17]

Maintenance of the Facilities

The responsibility of maintaining the capital assets providing drinking water and sewage disposal facilities, and of collecting water taxes and user charges, lies with the local government. In situations where local bodies are financially or organisationally weak, state government departments or state-level boards take up the maintenance responsibility for short or long durations. In some states, the state-level boards construct as well as maintain the water works, including organising bulk and retail sales. They also maintain the old water delivery systems that were transferred to them by the state governments when they were first set up. In the small and medium towns of Madhya Pradesh, where, of late, water supply projects have been undertaken through World Bank assistance, the state government maintains them, although revenue is usually collected by the municipalities. Maintenance of water supply and sewerage systems directly by the state governments or indirectly through boards and other bodies at the state level is, therefore, not uncommon.

Resources of the Local Government

It would be worthwhile to examine the financial condition of urban local bodies in some detail since they have the major responsibility of maintaining water supply and sanitation facilities. These bodies have both external and internal resources of revenue to meet their capital and current expenditures. External sources include grants and borrowings from central and state governments, national-level agencies such as the LIC, GIC and HUDCO, and state-level municipal finance corporations. Grants from the central government can be categorised as follows:

(*i*) compensation in lieu of octroi in the states where this has been abolished; and

(*ii*) plan grants for centrally sponsored schemes. Grants so far have been routed through the state governments and the centre has been cautious in not intervening directly or indirectly in municipal administration.[18]

Fiscal transfers from states to municipal authorities take place under several heads:

— assigning of tax revenue and sharing of taxes;
— specific grants;
— revenue grants; and
— plan assistance.

Assigning a fixed amount in lieu of tax or sharing certain taxes is basically compensatory in nature and local bodies have a right over it. This is done in the case of receipts of fines for breach of municipal laws in most states, for the proceeds of entertainment tax in Tamil Nadu and Andhra Pradesh, for land revenue in Gujarat, entry tax in Madhya Pradesh, and so on. Sharing of earnings is done for the motor vehicle tax, entertainment tax, land revenue and property revenue fees in most states. At present such sharing is not based on any compensation principle or on an assessment of loss of revenue owing to transferring of taxes, but on certain equalisation criteria. Specific grants are also compensatory in nature. These are given either for the expenditure incurred in managing the state government functions such as health or education, or in lieu of specific municipal taxes transferred from the local bodies to the state. The revenue grant, on the other hand, is discretionary in nature and belongs to a category different from those discussed above. It has a high degree of flexibility as it can be linked to the needs of municipal bodies and not necessarily to the loss of revenue in the past. This grant can, therefore, be used as an instrument for strengthening weaker municipal bodies and bringing about balanced regional development. Finally, plan assistance is given for development expenditure in projects approved by the state government. Presently, no block grant is given to municipalities for financing their own plans since the 'municipal development sector is not recognised for plan assistance' (Planning Commission 1983).

Urban local bodies can borrow from the state governments and from the various national- and state-level agencies mentioned earlier to meet their current expenditure. So far the LIC has had a dominant share in the total loans disbursed to the municipal bodies, second only to that of the state governments. Any borrowing from the LIC or any other public sector agency, however, must be done with the approval of the state government when the loan amount is more than Rs. 5 lakhs and the repayment period less than thirty years.[19] Barring a few premier corporations such as Bombay, Calcutta and Madras, others do not borrow from the public. Legislations relating to the functioning of the corporations often set limits to public borrowings up to certain fixed amounts (Rs. 5 lakhs when borrowing in the open market and Rs. 25 lakhs when borrowing from the state government) or a percentage of the annual rateable value of the properties within the corporation, and specify the terms and conditions for it. While borrowing from the open market, corporations have to satisfy the central and state governments, the Reserve Bank of India and sometimes the Central Ministry of Finance with regard to the legitimacy of the purpose. In case of exigency, however, municipal authorities can borrow from commercial banks or obtain ways-and-means loans from the state governments. Needless to say, the smaller corporations and other local bodies borrow only from the state governments.

Besides the restrictions imposed through the Local Authorities Loans Act (1914) which fixes the upper limit, state governments also determine the rate of interest, duration and other terms and conditions for municipal borrowing. The interest rate charged by the state governments is generally the bank rate plus 1 per cent guarantee charge. It is, thus, clear that state governments exercise considerable control over all municipal borrowings.

There are no definitive norms for the disbursement of grants or loans by the state governments except in states where Municipal Finance Commissions have been set up and their recommendations are accepted. The states of Gujarat, Maharashtra, Karnataka, West Bengal, Andhra Pradesh and Orissa have, to varying degrees, streamlined the procedures for fund disbursement following the recommendations of their respective commissions.[20] And still, resource transfers to urban local bodies continue to be ad hoc in nature and subject to political pressures. In fact, municipal development plans are not an integral part of the state or the national developmental plan partly because of this ad hoc nature of resource transfers and partly because the resources involved are meagre. Most local bodies do not have enough funds to meet their current expenditure and have to perpetually depend on the state government, even for the disbursement of salaries of their regular staff.

The analysis of the structure of internal resources and changes in the urban local bodies provides interesting insight. The share of these bodies in the total public sector expenditure declined from about 8 per cent in the early 1960s to about 4 per cent in the early 1980s, basically because of their inability to generate resources internally. The surplus in the current accounts of several municipalities, in spite of their inability to fulfil their obligatory functions, can be explained in terms of the statutory requirement in most states to balance their annual budgets.

Variation in per capita revenue and expenditure of the urban local bodies across states and size (population) categories can be attributed to differences in their economic base and tax-raising capacity. The municipalities in the developed states of Maharashtra, Gujarat and the union territory of Delhi, for example, enjoy a per capita income (excluding grants) more than five times that of the poorer states such as Bihar, Assam and Rajasthan. Similarly, Class I cities (with a population of more than 1 lakh) have a stronger economic base and generate larger revenues. These are, therefore, in a position to provide a higher level of municipal services to their population.

As the growth in tax and non-tax revenue has failed to keep pace with other revenue sources, the municipalities have come to depend increasingly on grants. This is true, although to a smaller degree, for corporations as well, where a fall has occurred only in the share of tax revenues (in the total municipal revenues). With the abolition of octroi and the inadequate compensation made for it by the central government, the financial base of urban centres in general and that of smaller towns in particular has been further eroded since the earning from this source constituted about half the total tax revenue in several states. Increase in property values and property tax has occurred only in a few large cities. In others, this has not shown any significant rise which has adversely affected the level of municipal services, including the provision of water, sewerage, sanitation and other related facilities.

Among the various items of tax revenue, water and sewerage/sanitation taxes need to be discussed in some detail. While the general purpose property tax or house tax can be related to the provision of these facilities only indirectly, water tax, sewerage tax, scavenging tax and conservancy tax are those that are linked directly. As per the Municipal Acts in different states, property tax is a statutory local tax and has the following components: (a) general purpose tax or house tax, (b) water and drainage tax, (c) lighting tax, and (d) scavenging tax. In addition to the above, some states levy education tax and library tax as a part of property tax. Finally, there are non-tax revenues like user charges for water, sewerage and conservancy services. There are different methods of determining user charges and these are discussed in the following pages.

Pricing Systems

At present, the pricing system for water supply in different states and cities varies significantly. Often two or more systems prevail within a single city.

Flat Rate System

This system is adopted in towns and cities or in those parts of cities that do not have metered connections. A fixed amount per month or per quarter is charged from each household. The amount may be uniform or may vary depending on the value of the property and/or ferrule size but does not directly depend on the quantum of water consumed. This system exists in most small towns as also in a few large cities, because it is easy to administer and relatively inexpensive.[21] This, however, does not permit any progressivity in pricing the facility.

Uniform Rate Structure

Under this system, the rate per unit of water remains constant and each household pays an amount which is computed by multiplying the quantity of water consumed by the uniform rate. Obviously, metering is necessary for administering the system which in turn can reduce wasteful consumption.

Increasing Block Rate Schedule

This system envisages a higher price per unit at a higher level of consumption. The increase in price, however, is not smooth over consumption amount but takes place across a few slabs.[22] The objective of this system is obviously to provide water for essential consumption at low rates and discriminate against large consumers. The system can, therefore, be considered as progressive in nature since the poor with a low consumption rate of water pay a lower rate. This is adopted in most of the cities and towns in India where water connections are metered. The number of slabs and their limits, however, varies from city to city. The number is only two or three in most states and cities, which is a handicap in bringing about progressivity in pricing.

Besides the quantity of water consumed, there is yet another factor determining the water rate—the purpose for which it is used. Industrial and commercial consumers pay different rates which are often significantly higher than the domestic rates.[23]

The user charge for sewerage is usually collected as a (sewerage) surcharge from households connected to the sewerage system. In some cities, it is related to the amount of water consumed and is collected as a percentage of water charges.[24] However, barring a few large cities, sewerage charges have not been imposed by the local bodies even when the facility exists in several parts of the cities. Charges are levied indirectly in the form of drainage tax, scavenging tax, conservancy tax, etc., charges that are dependent on the annual rateable value of the property.

An analysis of the pattern of municipal expenditure and earnings from water supply and sanitation facilities reveals that only a fraction of the maintenance cost is realised through relevant taxes and user charges.[25] These, 'in most municipalities do not meet even the cost of routine maintenance' (National Commission on Urbanisation 1988). This adversely affects the availability of funds for undertaking capital projects and thereby the quality of services. The need to improve the facilities and generate more internal revenue through higher user charges, higher tax rates, a better recovery rate and efficient management of the systems cannot, therefore, be overemphasised.

Access of the Poor to Water Supply and Sanitation

The organisational structure discussed so far is entrusted with the investment and maintenance responsibilities of water supply and sewerage/sanitation facilities for both the poor and non-poor in urban India. In the case of a few cities, specific capital projects in slum colonies are undertaken either by the concerned state government departments or by state-level slum boards. The responsibility of maintenance generally lies with the local authorities. The role of vested interests and local elites in the selection of infrastructural projects and their locations within the cities cannot be ruled out, as in any other decision-making process in the country. One therefore finds a significantly higher investment in per capita terms and better maintenance of the facilities in relatively well-off areas. The distributional network by its very design tends to discriminate against the low income colonies, particularly those residing away from posh localities (Misra and Sharma 1979).

In a few states, Slum Clearance Boards have been set up that relocate pavement dwellers and shanty settlements from the dense areas of the cities to the peripheries. They take up integrated housing projects for the poor that include provision of water supply and sanitation. In some of the metropolitan cities, there are slum and squatter wings within the development authorities, like the Slum Wing of the DDA, currently with the DMC, or the Municipal and *Anchal* Development Sector of the CMDA. In other large cities, development work in slums is undertaken by the regular departments of the municipality or its special Slum Wing or *Bustee* Cell. The responsibility of reaching the services to the poor, however, lies primarily with the local bodies.

It is evident that most of the urban poor draw water from public stand posts (PSP) managed by urban local bodies. People in regularised slums as also in certain unauthorised colonies have this facility within the locality while others have to either get it from a PSP outside the locality, from households that have domestic connections, and from ponds and *nallahs* in the neighbourhood.

It is not always possible to provide water through public stand posts to all slum localities, owing to their distance from the existing pipelines or because of inadequate supply of water. It is then made available through tubewells or handpumps. This is of course more common in cities where the water table is reasonably high. The Calcutta Municipal Corporation, for example, has a separate department responsible for the installation and upkeep of small-diameter tubewells all over the city. In addition, it installs large-diameter tubewells in a few water-scarce pockets. In Delhi, too, both the DDA and the DMC have installed a large number of tubewells for the slum and pavement population.

In a few large cities, tankers are used either regularly or during periods of scarcity to provide water to colonies not covered or inadequately covered through the piped system or in areas where ground-water is not potable. In Madras, Delhi and several large towns in Karnataka, water is supplied to a section of the urban poor through tankers.

What are the problems the poor face in obtaining water through the public delivery system? It may be noted that water is available through the PSP for short durations at a low pressure and the supply is often erratic. As the number of persons per PSP or per tubewell is also very high in the low income colonies, long queues and hours of waiting often result in rising tempers and quarrels. When there is no tap in the locality, water has to be brought from great distances. As a result, the per capita water consumed in localities without tap connections is very small as compared to the others.

Households without domestic connections do not pay any user charges but in certain cities they have to pay a water tax (which is included in the property tax) if they live in localities covered by the distribution system. The charges, however, are nominal and are less than Rs. 10 a year.

A section of the urban poor has domestic connections for water supply. Most of these are unmetered and therefore the payment is minimal, generally less than Rs. 10 a month. Even for metered connections, the payment works out to be about the same since the poor belong to the lowest consumption category. The problem, therefore, is not one of non-affordability of the current expenses. On the other hand, since the user charge is low and does not show significant progressivity (with increases in consumption, ferrule size or value of property), non-priority use of water or its wastage rises. In many states the exemption limits fixed by the authorities are high, which enables the urban rich not to pay for a substantial part of their water consumption. It is unfortunate that pricing of water has not been applied as an instrument to rationalise its use which could have increased water availability in the slums through public stand posts.

The problem of affordability is, however, important for the poor in the context of the capital expenditure involved in obtaining a new domestic connection. In the old parts of large cities, several households with domestic connections need to replace their local pipelines. There is a great risk of epidemics due to the seepage of sewer water through corroded pipes. The cost of a new connection or of replacement even at subsidised rates works out to a figure between Rs. 300 and Rs. 500 per household. The poor cannot afford this expenditure. Many among them are not able to perceive the imminent dangers while others believe that such expenditure should be borne by the government. In certain large cities, the risk of epidemics is high due to shallow tubewells. The local authorities generally become sensitive to the dangers caused by these tubewells owned privately or publicly, only after the damage is done and a few hundred lives are lost.

As far as sanitation facilities are concerned, the poor generally use the free community toilets provided by local bodies or open spaces for defecation. Slums either have open drains or are bereft of any drainage facility. Even in large cities, which are reported to have been fully or partially covered by the underground system, most of the slum colonies remain unsewered.

The number of public toilets in low income colonies is quite inadequate to meet the needs of the population. This results in long queues and use of public spaces for defecation. Because of lack of proper maintenance, many of these toilets are rendered unusable. Owing to the non-availability of water near the toilets, negligence, inadequate sanitary staff and other such problems, many of these remain choked for several days in a month. Defecation in open spaces, along with the overflowing toilets and drains, poses a major health problem, particularly during the rainy season.

A few among the urban poor have toilets in their houses. These are mostly dry latrines cleaned by the municipal staff but sometimes privately as well. Their maintenance is not very satisfactory because of paucity of funds with the local bodies. The sanitation tax and the user charges together work out to be no more than Rs. 5 per month in most cities. Besides, the recovery rate is also very low.

The major problem with private latrines is not their current but capital cost which, even with a subsidy component, works out to a few hundred rupees, as noted earlier. The poor do not get individual connections because they cannot afford them and they are also unable to appreciate the necessity. Also, the conversion of dry latrines into water-borne has been extremely tardy despite the subsidy component in the schemes.

Given the high cost of construction and maintenance of flush or dry latrines, sanitary toilets with septic tanks have emerged as a low-cost alternative. Here, the responsibility of the local bodies is much less as the tanks need cleaning only once in a period of five to ten years. In many cities and towns, local bodies are now permitting the construction of dwelling units only when the individuals or cooperatives undertake to build their own tubewells and septic tanks, placing no extra demand on the existing system. The inability to meet this municipal requirement often puts the settlements of the urban poor into the unauthorised or illegal category.

In recent years, some efforts have been made by the state-level bodies or municipalities to extend sewer lines or provide open drains to the slum colonies. The dim prospects of cost recovery and lack of funds for urban development, particularly for 'uneconomic projects', have hindered progress in this direction. Governmental efforts through environmental improvement schemes have, therefore, been sporadic, often linked with the outbreak of epidemics or an impending election, and have not been carried out on a sustainable basis.

Health Care Delivery System

Levels of Health Care Services

According to the Constitution, health care is the responsibility of the state government, although in certain limited areas, the central government exercises its direct control. The central list of legislative functions includes aspects of international health, prescription and enforcement of medical standards with respect to medical education, besides the management of central health agencies and a few institutions of research. Legislative as well as executive functions related to these are the responsibility of the central government. The Concurrent List includes prevention of infectious and contagious diseases, lunacy and mental deficiency, regulation of births and deaths, control of adulteration of foodstuffs and other goods. Provision of medical facilities and preventive health care to the people is the direct responsibility of the state government or the union territory administration. In addition, medical facilities are provided by local bodies and voluntary agencies.

The delivery of health care services to people takes place at three levels: (*a*) the grass-roots level, (*b*) the intermediate level, and (*c*) the apex level.[26] Agencies at the grass-roots level provide the first point of contact between individuals and the delivery system where people obtain primary health facilities. These are primary health centres, sub-centres and dispensaries in the rural areas and dispensaries and hospitals in urban areas. Besides providing basic medical care, these centres also have facilities for preliminary investigations.[27]

When the facilities at the first point of contact are inadequate, individuals are referred to agencies at the intermediate level that generally provide better curative services and testing facilities of a higher order. These include, among others, bio-chemical tests, blood and urine culture, blood urea, ultrasound and ECG.

At the apex level, health institutions provide specialised medical care and special services such as cardio-therapic surgery, neuro-surgery and plastic surgery, besides conducting medical research.

Intervention by the centre

The central Ministry of Health and Family Welfare is the ultimate authority responsible for setting standards of health facilities, implementing national-level health programmes, besides the management of its own health delivery system. The Director General of Health Services (DGHS) is the technical wing of the Ministry and implements programmes on its behalf. The Director General advises the Minister on health and allied matters, coordinates programmes and policies and provides technical information and assistance.

In the provision of health care facilities, the central government intervenes through the following agencies:

— hospitals for the general public;
— hospitals/dispensaries for central government employees and their families;
— departmental hospitals for employees of the respective departments; and
— centres for medical education, research and training.

Hospitals for the General Public

There are only a few central government hospitals located in Delhi that provide medical facilities to the general public. The Safdarjang, Ram Manohar Lohia,[28] Sucheta Kripalani and Kalavati Saran Hospitals are directly under the control of the Director General of Health Services. While the first two provide general facilities to the people, the latter two are meant specially for women and children, respectively.

Besides these, the central government also provides full financial support to a few autonomous institutes considered to be of national importance. These provide medical care to people as part of their programmes of medical education and research. These institutes also receive fees from undergraduate and post-graduate students as per their prescribed schedules. The hospitals associated with these institutes also charge certain fees (highly subsidised) for treatment/services rendered to the patients. The All India Institute of Medical Sciences (AIIMS), New Delhi, the Post-Graduate Institute of Medical Education and Research (PGIMER), Chandigarh, and the Jawaharlal Institute of Post-Graduate Medical Education and Research (JIPMER), Pondicherry, are examples. These are considered to be quasi-government institutes and provide medical facilities at all the three levels.

There are a few central government-aided organisations that provide only apex-level medical facilities to people. The Vallabhai Patel Chest Institute, Delhi, the Mahatma Gandhi Institute, Sewagram (Wardha) are examples. These are not directly administered by the central government but the latter shares the expenditure along with the state government and the organisations responsible for their management.[29]

Health Services for Central Government Employees

The central government intervenes directly in providing health care facilities to its own employees and their families through a network of dispensaries under a contributory scheme known as the Central Government Health Scheme (CGHS).[30] These dispensaries are located in the national capital and in fifteen other cities in the country which have a sizeable number of central government employees.

The facilities under the scheme include out-patient care provided through a network of allopathic dispensaries. Ayurvedic, homeopathic and unani medical care are available in certain specified hospitals. *The nature of accommodation and associated facilities in case of hospitalisation depends on the salary slab of the individual concerned.*[31] Under the CGHS, the government also runs specialised services such as maternity hospitals.

At the intermediate level there are CGHS polyclinics in a few cities[32] with a sizeable number of central government employees. At places where there are no central government hospitals, patients are referred to the state government hospitals. In case of hospitalisation, patients can be referred to private hospitals recognised[33] under the scheme.

Departmental Hospitals for Employees

Some of the ministries and departments of the central government have their own hospitals for the provision of medical services to their employees. Significant among them are the Railways and the Defence Services. The medical system in the Railways is organised in nine zones and services are provided through a three-tier system in each zone. At the grass-roots level there are health units/dispensaries located at points of concentration of railway staff, the maximum distance between any two units/dispensaries being 80 km. The health units, manned mainly by general duty doctors, cater largely to out-patients. The facilities for investigation available at these units are very limited.

At the intermediate level, there are sub-divisional or divisional hospitals where junior specialists of all major branches of medicine are available to render routine care. The laboratory and X-ray facilities provided at these hospitals meet about 80 per cent of the investigational requirements of the patients. These hospitals are located at large work spots and divisional headquarters.

At the apex level, there are zonal hospitals where more experienced and better qualified doctors take care of complicated cases. These hospitals function under the control of Additional Chief Medical Officers or the Chief Hospital Superintendents.

It is important to note that the three-tier system functions much more effectively in the case of the Railways than in other organisations. However, their horizontal linkages are extremely limited within a city and patients often have to go to other cities for higher-level facilities. Furthermore, only in the case of an emergency are the doors of railway hospitals open to the general public.

The Defence Services also have their own system of medical care, the 'Armed Forces Medical Services'. The services are provided through clinics and hospitals at various levels. The system, similar to that of the Railways or the CGHS, is open to the general public only in exceptional cases. Thus, access of the urban poor to the central government medical facilities, except in general hospitals located in Delhi and in a few other cities, is extremely limited.

Delivery System at the State Level

As at the centre, the Department of Health and Family Welfare of the state government also has a technical wing, the Directorate of Health Services headed by a Director. However, in some states, as in Tamil Nadu, there is a separate Director for Medical Education as well. The organisational structure within the Directorate varies from state to state. In most cases, the district-level administration functions directly under the state Health and Family Welfare Department. However, in some states like Madhya Pradesh, Uttar Pradesh and Bihar, the district administration is linked to the state through a structure at the divisional level headed by Additional/ Joint Directors.

The Chief Medical Officer or District Medical Officer is responsible for managing the health system in the district, except the hospital at the district headquarters which is under the direct control of the Civil Surgeon or his counterpart. In some states, however, there are Block Medical Officers/*Taluka* Medical Officers who provide a decentralised base for health administration.

The health delivery system in urban areas in most of the states and union territories operates through a hierarchy of agencies that may be categorised as follows:

Hierarchy of Settlements	*Agencies*
state headquarters	well-equipped hospitals and hospitals associated with medical colleges
district headquarters/ large towns	civil hospitals with high-level investigative facilities
taluka headquarters/ small towns	general hospitals/*taluka* hospitals and dispensaries depending on the population size

It is evident that the state health delivery system operates at all the three levels discussed earlier. The grass-roots level constitutes the first point of contact between the individual and the health delivery system where the individual obtains basic health care. In general, dispensaries and hospitals in small towns and *taluka* head-quarters provide this contact point.[34] The facilities available at this level are supposed to be adequate for the treatment of cases of general sickness but can only provide immediate relief if the ailment is of a serious nature. Many of these units do not have facilities for even preliminary blood/urine tests.

At the intermediate level, there are hospitals with specialised facilities to cater to the requirements of a large population and for special laboratory tests. These are generally located in district headquarters or in large towns. These hospitals are expected to provide medical care for all ailments except those requiring specialised treatment, such as cancer, heart disease and neurological problems.

The delivery system at the apex level consists of hospitals attached to the medical colleges[35] and certain specialised hospitals. It is important that the facilities at the intermediate and apex levels are available to people with or without references from a lower level. These hospitals are accessible for normal medical care as well as specialised facilities. However, there are certain hospitals that are exclusively referral—the G.B. Pant hospital run by the Delhi Administration is one such example.

As in the case of the central health delivery system, in the states also hospitals are of two types: (*a*) state public and (*b*) state special.

State Public

State public hospitals are those which cater to the needs of all sections of the population. Besides the three-tier system discussed earlier, these include certain specialised hospitals such as for T.B. and maternity hospitals at the apex or intermediate levels.

State Special

State special institutions are those which are run by specific departments of the state government and are meant for their staff, persons directly connected with the department and their family members. Jail hospitals fall in this category.

Employees' State Insurance (ESI) hospitals have been established under the Employees' State Insurance Act of 1948 to provide health care facilities to workers in the organised sector. This is a contributory scheme that covers workers in factories registered under the Factories Act (1948):

— manufacturing units employing more than twenty persons;
— units using electricity and employing ten to nineteen persons;
— shops, hotels, restaurants, cinemas, road transport organisations, newspaper establishments and such others employing twenty or more persons.

Employees drawing a salary of Rs. 1,600 or less per month are entitled to ESI. Contributions are taken at the rate of 2.25 per cent of the basic salary from the employees and at the rate of 5 per cent from the employers for all employees covered under the scheme. Employees earning less than Rs. 6 per day are not required to pay any contribution, but the employers have to pay their share. The state governments contribute 12.5 per cent of the total expenditure under the system in all the states. Besides the medical facilities, workers are entitled to benefits for sickness, disablement and rehabilitation under the scheme.

The total expenditure on the health delivery system in the states is borne by the state governments. A small portion of this expenditure is raised through registration fees, investigation charges, and so on. The medical colleges under the state governments raise a substantial portion of their funds through tuition fees from undergraduates, post-graduates and research students, and from research projects, as in the case of those under the central government.

Contribution of Local Bodies

Certain local bodies such as municipal corporations and municipal committees also provide medical facilities. Most local bodies in metropolises and in other large cities run hospitals and dispensaries on their own. In the states of Andhra Pradesh, Gujarat, Maharashtra, Tamil Nadu, Uttar Pradesh, West Bengal, and in the Union territory of Delhi, a sizeable number of hospitals and dispensaries are run by local bodies. On the other hand, there is not a single health facility run by local bodies in Arunachal Pradesh,

Assam, Goa, Daman and Diu, Jammu and Kashmir, Kerala, Meghalaya, Mizoram, Nagaland, Sikkim, Tripura, Andaman and Nicobar Islands, Chandigarh, Dadra and Nagar Haveli, Lakshadweep and Pondicherry.

The contribution of local bodies in the total health delivery system at the all-India level is shown in Table 3.1.

Table 3.1: *Hospitals/Dispensaries Run by Local Bodies as on 1 January 1988*

	Total	Contribution of Local Bodies	% Share of Local Bodies
No. of hospitals	9831	292	2.97
Bed strength	585889	20220	3.45
No. of dispensaries	27495	3071	11.17
Bed strength	23846	2672	11.20

Source: **Ministry of Health (1988).**

The hospitals and dispensaries run by these organisations are similar to those of the state government. These provide medical facilities to the general population which includes free consultation, free clinical tests and free medicines that are available with them.

Private and Public Undertakings

The large public and private sector undertakings engaged in manufacturing and service activities often provide medical facilities at the grass-roots and intermediate levels for their own employees. Obviously, the nature of medical facilities depends on the status of the undertaking and the number of employees. In major public sector projects a town or a township is created through the location of a public sector undertaking and here the level and quality of services are usually quite satisfactory. Non-employee populations in these townships and their surrounding areas also get partially served by these. Facilities created at Dhanbad for Coal India Limited, at Korba for the National Thermal Power Corporation (NTPC), at Bhilai for the Steel Authority of India, and at Pilani for Bharat Heavy Electricals Limited (BHEL) are some important examples. In cases where the employees with an undertaking constitute only a small fraction of the town population, only grass-roots facilities are created for them. Facilities at the intermediate level are provided through arrangements with state governments or other organisations. A large number of small public undertakings that do not have their own dispensaries/hospitals provide medical facilities through a system of reimbursement.

Large private companies such as the Modis and Tatas have also created a network of medical facilities to serve their employees. For example, the township of Modinagar originally built by the Modi Group of Industries, and Tatanagar built by the Tatas, are served by medical institutions set up and managed by these industrial houses. Significantly, these institutions offer certain facilities to non-employees as well. There are several other smaller companies that have established hospitals/dispensaries for their employees and family members (as also for non-employees)—for example, Escorts. Most small private organisations, however, provide medical facilities to their employees either through reimbursement of medical expenses or through fixed medical allowances, as discussed in a later section.

Support Services through Voluntary Agencies

Although health delivery is basically the responsibility of the state, voluntary organisations have joined hands in this. These organisations, registered under the relevant state Acts, constitute an extremely heterogeneous category. Owing to the diversity in their constitution and functioning, the role of voluntary agencies in various developmental and welfare activities, including health, has become a controversial issue. In the health sector there are a variety of organisations which provide facilities to people in different income and social classes. Several among these organisations basically serve the urban middle and upper classes but extend only minimal facilities to the urban poor in order to fulfil registration or grant requirements.

One also finds the mushrooming of clinics managed by voluntary organisations in cities, many of which function virtually as private nursing homes for the urban elite. On the other hand, there are agencies engaged in the service of the general population with a special concern for the poor, physically handicapped and those suffering from diseases to which a social stigma is often attached. The institutions in the latter category are generally run by churches, missionaries and charitable organisations. Some of the voluntary organisations operate in remote areas where the state health system has not yet reached. Quantitatively, the contribution of the voluntary agencies is quite significant: currently as many as 1,355 hospitals with more than six beds and 692 hospitals with less than six beds are managed by them.[36]

These organisations raise funds from different sources within the country and abroad. The central government provides assistance to them under different schemes. Non-recurring central government grants are given for the purchase of essential hospital equipment. The central government also provides assistance for the purchase of vans and materials to support voluntary blood donation programmes.

A large part of the governmental grants to the voluntary agencies comes from the states and union territory administrations which have their own norms for this purpose. Grants are generally provided for specific purposes and under definite conditions. For example, Delhi Administration provides grants-in-aid to institutions that reserve a certain number of beds for the general public on a no-payment basis.[37] Most of the institutions claim to earmark these beds for the poor. There is, however, no proper control over the number of beds kept for the purpose or the actual income level of the patients benefiting from the system. In Tamil Nadu, the state government gives grants-in-aid only for maintenance and equipment. In Meghalaya the criteria for grants-in-aid are based on the area covered and services rendered by the organisation on the recommendations of the Civil Surgeon. Arunachal Pradesh provides a 100 per cent grant to hospitals run by the Ramakrishna Mission.

Systems of Reimbursement Complementing the Medical Facilities

Large autonomous bodies and public and private undertakings that do not have their own health care facilities generally adopt a system of reimbursement for medical expenditure. Undertakings with limited medical facilities also adopt such a system as an alternative or as complementary to their facilities. Even in the case of central and state government employees, there is a system of full or partial reimbursement and employees can benefit from it under special circumstances. They can, for example, buy the medicines not available in their dispensaries from the Super Bazar. The employees of the Reserve Bank of India can, under similar situations, purchase medicines from any chemist listed on a panel specified for each locality. Similarly, expenses incurred in recognised hospitals on tests and treatment that are not available within the government system are also reimbursable through certain specified procedures. The system is generally more liberal in the case of public sector undertakings than within the government, particularly at the state level. The system has several variations:

i. The most common system of reimbursement employed by organisations is that of proposing a panel of doctors to provide free consultation to their employees. Employees can purchase medicines in the open market and claim reimbursement for them. Most public sector undertakings such as Air India, Indian Airlines, International Airports Authority of India, National Thermal Power Corporation, and several autonomous colleges and schools all over the country have adopted this system for their employees.

ii. Organisations sometimes propose a panel of doctors and chemists where employees do not have to make cash payments for consultation and medicines. The organisations issue slip-pads that are handed over by the patients to the doctors and chemists who in turn claim the amount from the organisation. The Delhi Development Authority, the Mineral and Metal Trading Corporation, and the State Trading Corporation, for example, follow this system.

iii. Under a somewhat more liberal system, employees can go to any doctor, purchase medicines from any store and get the expenses reimbursed. Employees of the Coal Authority of India, Steel Authority of India, and Engineers India Limited are covered by this system. While adopting this system some organisations like the Delhi Transport Corporation have imposed a ceiling on the total yearly claims that can be made by the employees.

iv. Some organisations employ doctors who are designated as Authorised Medical Attendants and who are available during fixed hours for free consultation by the employees. On the recommendation of these doctors, they can purchase medicines from any store and obtain reimbursement. Employees of the Damodar Valley Corporation and Indian Tobacco Company are covered under such a system.

v. Several organisations pay a fixed amount as medical allowance to employees—in commercial banks, a few public sector organisations and autonomous institutions. The option of accepting a fixed allowance is also given to employees in organisations that have a system of reimbursement of actual expenses. The upper limit of reimbursement is sometimes linked with the basic salary of the employee which makes the system regressive in the nature.

Health Delivery System and the Poor

The foregoing analysis of the organisational structure in the sectors of housing, water supply and sanitation reveals that although the per capita availability of these facilities is higher in the relatively better-off localities and households, there are norms and statutory provisions in their distributional system stipulating easy access of the poor to such facilities. Also, separate agencies have been set up to meet the special problems of the urban poor. In the health sector, however, such biases in favour of the poor are almost non-existent.

The Central government and some of the public and private corporations/companies have developed comprehensive health care systems for their employees. A referral system has been built into it which gives an employee or his/her family members access to qualified medical personnel and technical facilities of a high level.[38] Unfortunately, a similar system does not exist for those working with the state governments or union territory administrations. They use the hospitals and dispensaries meant for the general public which are managed by the state government or union territory and are often inadequately equipped to deal with complicated cases. Besides these, all the agencies mentioned above have adopted some schemes for reimbursement of medical expenditure when the required facilities or medicines are not available in their hospitals. Unfortunately, the benefits of such schemes are cornered by a small section of the employees in the highest income bracket.

The component of facilities open to the general population thus works out to be very small in the health sector. This, to a certain extent, is true for housing as well, but much less for water supply and sanitation. It is important to note that the urban poor who are excluded from the special category hospitals do not get any preference in the general health system. Here, they must compete with the rest of the population. Thus, the public health delivery system by its very design is biased in favour of the rich and organised working class. It discriminates between employees of the central government and those of the state governments; between employees of different public and private sector companies; between employees at different income levels; and, most importantly, between organised and unorganised workers. The urban poor evidently figure at the bottom of the hierarchical system and therefore get only a small share of the facilities open to the general population.

It is true that public sector facilities are provided free of cost (except for a registration fee of 50 paise or Re. 1 in some cases) to the poor while the non-poor (who declare their income to be above a certain level) are required to make payments for them. It must however be added that no strict procedure is followed when identifying the poor[39] and the hospitals have been quite generous in extending free medical services to many among the non-poor. Besides, the charges are very low, covering only a small proportion of the cost of providing the services. It is thus evident that pricing of services has not been used to restrict their use by the non-poor, thereby increasing their availability to the poor.

Unlike water supply, sewerage and sanitation facilities, health care in the public sector is not provided at the doorstep. While grass-roots level facilities are available to the people in small and medium towns at distances of 2 to 3 km., for higher-level facilities they must go to hospitals in the neighbouring class I cities. People residing in the latter can get the facilities within the cities but at an average distance of 6 to 8 km. It is important to note that distance decreases accessibility much more for the poor than for the richer sections of the population.

An overview of the medical system organised by different agencies suggests that the central government facilities reaching the poor are negligible. There are only a few hospitals in Delhi and in other cities which are open to the general public. The problems here obviously are physical access as the cost of travel and stay would preclude the urban poor, living in any other city, making use of the facilities. Even in cities such as Delhi, only very few of the poor manage to reach these hospitals because of physical distances and various administrative and other difficulties.

The only facilities used by the urban poor are the dispensaries and hospitals at the grass-roots level run by the state or local governments. As a result of improvements in the health delivery system in the country over the past four decades, the small and medium towns now have at least one dispensary and/or a hospital, while large cities have a number of them located in different localities. The major problem here is that of quality and quantity. Reaching the hospitals in medium towns using the intermediate public transport (in the absence of a mass transport system) is an expensive proposition. In large cities, too, the poor may find it difficult to stay away from work for half a day in order to avail themselves of the medical facility in the nearest hospital or dispensary. Often there are pressures on the limited facilities available resulting in a long wait and an indifferent attitude among the medical personnel, which, in turn, discourage their use by the poor. The more important problem here, however, is the low quality of services, non-availability of medicines and basic testing facilities, and the non-functioning of a referral system.

At the intermediate and apex levels, the pressure of demand is several times more than at the primary level. The investments for strengthening the middle- and higher-level facilities (except research) have not kept pace with population growth over the past few decades. As a result, most of the state government hospitals at these levels are either not equipped to treat complicated cases or do not have adequate facilities. After providing consultation, a few routine tests and elementary drugs, patients are often advised to go to non-governmental clinics. In such situations of extreme scarcity it is natural that personal relations, bureaucratic linkages and corruption would determine access to these facilities. This obviously puts the poor at a serious disadvantage since most of them neither have the necessary connections nor can they afford these privately. Thus, they often remain outside the public health delivery system with respect to higher-level facilities.

As a result of the deterioration in the quality of general medical facilities, government employees and those working in large public and private corporations have demanded and have often succeeded in getting separate systems for themselves. This is responsible for a still lower quantum of resources being made available for the general facilities. Various reimbursement schemes have also been introduced for the workers in the organised sector which have resulted in employees, particularly those in higher categories, switching to the private medical system. In a vicious circle, this has caused further deterioration in the health facilities provided to the public in the urban areas.

It is observed that as one moves from a large city to a small town, the quality of medical services declines. People in metropolitan and other large cities can directly avail themselves of the facilities at all the three levels discussed earlier. Specialised hospitals with qualified personnel for different ailments and advanced technology can be approached when needed without much loss of time. Besides the state-run institutions, certain hospitals funded by the central government also exist in most of these cities. Although the latter cater basically to the needs of central government employees, certain benefits reach the general public as well. Even the local bodies which are financially strong often run fairly well-equipped hospitals for the common people in some of these cities. Finally, there are hospitals and dispensaries run by voluntary agencies in these cities, their incidence being much less in small urban centres. These centres, on the other hand, have either a dispensary or a hospital with a limited supply of medicines, a few medical personnel and inadequate infrastructure. Thus, the access to medical facilities to a certain extent depends on the location of the person since the possibility of his/her getting the higher-level of facilities is far greater in large cities.

In the provision of basic medical facilities to the poor, the major problem is that of physical access. In some cities this problem has been met by the extension of the facilities to slum colonies through mobile vans. This, besides making it possible for the slum dwellers to receive medical care at their doorstep, increases their access by cutting down the administrative formalities.

The role of voluntary agencies in the health sector is extremely important, much more than in the housing, water supply or sanitation sectors. Several agencies funded by international organisations have succeeded in mobilising people's enthusiasm and support for their activities by locating the dispensaries and medical camps within the slums. The government has recognised the success of these agencies in providing services in a cost-effective manner and have extended financial and other support to them.

The possibility of reducing the cost of providing health facilities by involving voluntary agencies has made them very popular with the government. They can cut down their expenses by motivating doctors and others to work for them gratis or for marginal payment. They are not obliged to pay government scales or provide other facilities to their employees and often invite doctors to work on a voluntary basis, with or without a token honorarium. They employ persons from within the locality as nurses or attendants by providing some limited training. The standards of the hospital building, the equipment, etc., are mostly lower than those in government hospitals. The World Bank's philosophy of lowering the standards of services to match the affordability of the community is achieved effectively through these agencies to the advantage of the poor.

With the growing importance of voluntary agencies in the health sector, it is important to guarantee the minimum level of quality through a system of checks. At the same time, it must be ensured that excessive bureaucratic control does not dampen the spirit of the workers. The other important component is to build up a referral system to support the grass-roots institutions organised by these agencies. This would be important to integrate the isolated efforts of the individuals or agencies into a comprehensive medical system.

Public Distribution System

The public distribution system (PDS) involves the procurement of foodgrains and a few other items by the central or state government departments/agencies at certain predetermined prices, storage and transportation to different parts of the country, and distribution among consumers through a system of fair price shops. The recent controversy relating to its functioning and the financial losses incurred therein, raised in the context of the process of structural adjustment in the country, clearly reveals that the economic aspects of the PDS cannot be analysed independent of its political implications. It would, therefore, be interesting to examine the evolution of the system with different governments at the centre.

Evolution

The PDS was started[40] as an emergency measure to make a few essential commodities, including foodgrains, available to all sections of the population during the Second World War. Following the national debate created through several Price Control Conferences[41] and All-India Food Conferences between 1941 and 1943, the Foodgrains Policy Committee (1943) was appointed. Based on the guidelines emerging from these Conferences and, more specifically, the Foodgrains Policy Committee Report,[42] the provincial governments in British India introduced the rationing system in the country, the Madras and Bombay governments being the pioneers in the field. In the initial years, however, the major beneficiaries were the employees of the central and state governments and the industrial labour.

The Foodgrains Procurement Committee (1950) reviewed the situation prevailing between 1947 and 1950 and proposed measures for effective coordination and improvement in the delivery system. Rationing continued during the period 1950 to 1954, with the objective of curbing inflation and making essential items available to certain targeted groups of the population, largely through imports. Subsequently, however, with the decline in open market prices, many of the controls were withdrawn. By the end of 1954, trading in foodgrains became almost free. This was, however, shortlived because in the latter half of 1955 food prices rose sharply, particularly the price of coarse grains. This necessitated the reimposition of some of the controls.

The Essential Commodities Act was passed in 1955 which empowered the central government to levy taxes and take over the trading activities or stocks of the hoarders. The Act has been modified from time to time in a manner that has in a way increased the possibility and areas of state intervention. Selective credit control adopted by the banking system under the overall supervision of the Reserve Bank of India has also been used to help the cooperatives obtain subsidised finance for storage and trading operations. The credit policy has also been used to discourage speculation and increase the supply of essential commodities in the free market.

India received foodgrains from the United States under PL480 which changed the complexion of the PDS (Srivastava 1968). As the supply was assured to the government, the objective shifted from administering regulatory controls on the market to increasing the supply through 'ration shops'. The Foodgrains Enquiry Committee (1957) supported the import policy and recommended the continuance of the scheme.

In the early 1960s, a new contract was signed with the American government to supply 16 million tonnes of wheat and 1 million tonnes of rice during the next four years. This benefited a large section of consumers as the cereals were sold at prices significantly lower than in the market. Commending the performance of the system in the early 1960s, the Dandekar Committee (Ministry of Food and Agriculture 1966) observed that foodgrains 'were available to anybody who needed them and they were available in sufficient quantities.' Rationing in terms of quantity was, therefore, almost non-existent.

The supply of foodgrains became difficult in the mid 1960s (Ministry of Food and Agriculture 1968), as a result of which the government had to reintroduce the 'rationing system'. The Food Corporation of India (FCI) and Civil Supplies Organisation were established during this time to meet the emerging challenge. The major objective of the Corporation was to build buffer stocks largely through internal procurement at prices determined by the central government. The Civil Supplies Organisation, on the other hand, did not have any statutory power and could only make requests and suggestions to concerned state government departments. Around 1967–68, the 'fair price system' was renamed the public distribution system. It was in principle a temporary programme and it was only in 1969 that the PDS was incorporated on a regular basis under the Fourth Five-Year Plan. The objectives were to control inflationary pressures and meet exigencies arising out of crop failures, largely through internal procurement.

In the early 1970s, the food stock with the FCI was comfortable and off-take was less, thanks to the good harvest. The government, therefore, did not consider strengthening the PDS. However, in 1973, which was a year of deficit, the government took over the monopoly control of wheat trade, although without much success. A committee on Essential Commodities and Articles of Mass Consumption was constituted under the Chairmanship of Mr. Mohan Dharia, the then Minister of Planning. In the meantime, schemes were launched to cover a few large cities (about thirty) in the country in a comprehensive manner. The facility was to be extended to other areas over a period of time.

In October 1974, the Department of Civil Supplies was created. In 1975, the National Commission on Agriculture made a strong plea for protecting the vulnerable sections of the population in rural areas, particularly in the drought- and flood-prone areas. In the same year, the (Congress) government launched a national programme for revamping the PDS, as per the blue prints prepared at the Narora Congress Camp. In 1976, the Ministry of Industries, Civil Supplies and Cooperation was bifurcated and the Ministry of Civil Supplies and Cooperation was established separately from the Ministry of Industries. All these reflect the growing recognition of the importance of public intervention in the provision of essential items in the mid-1970s.

The Janata Government came to power in 1977 and made a commitment to strengthen the PDS, particularly by providing one fair price shop for a population of 2,000. In the face of sharp criticism from the Federation of Indian Chambers of Commerce and Industries (FICCI), a comprehensive programme was launched on 1 July 1979 under the leadership of Mr. Mohan Dharia who had become the Minister for Civil Supplies and Cooperation. Although the government had initially promised to cover a large number of commodities, only a few items could be taken up in the first phase and the government did not survive long enough to take the programme into its next phase. It is, however, important to note that the percentage of PDS sales to total sales remained at around 10 per cent despite the launching of 'new programmes' and attempts to strengthen the system from time to time.

The Congress government came back to power in 1979, not wanting to minimise the importance of the PDS. It maintained the norms of the previous government for the setting up of fair price shops. It also announced a plan to take over the wholesale trade of essential commodities. The Sixth Five-Year Plan envisaged that the PDS would be 'a stable and permanent feature of our strategy to control prices, reduce fluctuations in them and achieve an equitable distribution of essential consumer goods.'

In the Seventh Plan, the Essential Supplies Programme (Planning Commission 1985) was introduced in January 1982 as a part of the New Twenty-Point Programme (point no. 17). The objectives were to extend the facility of the PDS to certain target groups of the population—the economically vulnerable sections, industrial workers, students, etc.—strengthen the distributive network in rural, backward and remote areas, and promote a consumer move-ment. Further, in 1987–88, the PDS was added as a new item in the Minimum Needs Programme. The objective was to ensure at least minimum food consumption in all regions of the country.

The process of economic liberalisation and the consequent structural adjustment that started in the early 1980s have serious implications for the PDS. With the squeeze on resources, the government has shown determination to cut down non-plan expenditure and subsidies in various sectors of the economy. Naturally, the PDS has came under sharp criticism (Bhatia 1990) since the direct subsidy involved in the scheme has risen from Rs. 100 crores in 1966–67 to Rs. 2,600 crores in 1991–92.[43]

The budget for the year 1991–92 envisages removing the subsidy on sugar as it is not considered essential for survival and a large percentage of its off-take is by the rich. Also, the fertiliser subsidy has been abolished and the farmers have been promised a higher procurement price in compensation. A simple calculation would indicate that the total food subsidy needed to achieve the stated objectives is far higher than what is proposed in the budget of 1991–92 by increasing the amount from Rs. 2,450 crores in 1990–91 to Rs. 2,600 crores in 1991–92.

In January 1992, it was proposed to revamp the PDS in 1715 blocks located in the backward and hill areas. Currently, 167 million people living in these blocks, with 24.9 million ration cards, are being served by 79,000 fair price shops. It is proposed to set up 11,000 additional fair price shops and issue another 2.36 million cards for this purpose. The moot question remains: How can the financial requirements of this enlarged PDS be accommodated within the present budgetary stipulations without affecting the access of the 'non-targeted population'?

Organisational Structure

The PDS is the joint responsibility of the central, state/union territory and district administration.[44] The central government undertakes the basic tasks of determining the support prices, procuring foodgrains, transporting and storing these in godowns and allocating quotas among states and union territories. Different agencies have been created to perform these functions. The central government also recommends retail prices, transport and storage charges, dealer's commissions, etc., to the concerned state-level organisations.

The responsibility of distributing the essential commodities among consumers is that of the states. As a result, considerable variation exists in the administrative structure, retail prices, and the system of issuing ration cards and rations across the states, as discussed later. Tables 3.2 and 3.3 provide an overview of the functional hierarchy as also identify the areas of authority and responsibility at different levels of administration.

Table 3.2: *Administrative and Functional Structure of the PDS*

Central Government
1. Obtaining supplies, procurement and imports
2. Determining procurement prices, issue prices (to states) and subsidies
3. Allotments to states
4. Deciding the guidelines for the structure of the PDS at state level

State Governments
1. Receiving the central allocation of foodgrains
2. Procurement in the state
3. Purchases from other states
4. Warehousing
5. Determination of:
    (*i*) Consumer issue price
    (*ii*) Commodity coverage
    (*iii*) Ration scales
    (*iv*) Rules for issue of ration cards, licences for fair price shops
    (*v*) Profit margins
    (*vi*) Periodicity of sale to consumers
6. Allotment to Districts and making transport arrangements

District and Local Agencies
1. Lifting of stocks; Warehousing
2. Issuing of ration cards
3. Licensing of dealers of fair price shops
4. Arranging/ensuring lifting by dealers of fair price shops
5. Enforcement, inspection and vigilence

Source: Kabra and Ittyerah (1986).

Table 3.3: *Areas of Decision-Making at Various Levels*

Centre
1. Commodity coverage
2. Total PDS supplies: procurement, import/exports and inventories
3. Size of covered population: exclusions
4. Nature of PDS support—total or supplementary
5. Areas or population groups identified for preferential treatment
6. Difference between open market price and PDS issue price
7. Amount of subsidy

Table 3.3 (Contd.)

States

1. Matching of supplies with needs through procurement within the state
2. Adequate and well-dispersed warehousing
3. Capacity to buy from other states
4. Inclusion of additional items under the PDS
5. Determining the issue price taking the profit margin and open market prices into consideration
6. Commodity coverage
7. Periodicity
8. Ration scale
9. Cost and procedures of issuing ration cards
10. Location and performance of fair price shops
11. Adequacy and regularity of allotment
12. Public, private or cooperative transport of stocks to fair price shops
13. Transport charges; zoning for the purpose

District and Local Agencies

1. Ensuring quality and quantity in the delivery to fair price shops
2. Overviewing storage by fair price shops
3. Costing of the products and services
4. Varying the scale determined by the state government
5. Ensuring regularity in lifting of stocks by fair price shops for round-the-year availability
6. Keeping reserve stocks; rate of state deliveries to fair price shops
7. Monitoring of stocks and sales performance of fair price shops

---

Source: Kabra and Ittyerah (1986).

Central Level

The task of the central government was restricted primarily to distribution in the early 1960s when a large amount of foodgrains was imported under PL480. With the decline in this food aid from the United States during the mid- and late 1960s, as discussed earlier, internal procurement became a major challenge. The Food Corporation of India was established under the Food Corporation Act of 1964 for this purpose.

An Advisory Council headed by the Union Minister of Food and Civil Supplies has been constituted to review the functioning of the PDS. The concerned ministers in the states and union territories and a few central ministers are the members of the council. The functioning of the PDS under the Twenty-Point Programme is, however, reviewed by a Standing Committee under the

Chairmanship of the Secretary to the Department of Civil Supplies in the central government.

For procurement and distribution of foodgrains, the FCI divides the country into four zones and nineteen regions. Most of the large states are recognised as FCI regions and the regional offices are located in the state capitals.

The central government currently supplies only seven commodities to the states. These are: (a) wheat, (b) rice, (c) levy sugar, (d) kerosene, (e) imported edible oil, (f) soft coke, and (g) controlled cloth. The state governments, however, are free to include any other commodity. Some states like Gujarat and Maharashtra procure coarse grains like maize, *jowar* and *bajra* for their PDS. The other commodities included in the PDS list are pulses, *vanaspati*, toilet soap, cycle tyres and tubes, torch cells and soda ash. These vary from state to state. The central government helps the states in procuring some of the commodities at wholesale prices.

The procurement of foodgrains is done by the FCI with support from the state government administration. In procuring sugar, the State Civil Supplies Corporations assist the FCI in several states. The task of importing sugar and edible oil is that of the State Trading Corporation. The procurement prices are determined by the Commission on Agricultural Costs and Prices. Foodgrains are procured at regulated markets and *mandis*. The levy sugar is lifted by concerned state-level agencies directly from the factories, as per their allotment.

The major part of the storage is done by the FCI in its own godowns, although in some states it rents in the facilities from the Warehousing Corporation of the central government, Food and Civil Supplies Corporations and the Warehousing Corporations of the state governments and private agencies.

State Level

There exists a two-tier system in most of the states to administer the PDS at the state and district levels. In some states, as in Punjab, Maharashtra and Bihar, however, there is an intermediate administration at the divisional level.

The Secretary of the Food and Civil Supplies Department is in charge of the programme at the state level. He is assisted by the

Commissioner and Director of the Department, as in the case of Andhra Pradesh, Kerala, Tamil Nadu and Rajasthan. However, in Bihar, Maharashtra, Punjab, Gujarat and Uttar Pradesh, the Secretary-cum-Commissioner heads the department. Similarly, in Haryana, Madhya Pradesh, West Bengal, Himachal Pradesh, Manipur and Tripura, the Director administers at the apex level. The responsibility of determining the policy of procurement and distribution at the state level, thus, lies with the Department of Food and Civil Supplies (Planning Commission 1985).

The central government makes allotments to different states every month, keeping in view their requirements and the size of the central pool. The indent for the quantity allotted to each district (by the state governments) is sent to the FCI under intimation to the Regional Food Controller and the District Magistrate/Collector. The allotted quota of foodgrains is lifted from the godowns of the FCI and of sugar from the State Cooperative Federations or the factories, as noted earlier.

Several states have established Civil Supplies Corporations for the purpose of distributing the commodities under the overall supervision of the Department of Food and Civil Supplies.[45] Consumer Federations, Marketing Federations, etc., also have a share in this responsibility. In Andhra Pradesh, the State Essential Commodities Corporation and the State Civil Supplies Corporation and in Bihar, the State Food and Civil Supplies and Federation of Consumer Corporation Limited are responsible for the distributional network. These agencies lift the supplies made available at the warehouses/factories, move these to district or block stockist points and finally to the fair price shops.

District Level

The District Magistrate/Collector is the overall in charge of the programme at the district level. In Manipur and Tripura, however, there exists no separate administrative structure at the district level. Here, the State Directorate of Food and Civil Supplies directly looks after the administration in urban areas. In rural areas, revenue officials are entrusted with this responsibility. In Maharashtra, the programme is implemented through *tehsildars* at the *taluka* level.

It is the job of the district administration to make arrangements for transportation of the commodities from the FCI godowns, in receipt of their allocation from the state government. This is done mostly through private agencies and the expenses are borne by the states.

Licences to dealers and ration cards to consumers are issued by the authorities at the district level under certain terms and conditions. Enforcement, inspection and vigilance are also organised by the officers of the Department of Food and Civil Supplies working at the district level. Violation of rules and regulations carries penalties, including suspension of fair price shop licences. *Tehsildars* and Block Development Officers are in charge of the programme at the *taluka*/block levels. The Collector or Sub-divisional Officer (SDO) allots quotas to towns, villages or retail outlets in consultation with sub-divisional committees.

Fair Price Shops

The fair price shops are the last but very crucial link in the administrative hierarchy of the public distribution system. As mentioned earlier, the central government laid down the norm of one fair price shop for every 2,000 persons in 1979 which is in force even today. Furthermore, no consumer is normally expected to travel more than 3 km. to reach his or her fair price shop (Ministry of Food and Civil Supplies 1987). In areas that cannot be covered through regular fair price shops, the provision of mobile vans has been made, particularly in hill, remote and desert areas. Emphasis is given to opening of fair price shops in Harijan *bastis* and weekly *haats* (markets) located in tribal areas. Above all, campaign sales are organised for items like controlled cloth and edible oils during the festival season.

In all, there are 5,196 PDS blocks in the country. The retail outlets or fair price shops are managed by the Departments of Civil Supplies, cooperatives and private entrepreneurs. Of the 375,000 outlets, as reported on 31 December 1990 (the revised figure in June 1991 being to 397,000), 285,000 were in rural areas and 90,000 in urban areas. The percentage of cooperatives to the total outlets was 23.7 in rural areas and 21.5 in urban areas. They function basically through community participation. In several states, cooperatives are preferred in running the retail outlets. A few voluntary agencies, particularly women's organisations, have been brought into the cooperative system. Besides the share contribution of the members, these cooperatives receive loans from banks.

The shops run by state government departments are largely in the states of Jammu and Kashmir and Tamil Nadu. Consumer Advisory Committees have been set up at district, block and *tehsil* levels in almost all the states to oversee the functioning of the system.

The largest number of fair price shops are, however, run by private individuals who are authorised by the State Civil Supplies Department. Many state governments have laid down clear guidelines for selecting the authorised dealers. Preferance has generally been given to people belonging to Scheduled Castes and Scheduled Tribes, unemployed persons, ex-servicemen, war widows, etc. As regards their functioning, the fair price shops managed by the cooperatives are not more efficient than those run by private entrepreneurs. Indicators pertaining to the lifting of stocks from wholesale agencies, maintenance of books and accounts, regularity of opening hours, etc., have not revealed any significant difference between them. The departmental shops, on the other hand, are noted to function efficiently both in terms of providing services and financial management only in Tamil Nadu and Jammu and Kashmir.

The profit margin in the PDS operations is also decided by the State Civil Supplies Department, taking the suggestion of the central government into consideration. This is kept at a low level. However, there is no risk involved in this when undertaken by a private dealer, except for the fluctuating level of off-take by the consumers.

The PDS and the Poor

The working of the fair price shops is, to a large extent, determined by the rules laid by the Department of Civil Supplies, as noted earlier. This includes matters concerning business hours, issue of ration cards, giving receipts to buyers, maintenance of account books, periodicity of sale, method of arranging supplies from wholesale depots to fair price shops, etc. These procedures are determined by taking into consideration the needs and preferences of the average urban dwellers and therefore are not sensitive to the requirements of the poor. This issue can be analysed appropriately only when we consider all the operational aspects of the system, which has been done in the next chapter. A detailed discussion on the issue of the sensitivity to the poor has also been attempted therein.

Notes

1. According to the *World Development Report 1992* (annual publication of the World Bank), India ranks twenty-first from the bottom among forty-three low income countries with a per capita GNP of US $350 against the same average figure for all the low income countries.
2. In the rural areas, the useable housing stock comprises *pucca, semi-pucca* and serviceable *katcha* structures, while in the urban areas only *pucca* and semi-*pucca* structures are included in this category.
3. This estimate is based on the assumption that a *pucca* dwelling unit is adequate for a household with five persons. Using the norm of five persons per dwelling unit, and making an allowance for sub-standard units, the BISR gave an alternate estimate of the shortage at 44.9 million—35.3 million in rural and 9.6 million in urban areas.
4. The only difference in the methodology used to arrive at the two estimates by the IIMA is that in the first, one household per house is taken as the norm whereas in the second, the norm is five persons per house.
5. Persons working for the government, semi-government organisations, public sector undertakings and large private companies generally obtain housing loans from their own organisations or public sector agencies like the Life Insurance Corporation (LIC) or commercial banks. They also borrow from private individuals or private financial institutions. The rest of the population depends largely upon borrowings from relatives, friends and money-lenders, although a small proportion of (public sector) institutional funds also reaches them.
6. See Planning Commission (1983). The 1976–77 Survey by the NSSO (1980) of eight metropolitan cities estimated that 17 per cent of the population in these cities lived in slums. This figure is considered to be an underestimate of the actual slum population. The NBO estimated that 30 million lived in slums in urban areas in 1981, which works out to nearly 19 per cent of the total urban population.
7. According to the Delhi Cooperative Housing Society Act, the Gujarat Co-operative Society Act and the Maharashtra Cooperative Society Act, for example, a minimum of ten persons from ten households are required to form a primary cooperative housing society.
8. During the First Five-Year Plan, the housing schemes were the Subsidised Industrial Housing Scheme and the Slum Clearance Scheme. In the Second Five-Year Plan, schemes for plantation labour, population in low and middle income groups in union territories, and rental housing schemes for state government employees were introduced along with those of the First Five-Year Plan. In the Third Five-Year Plan, schemes for dock labour housing, slum improvement and construction of night shelters for pavement dwellers were introduced, besides maintaining the schemes of the earlier plans.

9. The LIC accounts for about 70 per cent of the total indirect institutional finance in housing but housing loans constitute about 11 per cent of its total lending.

10. According to the recommendations of the Group, loans up to 50 per cent of the total cost of the house could be given to individuals at a 12 per cent rate of interest, with 0.5 per cent rebate for regular payment. The loan period was seven years, extendable by another three years in exceptional cases. Economically weaker sections, low income groups, Scheduled Castes (SCs) and Tribes (STs) could, however, get 80 per cent of the project cost as loan. SCs and STs could get loans at 4 per cent interest if the amount was less than Rs. 2,500. In the case of builders, banks would advance loans at commercial rates up to 40 per cent of the project cost. In exceptional cases, the amount could be raised to 50 per cent.

11. A period of two years is considered as the construction period, and is deducted from the total repayment period. Effectively, the beneficiary has to repay the loan in twenty years, whereas the housing agency repays it in twenty-two years.

12. The Tamil Nadu Housing Board (TNHB) was able to acquire land outside the Madras Municipal Corporation limit at Rs. 450 to Rs. 700 per sq. m. in 1987–88. The price of a 20 sq.m. plot would, thus, vary from Rs. 9,000 to Rs. 14,000 (data collected from the land acquisition department of the TNHB). In the main residential areas of Calcutta city, land is available for Rs. 7,000 to Rs. 8,000 per sq. m. The cost of a plot of 20 sq. m. will, therefore, range from Rs. 140,000 to Rs. 160,000.

13. Although the municipal corporations undertake capital projects in all these cities, their organisational structures differ significantly. The Municipal Corporation of Delhi (MCD), for example, discharges these duties through a separate agency, the Delhi Water Supply and Sewage Disposal Undertaking (DWS and SDU). It is a wing of the corporation but works like a state-level water board. Besides consumers in the MCD area, it supplies water in bulk to the New Delhi Municipal Committee (NDMC) and Delhi Cantonment. It is also responsible for sewage disposal in the entire metropolitan area.

14. The DWS & SDU, however, receive funds for capital expenditure directly from the Ministry of Urban Development, routed through the Delhi Administration. Only loans (and not grants) are made available in instalments to the Board for capital projects on the basis of the progress report submitted to the Delhi Administration. The loans are repayable, with interest, within a period of thirty years.

15. The LIC provides loans up to the maximum of two-thirds for the first one crore of the project cost, 50 per cent for the next one crore, 40 per cent for the next 3 crores and 25 per cent in excess of 5 crores. Usually 8 per cent of LIC's investible funds are earmarked for water supply projects.

16. In Maharashtra, for example, public contribution constitutes a significant portion of the total funds. The combination of loan, grant and public contribution varies in the following proportion:

Class of Municipal Council	Percentage Distribution of Funds from		
	State Govt.	LIC	Public Contribution
Corporations (excluding Bombay Municipal Corporation)	23.3	66.7	10
A class (pop. more than 75,000)	23.3	66.7	10
B class (pop. between 30,000 and 75,000	40	50	10
C class (i) pop. 15,000 to 30,000	50	40	10
(ii) pop. less than 15,000	90	–	10

Source: Maharashtra Water Supply and Sewerage Board (1988).

17. The World Bank's commitment for urban water supply and other urban development projects totals US $2.25 billion. In India, thirteen such projects have already been completed and twelve more are under implementation.

18. The Task Forces on Urban Development (Planning Commission 1983), however, anticipated the possibility of 'direct' federal involvement in urban affairs in India as has happened in most of the urbanised federations such as in the USA and Australia. It argued that the 'central concern to improve the quality of life would certainly increase and attempts are likely to be made to marshal more central funds for the purpose of augmenting urban finances.'

19. Central approval is necessary under a central legislation, the Local Authorities Loans Act, 1914.

20. To stop the ever-increasing dependence on state government grants/transfers, the Municipal Finance Commission of West Bengal evolved the methodology of the Revised Grant Structure (RGS) under which the municipal bodies are required to improve their fiscal performance both in revenue collection and revenue expenditure. According to norms set by the government, the individual municipal body's revenue income and expenditure are projected and the revenue gap is worked out much before the beginning of the year. After deducting the share of entry tax from the projected gap (which is the statutory entitlement of a municipal body), the remaining gap is bridged by the state's 'gap-filling grant'. Since the RGS includes a gap-filling grant as well, a municipality is not entitled to any other revenue grant from the state government.

21. In the cities and towns of West Bengal, for example, this system prevails for domestic consumers. In Calcutta the rate is based on the ferrule size. For connections with a ferrule size of 20 mm., the charge is Rs. 120 per quarter; the rate being Rs. 195 for connections with a ferrule size of 25 mm. Domestic consumers who have a ferrule size of less than 20 mm. are exempt from paying any user charges. A large number of consumers with ferrule sizes of 20 mm. and above were, until recently, exempt from paying water charges. The above rates were introduced at the insistence of the World Bank from 1 January 1986. Even then, out of nearly 2.5 lakh households with water connections, only about 35,000 pay water fees in Calcutta city (Bhattacharya 1985).

22. In Bangalore, for example, for domestic consumers the rates vary with blocks of water consumed as follows:

Consumption per Month (Litres)	Rate per 1000 Litres (Rs.)
Up to 10,000	0.35
10,000–25,000	0.45
25,000–50,000	0.75

Source: Unpublished data from the Bangalore Water Supply and Sewerage Board (1989).

In Delhi nearly 90 per cent of the connections are metered but households with unmetered connections are required to pay rates varying with ferrule size and number of taps. In both cases a progressive rate structure is maintained. After the revision of water rates in March 1990, the consumers with metered connections are required to pay at the rate of 35 paise per kilolitre (KL) up to 10 KL per connection per month and 70 paise per KL up to a 20 KL limit. For consumption beyond that, the consumers have to pay 84 paise per KL. For domestic consumers with unmetered ferrule connections the rates are as follows:

Amount to be paid by
Households per Month (Rs.)

	Ferrule Size (inches)		
	1/4	3/8	1/2
Up to 3 taps	9	15	30
For every additional tap	2	3	4

Source: Unpublished data from the Delhi Water Supply and Sewage Disposal Undertaking (1990).

23. In Bombay, consumers pay Re. 1 per 1,000 litres for domestic use but Rs. 10 and Rs. 18 for commercial and industrial uses, respectively (Source: Maharashtra Water Supply and Sewerage Board 1988). In Delhi, non-domestic users are placed in two categories and pay different rates. For the first category (shops, offices, households, industries, hospitals, etc.), present rates are Rs. 2.40 per KL up to 50 KLs and Rs. 3.60 per KL for any additional consumption per connection per month. For the second category (cinema halls, large factories, railway stations, etc.), the rates are as follows:

Rs. 3.60 per KL up to 50 KL per month per connection;
Rs. 4.80 per KL from 50 to 100 KL; and
Rs. 6 per KL for consumption beyond 100 KL

Source: Unpublished data from the Delhi Water Supply and Sewage Disposal Undertaking (1990).

24. In Bangalore, for example, the sewerage charge is 10 per cent of the water charges, subject to a minimum of Rs. 2 per month (Source: unpublished data from the Bangalore Water Supply and Sewerage Board). In Bombay too the sewerage charge is related to the water charge, the former being about 50 per cent of the latter (Source: unpublished data from the Bombay Municipal Corporation). In the recent budget (1990–91) of the Delhi Water Supply and Sewage Disposal Undertaking, a surcharge of 20 per cent has been levied as

waste water disposal expenses on those whose water bills exceed Rs. 7.50 a month. In March 1993, the water rates in areas maintained by the DDA were brought down at par with the MCD rates.

25. A recent study reported in *India Today* (31 January 1988) reveals that in Bangalore the cost of water supply per 1,000 litres is Rs. 8 while the average charge for it is only Rs. 1.75.

26. The three levels identified generally represent a hierarchy of health institutions although one may observe some deviations—primary health facilities made available to the local population through the intermediate and apex institutions in big cities.

27. These investigations generally include TLC, DLC, HB and routine urine and stool examinations. These centres also provide facilities for vaccination against communicable diseases and immunisation of children.

28. Safdarjang Hospital has only general wards whereas Ram Manohar Lohia Hospital has a nursing home and a maternity ward that are open to the general public on payment. Central government employees with a basic salary of Rs. 2,500 and above can avail themselves of these facilities free of cost, while others are required to pay under the Central Government Health Scheme.

29. The V.P. Chest Institute is administered and controlled by the Executive Council, University of Delhi, while the Mahatma Gandhi Institute of Medical Sciences, Sewagram (Wardha) is run by the Kasturba Health Society, Sewagram (Wardha) and is controlled by Nagpur University.

30. Contributions are determined on the basis of the basic salary of the employees.

Pay in the Revised Scale (Rs.)	Contribution
Up to 1,200	Re. 1.00
1,200 – 1,500	Rs. 2.00
1,500 – 1,800	Rs. 3.00
1,800 – 2,500	Rs. 4.00
2,500 – 3,200	Rs. 5.00
3,200 – 4,000	Rs. 6.00
4,000 – 5,000	Rs. 9.00
above 5,000	Rs. 12.00

31.

Salary Slab	Nature of Hospital Accommodation
Pay up to Rs. 2,500	General ward
Rs. 2,500 – Rs. 3,500	Semi-private ward
Rs. 3,500 above	Private ward

Employees drawing a basic salary above Rs. 2,500 have access to nursing home facilities in government hospitals as well.

32. There are thirteen polyclinics functioning in different cities of the country for central government employees.

33. Recognised hospitals include central and state government hospitals as well as those managed by quasi-government and private agencies.

34. In some cases civil hospitals or medical colleges may also provide the first

contact point if they are easily approachable. In Haryana, sub-divisional hospitals, and *taluka*-level hospitals in Kerala provide the first point of contact with the patients.

35. Different states follow different norms for setting up medical colleges. Usually the divisional headquarters had medical colleges but with the creation of several new divisions this is no longer possible. In Madhya Pradesh, for example, eight divisional headquarters have a medical college but none of the recently created divisions has a medical college.

36. Based on the Hospital Directory of Voluntary Organisations published by the Voluntary Health Association of India, New Delhi.

37. Free beds include free accommodation and free medical treatment, including medicines, investigations and food.

38. It is, however, true that these high-level facilities are not available to all the government employees for the simple reason that there are not enough of them. Employees in the higher categories are able to claim larger shares of the facilities through their personal influence and connections. Furthermore, there is a built-in bias in the system in their favour. Persons at certain levels are entitled to higher facilities, such as nursing home facilities free of cost, while the others are required to pay for the same.

39. Hospitals often accept the income level as declared by the patient. Sometimes an income certificate is required to be produced from the local municipal councillors who are often generous in issuing it.

40. The system of fair price shops was introduced in 1939 while the rationing system was lunched in 1942.

41. The Committee was headed by Sri T.N. Gregory and its main objective was to propose measures to ensure adequate supply and equitable distribution of foodgrains.

42. For details see Joseph (1961).

43. It is important to note that food subsidy has two components: direct subsidy to consumers and cost of buffer stock operation. The second component, constituting 28 per cent of the total cost, may be considered an indirect subsidy to consumers. Bhatia (1990), however, views this as a subsidy to the Food Corporation of India for its inefficiency.

44. The responsibility of organising the public distribution system is mentioned in the Concurrent List (items thirty-three and thirty-four) of the Constitution. It, however, appears as an important item in the State List.

45. The Corporations are autonomous bodies established through statutes and thus remain relatively independent of the state governments. They obtain share capital from the state and, therefore, are accountable to the government in financial matters.

References

Bhatia, B.M. (1990). 'PDS is a Burden on the Economy', *Times of India*, 23 January.

Bhattacharya, Swadesh Kumar. (1985). 'Pricing Urban Domestic Water Supply in Developing Countries', *Journal of Institute of Public Health Engineers India*, April–June.

Central Public Health and Environment Engineering Organisation. (1983). *National Master Plan, India—International Drinking Water Supply and Sanitation Decade 1981–90.* Ministry of Works and Housing, Government of India, New Delhi.

Housing Development Finance Corporation Limited. (1988). *Eleventh Annual Report, 1987–88.* Housing Development Finance Corporation Ltd. Bombay.

Joseph, S.C. (1961). *Food Policy and Economic Development in India.* Allied Publishers, Madras.

Kabra, K.N. and A.C. Ittyerah. (1986). *The Public Distribution System.* IIPA; New Delhi.

Lee, Michael. (1986). 'The Mobilisation of Informal Sector Savings: The USAID Experience', paper presented at the workshop on Informal Sector Savings, 8–12 December. Society for Development Studies, New Delhi.

Maharashtra Water Supply and Sewerage Board. (1988). *Annual Report, 1987–88.* Maharashtra Water Supply and Sewerage Board, Bombay.

Ministry of Food and Agriculture. (1966). *Report of the Study Team on Fair Price Shops.* Government of India, New Delhi.

———. (1968). *Report of the Jha Commission on Foodgrain Prices for 1964–65.* Government of India, New Delhi.

Ministry of Health. (1988). *Health Information, India.* Government of India, New Delhi.

Ministry of Urban Development. (1988). *Report, 1987–88.* Government of India, New Delhi.

Misra, Girish, K. and K.S.R.N. Sharma. (1979). *Distribution and Differential Allocation of Public Utilities in Urban Delhi.* IIPA, New Delhi.

National Building Organisation. (1984). *Handbook of Housing.* Government of India, New Delhi.

National Commission on Urbanisation. (1988). *Report of the National Commission on Urbanisation.* Vols. I & II. National Commission on Urbanisation, New Delhi.

National Housing Bank. (1989). *Guidelines for Land Development and Shelter Projects.* National Housing Bank, New Delhi.

National Sample Survey Organisation. (1980). 'Economic Condition of Slum Dwellers in Cities', *Sarvekshana,* 3(4).

Planning Commission. (1983). *Task Forces on Housing and Urban Development.* Vols. I–IV. Government of India, New Delhi.

———. (1985). *Evalution Report on Essential Supplies Programme.* Programme Evalution Organisation, Government of India, New Delhi.

Reserve Bank of India. (1987). *All India Debt and Investment Survey 1981–82—Assets and Liabilities of Households as on 30th June 1981.* Reserve Bank of India, New Delhi.

United States Agency for International Development. (1989). 'An Urban/Shelter Strategy for India', *Urban India Today,* United States Agency for International Development, New Delhi, January.

Verma, H.S. (1985). *Bombay, New Bombay and Metropolitan Region-Growth Processes and Planning Lessons.* Concept, New Delhi.

Srivastava, V. (1968). 'The Impact of Public Law 480 on Price and Domestic Supply of Cereals in India: Comment', *American Journal of Agricultural Economics,* 50(1).

4

Programmes for Formal Housing, Shelter and Basic Amenities

Formal Housing Schemes

Housing schemes for the poor, initiated and implemented by public housing agencies in different states, have largely depended on the central government guidelines issued from time to time in various Five-Year Plans and other policy documents. These guidelines have been mainly with regard to how the schemes need to be financed and who would share this burden. Hence, these have ultimately determined the method of financing the schemes, which, in turn, has led to the creation of new linkages among agencies and sometimes even to the creation of new institutions. The housing schemes discussed here have therefore been classified according to the financing systems and the supporting institutions (see Table 4.1). An attempt will be made, however, to analyse how the financing agencies have moved from one system of financing to another with the changes in the government's attitude to developmental policies.

There are six types of public sector systems through which an individual can obtain a house in India. These are:

(i) Rental housing
(ii) Hire-purchase
(iii) Self-financing
(iv) Housing loan
(v) Savings linked loan
(vi) House rent allowance

Under the first three systems, the public housing agencies undertake the responsibility of providing a house or a plot and in addition help arrange the necessary finance at a subsidised rate.

Table 4.1: *Financing of Formal Housing Schemes*

Financing Systems for Obtaining a House	Central Government	State Government	Local Authority	HUDCO	NHB	LIC	Commercial Banks	HDFC
1	2	3	4	5	6	7	8	9
Rental housing	(a) SIHS/ISHS (b) Slum clearance schemes (c) Staff housing	(a) Staff housing (b) Night shelter	(a) Staff housing (b) Night shelter	(a) Staff housing	(a) Staff housing	(a) Staff housing	(a) Staff housing	–
Hire-purchase	(a) LIG & MIG before setting up of HUDCO			(a) Urban housing schemes– – EWS-II – LIG-I&II – MIG-I&II – HIG (b) Staff housing (c) Co-operative housing (d) Repairs, additions scheme				
Self-financing schemes				(a) Urban housing schemes – LIG, MIG				

(Financing Agencies — columns 5 to 9)

Housing loan	(a) Loan to employees	(a) Loan to employees	(a) Cash loan scheme	(a) Loan to employees	(a) Loan to employees	(a) Loan to employees (b) Housing loan scheme	(a) Home loan scheme (b) Step-up repayment facility (c) Telescopic loan (d) Short-term bridging loan (c) Corporate loan
Savings linked loan				(a) Home loan account	(a) Own your home scheme (b) *Bima niwas yojna*		(a) Home saving plan (now discontinued) (b) loan linked deposit scheme (c) Cumulative interest scheme (d) Certificate of deposit scheme
House rent* allowance	(a) HRA to employees	(a) HRA to employees	(a) HRA to employees	(a) HRA to employees	(a) HRA to employees	(a) HRA to employees	(a) HRA to scheme employees

Source: Based on publications of HUDCO, NHB, and HDFC and discussions with the officials of these agencies.

Note: * Under this, individuals obtain houses from private agencies but the financial support comes from the public sector.

Whereas in the first type of scheme the government assumes the role of a provider in the housing sector owning the entire housing stock, in the next two schemes the government initially acts as a provider but subsequently transfers the ownership on a freehold or a leasehold basis to the individuals. Costs are recovered over a long period in hire-purchase schemes while under the self-financing system the period of recovery is short. In the last three systems, the public agencies only give finance in the form of loans and the responsibility of providing a house or a plot is passed on to the private sector. It may, however, be noted that in the National Housing Bank's (NHB) scheme coming under the savings-linked loan system, the responsibililty of providing a house or a plot is partly retained by the public sector since account holders receive preferential allocation in public housing projects. Nevertheless, the responsibility of raising the finance is passed on to the individual. There has been a shift from the first two to the last four types of schemes during the past forty or more years of planning, primarily due to the resource crunch. This shift in policy has come about for all sections of the population including the poor. As a result, the latter have lost the preferential treatment in housing enjoyed by them during the first three Five-Year Plans and are now obliged to compete with other sections of the population, as can be seen in the analysis which follows.

Rental Housing

Under the rental housing schemes undertaken during the 1950s and 1960s, units were constructed by public agencies with finance advanced largely by the central government[1] and given to targeted groups of the population on a rental basis. The Subsidised Industrial Housing Scheme (SIHS), Integrated Subsidised Housing Scheme (ISHS), Slum Clearance Scheme (SCS), Dock Labour Housing, Night Shelters for the pavement dwellers and such others belong to this category. The targeted groups, belonging mostly to the category of the poor, were entitled to houses on payment of a nominal rent and maintenance charges. The responsibility of capital investment, in this case, was that of the government.

The SIHS and ISHS were meant for workers whose monthly household incomes did not exceed Rs. 350. The workers could live in these houses till their household incomes reached Rs. 500 per month, after which they had to either vacate the premises or pay an enhanced rent. The schemes were being implemented through state housing boards, employers and registered cooperative societies of industrial workers. These organisations were also responsible for collecting the rents.[2] These schemes were discontinued in the 1970s.[3]

Slum clearance schemes (SCS) were taken up in urban areas with the objective of providing better living conditions to slum dwellers and removing unauthorised hutments from the heart of cities and other congested areas. The schemes were launched in 1956 and continued until the mid-1970s. Central government finances were available to the tune of 87.5 per cent of the approved cost,[4] 50 per cent as loan and 37.5 per cent as subsidy. The remaining 12.5 per cent was expected to come from the state government as subsidy. The subsidy was available to households with incomes up to Rs. 2,000 per year.

The SCS were implemented mostly by the state housing boards[5] but after the creation of the Slum Clearance Boards (SCB) these were transferred to the latter.[6] The rents collected by the implementing agency for the units constructed under the schemes varied from state to state.[7] In some cities dwelling units were given to the urban poor on a hire-purchase basis as well under the scheme. This has been discussed in the following section.

Schemes for constructing night shelters for pavement dwellers and the floating population in large cities have been taken up by the local authorities in some cities. Any person can use the facility by paying a nominal charge on a daily basis. In Delhi, for example, night shelters have been constructed by the Slum Wing of the DDA and a payment of Re 1 per night entitles the person to the use of bedding and toilet facilities within the complex.

Lastly, central and state governments and large public and private sector undertakings have rental housing schemes for their own employees. These schemes cannot obviously be for the poor since not many among their employees are likely to be below the poverty line.

Hire-purchase

During the 1950s and 1960s, there did exist a hire-purchase system of obtaining a house for low and middle income groups but this was available only to a few. With the setting up of HUDCO in 1972, it became the predominant system of financing. Under this system, a household could occupy a house on payment of a small part of the total cost. The balance could be paid at a low interest rate in equal monthly or quarterly instalments over a stipulated period. Here, the housing agencies draw up schemes and make capital investments either by borrowing from public sector financing agencies or out of their own funds, a small portion of it coming from the beneficiaries. The title of the plot or dwelling unit is generally transferred to the buyer only when all the instalments are paid.

As already discussed, preferential treatment was given to sections of the urban poor through rental housing schemes. This was withdrawn in the early 1970s and the poor, like any other section of the population, were required to purchase the houses. However, the hire-purchase system was considered appropriate for the urban poor because they could start living in the house after paying only a small part of the total cost. They could pay the remaining amount in small instalments over a long period of time at a low rate of interest. It may be noted that among the total units financed by HUDCO, around 75 per cent are supposed to be for EWS and LIG categories.

The hire-purchase schemes currently being implemented by the public agencies are financed by HUDCO and in some cases by the central government. There are some developers and builders who also provide houses on a hire-purchase basis for a short duration but these are not meant for the poor since the total cost or the monthly instalments are beyond their affordability.

All the schemes under which houses are available on a hire-purchase basis have been listed in Table 4.1 against the agencies financing them. Table 4.2 gives the terms and conditions for obtaining benefits under each scheme. Amongst the Urban Housing Schemes, EWS-II appears to be extremely important in the context of housing for the urban poor. It is, therefore, discussed here in some detail.

Urban Housing—EWS–II

Under urban housing schemes, which are mainly financed by HUDCO, housing units are constructed by public agencies and allotted to those registered with them as per the norms and conditions presented in Table 4.2. The system has changed significantly during the late eighties and early nineties. Presently the households are categorised into four groups based on their monthly incomes. These are (a) the economically weaker section (EWS) with incomes of Rs. 1,250 or less, (b) the low income group (LIG) with income between Rs. 1,251 and Rs. 2,650, (c) the middle income group (MIG) with income between Rs. 2,651 and Rs. 4,450, and (d) the high income group (HIG) with income above Rs. 4,450. Households with monthly incomes of Rs. 1,200 or less can be categorised as poor and EWS-II supported by HUDCO is a scheme meant for them.

HUDCO funds are allocated among schemes based on certain equity criteria. Currently, 30 per cent of its total resources are reserved for the EWS schemes which compares favourably with the figure of 25 per cent maintained up to 1975–76.[8] It may be noted that up to the year 1978–79, the HUDCO funds were going to urban areas alone. However, with the introduction of rural schemes for the EWS category in that year, the share of urban EWS housing came down to 15 per cent. Moreover, owing to increases in the cost of land and construction, it had become almost impossible for public agencies to stay within the cost ceilings specified by HUDCO, particularly for the EWS houses. The revised cost ceilings (1992) are: Rs. 22,000 for EWS, Rs. 50,000 for LIG, Rs. 1,75,000 for MIG and none for HIG. The new interest rates are 8.0 per cent, 11.5 per cent, 14 per cent and 16 per cent, respectively. In fact, the MIG pays an interest rate of 12.0 and 13.0 per cent only when the costs are less than Rs. 60,000 and Rs. 80,000, respectively. Similarly the HIG pays 14 and 15 per cent interest rate when the costs are less than Rs. 1,15,000 and Rs. 1,50,000, respectively. Of late several housing boards have obtained HUDCO loans under the EWS category and subsequently revised their scheme to LIG and pay a higher interest rate. These cases are, however, retained in the HUDCO records as EWS which implies that the figures of loans reportedly sanctioned to EWS are overestimates (Table 4.3).

The monthly instalments under all the schemes discussed above are equally distributed over the repayment period. For a loan amount of Rs. 1,000, the instalment works out to be the lowest for the EWS scheme which is around Rs. 8.06 per month at an interest rate of 8 per cent per annum (see Table 4.3). For a dwelling unit

Table 4.2: Details of Schemes Under the Hire-Purchase System in the Late 1980s

Scheme	Financing Agency	Eligibility Criteria	Security	Cost Ceiling Land Cost (Rs.)	Loan Ceiling as Per Cent of Project Cost	Net Rate Interest (%)	Repayment Period (Yr.)	Remarks
Urban housing schemes	HUDCO	Income (Rs.)						
(i) EWS-II		up to 700	Government	15,000	90	7.0	22	–
(ii) LIG-I		700–1500	guarantee	20,000	85	8.5	15	–
(iii) LIG-II		700–1500	and bank	30,000	85	9.0	15	–
(iv) MIG-I		1501–2500	guarantee	60,000	75	11.0	15	–
(v) MIG-II		1501–2500		100,000	75	12.5	15	–
(vi) HIG		Above 2500		250,000	60	13.5	15	–
Staff housing	HUDCO	Income (Rs.)						Three years
(i) Ownership housing		as stated in (i) to (vi)						moratorium
(ii) Central government employees scheme		up to 800	Govt. security	above 125,000	90	12.0	20	
		801–1700		200,000	90	12.0	20	
Cooperating housing	HUDCO	Income (Rs.)	Government	same as from (i) to (vi)				
(i) EWS		up to 700	security		75	7.0	22	–
(ii) LIG		701–1500	& mortgage,		75	8.5/9.0	15	–
(iii) MIG		1501–2500	if financed		60	11.0/12.5	15	–
(iv) HIG		Above 2500	through		60	13.5	15	
Hsq. financed			Apex coop. Society or else bank guarantee required					

Repairs & renewal scheme	HUDCO	Income	--- Same as urban housing schemes ---		
Repair/addition scheme	HUDCO	Income (Rs.)			
(i) EWS		up to 700	--- Same as urban housing ---	72	-- Same as urban-
(ii) LIG		701–1500	schemes	68	housing schemes
(iii) MIG		1501–2500		60	
(iv) HIG		Above 2500		48	

Source: Based on publications of HUDCO.

Note: The Table presents the system as prevailing in 1988–89. There have, however, been significant changes in it, as discussed in the text.

Table 4.3: *Terms and Conditions at which Public Housing Agencies Get HUDCO Loans under the Hire-Purchase System, Revised up to September 1992*

Scheme	Monthly Income (Rs.)	Maximum Cost Ceiling (Rs.)	Loan Ceiling (Rs.)	Extent of Finance (Per cent)	Net Rate of Return (Per cent)	Repayment Period (Years)	Monthly Instalment on Loan of Rs. 1000 (Rs.)
EWS							
Housing	Up to 1250	22,000	19,500	90	8.0	22	8.06
Repairs and additions	As above	11,000	9,500	90	8.0	10	12.13
LIG							
Housing	1251–2650	50,000	42,000	85	11.5	15	11.68
Repairs and additions	As above	25,000	21,000	85	11.5	10	14.06
MIG							
Housing I	2651–4450	1,75,000	60,000	75	12.0	15	12.00
Housing II	As above		80,000	75	13.0	15	12.65
Housing III	As above		1,15,000	75	14.0	15	13.32
Repairs and additions							
I	As above	85,000	30,000	75	12.0	10	14.34
II	As above		40,000	75	13.0	10	14.93
III	As above		55,000	75	14.0	10	15.53
HIG							
Housing I	Above 4450	None	1,15,000	60	14.0	15	13.32
Housing II	As above	–	1,50,000	60	15.0	15	14.00
Housing III	As above	–	2,00,000	60	16.0	15	14.69
Repairs and additions							
I	As above	–	55,000	60	14.0	10	15.52
II	As above	–	75,000	60	15.0	10	16.13
III	As above	–	1,00,000	60	16.0	10	16.75

costing Rs. 22,000, and a loan of Rs. 19,500, that are the ceilings for EWS prescribed by HUDCO, the monthly instalment is around Rs. 156. It may be noted that when the loan is passed on to the allottee after the hire-purchase document is signed, the gross interest charged by the housing agency is 0.5 per cent higher than that charged by HUDCO. Similarly, the period of loan repayment is reduced by at least two years as this period is considered necessary for completing administrative procedures and construction of the house.[9] Consequently, the monthly instalment for an amount of Rs. 1,000 would work out to be significantly higher than Rs. 8.20. The instalment amount will go up further if the time spent in completing procedural formalities and construction exceeds two years.

The down payment taken by the housing agencies can be anything between 10 per cent and 40 per cent, depending on the policy of the agency and the income category of the beneficiary.[10] The payment known as the hire-purchase cost is the least for the EWS schemes. This can be 10 per cent or more of the final cost of the dwelling unit. The down payment taken is, thus, generally higher than that stipulated by HUDCO under all schemes except the EWS. Effectively, the instalment for an EWS unit costing Rs. 19,500 works out to more than Rs. 200 per month.[11]

The method of calculating the cost of a housing unit is quite elaborate and varies from agency to agency. The total cost includes establishment charges, interest on land from the date of acquisition, interest on capital invested in the building during the construction period[12] and the profits. Establishment charges, alternatively known as administrative charges, are taken at a flat rate from all categories of schemes by some agencies whereas others charge differential rates.[13] However, profits are generally taken from MIG and HIG schemes only and not from LIG and EWS schemes. The only exception to this seems to be the Gujarat Housing Board which charges profit from the LIG scheme as well.[14]

It is clear from the foregoing discussion that all the public housing agencies subsidise their EWS schemes. The method of pricing adopted by these agencies and the differential rates of interest at which they obtain funds often result in schemes for higher income groups subsidising those for the poor. Even so, as shown earlier, the monthly instalment payable for EWS housing comes to at least Rs. 180, which is about 20 per cent of the income for households at the poverty line in the year 1986–87. People at or below the poverty line are unlikely to spend more than 10 per cent of their income on housing, as noted in Chapter 2. Thus, because of the very design, urban housing schemes, even under extremely favourable circumstances, fail to reach the poor. The subsidy given to EWS schemes, therefore, flows to the population in higher income brackets through regular or irregular transfer of the properties.

Self-Financing

Public housing agencies have gradually shifted their thrust towards self-financing schemes (SFS), particularly since the early 1980s. Under it, the house allottee (buyer) is required to pay the cost of the unit at different stages of house construction. The entire cost of the unit is, thus, recovered by the agency before it gives possession to the allottee. Thus, unlike the hire-purchase schemes, these do not keep the funds of the housing agencies blocked over long periods.

Like the hire-purchase schemes, self-financing schemes are also designed for people in different income categories as specified by HUDCO, except the EWS category. A subsidy amount is generally built into the schemes for all the income categories, namely, the LIG, MIG and HIG, since finance and sometimes land are made available to housing agencies at concessional rates. Also, the profits charged by public agencies are often lower than those of private builders. It may be noted that pricing of houses is done in a manner so as to subsidise the LIG scheme more than the MIG and HIG schemes. However, since the total price of the house is to be paid within a very short period, people in lower income brackets have not been able to take advantage of it. Only those who have accumulated savings or can obtain long-term housing loans from sources such as the HDFC, commercial banks, public and private sector employers, and relatives can benefit from the scheme.

A new model in SFS has been introduced by certain development authorities where the household wanting to buy a house is required to deposit its savings with the authority for a certain minimum period, varying between ten and fifteen years. The balance has to be paid as a down payment at the time of taking possession of the house. The Kalpataru and Kuber schemes floated by the Jaipur Development Authority are examples in this category.

The Housing Loan System

A person can purchase a house or a plot from the open market, that is, from private builders, developers, individual house owners, and so on, for which loans can be obtained from public financing agencies. In this case, he/she does not get the benefit of the subsidised housing scheme of the public agencies. Nonetheless, funds available for housing from government institutions are cheaper than in the open market. The basic idea behind these loan schemes is to shift the housing responsibility from the public to the private sector.

Housing loan schemes for employees in government, public and private enterprises, schemes for the general population and for socially and economically weaker sections offered by commercial banks, loan schemes of the HDFC, the cash loan scheme recently introduced by HUDCO and such others come under this category, as seen in Table 4.1. It may be noted here that apart from the housing loans provided by employers to their staff, the HDFC is the major agency lending to individuals or to groups of individuals.

The government has initiated several measures to strengthen the housing loan system since the mid-1970s. The Seventh Plan document lauds the role of the HDFC as a private sector financing institution and advocates the multiplication and expansion of such housing finance agencies. In view of the shift in the government's policy from construction of houses to provision of housing loans, HUDCO introduced a cash loan scheme in 1986 whereby an individual can get a loan through the public housing agencies to construct a house. The prerequisite for obtaining this loan is ownership of a plot. Finally, the Reserve Bank of India, at the instance of the Government of India, has recently instructed commercial banks to increase their lending to the housing sector. The terms and conditions of the loans offered by different agencies is given in Table 4.4.

It can be argued that the housing loan schemes are generally beyond the affordability of the poor. HUDCO's cash loan scheme is, however, the one which has been designed specifically for the poor. Here, the rate of interest and period of repayment are dependent on the income of the applicant which places the economically weaker sections at a distinct advantage. However, getting loans at concessional rates alone may not be a great help for the

Table 4.4: Details of Schemes Under the Housing Loan System

Scheme	Financing Agency	Eligibility Criteria	Security	Loan Ceiling	Net rate of Interest (Per cent)	Repayment Period (Yrs)	Remarks
1	2	3	4	5	6	7	8
1. Cash loan scheme	HUDCO	Income		As per urban housing schemes Design to be chosen as per HUDCO specifications			Given to only those who have a plot
2. Home loan scheme	HDFC	For construction of new residential units	First mortgage, bank guarantee, LIC policies, guarantee from sound & solvent guarantor, shares, etc.	Repayment capacity, 85% of project cost including land cost or Rs. 250,000, whichever is less	Related to loan amount up to Rs. 20,000, 12.5% Rs. 20,001–50,000, 13.5% Rs. 50,001–100,000, 14% Above Rs. 100,000, 14.5%	Between 5 to 20 yrs. and not to exceed age or retirement	Now discontinued
3. Step-up repayment facilities	HDFC	Regular employment in reputed co. or self-employed as professional	Same as in 2	Higher loan amount than the eligible amount stated in 2	Same as in 2	Same as in 2	Instalments stepped up after certain intervals which can enable a person to take more loan than he/she is eligible for
4. Telescopic loan	HDFC	To those whose repayment capacity is	Same as in 2	Rs. 250,000 or repayment capacity	Same as in 2	Maximum initial repayment period of 30 yrs.	Those in lower income brackets likely to move

No.	Type	Source	Eligibility	Security	Loan amount	Interest	Repayment	Remarks
	(continued from previous entry)		expected to increase in future				which can be reduced later	up in future can initially take loans for longer period and gradually reduce the period
5.	Short-term bridging loan	HDFC	To those who already own a house	Same as in 2	Same as in 2	Simple interest of 15.5 per cent per annum	In lumpsum or in instalments at the end of agreed term between 6–20 months or when existing house is sold	With the loan, people may buy/construct a new unit. During the loan period, insurance of both the existing and new houses is necessary
6.	Corporate loan (i) Employer-owned housing	HDFC	Only companies are eligible	Same as in 2	50 per cent of the construction cost or purchase price or value of property whichever is less or Rs. 100,000	Minimum 14.5%; depends on the extent of financing, repayment period and cost of unit and is subject to change	3 to 7 years	0.5 per cent interest concession to those holding HDFC shares
7.	(ii) Employee-owned/line of credit a) Loan through co.		Employees of reputed co.	As stated in 2 plus co. guarantee	90 per cent of dwelling cost or maximum Rs. 250,000	—		Maximum 20 yrs. or retirement age

Table 4.4 (contd.)

Scheme	Financing Agency	Eligibility Criteria	Security	Loan Ceiling	Net rate of Interest (Per cent)	Repayment Period (Yrs)	Remarks
1	2	3	4	5	6	7	8
b) Loan to co.			As stated in 2 plus bank guarantee		As per loan amount up to Rs. 20,000, 12.5% Rs. 20,001–50,000, 13.5% Above Rs. 50,000, 14%		Maximum 20 yrs. or average repayment term offered by co. under its housing rules
8. Housing loan scheme	Commercial banks	(a) Anyone who can furnish required security (b) SC. ST. EWS & LIG	Same as in 2 Same as in 2	50 per cent of total cost 80 per cent of total cost	Over 16 per cent 4 for SC & ST if loan amount less than 2,500, for the EWS & LIG, about 12 per cent		

Source: Based on the publications of HUDCO, HDFC and commercial banks.

urban poor because first, most of them cannot afford to buy land from the market. Second, even if they are given plots under the Sites and Services (S&S) Schemes, they are required to pay back the cost of the land in instalments which often work out to be higher than those of HUDCO's EWS-II scheme, as discussed later.

Savings Linked Loan

The provision of loans linked to amount saved over a given period of time was in the domain of the private sector until the mid-1980s but is now being talked about as a major instrument for financing public sector housing. Under this system, an individual can buy a house or a plot from a public agency or the market after paying the full price of the house/plot, as in the case of a home loan scheme (HLS). However, unlike in the HLS, he/she is required to deposit a certain amount as savings with the financing agency in order to be eligible for a loan. Here, not only is the responsibility of housing passed on to the individual but, more importantly, the responsibility of mobilising resources is also partly shifted to him/her. The objective of this system is to encourage resource mobilisation for housing through the savings of the households seeking shelter and thereby reduce the financial burden on the government. The NHB, HDFC and LIC offer schemes for acquiring houses under this system.

The HDFC was the first among the formal financial institutions to introduce this system. Four of its schemes, the Loan-Linked Deposits Scheme, Cumulative Interest Scheme, Certificate of Deposit Scheme and Home Savings Plan (HSP) belong to this category (see Table 4.5). It is generally argued that the HSP, which has been recently introduced and which carries the lowest rate of interest (amongst the HDFC schemes) of 8.5 per cent, is designed for the poor. However, the HDFC pays interest at the rate of 6.0 per cent only on the savings under the scheme and the period of loan repayment is restricted to fifteen years. In the first three HDFC schemes, the interest paid on household savings is higher and the maximum period of repayment is longer, that is, twenty years. The major difference between the first three schemes and the HSP is that under the former, the depositor merely enjoys a priority amongst the applicants whereas under the latter,

Table 4.5: Details of Savings-Linked Loan Schemes in the Late 1980s

Scheme	Funding Agency	Eligibility Criteria for Loan	Security for Loan	Minimum Deposit Amount (Rs.)	Loan Ceiling	Net Rate of Interest (per cent)		Repayment Period (Years)	Remarks
						On savings	On loan		
1	2	3	4	5	6	7	8	9	10
1. Loan-linked deposit scheme	HDFC	Savings under this scheme	As other HDFC loan schemes	200 at a time (flexibility in period and amount)	Same as other HDFC loan schemes	9.0	As per other HDFC loan schemes	As per other HDFC loan schemes	Preference in loan processing for depositors
2. Certificate of deposit scheme	HDFC	Savings under this scheme	As other HDFC loan schemes	2,000	Same as other HDFC loan schemes	As per maturity period Months R.I.** (%) 6 9.5 12 10.5 24 11.0 36 11.5 60 12.0	Same as other HDFC loan schemes	Same as other HDFC loan schemes	
3. Cumulative interest scheme	HDFC	Savings under this scheme	As other HDFC loan schemes	1,000	Same as other HDFC loan schemes	11.0–12.0	Same as other HDFC loan schemes	Same as other HDFC loan schemes	
4. Home savings plan	HDFC	Regular monthly savings for certain acceptable period	As other HDFC loan schemes	Flexible	Same as other HDFC loan schemes	6.0 Loan given only when funds are available through deposits under the scheme	8.5	15	Available for buying or constructing a house, presently discontinued

						R.I.	Related to loan amount (Rs.)	R.I.
								15
5. Home loan account	NHB	Regular monthly savings for five years*	As per RBI guidelines	30 p.m. (the savings amount to be in the multiple of 10)	2.5 times annual income or Rs. 300,000 or multiple of amount saved whichever is less savings loan built up space times sq.m. up to 40-4 times 41-80-3 times Above 80-twice	10.0	up to 50,000	10.5
							50,001-100,000	12.0
							100,001-200,000	13.5
							200,001-300,000	14.5
6. Own your home scheme	LIC	LIC policy holder	LIC policy, mortgage & bank guarantee	–	–	12.0	–	
7. Bima Niwas Yojna	LIC	LIC policy holder in four metros Delhi, Bombay, Madras, Calcutta	Same as in 6	–	Rs. 200,000 (extendable up to Rs. 300,000 or 55–75 per cent of total cost	12.0–15.0	–	

Source: Based on the publications of HDFC and NHB.
Note: * Recently changed to three years.
    ** Rate of interest.

the depositor is somewhat certain of getting a housing loan (generally not more than twice the amount saved) but only after saving for a period considered reasonable by the HDFC. However, the major hurdle in this scheme reaching the poor is the security for the loan that is as rigorous as for any other HDFC scheme. Only those who can furnish the required security are allowed to save under the HSP, which effectively restricts the entry of the poor.

The NHB has also introduced a similar scheme, the Home Loan Account (HLA), which is being projected as a major instrument to achieve the objective of providing housing to the poor and the shelterless by the year 2001. The NHB insists that public housing agencies seeking loans from it should have at least 75 per cent of the total plots in the smallest size category, that is, less than or equal to 60 sq.m. Similarly, 75 per cent of the houses built must have areas less than or equal to 40 sq.m. Through this restriction, the NHB hopes to increase the supply of small housing units and stabilise the real estate prices in favour of the poor.

Under the HLA scheme of the NHB, an individual is required to save a certain minimum amount—Rs. 30 per month—with any branch of the designated scheduled banks for at least three years.[15] Only then does the individual become eligible for the loan. The maximum permissible loan depends on the accumulated savings as well as the built-up accommodation of the proposed housing unit. For a unit up to 40 sq.m., an individual can obtain four times his total savings as a loan; from 40 to 60 sq.m., three times the savings; and for more than 80 sq.m., twice the savings. The amount saved is, thus, an important factor determining the amount of the loan and size of the built up area.

The interest paid on the savings by the NHB is 10 per cent which is higher than that of the HDFC under a similar scheme discussed above. The rate of interest charged by it on loans up to Rs. 50,000 is 10.5 per cent, which is much higher than that charged by the HDFC under the HSP. Also, the interest rate increases with the loan amount, ulike the HSP. For an amount between Rs. 50,001 and Rs. 100,000, the interest rate is 12 per cent, between Rs. 1 lakh and Rs. 2 lakhs it is 13.5 per cent; and between Rs. 2 lakhs and Rs. 3 lakhs it is 14.5 per cent (see Table 4.5).

The monthly instalment for the NHB loan of Rs. 1,000 comes to Rs. 11.28, the corresponding amount being around Rs. 10.04 for the HDFC loan. This difference is due to the lower interest rate charged by the HDFC, as discussed above. The difference comes out sharply when instalments on loans taken from the two sources, after certain years of uniform deposit, are compared. For example, if an amount of Rs. 30 per month is saved under both the schemes for five years, the total savings including the interest at the end of the period would be Rs. 2,300 under the HLA, and Rs. 2,150 under the HSP. Under the HLA the maximum loan entitlement is Rs. 9,200 and, including the accumulated savings, an individual can get Rs. 11,500 to purchase a house/plot or construct a house. For the same amount (of Rs. 11,500), the loan required under the HSP would be Rs. 9,350, assuming that like the NHB scheme, the savings are also allowed to be withdrawn along with the loan. If the HDFC gives this loan, amounting to 4.3 times the accumulated savings, the monthly instalments for the next fifteen years would work out to Rs. 94. This is much less than that under the HLA, which is Rs. 104. It can, thus, be shown that if the monthly savings under both the schemes are the same and if both the NHB and HDFC give about four and a half times the amount saved as a loan, the HDFC scheme will be cheaper. However, the HDFC could not meet the massive demand for loans against the small savings under the scheme, which was consequently discontinued. Also, as noted earlier, individuals holding an HLA would get preference in the allotment of plots or houses by the public housing agencies borrowing funds from the NHB, a facility which was not available to the account holders of HDFC.

House Rent Allowance

There is a system of providing house rent allowance (HRA) for a section of employees in the organised sector. Workers in government and semi-government organisations and undertakings and in a few large private companies are entitled to a certain percentage of their salary as a rent allowance in lieu of rental housing facility. The allowance being linked to the basic salary, employees with higher incomes get larger benefits. Workers in the unorganized sector, to which most of the urban poor belong, do not get this facility.

It may be argued that the HRA system, available to public sector employees who do not get government accommodation, encourages private entrepreneurs to invest in housing. A part of the finance eventually comes from the public sector through HRA on a monthly basis. It is, thus, a case of the public sector facilitating a section of its own employees (who are economically better off than the average population in the country) and individual house owners to work out private solutions to the housing problem because of the incapacity of the public sector to solve it.

Programmes for Shelter and Basic Services

It has been argued earlier that the formal housing schemes in the public sector do not reach the poor as they cannot pay the high instalments. The Task Force on Urban Development acknowledges the fact that 'over a period of time even the cheapest house built by public agencies (has been) way beyond the means of the Economically Weaker Sections and Low Income Groups . . . despite objectives in favour of the poor stated in the Plan Documents, there is insufficient evidence as to the extent that the urban poor have benefited from these schemes' (Planning Commission 1983). The inability of the government to provide minimum housing and basic services to all sections of the population, particularly the poor, has been explicitly noted by the Task Forces as also the Sixth and Seventh Five-Year Plans. To quote the Task Force report, 'one of the key challenges for urban policy over the next couple of decades will be a search for means to provide for the possibility of giving access to the poor to adequate shelter. If it is not possible to provide everyone with housing of a high standard it should at least be possible to make provision for a healthy environment in areas which are normally called slums' (Planning Commission 1983).

It has been recognised that the provision of the minimum (acceptable) housing and water supply and sewerage facilities to the urban poor who have a very low paying capacity involves massive subsidies. This would require a substantial portion of the planned resources to be allocated to these sectors. During the Fourth Plan itself, the need to lower the standard of minimum housing was accepted implicitly through the introduction of the Sites and Services and Slum Improvement Schemes. The recognition of the resource crunch and the emphasis on the provision of land and basic services rather than formal housing to the poor can be clearly seen in the Sixth and Seventh Plans. The Sixth Plan noted that 'in view of the severe constraints of public resources . . . the resources of institutional agencies like HUDCO and state housing boards will need to be augmented to enable them to provide infrastructural facilities as a means of encouraging housing in the private sector' (Planning Commission 1980).

It was argued that not only was a large segment of the population in urban India deprived of the minimum acceptable housing but an equally large segment had remained without access to safe drinking water and sanitation facilities. Keeping this in view, many urban development programmes were designed in the 1980s with water supply and sanitation as their major components. The term 'shelter', implying a plot of land with a temporary roof and certain basic services like water supply and sanitation, was coined during this period. It was recognised that a poor country like India can only afford the provision of shelter and basic services and not a formal house to its vast majority of poor, at least for the time being. These urban development programmes sought to cover a substantially larger segment of the uncovered population than did the formal programmes on housing and basic services. This policy shift brought the costs of the facilities within the affordable limits of the poor households and the government, a condition necessary for cost recovery and the long-term sustenance of the programme.

The programmes for shelter and minimum basic services can thus be seen as an extension of the programme of housing. The responsibility for these has been taken up by, besides the local authorities, the state-level housing boards, slum clearance boards and others. These programmes can be classified as:

1. Basic Services Programmes through which only services are provided in deficient slum areas or settlements, without altering the physical structure of the houses.
2. Shelter-cum-Services Programmes under which serviced land, security of tenure and certain basic services are made available.

These programmes can be further classified (Table 4.6) based on their system of management, the levels of cost recovery, methods of implementation, namely, whether implemented through the local community or the government machinery, and forms of tenurial right, as discussed below:

a. Basic Services Programmes comprising
   — Environmental Improvement of Urban Slums (EIUS)
   — Urban Basic Services (UBS)
   — Urban Community Development (UCD)
   — Special Schemes
b. Integrated Development of Small and Medium Towns (IDSMT) programme comprising schemes of slum improvement and low-cost sanitation.
c. Low-Cost Sanitation Programme (LCS)
d. Shelter-cum-Services Programmes which consist of
   — Sites and Services Schemes
   — Slum Upgradation-cum-Improvement Schemes

The programmes mentioned under (*a*) and (*b*) are sponsored by the central government. The EIUS, UBS and UCD are designed exclusively for the poor and localised in slums. On the other hand, the IDSMT has been introduced to arrest the growth in large cities

Table 4.6: *Details of the Programmes for Shelter and Basic Services*

Programmes	Components	Financing Agencies	Mode of Finance
1	2	3	4
I. Central Sector			
(*a*). Basic services			
(*i*) Environmental improvement of urban slums (EIUS)	(*i*) Water supply (*ii*) Sanitation	(*i*) Central govt. (*ii*) State govt.	Grant
(*ii*) Urban basic services (UBS)	(*i*) Water supply (*ii*) Sanitation (*iii*) Health (*iv*) Education	(*i*) Central govt. (*ii*) State govt. (*iii*) UNICEF	Grant-cum-loan
(*iii*) Urban community development (UCD)	(*i*) Water supply (*ii*) Sanitation (*iii*) Health (*iv*) Education (*v*) Shelter (*vi*) Employment	(*i*) Central govt. (*ii*) State govt. (*iii*) Local authority (*iv*) Overseas development administration	Grant-cum-loan

Table 4.6 (Contd.)

Programmes	Components	Financing Agencies	Mode of Finance
1	2	3	4
(*iv*) Special schemes	(*i*) Water supply (*ii*) Sanitation	Central govt. (PM's fund & ninth finance commission)	Grant
(*b*) Integrated development of small & medium towns (IDSMT)	(*i*) Water supply (*ii*) Sanitation (*iii*) Shelter (*iv*) Industrial development (*v*) Commercial development	(*i*) Central govt. (*ii*) State govt.	Loan
II. Outside Central Sector (*c*) Low-cost sanitation	(*i*) Sanitation	(*i*) State govt. (*ii*) HUDCO (*iii*) World Bank (certain schemes by central govt.)	Loan-cum-grant
(*d*) Shelter-cum-basic services 1. Sites & services	(*i*) Water supply (*ii*) Sanitation (*iii*) Shelter	(*i*) Central govt. (*ii*) State govt. (*iii*) HUDCO (*iv*) World Bank	Loan
2. Slum improvement and upgradation (*i*) SIP-I	(*i*) Water supply (*ii*) Sanitation (*iii*) Health (*iv*) Employment	(*i*) State govt. (*ii*) Local authority	Grant
(*ii*) SIP-II (*iii*) SUP-I (*iv*) SUP-II	(*i*) Water supply (*ii*) Sanitation (*iii*) Shelter	(*i*) HUDCO (*ii*) World Bank	Loan-cum-grant

and has only certain components for the poor and slum dwellers. It may be mentioned that these programmes for providing basic services were initially launched by the central government. Barring the Urban Community Development (UCD) Programme, the responsibility of monitoring progress still lies with the central Ministry of Urban Development, although the financing responsibilities have gradually been passed on to the state governments and the local bodies. The responsibilities of project formulation, coordination and of mobilising funds from various sources are, however, those of the state governments. Although partial funding is available from the centre, finances are provided in the state budget as grants or loans for these programmes.

Besides these programmes, special grants from the Prime Minister's Fund, the Ninth Finance Commission, and so on, have been available in the recent past in some cities for undertaking extension, augmentation and development of basic services in slum areas.

The Low-Cost Sanitation (LCS) Programme has been launched by several state governments availing themselves of funds from HUDCO or the World Bank besides their own resources. It may also be noted that the central government had launched a sanitation programme in 1967 on the eve of the birth centenary of Mahatma Gandhi to convert dry latrines into pour-flush latrines. The LCS, like shelter schemes, is a component of programmes such as the IDSMT.

As far as the Shelter-cum-Services Programmes are concerned, direct central government involvement is minimal. Funds have been provided to these programmes through apex public sector institutions like HUDCO and also the World Bank. Initiative for these programmes, therefore, rests solely with the state governments and are taken up only in some states and cities unlike the Basic Services Programmes that are sponsored by the central government and have a wider coverage. Nevertheless, these programmes have come into existence through the policies and often the initiatives of the central government.

Central Sector Programmes

The central government programmes have played a major role in determining the accessibility and availability of shelter and basic services to the urban poor. These programmes have, therefore, been discussed here in greater detail.

Basic Services Programmes

Environmental Improvement of Urban Slums (EIUS)

A programme for slum clearance and improvement was launched during the Second Five-Year Plan, which aimed at providing alternate shelter to slum dwellers, as discussed in the previous section. This included provision of a plot with water supply, drainage and sanitation facilities at sites away from the existing location of the slums. The programme continued till the Fourth Plan. The major problems faced in its implementation were paucity of funds and availability of developed land. It was realised that given the resources, a larger number of people could be covered through upgradation or renovation schemes than was possible through resettlement schemes. In Calcutta, the *Bustee* Improvement Programme was alread; being implemented and under it, squatter settlements were provided with basic sanitation and water supply facilities as a stop-gap arrangement (although its ultimate objective was clearance of slums by providing alternate sites). It was against this background of the failure of the resettlement policy and the moderate success of slum improvement schemes (in Calcutta) that the EIUS programme was launched in 1972 with full central assistance. It was transferred to the state sector under the Minimum Needs Programme (MNP) during the Fifth Plan and in 1986, its importance was emphasised by including it in the (Prime Minister's) Twenty-Point Programme.[16] The Sixth and the Seventh Plans placed further emphasis on the programme by allocating a substantially large share of funds so as to cover a greater population.[17] The allocation for this in the Eighth Plan has, however, been less in relative terms.

Presently, the EIUS is a major programme of the central government, designed solely for the physical improvement of slums through the provision of basic facilities. The following six services are provided to slum dwellers:

(*i*) one water tap for 150 people;
(*ii*) open drains for outflow of waste water;

(*iii*) storm water drains for quick draining out of rain water;
(*iv*) one community bath for twenty to fifty people;
(*v*) one lavatory seat (in community latrines) for twenty to fifty people;
(*vi*) widening and paving of the existing lanes; and
(*vii*) poles, 30 metres apart, for street lighting.

The programme was initiated in eleven major cities with populations above 3 lakhs. Subsequently, however, all urban centres, irrespective of their size, were brought under its purview. The per capita amount sanctioned was only Rs. 120 in the initial years which was later increased to Rs. 150. In view of the slow progress in the programme during the first three years of the Sixth Plan, a scheme of central grants was introduced under the MNP in 1983–84 to supplement the state government funds. This continued up to 1985. The per capita expenditure under the programme was raised to Rs. 250 in 1984, which was further revised to Rs. 300 in 1985 (all at current prices).

The Planning Commission specifies the target population to be covered under the MNP in consultation with state governments. The latter identifies the slums to be covered each year. These are selected according to the guidelines issued by the central government. Following these, slums in which two-thirds of the families earn less than Rs. 250 per month were selected for improvement in the Seventh Plan. Generally, the schemes are restricted to slums located on government lands where there is no possibility of undertaking a slum clearance or redevelopment scheme in the following fifteen years in the case of *pucca* built-up tenements and ten years for hutment-type tenements. This ensures that the period of benefit of the project is long enough to justify the capital expenditures on it. Presently, however, slums on private lands are also being brought under the programme in a few cities where their number is large.

The state governments implement the scheme through Slum Boards (wherever they exist) and through local bodies. In some cities like Calcutta and Delhi, the development authorities have been given this responsibility. The maintenance of the facilities in the improved slums is undertaken by local bodies.

The programme was pursued during the Seventh Plan with great vigour. In many cases, security of tenure was given to the slum dwellers and the beneficiaries were entrusted with the responsibility of maintaining and improving the assets provided to them.[18]

Urban Basic Services

Since 1976, UNICEF has been supporting the efforts of the government to improve environmental conditions in slums. In January 1985, three UNICEF-assisted urban programmes, namely, Urban Community Development, Small and Medium Town Development and Low-Cost Sanitation, were brought together under a single programme called the Urban Basic Services. Under this programme, an integrated approach, as under the UCD programme, has been adopted implying management of the basic services and other socio-economic facilities through inter-agency coordination and community-based organisations. The programme components are:

(i) health and nutrition;
(ii) water supply and sanitation;
(iii) learning opportunities and education for children and women;
(iv) capacity building by training community volunteers; and
(v) community participation by providing community organisation in slums.

The focus of the programme is on women and children. However, the entire project population benefits from it, owing to the adoption of an integrated approach. Under the water supply and sanitation component, Mark II handpumps are installed and low-cost pour-flush latrines are provided to replace the existing dry latrines. The users have to share a part of the cost. The latrines up to plinth level are constructed with the programme funds while the superstructure is built by the user as per his/her affordability. The responsibility of maintaining the facililty is entirely that of the user.

The programme involves the financial participation of the central government, state government and UNICEF in the proportion of 20:40:40.[19] The most important feature of the project is its community-based approach involving the physical and financial participation of the beneficiaries. The programme has been taken up in thirty-six districts in twenty-three states and union territories. All the towns and cities in the selected districts are to be covered in a phased manner. The programme aimed to provide safe water and sanitary latrines to at least 80 per cent of the population in the project areas by the end of 1989. Subsequently, the UBS Programme was integrated with other government programmes such as ICDS, IDSMT and UCD in the Eighth Plan.

The municipalities and development authorities in the project towns cooperate with the UBS officials in the implementation of the programme. As the district is the unit under the programme, the District Collector or the Development Commissioner coordinates and oversees the progress while the Town and Country Planning Organisation (TCPO) monitors it at the national level.

Urban Community Development Programme

This scheme was launched as a centrally sponsored programme on an experimental basis in 1966, covering fourteen cities in different states in the first phase. Owing to paucity of funds, several states discontinued the programme, particularly after it was transferred to the state sector in 1969. However, a few projects were started even after central assistance ceased to be available: in Jamnagar, Surat, Baroda, Quilon and Guwahati. At the end of the Fourth Five-year Plan, only five UCD projects in Gujarat (Baroda, Rajkot, Surat, Jamnagar and Bhavnagar) and one in Andhra Pradesh (Hyderabad) were functioning. Vishakhapatnam, Madras and Calcutta are the three cities where the project has been started subsequently and is currently being implemented.

The programme was launched with the objective of involving municipalities in the provision of basic facilities in slum areas. It attempted to bring in community participation to reduce the expenditure in the maintenance of the assets and continuation of the development activities. UCD is an integrated programme, its components being slum improvement, low-cost sanitation, low-cost health services, and, in some cases, construction of dwelling units. Slum improvement includes provision of facilities such as sewer lines, public stand posts, roads and street lights. Again, owing to paucity of funds, investment in expensive infrastructure such as roads and sewer lines have not been undertaken under the project except in a few cities like Hyderabad and Vishakhapatnam.[20] Low-cost sanitation comprises conversion of dry latrines into pour-flush latrines and the construction of new latrines. Emphasis was placed on schemes pertaining to the health of women and children and female employment. The shelter component, which includes construction of EWS units, has been taken up only in the cities of Hyderabad and Vishakhapatnam.

UCD envisages a process of social transformation in urban areas through which people can organise themselves in communities, understand their local problems and work together for their solution. The programme is seen as a catalyst in the development process wherein the community is the most important actor with the local authorities and government playing, at best, a sponsoring and supervisory role.

Initially, the central government funded 50 per cent of the project cost, the remainder being shared equally by the municipality and the state government. Subsequently, UNICEF became a financing partner in some of the components of the project but its contribution varied from year to year. Presently, marginal central government or UNICEF funds are available for the project and municipalities are arranging resources either on their own or through the state governments and external agencies. The UCD programme in Andhra Pradesh, for example, is now continuing as a state plan scheme with an annual budget of about Rs. 4.5 lakhs, one-third of which is disbursed as a grant. The balance is met by the municipal corporations through loans from the UK Overseas Development Administration (ODA). In the case of Ahmedabad, 40 per cent of the expenditure is in the form of a grant which comes from the state government, the remaining 60 per cent being the contribution of the corporation.

Hyderabad and Vishakhapatnam UCD projects have been noted as success stories. In these, unlike in other UCD projects, the construction of shelters for the poor and improvement of slums have been taken up as major components. Under the Hyderabad UCD project, slum improvement was envisaged in three phases in the twin cities of Hyderabad and Secunderabad. The first phase, implemented during 1981 and 1983, was financed by the centre, the state and the municipal corporations. During Phase II (1983–84 to 1986–87), financial help was rendered by the ODA. Seventy per cent of the cost was borne by the state government which was subsequently reimbursed by the central government through ODA funds. The remaining 30 per cent was shared by the state government and the municipal corporation. Phase III of the programme began in 1988–89, and its financing pattern is almost the same as in Phase II. ODA assistance being in the form of 100 per cent grant, no improvement cost is charged to the beneficiaries.

In Vishakhapatnam, the project started in 1979 with partial assistance from UNICEF as in other cities. Through this, the municipal corporation made an effort to improve the living conditions in slums by providing basic services and shelter to the slum population. However, owing to financial constraints and a fast-growing slum population in the city, it did not make a significant impact. Since 1988, the Municipal Corporation of Vishakhapatnam has been receiving assistance from the ODA. Three thrust areas identified under the ODA-assisted slum improvement project are basic civic infrastructure, health and employment.[21]

Low-cost housing or the construction of EWS units is an important component of UCD. It is carried out in three major stages, namely, granting *pattas* (land rights) to the beneficiaries, designing the layout of the colony, and actual construction of the dwelling units.[22] It has been observed that because of the very design and method of implementation of the scheme, only those slum dwellers occupying government and quasi-government lands could be given *pattas* under the programme. While preparing the layout of the colony in the second stage, giving away a portion of private land for community use or marginal adjustments in the size of the individual plot often becomes necessary. In such situations, a solution acceptable to the affected households can be worked out through community participation. The technical assistance for the layout plan and dwelling unit design is provided by the engineering wing under the UCD department of the municipal corporation.

The third and most important stage of the programme is house construction for which the UCD cell arranges loans, ensures supply of materials at a low cost (especially cement at controlled prices) and motivates beneficiaries for active participation. In order to get a HUDCO loan, a project proposal is prepared by the Andhra Pradesh State Housing Corporation (APSHC) on behalf of the UCD cell. The loan,[23] which is routed through the APSHC, covers around 80 per cent of the cost, including the cost of land. The remaining amount comprises the government subsidy of around 10 per cent and the same contribution by the beneficiary. HUDCO loans are available on terms and conditions stipulated for the EWS-II scheme. Like in any other hire-purchase scheme, the land title is transferred to the beneficiary after the loan is repaid. The difference between this scheme and the urban housing scheme discussed earlier lies in the method of implementation. While the formal housing programmes are the responsibility of housing agencies, construction being done by contractors, the shelter component under UCD is implemented through local bodies based on a self-help approach.

Between 1981 and 1987, construction of EWS houses was taken up in slums but only 60 per cent of the proposed dwelling units could be completed. Owing to difficulties in plot adjustments, litigation, lack of motivation among the beneficiaries and their poor economic condition, 15 per cent of the proposed units could not be taken up for construction while the remaining 25 per cent faced an inordinate delay.

A special UCD cell—the project implementing agency—has been created within the municipal corporations. The staff in the cell are expected to provide an effective link between the local government and the target population. At the grass-roots level are volunteers and workers selected from the project areas who work in various schemes for a small honorarium. It is largely due to their involvement from the stage of planning to that of execution and maintenance (of the created assets) that the Hyderabad UCD project has been both popular and successful.

Two other innovative UCD projects have been taken up in recent years in Madras and Calcutta. Unlike the other UCD schemes, the Madras project is under the control of the Tamil Nadu Slum Clearance Board (TNSCB). The Madras Metropolitan Development Authority, Tamil Nadu Housing Board and a voluntary organisation, New Residents Welfare Trust, are cooperating with the TNSCB in its implementation. The Calcutta project, on the other hand, has been initiated by a consortium of voluntary agencies. It seeks to improve the economic condition of slum dwellers by providing funds to start small-scale industries and assist in self-employment. The Calcutta Metropolitan Development Authority (CMDA) is supervising and monitoring the project.

Special Schemes

In certain exceptional cases, the central government has given special funds to provide basic services to the poor. The Greater Bombay project with the Prime Minister's special grant of Rs. 100 crores is one such example. This is a multi-sectoral project and has three components: urban renewal, slum upgradation and Dharavi

Redevelopment. It proposes environmental improvement and granting of land lease to the beneficiaries as under the Bombay Urban Development Project (BUDP). Home improvement loans are also made available to the tune of Rs. 5,000 per household, repayable in twenty years with an interest rate of 5 per cent per annum which is much less than that under the BUDP. The Dharavi Redevelopment Scheme envisages the improvement of civic facilities available to the population in the area. The implementing agencies of this scheme are the Maharashtra Housing and Area Development Authority (MHADA), the Municipal Corporation and the Bombay Metropolitan Regional Development Authority (BMRDA).

Another special programme is being carried out in Bombay and Calcutta at the recommendation of the Ninth Finance Commission. At the instance of the Commission the central government has sanctioned a one-time grant of Rs. 50 crores to the governments of Maharashtra and West Bengal on condition that there is a matching grant from the respective states. This project aims at environmental improvement and the renovation/provision of community facilities in slums in these two cities.

Integrated Development of Small and Medium Towns (IDSMT)

The programme was mooted during the Fifth Plan to improve the quality of economic infrastructure and public utilities in a select set of towns to enable them to act as growth or service centres for their rural hinterlands and thereby reduce the migration towards the metropolises or a few other large cities. Although the programme was launched basically to restructure the hierarchy of urban settlements by promoting middle-order towns, it had two other objectives—to provide basic services to the poor and improve their economic conditions so that their migration towards metro cities could be arrested. Thus, although the IDSMT is not specifically meant to provide basic amenities in the slums or other low income colonies, these figure as its important components.

Initially, its scope was restricted to towns with populations below 1 lakh, as per the 1971 Census. Presently, however, a few towns with populations of more than 1 lakh but less than 3 lakhs have been brought under the programme. Incidentally, this was also one of the recommendations of the National Commission on Urbanisation

(1988). Fast-growing centres that are also district or sub-divisional headquarters have generally been selected under the programme. During the Sixth Plan, 235 towns were brought under it in twenty-two states and six union territories. The programme was further extended to 124 towns during the Seventh Plan.

The activities under the programme are placed in two categories, namely, central sector or Part A and state sector or Part B. Activities in part A envisage the development of economic infrastructure that will generate employment and income in the town. Acquisition of land for commercial and residential purposes, improvement in the traffic and transportation system, and sites and services schemes are included in it. (The discussion of sites and services has been taken up later along with the shelter programmes). Low-cost sanitation is another component which was brought under it in the year 1983–84. Part B of the programme includes activities to improve the physical environment in the towns that are not financially remunerative. Upgradation of slums, low-cost schemes of water supply, sewerage, drainage, sanitation, preventive medical facilities and health care are covered under it.

Standard norms have been fixed for the facilities provided under the programme. These norms have been kept low so as to cover a larger number of persons with the limited resources available for the purpose.[24] The schemes under Part A are assisted by the central government through provision of funds on a matching basis amounting to Rs. 40 lakhs or 50 per cent of the project cost, whichever is lower. For the low-cost sanitation programme, however, central assistance of Rs. 15 lakhs per town is available only if the state or union territory were to contribute Rs. 12 lakhs. During the Seventh Plan, central assistance was increased to Rs. 46 lakhs for Part A projects. Low-cost sanitation projects, on the other hand, are to be financed necessarily by the state government on a 50 per cent matching basis.

Central support to the IDSMT programme comes in the form of a soft loan carrying an interest rate of 5.5 per cent which was raised to 9.75 per cent in 1990, to be repaid in twenty-five years. Repayment starts five years after the receipt of the loan although interest has to be paid for the intervening period as well. However, it is very difficult to estimate the exact financial burden on the beneficiary household for each component of the programme.

The programme is generally implemented by the local bodies

although state government departments such as the Public Works Department (PWD), the Town and Country Planning Department, the Housing Board and the Slum Improvement Board share this responsibility. The scheme is coordinated and monitored at the town level by the Collector and at higher levels by the Development Commissioner and the Chief Secretary.

It may be noted that funds available under the programme could not be fully disbursed as the state governments did not or could not mobilise matching resources. During the Sixth Plan, a provision of Rs. 96 crores was made in the central sector. Nearly 50 per cent of the central assistance remained unutilised in the absence of corresponding amounts from the state governments. During the Seventh Plan, the central allocation was reduced to Rs. 88 crores, of which only Rs. 64.08 crores could be disbursed up to March 1989.

Low-Cost Sanitation Programme

The programme was initially directed towards the elimination of manual scavenging. With the announcement of the International Water Supply and Sanitation Decade in 1981, the goal of providing sanitation facilities to 80 per cent of the urban population was fixed.[25] In view of the dual objectives and the recognition that the provision of a sewerage system in the whole country would be impossible given the limited resources, low-cost alternatives were encouraged by the government under the programme. Technical assistance was provided by the United Nations Development Programme (UNDP). Different types of low-cost latrines, *Sulabh Sauchalayas*, for example, that do not need a sewerage network and have wide replicability,are now being adopted in different states by local bodies and other agencies like housing boards, development authorities and slum clearance boards to provide sanitation facilities to slums and other low income colonies.

The objective of the Programme for Water Supply and Sanitation to provide low-cost sanitation facilities to 80 per cent of the urban population is sought to be achieved by:

(*i*) converting all dry latrines into sanitary latrines;
(*ii*) providing pour-flush latrines with leach pits to individual households; and

(*iii*) providing well-maintained, low-cost community latrines to people without individual latrines (Ministry of Works and Housing 1983).

Funds for the programme are available from the following sources:

1. HUDCO loans are available to provide low-cost sanitation facilities in old city areas and slums under its Basic Sanitation Scheme. For individual toilets, 50 per cent of the total cost (of about Rs. 1,200) is available as a loan at 8 per cent rate of interest repayable in twelve years.
2. Low-cost water supply and sanitation projects are presently being implemented in select towns of Gujarat, Tamil Nadu, Madras, Kerala and Bombay, with financial support from the World Bank. A stipulated number of towns is proposed to be covered in each state.[26]

As mentioned earlier, the LCS programme was started by the central government in 1967. Presently, certain schemes aimed at elimination of manual scavenging are being supported by the Ministry of Human Resource Development through grants which cover 50 per cent of the project cost. The balance is arranged by the implementing agency and given as a loan to the beneficiary.

In towns where the LCS programme is made a part of the IDSMT, central assistance of Rs. 15 lakhs is given (exclusively for LCS), provided that matching funds are available from the state government.

Programmes Outside the Central Sector

Besides the programmes initiated by the central government, for which allocations are made under central and state plans, state and local governments also undertake schemes on their own to provide shelter and water supply and sanitation facilities to the poor. They launch projects for the provision of low-cost sanitation, shelter, sites and services, slum upgradation, etc., generally for the areas not covered by the central sector schemes. The funds for these schemes are obtained from internal as well as external sources.

While HUDCO is an important source of internal finance, the World Bank is the source of external finance for these programmes.

Shelter-cum-Basic Services Programmes

The Shelter-cum-Basic Services Programmes consist of the Sites and Services and the Slum Upgradation Schemes. Both these are taken up either at the initiative of the state-level housing agencies such as housing boards and slum clearance boards, or the city-level agencies such as development authorities and local authorities. Whereas the Sites and Services schemes are mainly implemented by the housing agencies and development authorities, the Slum Upgradation schemes are largely taken up by the agencies or departments specifically created for the purpose of slum clearance and improvement. The implementing agencies have been getting their funds mainly from HUDCO and the World Bank.

Sites and Services Schemes

It has been argued earlier that the houses constructed under the the EWS scheme with loans obtained from HUDCO and/or state governments on very generous terms and with some amount of cross subsidisation, as attempted by various public housing agencies, would still be beyond the affordability of the poor. On the other hand, it is believed that the poor have a considerable amount of unused labour and other non-financial resources which, if mobilised, can substantially bring down the cost of house construction. This would reduce the direct responsibility of the public agencies towards housing the urban poor, allowing their limited resources to be utilised for acquisition and development of land. Under this policy perspective, the Sites and Services (S&S) Programme was introduced during the Fifth Plan.[27]

The programme envisages the provision of small plots with certain minimum facilities to the urban poor on a hire-purchase basis. It is expected that they would construct their houses primarily through family labour and obtain some of the building materials from their old houses or from the community at nominal prices. Government agencies are expected to play an important role but only in the organisation of this effort and in the provision of technical support through voluntary agencies. The programme is, thus, designed to provide an opportunity to the urban poor to build their own shelters. The involvement of private builders and contractors is, therefore, expected to be marginal. The cost of construction under the programme is likely to be less than that of public agencies because of the use of free labour and other inputs from within the households, designing and supervision by the community, leading to savings in the establishment cost.

There is considerable variation within the S&S Programme since different levels of facilities are provided to the beneficiaries under different schemes: (*a*) developed plots, (*b*) plots with a sanitary core of bathing and toilet facilities, (*c*) plots with superstructure up to plinth level, (*d*) skeletal housing without ceilings, and (*e*) houses with ceilings but without inside walls, doors and other fixtures. Beneficiaries are, thus, required to take the responsibility from total to partial construction of the dwelling units, depending on the nature of the scheme.

Sites and Services Schemes are funded by HUDCO, the World Bank and even by the central government under the IDSMT, as mentioned earlier. Although HUDCO was the first financing agency to introduce these schemes in the country, impetus to them has been given by the World Bank. Presently, the major financial contribution for these schemes comes from the Bank.

HUDCO-financed sites and services scheme: HUDCO introduced the S&S Schemes under the head 'EWS-I'. The rate of interest charged for the loans given to the implementing agencies is 5 per cent for a period of 22 years which is significantly below the corresponding World Bank rate (see Table 4.7). However, the agencies normally charge a slightly higher interest rate (0.5 per cent more than the HUDCO rate) from the beneficiaries. When the cost of the plot is Rs. 6,000 (which is the ceiling) and 10 per cent of the amount is taken from the beneficiary as a down payment, the instalment at the interest rate of 5.5 per cent works out to Rs. 37.69 per month (see Table 4.8). This is much lower than the corresponding figure for the World Bank scheme. It works out to only 5 per cent of the monthly income for households at the poverty line, which is well within their affordability limit, as discussed in Chapter 2. The rate of interest has currently been revised to 7 per cent and the cost/loan ceiling to Rs. 7,500.

Table 4.7: Details of Shelter-cum-Services Schemes in the Late 1980s

Scheme	Financing Agency	Eligibility Criteria	Security	Cost Ceiling Including Land Cost (Rs.)	Loan Ceiling as Per cent of the Project Cost	Net Rate of Interest (%)	Repayment Period (Years)	Remarks
1	2	3	4	5	6	7	8	9
Sites and services								
(i) EWS-I	HUDCO	up to 700	Govt. Guarantee	6,000*	100	5.0	22	–
(ii) As a part of UD projects	WB							
(a) BUDP	WB	Income (Rs.) –	–	–	90	12	20	Full cost recovery and only cross-subsidy in land development through pricing of plots
(b) MUDP-I	WB	Income (Rs.)	–	Not specified	–	–	–	
EWS		up to 350			90	12	20	
LIG		351–600			90	12	15	
MIG		601–1000			90	12	12	
(c) MUDP-II	WB	Income			90	12	15	No core housing Five years moratorium on loan
(d) IDSMT	Central Govt.	N.A.	N.A.	N.A.	N.A.	N.A.		

Slum improvement and upgradation (SIP-II and SUP-I & II)	WB	Slum resident with identity card	–	Not specified	90	12	20	In slums where residents are willing buy land *pattas*
	HUDCO		Govt. guarantee	5000	50 for improvement 100 for up-gradation	6.25	22	In slums on public lands
Urban community development								
(*i*) Regular UCD	HUDCO	–	Govt. guarantee	6,200	70–75	7.0		
(*ii*) Habitat housing scheme	Commercial Bank	–	As above	–	80	8.0		

Source: Based on publications of the World Bank and HUDCO.

* Excluding land cost.

Table 4.8: *Details of Sites and Services Schemes as in the Late 1980s*

Scheme	Plot Type	Monthly Income (Rs.)	Plot Area (Sq.m.)	Total Cost Expected (Rs.)	Down Payment (Rs.)	Down Payment (%)	Net Rate of Interest (%)	Monthly Instalment (Rs.)	Monthly Instalment as per cent of Household Income (%)
1	2	3	4	5	6	7	8	9	10
World Bank financed-BUDP (Representative)									
	A_1	Up to 300	21.0	3,464	350	–	12.0	34.3	min 11
	A_2	301–500	24.5	5,938	500	–	12.0	59.9	12–20
	A_3	501–725	28.0	9,576	1000	–	12.0	94.4	13–19
	B	726–800	40.0	7,200	–	20	12.0	63.4	8–9
	C	801–1250	60.0	14,400	–	20	12.0	126.9	10–16
	D	1251–2500	100.0	32,130	–	20	12.0	283.0	11–23
	Cooperative	–	50	12,000	–	100	12.0	–	–
MUDP-I	EWS-A	151–200	40.0	1,975†	197.5	10	12.0	20	10–13
	EWS-B	201–300	46.5	3,002†	300.2	10	12.0	30	10–15
	EWS-C	301–350	46.5	6,647†	664.7	10	12.0	66	19–22
	LIG-D	351–450	74.5	3,690†	369.0	10	12.0	40	9–11
	LIG-E	451–600	139.4	5,435†	643.3	10	12.0	70	12–16
	MIG-F	600–1000	223.0	10,845†	1084.5	10	12.0	128	13–21

MUDP-II								
EWS	A$_1$	150–200	33.5	407* + 1100**	41	10	12.0	20.6***	10–14
	A$_2$	201–250	33.5	1683* + 1100**	168	10	12.0	30.8***	12–15
	A$_3$	201–250	35.5	2176* + 1700**	218	10	12.0	39.7***	16–20
	B$_1$	251–300	44.5	3712* + 800**	371	10	12.0	52.7***	18–21
	B$_2$	251–300	44.5	3712* + 800**	371	10	12.0	52.7***	18–21
	C$_1$	301–350	44.5	5261* + 500**	526	10	12.0	65.8***	19–22
	C$_2$	301–350	44.5	6598* + 500**	660	10	12.0	80.3***	23–27
LIG	I	351–450	74.0	3,700	370	10	12.0	43.0	10–12
LIG	II	451–600	140.0	7,700	700	10	12.0	86.2	14–15
MIG		600–1000	220.0	15,400	1540	10	12.0	169.3	17–28
HUDCO-financed-EWS-I		Up to 700		6,000‡	600	10	5.0	37.75	

Source: Based on publications of the World Bank and HUDCO.

Note: * Total cost of land development at 1979 prices.

** Optional shelter loan permitted.

*** Including instalments for optional shelter loan. Otherwise the instalments per month would come to Rs. 7.4, Rs. 22.2, Rs. 26.5, Rs. 43.1, Rs. 43.1, Rs. 59.8 and Rs. 74.3, respectively.

† At 1976 prices.

‡ Excluding land cost.

World Bank-financed sites and services schemes: The first multi-sectoral urban development programme was taken up in Madras in 1976–77 with partial funding from the World Bank. Known as the Madras Urban Development Project Phase I (MUDP-I), this had a provision for sites and services (with slum improvement and upgradation figuring as important components) which was implemented during the period 1976–77 to 1980–81 (for details see Slingsby 1989 and Vaessen 1989). Subsequently, the Bank took up several other S&S Schemes in different cities: in Kanpur in 1981–82, in Indore in 1982–83 and in a number of cities in Gujarat in 1985–86. In 1985–86, when the MUDP Phase-II came to a close, the programme[28] was extended to other major cities and towns in Tamil Nadu under the Tamil Nadu Urban Development Project (TUDP). The other major project financed by the Bank is the Bombay Urban Development Project (BUDP) during the period 1985–90 which includes S&S as well as slum improvement schemes. It may be noted that sites and services schemes are generally implemented by the state-level housing agencies whereas the slum improvement schemes are implemented through the slum clearance boards or slum wings of the development authorities/local bodies.

Sites and services schemes financed by the World Bank in India have several options relating to plot size for people in different income groups even within the EWS category. As a part of the scheme, serviced plots are provided for LIG and MIG housing as also for commercial and industrial use. In disposing of these semi-finished houses, the cost of the core housing is charged to the respective beneficiary groups while the cost of land development is distributed following certain equity criteria. As a result, commercial and industrial plots are priced at the highest rate while the smallest size EWS plot carries the lowest price. The land prices charged for different usages and from different income groups of beneficiaries are given in Table 4.8 under different schemes. The Table also furnishes details of the required down payment, loan amount and monthly instalments.

Unlike in the housing schemes, establishment costs or profits are normally not charged under the S&S programme. Also, the interest payment on the capital invested is relatively low. All these result in some amount of subsidisation of the facility. The interest charged under the World Bank S&S schemes is 12 per cent per annum (recently revised upward) which is the same as for the LIG and MIG population under its shelter programme. The repayment period for the former, however, is twenty years which is more than that for the other programmes offered by the Bank (see Table 4.7). It is also important that under MUDP-I, core housing was a part of the project whereas under MUDP-II only developed plots were made available and the allottees could apply for separate housing loans. This reflects the trend of transferring the responsibility of house construction from public agencies to the people even within the S&S Programme.

It may be seen in Tables 4.7 and 4.8 that the monthly instalments under certain S&S Schemes funded by the World Bank work out to be not much lower than that of the hire-purchase housing for the EWS population. In some of the schemes providing semi-finished houses, the monthly repayment works out to more than 20 per cent of the income for households at the poverty line. While paying this instalment, the households must also find additional resources to complete the house which may significantly add to their debt burden. The Sites and Services Schemes under the IDSMT also carry a higher interest rate (the same as under other schemes of the IDSMT with the same period of repayment) which is more than that under HUDCO schemes.

The foregoing discussion makes it clear that the responsibility of building dwelling units, including those for the poor, has been passed on, at least partially, to the people themselves and this has reduced the burden on the public exchequer. However, many among the beneficiaries, unable to mobilise their own resources to construct houses, are forced to live in makeshift arrangements on their plots for a long time. Also, since they borrow money from informal sources such as relatives, moneylenders and shopkeepers to complete the construction of their houses or pay their instalments, the interest rate often works out to be very high, which results in their losing possession of the land formally or informally. Not many loans have been made available to the beneficiaries by public agencies under the scheme for completing the houses. Thus, a shift to the S&S Programme from the hire-purchase system for the EWS category definitely implies transferring much of the housing responsibility to the poor.

Slum Upgradation-cum-Improvement Programme

The first Slum Improvement Programme (SIP) was introduced in Calcutta by the Metropolitan Planning Organisation (CMPO) in the 1960s, as mentioned earlier. This implied a shift of policy from clearance and resettlement of slums, as was pursued up to the Third Plan, to their upgradation and improvement. Since the Fourth Plan, the latter became the dominant approach to slum development, although the nature of the projects varied considerably from city to city and over the years.

Currently, three types of slum development programmes are being implemented in the country: (a) slum improvement, (b) slum upgradation, and (c) slum reconstruction. Their approaches vary depending on (a) the status of the land on which the slum development project is to be taken up, (b) the socio-economic conditions of the slum dwellers, and (c) the conditions laid down by the financing agency with respect to cost recovery.

The Slum Improvement Programme (SIP)

This programme involves merely physical improvement of the slum by the provision of a standard package of basic facilities. The schemes under it can be classified into two categories depending on whether or not the cost of providing the amenities is recovered from the beneficiaries. In the first type, termed here SIP-I, the facilities are provided without charging the cost to the beneficiaries. The EIUS programme launched during the 1970s by the central government belongs to this category in terms of the approach and has been discussed earlier. Quite often, the state governments implement such schemes through their own funds as in the case of the Accelerated Slum Improvement Scheme[29] taken up in Madras and implemented by the Tamil Nadu Slum clearance Board (TNSCB).

In the second category, described here as SIP-II, the cost of improvement is recovered from the beneficiary in instalments. World Bank-financed urban development projects which have SIP as a component, such as the Calcutta Urban Development Project (CUDP)[30] and TUDP Phase-III, belong to this category.[31] The Bank provides grants and loans to the implementing agencies through the Government of India to finance this component. The loan is passed on to the beneficiaries at a 12 per cent rate of interest repayable in twenty years. The second important source of finance for SIP-II schemes is HUDCO which gives half the cost of the project as loan at an interest rate of 8 per cent to be repaid over twenty-two years.

As noted earlier, the SIP is directed towards the improvement of the physical conditions of slums and does not include upgradation of housing conditions or reconstruction of individual houses. Further, it does not involve community participation as it is implemented through government agencies. It has, therefore, been regarded as a purely technical approach to slum development (Borst 1990).

Slum upgradation and reconstruction programmes can only be taken up in slums which are compatible with the zoning and land use restrictions, imposed for public purposes, in the development plan of the city. Besides, these slums should not be close to a *nallah*—that is, on land which can get water-logged—or near high-tension power lines, railway tracks, airports, sensitive defence establishments or on hill slopes (Sinha 1990). These slums are termed as unobjectionable and can be identified through a slum census in the city. However, by these criteria, around half the slums in the metro cities would be classified as objectionable and thus be disqualified for upgradation or reconstruction.[32] The population in the objectionable slums is to be shifted and resettled in some other parts of the city under the slum clearance or Sites and Services Schemes discussed earlier. Experience shows that as slum relocation is an expensive proposition, large sections of the affected population are not able or willing to pay for the new accommodation.[33] In such cases, improvement of slums is the only alternative which can be pursued.

The Slum Upgradation Programme (SUP)

This programme, for the provision of shelter and basic services, was started in the Fifth Plan at the instance of the World Bank. Currently, HUDCO also finances the SUP under its Slum Upgradation and Improvement Scheme. Like the S&S Schemes, it was first taken up in Madras as a component of MUDP-I in 1977. Usually the same facilities are provided under it as in the SIP. However, giving land *pattas* on a *leasehold or freehold* basis is a requirement which distinguishes it from the SIP. It may be noted that even under the central government's EIUS programme, the provision of land rights to the beneficiary is absent.

The SUP can also be classified into two depending on the degree of formalisation of land tenure. In the first type, the SUP-I, *pattas* are given to individual households on a freehold basis. MUDP-I and II undertaken in Madras during the late 1970s and early 1980s, as discussed earlier, and the Tamil Nadu Urban Development Project (TUDP) currently under implementation are examples. The programmes under which land is leased out to the community on a collective basis, as in the case of Bombay, are termed SUP-II. For the success of this programme, a higher level of community participation, as compared to SUP-I, is required. Needless to say, the SUP can be designed with the provision of land being given to individuals on a leasehold basis or to the community on a freehold basis.

Another important feature of the SUP which distinguishes it from the SIP is the availability of home improvement loan (HIL) to the beneficiary on an optional basis. HUDCO gives a loan upto Rs. 4,000 as per the norms of EWS housing under the scheme. The former also includes provision of certain basic services such as water supply, latrines, sewer connections, storm water drains, street lights pathways and shelter upgradation. The norms followed in providing the infrastructure vary from project to project.[34]

The prospective beneficiaries are required to clear their backlog of rent and other municipal charges at the time of their registration under the scheme. The agreement, known as the lease-cum-sale agreement (between the implementing agency and the beneficiaries), for land right is signed once 10 per cent of the infrastructural cost, termed as environmemt improvement charges, are paid by the beneficiaries. This also entitles the beneficiaries to a home improvement loan. The engineering works, infrastructural layout, etc., commence only after the land deeds are signed. It may thus be seen that unlike the SIP, there is no direct subsidy in this programme.

Under the SUP-I, each household individually enters into the lease-cum-sale agreement with the housing agency. Thus, once the household has paid the cost of land, infrastructure and shelter upgradation, the ownership deeds are transferred to it as in the hire-purchase system. In contrast, under the SUP-II, the cooperative society of the beneficiaries enters into a lease-cum-sale agreement with the housing agency and subsequently sub-leases the plots to its members at a nominal rate. In the case of the BUDP, the monthly payment for the lease is Re. 1 only for an initial period of thirty years.

The cost charged to the beneficiaries for upgrading their units[35] varies with the size of the hut, location of the slum and the use to which it is put. Sometimes it is possible that a portion of the land in the project (in the case of low-density slums) is put to commercial use and disposed of at a high price. The profits thus earned are used to cross-subsidise the residential units.

The terms and conditions of lending, both for the SUP-I and II, depend on the concerned financing agency, as in other schemes. These are taken up at the initiative of the state government as stated earlier. Today, the state- or city-level implementing agencies can seek finance from only two agencies: HUDCO and the World Bank. The HUDCO scheme is known as the Slum Upgradation and Environmental Improvement Scheme. The ceiling cost is stipulated at Rs. 5,000 per family, of which Rs. 2,000 is for the improvement of the environment and Rs. 3,000 for shelter upgradation. Only 50 per cent of the former is given as a grant to the beneficiary, the rest being a loan. The rate of interest for the loan is 8 per cent and the period of repayment is twenty-two years.

HUDCO finances improvement and upgradation of slums located on public lands where sewers, electricity mains and water, through pipes or wells, are available in close proximity. The local bodies, state-level agencies such as the slum clearance boards or other state government departments, can borrow from HUDCO with guarantee from the state government or any other authority acceptable to it (such as a scheduled commercial bank).

World Bank loans for slum upgradation are available at an interest rate of 12 per cent to be repaid in twenty years. The exception is the TUDP where the loan period is fifteen years. The monthly instalment varies between Rs. 12 and Rs. 70 under the TUDP (World Bank 1988), whereas under the BUDP it ranges from Rs. 21 to Rs. 88 (according to the Bombay Metropolitan Region Development Authority) for plots of different sizes. However, the range reported by Krishnamurthy (1988) for the BUDP is from Rs. 23.8 to Rs. 107.6

Although projects are implemented through the state government departments, slum clearance boards, development authorities and the local bodies, the Bank exercises control over procedural and operational details. It has, for example, insisted on lowering the standards and adopting low-cost solutions for shelter and basic services to make these affordable to the poor. It has also tried to create systems to ensure cost recovery so that the agencies providing the services can function on a self-sustaining basis. Besides, it has proposed measures to strengthen the existing organisational structures, introduce proper accounting systems and ensure community participation.

Slum reconstruction as an approach to slum development has been adopted in a few cities. Under it, the slum population is rehoused after reconstruction of the houses with a proper layout plan on the same site. This involves temporarily shifting the population to an alternate site. The scheme thus becomes similar to the slum clearance scheme with the difference that the affected population is rehoused on the same plot.

The scheme involves, in most cases, a substantial subsidy owing to the low affordability of the affected population. However, there are a few instances where the scheme is implemented with a self-help approach, resulting in significant reduction in costs and subsidies. The UCD projects in Hyderabad and Vishakhapatnam are examples of self-help slum reconstruction projects, as discussed earlier.

It is important to note that public investment in basic amenities under any of the three slum development projects provides a sense of security to the slum dwellers which motivates them to make private investment in housing. This is true even in the case of the SIP where formal land tenure is not given. As a result, wherever these programmes have been taken up, there has been a significant increase in land prices.

It has been recorded that the monthly instalments under the SUP work out to be quite high in certain projects. For example, under MUDP-I, about one-eighth of the households covered in the project paid more than 20 per cent of their monthly income, 'the upper affordability limit generally used by the World Bank' (Borst 1990), as instalment.

Studies have shown that wherever lease-cum-sale agreements were signed with individuals, as in Madras, most of the tenants were expelled by their plot owners at the onset of the project. This is due to the apprehension of the tenants being recognized as plot owners and thus getting a share of land under the scheme. 'According to unofficial government statements, the estimated level of displacement in all slums improved under MUDP-I is about 25 to 30 per cent' (Borst 1990).

It is important to note that while making public investment in basic amenities, if land titles are given to individuals, private investments in land and housing tend to be much higher, as in the case of the SUP-I, as compared to the SIP or SUP-II projects. Thus, under the former, land becomes an easily tradeable commodity resulting in large-scale displacement of low income households by those in higher categories.

The SUP-II requires a higher level of community participation because the lease-cum-sale agreement is not signed with individuals but with their cooperative societies. The latter has the responsibility of ensuring that all the past dues and the initial improvement charges are paid by the members and, after the completion of the scheme, the instalments are paid regularly. Besides, the individual must apply for a home improvement loan through the cooperative and repay it through the latter. A cooperative, thus, exercises considerable control over its members. As a result, under this programme, the problem of displacement is less serious than in the SUP-I, since community participation and control act as deterrents to property transfers.

An Assessment of the Programmes

An analysis of the programmes and schemes undertaken by the central, state and local governments to provide shelter and basic services to the poor reveals that the major concerns and the areas of emphasis have been changing from time to time with the changing policy perspective. However, success in terms of their targets has been extremely limited although certain states have done better than others, as discussed in the following chapters. This conforms to the assessment of the National Commission on Urbanisation (NCU) which observed that:

(a) the reach of the programmes was limited;
(b) even the main targets were missed;
(c) there was a high degree of inflexibility in the programme and schemes;
(d) there was a lack of convergence of programmes, and
(e) excepting the Hyderabad/Vishakhapatnam UCD projects, the programmes were taken up on a laboratory scale (NCU 1988: 99).

It has been seen that most of the programmes were financed

primarily by the central government in the initial years of planning. However, during the 1960s and 1970s, there was a shift of responsibility from the central to the state governments and local bodies. The EIUS and UCD were started with a central grant of 100 per cent and 50 per cent, respectively. These programmes are now being financed completely by the state and local governments. The UBS and IDSMT are comparatively new schemes that still enjoy a certain amount of central assistance, although much less than that provided in the earlier programmes. For UBS, for example, central assistance is only 20 per cent of the project cost. In the case of the IDSMT, a maximum of 50 per cent of the cost or Rs. 46 lakhs is the central component. The remaining 50 per cent is to be shared equally by the state and the local governments. It is, however, important that the central loan is available, as has been noted earlier, only for the Part A component of the programme. This also bears a relatively higher rate of interest (9.75 per cent) than that charged in the other schemes or in this very scheme in the initial years. The rate has been revised further in recent years.

Transferring the responsibility of financing (and also maintaining) the projects, at least partially, to the state and local bodies, when many of them are facing serious financial crises is responsible for their slow progress and tardy implementation. This, in turn, has adversely affected the availability of basic services to the urban population, particularly the poor.

Some of the state governments have closed down programmes like UCD with the discontinuation of central assistance. A few others have opted for institutional funds for the project at a high rate of interest instead of making budgetary provisions for it.

The weak financial position of the state governments, particularly that of the local bodies, has caused problems of delay in project implementation. It has been mentioned that the World Bank insists on the recovery of development costs under the slum upgradation/improvement schemes by increasing water rates, property taxes, and so on. Many local bodies have found it difficult to comply with this requirement.

HUDCO loans can indeed be availed of by the housing boards, slum clearance boards, development authorities, local bodies and others for upgrading and improving the basic services in slum areas at a rate (8.00 per cent) much cheaper than that of the World Bank. However, these loans are available only when the agency grants tenure rights of land for not less than twenty years, or when the state government guarantees that the occupants will not be removed until the loan is repaid. This condition has often come in the way of the local bodies and other authorities obtaining HUDCO loans for the slum colonies located within the cities.

The experience of the EIUS in many states shows that the ceiling on per capita expenditure, even after the recent revision, works out to only Rs. 300 which is inadequate for the services to be provided according to the stipulated norms. In many states, the actual expenditure has been much more than this ceiling.

In the states where additional resources could not be placed at the disposal of the project authorities, either the quality of the services has suffered or fewer people have been covered. If the ceiling on per capita expenditure remains fixed for a long period, the standard of the facilities would have to be lowered owing to cost escalation.

Low-cost sanitation facilities have been extended to the urban population under different state government schemes with 50 per cent of the cost coming to the beneficiary as a grant and the remaining as a loan at a low rate of interest. Yet, it has remained beyond the affordability of those below the poverty line. Further, where people have been provided with toilets, the recovery of the implementation charge or the loan has been very poor.

It is indeed true that when private organisations or non-governmental organisations (NGOs) such as Sulabh International have taken up the construction and maintenance jobs, the recovery rate has risen. It must, however, be noted that they charge certain administrative costs that become an additional burden on the local body as well as on the beneficiary. Sulabh charges 10 to 25 per cent of the project cost in the case of individual latrines and 20 per cent in the case of community latrines as their administrative cost. Besides, 80 per cent of the project cost, including the administrative cost, has to be paid in advance and the remaining 20 per cent within two months of completion. Sulabh makes different types of latrines, their costs ranging from Rs. 700 to Rs. 1,500. Given this cost and schedule of payment, not many among the urban poor can afford individual latrines even when 50 per cent of the cost comes as a subsidy.

In the case of community latrines, the maintenance responsibility remains with Sulabh which it undertakes on a 'pay and use' basis.

In several localities, where the resident population is extremely poor or unruly, it has failed to collect the user charges. In all such situations the maintenance expenditure is borne by the local bodies which becomes an additional burden for them.

Besides these financial constraints, the programmes have suffered because of administrative weaknesses. Multiplicity of agencies creates administrative difficulties at the implementation stage. Lack of coordination among agencies dealing with water supply, electricity, sewerage, etc., has emerged as a major problem. The development authorities, slum clearance boards and state government departments that generally take up environmental improvement projects in the slums hand over the created facilities to the local authorities after completion and the latter take up the responsibility of maintenance. The transfer has often not been very smooth and many of these facilities have not been functional for long periods in the absence of proper supervision or because of lack of coordination between the construction and maintenance agencies.

Undertaking the EIUS programme in the slums situated on private lands is yet another problem. Several conditions must be ensured before such slums can be included in the programme. Amendments in the existing laws and adoption of a new Act would be necessary to safeguard the slum dwellers from higher rentals being charged by the private owners after the improvement work. This involves a cumbersome procedure and requires a strong political will. As a result, barring a few cases, slums on private lands have not been taken up under the programme. This has left about 45 per cent of the slum population outside the purview of the EIUS.

The selection of towns under the IDSMT programme is often guided by political considerations as well as economic viability. It is seldom based on an analysis of infrastructural deficiency. As the state governments have to repay central assistance, only those schemes are selected that are remunerative and involve less risk. Slum improvement and provision of basic services that are included in Part B of the programme, therefore, are often left out. Unfortunately, unlike low-cost sanitation, no special allocation has been made for slum improvement under this programme.

It has been argued that Part A and Part B of the programme should be merged to give a wider choice to the local authorities.

This, it is hoped, will improve the financial viability of the programme and improve the recovery rate. With the acceptance of this, components such as slum improvement and provision of services that have low commercial viability will be accorded a still lower priority.

Under the IDSMT, towns are selected either at the state or at the central level. Further, the project outline is prepared by people who are not very familiar with the problems or the development prospects of the towns. The components of the programme are more or less standardised and no major departure to suit local requirements is permitted. As a result, activities are selected or designed under the schemes as an administrative formality without much concern for the needs of the people in the towns.

It should also be noted that at the beginning of 1980s, a concern for water supply and sanitation in the country was expressed and a sense of urgency shown by the central government with the adoption of the Master Plan for the Water Supply and Sanitation Decade. Ambitious targets were fixed to provide these services to the urban areas with special provisions to extend them to the fringe areas. Unfortunately, these were not matched by a corresponding allocation of resources or by the launching of major programmes, barring the few by the central government, as discussed earlier. Besides making certain policy statements from time to time, both at the central and state levels, no major attempts were made to strengthen the existing delivery system and ensure its better management. As a result, the water supply and sewerage-sanitation scenario at the end of the decade, particularly in terms of access of the poor, remained virtually unchanged.

Programmes for Health Care

The health care system in urban India, organised through government, semi-government, private and voluntary organisations, provides health services to the general public as well as to workers in the organised and unorganised sectors, as discussed in the previous chapter. In addition, the central government has launched special programmes to strengthen or augment the existing health facilities and to control and eradicate certain communicable diseases which take a heavy toll of human life. These programmes received an impetus with the establishment of the National Institute of Communicable Diseases whose basic responsibility was to plan and monitor the programmes related to communicable diseases.

India had a very high infant mortality rate of 134 per 1,000 live births at the time of Independence which was attributed to the prevalence of several communicable diseases on the one hand, and to poor health infrastructure on the other. Malaria, leprosy, tuberculosis, filariasis, *kala azar*, guinea worm and diarrhoeal diseases were the major health hazards that threatened the population both in rural and urban areas and led to high morbidity. Besides, a large section of the population was affected by various nutritional deficiencies such as vitamin A deficiency causing blindness, iodine deficiency leading to endemic goitre and physical and mental retardation in children, and iron deficiency leading to anaemia. The incidence of these is very high among the poor and those living in unhygienic environments.

In view of the inadequate health infrastructure available to the poor, the central and state governments intervened and launched drives for the eradication of these diseases and nutritional deficiencies. The major programmes of the government in existence today can be placed in two categories: (*a*) preventive and curative programmes; and (*b*) integrated programmes encompassing health, environment, education, family planning, and so on. Although preventive and curative programmes are not specifically targeted to the poor, they become the major beneficiaries because of their greater vulnerability to the diseases. At present, the following programmes are in operation under this category:

(*i*) National Leprosy Eradication Programme
(*ii*) National Guinea Worm Eradication Programme
(*iii*) Malaria Eradication Programme
(*iv*) Programme for the Control of Blindness
(*v*) Programme for Tuberculosis Control
(*vi*) Goitre Control Programme
(*vii*) STD + AIDS Control Programme
(*viii*) Cancer Control Programme
(*ix*) Diabetes Control Programme
(*x*) Universal Immunisation Programme
(*xi*) Mental Health Programme

Most of these programmes were initiated during the First and Second Five-Year Plans and have continued in the subsequent plans. The Malaria and Leprosy Eradication Programmes were started in the 1950s, whereas the Goitre Control and TB Control Programmes were initiated in 1962. From the Third Five-Year Plan, attention shifted from curative to preventive programmes. As a result, Programmes like Universal Immunisation and Mental Health were launched.

The Universal Immunisation Programme is the most important preventive programme launched by the central government in 1978. Earlier known as the Expanded Programme on Immunisation (EPI) with the objective of immunising eligible children and pregnant women against certain communicable diseases through hospitals and dispensaries in urban areas, the programme was later extended to rural areas in all the districts. It is now known as the Universal Immunisation Programme and is a component of the Technology Mission. The objective is to immunise all children against six most common diseases. The programme is being supported by the World Health Organisation (WHO) with help from UNICEF. The central government is assisting the state governments with the supply of vaccines, equipment and training of medical staff, while the state governments implement the programme and provide facilities through the existing health delivery system.

In all these centrally sponsored programmes the central government either bears the full cost or shares it with the state government on a 50:50 basis. In some cases, the financial responsibility of the centre has gone up over the years. For example, the National Leprosy Eradication Programme which was started in 1955 with a rural bias with partial central assistance was converted into a centrally funded programme in 1969–70 and extended to urban areas as well. For the Malaria and Guinea Worm Eradication Programmes, the costs are shared by the centre and the states on a 50:50 basis.

Bilateral and international finance is also available for some of the programmes. For example, the Tuberculosis Control Programme is supported by UNICEF and by the Swedish International Development Agency (SIDA). Different regulatory bodies have been set up from time to time to monitor these programmes. In the case of the Leprosy Eradication Programme, a National Leprosy Eradication Commission (NLEC) was set up during the Sixth Five Year Plan for guidance and surveillance and a National Leprosy Eradication Board was established to implement the programme. The

National Guinea Worm Eradication Programme is monitored by the National Institute of Communicable Diseases while the Directorate of the Malaria Eradication Programme at the central level and the Directorate of Health at the state level are responsible for implementing the Malaria Eradication Programme.

In addition to these preventive and curative programmes, certain integrated programmes are also in operation. With the announcement of the National Health Policy in 1982 which redefined the programme priorities and aimed at providing 'an integrated package of services to tackle the entire range of health conditions', the scope of these programmes has increased.

The Revised Family Welfare Strategy announced in 1986 is one such integrated approach to the problem of health. The Family Planning Programme was launched during the First Five-Year Plan and was initially aimed at only reducing the crude birth rate, death rate and infant mortality rate, and increasing the couple protection rate. It has now been integrated with the Maternal and Child Health Programme. It was also recognised that the programme should not be the responsibility of one department alone but should be implemented jointly through the concerned departments in the government.[36]

A few other integrated programmes that are not formally a part of the health sector also have the provision of health services as a major component. One such programme is the Integrated Child Development Services (ICDS). The programme was launched in 1975 by the Department of Women and Child Development, Ministry of Human Resource Development, on an experimental basis in pursuance of the National Policy for Children announced in 1974. It envisages the provision of services such as basic health, nutrition and pre-school education to children under 6 years of age and certain health facilities for pregnant and lactating mothers. Initially, thirty-three experimental projects were taken up covering rural and tribal areas and selected urban slums. With the success of these pilot programmes it was extended to several other areas in the Sixth Plan. Presently, there are 1,019 projects in the country. The programme aims at providing:

— supplementary nutrition;
— immunisation;
— Health Check-up; and
— Referral services for complicated cases.

The ICDS was declared a national programme in the Sixth Plan and is implemented through the state governments with complete central assistance. It may be noted that besides the Ministry of Human Resource Development, the Ministry of Food and Civil Supplies and the Ministry of Agriculture also cooperate in the implementation of the programme. UNICEF is supporting the programme and the Central Social Welfare Board, voluntary organisations, local bodies and others are involved in its implementation. The services are provided through *anganwadis* under the supervision of the *mukhya sevika* and the Child Development Project Officer. *Anganwadi* workers are local women who, after receiving basic training for a period of three months, are appointed on an honorary basis. The unique feature of the ICDS is that most of the centres for training the grass-roots workers are managed by voluntary organisations.

Programmes Focused on the Urban Poor—An Evaluation

Urban Basic Services (UBS) is yet another centrally sponsored integrated programme which is taken up in the urban slums. As discussed, UBS is not an exclusive health programme as it aims at improving the social and economic conditions of the slum dwellers by providing a minimum level of basic services. The programme was launched in 1985 by the central government in collaboration with UNICEF by combining three existing UNICEF-supported programmes, namely, Urban Community Development, Small and Medium Town Development and Low-cost Sanitation. The basic objective of the programme is to improve the living conditions of urban, low income families, especially the children and women, in selected less developed districts, through the provision of a package of services which includes (*a*) health and nutrition, (*b*) water supply and sanitation and (*c*) learning opportunities for children and women.

The health services under the programme include:

(*i*) immunisation;
(*ii*) improved infant feeding practices;
(*iii*) child growth monitoring;
(*iv*) home-based diarrhoea management; and
(*v*) health and nutrition education.

The aim is to strengthen and expand the existing health services to be managed by the state health departments and municipalities through inter-agency coordination and community support. All the grass-roots level functionaries are to be selected from the local communities. The programme is implemented through different types of functionaries: District Project Officer, Community Organiser, Resident Community Volunteers, Pre-school and Creche Workers, Health Volunteers and Para-medical Personnel (who are trained to work closely with the ICDS and the Health Ministry's National Immunisation Programme).

The financial liabilities under UBS are shared by the centre, state and UNICEF in the proportion of 20:40:40. It was initiated in 1985 and 200 towns were brought under it in the first phase. It aimed at covering at least 85 per cent of the children in the project towns by the year 1987 and Rs. 3 lakhs were allocated to each project town for this purpose.

An overview of these programmes at the national level reveals that the resources committed to these were too meagre to make any dent on the health problems of the poor. The scale of operation never went beyond the experimental stage. However, instead of launching the programme on a large scale after learning from these experiences, the government is now withdrawing due to the resources crunch. Under the policy of economic liberalisation, the specific programmes for the poor in the sector would be the worst casualty.

Several other urban development projects being implemented in slum areas in some cities also include a health component. The Urban Community Development (UCD) project, still in operation in a few cities and towns, has a major health component. In the cities of Hyderabad, Vishakhapatnam, Ahmedabad and Indore, UCD is implemented through the municipal corporation and the UCD wing (in the municipality) is viewed as an intermediary between the people and the corporation.

In Hyderabad, UCD covers child welfare activities, immunisation, balwadis, mid-day meal centres, medical check-up centres, etc. In Ahmedabad, on the other hand, UCD is playing an important role in providing immunisation and nutrition services to the urban poor. The UCD cell functioning under the municipal corporation helps in persuading voluntary organisations to open health camps, and in obtaining financial assistance and medicines from the state government and municipalities. The Vishakhapatnam UCD project is also giving special emphasis to the health component which includes health education. Primary health centres have been set up under the programme in slums with 500 families. One honorary medical practitioner works in each slum on a part-time basis. Resident community volunteers visit individual households. These centres provide preventive as well as curative care. Complicated cases are referred to higher levels, namely, to the municipal dispensaries and civil hospitals. The centres also organise food and nutrition camps to train mothers to prepare nutritious food in a clean environment.

By the end of the Seventh Plan, the programme was modified to include only the social components and consequently the physical inputs pertaining to sanitation facilities were excluded. The target shifted to the poor alone and the programme was renamed Urban Basic Services for the Poor. Despite this apparent concern, the funds allocated to the programme were minimal and could cover, under the most optimistic assumptions, not more than 10 per cent of the urban poor during the entire plan period.

Operational Aspects of the Public Distribution System

The effectiveness of the PDS and its capacity to serve the people in general and the weaker sections in particular[37] depends, to a large extent, on the operational system which differs from state to state. The distributional systems have been designed keeping the following objectives in view:

1. The method of identification of the beneficiaries and the issuing of ration cards should enable the poor to avail of the PDS supplies.
2. The commodities supplied by the PDS should cover most of the items required by the poor.
3. The amount of ration supplied should be adequate to meet the requirements, particularly those of the poor, so that their reliance on the open market is minimised.
4. The prices and periodicity of sale must be in tune with the incomes to the poor.

Keeping this in view, the following aspects of the operational system which have a direct bearing on the objectives have been analysed in the present section.

1. Issuing of ration cards, i.e., to whom to issue and the procedure of issuance.
2. Commodities covered.
3. Ration scale or the amount of supply.
4. Periodicity of sale
5. Issue price.

The method of issuing ration cards in almost all states has a provision to exclude access by the relatively better-off sections of society. The extent of exclusion, however, is not significnt. The procedure of differentiating the relatively poor from others varies across states. In fact, each state has separate norms that are incorporated in the system by (a) excluding those above a certain income, those with a certain level of sale/turnover or landholdings, (b) denying certain commodities to specific groups, (c) charging higher prices from richer sections of the population, (d) supplying particular income groups for only a limited period each year, and (e) restricting the number of family members eligible for rations. Some of these criteria have often been used in combination (Kabra and Ittyerah 1986).

In Punjab, for example, people below the poverty line, identified through a survey, have been given yellow cards. Others have white cards. Those with yellow cards get pulses and edible oil at subsidised rates that are not available to the white card holders. In Gujarat, people earning more than Rs. 800 per month are not given cereals under the PDS. Also, agriculturists with landholdings above a certain limit, manufacturers and businessmen with a sale/turnover above a certain limit, or those registered with the sales tax department are denied access to cereals. In Madhya Pradesh, families with a monthly income exceeding Rs. 1,000 do not have access to cereals. They, however, can buy sugar and edible oil from the PDS.

In Kerala, self-sufficient and surplus farmers are not eligible for cereals. Those producing only a part of their annual requirement get cereals for a limited period during the year. The self-sufficient and surplus farmers are also excluded from the PDS in Goa. In

Andhra Pradesh, no one is excluded from the PDS. Those earning below Rs. 600 a month are, however, eligible for green cards that entitle them to rations at lower rates. The rest of the population has yellow cards and the maximum entitlement is that of a family with five members. This puts large families with yellow cards at a disadvantage. Karnataka and Tamil Nadu have similar schemes of positive discrimination based on the income criterion.

West Bengal has a much more elaborate system. It has two methods of rationing, statutory and modified. Statutory rationing is operative in the cities of Calcutta, Durgapur and Asansol. The remaining part of the state is covered by the modified rationing system. In the statutory rationing areas, everybody is given a card and is entitled to a uniform quantity of rationed cereal. Under the modified system, households with landholdings above a specified limit cannot get cereals. Eligible families are divided into five categories and allowed cereal entitlements depending on their landholdings.

In Orissa, families with a monthly income in excess of Rs. 600 are issued B-class cards and are required to pay higher prices for their purchases as compared to those with A-class cards who have lower incomes. Jammu and Kashmir, too, has an elaborate system of differentiation among groups of consumers in terms of ration scale and issue price. Urban families with an income of Rs. 600 and above per month are charged a 'land cost price'. Families with lower incomes pay lower prices. Again, all the low income families are not charged uniformly for the total quantity of their entitlement. Prices also vary according to the amount purchased.

Despite the differentiated system of rationing followed in the states, the population excluded from the PDS constitutes only a minor proportion of the total. The state governments have mostly adopted the norm of universal coverage and over 80 per cent of the population is technically eligible for ration cards.

The procedure for issuing ration cards in urban areas is more or less the same in all states. Persons eligible under the system prevailing in the state apply to the civil supply authorities. The eligibility conditions mostly result in exclusion of people without a permanent address which implies discrimination against pavement and slum dwellers. The bureaucratic formalities also discourage the urban poor from applying for ration cards.

The coverage of commodities for distribution under the PDS is another important dimension with significant inter-state variations. At present, the central government procures and supplies seven commodities, as discussed in the previous chapter. The important omissions from the central list are coarse cereals (such as *ragi*, *bajra*, *jowar* and other millets) and pulses. A few states, namely Rajasthan, Gujarat and Maharashtra, undertake limited procurement of coarse grains. These, however, are not regular components of the state PDS and are used in special situations and on a limited scale. Pulses are included in the PDS in the states of West Bengal and Punjab. Since the distribution of coarse cereals and pulses does not enjoy the support of the central government, the states usually do not subsidise the issue price. Some states are, however, able to sell coarse cereals at less than their procurement price through cross-subsidisation, using the profit made on the distribution of edible oil and sugar. The exclusion of coarse grains and pulses leaves a large number of urban poor dependent on the open market.

The coarse grains, such as *jowar* and *bajra*, constitute a fairly significant portion of the consumption basket in several states, particularly in areas with low rainfall. The calorie content of coarse grains, purchased with a given sum of money, would be much higher than that of wheat and rice. Besides, the price of coarse grains and pulses, particularly that of the latter, is subject to fluctuations and inflationary pressures, like that of other essential commodities. Due to these reasons, several state governments have pleaded for the inclusion of coarse cereals and pulses in the list of centrally supplied commodities.

The other important aspects of the PDS relate to the periodicity of purchase, scale of ration (entitlement) and number of card holders per family. There are restrictions on the frequency and size of purchase. The states of West Bengal, Kerala and Tripura permit weekly purchases. In the union territory of Delhi, a fortnightly system exists. Most other states follow a monthly disposal system.

The variation in the per capita ration made available across the states, however, is much more pronounced than in the case of periodicity of purchase. The variation in the amount of ration is essentially the result of the demand and supply position in different states. On the demand side, the important factor is whether the concerned cereal constitutes the staple food of the people. On the supply side, factors such as production, availability and surplus determine the quantity of ration.

The last consideration in the operation of the PDS is the issue price to the consumers. The price charged by the central government from the states is dependent on the procurement price or support price. Various costs are added to the latter to obtain the ex-godown price for deliveries to state governments. These include transport and administrative overhead expenses incurred by the Food Corporation of India. However, the actual price charged from the state is low due to the central subsidies. The issue price to the consumer is arrived at by adding the interest, transport, handling and storage costs incurred by the state government and the margin given to fair price shop dealers, to the ex-godown price charged by the central government. Due to the differences in the costs incurred by the state governments, the final issue price paid by the consumers varies significantly from state to state.[30] Finally, there exists considerable variation in the open market price across states, so much so that in some states the PDS prices are at par with or exceed the open market prices.

Reaching Out to the Poor

The distribution of essential commodities at subsidised rates to people in general and to the poor in particular through the PDS has been viewed as an anti-inflationary and anti-poverty strategy. The main thrust has supposedly been on the poor. This is sought to be achieved through selectivity in issuing ration cards, coverage of commodities, system of issuing rations, the pricing policy, etc. The foregoing overview of the functioning of the PDS in different states, however, reveals serious inadequacies and constraints within the system that come in the way of the fulfilment of the objectives. The major shortcomings of the system have been analysed here in the context of the needs and affordability of the poor.

The procedure of issuing ration cards involves an implicit bias against the poor, illiterate, houseless, slum dwellers and temporary migrants. Most of these people do not satisfy the requirement of having legal ownership or tenancy over the place of their residence.

Many do not even have a permanent address. Besides, their capability to cope with the administrative requirements of the system is extremely limited due to their socio-economic background.

It has been noted that the poor are being pushed out of the posh and formal localities in most cities. A large number of them live in colonies at great distances from the office issuing ration cards. Most of these colonies do not have a fair price shop in the neighbourhood. Their real cost of obtaining ration cards and ration thus works to be significantly more than that for the non-poor population. The cumbersome and time-consuming process of completing the forms and repeatedly visiting the civil supply office puts the poor at a disadvantage.

Due to their low level of literacy, unfamiliarity with the rules and regulations and their inability to establish 'contacts' through friendship and family ties, the urban poor have no access to the bureaucracy. Finally, engaged in a struggle for survival, they do not have time to complete the bureaucratic requirements of obtaining a ration card.

The problem of bogus ration cards is indeed serious in several large cities. It is estimated that there are 2 lakh such cards in the national capital of India itself. Its incidence is, however, likely to be more among the middle income group with access to corridors of power and the poor will have only a small share in this.

Coarse cereals and pulses, which are not included in the central government supplies, claim a significant portion of the consumption expenditure of the poor in several states. The prices of coarse cereals such as *jowar* and *bajra* are less than those of wheat and rice, which tilts the preference of the poor in favour of the former. In the case of pulses, per capita consumption is not very different across the consumption fractiles. These constitute the major source of vegetable protein for a large number of urban poor. The exclusion of coarse cereals and pulses from the PDS in most states, thus, forces them to depend on the open market, further eroding their purchasing power.

Yet another aspect of the PDS, believed to be going against the poor, is the periodicity of sale. The study by Kabra and Ittyerah (1986) shows that the system of issuing rations on a monthly basis is founded on the assumption that the target populations under the PDS have regular incomes and can buy their provisions on a monthly basis. A large majority of urban workers are employed in informal activities associated with construction, trade and commerce, and have an irregular and uncertain flow of income. Many among them get their salaries on a weekly basis. They might also find it difficult to purchase their monthly requirements in one instalment. The weekly or fortnightly system is, therefore, believed to be better suited to the urban poor.

It may, on the other hand, be argued that the weekly disposal system increases the cost of delivery to the government, cooperative and private dealers. It may also be inconvenient to consumers as the dealer of a fair price shop may then insist on the consumer visiting the shop several times a month to collect his or her total quota. The risk appears as real in view of the irregularity of supply and the not-so-friendly attitude of the fair price shop personnel, against whom complaints are always being lodged in the concerned office. It would, therefore, be worthwhile to examine the preference of the poor in the context of their irregular income and implicit cost of visiting fair price shops several times each month. This has been attempted in Chapter 6.

Notes

1. From the Fourth Plan onwards, these schemes were placed under the state sector. However, the central government continued to give financial assistance in the form of block loans and block grants. Presently, the investments made under these are negligible.
2. The monthly subsidised rent charged by the Maharashtra Housing Board in Bombay was Rs. 22.5, besides some service charges. The total works out to about 5 to 7 per cent of the monthly income (Taleyarkhan 1964).
3. In Gujarat, the scheme continued until 1979–80, in Tamil Nadu until 1973–74 and in Maharashtra until 1969–70.
   (**Source**: Gujarat Housing Board, Tamil Nadu Housing Board and Maharashtra Housing and Area Development Authority, respectively).
4. In Maharashtra, the centre's contribution was 75 per cent of the cost—37.5 per cent as loan and 37.5 per cent as subsidy—and the remaining 25 per cent was to be divided between the state government and concerned municipality. (Taleyarkhan 1964).
5. In Maharashtra, the municipalities and municipal corporations have implemented the SCS. In the union Territory of Delhi, as already discussed earlier, the Slum Wing of the DDA was the implementing agency. In many other cities, the slum wings of the respective municipal corporations were assigned this responsibility.

6. For example, in Tamil Nadu and Karnataka, these schemes were handed over by the housing boards to the slum clearance boards. In Gujarat, however, the schemes were not taken up by the housing board. It was only after the establishment of the SCB that the scheme was designed and implemented.

7. The Tamil Nadu Slum Clearance Board (TNSCB) has been charging Rs. 20 as monthly rent from the households. For water supply and electricity, additional amounts of Rs. 2 and Rs. 3, respectively, are being charged. Only households with monthly incomes up to Rs. 350 were eligible for allotment under this scheme. The monthly rent, therefore, worked out to about 5 to 7 per cent of the household's income, which seems reasonable.

8. When HUDCO was set up, the only stipulation made was that at least 25 per cent of its disbursement would be for EWS housing. Subsequently, however, the responsibility of HUDCO for the provision of housing for lower, middle and higher income groups was also recognised. For the purpose of generating resources it also wanted to take up commercial and industrial schemes that assured a high rate of return. As a result, a formal structure of resource allocation was laid down in 1975–76 in which the share of EWS was 30 per cent and the shares of the LIG, MIG and HIG were fixed at 25, 25 and 20 per cent, respectively. All these schemes were mainly taken up in urban areas up to 1978–79.

9. This information is collected from the Gujarat Housing Board (GHB), TNHB, MHADA and the housing board of the Haryana.

10. For example, the GHB takes 10 per cent of the cost as down payment in schemes designed for people in reserved categories such as Scheduled Castes and Tribes, the blind, handicapped, Other Backward Castes and EWS. For the LIG, it takes 25 per cent and for other schemes, the percentage varies from 40 to 75 per cent depending on the preference of the allottee. The TNHB collects 20 per cent of total cost as down payment for EWS schemes, 33 per cent for LIG and 30 to 40 per cent for MIG and HIG schemes. If the cost of the dwelling unit exceeds Rs. 2 lakhs, 50 per cent is taken as the down payment. As against this the Jammu and Kashmir Housing Board takes a down payment as high as 50 per cent of the cost even under EWS schemes.

11. The monthly instalment is calculated at 8 per cent interest rate, twenty years repayment period and 10 per cent down payment for a unit costing Rs. 22,000.

12. One and a half years is assumed to be the average construction period and interest is charged for half the period, that is, for nine months at the rate charged for that particular scheme.

13. The Housing Boards of Haryana and of Jammu and Kashmir recover administrative charges at a flat rate of 10 per cent of the unit cost. In Gujarat, however, rates are different in different schemes; establishment charges are not recovered from sites and services schemes, whereas for EWS, LIG, MIG and HIG projects, 5, 10, 12 and 12 per cent of the unit cost, respectively, is charged. The TNHB charges a supervision cost of 10 per cent over and above the establishment charges of 12.5 per cent.

14. For example, the GHB charges 5 per cent of the cost as profits under the LIG schemes, the rate being 10 per cent and 15 per cent for MIG and HIG schemes, respectively.

15. The stipulation regarding the minimum saving period was five years which has recently been revised to three years by the NHB.

16. The Slum Improvement Programme (SIP) still continues in Delhi and in Madras (as the Accelerated Slum Improvement Scheme). This shall be discussed along with the schemes outside the central sector.

17. The Seventh Plan allocation was Rs. 269.55 crores against the Sixth Plan figure of Rs. 151.45 crores.

18. It is estimated that from the inception of the scheme till the end of March 1989, nearly 23.9 million slum dwellers had been covered.

19. The total outlay was estimated at Rs. 27.60 crores during the five-year period between 1984 and 1989 (at 1984 prices), out of which UNICEF's contribution was Rs. 11.04 crores.

20. In Hyderabad and Vishakhapatnam an integrated approach has been adopted wherein, besides providing for the basic urban services, attempts have been made to meet people's social and economic needs as well. The following components in the Hyderabad project show its integrated character:

   — family welfare activities which include immunisation, health check up and first-aid centres;
   — supplementary feeding programme;
   — youth and women's employment programme;
   — educational activities for small children;
   — environmental sanitation, water supply and physical improvement activities; and
   — shelter construction activities.

21. The scheme aimed to cover the entire slum population in the city in three phases: Phase I (1988–89), Phase II (1989–90) and Phase III (1990–91).

22. As per the survey conducted in 1979, 455 slums with a population of 4.2 lakhs were identified in the twin cities. After the increase of the slum population to 5.4 lakhs in 1981, an additional 275 slums were identified. Out of the 455 slums identified earlier, only 137 were located on government and quasi-government lands. Of the latter, as many as twenty were categorised as 'objectionable' slums to be relocated in the larger interest of the city population. However, 70 per cent of the total slums were on private lands where granting *pattas* was not possible. Up to 1985–86, *pattas* were given to households in 137 slums that were located on government and quasi-government lands. During 1985–86, an additional forty-eight slums were notified for acquisition under the Andhra Pradesh Slum Improvement (Acquisition of Land) Act, 1956. *Pattas* have already been given in eleven of them, taking the number of slums in which *pattas* have been given to 148 (20 per cent of a total of 730 slums).

23. From 1976 to 1981, loans were provided by commercial banks under the Habitat Housing Scheme initiated by the Reserve Bank of India (RBI). The ceiling cost of the house was fixed at Rs. 6,200, of which 80 per cent was given as a loan and the remaining 20 per cent was the contribution of the beneficiary in the form of money, material and labour (Table 4.7).

24. The norm for water supply, for example, was kept at 15 to 20 gallons per capita per day when the present average supply is 40 to 60 gallons. Similarly, preventive medicine is advocated and provided rather than expensive health care services. Most of the funds in the housing sector are to be spent on the sites and services schemes under the programme.

25. The International Water Supply and Sanitation Decade was declared by the

United Nations with the objective of covering the entire world population with safe drinking water and sanitation facilities. The Indian Chapter of the programme was started in 1981 and was to continue up to 31 March 1991. Under it, various initiatives were taken at central, state and local levels to remove the deficiencies in the provision of the services. The following decadal targets were fixed by the central government in consultation with the states and union territories for urban areas:

1. 100 per cent piped water supply to all communities with the average water supply being 140 lpcd (range being 70 to 250 lpcd); stand posts in fringe areas and at strategic locations to ensure average water supply of 40 lpcd (range being 25 to 70 lpcd).
2. 100 per cent coverage of Class I cities with sewerage treatment facilities and provision of community toilets in the fringe areas; low-cost sanitation facilities in all other towns with overall targets being coverage of 80 per cent of the population.

26. In Gujarat, for example, fifty-five towns have been identified for the conversion of dry latrines into water-borne latrines. In Tamil Nadu and Kerala the number of such towns is fourteen and ten, respectively. In Tamil Nadu, pilot projects of low-cost sanitation have been taken up in Madras city only.
27. The programme was introduced initially for the EWS population but has subsequently been extended to people in all income groups under the name 'plotted development'.
28. The World Bank prefers to call the Sites and Services Schemes a shelter programme (rather than a housing programme) since shelter also includes the informal structures built by individuals as temporary dwellings.
29. Under the Accelerated Slum Improvement Scheme the following standards were adopted:

   (*i*) one latrine for every ten families;
   (*ii*) one water tap for every twenty families;
   (*iii*) street lights at every 40 metres of road length.

   The cost per household was limited to Rs. 1,250.
30. In CUDP-III the parameters are:

   (*i*) one latrine for each hutment or for every twenty-five persons;
   (*ii*) water tap connections to individual huts or for every 100 persons with an average water supply of 90 litres per capita per day;
   (*iii*) surface drains; and
   (*iv*) paved roads, street lighting, etc.
31. The Kanpur Urban Development Project (KUDP) was another World Bank-assisted project which was completed in 1985–86.
32. For example, in Bombay, as per the Slum Census of 1976, out of a total of 1,680 slums, seventy-eight (4.6 per cent) were on private lands, 309 (18.4 per cent) on municipal lands and 591 (35.2 per cent) on government and government agencies' lands. In the last category, 331 slum pockets were further examined with respect to their compatibility with the development plan and their feasibility of development. It was found that 169 (51.1 per cent) slum pockets had to be relocated (Sinha 1990).

33. An evaluation of a slum resettlement project of the Pune Municipal Corporation, which involved shifting 10,600 families living in seven shanty settlements close to the inner city to Bibwewadi and Dhanakawadi near the fringe, showed that 56.4 per cent of the households did not wish to participate in the scheme and only 19.8 per cent had already shifted to new accommodations, the tenements priced between Rs. 14,750 and Rs. 18,300, and serviced plots priced at Rs. 5,500. Around 23.8 per cent of the households which were waiting for the construction had only paid up to Rs. 100 as down payment which showed their unwillingness to pay. The reasons given for non-participation were (a) unaffordability (b) unwillingness to pay because of already incurred expenses on existing structures (Bapat 1988).

34. Under the TUDP, facilities are provided in slums according to the following norms:

    (i) one bath for ten families;
    (ii) one toilet for ten families; and
    (iii) one public fountain for 40 metres of road.

Under the BUDP, the norms are:

    (i) all dwelling units should be within a distance of 55 metres of a 6 metre road;
    (ii) minimum provision of 1 metre stand pipe (45 lpcd)for fifteen households;
    (iii) one toilet for ten households;
    (iv) drains, street lights, etc.

35. The average improvement charge for a household in Madras varied from Rs. 1,000 to Rs. 1,200 at 1978–79 prices. In Bombay, this came to Rs. 2,000 at 1985–86 prices, which works out to roughly the same as in Madras.

36. Against the outlay of Rs. 1,078 crores during the Sixth Plan, the total allocation to the family planning sector was stepped up to Rs. 3,256 crores during the Seventh Plan. This is over and above the total health sector outlay of Rs. 3,392.89 crores.

37. It has been stated clearly in the policy documents issued by the Ministry of Food and Agriculture that the PDS is being 'run for the good of the general public or a specific group thereof.'

38. Lele (1971) argues that the 'Agricultu: ~ Price Commission has been attempting to equalise the procurement price of paddy and rice in various states without much success. With as little success, it has emphasised the desirability of having a standard set of margins for the distribution of foodgrains . . . the government has even less control over regional differences in price.'

References

Bapat, M. (1988). 'Critical Evaluation of Toeing Official Line? Report on a Rehabilitation Project', *Economic and Political Weekly*, 23(16).
Borst, Frank Jan. (1990). 'Slum Improvement in Major Cities of India: A Tentative

Evaluation of Some Distinctive Types', paper presented at 11th European Conference on Modern South Asian Studies, Amsterdam, 2–5 July.

Kabra, K.N. and A.C. Ittyerah. (1986). *The Public Distribution System—A Report on Target Group Orientation and the Viability of Retail Outlets*. Indian Institute of Public Administration, New Delhi.

Krishnamurthy, A.N. (1988). 'Slum Upgrading as a Strategy of Public Sector Intervention for Housing the Urban Poor', Project Work for Workshop on Urban Housing Programme and Policy, Institute for Housing Studies, Rotterdam.

Lele, V. (1971). *Foodgrain Marketing in India*. Popular Prakashan, Bombay.

Ministry of Works and Housing. (1983). *National Master Plan, India, International Drinking Water Supply and Sanitation Decade 1981–1990*. Government of India, New Delhi.

National Commission on Urbanisation. (1988). *Report*, Vol. II. National Commission on Urbanisation, New Delhi.

Planning Commission. (1980). *Sixth Five Year Plan 1980–85*. Government of India, New Delhi.

———. (1983). *Task Forces on Housing and Urban Development, Report*, Vol. IV Government of India, New Delhi.

Sinha, A.P. (1990). 'Slum Development—The Cafeteria Approach', *Shelter*, 4. January–March.

Slingsby, Michael, A. (1989). 'Development of Post War and Post Independence Housing Policies', in Michael Dewit and Hans Schenk (eds.), *Shelter for the Poor in India*. Manohar, New Delhi.

Taleyarkhan. (1964). *Maharashtra Housing Board—Achievements*. Maharashtra Housing Board, Bombay.

Vaessen, Thieu. (1989). 'The World Bank's Perspective on Self-help Housing—The Case of India', in Michael Dewit and Hans Schenk (eds.), *Shelter for the Poor in India*. Manohar, New Delhi.

World Bank. (1988). *Tamil Nadu Urban Development Project—Implementation Report*. World Bank, Washington.

5

Levels of Housing and Basic Amenities—An Inter-State Analysis

Scheme of Presentation

An attempt has been made here to analyse the levels of housing and other basic amenities in urban areas at the national and state/union territory levels. The analysis is based on the data brought out by the 38th and 42nd rounds of the National Sample Survey (NSS), the Census of India 1981, and other official publications of the concerned government departments.

The first section deals with the qualitative and quantitative aspects of housing facilities at the state level. The second section analyses the inter-state variations in water supply and sanitation facilities while the third section deals with the medical facilities. The variations in the availability of these facilities in different size classes of urban areas have also been examined. Finally, in the fourth section the dependence of the population on and its utilisation of the public distribution system (of foodgrains and sugar) has been analysed in different states of the country.

Quality of Housing

The survey conducted by the National Sample Survey Organisation (NSSO) in its 38th round solicited information on structural aspects and types of housing facilities, per capita floor area, rental values and the type of sanitation facilities. The information on rents was obtained from urban households only, whereas for other aspects of housing the data were collected and compiled both for rural and urban areas separately. The imputation of rents for self-occupied houses was done on the basis of the prevailing rent for similar dwellings in the particular locality.

For the purpose of the survey, the sample households were selected through a two-stage process of stratified sampling—urban blocks being selected in the first stage and households in the second. In order to select the blocks from towns and cities, the list of Urban Survey Blocks of the 1981 Decennial Census was used as the frame. In the central sample, a total of 4,572 blocks were taken, and within each block, ten households were identified for the survey. However, the total number of valid questionnaires came to 43,410, and constitute the sample for the following analysis.

It may be seen from Table 5.1 that more than half the households in urban India live in *pucca* houses (made of cement, concrete, etc.), and more than 85 per cent of the households residing in

Table 5.1: *Percentage Distribution of Households over Types of Houses (All India)*

Housing Types	Percentage of Households
1	2
Independent, *katcha*	9.64
chawl/bustee, *katcha*	5.98
flat, *katcha*	1.07
All katcha	*16.69*
Independent, semi-*pucca*	16.72
chawl/bustee, semi-*pucca*	7.47
flat, semi-*pucca*	2.47
All Semi-pucca	*26.66*
Independent, *pucca*	32.75
chawl/bustee, *pucca*	6.66
flat, *pucca*	17.22
All pucca	*56.63*
Total	100.00

Source: Based on National Sample Survey Organisation (NSSO 1987).

these houses occupy either an independent house or a flat. However, around 12 per cent of these households live in *chawl/bustee* (degraded settlements and slums) type structures. It can also be seen that 17 per cent of all households live in *katcha* (made of mud, thatch etc.) houses, amongst which independent houses comprise around 60 per cent of the stock. Households living in *chawls/bustees* make up one-fifth (20.11 per cent), and one-fourth of this housing stock is *katcha*. Thus, the problem of the quality of housing in terms of being either *katcha* construction or a *chawl/bustee*-type structure is quite serious in urban areas.

The average floor area occupied per person is 7.81 sq.m. which is somewhat higher than the average per capita norm of 6 sq.m. as specified by the National Building Organisation for low income groups. Around 60 per cent of the households live in self-occupied houses—only 37.56 per cent of the housing stock being rental dwellings. The major problem of housing in urban areas, therefore, is not the absence of any kind of structure (identified as a house by the NSS) for living but its poor quality and the non-availability of basic services. As per the estimates available from the NSSO, more than one-third (36.82 per cent) of the households have no access to latrines at all and another one-third share latrines. Further, 18 per cent of the total households have access to only service latrines. Finally, less than 41 per cent of the urban households have access to water-borne latrines (septic and flush), of which 58 per cent share the facility.

The Census data of 1981 show that only 0.70 per cent of the households are houseless and that only 0.52 per cent have no exclusive room to themselves. However, a very large percentage of households—45.28 per cent—have only one room, which indicates a highly congested living condition. The average per capita floor area as obtained from the 38th round of the NSS, however, does not indicate any significant shortage of space. It can, however, be argued that a high level of inequality exists in the distribution of housing space (floor area) between the rich and poor in urban areas. This observation will be further corroborated through the analysis of per capita floor area available to households in different expenditure classes in Chapter 6.

As discussed in Chapter 2, the share of rent in the monthly expenditure of an urban household works out to about 10 per cent on average. The average per capita actual rent is Rs. 17.28 while the imputed rent is Rs. 23.98 per month. This implies that households living in owner-occupied houses are generally better-off in terms of housing than those living in rental premises. It may be noted from Table 5.2 that more than half the households living in rented houses pay an actual monthly rent of less than Rs. 50. The corresponding figure (based on imputed rents) for households living in non-rented houses is 26 per cent only. The households paying an

Table 5.2: *Percentage of Households Residing in Rented and Non-rented Houses over Monthly Rent Categories*

Households Living in	Monthly Rent Class (Rs.)					
	0–20	*20–50*	*50–100*	*100–250*	*250 & Above*	*All*
Rented houses	18.14	33.89	25.25	17.50	5.22	100.00
Non-rented houses	8.69	17.52	18.53	24.13	31.13	100.00

Source: Based on NSSO (1987).

actual monthly rent of Rs. 100 or more constitute only 22.72 per cent whereas the figure for the corresponding category of imputed rent is 55.26. Also, the distribution of households over imputed rent classes is skewed much more to the higher side as compared to actual rent classes. This further confirms that the households living in owner-occupied houses have better housing than those in rented accommodation. It can also be argued that the housing problem at the all-India level is related to unequal distribution of floor area, ownership pattern of houses and access to services, and not simply to the average quality of houses.

The inter-state variation in the availability and quality of housing stock has been presented in Table 5.3. It may be noted that the percentage of *katcha* houses in the total housing stock is negatively associated with the level of urbanisation and economic development of the state. The states of Andhra Pradesh, Assam, Bihar, Orissa, Manipur, Nagaland and Tamil Nadu, and the union territories of Andaman and Nicobar Islands and Pondicherry have a higher percentage of *katcha* houses than the national average of 16.69. While the higher incidence of *katcha* houses in Assam, Manipur, Nagaland and Andaman and Nicobar Islands may be attributed to climatic conditions and availability of raw materials for constructing good *katcha* houses, the explanation for other states would be primarily economic in nature.

Table 5.3 also shows that the percentage of households living in *bustees/chawls* is positively related to the level of urbanisation and economic development. The exceptions to this are Madhya Pradesh, Nagaland, Orissa and Andaman and Nicobar Islands which are backward with low urbanisation levels but still have a high percentage of households living in *chawls/bustees*. In the highly urbanised states, such as Maharashtra, Gujarat, West Bengal and Karnataka (the exceptions are Haryana and Punjab where industrialisation is partly agro-based and spatially more dispersed), the percentage of households living in *chawls/bustees* is significantly higher than the national average. When the *chawls/bustees* are further classified by the quality of house structure, it is observed that in the urbanised states, the percentage of households living in *pucca chawls/bustees* is higher. This suggests that the process of urbanisation pushes a section of the non-poor as well into the *chawls* and *bustees* but their structures are *pucca* and permanent. A *pucca chawl/bustee* provides an important component of the housing stock in the urbanised states of Gujarat, Maharashtra and Karnataka, accommodating sections of the poor as well as the non-poor. The households living in *katcha chawls/bustees* are greater in the backward states such as Andhra Pradesh, Assam, Madhya Pradesh and Orissa and can be explained in terms of the incidence of poverty.

Table 5.4 is based on the Population Census data of 1981 as well as the NSS data. The Table gives the percentage of houseless households and households with no exclusive room or one room in the metro cities, Class I cities excluding the metropolises and Class II to Class VI urban centres in different states, along with the per capita floor areas. It can be seen that Andhra Pradesh, Karnataka, Madhya Pradesh, Maharashtra, West Bengal, Chandigarh, Delhi, Goa, Daman and Diu and Pondicherry have a higher percentage of houseless households than the all-India average. The figures are very high in the case of Delhi, Chandigarh and Pondicherry. Since the states and union territories mentioned above, with the exception of Andhra Pradesh and Madhya Pradesh, have very large cities, it can be argued that houselessness is a phenomenon associated with large cities. Analysed across the size class of the urban centres, it is noted that in Maharashtra and West Bengal, houselessness is the highest in metro cities, whereas in Karnataka, Gujarat, Haryana and Punjab it is in the Class II to Class VI towns. Houseless households are comparatively fewer in certain backward states such as Uttar Pradesh, Tripura and Tamil Nadu. In other backward states such as Orissa, Rajasthan and Bihar, houselessness is high in Class I cities. No definite pattern emerges with respect to the percentage of households with no exclusive room. The figures are high in the developed states of Maharashtra and Karnataka, as also in the backward state of Bihar.

Table 5.3: *Percentage Distribution of Households over Housing Types for each State/Union Territory in 1983*

State/Union Territory	Katcha				Pucca			
	Independent House	Chawl Bustee	Flat	All	Independent House	Chawl Bustee	Flat	All
1	2	3	4	5	6	7	8	9
Andhra Pradesh	12.53	8.53	4.09	25.15	30.99	2.63	18.38	52.00
Assam	33.25	8.19	0.36	41.81	23.25	1.93	7.83	33.01
Bihar	18.72	3.97	1.80	24.49	33.52	3.36	14.18	51.06
Gujarat	2.98	5.86	0.00	8.84	47.09	6.97	11.06	65.13
Haryana	3.16	2.28	0.88	6.32	60.18	2.63	17.54	80.35
Himachal Pradesh	11.92	2.17	0.81	14.91	40.65	1.90	13.55	56.10
Jammu & Kashmir	10.16	0.90	1.32	12.39	34.66	1.32	6.12	42.10
Karnataka	6.92	5.73	1.40	14.06	27.32	8.62	7.70	43.62
Kerala	12.16	3.18	0.50	15.84	48.51	0.42	6.65	55.59
Madhya Pradesh	10.49	7.05	0.22	17.76	26.62	10.23	7.27	44.13
Maharashtra	4.08	9.01	0.29	13.38	15.14	21.00	17.48	53.63
Manipur	41.84	8.16	0.51	50.51	3.23	0.00	0.00	3.23
Nagaland	4.09	18.87	0.63	23.58	8.80	0.63	16.35	25.79
Orissa	15.22	15.65	1.52	32.39	27.39	3.04	9.78	40.22
Punjab	4.06	0.94	0.67	5.68	57.99	4.34	18.03	80.36
Rajasthan	8.22	3.18	0.41	11.81	53.30	7.35	15.22	75.87
Sikkim	0.50	3.00	0.00	3.50	23.50	2.50	23.00	49.00
Tamil Nadu	10.00	8.10	1.90	20.00	33.91	2.24	19.83	55.99
Uttar Pradesh	8.99	2.87	0.64	12.51	39.22	3.98	21.20	64.39

West Bengal	5.09	5.62	0.79	11.51	23.20	8.42	31.32	62.94
Andaman & Nicobar	8.85	9.18	0.33	18.36	28.52	5.90	17.38	51.80
Chandigarh	4.00	0.67	0.00	4.67	48.67	0.00	36.00	84.67
Delhi	3.41	2.90	0.17	6.48	54.43	4.09	22.66	81.18
Goa, Daman & Diu	1.90	7.59	3.16	12.66	18.35	0.00	43.03	61.39
Mizoram	15.03	1.88	1.04	17.95	3.76	0.84	3.34	7.93
Pondicherry	18.24	10.06	3.77	32.08	22.64	1.89	23.27	47.80
All-India	9.64	5.98	1.07	16.69	32.42	6.66	16.22	55.30

Source: Based on NSSO (1987).

Table 5.4: *Percentage of Houseless Households, Households with no Exclusive Room, One Exclusive Room and Per Capita Floor Area by Size Class of Cities and Union Territory in 1981*

State/Union Territory	All Metro			Class I Excluding Metro			Class II to VI			All Urban			Per Capita Floor Area (Sq.m.) 1983
	Houseless Households	Households with		Houseless Households	Households with		Houseless Households	Households with		Houseless Households	Households with		
		No Exclusive Room	One Room		No Exclusive Room	One Room		No Exclusive Room	One Room		No Exclusive Room	One Room	
1	2	3	4	5	6	7	8	9	10	11	12	13	14
Andhra Pradesh	0.60	0.00	38.93	1.29	0.00	54.46	1.07	0.00	52.19	1.06	0.00	50.60	6.85
Arunachal Pradesh	–	–	–	–	–	–	0.18	0.04	36.72	0.18	0.04	36.72	–
Bihar	–	–	–	0.73	1.02	36.03	0.32	0.74	36.48	0.55	0.89	36.23	7.45
Gujarat	0.29	0.18	47.91	0.67	0.24	45.70	0.72	0.19	42.83	0.69	0.20	44.99	9.14
Haryana	–	–	–	0.34	0.09	39.33	0.49	0.11	04.11	0.43	0.10	39.81	7.76
Himachal Pradesh	–	–	–	–	–	–	0.53	0.23	42.73	0.53	0.23	42.73	10.13
Jammu & Kashmir	–	–	–	0.11	0.06	14.95	0.08	0.04	24.68	0.10	0.05	18.46	10.91
Karnataka	1.09	0.74	44.61	0.70	0.77	31.86	1.38	0.72	06.11	1.03	0.74	44.27	7.72
Kerala	–	–	–	0.45	0.24	17.08	0.57	0.24	15.14	0.51	0.24	16.18	10.03
Madhya Pradesh	–	–	–	0.79	0.11	38.15	1.07	0.08	34.45	0.94	0.09	36.13	10.97
Maharashtra	1.30	2.13	63.78	0.83	2.87	58.94	0.95	3.16	57.77	1.10	2.55	61.19	5.92
Manipur	–	–	–	–	–	–	0.39	0.17	17.01	0.39	0.17	17.01	13.56
Meghalaya	–	–	–	0.37	0.01	31.32	0.31	0.00	28.69	0.35	0.01	30.62	–
Nagaland	–	–	–	–	–	–	0.66	0.18	41.68	0.66	0.18	41.68	20.18
Orissa	–	–	–	0.92	0.05	40.44	0.65	0.06	34.03	0.76	0.05	39.57	7.87

State/UT												
Punjab	–	–	0.37	0.27	0.02	38.36	0.49	0.06	34.03	0.40	0.05	35.88
	7.28
Rajasthan	0.07	42.77	0.81	0.22	0.22	38.23	0.66	0.12	33.53	0.67	0.15	36.43
	7.50
Sikkim	–	–	–	–	–	–	2.03	0.00	51.15	2.03	0.00	51.15
	4.10
Tamil Nadu	0.24	45.50	0.25	0.01	0.01	50.72	0.27	0.02	51.61	0.26	0.01	49.72
	6.78
Tripura	–	–	0.19	0.19	0.00	68.13	0.19	0.02	77.09	0.16	0.01	71.96
	–
Uttar Pradesh	0.19	47.81	0.05	0.05	0.10	40.27	0.04	0.14	36.75	0.07	0.12	39.66
	8.39
West Bengal	1.03	55.13	0.66	0.66	0.02	42.86	0.62	0.13	51.00	0.89	0.05	52.54
	7.29
Andaman & Nicobar	–	–	–	–	–	–	–	–	–	–	–	–
	–
Chandigarh	–	–	–	–	–	–	1.09	0.00	45.65	1.09	0.00	45.65
	11.07
Dadra Nagar Haveli	–	–	–	–	–	–	1.40	0.06	43.37	1.40	0.06	43.37
	11.93
Delhi	1.34	54.27	–	–	–	–	1.69	2.15	46.82	1.69	2.15	46.82
	–
Goa, Daman & Diu	0.08	–	–	–	–	–	–	1.88	–	1.36	0.08	54.19
	8.60
Lakshadweep	–	–	–	–	–	–	2.20	1.75	34.80	2.20	1.88	34.80
	11.47
Mizoram	–	–	–	–	–	–	0.07	0.29	18.94	0.07	1.75	18.94
	5.64
Pondicherry	–	–	2.06	2.06	0.01	59.70	0.17	–	28.63	2.01	0.29	58.69
	13.35
All-India	–	–	–	–	–	–	–	–	–	0.70	0.52	45.28
	7.81

Source: Based on data from Census of India (1981) and NSSO (1987).

The percentage of households living in one-room houses is high in states with large metro cities, for instance, Maharashtra, West Bengal, Tamil Nadu, and the union territories of Delhi and Pondicherry. Besides these, in the metro cities of Gujarat, Karnataka and Uttar Pradesh, the percentages are higher than the national average. When comparisons are made across the size class of towns, it can be seen that in Gujarat, Maharashtra, Punjab, Rajasthan, Kerala, Madhya Pradesh, Uttar Pradesh, Orissa and Meghalaya, the percentage is high in metro cities or in Class I cities and it decreases with the size of the city. In Haryana, Tamil Nadu, Bihar, Jammu and Kashmir and Tripura, however, an opposite pattern is observed.

Table 5.4 also gives the average per capita floor area for different states and union territories. With the exception of Gujarat, Delhi and Chandigarh, the states for which the figures are higher than the all-India urban average are relatively backward. On the other hand, in the states of Maharashtra, Tamil Nadu, West Bengal and Karnataka which have metropolitan cities, the per capita floor area is significantly lower than the all-India average.

It can be seen from Table 5.5 that all the relatively developed states—Gujarat, Karnataka, Maharashtra, West Bengal and Tamil Nadu, and the union territory of Chandigarh—have a high percentage of households living in rented premises. Also, with the exception of Andhra Pradesh, Manipur, Sikkim, Nagaland and Tamil Nadu, the average imputed rental values (of non-rented houses) are higher than the actual rentals. This corresponds to the pattern noted for the country as a whole. It is important to note that in the developed states of Gujarat, Maharashtra, Haryana, Punjab and West Bengal, and the union territories of Delhi and Chandigarh, the average per capita imputed values are more than one and a half times the actual rents. This shows that with the increase in level of urbanisation and economic development, people residing in their own homes tend to have an advantage. Land values rise at a faster rate in large cities than in small towns. However, due to friction in the rental market, the difference between imputed and rental values is larger in the states with metro cities. Thus, the inequality in housing conditions between the households living in rental premises and self-occupied houses increases with urbanisation.

Table 5.6 gives the percentage distribution of households in rented houses over rent classes by states and union territories. A

Table 5.5: *Percentage of Households Residing in Rented Houses, Average Per Capita Monthly Rent Paid for Rented Houses, and Imputed Rent for Non-Rented Houses by States and Union Territories in 1983*

State/Union Territory	Percentage of Households Living in Rented Houses	Average Per Capita Monthly Rent (Rs.)	
		Actual (Rs.)	Imputed (Rs.)
1	2	3	4
Andhra Pradesh	38.07	18.96	17.94
Assam	27.65	19.83	22.07
Bihar	30.70	12.20	13.09
Gujarat	41.78	14.74	29.94
Haryana	31.83	20.10	29.16
Himachal Pradesh	47.32	22.98	26.46
Jammu & Kashmir	14.21	21.00	34.86
Karnataka	41.21	19.45	24.79
Kerala	16.30	24.17	25.35
Madhya Pradesh	33.61	13.58	15.90
Maharashtra	48.22	13.87	28.26
Manipur	4.10	16.68	2.88
Nagaland	51.09	28.22	10.49
Orissa	26.51	13.02	13.33
Punjab	32.29	20.83	32.98
Rajasthan	24.76	15.00	15.16
Sikkim	69.43	24.00	19.67
Tamil Nadu	43.41	20.22	19.10
Uttar Pradesh	29.84	13.84	18.04
West Bengal	45.83	15.51	29.01
Andaman & Nicobar	42.25	16.03	37.99
Chandigarh	77.38	33.82	145.85
Delhi	33.43	39.00	72.11
Goa, Daman & Diu	40.43	21.39	39.86
Mizoram	27.98	28.05	30.95
Pondicherry	25.74	16.84	28.69
All-India	37.56	17.28	23.98

Source: Based on NSSO (1987).

similar distribution of households living in owner-occupied houses over imputed rent classes is given in Table 5.7. From these two Tables it can be seen that in the relatively developed states and the union territories of Delhi and Chandigarh the concentration of households is more in the bottom two rental classes for rental

Table 5.6: *Percentage Distribution of Households Residing in Rented Houses over Monthly Rent Classes by State/Union Territory in 1983*

State/Union Territory	Monthly Rent Class (Rs.)					
	0–20	20–50	50–100	100–250	250 & Above	All
1	2	3	4	5	6	7
Andhra Pradesh	9.49	32.64	27.25	25.48	5.14	100.00
Assam	8.84	33.97	35.50	15.35	6.34	100.00
Bihar	22.01	36.36	27.37	12.20	2.06	100.00
Gujarat	24.93	32.48	17.96	19.64	4.99	100.00
Haryana	15.96	23.36	35.42	20.62	4.64	100.00
Himachal Pradesh	26.53	24.52	27.75	14.59	6.61	100.00
Jammu & Kashmir	10.34	21.03	37.16	28.46	3.01	100.00
Karnataka	9.38	31.60	30.09	21.22	7.71	100.00
Kerala	7.98	30.02	35.49	18.66	7.85	100.00
Madhya Pradesh	14.20	40.63	28.84	13.54	2.79	100.00
Maharashtra	22.57	35.73	25.18	12.51	4.01	100.00
Manipur	49.34	9.41	15.11	26.14	0.00	100.00
Nagaland	9.32	26.22	46.55	17.91	0.00	100.00
Orissa	30.40	31.11	23.15	13.06	2.28	100.00
Punjab	14.21	30.08	33.70	18.61	3.40	100.00
Rajasthan	18.02	29.94	29.56	20.94	1.54	100.00
Sikkim	10.29	14.22	42.71	23.50	9.28	100.00
Tamil Nadu	11.46	33.51	28.18	19.95	6.90	100.00
Uttar Pradesh	24.76	36.02	21.08	14.19	3.95	100.00
West Bengal	28.34	39.75	17.13	9.96	4.82	100.00
Andaman & Nicobar	4.84	25.29	38.03	24.10	7.74	100.00
Chandigarh	3.58	28.78	25.43	26.85	15.36	100.00
Delhi	7.50	16.20	22.29	39.29	14.72	100.00
Goa, Daman & Diu	12.10	29.47	24.49	26.24	7.70	100.00
Mizoram	0.85	3.71	39.20	50.91	5.33	100.00
Pondicherry	15.99	26.50	37.34	12.47	7.70	100.00
All-India	18.14	33.89	25.25	17.50	5.22	100.00

Source: Based on NSSO (1987).

premises, whereas for owner-occupied houses the concentration is in the upper classes. This shows that a large number of households cannot afford to pay even modest rents between Rs. 50 and Rs. 100. Also, the rapid increase in rent forces the households to opt for ownership housing. This category comprises illegal and informal structures set up by the poor as also the spacious and expensive

Table 5.7: *Percentage Distribution of Households Living in Non-Rented Houses over Monthly Imputed Rent Classes by State/Union Territory in 1983*

State/Union Territory	Monthly Imputed Rent Class (Rs.)					
	0–20	20–50	50–100	100–250	250 & Above	All
1	2	3	4	5	6	7
Andhra Pradesh	18.97	28.43	23.79	21.99	6.82	100.00
Assam	15.86	17.31	24.81	27.82	14.20	100.00
Bihar	34.25	24.12	17.17	18.01	6.45	100.00
Gujarat	15.56	12.18	20.86	30.34	21.06	100.00
Haryana	4.82	10.15	24.00	39.08	21.95	100.00
Himachal Pradesh	38.00	11.61	11.09	23.47	15.83	100.00
Jammu & Kashmir	17.09	5.29	14.19	35.15	28.28	100.00
Karnataka	16.49	20.62	22.82	24.34	15.73	100.00
Kerala	8.96	18.96	23.53	31.13	17.42	100.00
Madhya Pradesh	15.68	29.32	23.55	22.98	8.47	100.00
Maharashtra	10.71	23.08	24.98	24.05	17.18	100.00
Manipur	85.28	3.50	3.95	5.99	1.28	100.00
Nagaland	65.23	11.39	12.73	6.34	4.31	100.00
Orissa	31.52	26.89	17.59	19.87	4.13	100.00
Punjab	4.83	12.20	22.60	38.52	21.85	100.00
Rajasthan	15.20	27.54	26.32	23.59	7.35	100.00
Sikkim	52.32	6.66	14.33	14.32	12.37	100.00
Tamil Nadu	17.36	32.65	20.53	20.41	9.05	100.00
Uttar Pradesh	14.85	21.15	28.07	27.27	8.66	100.00
West Bengal	13.15	24.25	23.44	21.60	17.56	100.00
Andaman & Nicobar	4.59	18.04	16.32	40.70	20.35	100.00
Chandigarh	5.07	27.55	6.47	14.79	46.12	100.00
Delhi	8.12	7.37	10.55	32.57	41.39	100.00
Goa, Daman & Diu	1.94	23.40	24.81	33.03	17.18	100.00
Mizoram	9.70	3.65	16.96	55.42	14.27	100.00
Pondicherry	20.57	34.44	23.30	10.44	11.25	100.00
All-India	15.97	22.71	22.63	24.97	13.72	100.00

Source: Based on NSSO (1987).

houses of the rich. There exists a sharp inequality between the two types of houses and their households and it widens with the level of urbanisation.

The foregoing state-level analysis reveals that the problem of housing with respect to the quality of structures is acute in the backward states. However, the crux of the housing problem is reflected in the inadequacy of floor area—in the lack of access of around 50 per cent of the population to urban land. The figure is even higher in urbanised states and in large cities. With an increase in the level of urbanisation, the problem of space for the poor becomes more acute since urbanisation tends to accentuate inequality in the distribution of land.

Water Supply—Coverage, Sources and Agencies

Apart from the 42nd round of the NSS, two other sources, namely (*i*) State-Level Town Directories, Census of India (1981), and (*ii*) the Central Public Health and Environmental Engineering Organisation (CPHEEO), Ministry of Urban Development, have provided the data for this section. After an overview of the scenario at the national level, an attempt has been made to analyse inter-state variations and provide certain tentative explanations for them. Table 5.8 shows the percentage of urban population covered by a protected water supply at different points of time, available from the mid-term reviews of the International Water Supply and Sanitation Decade Programme. As has been noted in the previous chapter, the programme set out to cover 100 per cent of the urban population with a protected water supply by March 1991. At the time the programme was launched, in 1981, the population covered was 72.25 per cent. This implies that nearly 28 per cent of the population remained to be covered at the time. The percentage of uncovered population declined over time to 18 per cent in 1988. Thus, the increase in the population covered by a drinking water facility was only 10 per cent over a period of eight years, which is much below the target. Indeed the performance was very low in the initial years and the mid-term review of the programme in 1985 showed that the percentage of covered population increased by only 0.63 points over the first five-year period.

Town-level data available from the 1981 Census bring out a similar picture at the all-India level, as may be seen from Table 5.9. It is distressing to note that 38 per cent of the 3,790 towns (for which data are available) in the country, do not have taps while 17 per cent do not have either a tap or a tubewell. This implies that a sizeable section of the urban population has to fall back for drinking

Table 5.8: *Percentage of Urban Population Covered by a Water Supply System*

States/Union Territories	Percentage of Population Covered				
	1981	1985	1986	1987	1988
1	2	3	4	5	6
Andhra Pradesh	55.33	52.09	62.42	62.42	71.75
Arunachal Pradesh	47.61	88.46	100.00	100.00	100.00
Assam	25.89	37.53	37.53	37.53	37.53
Bihar	63.42	59.44	63.38	63.58	69.77
Goa	93.75	81.85	79.91	81.45	83.33
Gujarat	88.94	83.14	93.36	93.35	91.87
Haryana	39.97	69.09	100.00	100.00	100.00
Himachal Pradesh	100.00	89.07	92.87	100.00	100.00
Jammu & Kashmir	97.61	86.61	94.98	94.98	95.57
Karnataka	88.81	81.17	94.88	98.72	99.60
Kerala	59.73	64.50	63.81	65.62	68.21
Madhya Pradesh	67.06	79.68	80.00	80.48	81.00
Maharashtra	94.89	87.04	89.98	99.70	99.70
Manipur	69.33	51.48	75.47	75.47	68.49
Meghalaya	24.89	22.14	19.35	49.47	47.49
Mizoram	8.19	7.57	18.56	18.57	18.36
Nagaland	58.33	46.66	46.66	19.87	43.47
Orissa	34.40	38.10	37.11	37.11	37.80
Punjab	65.61	71.16	71.28	71.17	71.18
Rajasthan	56.31	56.00	56.06	54.53	98.59
Sikkim	46.15	89.02	55.88	67.12	69.33
Tamil Nadu	80.86	83.74	86.66	88.24	88.51
Tripura	48.67	51.50	53.19	53.19	53.19
Uttar Pradesh	70.30	70.09	69.29	69.29	69.99
West Bengal	60.01	63.65	67.16	68.29	69.34
Andaman & Nicobar	100.00	100.00	100.00	100.00	100.00
Chandigarh	94.11	100.00	100.00	100.00	100.00
Delhi	81.48	98.12	97.08	96.98	97.16
Pondicherry	56.96	76.30	100.00	100.00	100.00
All-India	72.25	72.88	77.25	79.24	82.28

Source: Based on information provided by the Central Public Health and Environmental Engineering Organisation, Ministry of Urban Development.

Note: The figures have been obtained by using the actual population of 1981 and the corresponding projected population of other years as on 31 March.

water upon sources that are neither reliable nor hygienic. Another important point emerging from the town-level data is that the percentage of towns not covered is inversely related to the size class of towns. While 18.18 per cent of Class I towns are not

Table 5.9: Percentage of Towns Without Protected Sources of Drinking Water in Selected States in 1981

States	Class I			Class II			Class III			Class IV & below			All Classes		
	No. of Towns	Not Served by Tap	Not Served by Tap/Tube-well	No. of Towns	Not Served by Tap	Not Served by Tap/Tube-well	No. of Towns	Not Served by Tap	Not Served by Tap/Tube-well	No. of Towns	Not Served by Tap	Not Served by Tap/Tube-well	No. of Towns	Not Served by Tap	Not Served by Tap/Tube-well
1	2	3	4	5	6	7	8	9	10	11	12	13	14	15	16
Andhra Pradesh	21	4.76	4.76	33	27.27	18.18	91	57.14	46.15	107	65.42	50.47	252	52.38	40.87
Bihar	14	14.28	–	25	40.00	12.00	75	36.00	13.33	106	54.72	26.41	220	44.10	18.64
Gujarat	11	36.36	18.18	27	22.22	7.21	56	44.64	28.57	160	55.62	40.62	254	48.82	33.46
Haryana	9	22.22	11.11	7	28.57	14.28	15	6.67	–	50	32.00	8.00	81	25.92	7.41
Karnataka	14	0.00	0.00	16	0.00	0.00	71	4.22	4.22	180	15.00	15.00	281	10.68	10.68
Kerala	6	0.00	0.00	8	0.00	0.00	64	15.62	15.50	28	39.29	32.14	106	19.81	16.04
Jammu & Kashmir	2	0.00	0.00	–	0.00	0.00	5	40.00	–	51	45.10	21.57	58	43.10	18.96
Maharashtra	29	0.00	0.00	25	0.40	0.40	89	15.75	15.73	164	23.17	23.17	307	17.26	17.26
Madhya Pradesh	14	7.14	0.00	27	33.33	0.00	48	12.50	–	238	40.34	22.27	327	34.25	16.51
Manipur	1	0.00	0.00	–	0.00	0.00	2	100.00	–	29	24.14	24.14	32	28.12	21.87
Orissa	6	0.00	0.00	8	0.00	0.00	26	7.69	7.41	68	29.41	8.82	108	20.37	5.55
Punjab	7	100.00	0.00	10	100.00	0.00	27	81.48	7.41	90	100.00	7.78	34	96.27	6.72
Rajasthan	11	90.91	45.45	10	100.00	50.00	55	85.45	40.00	125	90.40	62.40	201	89.55	54.73
Tamil Nadu	21	14.28	14.28	41	2.43	2.43	89	10.11	5.62	283	25.09	22.97	434	19.35	17.05
Uttar Pradesh	30	0.00	0.00	38	2.63	0.00	98	24.49	–	538	50.18	6.13	704	41.90	4.69
West Bengal	24	0.00	0.00	40	0.50	0.00	52	23.08	–	175	55.43	5.14	291	38.14	3.09
All India	220	18.18	5.45	315	19.36	6.36	863	29.89	14.14	2392	45.82	20.65	3690	38.13	17.10

Source: Based on data from Census of India (1981).

covered by tap water, the figure is as high as 19.36 for Class II, 29.89 for Class III and 45.82 per cent for other classes of towns.

The data from the 42nd round of the NSS, as analysed in Table 5.10, show the percentage of population served by tap water in the year 1986–87 to be only 72.43, which was lower than the coverage of 79.24 per cent reported for the same year by the CPHEEO. As the NSS data, collected by an independent agency through a questionnaire canvassed at the household level, would have greater reliability, one can argue that the actual situation was less satisfactory than was reported officially by the CPHEEO.

Table 5.10: *Percentage Distribution of Persons over Major Sources of Drinking Water for Selected States in 1986–87*

States	Tap	Tubewell Hand-pump	Pucca Well	Others	All
1	2	3	4	5	6
Andhra Pradesh	70.28	13.09	14.76	1.87	100.00
Assam	44.73	38.97	12.64	3.66	100.00
Bihar	48.87	25.76	21.96	3.41	100.00
Gujarat	91.62	4.85	1.36	1.17	100.00
Haryana	79.97	19.97	0.06	0.00	100.00
Himachal Pradesh	96.11	0.59	1.82	1.48	100.00
Jammu & Kashmir	93.56	3.52	0.21	2.71	100.00
Karnataka	83.05	5.44	9.72	1.79	100.00
Kerala	49.74	1.16	48.08	1.02	100.00
Madhya Pradesh	80.04	7.86	10.47	1.63	100.00
Maharashtra	92.83	1.54	4.72	1.21	100.00
Orissa	52.68	13.49	27.49	9.84	100.00
Punjab	61.33	38.57	0.10	0.00	100.00
Rajasthan	79.69	7.66	11.72	0.93	100.00
Tamil Nadu	70.66	13.78	11.32	4.24	100.00
Tripura	83.48	11.15	1.20	4.17	100.00
Uttar Pradesh	58.73	30.14	10.02	1.11	100.00
West Bengal	59.39	33.95	6.55	0.11	100.00
All-India	72.43	15.44	10.26	1.87	100.00

Source: Based on NSSO (1990a).

Table 5.11 presents the percentage distribution of urban population dependent on different agencies by major sources of drinking water. More than 85 per cent of the population dependent on tap water uses government sources. Similarly, about 80 per cent of

Table 5.11: *Percentage Distribution of Persons over Agencies of Construction and Major Sources of Drinking Water in Urban India in 1986–87*

Major Sources	Government	Community	Charitable Inst.	Others	Not Recorded	All
Tap	86.87	1.32	0.26	11.32	0.22	100.00
Tubewell/ Handpump	35.42	4.80	0.65	58.04	1.07	100.00
Pucca well	17.87	9.87	2.16	69.19	0.92	100.00
Tank/pond	26.96	5.54	0.00	64.82	2.60	100.00
Tankers	79.05	9.34	0.77	4.10	6.75	100.00

Source: Based on NSSO (1990a).

those who get water through tankers are also served by government agencies. The government's involvement is much less for the other sources.

The government's involvement in the provision of drinking water has been important, especially in urban areas, as shown in Table 5.12. It may be seen that 71.47 per cent of the urban population gets water from government agencies. The percentage of population dependent on other sources, i.e., facilities created through individual or private efforts, thus, works out to be as high as 25.22 per cent, the community and charitable institutions covering only 3.3 per cent of the population. This reflects the inadequacy of the public water supply system.

In providing water to the urban population, the efforts of the community as well as of charitable institutions are negligible as only 2.79 and 0.52 per cent of the population depends on these two sources, respectively. This would seriously discount the expectation of any major involvement of non-government organisations in providing potable water, as envisaged by the International Water Supply and Sanitation Decade Programme.

The inter-state scenario presented in Table 5.8 suggests significant regional disparity which does not appear to be declining over time. While Haryana, Arunachal Pradesh, Gujarat, Jammu and Kashmir, Maharashtra, Rajasthan and Chandigarh had achieved or were close to the 100 per cent target by 1987, Assam, Bihar, Orissa, Meghalaya, Mizoram, Nagaland, Manipur, Kerala and Andhra Pradesh had a coverage significantly below the national average. It

Table 5.12: *Percentage Distribution of Persons over Agencies of Construction of a Drinking Water System for Selected States in 1986–87*

States	Govern- ment	Community	Charit- able	Others	All
Andhra Pradesh	76.05	0.65	0.17	23.13	100.00
Assam	50.45	2.59	0.35	46.61	100.00
Bihar	50.76	5.66	0.58	43.01	100.00
Gujarat	88.86	1.89	0.40	8.85	100.00
Haryana	78.56	0.05	0.00	21.59	100.00
Himachal Pradesh	94.72	0.68	1.37	3.23	100.00
Jammu & Kashmir	95.68	2.30	0.00	2.02	100.00
Karnataka	83.16	1.54	0.17	15.13	100.00
Kerala	45.83	0.40	0.14	53.63	100.00
Madhya Pradesh	75.37	2.89	0.34	21.40	100.00
Maharashtra	87.45	1.68	0.54	10.33	100.00
Orissa	64.75	3.35	0.26	31.55	100.00
Punjab	55.30	7.28	2.03	35.61	100.00
Rajasthan	81.14	7.28	2.03	9.55	100.00
Tamil Nadu	75.30	0.73	0.45	23.52	100.00
Tripura	84.52	0.63	0.00	14.85	100.00
Uttar Pradesh	45.17	5.02	0.69	49.12	100.00
West Bengal	73.04	4.22	0.67	22.07	100.00
All-India	71.47	2.79	0.52	25.22	100.00

Source: Based on NSSO (1990a).

may be noted that these are either less developed states or else they fall in the hilly terrain where there are special geographical constraints in providing water supply. It is unlikely that these states would achieve the target set under the International Water Supply and Sanitation Programme in the near future. Besides, the performance of states such as Uttar Pradesh, West Bengal, Punjab and Andhra Pradesh leaves much to be desired.

The town-level data in Table 5.9 show that the variation in the percentage of population not covered by taps or tubewells across the size class of towns and states is very high. While in the southern states (except Andhra Pradesh) the percentage of population not served by taps varies between 10 and 20 per cent only, in Punjab and Rajasthan the corresponding figures are as high as 90 per cent. At the middle level there are states such as Andhra Pradesh, Gujarat, Bihar, Jammu and Kashmir and Uttar pradesh where the percentage ranges between 42 and 52. In the case of Punjab, Bihar and Jammu and Kashmir, the problem is alleviated to a certain extent because tubewells emerge as an important alternative and the percentage of towns not served by taps or tubewells comes down to less than or equal to the national average. Rajasthan, Andhra Pradesh and Gujarat seem to be the real problem states where the percentage of towns not served either by taps or tubewells is twice that of the national figure.

The percentage figures for urban population covered with tap water facilities in different states are given in Table 5.10 which shows that in the less developed states of Assam, Bihar, Kerala and Orissa, only about 50 per cent of the households are covered by this facility. The figure for UP is slightly higher at 59 per cent, but below the national figure of 72.43 per cent. The problem becomes less serious when one considers that the alternate source of drinking water—tubewells—is abundant in some of these states. One must, however, note that tap water is usually more reliable and hygienic than water from tubewells and handpumps that are often not very deep. Also, there is a substantial subsidy available through taps (provided largely by the government agencies) which is almost negligible in tubewells and handpumps (see Table 5.11). Again, the percentage of households drawing water from wells and other sources requiring individual effort is quite high in these states and in other less developed states such as Andhra Pradesh, Madhya Pradesh, Orissa, Rajasthan and Uttar Pradesh.

Table 5.12 indicates the involvement of the government and other agencies in providing potable water in different states of the country. It reveals that in states where the percentage of population served by tap water is low (see Table 5.10), the government's involvement is also less. For example, in Assam, Bihar, Orissa, Punjab, Uttar Pradesh and Kerala, the percentage served by government agencies is low and so is the percentage getting water from taps. In all these states a higher percentage of the population depends on sources constructed by the people themselves. Table 5.13 shows the percentage distribution of population with access to different sources of drinking water over the agencies of construction in different states. It is seen that in almost all the states, those using taps obtain water largely from government agencies. In some states, like Bihar and Uttar Pradesh, a low share of the population is served by the government's tap water facility, much less than the all-India average. Here, the proportion of population served by

Table 5.13: Percentage Distribution of Persons over Agencies and Sources of Drinking Water in 1986–87

States/Sources/Agency	Tap			Tubewell/Handpump			Pucca well			Tank/Pond Reserved for Drinking			Tankers		
	Govt.	Community & Charitable Inst.	Others	Govt.	Community & Charitable Inst.	Others	Govt.	Community & Charitable Inst.	Others	Govt.	Community & Charitable Inst.	Others	Govt.	Community & Charitable Inst.	Others
1	2	3	4	5	6	7	8	9	10	11	12	13	14	15	16
Andhra Pradesh	89.01	0.41	10.58	66.42	2.21	31.37	21.39	1.67	76.96	69.67	0.00	30.33	100.00	0.00	0.00
Assam	86.39	–	13.51	24.83	5.83	69.22	5.69	4.66	84.48	0.00	0.00	93.70	–	0.00	0.00
Bihar	73.97	0.12	24.99	33.39	9.69	56.72	20.39	14.47	65.14	77.43	22.57	0.00	–	53.24	0.00
Gujarat	92.49	2.18	4.61	22.23	2.68	28.56	81.79	8.42	9.78	100.00	0.00	0.00	–	0.00	0.00
Haryana	96.51	–	3.49	5.86	0.28	93.86	–	0.00	74.01	25.99	0.00	0.00	–	0.00	0.00
Himachal Pradesh	92.83	0.25	6.92	27.73	72.27	–	–	74.01	25.99	0.00	0.00	0.00	–	0.00	0.00
Jammu & Kashmir	99.13	–	0.87	7.80	67.75	24.45	–	0.00	0.00	0.00	0.00	100.00	86.67	–	13.34
Karnataka	99.19	1.48	6.97	85.79	0.27	13.94	23.14	4.71	72.15	0.00	0.00	100.00	–	–	–
Kerala	86.47	0.44	12.50	18.31	–	81.69	5.07	0.67	90.55	0.00	0.00	100.00	–	–	–
Madhya Pradesh	82.73	0.81	16.45	64.54	4.72	30.74	27.26	20.55	52.19	0.00	0.00	–	–	–	16.41
Maharashtra	91.24	2.00	6.63	51.52	0.74	46.71	26.84	5.54	66.83	0.00	0.00	–	36.91	38.48	–
Orissa	85.68	3.28	11.04	76.60	6.46	16.94	20.09	2.90	76.61	0.00	0.00	100.00	–	–	–
Punjab	88.83	0.55	10.61	2.10	1.95	95.95	–	–	100.00	0.00	0.00	0.00	0.00	0.00	0.00
Rajasthan	93.42	0.95	5.63	67.17	7.32	25.51	8.62	5.52	25.85	0.00	93.39	6.61	0.00	100.00	–
Tamil Nadu	86.95	0.43	12.59	60.10	2.90	37.01	18.93	3.97	75.76	57.39	0.00	42.61	94.13	–	4.55
Tripura	88.54	0.46	11.00	51.42	2.06	46.51	100.00	–	–	100.00	0.00	0.00	–	–	–
Uttar Pradesh	71.49	1.81	26.64	6.02	7.02	86.86	8.77	24.66	65.99	–	0.00	100.00	0.00	–	0.00
West Bengal	86.67	4.62	8.04	57.53	5.15	36.73	31.19	6.01	62.00	0.00	0.00	–	0.00	–	0.00
All-India	84.01	4.04	11.62	59.75	4.56	33.58	29.15	17.58	53.04	41.83	14.52	42.35	84.68	1.59	13.45

Source: Based on NSSO (1990a).

government tubewells or handpumps in the total population dependent on these sources is also very low: 33 per cent and 5 per cent, respectively. The other states where a low percentage of the population is served by government-constructed tubewells or handpumps are Haryana, Jammu and Kashmir, Punjab and Kerala. In Jammu and Kashmir, 67.75 per cent of the population dependent on these sources is served by charitable institutions. However, in Kerala, more than 80 per cent and in Punjab and Haryana more than 90 per cent of the population depends on the facilities constructed by 'others' which, as has already been mentioned, involves both private effort and expenditure. In states like Andhra Pradesh, Karnataka, Madhya Pradesh, Orissa, Rajasthan and Tamil Nadu, the percentages of the population served by government tubewells and handpumps are above the national average of 59.75 per cent.

Based on the above analysis, it is possible to argue that the water supply facility is highly correlated with the economic development of the state. State intervention, directly or through the local authorities, for the provision of water is reflected in the increased coverage of population through the tap water system. Evidently, poorer states have lower government participation and, as a result, a lower percentage of the population is covered by the piped water system. Finally, the smaller towns are generally worse-off than their larger counterparts within the state. This can be explained in terms of a low tax and non-tax revenue base and the high establishment costs (in per capita terms) in the case of the former, leaving few resources to improve their water supply systems.

Sanitation and Sewerage Facilities

The target to cover 80 per cent of the urban population through formal sanitation facilities and eradicate manual scavenging during the 1980s was set as part of the International Water supply and Sanitation Decade Programme, as mentioned in the previous chapter. Table 5.14 shows the coverage of population by sanitation facilities across the states at the time the programme was launched in 1981 and for a few subsequent years—1985, 1986, 1987, 1988— when the programme was reviewed. The all-India figures show

Table 5.14: *Percentage of Urban Population Covered by Sanitation Facilities*

States & Union Territories	Sanitation Coverage				
	1981	1985	1986	1987	1988
1	2	3	4	5	6
Andhra Pradesh	11.21	10.88	15.94	15.94	19.98
Arunachal Pradesh	47.61	38.46	100.00	100.00	100.00
Assam	14.65	15.72	15.72	15.72	15.72
Bihar	19.95	22.88	38.40	38.40	38.79
Goa	17.04	13.27	23.75	28.33	28.73
Gujarat	41.21	37.99	78.33	79.22	77.51
Haryana	12.38	28.38	31.84	35.34	100.00
Himachal Pradesh	15.33	13.66	20.00	18.57	21.72
Jammu & Kashmir	7.94	7.75	7.13	6.87	7.05
Karnataka	3.73	38.38	55.97	59.86	57.19
Kerala	6.29	28.17	29.67	29.60	31.78
Madhya Pradesh	5.10	7.81	9.66	9.73	10.32
Maharashtra	38.28	39.73	40.00	62.22	62.40
Manipur	NA	0.80	9.43	9.43	8.56
Meghalaya	NA	NA	21.50	20.90	21.28
Mizoram	NA	1.51	1.51	1.43	2.04
Nagaland	NA	NA	NA	6.21	6.21
Orissa	9.32	9.42	26.84	26.84	33.78
Punjab	35.28	48.46	51.05	51.03	52.36
Rajasthan	4.16	9.59	9.58	9.06	76.22
Sikkim	NA	32.92	26.81	26.02	33.33
Tamil Nadu	46.38	47.49	47.00	47.39	47.78
Tripura	4.42	13.15	11.33	11.33	11.33
Uttar Pradesh	12.86	14.01	13.98	13.98	14.04
West Bengal	15.50	19.43	39.49	39.60	32.12
Andaman & Nicobar	40.00	55.00	100.00	100.00	100.00
Chandigarh	94.11	100.00	100.00	100.00	100.00
Delhi	64.14	73.33	81.19	86.44	87.21
Pondicherry	37.97	39.88	38.56	38.60	38.84
All-India	25.04	28.39	36.57	40.37	43.51

Source: Based on data of the Central Public Health and Environmental Engineering Organisation.
Note: The figures have been obtained by using the actual population as on 31 March 1981 and the corresponding projected populations for other years.

that population coverage increased from 25.04 per cent in 1981 to 43.91 in 1988 (based on the projected population for that year). In the initial four years, the progress was slow, as was the coverage for water supply, registering a total increase of 3.35 percentage points only. However, the increase during 1985–86 was as high as 8.18 percentage points. Subsequently, the rate of increase in coverage came down to its previous level and, therefore, the sanitation target set for March 1991 under the programme remained unachieved.

Table 5.15 shows that the all-India figure (36.82 per cent) for households without a latrine facility is very high. Water-borne latrines or flush latrines and those with septic tanks together serve 64.58 per cent of the households with latrine facilities. This implies that as 35.42 per cent of the households have service or other types of latrines. Undoubtedly, a large majority of the households which do not have latrines or have service latrines belong to the low income and poor categories, as seen in the following chapter. The Table further shows that among the households which have some type of toilet/sanitation facility, only 42.40 per cent have it exclusively for their own use while 57.60 per cent share it with others. A large proportion of the households who share the latrine facility are obviously slum dwellers with access to only community toilets.

The state-level analysis shows that the incremental coverage of the population with sanitation facilities was very slow during the first four years of the Water Supply and Sanitation Decade Programme in almost all the states, as was the case with water supply (Table 5.14). From 1986 onwards, however, there has been a notable improvement in the coverage, particularly in Gujarat, Haryana, Rajasthan, Arunachal Pradesh and Andaman and Nicobar Islands. In the states of Karnataka, Maharashtra and in the union territory of Delhi as well the progress has been satisfactory. However, in the poorer states such as Andhra Pradesh, Assam, Jammu and Kashmir, Madhya pradesh, Nagaland, Tripura and Uttar Pradesh, the increase in coverage has been marginal.

Several states have a large percentage of service latrines (Table 5.15), among them the states of Assam, Haryana, Jammu and Kashmir, Madhya Pradesh, Punjab, Rajasthan, Uttar Pradesh and those in the north-eastern region. In all the developed states the share of service latrines is low. It can possibly be argued that the high incidence of service latrines occurs due to lack of initiative or resources of the state governments.

The percentage of households without latrines is very high in almost all the backward states such as Andhra Pradesh, Bihar, Rajasthan and Orissa (Table 5.15). But in some developed states like Punjab and

Haryana as well, the figure works out to be high. It is important that in most of the north-eastern states such as Manipur, Mizoram, Meghalaya and Assam, the percentage of households without a latrine facility is very low. These states, however, have a high percentage of households using 'other' types of latrines comprising informal and *katcha* structures. States like Kerala and West Bengal also have a fair percentage of households using 'other' latrines.

States with a high percentage of households using service latrines and a low percentage using with flush latrines are mostly less developed hill states such as Assam, Jammu and Kashmir, Meghalaya and Nagaland. The developed states and union territories such as Gujarat, Karnataka, Punjab, Tamil Nadu, Maharashtra, Chandigarh, Delhi and Goa, on the other hand, have a high percentage of households using flush latrines.

The state-wise distribution of households with shared and exclusive latrines as presented in Table 5.15 reveals a distinct pattern. The relatively developed states that have one or more metro cities, such as Maharashtra, West Bengal and Gujarat, show a very high percentage of households with shared latrines. The figure is very high for Delhi and Pondicherry as well. This can be attributed to the efforts of the respective governments and the local bodies in providing community latrines to the poorer sections of the population, especially to those residing in slum areas.

A major limitation of the 38th round of the NSS is that it does not provide any information on the types of sewerage and drainage facilities existing in different urban centres. The relevant data, however, can be obtained from the population census although the most recent data would be for the year 1981. Table 5.16 shows the types of sewerage and drainage systems existing in different size classes of towns. It is well-known that the underground sewerage system is the best and most hygienic method of disposing sewage and sullage water. However, only 12.18 per cent of the towns in the selected states have this facility and only a fraction of the population in these towns is covered by it. Most of the towns depend on open surface drains (OSDs) for disposal of waste water. In the absence of proper maintenance and cleaning the open drains pose a major threat to environmental hygiene in many of the urban centres. A small percentage of towns (4.35) have box surface drains (BSDs). The sewerage facilities in Class I cities are, however, better than in other classes of towns. The percentage of

Table 5.15: Percentage Distribution of Households by Latrine Facilities in States and Union Territories in 1983

State/Union Territories	Households with No Latrine	Households with Latrines		Service Latrine	Households Using		Others
		Using Shared Latrine	Having Exclusive Latrine		Septic Tank	Flush System	
1	2	3	4	5	6	6	8
Andhra Pradesh	51.77	61.91	38.09	25.86	51.00	19.19	3.94
Assam	6.99	34.69	65.31	39.02	34.60	2.36	24.00
Bihar	45.21	54.63	45.37	24.44	62.22	7.14	6.20
Gujarat	34.12	60.84	39.16	12.37	43.00	43.29	1.33
Haryana	42.80	42.44	57.56	59.56	5.59	33.22	1.64
Himachal Pradesh	39.13	49.16	50.84	4.79	16.29	44.16	2.71
Jammu & Kashmir	20.66	59.69	40.31	83.04	4.23	7.38	6.15
Karnataka	44.20	54.10	45.90	9.95	20.54	61.79	7.78
Kerala	26.67	23.44	76.56	3.03	53.00	6.52	36.94
Madhya Pradesh	47.48	51.43	48.57	42.49	27.08	19.46	10.99
Maharashtra	26.61	72.16	27.84	19.03	30.48	48.47	2.02
Manipur	1.90	62.76	37.24	32.77	5.54	3.67	58.83
Meghalaya	7.62	NA	NA	40.21	32.30	8.65	18.83
Nagaland	3.23	96.77	3.23	53.09	41.37	0.65	4.89
Orissa	56.13	38.23	61.77	25.71	61.94	7.21	5.14
Punjab	39.40	54.13	45.69	46.99	4.44	49.45	4.06
Rajasthan	49.07	56.13	43.81	37.09	25.17	30.69	7.05
Sikkim	28.40	62.09	37.91	14.24	84.11	0.75	0.89
Tamil Nadu	47.64	60.48	39.52	35.82	26.47	35.84	1.86

Uttar Pradesh	33.62	53.69	46.31	59.22	8.96	29.59	2.23
West Bengal	13.29	62.29	37.71	19.04	61.02	7.85	12.09
Andaman & Nicobar	30.39	58.84	41.16	37.49	55.81	4.76	1.92
Chandigarh	14.31	25.85	74.15	4.89	1.30	93.80	0.00
Delhi	27.28	50.62	49.38	19.35	6.35	68.22	6.08
Goa, Daman & Diu	52.21	42.48	57.02	2.34	3.34	48.98	15.27
Mizoram	10.29	30.75	69.25	4.16	10.27	0.59	84.98
Pondicherry	66.54	52.39	47.61	13.36	61.15	25.49	0.00
All-India	36.82	57.60	42.40	28.62	32.72	31.86	6.80

Source: Based on NSSO (1987).

Table 5.16: Percentage Distribution of Towns by Classes and Types of Sewerage/Drainage Facilities in Selected States, 1981

Class of Towns/States	Class I				Class II				Class III				Class IV & Below				All Towns			
	No. of Towns	% of Towns with BSD	OSD	S	No. of Towns	% of Towns with BSD	OSD	S	No. of Towns	% of Towns with BSD	OSD	S	No. of Towns	% of Towns with BSD	OSD	S	No. of Towns	% of Towns with BSD	OSD	S
1	2	3	4	5	6	7	8	9	10	11	12	13	14	15	16	17	18	19	20	21
Andhra Pradesh	21	–	95.24	21.42	33	–	96.92	24.24	91	–	95.60	25.22	107	–	86.91	30.84	252	–	92.86	31.35
Bihar	14	21.43	92.86	21.42	25	8.00	100.00	–	75	4.00	100.00	4.33	106	3.77	100.00	3.77	220	15.45	99.55	3.64
Gujarat	11	–	36.36	63.64	27	–	51.85	51.85	56	–	46.43	30.36	160	2.50	58.62	21.25	254	1.57	77.65	28.33
Haryana	9	–	88.89	88.89	7	–	71.43	85.71	15	–	80.00	66.67	50	–	88.00	20.00	81	–	85.10	41.97
Karnataka	14	7.14	92.86	85.71	16	37.50	75.00	31.25	71	28.17	88.73	8.45	180	21.67	91.11	7.78	281	23.49	89.68	13.17
Kerala	6	–	50.00	50.00	8	–	25.00	62.50	64	1.56	15.62	26.56	28	–	10.71	10.71	106	–	16.98	26.41
Jammu & Kashmir	2	50.09	100.00	–	0	0.00	0.00	0.00	5	40.00	100.00	–	51	13.72	98.84	–	58	15.52	98.27	–
Maharashtra	29	6.89	96.55	13.79	25	16.00	96.00	8.00	89	2.25	95.00	3.37	164	3.66	92.68	4.87	307	4.56	94.14	5.54
Madhya Pradesh	14	57.14	100.00	–	27	25.92	100.00	–	48	–	97.92	–	238	–	94.54	–	327	4.59	95.72	–
Manipur	1	–	–	–	0	0.00	0.00	0.00	2	–	–	–	29	–	–	–	32	–	–	–
Orissa	6	16.62	100.00	33.33	0	12.50	100.00	–	26	–	92.30	15.38	68	4.41	76.47	8.82	108	4.63	84.26	11.11
Punjab	7	–	100.00	100.00	10	–	100.00	80.00	27	–	96.24	77.72	90	–	98.89	4.11	134	–	98.51	54.48
Rajasthan	11	–	100.00	18.18	10	–	100.00	–	55	–	96.36	1.82	125	–	95.20	4.80	201	–	96.10	4.48
Tamil Nadu	21	9.52	71.43	23.81	41	2.44	92.68	4.88	89	–	79.77	3.37	283	1.06	78.09	4.24	434	1.38	79.49	5.07
Uttar Pradesh	30	13.33	90.00	46.67	38	10.53	100.00	15.79	98	2.01	94.90	9.78	538	0.74	99.07	3.90	704	1.99	98.15	7.09
West Bengal	24	33.33	91.67	37.50	40	17.50	85.00	10.00	52	5.77	84.61	2.69	175	–	66.28	2.28	291	6.87	74.25	7.22
Total	220	11.60	87.22	41.36	307	10.15	88.57	19.04	863	5.82	83.54	15.78	2392	2.90	85.61	8.02	3790	4.35	83.44	12.18

Source: Based on data from Census of India (1981).

Note: BSD = Box Surface Drains
OSD = Open Surface Drains
S = Sewerage

urban centres covered by an underground sewerage system in Class
I towns is 41.36, for Class II towns it is 19.04, for Class III towns it is
13,78 and for the lower classes of towns it is only 8.02 per cent. It
may be argued that only the better-off sections of the urban
population in our country who tend to be concentrated in metropolitan cities and in a few Class I cities manage to have access to
the sewerage system to the exclusion of all others.

This pattern noted at the national level holds good for almost all
the states. In Andhra Pradesh, Gujarat, Haryana, Karnataka and
Punjab, the percentage of Class I cities covered through a sewerage
system is very high. More importantly, with the exception of
Karnataka, the figures work out to be much higher than the
corresponding national average and for lower size classes of
towns.

In almost all the states, OSDs constitute the major system of
drainage in all size classes of towns, as 83.44 per cent of the urban
centres in the country are covered by it. The major exceptions to
this are Gujarat, West Bengal and Kerala where the percentage of
towns with OSDs is significantly below the national average. In
Kerala a comparatively larger percentage (26.41) of towns are
reported to have a sewerage system while only 16.98 per cent of the
towns have OSDs, a figure much lower than the all-India average.
This could be because the census has not provided the relevant
information for a large number of towns which have mostly OSDs.
In the case of Gujarat, a low coverage by OSDs (in every category
of urban centre) is ameliorated by a higher percentage of towns
having a sewerage system. In the case of West Bengal, however,
the problem is only with the smaller towns, that is, Class IV and
below, which reflects disparity in the availability of the facility
across the size class of urban centres.

A sewerage system as a method of night soil disposal is an
important component of sanitation facilities in the urban areas,
which has been analysed in Table 5.17 using the data from the
Population Census of 1981. It may be seen that only 8.97 per cent
of the towns have a sewerage system as a method of night soil
disposal. The corresponding figure for Class I towns is relatively
higher—26.36 per cent. The figures for all other classes of towns
are extremely low. The states in which the percentage of urban
centres with sewerage facilities is higher than the national average
are Gujarat, Haryana, Karnataka, Kerala and Punjab. This can be

Table 5.17: *Percentage of Towns with Sewerage as a Method of Night Soil Disposal in 1981*

States/Class of Towns/ Facilities	Class I		All Classes	
	No. of Towns	Towns with Sewerage	No. of Towns	Towns with Sewerage
1	2	3	4	5
Andhra Pradesh	21	23.81	252	4.76
Bihar	14	–	220	3.18
Gujarat	11	45.45	254	19.60
Haryana	9	33.33	81	17.28
Karnataka	14	78.57	281	12.81
Kerala	6	–	106	51.90
Jammu & Kashmir	2	–	58	–
Maharashtra	29	20.69	307	11.40
Madhya Pradesh	14	–	327	–
Manipur	1	–	32	–
Orissa	6	33.33	108	5.55
Punjab	7	28.57	134	26.86
Rajasthan	11	9.09	201	9.45
Tamil Nadu	21	9.52	434	0.23
Uttar Pradesh	30	16.66	704	5.68
West Bengal	24	12.50	291	4.81
All India	220	26.36	3790	8.97

Source: Based on data from Census of India (1981).

attributed to the provision of this facility generally in the Class I cities in these states (see Table 5.17). Orissa is the only state where the percentage figure for Class I cities is higher than the national average but the aggregative figure is lower. Based on the foregoing analysis, one can argue that sewerage and sanitation facilities in urban areas are highly inadequate and cover only a section of the well-to-do population in large cities.

Availability and Utilisation of Medical Facilities

The average level of health care in different states and union territories has been analysed based on information on the number and types of medical facilities obtained from the Population Census of 1981. The data on the utilisation of the facilities has been obtained from the 42nd round of the NSS. Besides the indicator relating to hospital beds, Table 5.18 presents composite indices constructed by giving weightages to different types of medical facilities and dividing the aggregate value by the population (in thousands) for different size classes of urban centres. The hospitals have been assigned a weightage of 4, dispensaries a weightage of 3, primary health centres a weightage of 2, and other types of facilities a weightage of 1. The weightages are based on our judgement regarding the quality of health care facilities and their coverage.

Table 5.18: *Select Indices of Health Facilities for States in 1981*

States	Beds per 1000 Population	Health Index			All Urban
		Class I Cities	Class II & III Towns	Class IV, V & VI Towns	
Andhra Pradesh	3.00	0.21	0.61	1.20	0.45
Bihar	3.29	0.36	0.62	0.40	0.59
Gujarat	2.79	0.19	0.41	0.74	0.35
Haryana	2.34	0.18	0.19	0.30	0.21
Jammu & Kashmir	3.74	0.10	0.24	0.62	0.24
Kerala	4.30	0.20	0.27	0.36	0.25
Madhya Pradesh	2.00	0.14	0.20	0.36	0.21
Maharashtra	2.13	2.30	1.40	1.50	2.10
Manipur	3.88	0.15	0.29	1.60	0.30
Orissa	3.00	0.29	0.39	0.52	0.38
Punjab	2.66	0.26	0.30	0.47	0.29
Rajasthan	2.50	0.30	0.43	0.52	0.39
Uttar Pradesh	2.39	0.19	0.30	0.56	0.31
West Bengal	2.74	0.13	0.21	0.29	0.18

Source: Based on data from Census of India (1981).

Kerala ranks first in terms of beds per 1,000 population. which confirms the common belief that the state has a well-developed health care system. Assam, Manipur and Jammu and Kashmir follow, and this can be explained in terms of the attempts of the respective governments in these hill states to organise health facilities in their capitals and the few urban centres with considerable central support. The composite health indices of some of these states are also very high.

It is quite clear that the level of economic development or that of urbanisation does not explain the variations in the health care facilities across the states. Some of the less developed states such as Bihar and Andhra Pradesh have a high health index along with certain developed states like Haryana, West Bengal and Maharashtra.

The variations across the size classes of urban centres also do not show a clear pattern, although it can be argued that the Class I cities have a lower health index than the smaller towns. Similarly, the figures for Class IV and Class V towns are higher than those for Class II and Class III towns in a large number of states. It is, therefore, possible to argue that if only the availability of hospitals and dispensaries is taken into consideration (and not the nature and quality of services provided) in constructing the index of health care, its value would be high for smaller towns. This reflects the government's success in covering a large segment of the urban population in the country, reaching small and medium towns through a decentralised health delivery system. The level and quality of the facilities are, however, very low and unsatisfactory at the lower level of the urban hierarchy, as discussed in Chapter 3.

The question of availability of medical facilities to people in different states has been examined using the data from the 42nd round of the NSS. The survey was conducted in a sample of 4,568 urban blocks. For the selection of households, the blocks were divided into two sub-strata—one containing households with at least one case of hospitalisation during the preceding 365 days from the date of enquiry, and the other comprising households (out of the households not included in the first category) with at least one case of ailment or injury (excluding childbirth) during the preceding thirty days. Thereafter, a sample of two households was selected from each sub-stratum systematically with a random start. The households excluded were those that did not report any ailment or injury during the reference period, which would not affect the analysis of the utilisation of medical facilities in any way.

It is important that hospitalisation cases per 1,000 population are higher for males than females, the figures being 30.06 and 23.54 for rural areas and 16.36 and 12.69 for urban areas. The male-female ratio among hospitalised persons thus works out to be 56:44 in both rural and urban areas. It is, however, surprising that the rate of hospitalisation is 26 per 1,000 population in rural areas as compared to the corresponding figure of 13 in urban areas (the aggregative figures reported by the NSS are, however, 28 and 17, respectively). This is because of the non-availability of out-patient facilities in the villages, forcing the patients to seek hospitalisation. The low rate of hospitalisation in urban areas is compensated by a significantly higher rate of out-patient treatment. This implies that urbanites can avail of the medical facilities without seeking hospitalisation.

The question of availability of health care services to people in different states can also be analysed by considering those who have received out-patient treatment as a percentage of those reporting ailments. The rate is significantly higher for urban areas (both for males and females) as compared to rural areas. The same is true for males as compared to females.

Table 5.19 presents the indicators of the facility of hospitalisation for different states of the country. It may be seen that in most of the smaller states in the north and north-east including Assam, Himachal pradesh and Jammu and Kashmir and in many of the less developed states such as Madhya Pradesh, Orissa and Rajasthan, there is a high rate of hospitalisation in public hospitals and primary health centres (PHCs). In the case of the small hill states this reflects the state governments' involvement through substantial financial support from the centre in the provision of medical services. As these states are small, the joint effort by the central and state governments results in higher hospitalisation coverage (through government agencies) for the urban as well as rural populations. The percentage of cases reporting non-payment exhibits a strong and positive correlation with the indicator of hospitalisation in public hospitals and PHCs. This can be explained in terms of the free medical facilities provided by the public health care system.

The average payment per hospitalisation case in public hospitals works out to about one-third that in private hospitals (Table 5.19). This is why people, particularly the poor, prefer government to private agencies. The inter-state variations in the average payment reveal a strong positive relationship with the level of economic development and urbanisation. Relatively developed states such as Gujarat, Karnataka, Maharashtra, Tamil Nadu and West Bengal, along with the hill states of Jammu and Kashmir, Meghalaya and Sikkim, report a high average expenditure both in public and

Table 5.19: *State-wise Indicators of In-Patient Hospital Facilities*

States	Percentage of Cases		Average Payment (Rs.) Per Case	
	Treated in Public Hospitals & PHCs	Reporting No Payment	Govt. Hospitals	Private Hospitals
1	2	3	4	5
Andhra Pradesh	37.98	40.85	113	576
Assam	82.33	76.13	159	1596
Bihar	45.71	56.92	257	619
Gujarat	59.21	39.02	481	1195
Haryana	55.31	52.35	101	927
Himachal Pradesh	80.98	76.76	347	305
Jammu & Kashmir	95.26	91.60	385	1860
Karnataka	42.90	36.31	525	1178
Kerala	55.85	45.00	223	552
Madhya Pradesh	76.98	73.34	197	587
Maharashtra	46.23	39.60	400	1928
Manipur	92.82	77.77	141	536
Meghalaya	53.41	37.34	440	501
Nagaland	83.74	76.34	123	927
Orissa	81.48	87.94	211	640
Punjab	48.77	46.10	278	1497
Rajasthan	85.62	84.79	351	490
Sikkim	95.87	82.83	1124	1491
Tamil Nadu	58.04	57.50	728	1070
Tripura	100.00	97.46	135	–
Uttar Pradesh	59.25	56.07	683	1104
West Bengal	73.90	69.30	378	2195
All-India	60.26	55.22	386	1206

Source: Based on NSSO (1989).

private hospitals. This is due to the higher average paying capacity of people in the developed states and the concentration of highly paid government jobs (with a low percentage of poor) in the cities and towns of the smaller states in the north and north-east.

The inter-state variations in the availability of treatment other than hospitalisation (Table 5.20) reveal a pattern similar to that of hospitalisation. Once again, the small hill states and the less developed states exhibit higher coverage of treatment through the public

Table 5.20: *State-wise Indicators of Out-patient Medical Treatment in 1986–87*

States	Percentage of Treatment in Public Hospitals & PHCs	Percentage of Cases Reporting No Payment	Average Payment (Rs.) Per Case		Percentage of Untreated Ailments due to Financial Reasons
			Govt. Hospitals	Private Hospitals	
1	2	3	4	5	6
Andhra Pradesh	20.55	38.45	42	86	7.96
Assam	29.60	49.44	225	88	3.68
Bihar	17.63	30.30	92	102	9.12
Gujarat	15.86	4.15	84	101	13.31
Haryana	17.00	34.01	60	83	7.13
Himachal Pradesh	47.71	49.19	116	132	NA
Jammu & Kashmir	47.04	78.38	118	85	4.49
Karnataka	29.94	37.57	68	75	11.26
Kerala	35.69	36.90	44	61	4.54
Madhya Pradesh	30.41	46.61	100	114	8.55
Maharashtra	24.15	17.60	93	137	8.15
Manipur	61.44	36.18	170	229	3.05
Meghalaya	26.02	29.40	121	96	1.86
Nagaland	30.60	34.82	153	235	NA
Orissa	46.45	66.18	40	84	12.09
Punjab	10.15	20.79	93	77	2.09
Rajasthan	57.21	72.02	129	115	11.17
Sikkim	87.20	68.72	282	459	–
Tamil Nadu	32.57	42.78	47	64	7.45
Tripura	25.18	44.69	84	54	16.10
Uttar Pradesh	15.93	40.84	198	120	15.11
West Bengal	20.84	63.29	80	100	11.82
All-India	25.54	42.26	103	91	9.57

Source: Based on NSSO (1989).

health care system. The significant addition to this list is Kerala. The percentage of cases reporting non-payment is multi-collinear with the percentage of treatment in public hospitals, PHCs, etc., as expected. Interestingly, the average payment for any treatment in public hospitals is slightly higher than that in private hospitals. This is because cases of free treatment have been excluded in computing the figures that are higher for government hospitals. It is well-known that only lower level medical facilities are made available free of cost in public hospitals. For clinical testing, X-ray and other higher levels of facilities and treatment, most of the patients are required to pay. It is, therefore, understandable that if the patients are required to pay they often prefer doctors or hospitals in the private sector as they get more personalised attention.

The payment per case of out-patient treatment in public hospitals is high in the case of the hill states and the relatively less developed states (except Orissa). The same is not true for the private hospitals. It is observed that the developed states of Gujarat, Maharashtra and West Bengal report high expenditure in private hospitals. Thus, the inter-state variation in the average payment in public hospitals is significantly different from that in private hospitals.

The percentage of ailments that could not be treated (Table 5.20) owing to financial reasons does not vary much across the states, except that the smaller states of Assam, Jammu and Kashmir, Manipur, Meghalaya and Kerala report lower figures. Furthermore, several developed as well as backward states report high values of this indicator. It is, therefore, not possible to explain the variation in non-treatment owing to financial reasons across the states in terms of their per capita state domestic product.

Use of the Public Distribution System

In 1990, there were 376,000 retail outlets for the distribution of commodities through the public distribution system in the country. Of these, 90,000 were in urban areas. About 77 per cent of the outlets were managed by private dealers, selling either only PDS commodities (at predetermined prices) or other items as well. About 24 per cent of the shops in rural areas and 21 per cent in urban areas were in the cooperative sector. There was, however, considerable inter-state variation in the scenario, as may be noted from Table 5.21.

The government is expected to provide one shop for every 2,000 persons. The average figure for urban areas, however, works out to be less than 0.9. It is satisfying to note that this norm is fulfilled in almost all the hill states—Sikkim, Assam, Himachal Pradesh,

Table 5.21: *Indicators Concerning Fair Price Shops, 1990*

State/UT	No. of Fair Price Shops				Shops Per 2,000 Persons (Urban)	Per cent of Co-operative to Total (Urban)
	Cooperatives		Others			
	Rural	Urban	Rural	Urban		
Andhra Pradesh	1831	797	27049	6006	0.76	11.72
Arunachal Pradesh	218	36	283	31	1.28	53.73
Assam	705	167	20926	2618	2.25	6
Bihar	2686	552	29671	6718	1.28	7.59
Goa	158	60	262	85	0.61	4.38
Gujarat	3157	516	6519	1914	0.34	21.23
Haryana	1131	126	3314	1961	0.52	6.04
Himachal Pradesh	2447	109	531	105	0.96	50.93
Jammu & Kashmir	182	–	1857	573	0.62	0
Karnataka	5284	1977	7275	2322	0.31	45.99
Kerala	–	1193	–	11814	1.39	9.17
Madhya Pradesh	9008	2290	9375	3374	0.74	40.43
Maharashtra	6856	2756	18053	7493	0.67	26.89
Manipur	19	11	1488	167	0.7	6.18
Meghalaya	37	18	2670	552	3.47	3.16
Mizoram	16	2	615	184	1.17	1.08
Nagaland	–	–	156	193	1.74	0
Orissa	3108	255	15828	2608	1.35	8.91
Punjab	2088	97	6021	2131	0.74	4.35
Rajasthan	5396	961	5075	2767	0.74	25.78
Sikkim	73	36	721	540	31.14	6.25
Tamil Nadu	17312	4396	73	155	0.48	95.59
Tripura	299	41	766	85	0.6	32.54
Uttar Pradesh	4902	2167	43265	8558	0.78	20.21
West Bengal	494	516	14646	4348	0.52	10.61
Andaman & Nicobar	56	13	155	53	1.76	19.7
Chandigarh	13	33	41	220	0.88	13.04
Dadra & N Haveli	41	–	–	–	–	16
Goa, Daman & Diu	14	7	4	14	0.89	33.33
Delhi	35	109	236	3215	0.79	3.28
Lakshadweep	18	12	–	–	0.83	1000
Pondicherry	149	135	18	55	0.74	71.05
All India	67733	19388	216893	71759	0.84	21.48

Source: Unpublished data of the Planning Commission.

Arunachal Pradesh, Nagaland, Mizoram and Meghalaya. Besides these, Bihar and Kerala too have figures above the norm. It is surprising that while the southern states of Karnataka and Tamil Nadu have a high coverage of population under the PDS, as discussed later, the norm for the average number of PDS outlets is not fulfilled at the state level. Gujarat and West Bengal too have very low figures of PDS outlets relative to their populations.

The role of the cooperatives in organising the PDS is very important in the state of Tamil Nadu and in the union territories of Lakshadweep and Pondicherry. The states where the cooperative movement is yet to make a dent on the PDS are Jammu and Kashmir, Assam, Sikkim, Punjab, Haryana, Bihar and West Bengal, besides the north-eastern states of Manipur, Meghalaya and Mizoram.

The average percentages of population covered partially or fully through the public distribution of wheat and rice are not very different (Table 5.22). The inter-state variations are, however, quite significant. The southern states in general have a much better coverage of population for both rice and wheat which reflects the initative and efforts of the state governments. In most of the rice-eating states in the north and north-east, like Jammu and Kashmir, Assam, Tripura and West Bengal, the percentage of the population served by the PDS is higher than the national average. The rice-eating states where the coverage (for rice) is extremely low (almost negligible) are Bihar and Orissa. In these two states an equally low percentage of the population is covered by the distribution of wheat through the PDS.

The inter-state variations in the coverage for wheat are quite different from that of rice (Table 5.22). In the wheat-eating states of Punjab, Haryana, Rajasthan, Madhya Pradesh and Uttar Pradesh, a low percentage of the population is covered for wheat under the PDS. The rice-eating states including the southern states (with the exception of Tripura, Assam, Bihar and Orissa), on the other hand, report a high coverage. It is interesting that in the above states, the percentage of the wheat-eating population completely dependent on the PDS is also high—much higher than the national (urban) average of 29.48 per cent. The figure ranges between 48 and 92 per cent—for Karnataka it is 48 per cent; for Andhra Pradesh 49 per cent; for Tamil Nadu 63 per cent; for West Bengal 69 per cent and for Kerala 92 per cent.

Table 5.22: *Percentage of Urban Population Served (Fully or Partially) by the PDS to All Persons Buying the Items in 1986–87*

States	Fully or Partially Served by PDS			Fully Dependent on PDS		
	Rice	Wheat	Sugar	Rice	Wheat	Sugar
1	2	3	4	5	6	7
Andhra Pradesh	50.23	51.18	77.35	5.13	48.57	51.25
Assam	46.07	5.13	68.79	3.10	3.10	16.66
Bihar	0.85	9.53	64.44	0.38	5.23	42.66
Gujarat	47.21	30.36	86.11	24.50	20.68	11.79
Haryana	13.43	0.00	79.59	10.71	0.00	4.07
Himachal Pradesh	33.63	9.64	74.15	19.94	7.45	8.99
Jammu & Kashmir	79.59	73.64	88.26	32.69	31.22	54.77
Karnataka	62.72	60.68	75.70	7.62	47.83	39.18
Kerala	87.15	94.68	91.72	3.98	91.75	16.19
Madhya Pradesh	21.96	11.21	70.56	13.37	5.96	25.03
Maharashtra	44.91	33.84	79.51	18.20	17.51	8.68
Orissa	0.81	22.83	64.34	0.81	19.51	45.75
Punjab	8.10	0.43	64.45	6.49	0.43	1.61
Rajasthan	5.08	6.46	52.44	4.61	4.98	18.67
Tamil Nadu	50.57	67.22	78.17	1.84	63.90	36.80
Uttar Pradesh	8.97	5.07	67.84	6.75	3.37	47.87
West Bengal	43.70	74.66	86.95	9.28	68.83	29.54
All-India	39.11	36.69	75.63	11.14	29.48	29.19

Source: Based on NSSO (1990b).

The percentage of population dependent entirely on the PDS for rice, however, shows a different pattern. Here, the wheat-eating states such as Gujarat, Himachal Pradesh, Madhya Pradesh and Maharashtra come in at the top. The rice-eating states, on the other hand, have very low figures. The high percentage of the population entirely dependent on the PDS for wheat in rice-eating states and for rice in wheat-eating states could be attributed to the fact that those eating a cereal which is not their first choice are economically worse-off and therefore are relatively more dependent on the PDS. It can also be attributed in part to better-off sections of the population finding even the limited supply from the PDS enough for their requirements. Jammu and Kashmir must be considered as a special case which reports a very high percentage of its population served by, as also fully dependent on, the PDS for both commodities. Based on this, it can be argued that the rice-eating states are somewhat better placed than the wheat-eating states in terms of the *coverage of population* by the distribution of cereals.

An analysis of the field data collected from 1,325 beneficiary households by the Programme Evaluation Organisation of the Planning Commission (1985) provides interesting insights into this issue. The beneficiaries not drawing wheat and rice from ration shops regularly are 37 per cent of the total. Among these, 35 per cent cite irregularity of supply as the reason for not drawing their entitlement of wheat while the corresponding figure for rice is 31 per cent. Furthermore, the percentages of beneficiaries reporting inadequate supply of wheat and rice are 74 and 70, respectively. These further support the proposition that the supply of rice through the PDS is relatively better than that of wheat.

For sugar the coverage is higher than for cereals (Table 5.22, cols. 2–4) largely because a section of the urban population—generally belonging to the higher income brackets—uses the PDS for sugar only. The inter-state variations for this indicator are not so significant. Here, the four states appearing at the bottom are Bihar, Orissa, Rajasthan and Punjab. These states (along with Haryana) report a very low percentage of population covered through the PDS by rice and wheat as well. For the states of Punjab and Haryana, this may not be a matter of grave concern since the marginal difference between the open market and PDS prices and the strong rural-urban linkage allow people in towns and cities to be less dependent on ration shops. Consequently, the PDS has not been developed in these states. In the other three states, however, the low coverage for both sugar and cereals reflects a major deficiency in their systems. This would pose serious problems for the poor whose purchasing power gets eroded as they are forced to buy the essential food items from the market.

The quantity purchased from the PDS as a percentage of total purchase of wheat and rice shows a variation corresponding to that of population coverage (Table 5.23). It may be seen that the three problem states of Bihar, Orissa and Rajasthan report low figures here as well. One can add the states of Madhya Pradesh and Uttar Pradesh in the list since these too show a very low coverage by the PDS and low purchase of cereals from the PDS, particularly rice.

The percentage of persons in urban areas reporting no purchase

Table 5.23: *Percentage of Quantity Purchased from the PDS to Total Purchase in 1986–87*

States	Urban		Rural	
	Rice	Wheat	Rice	Wheat
Andhra Pradesh	21.47	47.98	32.54	20.39
Assam	14.83	1.65	14.40	17.79
Bihar	0.29	7.05	0.42	1.51
Gujarat	26.21	19.63	46.53	37.02
Haryana	8.89	0.00	7.29	0.00
Himachal Pradesh	20.48	8.81	33.56	15.81
Jammu & Kashmir	63.87	58.54	31.56	18.65
Karnataka	25.69	43.78	22.22	49.86
Kerala	46.16	91.48	51.36	92.04
Madhya Pradesh	10.47	5.65	6.14	7.12
Maharashtra	27.77	21.45	27.45	43.13
Orissa	0.41	25.02	0.40	18.11
Punjab	5.15	0.05	–	0.68
Rajasthan	15.94	3.61	7.47	15.94
Tamil Nadu	12.17	63.48	18.66	12.17
Tripura	24.52	15.28	19.42	4.44
Uttar Pradesh	8.03	3.32	4.45	2.43
West Bengal	19.48	69.87	6.59	49.03
All-India	19.02	19.33	16.76	12.64

Source: Based on NSSO (1990b).

of rice and wheat from the PDS for the reason that these are not available in ration shops (Table 5.24) gives further insight into the functioning of the system. In all the problem states, the percentage figure is much above the national coverage of 19.35 for rice. In the case of wheat, the corresponding figure is equal to or higher than the national figure of 21.13 per cent in all these states.

Most of the southern states which already have a high coverage of population under the PDS for cereals surprisingly report a high percentage of people who consider not having a ration card as the reason for purchasing rice and wheat from the market. The figures are very high for the states of Andhra Pradesh, Karnataka and Tamil Nadu, although they have a fair coverage of the population under the PDS. One can, therefore, argue that because of the higher level of awareness regarding the PDS and the availability of rationed grains at a much cheaper rate, people appreciate its

Table 5.24: *Percentage of Persons not Fully Dependent on the PDS over Reasons for No Purchase and Partial Purchase in 1986–87*

States	No Ration Card		Not Available in Ration Shop	
	Rice	Wheat	Rice	Wheat
Andhra Pradesh	42.69	7.08	2.74	17.50
Assam	20.41	9.01	16.43	22.00
Bihar	11.40	8.22	58.43	46.33
Gujarat	15.70	13.27	6.73	5.02
Haryana	9.52	6.52	29.70	27.35
Himachal Pradesh	18.00	4.02	14.72	14.87
Jammu & Kashmir	12.23	4.16	5.08	13.17
Karnataka	22.08	22.15	4.06	7.88
Kerala	6.11	4.72	1.75	9.54
Madhya Pradesh	16.32	13.97	29.90	22.06
Maharashtra	14.96	14.38	2.27	2.29
Orissa	11.82	6.28	54.93	18.51
Punjab	19.74	4.01	28.39	31.64
Rajasthan	3.33	2.97	53.36	51.10
Tamil Nadu	21.29	13.36	2.24	8.14
Uttar Pradesh	10.76	10.43	44.67	43.87
West Bengal	13.96	17.16	7.89	10.38
All-India	16.76	11.18	19.35	21.13

Source: Based on NSSO (1990b).

relevance in these states and a large section of the uncovered population wishes to be covered by it. Gujarat and Maharashtra are the two other states (along with most of the problem states) where a high percentage of the population wants to be issued ration cards.

It is, therefore, possible to argue that low coverage of population and a low share of the PDS in total purchases go hand in hand across the states. Further, the reasons for non-purchase or partial purchase from the PDS are non-availability of items at the ration shops and, to a certain extent, the people not having ration cards. Based on the foregoing analysis, we may identify Bihar, Orissa, Rajasthan, Madhya Pradesh and Uttar Pradesh as the real problem states in the country that badly need improvements in their public distribution system through increase in the coverage of population as also the quantity of commodities supplied.

References

Census of India. (1981). *Housing Tables*. Government of India, New Delhi.

National Sample Survey Organisation. (1987). *Tables with Notes on Particulars of Dwelling Units*, 38th Round, January–December 1983, Number 339. Government of India, New Delhi.

———. (1989). *Morbidity and Utilisation of Medical Services*, 42nd Round, July 1986–June 1987, Number 364. Government of India, New Delhi.

———. (1990a). 'A Profile of Households and Population by Economic Class and Social Group and Availability of Drinking Water, Electricity and Disinfection of Dwelling', 42nd Round, *Sarvekshana*, 13(4). Government of India, New Delhi.

———. (1990b). 'Utilisation of Public Distribution System', *Sarvekshana*, 13(4), Government of India, New Delhi.

Planning Commission. (1985). *Evaluation Report on Essential Supplies Programme*. Programme Evaluation Organisation, Planning Commission, New Delhi.

6

Levels and Quality of Housing and Basic Amenities Available to the Urban Poor

Scope

In the preceding chapters, the organisational structures and the programmes for the provision of housing and other basic services, along with their availability at the national and state/union territory levels have been analysed. Although the sensitivity of the existing system to the urban poor has also been examined in some detail, the question of their access to these services has not. The present chapter is focused on this specific issue. Considering the population below the poverty line to be roughly between 35 and 40 per cent in urban areas, an attempt has been made to assess the quantity and quality of the facilities available to this section of the population.

The analysis of housing and sanitation facilities is based on the data provided by the 38th round of the National Sample Survey (NSS). The 42nd round of the NSS was devoted mainly to the enquiry on social consumption. Its objective was to assess the extent to which people in different economic and social strata have benefited from public expenditure in the fields of health care, education, public distribution of foodgrains and certain basic services like water supply. Several micro-level studies that have analysed the availability of these facilities to the poor and the slum populations in different cities have also been used for comparing and cross-checking the results. Finally, the information and impressions gathered through field visits to the slums in select cities such as Calcutta, Delhi, Ahmedabad, Nagpur, Goa, Chandigarh, Jammu and Vishakhapatnam, and through discussions with officials responsible for slum improvement programmes in these cities, have been used to corroborate or question the results obtained through the secondary data. It may be noted that a detailed field survey in limited slum pockets of Delhi was undertaken during December 1989. This questionnaire-based survey covered 169 randomly selected households from the slum localities of Jahangirpur, Timarpur, Rajiv Nagar, Jama Masjid, Nand Nagri, Sail-ul-Atab (Kalkaji), Tigri *Jhuggi Jhompri* (JJ) Colony, Shadipur Depot and Raghubir Nagar. The aspects covered were housing, water supply and sanitation, health and the public distribution system. In addition, eleven localities were visited and unstructured interviews were held with groups of residents, shop-keepers, slum *pradhans* (heads) and community workers. The discussions were essentially confined to various aspects of the above-mentioned facilities. The JJ colonies thus covered were Gautampuri under the ITO bridge, Ambedkar Camp and Navjeevan Camp in Kalkaji, Indira Colony near Saket, Mukherji Nagar and Patvakar Colony in Timarpur, Shastri Mohalla and Jawahar Mohalla in Padpadganj, and Laxmi Nagar on the river bank near ITO. Besides these, the resettlement colonies of Seemapuri and Trilokpuri were also covered in the survey.

The first section analyses the access of the urban poor to housing while in the second section the availability of water supply and sanitation facilities have been examined. The third and the fourth sections deal with the availability of health care services and the public distribution system (PDS), respectively.

Access to Housing

The analysis of the access of the bottom 40 per cent of the households to housing and sanitation in this as also in the following section is largely based on the data from the 38th round of the NSS, as noted earlier. Information on quality of housing available to different consumption brackets is available in Volume 339 of this round. Here the data have been tablulated by classifying the households in thirteen consumption classes with unequal intervals, as presented in the tables that follow. It is noted that 38.97 per cent of the households report a per capita monthly consumption expenditure of Rs. 125 or less (the urban poverty line in 1983 was Rs. 111.23). Considering this section of the households as the urban poor or at least with characteristics similar to the urban poor, a separate row of information has been added to every Table. A comparison of the quantity and quality of the facilities available to this segment with the total urban population has helped in highlighting the magnitude of disparity.

In the previous chapter, the problem of houselessness in urban areas was found to be negligible. This is so because households (including those living on pavements) with some kind of temporary or informal structures have been excluded from the houseless category. Attention must, therefore, be focused on the quality of the shelter, housing type, per capita space available, legality of the structure, cost of the unit and availability of essential services, while analysing the question of access of the poor to housing. The type of structure, for instance, whether *katcha* or *pucca*, reflects the degree of physical protection offered by it. The housing type, independent house or *chawl/bustee*, indicates, somewhat approximately, the environmental conditions of the dwelling in terms of congestion and availability of light and ventilation. The legal status of the dwelling unit would suggest the vulnerability of the households to eviction, demolition and harassment by the landlord, police, etc. The NSSO has unfortunately not collected any detailed information on the legal status of the household but the rental or non-rental status of the residents may be used to make inferences about this aspect. The rental houses, by and large, have a legal status whereas non-rented premises include all kinds of illegal structures. In fact, the latter are often rented out and the rents here are, on average, quite low.

The per capita housing space available is a direct measure of access to the most important urban resource, namely, land. The other important question with regard to housing is the locality where it is situated. No information was collected by the NSSO on this aspect. However, the cost of per capita floor area may indirectly reflect this locational parameter. The access to basic services like water supply and sanitation, which also indicates the quality of the environment in the locality, has been analysed in the following section.

In Tables 6.1 and 6.2, the quality of the dwelling units inhabited by households belonging to different expenditure classes has been shown. It may be seen from Table 6.1 that while the problem of *katcha* house structures is not severe at the aggregative level, for households with monthly per capita expenditure up to Rs. 125,

Table 6.1: *Percentage Distribution of Households by Monthly Per Capita Expenditure Class over Types of Houses in 1983*

Monthly Per Capita Expenditure Class (Rs.)	Types of Housing Structure			
	Katcha	Semi Pucca	Pucca	All
1	2	3	4	5
0–30	20.13	24.18	54.07	100.00
30–40	46.59	34.55	18.54	100.00
40–50	41.73	35.25	22.82	100.00
50–60	38.38	33.67	27.66	100.00
60–70	33.56	37.57	28.45	100.00
70–85	28.71	35.72	35.09	100.00
85–100	25.50	32.13	41.67	100.00
100–125	20.58	31.75	47.05	100.00
125–150	15.71	28.47	55.10	100.00
150–200	12.43	24.33	62.68	100.00
200–250	8.85	20.67	69.84	100.00
250–300	7.73	16.51	75.06	100.00
300 & Above	4.71	12.85	81.78	100.00
All Classes	16.43	25.72	57.20	100.00
Up to Monthly Per Capita Expenditure of Rs. 125	26.49	33.81	39.70	100.00

Source: Based on NSSO (1987).

that is, for roughly the bottom 40 per cent of the households, the problem is quite serious. Further, with the exception of the bottom-most class, the percentage of *pucca* houses increases with the level of expenditure. In the top two classes, the figures are as high as 75 per cent and 81 per cent, respectively. It may be noted that the figure for the bottom 40 per cent, that is, 39.70 per cent, is significantly below the national average of 57.20 per cent.

These arguments are further corroborated by the data in Table 6.2. The percentage share of households up to an expenditure of Rs. 125 (per capita per month) in *katcha* structures is higher than the figure for the total households. The pattern is the opposite in the case of *pucca* structures. Among the households living in *katcha* houses, around 63 per cent are below the poverty line. The corresponding figure is 27 per cent amongst those living in *pucca* houses. The slum surveys undertaken in Madras (MMDA 1986) and Ahmedabad (Ahmedabad Municipal Corporation 1976) also

Table 6.2: Percentage Distribution of Households by Nature of Structure and Housing Type over Monthly Per Capita Expenditure Classes in 1983

Monthly Per Capita Expenditure Class (Rs.)	Katcha				Semi-pucca				Pucca				Percentage of Households
	Independent House	Chawll Bustee	Flat	All	Independent House	Chawll Bustee	Flat	All	Independent House	Chawll Bustee	Flat	All	
1	2	3	4	5	6	7	8	9	10	11	12	13	14
0–30	0.31	0.31	0.19	0.33	0.24	0.28	0.25	0.25	0.20	0.25	0.35	0.25	0.27
30–40	1.18	1.20	1.27	1.19	0.72	0.32	0.44	0.56	0.13	0.06	0.17	0.14	0.42
40–50	2.97	2.18	2.24	2.61	1.44	1.01	2.49	1.41	0.46	0.37	0.22	0.41	1.03
50–60	5.90	4.77	4.72	5.38	3.46	2.53	1.99	3.01	1.31	0.89	0.85	1.11	2.30
60–70	7.90	7.48	6.00	7.60	6.47	4.13	3.60	5.43	2.24	1.60	1.20	1.83	3.72
70–85	13.73	13.93	7.23	13.33	11.94	8.33	10.06	10.60	5.65	4.78	2.90	4.68	7.63
85–100	13.42	14.36	11.59	13.65	12.70	8.61	8.70	10.99	7.33	5.70	5.04	6.40	8.79
100–125	19.42	16.89	20.88	18.55	18.38	18.59	17.02	18.28	13.86	11.86	9.29	12.17	14.81
125–150	11.40	11.79	10.79	11.51	12.99	13.60	14.35	13.32	12.54	12.96	9.34	11.58	12.03
150–200	11.87	13.32	16.42	12.76	14.97	17.54	16.53	15.95	19.68	17.55	16.71	18.47	16.86
200–250	5.04	5.93	7.87	5.59	7.14	9.87	10.24	8.32	11.95	13.37	13.57	12.64	10.36
250–300	2.97	3.21	5.09	3.22	3.83	4.94	5.87	4.39	7.82	9.15	10.93	8.96	6.83
Above 300	3.85	4.62	5.72	4.29	5.71	10.33	8.47	7.47	16.83	21.50	29.31	21.35	14.94
All Classes	100.00	100.00	100.00	100.00	100.00	100.00	100.00	100.00	100.00	100.00	100.00	100.00	100.00
Up to Monthly Per Capita Expenditure of Rs. 125	64.87	61.13	54.11	62.63	55.36	43.71	44.54	50.55	31.18	25.50	20.14	27.00	38.97

Source: Based on NSSO (1987).

showed a very high percentage of households living in *katcha* houses. In Madras 83 per cent of the structures in slums were *katcha* whereas in Ahmedabad only 56 per cent of the houses had *katcha* walls and 79 per cent had *katcha* roofs. During the primary survey conducted in 1989–90 for the present study in the slums of Delhi, it was observed that the house structures were largely *katcha* (mud walls with temporary roofs). Table 6.2 further indicates that amongst those living in *pucca chawls* and *bustees* there is a large proportion of the non-poor which discounts the popular belief that only the poor live in these settlements.

In Table 6.3, it can be seen that the per capita floor area available to households up to a per capita expenditure of Rs. 125 is significantly below the national average. The area occupied by the top-most class is about four times that of the bottom-most class. The unequal space distribution in urban areas also becomes evident from the fact that while the bottom 39 per cent of households occupy only 28 per cent of the floor area, the top 22 per cent claim a share as high as 56 per cent. Based on these figures it can be argued that the requirement of floor area is income elastic, that is, it rises more than proportionately with increase in income or consumption expenditure.

Table 6.3: *Per Capita Floor Area by Monthly Per Capita Expenditure Classes in 1986–87*

Monthly Per Capita Expenditure Class (Rs.)	Average Per Capita Floor Area (Sq.m.)
0–30	3.32
30–40	4.33
40–50	3.85
50–60	4.54
60–70	4.56
70–85	5.04
85–100	5.53
100–125	6.74
125–150	6.98
150–200	8.20
200–250	9.47
250–300	11.53
Above 300	15.54
All Classes	7.81
Up to Monthly Per Capita Expenditure of Rs. 125	5.68

Source: Based on NSSO (1987).

On average, the per capita floor area available to the bottom 40 per cent is 5.68 sq.m., which is significantly lower than the all-class average. Although per capita floor area figures given by the NSSO seem to be on the higher side (working out around 28 sq.m. for a household of five), the data do bring out the inequality in the distribution of urban space. Further, with the poor households by and large living in one-room dwelling units, as was observed in the Delhi survey as well, the figure seems to be on the higher side. Even the survey of Ahmedabad slums by the municipal corporation gave a very low figure of per capita floor area, that is, between 2.17 and 4.35 sq.m. for 53 per cent of the population and less than 2.17 sq.m. for the rest (Ahmedabad Municipal Corporation 1976).

Table 6.4 reveals that the phenomenon of renting increases with

Table 6.4: *Per Capita Rent, Percentage of Households in Rented Houses and Percentage of Expenditure on Rent by Monthly Per Capita Expenditure Class in 1983*

Monthly Per Capita Expenditure Class (Rs.)	Average Per Capita Monthly Rent (Rs.)		Per Cent Households Living in Rental Houses	Per cent Monthly Expenditure on Actual Rent
	Actual	Imputed		
1	2	3	4	5
0–30	3.91	8.05	10.83	13.03
30–40	3.46	6.78	14.78	9.89
40–50	3.67	6.36	19.03	8.16
50–60	4.33	7.84	15.83	7.87
60–70	4.81	8.67	19.84	7.40
70–85	6.16	9.99	23.60	7.95
85–100	6.90	12.10	27.53	7.46
100–125	8.81	16.36	30.82	7.83
125–150	10.42	19.67	36.16	7.58
150–200	14.60	27.62	40.44	8.34
200–250	20.75	37.43	45.98	9.22
250–300	26.37	50.86	51.04	9.55
Above 300	46.82	79.81	53.33	–
All Classes	17.28	23.98	37.56	–
Up to Monthly Per Capita Expenditure of Rs. 125	7.00	12.51	26.14	–

Source: Based on NSSO (1987).

the level of expenditure. While only 11 per cent of the households live in rented premises in the bottom-most class, the figure is more than 50 per cent for the top two classes. Among the poor, a very small percentage of households (26 per cent) live in rental premises. In the survey undertaken in Delhi's squatter settlements, it was found that only 8 per cent households lived in rented premises. However, in the slums of Madras (MMDA 1986), and Ahmedabad (Ahmedabad Municipal Corporation 1976), about 40 per cent households were living in rented premises.

Having access to rental houses also implies getting a legal status. As is well-known, and was also noted in the field surveys in Delhi and other large cities, the major hindrance for the poor getting ration cards is their not having a permanent (legal) address. Those who live in rented premises usually fulfil this requirement. A rent receipt immediately entitles them to ration cards. However, as rental housing is expensive, many among the poor remain out of the rental market. Further, when the land markets are buoyant, as in Delhi and several other large cities, the access of the poor to rental houses diminishes further.

It may be noted from Table 6.4 that the imputed values are, by and large, twice the actual rent for all expenditure classes, except the bottom-most class. This means that within an expenditure class, those living in their own premises have better houses than those living in rented premises. Those living in rented houses pay only 7 to 10 per cent of the monthly expenditure (income) on rent. On the other hand, the households living in self-occupied houses would have to pay around 15 per cent of their income on housing if they had rented the same type of house. Evidently, they cannot afford it and this forces them to seek ownership housing in the informal market or build illegally on public or private lands. However, this too is not free of cost. The field surveys undertaken in Delhi revealed that in the squatter settlements some illegal occupants had to regularly pay either the police or slum lords for their protection against fire, eviction and other harassment. Also, at the time of their initial construction/occupation they were required to pay certain sums either to the police, the local lord or the previous settler. Around one-third of the households had paid Rs. 1,500 to 2,000, another one-third between Rs. 1,000 and 1,500 and the rest less than Rs. 1,000, for constructing their huts. Unfortunately, these costs are not reflected in the NSSO data discussed above.

It was observed in the field survey of Delhi that the majority of families had occupied rented houses when they first came to Delhi. But as the rents were high—between Rs. 150 and 200 for a room— they were forced to shift to squatter settlements where, currently, they are illegally occupying public space. Some of them stayed with their relatives before resorting to illegal squatting. Table 6.4 further corroborates the fact that the capacity to pay for housing is income elastic. This implies that there is no need to subsidise housing for upper income classes, as has been done in the past decades (see Chapter 4).

Table 6.5: *Percentage Distribution of Households in Rented Houses over Monthly Rent Classes by Monthly Per Capita Expenditure Class in 1983*

Monthly Per Capita Expenditure Class (Rs.)	Percentage of Households in Monthly Rent Class (Rs.)		
	Up to 50	50–100	100 & Above
1	2	3	4
0–30	94.97	5.03	0.00
30–40	98.21	1.79	0.00
40–50	91.81	7.01	1.18
50–60	87.46	11.72	0.82
60–70	77.98	21.04	3.98
70–85	75.66	19.56	4.78
85–100	69.25	24.24	6.51
100–125	63.12	25.75	11.13
125–150	55.88	29.27	14.85
150–200	48.80	29.21	21.99
200–250	43.58	26.61	29.81
250–300	44.54	22.90	32.56
300 & Above	38.50	22.89	38.61
All Classes	52.03	25.25	22.72
Up to Monthly Per Capita Expenditure of Rs. 125	71.35	22.05	6.60

Source: Based on NSSO (1987).

Table 6.5 strengthens the argument relating to the low affordability of the poor with regard to housing. It can be seen that among those living in rental houses, the percentage of households paying a monthly rent up to Rs. 50 is very high in the lower expenditure classes, the figure decreasing in higher classes. On an average, around 70 per cent of the households at or below the expenditure level of Rs. 125 pay a monthly rent of Rs. 50 or less, which is about 8 per cent of the total monthly expenditure (taking the average size of a household to be five). This supports the observation made earlier with regard to the affordability of the poor.

It may be noted from Table 6.6 that self-occupancy of *katcha* houses is quite high (75 per cent as compared to 58 per cent in *pucca* houses). In the *katcha* houses occupied by the poor, 79 per cent of the households live in their own houses. The figure for self-occupancy of *pucca* houses occupied by the poor is somewhat lower, namely, 70 per cent. This suggests that the shelter to which the poor have access is owner-occupied, often illegal and *katcha* in nature. The Table further indicates that the phenomenon of renting increases with improvement in the quality of the structure.

Table 6.6: *Percentage of Households Living in Non-rented Houses among the Categories* Katcha, Pucca, Semi-pucca *and All Houses in 1983*

Monthly Per Capita Expenditure Class (Rs.)	Per cent of Households Living in			
	Katcha	Semi-pucca	Pucca	All Houses
1	2	3	4	5
0–30	91.30	75.00	93.65	89.17
30–40	78.82	92.06	88.24	85.22
40–50	79.57	82.80	80.39	80.97
50–60	83.21	81.55	82.97	84.17
60–70	82.99	79.74	76.92	80.16
70–85	81.39	75.15	73.32	76.40
85–100	74.31	72.84	70.63	72.47
100–125	77.17	66.88	66.88	69.18
125–150	73.78	62.07	61.45	63.84
150–200	70.00	55.47	58.74	59.56
200–250	68.44	49.73	53.07	54.02
250–300	59.39	44.29	48.45	48.96
Above 300	58.69	45.38	46.35	46.67
All Classes	75.29	63.41	57.92	62.44
Up to Monthly Per Capita Expenditure of Rs. 125	79.22	72.93	70.79	73.86

Source: Based on NSSO (1987).

Table 6.7: *Actual and Imputed Rent per Unit Area for* Katcha, Pucca *and All Categories of Houses over Per Capita Expenditure Classes in 1983*

Monthly Per Capita Expenditure Class (Rs.)	Rent in Rs. Per Sq.m. for					
	Katcha		Pucca		All	
	Actual	Imputed	Actual	Imputed	Actual	Imputed
1	2	3	4	5	6	7
0–30	1.07	0.97	1.30	3.36	1.18	2.42
30–40	0.83	1.14	0.57	2.96	0.80	1.57
40–50	1.14	1.27	1.29	2.64	0.95	1.65
50–60	1.00	1.24	0.92	2.57	0.95	1.73
60–70	1.16	1.18	1.13	2.69	1.05	1.90
70–85	1.16	1.25	1.28	2.65	1.22	1.98
85–100	1.12	1.43	1.29	2.79	1.25	2.19
100–125	1.09	1.39	1.62	3.33	1.31	2.43
125–150	1.34	1.74	1.64	3.33	1.55	2.82
150–200	1.63	1.87	1.87	3.95	1.78	3.37
200–250	1.75	1.90	2.29	4.38	2.19	3.95
250–300	2.93	2.32	2.31	4.66	2.29	4.41
Above 300	2.49	1.61	3.08	5.48	3.01	5.14
All Classes	1.56	1.47	2.40	3.90	2.21	3.07
Up to Monthly Per Capita Expenditure of Rs. 125	1.11	1.34	1.37	2.98	1.26	2.25

Source: Based on NSSO (1987).

In Table 6.7, the actual and imputed rental values for unit area are given for all expenditure classes, as also for *katcha* and *pucca* structures. It can be seen that these values increase with expenditure classes and that too, systematically after the class of Rs. 100 to 125. The difference between the bottom-most and the top-most class (for all houses as well as *katcha* and *pucca* structures) is higher for rental premises as compared to those occupied by owners. This again indicates that actual rents rise more sharply than the imputed values. However, rental values per unit area are greater in the higher expenditure class not only because of better quality of construction (which is partially reflected in the type of structure), but also because of better location. The latter would imply the availability of or proximity to a higher level of services, a better physical environment, etc., for the high income section of the urban population.

Table 6.8: *Percentage of Households with Monthly Per Capita Expenditure of Rs. 125 or Less by House Category in 1983*

State/Union Territory	Katcha	Pucca
1	2	3
Andhra Pradesh	34.80	39.55
Assam	61.03	16.10
Bihar	35.24	33.06
Gujarat	18.05	43.96
Haryana	10.38	70.00
Himachal Pradesh	38.02	30.04
Jammu & Kashmir	19.85	28.16
Karnataka	23.79	24.33
Kerala	25.79	36.80
Madhya Pradesh	23.71	27.98
Maharashtra	24.07	26.55
Manipur	68.99	2.96
Nagaland	51.43	8.37
Orissa	52.58	14.08
Punjab	9.21	69.39
Rajasthan	17.17	68.04
Sikkim	4.50	33.68
Tamil Nadu	31.68	40.66
Uttar Pradesh	17.00	50.81
West Bengal	21.37	42.63
Andaman & Nicobar	17.39	33.96
Chandigarh	13.61	54.49
Delhi	11.49	74.60
Goa, Daman & Diu	24.38	35.08
Mizoram	36.71	1.05
Pondicherry	43.68	25.20
All-India	26.49	39.70

Source: Based on NSSO (1987).

Tables 6.8 and 6.9 indicate the quality of housing available to households with a monthly per capita expenditure up to Rs. 125 in different states and union territories. In Andhra Pradesh, Assam, Bihar, Himachal Pradesh, Manipur, Nagaland, Orissa, Tamil Nadu, Mizoram and Pondicherry, there is a higher percentage of poor households living in *katcha* houses than the all-India figure. These states and union territories are either located in the hill regions or are economically less developed. This pattern, thus, corresponds with the average level of these facilities, as discussed in the previous chapter. The percentage of *pucca* houses occupied by the poor, on the other hand, is high in the developed states and union territories of Gujarat, Haryana, Punjab, Chandigarh and Delhi, along with the backward state of Rajasthan which is an exception. Surprisingly, the figure for Maharashtra is quite low and it is less than the national average for the percentage of *katcha* houses as well. This is because a large segment amongst the poor in the state lives in semi-*pucca* houses. One can, therefore, argue that the poor in backward states are, in general, worse-off in terms of the quality of housing structure than their counterparts in developed states.

The pattern emerging from Table 6.9 is once again similar to the average state-level scenario analysed in the previous chapter. It can be seen that the figures for per capita floor area for the bottom 40 per cent of households are equal to or higher than the all-India urban average for all backward states including the hill states of Himachal Pradesh, Jammu and Kashmir, Manipur and Nagaland. Also, the states which have metro cities, with the exception of Gujarat, have floor areas significantly less than the all-India average. It may be concluded that the poor in backward states are better placed in terms of access to urban land. With increasing urbanisation and development, however, inequality in the distribution of land increases, which reduces the availability of land to the poor.

Table 6.9 further reveals that in Kerala, Orissa, the smaller states of the north-east, those which have metro cities—like Andhra Pradesh, Karnataka and Tamil Nadu—and in the union territory of Delhi, the poor pay a rent (actual) higher than the national average. However, in Gujarat, Maharashtra and West Bengal the rents are less than the all-India average, which may reflect the fact that in these states benefits accrue to the poor owing to the implementation of the Rent Control Act. It is important to note that in all states and union territories, with the exception of Chandigarh and Delhi, around 60 to 70 per cent of the urban poor reside in non-rented premises.

With the failure of the existing organisational structure and formal housing schemes to reach the lower sections of the population, the urban poor have tried to find their own solutions. It is evident from the foregoing analysis that a large majority of them

Table 6.9: *Per Capita Floor Area and Actual and Imputed*
Monthly Rents and Rental Housing for
Households with Per Capita Monthly
Expenditure of Rs. 125 or Less by
States/Union Territories in 1983

State/Union Territory	Per Capita Floor Area (Sq.m.)	Per Capita Monthly Rent (Rs.)		Per Cent Households Living in Rented Houses
		Actual	Imputed	
1	2	3	4	5
Andhra Pradesh	5.22	8.07	12.12	27.59
Assam	6.00	7.81	15.72	5.13
Bihar	6.03	5.61	8.30	16.86
Gujarat	5.97	6.74	13.20	33.68
Haryana	5.17	5.76	18.38	16.25
Himachal Pradesh	5.99	3.83	10.71	19.30
Jammu & Kashmir	7.73	9.71	21.12	8.70
Karnataka	5.33	7.63	12.44	31.89
Kerala	7.40	8.69	14.06	5.17
Madhya Pradesh	7.46	6.09	8.99	22.08
Maharashtra	4.23	5.46	11.66	32.74
Manipur	7.53	10.04	2.48	3.76
Nagaland	13.32	9.82	3.24	17.43
Orissa	6.14	7.21	8.03	18.05
Punjab	4.36	7.19	14.27	20.11
Rajasthan	5.45	8.41	10.37	14.98
Sikkim	2.59	9.46	4.97	69.87
Tamil Nadu	4.44	7.66	10.25	33.67
Uttar Pradesh	6.71	6.57	12.30	20.93
West Bengal	4.18	5.27	13.48	35.17
Andaman & Nicobar	6.68	10.13	19.28	38.51
Chandigarh	4.10	9.78	17.32	74.29
Delhi	4.21	17.34	31.71	19.70
Goa, Daman & Diu	9.47	4.09	27.70	20.67
Mizoram	4.07	14.69	17.60	23.98
Pondicherry	5.77	5.33	7.32	22.51
All-India	5.67	6.99	12.49	26.14

Source: Based on NSSO (1987).

manage to live in urban areas, particularly in large cities, by constructing or 'buying' some kind of informal structure for which they are not required to pay any regular rent.

Access to Water Supply

The access of people in different consumption brackets to water supply facilities has been analysed based primarily on the 42nd round of the NSS data. The households covered by the NSS have been classified into ten fractiles in ascending order of monthly per capita expenditure, each comprising roughly 10 per cent of the households. The bottom-most and the top-most fractiles have further been divided into two, each comprising 5 per cent of the households. Information on water supply is provided by the NSSO for these twelve fractiles.

Table 6.10 shows the percentage distribution of persons using the major sources of drinking water over the fractile groups.

Table 6.10: *Percentage of Persons Using the Major Sources of Drinking Water to Total Persons Over Consumption Fractiles in 1986–87*

Fractiles	Tap	Tank & Pond	Tubewell/ Hand- pump	Pucca Well	River, Canal Spring	Tanker	Others
1	2	3	4	5	6	7	8
0–5	61.34	0.50	19.32	15.55	.82	0.53	2.50
5–10	63.06	0.67	17.43	17.20	.39	0.38	1.94
10–20	63.67	0.40	19.81	14.42	.35	0.30	1.75
20–30	68.69	0.31	18.15	11.41	.35	0.33	0.66
30–40	69.69	0.12	18.74	10.28	.77	0.20	1.99
40–50	70.77	0.19	15.80	11.87	.24	0.36	0.57
50–60	75.73	0.16	13.87	8.77	.28	0.42	0.48
60–70	76.94	0.20	13.45	8.04	.36	0.34	0.53
70–80	82.24	0.11	10.34	5.97	.16	0.32	0.48
80–90	84.28	0.07	9.51	5.00	.23	0.30	0.72
90–95	85.28	0.14	9.58	3.82	.14	0.02	1.35
95–100	89.23	0.10	6.26	3.05	.76	0.00	0.09
All	72.43	0.25	15.44	10.26	.40	3.32	1.02

Source: Based on NSSO (1990a).

Undoubtedly, taps that provide treated water through pipes are a hygienic, convenient, and the most subsidised system as far as urban water supply is concerned. It may be noted that, on an average, 72.43 per cent of the urban population in the country uses taps as the major source of drinking water. There is, however, significant variation in the availability of tap water facilities across the consumption fractiles. The population served by tap water increases steadily from 61.34 per cent for the lowest fractile to 89.23 per cent for the highest fractile. It is true that a substantial proportion of the population in the bottom three fractiles has access to tap water but the percentage figure is much lower than the average for all classes. It was observed in the preceding chapter that among those using tap water facilities, 87 per cent are served by public sector agencies. It can, therefore, be argued that the richer sections of the population benefit more than the poor from this heavily subsidised source provided largely by the government.

It can be seen (Table 6.10) that while 19.32 and 15.55 per cent of the population in the bottom fractile depend on handpumps and *pucca* wells, respectively, the corresponding percentages are 6.26 and 3.05 for the top fractile. It has been mentioned in the previous chapter that in obtaining water from these two sources, capital and current expenditures on the part of the individual are generally very high. It is thus evident that a higher percentage among the poorer households are obliged to find their own sources of drinking water instead of depending on the government system. The opposite is true for households in higher consumption fractiles.

Table 6.11 shows the specialisation index for the major sources of drinking water. The index indicates the relative dependence of people on different sources of drinking water. This has been worked out by dividing the percentage share of each fractile among the persons using a particular source by the share of that fractile in the total population. The index *sij/* for the *ith* fractile and the *jth* source of drinking water may be shown as:

$$S_{ij} = \dfrac{\dfrac{\text{Persons in the } ith \text{ fractile using the } jth \text{ source}}{\text{All persons using the } jth \text{ source}}}{\dfrac{\text{Persons in the } ith \text{ fractile}}{\text{All Persons}}}$$

Table 6.11: *Specialisation Index for Major Sources of Drinking Water over Consumption Fractiles in 1986–87*

Fractiles	Tap	Tank & Pond	Tubewell	Pucca Well	River, Canal	Tanker	Others
1	2	3	4	5	6	7	8
0–5	0.85	2.00	1.25	1.52	2.07	1.65	2.44
5–10	0.87	2.68	1.13	1.67	0.98	1.18	1.90
10–20	0.88	1.58	1.28	1.41	0.88	0.95	1.71
20–30	0.95	1.25	1.17	1.11	0.87	1.04	0.65
30–40	0.96	0.49	1.21	0.93	1.93	0.63	1.17
40–50	0.98	0.75	1.02	1.16	0.62	1.13	0.56
50–60	1.09	0.62	0.90	0.85	0.71	1.32	0.47
60–70	1.07	0.78	0.87	0.78	0.91	1.07	0.52
70–80	1.13	0.43	0.66	0.58	0.41	1.00	0.47
80–90	1.16	0.26	0.61	0.49	0.58	0.93	0.70
90–95	1.18	0.58	0.62	0.37	0.36	0.06	1.32
95–100	1.23	0.42	0.40	0.30	1.93	–	0.09

Source: Based on NSSO (1990a).

Table 6.11 shows that the values of the index for taps increase smoothly from lower to higher fractiles. This corroborates the argument (based on Table 6.10) that people in the higher fractiles have an advantage over those in the lower fractiles in their access to tap water. The value of the index exceeds unity in the expenditure fractile 50 to 60 and increases steadily to 1.23 for the top-most fractile. For all other sources of drinking water the pattern is quite the opposite. Poorer people, thus, obtain water from sources that are generally less hygienic, less reliable and more expensive.

Disparity among different classes in their access to the sources of water comes out more sharply in Table 6.12 where the figures of the bottom five fractiles are clubbed together. This Table thus provides information regarding the access of the bottom 40 per cent of the households to different sources of drinking water across the states. The Table shows that 66.01 per cent of the population among the bottom 40 per cent of households has access to tap water whereas the corresponding figure for all fractiles is as high as 72.43 per cent. For sources of water other than taps, the figures for this category of population are higher than those for the total urban population. Among the bottom 40 per cent of households,

Table 6.12: *Percentage of Persons by Major Sources of Drinking Water among Households belonging to the Bottom 40 Per cent Expenditure Fractile to All Persons in the Same Fractile in 1986–87*

States	Tap	Tubewell/ Hand-pump	Pucca Well	Tank/ Pond	River/ Canal	Tankers
1	2	3	4	5	6	7
Andhra Pradesh	70.63	14.81	16.70	0.40	0.37	0.76
Assam	33.34	49.10	11.81	1.18	1.65	–
Bihar	36.02	34.13	26.98	0.82	–	0.21
Gujarat	90.27	6.00	1.74	–	–	–
Haryana	78.01	21.99	–	–	–	–
Himachal Pradesh	93.30	1.02	3.10	–	2.59	–
Jammu & Kashmir	91.21	31.63	0.42	–	3.28	1.76
Karnataka	78.52	6.93	11.45	1.96	–	–
Kerala	43.52	0.52	54.48	1.08	–	–
Madhya Pradesh	76.39	8.80	13.42	–	0.65	–
Maharashtra	90.26	2.08	7.09	–	0.11	0.05
Orissa	42.33	15.18	35.00	2.83	5.06	–
Punjab	52.75	47.05	0.20	–	–	–
Rajasthan	74.64	9.01	15.41	–	–•	–
Tamil Nadu	67.54	17.78	10.17	3.90	1.43	2.10
Tripura	77.36	16.14	19.54	2.01	–	–
Uttar Pradesh	47.85	35.77	14.67	–	0.22	–
West Bengal	60.50	42.77	8.35	–	–	0.02
All-India	66.01	18.74	12.99	0.36	0.52	0.32

Source: Based on NSSO (1990a).

18.74 and 12.99 per cent of the population gets water from hand-pumps and *pucca* wells, respectively, whereas the averages for all fractiles are 15.44 and 10.26 for these two sources.

It has been indicated in the previous section that the level of development of the state bears a direct relationship with the proportion of population covered by the formal water supply system. It was seen in Table 5.11 in the preceding chapter that in less developed states such as Assam, Bihar, Kerala, Orissa and Uttar Pradesh, the percentage served by tap water is much lower than the national average. Table 6.12 shows that the percentage belonging to the bottom 40 per cent served by tap water in these states is also less than the state averages. On the other hand, in Gujarat,

Maharashtra, Haryana, Himachal Pradesh and Jammu and Kashmir, where the coverage of population by tap water facilities is high, a larger percentage among the poor also derive this advantage, as the state figures are higher than the national average. There is, thus, a positive relationship between the coverage of persons and the coverage of the poor with the formal water supply system. However, in relation to the population belonging to the higher fractiles in the same state, the share of the poor is definitely lower as inferred through a detailed analysis of the NSS data.

It is, thus, evident that about 34 per cent of the urban poor are not covered by piped water supply and are obliged to draw water from sources that are mostly private and at a cost higher than that of the piped system. In the relatively less developed states, the percentage of poor outside the tap water system is very high—over 60 per cent. Furthermore, the variation in coverage of population by taps between the lower and upper fractiles is significantly high in the less developed states.

The major limitation of the 42nd round of the NSS data is that it does not indicate the quality and quantity of water available to the households. Access to any source of water does not indicate its adequacy or its potability. Further, the NSS provides no information on the labour or time spent in obtaining the daily water requirements. An attempt, therefore, has been made here to supplement the data on access through field surveys in selected cities and also through the information available from surveys and studies conducted by other researchers. A study by the National Institute of Urban Affairs (NIUA 1988) showed—based on information supplied by the Government of Madhya Pradesh—that the supply through public stand posts (which is usually the source of tap water for a majority of the urban poor) varied between 22 lpcd and 36 lpcd, whereas the supply through domestic connections varied between 36 lpcd and 120 lpcd. The study further showed that in the sample towns of Karnataka, the percentage of population dependent on public stand posts and receiving a supply of less than 20 lpcd varied between 14 and 70. The National Commission on Urbanisation (1988) noted that 'the per capita water consumption was reported to be between 10 to 23 litres per day in slum areas of Bangalore.' It is, therefore, evident that in most cities, per capita water supply to the poorer sections of the population is much below the recommended minimum. The discussion with concerned officials of the

"Evenin', sir. I'm Deputy Dwight Harris. From the sheriff's office over in Savannah."

The man leaned forward slightly and glanced past him toward the golf cart parked at the end of the path. To discourage tourism and unwelcome visitors to the island, there wasn't a ferry to St. Anne from the mainland. Anyone coming here came by a boat they either owned or chartered. When they arrived, they either walked or rented a golf cart to get around the island's nine thousand acres, give or take a few hundred. Only permanent residents drove cars on the narrow roads, many of which had been left unpaved on purpose.

The golf cart wasn't as official-looking as a squad car, and Harris figured it diminished his authority a bit. To stoke his self-confidence, he hiked up his slipping gun belt.

The man behind the door asked, "How can I help you, Deputy Harris?"

"First off, I apologize for disturbing you. But I got a call earlier this evening. From a gal up in New York." The man waited him out, saying nothing. "Said she was trying to track down somebody who goes by the initials P.M.E."

"Really?"

"That's what she said. I didn't let on like the name registered with me."

"Did it?"

"Register, you mean? No, sir. Can't rightly say it did."

"Nevertheless, you're here."

"I'll admit she got my curiosity up. Never knew anybody to go only by his initials, you see. Don't worry, though. 'Round here, we respect a person's privacy."

"An admirable practice."

"St. Anne has a history of folks hiding out on her for one reason or another."

The moment it was out, Harris wished he hadn't said it. It smacked of an accusation of some sort. A long silence ensued. He cleared his throat nervously before continuing. "So anyhow,

tip of the island, situated on a little finger of land that pointed out toward Africa. Some of the tales he'd heard about the place stretched credibility. But the descriptions of the house were, by God, damn near accurate.

Typical of colonial Low Country architecture, the two-story white frame house was sitting on top of an aged brick basement. Six broad steps led up to the deep veranda that extended all the way across the front of the house and wrapped around both sides. The front door had been painted a glossy black, as had all the hurricane shutters that flanked the windows on both stories. Six smooth columns supported the second-floor balcony. Twin chimneys acted like bookends against the steeply pitched roof. It looked pretty much like Deputy Harris had imagined it would.

He hadn't counted on it looking so spooky, is all.

He jumped and uttered a soft exclamation of fright when a raindrop landed on the back of his neck with a hard splat. It had dripped from a low-hanging branch of the tree under which he was standing. Wiping the wetness away, he replaced his hat and glanced around to make sure no one had seen his nervous reaction. It was the gathering dusk and the inclement weather that was giving the place an eerie feel. Cursing himself for behaving like a coward, he forced his feet into motion.

Dodging puddles, he made his way up the crushed-shell path, which was lined by twin rows of live oaks, four to a side. Spanish moss hung from the branches in trailing bunches. The roots of the ancient trees snaked along the ground, some of them as thick as a fat man's thigh.

Altogether, it was an impressive front entry. Majestic, you might say. The back of the house, Harris knew, overlooked the Atlantic.

The house hadn't started out this grand. The four original rooms had been built more than two centuries ago by the planter who'd bought the island from a colonist who decided he preferred dying of old age in England to succumbing to yellow fever in the newly founded American nation. The house had expanded with the plantation's success, first with indigo and sugar cane, then with cotton.

Several generations into the dynasty, those first four rooms were converted into slave quarters, and construction of the big house was begun. In its day, it was a marvel, at least for St. Anne Island. Building materials and all the furnishings had been shipped in, then dragged on sleds pulled by mules through dense forests and fertile fields to the home site. It had taken years to complete, but it had been sturdily constructed, withstanding Union army occupation and the lashings of a couple dozen hurricanes.

Then it succumbed to a bug.

Around the beginning of the twentieth century, the boll weevil ruined more than the cotton crop. More damaging than weather and war, the boll weevil crushed the local economy and destroyed life as it had been lived on St. Anne.

A descendant of the plantation's original owner had correctly forecast his imminent doom and hanged himself on the dining room chandelier. The rest of the family stole off the island in the middle of the night, never to be heard of again, leaving debts and unpaid taxes.

Decades passed. The forest eventually reclaimed the property surrounding the house, just as it did the fields once white with cotton. Varmints occupied rooms once inhabited by aristocracy and visited by one United States president. The only people to ever venture inside the dilapidated mansion were crazy kids accepting a dare or an occasional drunk looking for a place to sleep it off.

It remained in ruin until a little over a year ago when an outsider, not an islander, bought it and commenced a massive renovation. Harris figured he was probably a northerner who'd seen *Gone With the Wind* several times and wanted himself an antebellum mansion on southern soil, a Yankee with more money than good sense.

Word around the island, though, was positive about th new owner. He'd made noticeable improvements on the plac folks said. But in Harris's opinion there was still a lot to done if it was going to shine as it had in its heyday. T deputy didn't envy the new owner the monumental task the expense involved in such an undertaking. Nor was he vious of the bad luck that seemed to go hand in glove with place.

Legend had it that the hanged man's ghost still resid the old house and that the dining room chandelier swung the ceiling for no reason that anybody could detect.

Harris didn't put much stock in ghost stories. He'c flesh-and-blood people do much scarier stuff than any m a ghost could drum up. Even so, he would have welcome tle more illumination as he mounted the steps, crossed randa, and approached the front door.

He tapped the brass knocker tentatively, then hard onds ticked by as ponderously as rain dripped from th It wasn't that late, but maybe the resident was alread Country folk tended to turn in earlier than city didn't they?

Harris considered leaving and coming back so time—preferably before the sun went down. But then approaching footsteps. Seconds later the front door open from the inside—but not by much.

"Yes?"

Harris peered into the crack formed by the open d psyched himself up to expect anything from the har to the twin barrels of a sawed-off shotgun aimed at a disgruntled homeowner that he'd unnecessarily of bed.

Thankfully he was greeted by neither, and the reasonably friendly. Harris couldn't see him well and of his face blended into the shadows behind him, sounded pleasant enough. At least he hadn't cusse

I thought I should oblige this lady. Came over in the department's motor launch. Asked around at the landing and was directed here."

"What did this lady from New York want?"

"Well, sir, I don't rightly know. She said it wasn't a legal matter or nothing like 'at. Just that she had business with P.M.E. I thought you might be a big winner in one of those sweepstakes, thought Ed McMahon and Dick Clark might be looking for you."

"I've never entered a sweepstakes."

"Right, right. Well, then . . ."

Harris tipped his hat forward so he could scratch the back of his head. He wondered why in hell the man hadn't invited him in or, short of that, why he hadn't turned on any lights. Pussyfooting hadn't gotten him anywhere, by God, so he bluntly asked, "You P.M.E. or what?"

"Did she leave her name?"

"Huh? Oh, the lady? Yeah." Harris fished a piece of notepaper from the breast pocket of his uniform shirt, which he was embarrassed to discover was damp with sweat. However, the man seemed not to notice or care about the dampness as he took the sheet and read what Harris had written down.

"Those're her phone numbers," Harris explained. "All of 'em. So I figured this business of hers must be pretty important. That's why I came on out tonight."

"Thank you very much for your trouble, Sheriff Harris."

"Deputy."

"Deputy Harris."

Then, before Harris could blink, the man closed the door in his face. "Good evenin' to you, too," he mouthed as he turned away.

His boots crunched the shells of the path. The evening had deepened into full-blown darkness, and it was even darker beneath the canopy of live oak branches. He wasn't afraid, exactly. The man behind the door had been civil enough. He hadn't been what you'd call hostile. Inhospitable, maybe, but not hostile.

All the same, Harris was glad to have this errand over and done with. If he had it to do over again, he might not assign himself this duty. What was it to him if some lady from up north was successful or not with her unspecified business?

When he sat down on the seat of the golf cart, he discovered it had been dripped on from the tree overhead. His britches were soaked through by the time he reached the landing where he'd tied up the boat.

The man from whom he had borrowed the golf cart—no charge for lawmen—eyed him distrustfully as Harris returned the key. "Find him?"

"Yeah, thanks for the directions," Harris replied. "You ever see this guy?"

"Now and again," the man drawled.

"Is he a weird sort?"

"Not so's you'd notice."

"He ever make any trouble around here?"

"Naw, he stays pretty much to hisself."

"Island folks like him okay?"

"You need any gas before headin' back?"

Which was as good as an invitation to leave and take his nosy questions with him. Harris had hoped to get a clearer picture of the man who occupied the haunted mansion and hid behind doors when folks came calling, but apparently he wasn't going to get one. He had no cause to investigate further—beyond his natural curiosity as to why a man went only by his initials and what a woman in New York City was wanting with him.

He thanked the islander for the use of the golf cart.

The man spat tobacco juice into the mud. "No problem."

CHAPTER 3

J ust one more picture, please, Mr. and Mrs. Reed?"

Maris and Noah smiled for the photographer who was covering the literary banquet for *Publishers Weekly*. During the cocktail hour, they'd been photographed with other publishers, with
their award-winnng author, and with the celebrity emcee. The
former women's tennis champion fancied herself an author
now that she'd had a ghostwriter pen a roman à clef about her
days on the professional circuit.

The Reeds had been allowed to eat their dinner in relative
peace, but now that the event had concluded, they were once
again being asked to pose for various shots. But, as promised,
the photographer snapped one last picture of them alone, then
scuttled off to catch the exercise guru whose latest fitness book
topped the nonfiction bestseller list.

As Maris and Noah crossed the elegant lobby of the Palace
Hotel, she sighed, "At last. I can't wait to get into my jammies."

"One drink and we'll say our good nights."

"Drink?"

"At LeCirque."

"Now?"

"I told you."

"No, you didn't."

"I'm sure I did, Maris. Between the main course and dessert, I whispered to you that Nadia had invited us to join her and one of the award recipients for a drink."

"I didn't know you meant tonight."

Maris groaned with dread. She disliked Nadia Schuller intensely and for this very reason. The book critic was meddlesome and pushy, always roping Noah and her into a commitment from which there was no graceful way out.

Nadia Schuller's "Book Chat" column was syndicated in major newspapers and carried a lot of weight—in Maris's opinion simply because Nadia had ramrodded herself into being the country's only book critic whose name was recognized by the general public. Maris held her in low regard both professionally and personally.

She was adroit at making it seem as though this sort of arranged meeting were for the benefit of the parties she was bringing together, but Maris suspected that Nadia's matchmaking was strictly self-serving. She was a self-promoter without equal and refused to take no for an answer. Whatever her request, she extended it assuming that it would be granted without a quibble. Noncompliance to her wishes was met with a veiled threat of consequences. Maris was wise to her manipulations, but Noah seemed blind to them.

"Please, Noah, can't we decline? Just this once?"

"We're already here."

"Not tonight," she implored.

"Tell you what. Let's compromise." He pulled her around to face him and smiled affectionately. "I think this might be an important meeting."

"Nadia always makes it sound not just important but imperative."

"Granted. But this time I don't think she's exaggerating."

"What's the compromise?"

"I'll make your excuses. I'll tell Nadia that you have a head-ache or an early breakfast appointment tomorrow morning. Have the driver take you home. After one drink, I'll follow you. Half an hour, max. I promise."

She slid her hand inside his tuxedo jacket and stroked his chest through the stiffly starched shirt. "I have a better com-promise, Mr. Reed. I'll tell Nadia to take a flying leap into the East River. Then let's go home together. Those jammies I men-tioned? They can be dispensed with."

"You ended your sentence with a preposition," he noted.

"You're the writer. I'm a mere editor."

"I'm a *former* writer."

"There's no such thing." She took a step closer and aligned her thighs with his. "What do you say? About the jammies."

"Noah? We're waiting."

Nadia Schuller approached with the bearing of a military general about to address the troops, except that she was better dressed and had her phony smile in place. She was skilled at turning on the charm at will—to intrude, disarm, and promote herself. Many fell for it. She was a frequent and popular guest on talk shows. Letterman loved her, and he was just one of her celebrity friends. She made it her business to be photographed with actors, musicians, supermodels, and politicians whenever possible.

She had elevated herself to heights that Maris felt were un-deserved. She was a self-appointed, self-ordained authority with no meaningful credentials to support her opinions on ei-ther writing or the business of publishing. But authors and publishers couldn't afford to offend her or they risked their next book being slammed in her column.

Tonight her arm was linked with that of a bestselling novelist who looked a little dazed. Or stoned, if the gossip about him was true. Or maybe he was only dizzy from being propelled through the evening by the turbo engines of Nadia's personality.

"They won't hold our table forever, Noah. Coming?"

"Well . . ." He hesitated and glanced down at Maris.

"What's the matter?" Nadia asked in a voice as piercing as a dentist's drill. She addressed the question to Maris, automatically assuming that she was the source of the problem.

"Nothing's the matter, Nadia. Noah and I were having a private conversation."

"Oh, my. Have I interrupted one of those husband/wife things?"

The critic could have been pretty if not for her edge, which manifested itself in the brittleness of her smile and the calculation in her eyes, which seemed to miss nothing. She was always impeccably dressed, groomed, and accessorized in the best of taste, but even arrayed in fine silk and finer jewelry there was nothing feminine about her.

It was rumored that she went through men like a box of Godivas, chewing up and spitting out the ones who didn't challenge her or who could do nothing to further her career— in other words, the ones with soft centers. Maris had no problem believing the gossip about Nadia's promiscuity. What surprised her was the number of men who found her sexually appealing.

"Yes, we were having a husband and wife *thing*. I was telling Noah that the last thing I want to do is join you for a round of drinks," Maris said, smiling sweetly.

"You do look awfully tired," Nadia returned, her smile just as sweet.

Noah intervened. "I'm sorry, Nadia. We must decline tonight. I'm going to take my wife home and tuck her in."

"No, darling," Maris said. She wouldn't play the wounded wife in front of Nadia Schuller. "I wouldn't dream of keeping you from this obligation."

"It's hardly that," Nadia snapped. "More like a rare opportunity to talk shop with one of publishing's most exciting novelists."

The exciting novelist had yet to utter a peep. He was bleary-eyed and seemed oblivious to their conversation. Maris gave

Nadia a knowing look. "Of course it is. That's what I meant."
Back to Noah, she said, "You stay. I'll see myself home."

He regarded her doubtfully. "You're sure?"

"I insist."

"Then it's settled." Nadia gave the writer's arm a sharp tug.
Like a sleepwalker, he fell into step beside her. "You two say
your good-byes while we go claim the table. Shall I order your
usual, Noah?"

"Please."

Then to Maris she called back airily, "Get some rest, dear."

Parker Evans stared out the window into nothingness.

He couldn't see the shoreline from this vantage point, but if
he concentrated, he could hear the surf. Rain clouds obscured
the moon. There was no other source of light, natural or man-
made, to relieve the darkness.

From this first-floor window overlooking the rear of his
property, Parker could see across a breast of lawn to the point
where it sharply dropped off several degrees before sloping
more gradually toward the beach. That edge of the lawn appeared to be the threshold of a black void that melded with the
ocean farther out. No wonder ancient sailors had feared the
unknown terrors that lay beyond the brink.

The room behind him was also dark, which wasn't an oversight. He had deliberately left the lights off. Had they been on,
his reflection would have appeared in the window glass. He
preferred looking at nothing to looking at himself.

Anyway, he didn't need a light in order to read the list of telephone numbers he held in his hand. In fact, he no longer needed
to read them at all. He had committed them to memory.

His six months of waiting had finally paid off. Maris
Matherly-Reed was trying to contact him.

As recently as yesterday, Parker had come close to scratching
his plan and devising another. After months of not hearing
from her, he figured that she had read the prologue of *Envy*,

hated it, tossed it, and hadn't even had the courtesy of sending him a rejection notice.

It had also occurred to him that the partial manuscript had never reached her desk, that mailroom staff had misdirected it or hurled it into a Dumpster within minutes of its delivery. Few of the major publishing houses even had slush piles anymore. Manuscripts either got in through literary agents or they didn't get in at all.

If his pages had survived that first selection process, a junior editor who was paid to cull material from slush piles could have deep-sixed the *Envy* prologue before it ever got to her office. In any case, he'd almost convinced himself that this plan was a bust and that it would be necessary to plot another.

That was yesterday. Just went to show what a difference a day could make. Apparently the pages *had* made it to her desk, and she *had* read them, because today she *had* tried to contact him.

Marris Madderly Reade. The deputy had misspelled all three of her names. Parker hoped he was more adept at taking down telephone numbers.

Business, she had told Deputy Dwight Harris when he had asked why she was looking for P.M.E. She had business to discuss. Which could mean good news for Parker. Or bad. Or something in between.

She could be calling to say that his writing stunk and how dare he presume to send her prestigious publishing house such unsolicited shit. Or maybe she would take a softer approach and say that he had talent but that his material didn't fit their present publishing needs, and wish him luck at placing his book with another house.

But those responses usually came in the form of rejection letters, written in language firm enough to discourage another submission but with enough encouragement to keep the rejected writer from jumping off the nearest bridge.

Ms. Matherly-Reed didn't know where to address such a letter to him, however. He'd made certain that she couldn't reach him by mail. So if her intention had been to reject *Envy*, he probably would never have heard from her at all. Instead, she had tried to track him down. From that, he deduced her response must be favorable.

But it wasn't yet time to ice down the champagne. It was a little early to award himself a gold star for being such a clever boy. Before he got too carried away, he forced himself to keep his heartbeat regular, his breathing normal, and his head clear. Success or failure hinged not on what he'd done up to this point but on what he did next.

So instead of celebrating this milestone, he had stared for hours out this window into the rainy, moonless night. While the calm surf swept the shoreline, he weighed his options. While his distant neighbors on St. Anne slept, or watched late-night TV, or made love under their summer-weight bedcovers, Parker Evans plotted.

It helped that he already knew the ending to this story. Not once did he consider changing the outcome from his original plot. He never considered letting Maris Matherly-Reed's attempt to reach him go unacknowledged, never thought about dropping this thing here and now.

No, he'd come this far, he was committed to seeing it all the way through the denouement. But between here and there, he couldn't make a single misstep. Each chapter had to be carefully thought out, with no mistakes allowed. It had to be the perfect plot.

And if his resolve to finish it ever faltered, he had only to remember how fucking long it had taken him to reach this point in the saga. Six months.

Well . . . six months and fourteen years.

Maris groped for the ringing telephone. She squinted the lighted clock on her nightstand into focus. Five-twenty-three. In the morning. Who—

Then panic brought her wide awake. Was this that dreaded, inevitable phone call notifying her that her father had suffered a coronary, stroke, fall, or worse?

Anxiously she clutched the receiver. "Hello?"

"Maris Matherly-Reed?"

"Speaking."

"Where do you get off screwing around with my life?"

She was taken completely off guard and it took a moment for the rude question to sink in. "I beg your pardon? Who is this?"

She sat up, switched on the lamp, and reached out to rouse Noah. But his side of the bed was empty. She gaped at the undisturbed linens, at the pillow that was still fluffed.

"I don't appreciate you calling the sheriff," the caller said hotly.

Where is Noah? "I'm sorry . . . I was . . . you caught me asleep. . . . Did you say sheriff?"

"Sheriff, *sheriff.* Ring any bells?"

She sucked in a quick breath. "P.M.E.?"

"A deputy came to my house, snooping around. Who the—"

"I—"

"—hell do you think you are?"

"I—"

"To mess with people's—"

"You—"

"—lives. Thanks for nothing, lady."

"Will you please be quiet for one second?"

Her raised voice brought him to an abrupt silence, but Maris sensed waves of resentment pulsing through the line. After taking a couple of calming breaths, she assumed a more reasonable tone. "I read your prologue and liked it. I wanted to talk to you about it, but I had no way of contacting you. You *left* me no way to contact you. So I called the sheriff's office in the hope that—"

"Send it back."

"Excuse me?"

"The prologue. Send it back."

"Why?"

"It's crap."

"Far from it, Mr.—"

"I shouldn't have sent it."

"I'm glad you did. These pages intrigue me. They're compelling and well written. If the rest of your book is as good as the prologue, I'll consider buying it for publication."

"It's not for sale."

"What do you mean?"

"Look, I've got a southern accent, but I'm still speaking English. Which part didn't you understand?"

His voice was geographically distinctive. Usually she found the soft *r*'s and slow drawl of southern regions engaging. But his manner was abrasive and disagreeable. If she hadn't seen real potential in his writing, recognized an untapped talent, she would have ended the conversation long before now.

Patiently she asked, "If you didn't want your book published, why did you submit the prologue to a book publisher?"

"Because I suffered a mental lapse," he answered, imitating her precise enunciation. "I've since changed my mind."

Maris took another tack. "Do you have a representative?"

"Representative?"

"An agent."

"I'm not an actor."

"Have you ever submitted material before?"

"Just send it back, okay?"

"Did you multiple-submit?"

"Send it to other publishers, you mean? No."

"Why did you send it to me?"

"You know what, forget sending it back. Toss it in the nearest trash can, use it for kindling, or line your birdcage with it, I don't care."

Sensing he was about to hang up, she said quickly, "Just one more moment, please."

"We're on my nickel."

"Before you decide against selling your book, a decision I think you'll regret, I'd welcome the chance to give you my professional opinion of it. I promise to be brutally honest. If I don't see any merit in it, I'll tell you. Let me decide if it's good or not. Please send me the entire manuscript."

"You have it."

"I have it?"

"Did I stutter?"

"You mean the prologue is all you've got?"

"It's not all I've *got*. It's all I've *written*. The rest of the story is in my head."

"Oh." That was disappointing. She had assumed that the remainder of the book was completed or nearly so. It hadn't occurred to her that the manuscript consisted of only those first twelve pages. "I urge you to finish it. In the meantime—"

"In the meantime, you're running up my long-distance bill. If you don't want to spend any money on return postage, then shred the damn thing. Good-bye. Oh, and don't send any more deputy sheriffs to my door."

Maris held the dead phone to her ear for several seconds before thoughtfully hanging up. The conversation had been almost surreal. She even thought that perhaps she had dreamed it.

But she wasn't dreaming. She was wide awake. By Manhattan standards, it was practically the middle of the night—and her husband wasn't in bed with her. If the strange telephone call weren't enough to wake her up, then Noah's unexplained absence certainly was.

She was concerned enough to call the hospital emergency rooms. But when she'd last seen Noah, he'd been in the company of Nadia Schuller. Which made her angry enough to throw something against the wall.

In either case, her night had ended and she was up for good. Throwing off the covers, she got out of bed and was reaching for her robe when Noah strolled into the bedroom, politely covering a wide yawn with his fist. He was still dressed in his tuxedo trousers and shirt, although he had removed the studs and his shirttail was hanging out. His jacket was slung over his shoulder. He was carrying his shoes.

He said, "Did I hear the telephone ring?"

"Yes."

"Was it Daniel? There's nothing wrong, I hope."

She was greatly relieved to see him, but dumbfounded by his nonchalance. "Noah, where in God's name have you been all night?"

Her tone stopped him in his tracks. He looked at her with puzzlement. "Downstairs on the sofa in the den."

"Why?"

"You were already asleep when I came in. I hated to disturb you."

"What time did you get home?"

He arched an eyebrow in silent disapproval of the third-degree tone of her questions. "About one, I think."

His calm manner only fueled her irritation. "You said—you promised—you'd be half an hour behind me."

"We had two rounds of drinks instead of one. What's the big deal?"

"The big deal is that I was awakened at five-twenty-something in the morning, and I was alone in bed," she exclaimed. "Call me irrational, but unless I know the reason why not, I expect my husband to be sleeping beside me."

"Obviously I wasn't missed until you were awakened."

"And who's fault is that?"

Her voice had gone shrill. It was the voice of a ranting wife. It called to mind the caricature dressed in a shapeless flannel robe and fuzzy scuffs, curlers in her hair, holding a rolling pin above her head as she caught her cheating husband sneaking in the back door.

She took a moment to get her temper under control, although she was still bristling with anger. "If you'll recall, Noah,

I tried to seduce you into coming home with me straight from the office. But you elected for us to go to that interminably long banquet instead. Following that, I tried to talk you into salvaging at least part of the evening just for us, but you chose to have drinks with Vampira and that dopehead."

He dropped his shoes to the floor, removed his shirt, then unzipped his trousers and stepped out of them. "Each book that 'dopehead' writes sells over a half million copies in hardcover. His paperback sales are triple that. But he thinks he can get even higher numbers. He's unhappy with his present publisher and is considering moving to another.

"'Vampira' set up the date for drinks, thinking that it would be a beneficial meeting for both parties. Indeed it was. The author agreed to let us work up a publishing proposal. We'll be hearing from his agent to discuss terms. I had hoped to surprise you and Daniel with this good news tomorrow, but . . ." He shrugged eloquently, then moved to the bed and sat down on the edge of it.

"And just to come completely clean with you," he continued, "I confess that the dopehead got so drunk we couldn't conscientiously put him into a taxi by himself. Nadia and I accompanied him to his apartment and put him to bed. Not a pleasant chore, I assure you. Then she and I shared a taxi back uptown. I dropped her off at Trump Tower, then after arriving home I came upstairs, saw you sleeping soundly, and decided not to disturb you.

"Throughout the evening, I was acting in what I thought was your—our—best interest." He placed his hand over his heart and bowed his head slightly. "Forgive me my thoughtlessness."

Despite his logical explanation, Maris still believed she had a right to be angry. "You could have called, Noah."

"I could have. But knowing how exhausted you were, I didn't want to disturb you."

"I don't like being obligated to Nadia."

"I don't like being obligated to anyone. On the other hand,

it's not very smart to intentionally alienate Nadia. If she likes you, she bestows favors. If she dislikes you, she can inflict serious damage."

"And either way—if you're a man—you get screwed."

That caused him to smile. "Why is it that a woman, and especially you, is never more beautiful than when she's angry?"

"I was."

"I know."

"I *am*."

"Don't be. I'm sorry I worried you. I didn't mean to." He looked at her and smiled gently. "You have no reason to be jealous, you know."

"Oh, really?" she asked, deadpan. "I think I have every right to be paranoid, considering the number of affairs you had before we were married."

"You had affairs, too, Maris."

"Two. You had that many a week, and you had a ten-year head start."

He grinned at her exaggeration. "I'm not even going to honor that with a comment. The point is that I married you."

"Sacrificing all that fun."

Laughing, he patted the spot beside him on the bed. "Why don't you stop this nonsense, retract the talons, and simply forgive me? You know you want to."

Her eyes narrowed with feigned malevolence. "Don't push it."

"Maris?"

Reluctantly she moved toward him. When she was still a distance away, he reached out far enough to take her hand and draw her down beside him on the bed. He tucked a strand of her hair behind her ear and kissed her cheek. She put up token resistance, but not for long.

When their first long kiss ended, she whispered, "I hankered for this all day yesterday."

"All you had to do was ask."

"I did."

"So you did," he said with a regretful sigh. "Let me make it up to you."

"Better late than never."

"Didn't you say something earlier about dispensing with these jammies?"

Moments later they were both down to their skin. Nibbling her neck, he asked, "Who called?"

"Hmm?"

"The telephone call that woke us up. Who was it?"

"That can wait." Seizing the initiative, she guided his hand down her belly to the notch of her thighs. "If you want to talk now, Noah, talk dirty."

Daniel Matherly laid aside the manuscript pages and thought-fully pinched his lower lip between his thumb and fingers.

"What do you think?" Maris asked. "Is it my imagination or is it good?"

Taking advantage of the mild morning, they were having breakfast on the patio of Daniel's Upper East Side town-house. Terra-cotta pots of blooming flowers provided patches of color within the brick enclosure. A sycamore tree shaded the area.

While Daniel was reading the *Envy* prologue, Maris had helped Maxine put together their meal. Maxine, the Math-erlys' housekeeper, had been practically a member of the family a full decade before Maris was born.

This morning she was her cantankerous self, protesting Maris's presence in her kitchen and criticizing the way she squeezed the fresh orange juice. In truth, the woman loved her like a daughter and had acted as a surrogate since the death of Maris's mother when she was still in grade school. Maris took the housekeeper's bossiness for what it was—an expression of her affection.

Maris and Daniel had eaten their egg-white omelets, grilled tomatoes, and whole-wheat toast in silence while he finished reading the prologue. "Thank you, Maxine," he said now when she came out to clear away their dishes and pour refills of coffee. "And yes, dear," he said to Maris, "it's good."

"I'm glad you think so."

She was pleased with his validation of her opinion, but she also valued his. Her father was perhaps the only person in the world who had read and reread more books than she. If they disagreed on a book, allowances were made for their individual tastes, but both could distinguish good writing from bad.

"New writer?"

"I don't know."

He reacted with surprise. "You don't know?"

"This wasn't a typical submission by any stretch." She explained how she had come to read the prologue and what little she had learned about the elusive author. She ended by recounting her predawn telephone conversation with him.

When she finished, she asked crossly, "Who goes strictly by initials? It's juvenile and just plain weird. Like The Artist Formerly Known as Prince."

Daniel chuckled as he stirred cream substitute into his last permitted cup of coffee for the day. "I think it adds a dash of mystery and romance."

She scoffed at that. "He's a pain in the butt."

"No doubt. Contrariness falls under the character description of a good writer. Or a bad one, for that matter."

As he contemplated the enigmatic author, Maris studied her father. *When did he get so old?* she thought with alarm. His hair had been white almost for as long as she could remember, but it had only begun to thin. Her mother, Rosemary, had been the widowed Daniel's second wife and fifteen years his junior. By the time Maris was born, he was well into middle age.

But he'd remained physically active. He watched his diet, grudgingly but conscientiously. He'd quit smoking cigarettes years ago, although he refused to surrender his pipe. Because he had borne the responsibility of rearing her as a single parent, he had wisely slowed down the aging process as much as it was possible to do.

Only recently had the years seemed to catch up with him. To avoid aggravating an arthritic hip, he sometimes used a cane for additional support. He complained that it made him look decrepit. That was too strong a word, but secretly Maris agreed that the cane detracted from the robust bearing always associated with him. The liver spots on his hands had increased in number and grown darker. His reflexes seemed not to be as quick as even a few months ago.

But his eyes were as bright and cogent as ever when he turned to her and asked, "I wonder what all that was about?"

"All what, Dad?"

"Failing to provide a return address or telephone number. Then the telephone call this morning. His claims that the prologue was crap. Et cetera."

She left her chair and moved to a potted geranium to pluck off a dead leaf that Maxine had overlooked. Maris had urged the housekeeper to get eyeglasses, but she claimed that her eyesight was the same now as it had been thirty years ago. To which Maris had said, "Exactly. You've always been as blind as a bat and too vain to do anything about it."

Absently twirling the brown leaf by its stem, she considered her father's question. "He wanted to be sought and found, didn't he?"

She knew she'd given the correct response when Daniel beamed a smile on her. This was the method by which he had helped her with her lessons all through school. He never gave her the answers but guided her to think the question through until she arrived at the correct answer through her own deductive reasoning.

"He didn't have to call," she continued. "If he hadn't wanted to be found, he could have thrown away my telephone numbers. Instead he calls at a time of day when he's practically guaranteed to have the advantage."

"And protests too loudly and too much."

Frowning, she returned to her wrought-iron chair. "I don't know, Dad. He seemed genuinely angry. Especially about the deputy sheriff."

"He probably was, and I can't say that I blame him. But he couldn't resist the temptation to establish contact with you and hear what you had to say about his work."

"Which I think is compelling. That prologue has me wondering about the young man in the boat. Who is he? What's his story? What caused the fight between him and his friend?"

"Envy," Daniel supplied.

"Which is provocative, don't you think? Envy of what? Who envied whom?"

"I can see that the prologue served its purpose. The writer has got you thinking about it and asking questions."

"Yes, he does, damn him."

"So what are you going to do?"

"Try and establish some kind of professional dialogue. If that's possible to do with such a jerk. I don't fool myself into thinking it will be easy to work with this character."

"Do you even know his telephone number?"

"I do now. Thanks to caller ID. I checked it this morning and recognized the area code I called yesterday."

"Ah, the miracles of advanced technology. In my day—"

"In your day?" she repeated with a laugh. "It's still your day."

Reaching for his speckled hand, she patted it fondly. One day he would be gone, and she didn't know how she was going to survive that loss. She'd grown up in this house, and it hadn't been easy to leave it, even when she went away to college. Her bedroom had been on the third floor—still was if she ever wanted to use it. Daniel's bedroom was on the second floor, and he was determined to keep it there despite the pain involved in getting up and down the stairs.

Maris recalled Christmas mornings, waking up before daylight, racing down to his room and begging him to get up and go downstairs with her to see what Santa Claus had left beneath the tree.

She had thousands of happy and vivid recollections of her childhood—the two of them ice-skating in Central Park, strolling through street fairs eating hot dogs or falafel while rummaging in the secondhand book stalls, having high tea at the Plaza following a matinee, reading in front of the fireplace in his study, hosting formal dinner parties in the dining room, and sharing midnight snacks with Maxine in the kitchen. All her memories were good.

Because she had been a late-in-life only child, he had doted on her. Her mother's death could have been a heartache that wedged them apart. Instead, it had forged the bond between father and daughter. His discipline had been firm and consistent, but only rarely necessary. Generally, she had been obedient, never wanting to incur his disfavor.

The most rebellious offense she'd ever committed was to sneak out one night to meet a group of friends at a club that Daniel had placed off-limits. When she returned home in the wee hours she discovered just how vigilant a parent her father was—the kitchen window through which she had sneaked out had been locked behind her.

Forced to ring the front doorbell, she'd had to wait on the stoop for what seemed an excruciating eternity until Daniel came to let her in. He didn't yell at her. He didn't lecture. He simply told her that she must pay the consequences of making a bad choice. She'd been grounded for a month. The worst of the punishment, however, had been his disappointment in her. She never sneaked out again.

She'd been indulged but not spoiled. In exchange for spending money, she was required to do chores. Her grades were closely monitored. She was praised for doing well more frequently than she was punished for mistakes. Mostly she had been loved, and Daniel had made certain every day of her life that she knew it.

"So you think I should pursue *Envy*?" she asked him now.

"Absolutely. The author has challenged you, although he might not have done it intentionally and doesn't even realize that he has. You, Maris Matherly-Reed, can't resist a challenge." He'd practically quoted from an article recently written about her in a trade journal.

"Didn't I read that somewhere?" she teased.

"And you certainly can't resist a good book."

"I think that's why I'm so excited about this, Dad," she said, growing serious. "In my present capacity, most of my duties revolve around publishing. I work on the book once all the writing and editing have been done. And I love doing what I do.

"But I didn't realize until yesterday when I read this prologue how much I'd missed the editing process. These days I read the final, polished version of a manuscript just before I send it to production. I can't dwell on it because there are a million decisions about another dozen books that are demanding my attention. I've missed working one-on-one with an author. Helping with character development. Pointing out weaknesses in the plot. God, I love that."

"It's the reason you chose to enter publishing," Daniel remarked. "You wanted to be an editor. You were good at it. So good that you've worked your way up through the ranks until now your responsibilities have evolved away from that first love. I think it would be stimulating and fun for you to return to it."

"I think so too, but let's not jump the gun," she said wryly. "I don't know if *Envy* is worth my attention or not. The book hasn't even been written yet. My gut instinct—"

"Which I trust implicitly."

"—tells me that it's going to be good. It's got texture, which could be fleshed out even more. It's heavy on the southern overtones, which you know I love."

"Like *The Vanquished*."

Suddenly her balloon of enthusiasm burst. "Yes."

After a beat or two, Daniel asked, "How is Noah?"

As a reader, as well as his wife, she'd been massively disappointed that Noah hadn't followed his first novel with a second. Daniel knew that, so mentioning the title of Noah's single book was a natural segue into an inquiry about him.

"You know how he is, Dad. You talk to him several times a day."

"I was asking as a father-in-law, not as a colleague."

To avoid her father's incisive gaze, her eyes strayed to the building directly behind them. The ivy-covered brick wall enclosing Daniel's patio blocked her view of the neighboring building's ground floor, but she watched a tabby cat in a second-story window stretch and rub himself against the safety bars.

Maxine poked her head outside. "Can I get either of you anything?"

Daniel answered for both of them. "No, thank you. We're fine."

"Let me know."

She disappeared back inside. Maris remained quiet for a time, tracing the pattern of her linen place mat with the pad of her index finger. When she raised her head, her father had assumed the listening posture he always did when he knew there was something on her mind. His chin was cupped in his hand, his index finger lay along his cheek, pointing toward his wiry white eyebrow.

He never pried, never pressured her into talking, but always patiently waited her out. When she was ready to open up, she would, and not a moment before. It was a trait she had inherited from him.

"Noah came home very late last night," she began. Without going into detail, she gave him the gist of their argument. "We ended up lovers and friends, but I'm still upset about it."

Hesitantly Daniel asked, "Did you overreact?"

"Do you think I did?"

"I wasn't there. But it sounds to me as though Noah had a logical explanation."

"I suppose."

He frowned thoughtfully. "Are you thinking that Noah has reverted to the habits he had while living a bachelor's life?"

Knowing the admiration and respect her father had for Noah, she was reluctant to recite a litany of complaints against him, which, when spoken aloud, would probably sound like whining at best and paranoia at worst. She could also appreciate that using her father as a sounding board placed him in an awkward position. He wasn't only Noah's father-in-law, he was his employer.

Daniel had brought Noah into their publishing house three years ago because he had proved himself to be the smartest, shrewdest publisher in New York, save Daniel himself. When Maris and Noah's relationship became more social than professional, Daniel had expressed some reservations and cautioned her against an office romance. But he had given his approval when Noah, after being with Matherly Press for one year, confided in Daniel his plans to marry his daughter. He had even offered to resign in exchange for Maris's hand. Daniel wouldn't hear of it and had embraced Noah as his son-in-law with the same level of enthusiasm as he had hired him as vice president and business manager of his publishing house.

For almost two years, they had successfuly managed to keep their professional and personal roles separate. Airing her wifely grievances could jeopardize the balance. Daniel wouldn't want to say too much or too little, wouldn't want to choose one side over the other or trespass into marital territory where a father-in-law didn't belong.

On the other hand, Maris needed to vent, and her father had always been her most trusted confidant. "In answer to your question, Dad, I'm not thinking anything that specific. I don't believe that Noah's having an affair. Not really."

"Something's bothering you. What?"

"Over the last few months, I don't feel like I've had Noah's full attention. I've had very little of his attention," she corrected with a rueful little laugh.

"The champagne fizz of a honeymoon doesn't last forever, Maris."

"I know that. It's just . . ." She trailed off, then sighed. "Maybe I'm too much a romantic."

"Don't blame yourself for this stall. It doesn't have to be anyone's fault. Marriages go through periods like this. Even good marriages. Dry spells, if you will."

"I know. I just hope he isn't getting tired of me. We're coming up on our two-year anniversary. That's got to be some kind of record for him."

"You knew his record when you married him," he reminded her gently. "He had a solid reputation as a ladies' man."

"Which I accepted because I loved him. Because I had been in love with him since I read *The Vanquished*."

"And out of all those women, Noah returned your love and chose to marry you."

She smiled wistfully, then shook her head with self-deprecation. "You're right, Dad. He did. Chalk this up to hormones. I'm feeling neglected. That's all."

"And I must assume some of the blame for that."

"What are you talking about?"

"I've vested Noah with an enormous amount of responsibility. He's doing not only his job, which, God knows, is demanding enough, but he's begun taking up the slack for me as well. I've slowed down, forcing him to accelerate. I've suggested that he hire someone to shoulder some of his duties."

"He has difficulty delegating."

"Which is why I should have *insisted* that he bring someone else on board. I'll make a point to see that he does. In the meantime, I think it would be a good idea for the two of you to go away together for a few days. Bermuda, perhaps. Get some sun. Drink too many tropical drinks. Spend a lot of time in bed."

She smiled at his candor, but it was a sad smile. He'd said practically those same words last year when he'd packed them off to Aruba for a long weekend. They'd gone in the hope of returning pregnant. Although they'd made every effort to conceive and had enjoyed trying, they hadn't been successful. Maris had been greatly disappointed. Maybe that's when she and Noah had started drifting apart, though the rift had only recently become noticeable.

Daniel sensed that he'd touched on a topic best forgotten, or at least left closed for the present. "Take some time away together, Maris," he urged. "Away from the pressures of the office, the zaniness of the city. Give yourselves a chance to get back on track."

Although she wouldn't say this to Daniel, she didn't share his confidence that spending time in bed would solve their problem and set things right. Their disagreement this morning had ended with sex, but she wouldn't call it intimacy. To her it had felt that they were doing what was most expedient to end the quarrel, that they had taken the easy way out. Their bodies had gone through the familiar motions, but their hearts weren't in it.

Noah had defused her with flattery, which, in hindsight, seemed ingratiating and patronizing. She'd been genuinely angry, which wasn't an ideal time to be told how beautiful she was. Falling into bed together had been a graceful way to end an argument that neither had wanted to have. She hadn't wanted to accuse him further, and he hadn't wanted to address her accusations, so they'd made love instead. The implications of all that were deeply troubling.

For Daniel's benefit, she pretended to think over his suggestion of a tropical vacation, then said, "Actually, Dad, I was thinking of going away by myself for a while."

"Another good option. To the country?"

Frequently, when the city became too claustrophobic, she went to their house in rural western Massachusetts and spent long weekends catching up on paperwork and reading manuscripts. In the Berkshires, without the constant interruptions imposed on her in the office, she could concentrate and accomplish much in a relatively short period of time. It was natural for Daniel to assume that she would choose their country house for her retreat.

But she shook her head. "I think I'll go to Georgia."

Noah took it with equanimity. "I'm all for your getting away for a few days," he told her when she announced her intention to take a trip south. "A change of scenery will do you good. But what in heaven's name is in Georgia? A new spa?"

"An author."

"You'll be working? The whole point of taking a few days off is to relax, isn't it?"

"Remember the prologue I told you about yesterday?"

"The one from the slush pile?"

She ignored the skeptical slant of his grin. "I had difficulty locating the author but finally did."

"Difficulty?"

"Long story, and we've got that meeting in ten minutes. Suffice it to say he's not your routine writer trying to get published."

"In what way is he different?"

"Recalcitrant. Rude. And unenlightened. He doesn't realize how good his writing is. He's going to need some stroking, possibly some coaching, and a great deal of coaxing. I think a face-to-face meeting will yield more than telephone calls and faxes."

Noah was listening with only one ear. He was shuffling through a stack of telephone messages that his assistant had discreetly carried in and laid in front of him before slipping out. Then, checking his wristwatch, he stood up and began gathering materials off his desk for the upcoming meeting. "I'm sorry, darling, but a continuation of this conversation will have to wait. This meeting won't keep. When do you plan to leave?"

"I thought I'd go tomorrow."

"So soon?"

"I need to know if I should get excited about this book or drop it. The only way to find out is to talk to the author."

He rounded his desk and gave her a perfunctory kiss on the cheek. "Then let's go out tonight, just the two of us. I'll have Cindy make reservations. Where would you like to go?"

"My choice?"

"Your choice."

"How about having Thai brought in? We'll eat at home for a change."

"Excellent. I'll pick the wine."

They were almost through his office door when he drew up short. "Damn! I just remembered, I have a meeting tonight."

She groaned. "With whom?"

He named an agent who represented several notable authors. "Join us. He'd be delighted. Then we can go somewhere alone for a nightcap."

"I can't be out all evening, Noah. I have things to do before I can leave town, packing included."

"I've postponed this engagement twice," he said with regret. "If I ask for another rain check, he'll think I'm avoiding him."

"No, you can't do that. How late will you be?"

He winced. "As you know, this guy likes to talk, so it might be late. Certainly later than I'd like." Sensing her disappointment, he stepped closer and lowered his voice. "I'm sorry, Maris. Do you want me to cancel?"

"No. He's an important agent."

"Had I known you planned to go away, I—"

"Excuse me, Mr. Reed," his assistant said from just beyond the doorway. "They're waiting for you and Mrs. Matherly-Reed in the conference room."

"We're coming." Once his assistant had withdrawn, he turned back to Maris. "Duty calls."

"Always."

"Forgive me?"

"Always."

He gave her a hard, quick hug. "You're the most understanding wife in the history of marriage. Is it any wonder I'm crazy about you?" He kissed her briskly, then nudged her toward the door. "After you, darling."

Members of the fraternity thought it brilliant of their chapter founders to have designed and built their residence house to correlate with the diamond shape of the fraternity crest.

But what they attributed to genius had actually come about by happenstance.

When shopping for a lot on which to build their fraternity house, those thrifty young men in the class of 1910 had purchased the least expensive property available, a deep corner lot a few blocks from campus whose owner was eager to sell. Its appeal was not its shape or location but its price. They acquired it cheaply.

So the lot came first, not the architectural renderings. They designed a structure that would fit on their lot; they didn't choose a lot that would accommodate their design. After the fact, some members might have noticed that the house was indeed diamond-shaped like their crest, but the similarity was coincidental.

Then, in 1928, a university planning and expansion committee fortuitously decided that the main avenue bisecting the campus should be converted into a landscaped mall open only to pedestrian traffic. They rerouted motor traffic onto the street that passed in front of the unusually shaped chapter house.

Consequently, through no genius of the founders, this location at a key intersection gave the fraternity a commanding presence on campus that was coveted by every other.

The front of the three-story house faced the corner, with wings extending at forty-five-degree angles from either side of it. Between the wings in the rear of the building were a limited and insufficient number of parking spaces, basketball hoops sans baskets, overflowing trash cans, two rusty charcoal grills, and a chain-link-fence dog run that was occupied by Brew, the fraternity's chocolate Lab mascot.

The building's facade was much more imposing. The stone path leading up to the entry was lined with Bradford pear trees that blossomed snowy white each year, providing natural decoration for the fraternity's annual Spring Swing formal.

Photographs of these trees in full bloom frequently appeared on the covers of university catalogues and brochures. This bred resentment in rival fraternities. Whenever threats of chain saws circulated, pledges were ordered to post twenty-four-hour guard. Not only would the fraternity lose face on campus if their trees were cut down, their residence hall would look naked without them.

In autumn the leaves of the Bradford pears turned the vibrant ruby red they were on this particular Saturday afternoon. The campus was uncharacteristically quiet. The football team was playing an away game. Had the team been at home, the front door of the fraternity house would have been open. Music would have been blaring from it. It would be a raucous gathering place for the members, their dates, their parents, and their alums.

Game-day traffic would be backed up for miles, and because every vehicle had to pass through this crossroads to reach the stadium, the members would enjoy a front-row seat for this bumper-to-bumper parade. They'd jeer at the rival team's fans and flirt with the coeds, who flirted back and sometimes, upon a spontaneous invitation, would leave the vehicles they were in to join the party inside the house. It was documented that several romances, and a few marriages, had originated this way.

On game days, the campus was drenched in crimson. If the school color wasn't worn, it was waved. Brass and drums from the marching band echoed across campus for hours prior to kickoff. The campus was energized, hopping, festive.

But today it was practically deserted. The weather was rainy and dreary, incompatible with any sort of outdoor activity. Students were using the day to catch up on sleep, study, or laundry—things they didn't have time to do during the week.

The halls of the fraternity house, smelling dankly of beer and boys, were dim and hushed. A few members were gathered around the large-screen TV that a prosperous alum had donated to the house the year before. It was tuned to an NCAA football game on which money was riding. Occasionally either a cheer or a groan filtered up the staircases to the resident rooms on the second and third floors, but these sounds did little to compromise the sleepy quiet of the corridors.

A quiet that was punctured by, "Roark! You asshole!" followed immediately by a slamming door.

Roark dodged the wet towel hurled at his head and started laughing. "You found it?"

"Whose is it?" Todd Grayson brandished a Sytrofoam cup that contained his toothbrush. Which wouldn't have been remarkable except that the cup had been used as a spittoon. The bristles of Todd's toothbrush were steeping in the viscous brown fluid in the bottom of the cup.

Roark was reclined on the three-legged sofa beneath their sleeping lofts, which were suspended from the ceiling by short chains. To maximize the small room's floor space, the lofts had been designed and constructed by the two young men in direct violation and defiance of fraternity house rules against any alteration to the structure of the building.

A couple of stacked bricks served as the sofa's fourth leg, but the eyesore was the focal point of their habitat, the "nucleus of our cell," Todd had intoned one night when he was particularly drunk. When furnishing their room, they'd found the atrocity in a junk store and bought it for ten bucks apiece. The upholstery was ripped and ratty and stained by substances that remained unidentified. The sofa had become so integral to the overall ugliness of their room, they had decided to leave it there upon their graduation as a legacy for the room's next occupants.

But Todd, who had once waxed poetic about the sofa, was so angry now that every muscle in his body was quivering. "Tell me. Whose spit cup is this?"

Roark was clutching his middle, laughing. "You don't want to know."

"Brady? If it's Brady's, swear to God I'll kill you." Brady lived down the hall. He was a terrific guy, an ideal fraternity brother, the type who, on a moment's notice and without any complaint, would come out and get you if your car broke down on a snowy night. Brady had a heart of gold. Personal hygiene, however, wasn't one of his strong suits.

"Not Brady."

"Castro? Jesus, please tell me it's not Castro's," Todd groaned. "That fucker's diseased!" The second man under consideration wasn't Cuban. His real name was Ernie Campello. He'd been dubbed Castro because of his talent for growing curly black hair, not only on his head and the lower half of his face, but all over his body. "God only knows what's crawling around in that pelt of his."

Roark laughed at that, then said, "Lisa somebody called."

The casual statement instantly doused Todd's anger. "Lisa Knowles?"

"Sounds right."

"When?"

"Five minutes ago."

"Did she leave a message?"

"Do I look like a secretary?"

"You look like an asshole with teeth. What'd she say?"

"She said you had a pencil-dick. Or did she say needle-dick? Gee, Todd, I can't remember. Sorry. But I did write down her number. It's on your desk."

"I'll call her later."

"Who is she? Is she hot?"

"Yeah, but she's seeing some Delt. She's in my North American history class and she needs notes."

"Too bad."

Todd shot his grinning roommate a dirty look, then tossed the offensive cup into their trash can. He'd been showering in the communal bathroom down the hall when Roark sneaked in and put his toothbrush in tobacco-laced sputum.

"Don't be pissed," Roark said as Todd rummaged in a bureau drawer for a pair of boxers. "It was a damn good joke and worth the expense of a new toothbrush. It was worth twice the expense."

"Are you going to tell me whose it was?"

"Don't know. Found it on a windowsill on the third floor."

"Jesus. It could be anybody's."

"That was the general idea."

"I'll get you back," Todd threatened as he pulled on a T-shirt. "I mean it. You've just screwed yourself but good, buddy."

Roark merely laughed.

"Didn't you have anything better to do? You've been lying on your ass all day."

"Gotta finish this over the weekend." Roark held up a paperback copy of *The Great Gatsby*.

Todd snorted scornfully. "The most pussy-whipped character in the history of American fiction. Want to go get something to eat?"

"Sure." Roark rolled off the sofa and shoved his feet into a pair of sneakers. As they went through the door, he and Todd ritualistically kissed their fingers and slapped them against the Playmate of the Month on their calendar. "Later, sweetheart."

It was their place. They were regulars. The moment they cleared the door of T.R.'s, T.R. himself drew them a pitcher of beer and delivered it to their booth.

"Thanks, T.R."

"Thanks, T.R."

There were no menus, but it wasn't even necessary for them to order. Knowing what they liked, T.R. waddled back behind the counter and started building their pie. It and their beer would go on their joint account, which they would pay when they got around to it. T.R. had been providing his customers with this kind of personalized service for thirty-something years.

The story was that he'd enrolled in the university as a freshman, but ended his first term by skipping finals. He used his second-semester tuition money to make a down payment on this building, which was then on the verge of being condemned. T.R. hadn't bothered to make renovations and it stood today as it had when he assumed occupancy. Engineering and architectural instructors continued to use the building as a case study for load-bearing beams.

The light fixtures were layered with generations of greasy dust. The linoleum floor was slick in some spots, gritty in others. No one dared look beneath the tables for fear of what he would find, and only in emergency situations did beer-bloated bladders seek relief in the restroom.

It wasn't much of a place, but it was an institution. Every guy on campus knew T.R.'s because it provided two basic needs of the male collegiate—cold beer and hot pizza.

By midterm, T.R. could call every customer by name, and even if the name escaped him, he knew how he liked his pizza. Todd's and Roark's never varied—thick crust, pepperoni, extra mozzarella, with a little crushed red pepper sprinkled on top.

Roark ruminatively chewed his first wonderfully cheesy bite. "You really think so?"

"Think what?"

"That Gatsby was a puss."

Todd wiped his mouth with a paper napkin from the table dispenser, took a gulp of beer. "The guy's rich. Lives like a frigging prince or something. He has everything a man could want."

"Except the woman he loves."

"Who's a selfish, self-centered airhead, borderline if not full-fledged neurotic, who continually craps on him."

"But Daisy represents to Gatsby what his money couldn't buy. The unattainable."

"Respectability?" Todd lifted another slice of pizza from the bent metal platter and took a bite. "With his money, why should he give a shit whether or not he's accepted? He paid the ultimate price for an ideal." Shaking his head, he added, "Not worth it."

"Hmm." More or less agreeing, Roark drank from his frosted mug. They discussed the merits of Gatsby, then of Fitzgerald's work in general, which brought them around to their own literary aspirations.

Roark asked, "How're you coming on your manuscript?"

A novel of seventy thousand words, minimum, was their senior project, their capstone prior to receiving a bachelor of arts degree. The one obstacle standing between them and graduation was the scourge of every creative writing student, Professor Hadley.

Todd frowned. "Hadley's up my ass about characterization."

"Specifically?"

"They're cardboard cutouts, he says. No originality, spontaneity, depth, blah, blah, blah."

"He says that about everybody's characters."

"Yours included?"

"I haven't had my critique yet," Roark replied. "Next Tuesday, bright and early, eight o'clock. I'll be lucky to escape with my life."

The two young men had met in a required composition class their first semester as freshmen. The instructor was a grad student, who they later decided didn't know his dick from a dangling participle. The first week of class, he assigned a five-page essay based on John Donne's *Devotions*.

Taking himself far too seriously, the instructor had assumed a professorial stance and tone. "You may not be entirely familiar with the text, but surely you'll recognize the phrase 'for whom the bells toll.'"

"Excuse me, sir." Todd raised his hand and innocently corrected him. "Is that the same as 'for whom the bell tolls'?"

Recognizing a kindred spirit, Roark introduced himself to Todd after class. Their friendship was established that afternoon. A week later, they negotiated a swap with the roommates the university had randomly assigned them. "Suits me," Roark grumbled when they proposed the idea to him. He gave Todd a word of warning. "He pecks on that goddamn typewriter twenty-four hours a day."

They received the two highest grades in the class on that first writing assignment. "The jerk wouldn't dare award an A," Roark sourly observed. Scrawled on the cover of his blue book was a large B+.

"At least you got the plus sign after yours," Todd remarked of his B.

"You would have if you hadn't been a smart-ass that first day. That really pissed him off."

"Fuck him. When I write the Great American Novel, he'll still be grading freshmen writing assignments."

"Ain't gonna happen," Roark deadpanned. Then he flashed a wide white smile. "Because *I'm* going to write the Great American Novel."

Love of books and the desire to write them was the foundation on which their friendship was built. It was a few years before cracks were discovered in that foundation. And by the time those fissures were discovered, massive damage had already been done and it was too late to prevent the structure's total collapse.

They were well-rounded students, maintaining good grades in the required subjects, but excelling in the language arts. Their second semester, they pledged the same fraternity. They were avid sports enthusiasts and good athletes. They played on their fraternity football and basketball teams, sometimes competing with each other as avidly as with rival teams.

They were active and well-known on campus. Todd was elected to the Student Congress. Roark organized a campus-wide food drive to benefit a homeless shelter. Both wrote occasional editorials, articles, and human interest stories for the student newspaper.

After one of his stories was published, Roark was approached by the dean of the journalism school. He was highly complimentary of Roark's work and asked him to consider switching the focus of his endeavors from creative writing to journalism. Roark declined. Fiction was his first love.

Roark never told Todd about that conversation, but he celebrated when Todd won first place in a national collegiate fiction-writing competition. Roark's submission hadn't even earned an honorable mention. He tried to conceal his jealousy.

They caroused and partied with their fraternity brothers. They drank enough beer to float a fleet. Occasionally they shared a joint, but they didn't make a habit of it and never tried hard drugs. They nursed one another's hangovers, loaned each other money during temporary financial crises, and when Roark contracted strep throat and his temperature shot up to one hundred and three, it was Todd who rushed him to the campus infirmary.

When Todd was notified of his father's sudden death, Roark drove him home across two state lines, and then stayed on through the funeral to lend the emotional support his friend needed.

Disagreements arose now and then. Once, when Roark borrowed Todd's car, he backed into a fireplug and dented the rear fender. Todd asked several times when he planned to have it repaired. He asked so frequently that it became a touchy subject.

"Will you get off my goddamn back about that?" Roark snapped.

"Will you fix my goddamn car?"

That heated exchange was the extent of the disagreement. Roark took the car to be repaired the following day, and Todd never mentioned it again.

And then there was the case of the missing Pat Conroy.

Roark drove to a bookstore in Nashville and stood in line for over two hours to meet the author and obtain a signed copy of *The Great Santini.* He admired Conroy more than any other contemporary novelist and nearly embarrassed himself when Conroy wished him good luck with his own writing pursuits. The autographed book was his most prized possession.

Todd asked to borrow it. He claimed that when he finished reading it, he replaced it in Roark's bookshelf. It never turned up, not even when Roark practically tore their room apart searching for it.

What happened to the book remained a mystery. They eventually stopped arguing about it, but Roark never loaned Todd a book again, and Todd never asked to borrow one.

They were good-looking, each in his own way, so there was never a shortage of girls. When they weren't talking about books, chances were very good that the subject was women. If one of them got lucky and a young lady stayed over, the other bunked down in a neighboring room.

One morning after a young lady had taken the "walk of shame" down the hallway of the fraternity house on her way out, Todd looked over at Roark and said morosely, "She wasn't all that hot, was she?"

Roark shook his head. "Last night you were looking at her through beer goggles."

"Yeah," Todd sighed. Then with a sly smile he added, "But it all feels good in the dark, doesn't it?"

They talked about women tirelessly and shamelessly, unabashedly adhering to the double standard. Only Roark came close to having a serious relationship, and only once.

He met her during his food drive. She had volunteered to help. She had a beautiful smile and a slender, athletic body. She was a smart and conscientious student and could converse intelligently on any number of subjects. But she also had a good sense of humor and laughed at his jokes. She was an excellent listener who focused on the topic when it turned to something serious. She taught him how to play "Chopsticks" on the piano, and he persuaded her to read *The Grapes of Wrath*.

She was a passionate kisser, but that's as far as she would go. She clung to a strict moral code, founded on her religion, and she didn't intend to break it. She hadn't in high school with her longtime sweetheart, and she wasn't going to until she knew she was with the man she would marry and grow old with.

Roark admired her for it, but it was damned frustrating.

Then she called him one night and said she had just finished reading the Steinbeck classic, and if he wasn't busy, she would like to see him. He picked her up, they went for a drive, then parked.

She had loved the classic novel and thanked him for sharing it with her. Her kisses that night were more passionate than ever. She raised her sweater and pressed his hand against her bare breast. And if caressing her and feeling her response wasn't the most physically gratifying sexual experience Roark had ever had, it was certainly the most meaningful. She was sacrificing something of herself to him, and he was sensitive enough to realize it.

He wondered if he was falling in love.

A week later, she dumped him. He was tearfully informed that she was resuming the relationship with her high school sweetheart. He was dumbfounded and not a little angry. "Do I at least get to ask why?"

"You're going to be somebody great, Roark. Famous. I know

it. But I'm just a simple girl from small-town Tennessee. I'll teach elementary school for a couple of years, maybe, then become a mother and the president of the PTA."

"There's nothing wrong with that."

"Oh, I'm not apologizing for it. It's the life I choose, the life I want. But it's not the life for you."

"Why do we have to plan the rest of our lives now?" he argued. "Why can't we hold off making major decisions and just continue to spend time together, enjoy each other, wait and see what happens?"

"Because if I continue seeing you, I'll sleep with you."

"Would that be so terrible?"

"Not at all terrible. It would be . . ." She kissed him deeply, her sweet mouth tugging on his with the restrained passion he had come to expect. "I want to," she whispered against his lips. "I want to so bad. But I made a pledge of abstinence. I can't break it. So I can't see you anymore."

To his mind, that was totally irrational, but she would not be dissuaded. He was depressed and testy for weeks. Todd, sensing that the budding romance had suddenly withered and died, walked on eggshells around him.

Finally, however, he'd had all the moodiness he could stand. "Christ, get over it already." He insisted that the only cure for one woman was another woman. He practically dragged Roark from their room. They got drunk and got laid that night.

Roark wasn't "cured," but eventually he came around because he had no choice. And, in retrospect, everything she had said was right. Maybe not the part about his guaranteed greatness. That remained to be seen. But regarding everything else, she had been inordinately insightful.

At the end of the semester, she transferred to a college nearer her hometown, where the boyfriend was attending. Roark wished her well and told her that her sweetheart was the luckiest bastard on the planet. She blushed, thanked him for the compliment, and said she would be watching for his name in print.

"I'll buy a dozen copies of your books and distribute them to

all my friends, and boast that I once dated the great Roark
Slade."

That was as close as either he or Todd came to having a
serious romantic entanglement. But women consumed their
thoughts and fueled their lusts, and on that rainy Saturday
evening, it was a girl that brought to a close their conversation
about Professor Hadley's grueling, demoralizing critiques.

A pair of coeds were actually brave—or brazen—enough to
enter the testosterone-charged sanctum of T.R.'s just as Roark
was advising Todd to deflect Hadley's comments. "After all,
they're just his opinion."

Todd, who was facing the door, changed the subject by saying, "Well, it's my opinion that that is one hot chick."

Roark glanced over his shoulder at the two girls. "Which
one?"

"Blue sweater. Packing Tic Tacs." That was their coded reference to evident nipple projection.

"She's hot, all right," Roark agreed.

Todd grinned at her and she grinned back.

Roark said, "Hey, Christie."

"Oh, Roark, hi." Her drawl stretched the single-syllable
words into roughly three apiece. "How are you?"

"Great. You?"

"Couldn't be better."

When Roark came back around, Todd was swearing into his
beer mug. "You son of a bitch. I might've known."

Roark merely smiled and sipped his beer.

Todd continued to ogle. "She's a fox. I don't remember you
ever going out with her."

"We didn't go out."

"Casual acquaintance?"

"Something like that."

"My ass," Todd scoffed. "You got on her."

"I—"

"Didn't you?"

"Maybe. Once. I think. We might've just mugged during a party."

The girls were now receiving instruction from several other customers on how to line up a pool shot. The lesson required bending over the billiard table, which provided Todd an anatomical perspective of Christie that actually caused him to moan. "Damn."

"Try not to drool, okay?" Roark admonished. "It's embarrassing."

He slid from the booth and approached the laughing group. The other men eyed him resentfully when he took Christie's elbow and steered her toward the booth. "Christie, Todd, my roommate. Todd, this is Christie."

Roark ushered her into his side of the booth, so that they were seated across from Todd. "Hi, Christie."

"Hi."

"Would you like a beer?"

"Love one."

Todd signaled T.R. to bring another pitcher and a third mug. "Pizza?"

"No, thanks."

Roark waited through the pouring of the beer before saying to Christie, "Listen, this is a bitch, but I gotta split. Are you okay with me leaving you in Todd's company? He's fairly harmless."

Her pout could have sold a million tubes of L'Oréal lipstick— to men. "It's Saturday night, Roark," she whined. "Where do you hafta go?"

"I left Gatsby, Daisy, and the gang waiting on me. I need to get back to them." He tilted his head toward Todd. "If he gets out of line, let me know. I'll knock him around for you."

She glanced flirtatiously at Todd. "I can handle him just fine."

"I bet you can," Todd said, bobbing his eyebrows. "Anytime, sweetheart."

Roark left her giggling over the innuendo. It was hours later before he returned to his and Todd's room. After listening at the door for several moments, he knocked tentatively.

"Huh?"

"Okay if I come in?"

"Yeah."

Todd was alone in his loft, lying on his back, one bare leg and foot dangling over the side. He looked completely done-in but managed to mumble, "Thanks for keeping your distance. Where've you been all this time?"

"The library."

"How's Gatsby?"

"No more pussy-whipped than you, ol'boy. When did Christie leave?"

"About ten minutes ago. Your timing was perfect."

"Happy to oblige."

"You know, she actually asked if they were friends of yours."

"Who?"

"That's what I asked. And she said, 'Those people waiting for him.'"

"You're kidding."

"Nope. Never heard of Gatsby. But who the hell cares? She fucks like she invented it."

Roark crossed to the window and opened it. "Smells like sex in here."

"Oh, before I forget, our favorite professor called and left you a message."

"Hadley?"

"Said he has a conflict at eight, so he bumped your appointment up to nine o'clock Tuesday morning."

"Fine by me. I won't have to get up so early."

Todd yawned and turned toward the wall. "Thanks again for Christie. She was something else. G'night."

Following the meeting that she and Noah had been required to attend, Maris went home from the office alone.

There was a moment, while she was getting mail from their box, that she was tempted to ask the night-duty doorman if he had noticed what time Noah had come in that morning, but she couldn't think of a way to ask without embarrassing both of them, especially herself.

She had a Thai dinner delivered. As she ate, she reviewed the revisions an author had made to her manuscript, signed off on them, and marked the manuscript ready to go to a copy editor.

She checked her calendar one final time to make certain that she and her assistant hadn't overlooked an appointment that needed to be rescheduled. She had blocked out the remainder of the week for her trip to Georgia, which might be a tad optimistic considering that the author hadn't been notified of her pending visit.

But in this instance, begging forgiveness was preferable to asking permission. She had to be assertive. With him, her approach must be proactive and aggressive. Timidity wouldn't make a dent. Rearranging her busy schedule and making travel arrangements had cemented her determination to go and see him whether or not he was agreeable.

Having put off for as long as possible the unpleasant chore of alerting him to her arrival, she dialed the number that had appeared on her caller ID machine that morning. The telephone rang four times before it was answered.

"Yeah?"

"This is Maris Matherly-Reed."

"Jesus."

"No, Maris Matherly-Reed."

He said nothing to that, not even a cranky *What do you want?* although his hostile silence spoke volumes.

"I was thinking . . ." She halted. Wrong tack. *Give him no outs, Maris, not even wiggle room.* "I'm coming to St. Anne Island to see you," she declared.

"I beg your pardon?"

"I was speaking English, wasn't I? Which part didn't you understand?"

After a moment, he made a gruff sound that could have passed for a laugh. "That's two. You're on a roll tonight."

"Well, I try."

"So you're coming to St. Anne."

"Yes, I am."

"I gotta warn you, it's different from what you're used to. Folks like you—"

"Folks like me?"

"—usually vacation on the more developed islands. Hilton Head. St. Simons. Amelia."

"This isn't a vacation trip."

"No?"

"I'm coming to talk to you."

"We've talked."

"Not face-to-face."

"What've we got to talk about? The flora and fauna of Georgia's sea islands?"

"Your book."

"I've already told you that my book isn't for sale."

"You also told me that there is no book. Which is it?" She had trapped him. His stony silence indicated that he knew it. "I'll be arriving tomorrow evening."

"It's your money."

"Could you recommend a—" She was talking to a dead line. He'd hung up on her. Stubbornly she dialed him back.

"Yeah?"

"I was asking if you could recommend a hotel in Savannah?"

When he hung up on her again, Maris laughed. As her father had said, he was protesting too loudly and too much. Little did Mr. P.M.E. know that the more he balked, the more determined she became.

She had just slid her suitcase from beneath the bed to begin packing when the telephone rang. She expected it to be the author. He'd probably invented some very good reasons why it was inconvenient or impossible for him to see her when she arrived tomorrow.

Bracing herself for a barrage of excuses, she answered with a cheerful, "Hello." To her surprise, a man with a broad Brooklyn accent asked to speak with Noah. "I'm sorry, he isn't here."

"Well, I gotta know what to do with this key."

"Key?"

"We don't make house calls after hours, ya know. Only, see, Mr. Reed give me twenty extra bucks to get it here tonight. You his ol' lady?"

"Are you sure you have the right Noah Reed?"

"Deals with books or something?"

"Yes, that's my husband."

"Well, he give me this address in Chelsea, said—"

"What address?"

He recited an address on West Twenty-second. "Apartment three B. He axed me to change out the lock yesterday, on account of he'd already moved some stuff in there and didn't want old keys floating 'round, ya know? Only I didn't bring an extra key yesterday, and he said he needed at least one extra. So I tole him he'd have it tonight.

"I'm here with the key, but the super's out for the evening. There's a note on his door, says call, but a call ain't gonna help me, is it? I don't trust leaving a key to Mr. Reed's apartment with the neighbors. You never know about people, am I right?"

"What kind of stuff?"

"Huh?"

"You said some stuff had already been moved into the apartment."

"Stuff. Furniture. You know, the kinda stuff rich folks have in their places. Rugs and pictures and shit. Could I afford nice stuff like that? Forget about it. All I know is, I'm ready to get my butt home and in my lounger on account of the Mets game. Only I don' wanna offend Mr. Reed. He give me twenty extra—"

"Bucks. So you said. I'll give you twenty more if you'll wait for me. I'll be there in fifteen minutes."

Maris left her building and practically ran the two blocks to the subway station at Seventy-second and Broadway. A taxi would take too long to get downtown. She wanted to see sooner rather than later the nice stuff that Noah had moved into an apartment in Chelsea that she knew nothing about. She wanted to learn sooner rather than later why he needed an extra apartment. And she wanted to know for whom he was having an extra key made.

Ivy clung to the old brick, contributing warmth and charm to the building's exterior. Flowers bloomed in window boxes on either side of the narrow stoop, which was separated from street level by eight steps. The block was lined with similar buildings that had been quaintly refurbished by urbanites trying to create a neighborhood feel and recapture the spirit of a kinder, gentler, bygone New York.

The leaded glass entrance door was unlocked. The locksmith was waiting for Maris in the foyer. Somehow he had managed to zip a khaki jumpsuit over a belly that extended a good two feet beyond his chest. "Who buzzed you in?" she asked him after introducing herself.

"I ain't a locksmith for nothin'," he said with a snort. "Only, truth be told, it wasn't locked. Too hot to wait outside. I was sweating like a pig."

The air-conditioning was cooling her own damp skin, a dampness she attributed to being in close confines with other sticky passengers on the subway train. The stations were notorious for being drafty and frigid in the winter and completely airless in the summer. But she was also sweating anxiously over what she would find on the third floor in Apartment B.

"You wanna settle up with me?"

She looked at him quizzically, then remembered the promised twenty dollars. After paying him, she asked for the key.

"I gotta check it out first," he told her. "It ain't as easy as people think, making keys. I never leave one with a customer before seeing if it works okay."

"All right."

"There ain't no elevator. We gotta climb."

She nodded for him to precede her up the staircase. "Why didn't you just go up, test the key, and then leave it in the apartment? Wouldn't the door have locked behind you when you left?"

"Not the deadbolt. Besides, that's all I need," he said, speaking to her over his shoulder as they rounded the second-floor landing. "Something turns up missing, I'm the first one accused of stealing."

"I doubt that."

"I ain't taking no chances goin' into a man's apartment when he ain't there. Forget about it."

He was huffing and puffing by the time they reached the

third level. As he approached the door, he withdrew the spare key from the pocket of his jumpsuit and slipped it into the lock. "Pouyfect," he said as he swung open the door. Then he stood aside and motioned for Maris to go in. "The light switch is there on your right."

She felt for the switch and flipped it on.

"*Surprise!*"

The shout went up from fifty or so people, all of whom she recognized. Her mouth dropped open like a trapdoor. She pressed a hand to her lurching heart. Everyone was laughing over her dumbfounded expression.

Noah separated himself from the others and came toward her, grinning from ear to ear. He embraced her tightly, then soundly kissed her mouth. "Happy anniversary, darling."

"B-but our anniversary isn't until—"

"I know when it is. But you always catch on to my attempted surprises. This year I thought I'd get the jump on you. Judging by your reaction, I'd say I was successful." He looked beyond her shoulder and addressed the locksmith. "You were terrific."

As it turned out, he was an actor hired to play the role. "You had me convinced that I was about to catch my cheating husband," Maris told him.

"Happy anniversary, Mrs. Reed," he said in a voice that resonated with the Queen's English. It was explained to her later that his most notable role was Falstaff. Now he reached for her hand and kissed the back of it. "Enjoy your special evening."

"Don't go. Stay and enjoy the party." She prevailed upon him, and he accepted her invitation.

"It's okay, isn't it?" she asked Noah when the actor joined the other guests in line at the buffet.

"Whatever makes you happy, darling."

"Whose apartment is this?"

"That part of his dialogue was true. It's mine."

"It really is?"

"Whose did you think it was?"

"I—"

"You need some champagne."

"But Noah—"

"You'll get a full explanation later. I promise."

After seeing to it that she had a brimming flute of bubbly, he maneuvered her through the crowd to greet their guests, which included most of the editorial staff of Matherly Press. Many remarked on how difficult it had been to keep the secret. One confessed to almost asking her what she was going to wear. "Noah would have killed me if I'd spoiled the surprise."

"And look what I turned out in," Maris groaned. "A wrinkled business suit and a shiny face. I didn't know I was coming to a party."

"I would kill to look like you on your worst day," the woman said.

Among the guests were also a handful of local authors with whom Maris worked, and friends whose careers were in other areas entirely, including an anesthesiologist and her husband who taught chemistry at NYU, a stockbroker, and a movie producer who had turned one of the books Maris had edited into a gripping feature film.

Then the crowd parted to reveal Daniel. He was seated with one hand resting on the engraved silver head of his cane while the other was saluting her with a glass of champagne.

"Dad!"

"Anniversary wishes a few weeks early, sweetheart."

"I can't believe you were in on this!" She bent down to kiss his cheek, which glowed with a champagne flush. "You gave nothing away this morning."

"Which was hard, considering the topic of our conversation." His meaningful look reminded her of the marital concerns she had shared with him.

Feeling her own cheeks grow warm with embarrassment, she said softly, "This explains why Noah has been distracted lately.

I feel like a fool now."

"Don't," Daniel ordered, his brows lowering sternly. "A fool is someone who ignores warning signs."

She kissed him again quickly before being pulled away to mingle. Noah had done an outstanding job, not only of putting over the surprise, but of planning a wonderful party. The chef of her favorite restaurant had prepared the food and was on hand to see that it was properly served. Champagne was poured liberally. The music got louder as the evening progressed, and, although it was a weeknight, guests stayed late. Eventually, however, they said their good nights.

Daniel was the last to leave. "Age has its benefits," he told Maris and Noah at the door. "Not many, mind you, but a few. One is that you can get tipsy on a weeknight and sleep late in the morning because there's nowhere you absolutely must be."

Maris hugged him exuberantly. "I love you, Dad. And I learn something new about you every day."

"For instance?"

"That you're damn good at keeping secrets."

"Watch your language, young lady, or I'll have Maxine wash your mouth out with soap."

"It wouldn't be for the first time," she said with a laugh. After another hug, she asked Daniel if he could manage the stairs all right.

"I got up here, didn't I?" he growled querulously.

"Sorry I asked." Even so, she motioned for Noah to accompany Daniel down. "Is a car waiting to take him home?"

"It's at the curb," Noah assured her. "I've already checked."

"Good. Dad, remember I'll have my cell phone with me in Georgia. I told Maxine to call—"

"And she will, the old busybody. Get me out of here, Noah. Please. Before Maris decides I'm ready for adult diapers."

Noah guided him down the hallway toward the staircase. "I'll be right back, darling," he called to Maris. "I haven't given you your present yet."

"There's more?"

"Just wait. And no snooping!"

Now that the apartment was empty of guests, she could see it well for the first time. Tall windows on the far wall of the living room overlooked the rooftop garden on the next building. The "stuff" was nice, but not as pricy as the "locksmith" had implied. There were pictures on the walls, and an area rug beneath the seating arrangement of chairs and sofas, but the emphasis was on fuctionality and comfort.

The galley kitchen was narrow, even by New York standards. Off the living room, a closed door led to what she assumed was a bedroom. She was making her way toward that door when hands seized her around the waist.

"I thought I told you not to snoop," Noah said, nuzzling her ear.

"I didn't know that I was. When are you going to tell me why you leased this apartment?"

"In good time. Be patient."

"Is my present behind door number one?"

"Let's take a look." He walked her toward the door. "You may open it now."

The room was a small cubicle, but a generous window made it appear larger. It was furnished with a desk, a leather swivel chair, and shelves only partially filled with books. It was further equipped with a telephone, a computer and printer, and a fax machine. A yellow legal tablet lay on the desk beside a metal pencil holder filled with sharpened pencils.

Maris took in every detail, then turned and looked at Noah.

He laid his hands on her shoulders and massaged them gently. "I know you've wondered about the late hours I've been keeping, as well as the unaccounted-for time I've spent away from home and office."

"I confess."

"I apologize for causing you to worry. I wanted this place to be completely set up before you saw it. It's taken me weeks to get it ready. Months, if you factor in the time I spent searching for a suitable space."

"A suitable space for what?"

"Well, not for conducting the illicit affair you thought I was having."

She lowered her eyes. "Again, I confess."

"With Nadia?"

"She topped the list of suspects."

"Maris," he said reproachfully.

She tossed her head back and shook out her hair, as though freeing herself of a burden. "God, I'm glad it's not that."

"Feel better?"

"Immeasurably. But, if this apartment wasn't designated as a love nest, what did you lease it for?"

He ducked his head in what could only be described as shyness. "Writing."

"Writing?" she repeated on a thin breath.

"That's your anniversary present. I've begun writing again."

For several moments she was too stunned to speak, then she threw herself against him. "Noah! That's wonderful. When? What made you . . . You always get so defensive whenever I mention it. Oh, I'm thrilled. Thrilled!"

She rained kisses over his face. He laughed and indulged her enthusiasm. Finally he set her away, keeping her at arm's length. "Don't get carried away. I'll probably fail miserably."

"You won't," she said adamantly. "I don't believe for a moment that you're the one-book wonder you fear you are. The author of *The Vanquished*—"

"Which I wrote years ago, Maris, when I was full of passion, a young man with stars in his eyes."

"And *talent*," she stressed. "Talent like yours isn't depleted by one book, Noah. It doesn't simply disappear. On the contrary, I think it ripens with age and experience."

"We'll see." He glanced at the computer dubiously. "In any case, I'm willing to test your theory. I'm going to give it a shot."

"You're not just doing it for me, are you?"

"I couldn't do it just for you. Writing is damn hard work. It's borderline masochistic. If your heart's not in it, you're doomed before you start." He rubbed his knuckles against her jaw. "This is something I want to do. Very much. And if it pleases you, that's a bonus."

"It pleases me very much. I couldn't be more pleased." She hugged him tightly, then kissed him with more heat than she could remember feeling for a long time.

As their lips clung, Noah slipped off his jacket. Her heart quickened. The surroundings were unfamiliar and untried. It would feel a shade illicit if they made love in this new apartment, on the sofa, on the rug. Hell, on the desk. Why not? They were grown-ups.

She slid her hands up his chest and began working on the knot of his necktie. But he moved her aside, sat down at the keyboard, and booted up the computer.

"I'm so anxious to get started."

"Now?"

He swiveled his chair around and looked up at her, grinning sheepishly. "Do you mind? It's taken me weeks to set up my new playground, but I haven't had time to play in it. I barely got the finishing touches put on this afternoon before the chef and waiters arrived. I'd like to install my software and maybe jot down a few notes. I've been toying with an idea. I'm afraid if I don't commit it to paper, it'll vanish. Do you mind if I work awhile?"

She forced herself to smile. "No. Of course not. Not at all."

There wasn't to be a romantic conclusion to the evening, and that was disappointing. But, fairly, she couldn't complain. This was what she had wanted. This was what she had been encouraging him to do for years.

"I'll say good-bye and leave you to your work."

"You don't have to go, Maris. You can hang around if you like."

She shook her head. "I don't want to be a distraction. Besides, I need to go home and pack for my trip."

He took her hand and kissed the palm. "Will you be all right hailing a cab?"

"Don't be silly. Of course." She leaned on the arms of his desk chair, bringing her face down to the level of his. "It was a lovely surprise party, Noah. Thank you for everything, but especially for this. I can't wait to read your next novel. Look what happened after I read the first one."

As they kissed, his hand followed the curve of her hip down to the back of her thigh. When she withdrew, he continued to stroke her leg. "On second thought, maybe I'll postpone starting until tomorrow."

She aimed her finger at the computer keyboard. "Plot!"

Fifteen minutes later, Noah let himself into another apartment. It was half a block away—seventy-seven steps, to be exact— from the one where he had set up an office he planned never to use. He dropped his key onto the console table in the short entry hall and moved into the living area, where he drew up short.

"I started without you," Nadia said.

"So I see."

She was lying on the sofa, one foot on the floor, naked except for a royal blue silk robe that lay open. Her eyes were half closed. Her hand was rhythmically moving between her thighs. "I'm close. You'd better hurry if you want to get in on this one."

He sauntered over to the sofa, reached down, and fingered her stiff nipple. It was enough to make her come. Smiling as he watched, Noah continued tweaking her until her arching body had squeezed every bit of pleasure it could from the orgasm, then relaxed and resettled into the sofa cushions.

"You're shameless, Nadia."

"I know." She raised her arms above her head and stretched. "Isn't it delicious?"

He began undressing. "The surprise party was a stroke of genius. Maris is now completely defused."

"Ooh, tell me."

"She admitted to harboring a suspicion that I was having an

extramarital affair."

"And who, pray tell, was the suspected correspondent?"

He gave her a look that caused her to purr with wicked satisfaction.

Continuing his account, he said, "Now that my wife has seen my writer's retreat, which made her positively misty, I can use it as an excuse to get away at any time of day or night."

"For this."

"Definitely for this. Along with the other business in which we're involved."

"Maris is only half the problem, though. What about Daniel?"

"He's an old man, Nadia. In his dotage."

"He'll never sell Matherly Press. He's gone on record a thousand times."

Nonchalantly Noah pulled his belt through the loops of his trousers and lightly spanked her thigh with it. "Not to worry, my dear. I'll have Matherly Press sold before either of them knows what's what. Maris is hot for a new author she's discovered in her slush pile. That'll keep her distracted. Daniel has virtually retired, entrusting the company's business dealings almost entirely to me. The first they hear of the pending sale will probably be when they read about it in *Publishers Weekly*, and then it'll be too late to stop it. I'll have Daniel's position and all the benefits that go with it, along with ten thousand shares of WorldView stock in my portfolio, and a cool ten million in my bank account."

"And the Matherlys will be left with only each other."

"I suppose. I really couldn't care less."

He stepped out of his trousers and underwear. Nadia's eyes widened with appreciation for his jutting penis. "Is Maris responsible for that? Remind me to thank her."

"Nothing to thank her for."

"You didn't get any tonight?"

"This morning."

"I thought tonight's party was an anniversary celebration."

"Maris has her way of celebrating, and I have mine."

Laughing, she encircled his penis with her hand and stroked it. "Sometime you must tell me all about it."

"Nothing much to tell."

She rolled her thumb over the smooth bulb. "Miss Maris doesn't fuck dirty?"

"Miss Maris doesn't fuck." He knelt between Nadia's thighs and pushed them wider apart. "She makes love."

"How sweet."

"That's what I like about you, Nadia."

"There's a lot you like about me. You'll have to be more specific."

He jammed himself inside her. "You're never sweet."

CHAPTER 6

The roads on St. Anne Island were banked on either side by woods that were deeper and darker than any Maris had seen in the Berkshires near their country house, deeper and darker than any she had seen anywhere. They were as deep and dark as the menacing forests described in a story written by the Brothers Grimm.

The undergrowth was dense and the trees were towering, making the shadows beneath them impenetrable. Occasionally the rustling of leaves in the thick brush alerted her to the presence of animals, the species and level of danger to human beings unknown. Afraid of what she might see if she looked too closely, she felt safer keeping her eyes fixed on the road.

She had arrived later than anticipated. Stormy weather in Atlanta had delayed her connecting flight to Savannah for three hours. By the time she checked into a hotel and made arrangements for transportation to the island, the sun was setting. The sea island would have been alien territory to her in broad daylight, but the gloaming exaggerated its strangeness and lent it a sinister quality that filled her with misgivings.

As she chugged along in her rented golf cart, she felt extremely vulnerable. The menacing woods intimidated her. They were as unfriendly as the man at the landing from whom she had rented the golf cart.

When she asked him for directions to the home of the local writer, he had responded with a question of his own. "Whada ya want with 'im?"

"Do you know him?"

"Yeah."

"Do you know where he lives?"

"Sure do."

"Can you give me directions, please? He's expecting me."

He looked her up and down. "Is that right?"

She'd unfolded the crude map of the island, given to her by the pilot of the small boat she had hired to bring her over from the mainland. "I'm here, right?" She indicated on the map the landing where the boatman had docked only long enough for her to disembark. "Which way do I go from here?"

"Well, there's only one road leading outta here, ain't there?"

"I can see that," she said with strained patience. "But according to the map the main road branches off in three directions. Here." She pointed out the marking to him.

"You ain't from around here, are you? You from up north someplace?"

"What difference does it make?"

He had snorted a derisive sound and spat tobacco juice into the dirt, then a stained, chipped fingernail traced the fork she should take. "You go along, hmm, 'bout three-quarters of a mile beyond the split. A turnoff to the left takes you straight to the house. If you wind up in the 'lantic, you've done went too far." His grin revealed large gaps where teeth should have been.

She had thanked him curtly and set out on the final leg of her trip. The landing's "commercial district" was limited to two places of business—the cart rental, and Terry's Bar and Grill. So read a hand-painted sign nailed above a screened door.

Terry's was a circular structure with a corrugated tin roof.

The top two-thirds of the exterior walls were screened, but the interior lighting was so dim that all Maris could see was the glow of neon beer signs on the far wall and light fixtures hanging from the ceiling, the kind usually suspended above pool tables. Several vehicles, mostly pickup trucks, were parked at one side of the building. Recorded music emanated through the screened walls.

Out front, a man, presumably Terry, was cooking meat on a large grill while sipping from his longneck bottle of beer. Even after she drove past, she could feel his eyes boring holes in her back until she rounded a bend in the road and was no longer in sight.

She had the road all to herself. No cars or trucks had passed. It seemed the dock was the last outpost of civilization. Having endured this harrowing—and she felt that was a fair adjective—journey, she wished she could look forward to being graciously received when she arrived at the author's home. Unfortunately, her expectations of how she would be greeted were very low.

Eventually she detected salt air over the dominant scent of evergreens. Realizing that the beach couldn't be much farther, she began looking for the turnoff, but when she reached it, she overshot it. There was no sign to mark it. It was so narrow and so well camouflaged by foliage that had she not been specifically looking for it, she would have missed it altogether.

Executing a tight U-turn, she steered the cart into the lane. The roadbed was rougher than the main road. The cart jounced over potholes. Tree branches formed an opaque canopy overhead. The forest here was even thicker, more silent, more foreboding.

She was beginning to think that this venture was foolhardy, that she should be sensible and retreat to the safety of her hotel room in gracious and hospitable Savannah. She could have a room-service meal, a bubble bath, a glass of wine from the mini bar. Thus restored, she could call and try to persuade the author to meet her on neutral turf.

But then she caught her first glimpse of the house and was instantly enchanted.

It was beautiful. Poignantly so. Beautiful in the way that evokes sadness. An aging film star whose once-gorgeous face now evinced the passage of decades. An antique wedding dress, its lace now yellowed and tattered. A gardenia whose creamy petals had turned brown. The house showed visible signs of former grandeur now lost.

But with its obvious flaws softened by the waning light, it was as lovely as a watercolor painted from a faded but fond memory.

Maris stepped out of the cart and followed a pathway marked by twin rows of spectacular, moss-shrouded live oaks. She climbed the steps as soundlessly as possible. When she reached the veranda, she had a silly urge to tiptoe across it as Jem Finch had done in *To Kill a Mockingbird,* so as not to alert the spooky Boo Radley to his presence in a place where he was a trespasser, where he didn't belong, and where he wasn't welcome.

Instead she bolstered herself with a deep breath and walked boldly to the front door and reached for the brass knocker.

"Maris Matherly-Reed?"

Startled, she jumped. The knocker dropped against the metal plate on the door with a loud clatter. Following the direction from which the unexpected voice had come, she stepped back and looked down the long veranda. A face was peering at her through one of the tall front windows.

"So," he said, "you really came."

"Hello."

He continued to stare at her through the screen, putting her at a distinct disadvantage. She was aware that he could see her much more clearly than she could see him, but she stood her ground. She had come this far.

Finally he said, "Come on in."

She pushed open the glossy black front door and stepped into a wide foyer. He emerged from one of the rooms opening off it, wiping his hands on a stained rag. He was dressed in khaki shorts and an ordinary chambray work shirt, the sleeves rolled up to his elbows. Both articles of clothing were rather baggy and as stained as the rag. On his feet he wore a pair of sneakers that had seen better days.

He glanced beyond her. "You came alone?"

"Yes."

"Mosquitoes are getting in."

"Oh. Sorry." She turned and closed the front door.

"No deputy sheriff along for the ride?"

His voice contained a trace of admonishment. She felt an explanation was called for. "I resorted to calling the sheriff's office out of desperation. I asked Deputy Harris if he knew anyone living in his county who went by the initials P.M.E. I had no idea he would conduct a search, and I apologize for any embarrassment that caused."

He harrumphed, but whether to accept her apology or dismiss it, she couldn't tell. She was just relieved that he hadn't cursed her and ordered her out. He wasn't as intimidating as she had anticipated. He was older and less physically imposing than his telephone voice had suggested. The drawl was there, but not the brusqueness.

However, he wasn't being overly friendly. His blue eyes were regarding her warily.

"I wasn't sure what to expect when I arrived," she said, hoping to disarm him with her honesty. "I was afraid I wouldn't even be invited inside."

He gave her a once-over that made her rethink her decision not to take the time to freshen up in Savannah. Now she wished she had at least changed clothes. Her traveling suit had been seasonally lightweight for New York, but was too heavy for this climate. It looked citified and grossly out of place. It was also wrinkled from rides in taxis, planes, and a boat.

"You're a long way from Manhattan, Mrs. Matherly-Reed."

His remark more or less summed up everything she'd been

thinking. "More than just geographically. Except for the golf carts, St. Anne could be in another century."

"The island is primitive in many ways. The people who live here want to keep it that way."

From that she inferred that she was an outsider whom they would have rather remained outside. Feeling self-conscious and wanting to divert attention away from herself, she took a quick look around.

A commanding, unsupported staircase swept upward from the floor of the foyer, but the second story was dark. A dozen questions about the history of the house sprang to mind, but, not wanting to press her luck at having gotten this far, she merely said, "The house is extraordinary. How long have you lived here?"

"A little over a year. It was in total disrepair."

"Then you've already done a lot to it."

"There's still a lot to be done. In fact, I've been working on a project in the dining room. Would you like to see it?"

"Very much."

He smiled at her, and she smiled back, then he turned and made his way back into the room from which he'd come. The crystal chandelier in the center of the ceiling was swinging slightly. He caught her looking at it.

"One of the first renovations was to install central air-conditioning. The vent blows directly on the chandelier and causes it to sway. At least that's what I choose to believe." He gave an enigmatic laugh, then motioned toward the fireplace.

The ornately carved mantel had been stripped down to the naked wood and was being prepared for refinishing. "It's become more of a project than I had counted on," he admitted. "Had I known how many layers of varnish and paint former owners had applied, how painstaking and time-consuming it was going to be to strip it all off, I would have hired a professional to do it."

She moved to the mantel and reached out to touch it, then

hesitated and looked back at him. "May I?" He motioned for her to go ahead, and she ran her fingertips over the intricate carving of a flowering vine.

"The owner who built the house kept a detailed diary of its construction," he explained. "A slave carved that mantelpiece as well as the balustrade of the staircase. His name was Phineas."

"It's lovely. I'm sure it will be even lovelier when you're finished."

"Parker's expecting it to be. He's a perfectionist."

"Parker?"

"The owner."

She dropped her hand and turned back to him. "Oh. I assumed you owned the house."

He shook his head in amusement. "I only work here."

"That's awfully generous of him."

"Generous of who?"

"Of Mr. Parker. That he opens his home to you and lets you write here."

He stared at her with perplexity for a moment, then began to laugh. "Mrs. Matherly-Reed, I'm afraid that you're operating under a misconception here, and it's entirely my fault. Obviously you've mistaken me for Parker, the man you've come to see. Parker Evans."

It took a second for her to process, then she smiled with chagrin. "Parker Evans. Middle initial *M*."

"You didn't know his name?"

"He didn't tell me."

"You've never heard his name before?"

"Not that I recall. Should I have?"

He studied her for a long moment, then smiled and extended his hand. "I'm Mike Strother. Forgive me for not making that clear to you when you arrived. I thought you would know immediately that I wasn't Parker."

"I'm pleased to meet you, Mr. Strother."

"Mike."

She smiled at him, liking the older gentleman and wondering how she could have mistaken him for the abrasive individual she had spoken to on the telephone. His eyes were kind, although she sensed that he was still taking her measure, sizing her up, appraising her. His wariness of her had diminished somewhat, but it was still there. Of course, there was no telling what his boss had said about her. It couldn't have been flattering.

"Are you the contractor in charge of the house's restoration?"

"Lord, no. I'm just trying my hand at this refinishing. I've worked for Parker since long before he bought this place."

"In what capacity?"

"I do a little bit of everything," he explained. "I'm the chief cook and bottle washer, housekeeper, gardener, valet."

"Is he a demanding taskmaster?"

He chuckled. "You have no idea."

Apparently she didn't. Her preconceptions of Parker M. Evans were being dispelled one by one. He certainly hadn't sounded like a man who would have a manservant at his beck and call. "I'm looking very forward to meeting him."

Mike's eyes shifted away to avoid looking directly at her. "He's not here."

Although she had already gathered that, having it confirmed was not only a crushing disappointment, it was perturbing. "He knew I was coming."

"Oh, he knew, he knew," Mike said, nodding. "He said you sounded just stubborn enough to travel all this way even after he'd told you it would be a waste of your time. But nobody on earth can outstubborn Parker. He didn't want to be sitting around here when you arrived as though he were waiting on you. So he went out."

"Out? Where?"

*　*　*

Maris angrily marched up to the man who'd rented her the golf cart. "Why did you send me all the way out to Mr. Evans's house?"

He smirked. "Knew you's lying 'bout him expecting you."

"Why didn't you tell me he was here?"

"Don't recollect you askin'."

She was seething, but he was too coarse and stupid to waste her anger on. She would save it for Mr. Parker Evans. She had a lot to say to him. He had probably known about the wild goose chase she'd been sent on. Terry, the cook, surely had. His charcoal grill had gone cold, but he was tending bar when she pulled open the squeaky screen door to his establishment and went inside.

She crossed a bare concrete floor, splashed through a puddle of what she hoped was beer, and strode past the pool tables straight to the bar at the back of the room. The man who had rented her the cart followed her inside.

Billiard balls stopped clacking. Conversations died. Someone turned off the boom box. The floor show was about to begin, and the angry New Yorker was the featured act.

Terry was grinning at her sardonically.

"Give me a beer."

His grin slipped a notch. He hadn't expected that. But he reached into an ice chest and pulled out a longneck bottle of beer. He uncapped it and passed it to her. Foam oozed from the neck. Maris shook it off her hand, took a long drink, then set the bottle on the bar with a hard thump.

"I'm here to see Parker Evans," she announced.

Terry planted his hairy forearms on the bar and leaned across it toward her. "Who should I say is calling?"

His customers guffawed. Terry basked in the success of his clever comeback. He laughed louder than anyone. Maris spun around and confronted the room at large. The interior was thick with tobacco smoke despite the screened walls and the overhead fans. Their desultory rotations didn't eliminate the smog but only stirred it into the warm, humid air.

A dozen pairs of eyes were focused on her. There was only one other woman in the place. She was wearing crotch-hugging shorts and a clinging tank top that barely contained her pendulous breasts and the tattooed cobra whose flared head and wicked tongue rose out of her cleavage. One hand was insolently propped on her hip, the other held a smoldering black cigarette.

The tavern smelled of beer and grilled meat, tobacco smoke and male sweat. Maris drew a deep breath and tasted those essences in the back of her throat.

"Isn't this rather juvenile, Mr. Evans?"

No one said a word. There was little movement beyond one man glancing at another, jabbing him in the ribs and winking. Another gave her a mocking salute with his beer bottle. One sitting near a pool table idly chalked the tip of his cue.

"To say nothing of rude," she continued.

Forcing herself to move away from the false security of the bar, she approached a group of three men sitting around a table. She looked at each of them carefully. Judging from their moronic leers, she doubted any of them could read without moving his lips, much less write fiction.

"I've come an awfully long way to see you."

"You can go back the same way." The voice issued from a shadowed corner and elicited more chuckles.

She gazed into the face of a man sitting alone. He was about Mike Strother's age, with a neglected white beard and the weather-beaten face of a seaman. He seemed not to be aware of her or anyone else. His rheumy eyes were fixed on the glass of dark liquor cradled between his callused hands.

"Mr. Evans, the least you could do is give me ten minutes of your time."

"Come on over here and bend over, honey," a nasally voice invited. "I'll give you the best ten minutes you've ever had."

"In your dreams, Dwayne," the tattooed woman drawled. "You can't keep it up more'n two."

Laughter erupted, louder than before. The woman was high-fived by the man standing nearest her, but he said, "Ol' Dwayne's got the right idea, though."

"Yeah, Yankee lady. You don't know what you're missin' till you've been rid hard by a horny southern boy."

Maris had experienced catcalls from construction workers made anonymous by distance and hard hats. She had received obscene propositions by crank callers and men lurking in recessed doorways on the sidewalks of the city. When she was seventeen, she had been groped in the subway, and to this day the memory of it made her skin crawl.

But having been the victim of crude behavior hadn't made her immune to it. Their vulgarity got to her, but not in the way they expected. It didn't frighten her; it made her angry. In fact, it made her mad as hell.

Not even attempting to disguise her contempt, she said, "Whoever you are, Mr. Evans, you're a damn coward."

The snickering ceased abruptly. Silence fell like a lead curtain. Any other insult was pardonable, but apparently cowardice wasn't. Name-calling couldn't get more serious than that.

Using it as her exit line, she made a beeline for the door. As she passed a billiards table, a pool cue arced down in front of her like the arm of a toll gate. She ran into it, connecting with her pelvic bones hard enough to make a smacking sound.

She pitched forward, but broke her fall against the stick. She took hold of it in a tight grip and tried to shove it out of her way, but it was unyielding. Turning her head toward the man holding it, she realized he was the one she'd noticed earlier chalking the pool cue.

"I'm Parker Evans."

Maris was astonished. Not by his audacity or the hostile eyes that reflected the red glow of a neon sign as they glared up at her.

What astonished her was the wheelchair in which he sat.

The contraption was green, a cross between a golf cart and a pickup truck. Maris learned later that it was called a Gator, but she had never seen one before Parker Evans nodded her toward the one parked outside Terry's Bar and Grill. He invited her to get in.

Still reeling from the shock of finding him in a wheelchair, she did as he requested and climbed into the passenger seat. She kept her head averted as he used his arms to lift himself onto the driver's seat. Then he leaned down, folded his chair, and swung it up into the shallow trailer.

The Gator had been reconfigured for him. The brake and accelerator were hand-controlled. He handled the vehicle with an ease that comes from practice as he steered it away from Terry's and headed it toward the dock.

"I can take you only as far as the ramp," he said. "It's too steep for my chair. I'd make it down okay, but I might have trouble stopping and would wind up in the drink. Which you probably think I deserve."

She said nothing.

"But even if I didn't go hurtling into the sound, I couldn't get back up the ramp on my own."

Maris was at a complete loss. "Ramp?"

"Down to the dock. Where you left your boat."

"I don't have a boat. I paid someone to bring me over."

"He didn't wait to ferry you back?"

"I didn't know how long I'd be here. I told him I'd call."

He brought the Gator to a stop, looking displeased that he wasn't going to shake her as soon as he thought. His shirt was chambray like Mike's, except that the sleeves had been cut out of Parker Evans's, revealing muscled arms that compensated for the limitations his legs imposed. Those muscles went to work as he pulled the steering wheel into a sharp turn.

"Shouldn't take a boat long to get over here. Terry will call for one. You got the number?"

"Couldn't we talk for a while, Mr. Evans?"

He braked the Gator again. "About what?"

"Look, be obtuse on somebody else's time. I've come a very long way—"

"Without an invitation."

"You invited me when you sent me that prologue."

He registered mild surprise over her snappishness and raised his hands in mock surrender.

She took a moment to collect herself, then continued in a more conciliatory tone. "It's been a very long day for me. I'm tired. A hot bath and cool sheets sound wonderful. But I'm here, so I'd like to make this trip worth my time, trouble, and expense by having a civil conversation with you before I leave."

He folded his arms across his chest in what she supposed could be viewed as a civil gesture. But it also looked smart-alecky, and that, she thought, was probably closer to his intention.

Doggedly she continued. "You sent me your work. You meant for me to read it or you wouldn't have sent it. Despite your claims to the contrary, you want this book to be published. I publish books. We could work together. You don't even have to meet me halfway. I'll go three-quarters of the way. In fact, I believe I already have by coming here. So could we please have that conversation?"

Despite his arrogance, he had a disconcerting way of staring. His expression was inscrutable, giving no indication of what he was thinking. He could have been seriously weighing her arguments or planning to toss her out of the Gator and letting her swim back to the mainland. One was as viable a guess as the other. Or he might have been thinking neither.

Taking his silence as permission for her to continue, she did. "I know it's rather late in the day to be talking shop, but I promise not to take up too much of your time. Mike said he would—"

"I know what Mike said. He called me at Terry's after you left the house. He's acting like a complete fool."

"He didn't strike me as a fool. Anything but."

"Ordinarily, no. Ordinarily he's levelheaded, calm, cool, and collected, the voice of reason, a goddamn pillar of sensibility. But you've got him in a dither. He's tearing around straightening up the house, fixing supper, acting like an old maid about to receive her first gentleman caller." His eyes were shadowed, but she could tell they were moving over her. "You must've laid on the charm double thick."

"I did nothing of the sort. Mike is just a nice man."

He barked a harsh laugh. "Unlike me."

"I didn't say that."

"Well," he drawled, "you just as well have, because it's true. I'm not at all nice."

"I'm sure you could be if you wanted to."

"See, that's the kicker. I don't want to."

Then, before she could prepare herself, he reached across the space separating them, hooked his hand around the back of her neck, and yanked her forward, bringing her mouth up to his. It was more an assault than a kiss. Hard, grinding, insistent. His tongue stabbed at the seam between her lips until it forced them apart.

Making angry sounds of protest, she pushed against his chest, but he didn't stop. Instead he continued to plumb her mouth forcefully as his lips twisted upon hers. Imperceptibly the thrusts became slower and gentler, more exploratory than invasive. His thumb stroked the underside of her chin, her cheek, and very near the corner of her lips. Her anger shifted into distress.

When he ended the deep kiss, he rubbed his lips against hers lightly before breaking contact with them, and even then they remained close, merely a breath apart. Only after he let his hands fall away did he pull back.

Maris turned her head away. She stared out across the water of the sound. It was relatively calm compared to the choppy currents circulating through her bloodstream. The lights on the shore of the mainland seemed very distant. Much farther than before. Now a world away. She felt strangely disconnected, as though that narrow body of water had widened into a gulf that couldn't be spanned.

Somewhere out on the sound a boat's horn bleated a warning. Inside Terry's, the boom box had been restarted and was playing a wailing song about a love gone wrong. Closer, she could hear the gentle slap of the water against the rocky beach at the bottom of the steep ramp that Parker Evans was unable to navigate in his wheelchair.

"It won't work, Mr. Evans," she said quietly. "I'm not going to flee in terror of you."

She turned then to look at him and was surprised by the absence of smugness in his expression. He didn't look contrite or apologetic, either, but he wasn't wearing the triumphant sneer she had expected. He was staring at her in the same disconcerting, inscrutable way as before.

"I ignored the vulgarities inside Terry's, just like I'm going to ignore that kiss. Because I know why you subjected me to that," she said, hitching her head in the direction of the bar, "and I know why you kissed me."

"You do."

"I'm calling your bluff."

"Bluff."

"You kissed me to scare me off."

"All right."

" 'All right'?"

"You can think that if you want to." He held her gaze for several seconds, then put the Gator into forward motion. "Did Mike happen to mention what's for supper?"

It turned out to be smoked ham sandwiches served in a casual room on the back of the house. Mike referred to it as the solarium.

"Fancy name for a glassed-in porch," Parker commented wryly.

"It was a porch," Mike explained to Maris as he spooned potato salad onto her plate. "You can't tell, now that it's dark, but this room overlooks the beach. Parker decided to enclose it with sliding glass panels that give us the option of closing it completely or opening it up. Now he can write in here during any kind of weather."

Maris had pretended not to notice the computer setup in one corner of the room, which was otherwise furnished with rattan pieces. Nods toward decoration were limited. A few throw pillows. One struggling potted plant that looked doomed to lose the struggle. That was all. It was a bachelor's room. A writer's retreat.

Stacked around the computer terminal, on the stone tile floor, in shelves, on every conceivable surface, were books. Reference books, literary novels and classics, mysteries, romances, science fiction, horror, westerns, autobiographies, biographies, poetry, childrens' books, histories, self-help, and inspirational. Every kind of book imaginable, some in hardcover, some in paperback, some of which, she was pleased to see, bore the Matherly Press imprint on the spine. Gauging by the worn appearance of the books, his library wasn't just for show. Parker Evans was well read.

"Whatever you call this room, I like it," she told them. "It's a wonderful place to read. And write." She gave Parker a sly glance, which he chose not to see as he spread mustard onto his sandwich.

After serving them, Mike sat down across the table from her, confirming what she had guessed, that he was as much a friend and companion as he was a valet—the need for which was now sadly apparent. "You went to far too much trouble, Mike."

"No trouble. We planned to have a late supper anyway, and I'm awfully glad to have a guest in the house. Parker isn't always the best company. In fact, when he's writing, he sometimes doesn't speak for hours, and when he does, he can be a real grouch."

Parker shot him a sour glance. "And you're a perpetual pain in the ass."

Maris laughed. Despite the swapped insults, the affection between them was obvious. "I've experienced Mr. Evans's grouchiness firsthand, Mike, but I don't take it personally. I'm used to it. I work with writers every day. A gloomy bunch, for the most part. I probably don't catch the verbal abuse their agents do, but I get my share."

Mike nodded sagely. "Artistic temperament."

"Precisely. I'm not complaining. Based on my experience— and confirmed only yesterday by my father—bad temperament is often an indicator of good writing."

She blotted her lips with her napkin and was shocked to realize that they were still tender. She'd checked her reflection in the framed mirror above the basin when Mike kindly directed her into the powder room shortly after she and Parker arrived. The only visible trace of the kiss was a slight abrasion above her upper lip. She'd applied powder to the whisker burn and then quickly switched off the light, afraid she would see in her eyes even more telling evidence of the kiss, which she had resolved to deny—a resolve jeopardized by whisker burns and such.

She and the author had spoken little on the drive to his home. She had kept her eyes trained on the twin beams the

Gator's headlights cast onto the road. The darkness within the forest made it easier to ignore, although at one point she couldn't resist taking one furtive glance into the trees.

"Oh!" she exclaimed.

"What?"

"Fireflies. There in the woods."

"Lightning bugs," he said. "Down here, we call them lightning bugs."

"I haven't seen any in years."

"Insecticides."

"Unfortunately. When I was little, I used to see them around our house in the country. I'd catch them and put them in a glass and keep it on my nightstand overnight."

"I did that, too."

She turned to him in surprise. "You did?"

"Yeah. The kids in my neighborhood used to hold contests to see who could catch the most."

So he had been able to chase fireflies. He hadn't always been confined to a wheelchair. Naturally she was curious about the nature of his disability, but she was too polite to ask.

He wasn't the first person she had known who was similarly incapacitated. She had enormous respect for those individuals who had made the best of their misfortune. Some were the most optimistic, upbeat people she had ever had the pleasure of knowing. What they lacked in physical stamina and strength, they made up for with courage and spiritual fortitude.

Parker Evans seemed to have the raw power of physically challenged triathletes who competed in the Ironman competitions, men and women who achieved Herculean feats with the strength of their arms—and willpower—alone. Frequently they were athletes or otherwise active young people whose pursuits had been ended in one fateful second, victims of tragic accidents. She wondered what had happened to Parker to change his life so dramatically.

She glanced across the table at him now. He was picking at

the bread crust on his plate but, as though feeling her eyes, raised his and caught her looking at him. He gave her a frank return stare.

He was undeniably attractive, although years of pain or unhappiness or disillusionment or a combination thereof had etched lines into his face, making him appear older than he probably was. His rare smiles were tainted by bitterness. His brown hair was thick and threaded with gray. Grooming it would probably be an afterthought. He was wearing two days' worth of stubble.

His eyes weren't a definitive color like blue or green or brown. They were best described as hazel and would have been unremarkable except for the occasional amber spots that flecked the irises. That unique feature, coupled with his amazing ability to remain focused on something for an incredible length of time, made his eyes compelling.

Staring at her now, he seemed to know exactly what she was thinking. His eyes were issuing a challenge. *Go ahead,* they seemed to say. *You're dying to know why I'm in this chair, so why don't you just ask?*

She wasn't going to take up that dare. Not now. Not until she knew him better, or not until she got at least a verbal commitment from him that he would finish his book.

"Have you written any more, Mr. Evans?"

"Want a refill of iced tea?"

"No, thank you."

"Another sandwich?"

"I'm full, thank you. Have you got more for me to read?"

He looked pointedly at Mike, who took the hint. "Excuse me. I need to put some things away." The older man got up and left the room through a connecting door.

As soon as Mike was out of earshot, he said, "You're a very determined woman."

"Thank you."

"I didn't mean it as a compliment."

"I know."

He backed away from the table, turned his chair, and stared through the glass as though he could penetrate the darkness and see the surf. Maris gave him this time. If he was balancing the pros and cons of a decision, she wanted to say nothing that might tip the scales against her.

After a time, he turned back. "Do you really think it's that good?"

"Do you think I would travel to a remote spot on the map if I'd had a lukewarm response to your writing?"

"In plain English, please."

"Yes, Mr. Evans, it's good."

He looked at her with exasperation. "My tongue has been inside your mouth, which makes the 'Mr. Evans' a bit ridiculous, don't you think? My name is Parker. Call me that, okay?"

She swallowed but refused to look away from him. "Okay. And you can call me Maris."

"I planned to."

He seemed determined to provoke her one way or the other, but she was equally determined not to let him. "Where are you from, Parker? Originally. The South, I know that."

"Shoot! What gave me away?" He spoke in an exaggeration of his natural drawl.

She laughed softly. "Well, there is the accent, but Yankees have a hard time distinguishing regional nuances. For instance, Texans don't sound like South Carolinians, do they?"

"Texans don't sound like anybody."

Again she laughed. "Where did your particular accent originate?"

"Why is that relevant?"

"Some of the words you use . . ."

"Like?"

"Like 'fixing' instead of preparing or cooking supper. And the word 'supper' itself, instead of dinner. 'Dither,' 'gentleman caller,' things like that."

"I guess those colloquialisms crop up now and then in my speech. I try and keep them out of my writing."

"Don't. They season it."

"A little seasoning goes a long way."

She acknowledged his point with a nod. "I see you've thought about it. You're conscientious about using idioms in your prose." Propping her arms on the table, she leaned forward. "You put a lot of thought and hard work into your writing, Parker. Why are you reluctant to have it read?"

He had the answer ready. "Fear of failure."

"Understood. Creative people are cursed with self-doubt. It's the nature of the beast." She gestured toward his bookcase. "But aren't we glad that most don't submit to it?"

"Many do, though, don't they?" he argued. "They couldn't stand the ridicule of critics, or the fickle whims of the buying public, or the pressure of living up to expectations, or the darkest goddamn doubt of all, which is that they had no talent to begin with and that exposure of that reality is just around the corner. How many writers can you name who drank themselves to death? Or made it quick and blew their brains out?"

She thought the question over, then said, "Tell me, Parker, does that require more courage, or less, than becoming a recluse on an out-of-the-way island?"

The shot struck home. For several long moments he seemed to wage a battle with himself, then he whipped his chair about and rolled it to the worktable. He booted up the computer, saying to her over his shoulder, "This means nothing, understand?"

She nodded agreement, although she was certain that they were both lying. Whatever *this* was, it meant *something*.

"I've written a first chapter."

"In addition to the prologue, you mean?"

"Correct. If you want to read it, I'll let you. With the understanding that I'm under no obligation to you. Whether you like the material or not, I'm making you no promises."

Maris moved beside his chair and together they watched the pages as they rolled out of the printer. "Does the first chapter start where the prologue left off?"

"No. The scene in the prologue comes toward the end of the story."

"So you go back and bring the reader forward?"

"Right."

"How far back?"

"Three years. Chapter one takes place when Roark and Todd are college roommates."

"Roark and Todd," she repeated, trying out the character names and deciding she liked them. "Which is which?"

"What do you mean?"

"Which one do we see in Hatch Walker's office in the prologue? Who crashes the boat and who has gone overboard?"

This time his grin was free of bitterness.

"You're not going to tell me, are you?" she asked.

"If I did, what would be the point of your reading the rest of the book?"

"The rest? So you *are* planning to finish it?"

His grin slipped a fraction. "Let's see what you think first."

"I can't wait."

"Don't get too excited, Maris. It's only one chapter."

He removed the pages from the tray on the printer, then tapped the edges on the table to even them up before passing them to her. She grasped them, but he continued to hold them. She looked at him expectantly.

"When I kissed you? It didn't have a damn thing to do with trying to scare you off."

Before she could respond, he released the pages and shouted for Mike. "Bring her a phone so she can call for a boat," he told the older man when he appeared in the doorway. "It'll take about as long for it to get to the island as it takes for you to get her back to the landing. Should time out just right."

"But it's after eleven o'clock," Mike exclaimed. "You can't send her back at this time of night."

Maris, flustered, said a little too quickly and loudly, "It's fine, Mike. I'll be fine."

"I won't hear of it." Ignoring Parker's warning look, Mike declared, "You'll stay here tonight. In the guest house."

To avoid the parties being seen together in a public restaurant, the luncheon meeting was held in a private dining room on the thirty-first floor of WorldView Center. The paneled room was discreetly and expensively furnished. The hand-woven carpet was thick and sound-absorbing, the floral arrangements were elaborate and still dewy, the lighting was indirect and subdued. To add to the dignified ambience, heavy draperies had been drawn across the expansive windows, which ordinarily would have provided a magnificent view of the Midtown skyline.

The host, seated at the head of the dining table, asked politely, "More coffee, Nadia? Mr. Reed?"

Nadia Schuller indicated to the white-gloved waiter that she would like her cup refilled. Noah declined. They had dined on vichyssoise, lobster salad, and marinated asparagus. Strawberries Romanoff and selected chocolates had been served for dessert.

Noah thanked their host for the sumptuous meal. "It was excellent."

"I'm glad you enjoyed it." Morris Blume thanked and then dismissed the servers.

As Nadia idly stirred cream into her coffee, Noah exchanged a look with her that said social hour was over and business was about to commence.

In addition to Morris Blume, five other representatives from WorldView were seated around the table. Six months earlier, Nadia had arranged an introductory meeting between Blume and Noah. Blume hadn't been coy at that initial meeting. Rather, he had stated plainly that he wished to acquire Matherly Press for WorldView.

Immediately upon adjournment of that meeting, his corporate lawyers had begun working feverishly on an acquisition proposal. After months of researching and analyzing, drafting flow charts, drawing market-share graphs, and making projections, the final rendition had been delivered to Noah in an enormous three-ring binder. This meeting was for the purpose of hearing his response to it.

"You've had a month to study our syllabus, Mr. Reed," Blume said. "I'm eager to hear your impressions."

Morris Blume was whipcord thin and strikingly pale, a feature emphasized by his prematurely bald head. A rim of sparse hair continued to grow from his scalp, but he shaved it every morning, which left a gray shadow beneath his shiny dome. He wore eyeglasses with silver wire frames and always dressed in conservative gray. The man seemed to have an innate aversion to color.

He had been at the helm of the international media conglomerate since his hostile takeover four years ago. Only thirty-six at the time, he had ruthlessly ousted his predecessor along with anyone on the board of directors who adhered to what Blume termed "archaic and unenlightened mindsets."

Under his leadership, WV, as it was affectionately known on the stock exchange, had expanded from its base entertainment and broadcast entities into Internet commerce, satellite communications, and fiber-optics technology. Blume had catapulted

WorldView into the twenty-first century, increasing its worth from a mere billion dollars to nearly sixty billion in only forty-eight months. Stockholders easily forgave his brash methods of doing business.

So what did a mammoth like WorldView want with a gnat like Matherly Press?

That was the question Noah now posed to Blume.

"Because it's there?" the pale CEO glibly replied. Everyone at the table laughed, including Noah. He could appreciate the son of a bitch's arrogance because he was an arrogant son of a bitch himself.

"You've already acquired a publishing house in the U.K.," Noah pointed out. "The ink is barely dry on that contract."

"True." Blume nodded solemnly. "Platt/Powers will be a good investment for us. Their magazine division is the strongest in the British Isles. They distribute everything from a well-respected world news weekly to the sleaziest of sleazy porno." He gave Nadia a smile that was disturbingly reptilian. "I assure you, Nadia, that I'm far more familiar with the former than the latter."

She looked at Blume over the rim of the china cup as she took a sip of coffee. "How disappointing."

Blume let the resultant laughter wane before he resumed. "Platt/Powers had twelve bestsellers in hardcover last year."

"Thirteen," one of the bean counters at the table supplied.

"More than that in paperback," Blume continued. "As part of WorldView, it will dominate the bestseller lists this year. We've got the know-how and the budget to make that happen."

"I've already interviewed two writers whom you pirated from their former publishers," Nadia remarked. "They're very excited about your marketing strategies, particularly the ones that will give them greater exposure here in the States."

"We utilize our media resources," Blume explained. "All of them. They are vast and unmatchable."

He folded his bloodless hands together on the table and assumed an earnest demeanor. Focusing on Noah, he said, "By buying Platt/Powers, WorldView acquired a healthy publishing house. But the U.K. market is smaller than the American market. Significantly so. We want one on this side of the pond. We want Matherly Press.

"You publish books with mass appeal. Moneymakers, if you will. But you also publish literary works. Without question yours is a profitable house. It's also a venerable publishing institution. It has a cachet of respectability. We'd like that for our little company."

The fatuous understatement elicited a twitter from the WV group, but Noah let it pass without even a smile. Blume seemed to take that as a sign that he should stop and let the other side talk for a while.

"I've studied the proposal thoroughly," Noah began. "You did your homework. The research was impressive. The projections are exciting but within the realm of achievability."

"This is sounding very good," Blume said, throwing grins all around.

Noah held up a cautionary hand. "However, before we move forward, there are a couple of points that must be addressed."

"That's the purpose of this meeting."

"First, what about antitrust laws? Are you going to be in violation? I don't want to become embroiled in a protracted legal dispute with the federal government."

"I assure you that we don't, either, and we've taken every precaution to avoid it."

One of the lawyers was given the floor to explain why the probability of that happening was slim. Noah asked several questions, which he didn't allow to be dismissed with legal double-talk. He kept at the counsel until his concerns were addressed and given the attention they deserved.

"Good," Blume said when explanations had been provided to Noah's satisfaction. "What's your second point?"

Noah plucked an invisible piece of lint off the sleeve of his suit jacket, then looked over at Blume and said blandly, "Matherly Press isn't for sale."

"To which he said?" Daniel Matherly asked.

"Nothing that bears repeating," his son-in-law replied.

"Something about stubborn old men who refuse to see the light, I'd bet."

"Nothing that blatant, but definitely along those lines."

They were having drinks together in Daniel's home study. Maxine had poured them the first round. "One is his limit. He can't have another," she told Noah before leaving them.

"I'll see that he doesn't," he called after her as she left the room. But a conspiratorial wink at Daniel nullified his promise to the housekeeper.

Now, a half hour later, they were enjoying their second round. "Fetch me my pipe, will you, please?"

Noah retrieved Daniel's pipe from where he'd left it on the desk. He delivered it and a tobacco pouch to the large leather wing chair where Daniel sat with his feet propped on an ottoman. Methodically he packed his pipe and put a match to it.

"If Maxine smells that smoke—"

"I'll claim it was you who was smoking." He exhaled a plume of smoke toward the ceiling. Thoughtfully, his eyes remained fixed on the crown molding. "The mongrels are closing in on us, Noah. They're mean and they have sharp teeth."

Noah sipped his scotch. "WorldView?" He made a negligent gesture. "I don't know how I could have stated it any more plainly. Matherly Press isn't for sale."

"They'll persist. Particularly that Blume bastard."

"It's said he pisses ice cubes."

Daniel chuckled. "I don't doubt it." He puffed on his pipe for a moment. "Even if Morris Blume falls by the wayside or gives up and goes away, another mongrel, even meaner than he, won't be far behind."

"Let them come. We can stave them off."

Daniel smiled at his son-in-law's confidence. Everyone in the industry had become acquainted with Noah Reed a decade ago following the publication of *The Vanquished*. The novel, set during the Reconstruction, had taken the nation by storm. There wasn't a publisher in New York who hadn't wished he'd been lucky enough to nab it, Daniel Matherly included.

But to everyone's surprise, and his new fans' dismay, Noah's ambitions lay not in writing, but in publishing. He had followed every step of the publishing process on *The Vanquished* and had derived more enjoyment out of that than he had from writing the novel.

He was an engaging young man with superior intelligence and razor-sharp instincts. Some of his ideas on how best to market his book had been implemented by his publisher, and they had worked. The house reasoned that Noah would be equally successful publishing other books and had hired him.

The junior editor had quickly proved his mettle. During his first year, he acquired an obscure manuscript from an unknown author, who became a bestseller with that first novel and remained one to this day.

Noah had been a quick study editorially, but the business side of the industry was where he truly distinguished himself. His inventive marketing strategies were so successful that they were blatantly copied by other publishers.

He was a fearless negotiator, whom literary agents admired but dreaded facing across the bargaining table. He was a born leader. Once, on the eve of a labor strike, he had traveled to a printing company in Pennsylvania to personally appeal to the disgruntled workers. Acting as a mediator between them and plant management, he helped settle the dispute, quelled the strike, and prevented an industry crisis.

Noah Reed was bright, ambitious, even shrewd. Daniel had been rightly accused of being shrewd himself, so he didn't regard it a derogatory term. So when, to Daniel's surprise, Noah

had come to him three years ago, covertly expressing his unhappiness with the limits placed upon him by his present employer and boldly stating his desire to make a move, Daniel had
listened with interest. Noah's ideas were innovative but didn't
conflict with the ideals on which Daniel's ancestors had
founded Matherly Press. Indeed, Noah shared them.

Additionally, Noah had appealed to Daniel's vanity, though
he would never admit it. The younger man had reminded him
of himself when he'd been that age—aggressive, determined,
confident to the point of conceit, which Daniel also regarded
more a virtue than a vice.

Daniel told Noah he would need a few days to think it over.
He was reluctant to bring in someone who wasn't family and
install him in a position of authority. On the other hand, the
business had expanded to the point where he and Maris
needed another pair of hands at the helm.

For Maris's part, she was positively giddy over the possibility
of working daily with the author of her favorite book. Though
she'd met Noah only once, at a literary function, she held him
in high esteem and had harbored a secret romantic crush on
him for years.

With her urging, Daniel created the job of vice president of
business affairs for Noah. He'd never regretted that decision.

"You still agree with it, don't you?" Daniel asked him now.

"With what?"

"The company philosophy."

He gave his father-in-law a retiring look. "From the beginning of our association, I've known how you felt about mergers,
Daniel. Unquestionably there would be benefits. We would
have more funds at our disposal, more venues for marketing
and promotion."

"But we'd no longer be autonomous."

"Which was the point I was about to make," Noah said. "Au-
tonomy was the basis on which Matherly Press was founded. I
knew the family mantra even before I married into it."

When Maris began seeing Noah outside the office, Daniel had nursed some reservations. He had been concerned on several levels. First, their ten-year age difference bothered him, but not overly so. Second, Noah's business acumen wasn't the only thing on which he'd built a solid reputation. It was rumored that he was a notorious womanizer. With so many rumors circulating for that many years, Daniel had to believe there was some basis for them. His greatest concern, however, was Noah's personal agenda. By marrying the last eligible Matherly, his career would receive a distinct boost.

Of course, when it came right down to it, it wasn't Daniel's decision to make. It was his daughter's, and Maris wanted Noah for her husband. Because of her mother's untimely death, she had always been mature beyond her years. Necessity had forced her to grow up quickly. She had begun forming her own opinions and making her own decisions at an early age. He had reared her to think for herself and to trust her instincts. It would have been wrong of him to second-guess her choice of a life partner.

To his credit, Noah had, without Maris's knowledge, approached his future father-in-law and told him that if he entertained any doubts regarding the marriage, it would never take place. He loved Maris to distraction, he had said, but he would walk away, forsake his position at Matherly Press, and disappear from her life unless Daniel could give his wholehearted approval of the union.

Daniel had given the couple his blessing, but, where Maris's happiness was concerned, he remained a vigilant watchdog. Yesterday, she had been a bit downcast, although the surprise party was a logical explanation for Noah's recent inattention.

Maris didn't talk about it, but Daniel also sensed that she was ready for children and was slightly disappointed that she hadn't become pregnant. It was too early to worry unnecessarily about that. Maris was still young. Noah had expressed a desire for children on numerous occasions. There was plenty of time for them to have a family.

Selfishly, Daniel wished for grandchildren soon. He would enjoy bouncing the next generation on his knee before he checked out.

Thinking of his daughter now, he asked, "Have you heard from Maris?"

"Not since she left this morning." Noah checked his wristwatch. "She should be there by now. It was a long way to travel and I'm afraid it will turn out to be a bust."

"Hopefully not. She seems very excited about this writer. Speaking of which, she told me about her present."

"Present?"

"Last night."

"Oh." Noah smiled with chagrin. "She's awfully easy to please, isn't she?"

"Your writer's cell is no small thing to her, Noah. She called from the airport this morning just prior to boarding her flight. If you'd given her a diamond ring, she couldn't have been happier. She's always wanted you to resume writing."

Noah frowned. "I hope she doesn't expect too much from me. I'll probably disappoint her."

"Your effort alone will make her happy."

"I'd like to get in a few hours of effort tonight." Noah set his empty tumbler on the end table and stood up.

"Stay and have dinner with me. We'll play chess afterward."

"Tempting, Daniel. But I should use this time that Maris is away to crank out a few pages. There's only one way to write, and that's to write," he said with a smile. "Can I refresh your drink before I go?"

"Thanks, no. Maxine will be measuring the amount left in the decanter as it is."

"Then I for sure want to clear out before the fireworks start." Noah pulled on his suit jacket and retrieved his briefcase. "Anything else I can do for you?"

"As a matter of fact, there is," Daniel said. "The next time someone approaches you with an offer to buy my publishing house, tell him to fuck off."

Noah laughed. "Shall I quote you?"

"Absolutely. In fact, I would prefer it."

Two vodka martinis hadn't dulled the edges of Nadia's nerves. They seemed to be on red alert and had been since Noah had recounted for her his conversation with Daniel.

For half an hour she'd been pacing the hardwood floor of her Chelsea apartment, which was used strictly for romantic trysts. The apartment she owned in Trump Tower was her official address. Not even her accountant knew about this apartment.

"No matter how blasé he seems, I don't trust the old codger," she said. "How do you know he can't see through your act?"

"Because he isn't looking." Noah's voice conveyed his impatience.

"I don't mean to question your perception, Noah."

"Don't you?"

"No. I'm just afraid that something might go wrong. I want this deal so badly for you."

"I want it for *us*."

Her anxiety dissolving, she stopped pacing and moved to where he stood. Coming close, she rested her hands on his shoulders. "Damn you," she said softly. "By saying that, you've completely disarmed me."

Their kiss was passionate and deep. She unbuttoned his shirt and slipped her hand inside. When they pulled apart, she continued to tweak his chest hairs. "It's just that Daniel Matherly has been overseeing that publishing house for . . . how long?"

"He's seventy-eight. His father died when he was twenty-nine. Daniel's been in control since then."

"So almost fifty years."

"I can subtract, Nadia."

"All I'm saying is this: He hasn't made himself into a living legend by being a dimwit. He didn't become successful by misreading people. He's smart. He's savvy. He's—"

"Not as sharp as he used to be."

"Maybe. Or maybe he just wants you to think so."

Noah disliked being second-guessed and resented even a hint of criticism. Pushing her away, he moved into the kitchen, where he refilled his highball glass with ice cubes and splashed scotch over them. "I think I know my father-in-law at least as well as you do, Nadia."

"I'm sure—"

"If you were sure of me, you wouldn't be nagging me about this." He treated his drink like a shot, then set his glass on the countertop and took a moment to contain his temper before turning back to her. "Your job is to keep Blume and company pacified and reassured."

"I'm having dinner with Morris tomorrow night. The Rainbow Room."

"Good. Be a knockout. Eat, drink, and dance. Blow in his ear. Keep him happy. Let me handle the Matherlys. I've been handling them quite well for three years. I know how they think. I know how they react to given situations. This must be carried out with extreme delicacy. It can't be rushed or the whole thing could blow up in our faces."

His timetable had been in place for years. Now that the finish line was in sight, he wasn't going to sacrifice all his careful planning and strategizing to recklessness. By doing it his way, on his schedule, everything had gone according to plan.

The first step had been accomplished when Daniel Matherly hired him. By toeing the company line, he had earned the old man's trust. A major hurdle had been cleared when he married Maris, further solidifying his position. Then, when the time was right, he had subtly, through Nadia, telegraphed to Blume his interest in a merger. Blume was still working under the misconception that the idea had originally been his. Not at all. WorldView had been in Noah's game plan from the start.

Up to this point everything had been done Noah Reed's way, the only way that Noah Reed would have it. He wasn't going to screw himself now by rushing toward a quick finish.

"I don't know why you're being testy with me," Nadia said. "Morris issued the deadline today, not I."

That had been the one crimp in Noah's plan that he hadn't seen coming, and the reason for his querulousness tonight. Throughout his cocktail hour with Daniel, he'd been only half listening to the old man's rambling speech. Instead he'd been remembering Blume, with his lizardlike smile, imposing on him a two-week deadline to either fish or cut bait.

Blume had reminded Noah that he had been extended ample time in which to review the proposal, that either he was interested enough to move forward and make this deal happen or he wasn't. Noah had reminded him that his father-in-law wasn't a minor stumbling block but a major obstacle. "Daniel has stated unequivocally that his company is not for sale."

"Then you must take bold steps to see that he changes his mind, mustn't you?"

Blume concluded the meeting by reminding Noah that there were other publishing companies, almost as prestigious as Matherly Press, that would leap at the chance of becoming part of WorldView.

The hell of it was, Noah knew that Blume's threat was viable. Many smaller publishing houses were hanging on by a thread. They couldn't compete with the distribution capabilities and robust publicity budgets of media giants. They would welcome the financial relief and stability that WorldView would bring to them. Unlike Daniel, their primary concern was survival by any means possible, and to hell with sentiment.

There wasn't a sentimental bone in Noah's body, but he was well acquainted with Daniel's fanatical adherence to tradition and his family's history. The old man wasn't going to let go easily. It was an intricate complication that seemed beyond Blume's understanding.

"I'm well aware of Blume's deadline," Noah told Nadia now. "I'll see that it's met."

"What about Maris?"

"She's busy in Florida."

"Georgia."

"What?"

"You told me she went to Georgia."

"Whatever. I'm going to chip away at Daniel while she's gone. I began tonight by pointing out the advantages of Blume's offer."

"What happens when Maris gets back?"

"She'll go the way Daniel goes."

"That wasn't what I was talking about."

I should be so lucky. Sighing wearily, Noah closed his eyes and pinched the bridge of his nose. Jesus, he didn't need a discussion of this right now. He had enough to deal with.

"I know what you were talking about, Nadia." Lowering his hand and opening his eyes, he looked at her. "Think about it. Does it make sense for me to ask Maris for a divorce now? No. I can't do that until I have that WorldView contract signed, sealed, and delivered."

He expelled a breath of exasperation. "Do you think I've enjoyed being married to her? Do you think I've liked kissing Daniel's ass all these years?"

"That's a revolting thought."

"Isn't it? So imagine it from my perspective." He hoped the remark might cause her to smile; it didn't.

"And Maris?" she asked. "Will you miss kissing her ass?"

He gave a dry laugh. "I won't miss my wife, but I'll regret losing a good editor. However, with the operating budget Blume has promised me, I'll be able to hire three of her. Five of her. And even if none prove to be as good as she, I'll have my ten million to console me."

She held his gaze for a moment, her expression turning sulky. "You really don't mind my blowing in Morris Blume's ear?"

"Figure of speech."

"So what you said earlier . . ."

"About?"

"About your wanting this deal for *us*. Did you mean it?"

By way of answer, he pulled her against him and kissed her.

She finished unbuttoning his shirt, then spread it open and put tongue to nipple, flicking it lightly. "You did?"

"Right now I'd swear to anything."

Laughing huskily, she stroked him through his trousers. "I don't like sharing you with Maris. I'm impatient to have this all to myself."

"I'm rather impatient myself." He unzipped his trousers and pushed down his shorts. Nadia dropped to her knees and nuzzled him. She traced the length of his erection with her tongue before taking him into her mouth. Noah grunted with satisfaction.

"You stick to doing what you do best, Nadia, and leave the problem of the Matherlys to me."

Parker was at his computer. He'd been up for hours. His mind was skipping like a stone over water.

Mike delivered a third cup of coffee to him. "Your guest just left the cottage. She's dawdling along the way, taking in the seascape, but she'll soon be making an entrance."

He had asked Mike to be on the lookout for her and acknowledged the report with a nod.

Mike was uncharacteristically careless as he replaced Parker's empty coffee mug with the full one. Hot coffee sloshed out. The spill spread across the table and stained several sheets of handwritten notes. Parker stared at the mess, then raised his head and gave the older man a look.

"Sorry," Mike said.

"I'll bet."

Mike snorted.

"Look, if you've got something to say, why not act like a grown-up and just say it?"

"I think you know what I have to say, Parker."

"How about 'congratulations'?"

"How about 'get real'? Do you really expect me to congratulate you?"

"She's here, isn't she?"

"Yes. She's here." Mike looked none too happy about it, though.

Parker raised his shoulders in a shrug, asking impatiently, "What? The reverse psychology worked. She took the bait. Which is what we hoped she would do. If you had qualms, you should have thrown away her phone numbers when that deputy gave them to you. But you didn't. You passed them on to me. I called her and she came. So what's eating you?"

Mike turned away and stamped back into the kitchen. "My biscuits are burning."

Parker returned to his computer screen, but the interruption had log-jammed his creative flow. He couldn't focus on the last few sentences he'd written. They now seemed a jumble of words and phrases beyond translation. In an effort to assign them meaning, he forced his eyes to stop on each word separately. But no matter how hard he concentrated, he couldn't make sense of them. They could have been written in Sanskrit.

And then he realized why reading and understanding his own words had suddenly become a challenge: He was nervous. Which was odd, considering that everything had fallen into place more or less as he had planned. He'd made a few spontaneous adjustments to accommodate Maris Matherly-Reed's personality, but she was responding to him and his situation even better than he had dared hope she would.

Now that he thought about it, getting her here had been almost too easy. He had pulled the strings, and, like a puppet, she had made the correct moves. He figured that's what had Mike's shorts in a wad this morning. Her innocent cooperation had lent her a certain vulnerability and made her seem almost a victim.

But she isn't, he told himself stubbornly.

Yeah, he had tugged some strings to guide her in the direction he wanted her to go, but ultimately she was in control. Everything depended on how well she liked *Envy*, or if she liked it at all.

And that's what had *his* shorts in a wad. Not only from the standpoint of the overall plan, but as a writer, he was nervous to hear what she thought of the pages she had curled up with last night. What if she thought they stunk? What if she thanked him for the opportunity to review more of his work but declined it and said her good-byes?

His plot would be screwed, and he would feel like shit.

Agitated, he turned his wheelchair on a dime and saw her picking her way along the path between the main house and the cottage. Originally it had been the detached kitchen of the plantation house. Parker had converted it into a guest house. Not that he entertained a lot of guests. Not that he planned to in the future. Nevertheless, the interior of the structure had been gutted and he had spared no expense to have it completely and comfortably renovated.

Accomplished with only one guest in mind—the one presently occupying it.

Maris glanced up and saw him watching her from behind the glass panels of the solarium. She smiled and waved. Waved? He couldn't remember the last time someone had waved at him. Feeling rather goofy, he raised his hand and waved back.

She let herself in through the sliding door. "Good morning."

"Hi."

Her skin looked dewy. She smelled like floral-scented soap. Magnolia, maybe. She had his manuscript pages with her.

"It's gorgeous here, Parker," she exclaimed a bit breathlessly. "Last night it was too dark for me to fully appreciate the property. But seeing it in daylight, I understand why you fell in love with this place." She looked out across the expanse of green lawn, the sugary beach, and the sparkling Atlantic. "It's wonderful. So peaceful."

"I forgot a hair dryer."

Self-consciously she tucked a strand of damp hair behind her ear. "I searched but couldn't find one. Actually, it's such a warm morning, it felt good to leave it wet. A hair dryer is all the cottage lacked, however. You did an excellent job on it."

"Thanks."

He continued to scrutinize her, and, as he intended, his scrutiny increased her self-consciousness. "The furnishings are charming. I especially like the iron headboard and the claw-footed bathtub."

"Mike's ideas."

"Good ones."

"Yeah, he's into all that. Iron beds. Bathtubs. Mantels."

"He has an eye for detail."

"I guess."

The conversation lagged for several moments, then they spoke at the same time.

He said, "Your blouse is wet."

She said, "I read the new pages."

"What'd you think?" he asked.

"My blouse?"

"It's damp."

She looked down and saw what had held Parker's attention from the moment she stepped inside. She was dressed in the same skirt and blouse she had arrived in. Following supper last night, Mike had wheedled and pleaded, then insisted that she stay in their guest house. She had finally accepted the invitation, but because of the hour, it had been impractical to try and retrieve her luggage from the hotel in Savannah.

Consequently she had dressed in the same clothes this morning, except for her suit jacket, which she'd left off in deference to the climate. A damp pattern had appeared on the front of her blouse in the exact shape of her bra.

She rolled the sheets of manuscript into a tube, probably to stop herself from using them to shield her chest. "I washed out some things last night."

Things, plural. If she'd washed out *things,* what had been left for her to sleep in? Surmising made Parker go a little dewy himself.

"I guess they didn't get quite dry," she explained lamely.

"The humidity."

"I suppose."

Their eyes connected but only for a millisecond before she looked away. She was embarrassed, and that was good. In fact, that was excellent. He wanted to keep her rattled and off balance. Too fucking bad if Mike disapproved of the strategy.

Leaning forward from the wheelchair, he reached out and took the rolled pages from her. "You read them?"

"Three times."

He raised his eyebrows inquiringly.

"I have some comments."

His chin went up defensively.

"Who's ready for breakfast?" Mike asked.

He appeared in the doorway pushing a wheeled cart on which were platters of scrambled eggs, bacon, and wedges of pastel melons. Fresh from the oven, the biscuits had been wrapped inside a towel and placed in a wire basket. A gravy boat was filled to the rim, and a dish of steamy grits had an island of melting butter in its center.

Parker's stomach growled and his mouth began to water, but Mike's timing couldn't be worse, which Parker was sure had been deliberate. Mike avoided making eye contact with him until Parker said, "I'm on to you, old man."

"What?" Mike asked innocently.

Parker shot him a wry look, which Mike ignored and instead motioned Maris toward a small table on which Parker sometimes took his meals when he was writing.

"Good Lord." She watched in dismay as Mike filled her plate. "A bagel and coffee usually do it for me."

Scoffing, Mike reminded her that breakfast was the most important meal of the day. "Do you like grits?"

"I'm not sure. What exactly is a grit?" Parker laughed along with Mike as she took her first tentative bite, which she gamely swallowed. Politely she said, "Maybe it's an acquired taste."

"Break open your biscuit and let me ladle gravy over it," Mike told her.

Bacon gravy was also new to her, but she declared it delicious. "Do you eat like this every morning?"

"This is a special occasion," Mike said.

"He's trying to impress you," Parker told her.

"It worked."

She flashed a smile at Mike that should have caused his heart to melt and made Parker irrationally jealous. He grumbled into his plate, "You could've impressed her by remembering to put a hair dryer in the guest cottage."

She and Mike took their time, chatting about this and that as they ate, but he cleaned his plate in record time. Feeling fidgety, he wheeled himself into the kitchen—"No, don't bother," he told Mike when he was about to get up. "I'll get it."—and returned with the carafe of coffee riding on a tray on his lap.

He refilled their cups, then impatiently sipped from his while they exhausted the topic of cultivating rhododendrons, as if flower bushes mattered a shit. He lasted through a discussion on the merits of *Cats* over *Sunset Boulevard* and a heated debate over whether women should be allowed to play in the NBA before he rudely interrupted.

"Can we talk about my book now?"

"What's your rush?" Mike asked.

"We're not running a bed and breakfast here."

"I wish we were." Mike began collecting their used dishes and loading them onto the service cart. "At least I'd have someone pleasant to talk to now and then."

"I'm pleasant."

"As a skin rash."

Laughing, Parker balled up his napkin and tossed it onto the cart as though shooting a free throw. "Hurry up with those dishes and get back in here. You've been a good and gracious host, but I know you're itching to hear what Maris has to say about *Envy*."

Mike went out, muttering under his breath.

"Bet I came out none too well in that monologue," Parker said when Mike was out of earshot.

"Are you two related?"

"Not by blood."

"He loves you."

Parker looked at her sharply. When he saw that she wasn't being caustic, he bit back a snide retort. He pondered her simple statement, then said slowly, "Yes, I suppose he does."

"You never considered it?"

"Not in words."

"Has he always taken care of you?"

"Not always."

"I meant since your accident."

"Accident?"

She gestured toward his wheelchair. "I assumed . . ."

"What made you assume it was an accident?"

"Wasn't it?"

Mike reappeared but, sensing that he'd walked in on a serious conversation, hesitated on the threshold. Parker waved him forward, this time grateful for the man's timing. Again, he figured it was intentional. Not much escaped Mike Strother.

Parker took a deep breath, blew it out, and, turning to Maris where she had sat down on the rattan sofa, said, "Okay, let's get this over with."

She laughed lightly. "It's not an execution, Parker."

"It's not?"

"Not at all. What you've written is good. Very good." She paused, glancing from him to Mike and back to him.

"Why do I feel that there's a 'however' in my near future?"

She smiled, then said quietly, "You've written a terrific outline."

Mike coughed softly and stared down at his shoes.

"Outline?"

"What you have is excellent." She wet her lips. "But it's . . .
It skims the surface. You haven't delved deeply enough."

"I see."

"This isn't bad news, Parker."

"It's pretty bad."

Turning his chair around, he rolled it closer to the wall of
windows and watched the shallow waves break against the
sand. St. Anne Island didn't have much of a surf at any time,
but especially not on a day like today, when the wind would
barely qualify as such and there wasn't an offshore low pressure system churning up the elements.

"I'm not in the least bit discouraged by what I've read so far,"
Maris said. "Quite the contrary."

Her voice was even quieter now than before and sounded
timid in the uncomfortable silence. From the kitchen came the
swishing gurgles of the dishwasher, but otherwise the house
was hushed.

Parker's shoulders began to shake. He covered his mouth to
trap in the sound that issued up out of his chest.

Maris was instantly alarmed. "Oh, Parker, please don't."

Suddenly he spun his wheelchair around and looked at Mike,
who joined in his laughter. "You win, you old son of a bitch.
Fifty fucking bucks."

"I told you," Mike said, chuckling. "I've got great gut instincts."

"Along with a knack for alliteration."

Mike executed a neat, quick bow.

Maris, who had come to her feet, divided an angry look between them. She planted her hands on her hips—which she
really shouldn't have done since the stance drew the damp
cloth tighter across her chest, detailing lace beneath it.

"Obviously I'm the butt of an inside joke. Would you kindly
let me in on it?"

"Not exactly a joke, Maris." Mike curbed his laughter and

even looked a little sheepish. "It was more like an experiment. A test."

"Test?"

"A few months back we read the article about you in the publishing magazine. To me you came across as a knowledgeable editor and publisher. But Parker said that your daddy probably paid for the article—"

"I said bribed."

"—then commissioned your publicity department to write the piece."

"Which explained why it was so flattering."

"He said that you were no doubt riding on the coattails of your daddy's reputation, that you looked too young and . . . uh . . . inexperienced—"

"Actually, the word I used was 'shallow.'"

"—to know good writing from bad. That your reading was probably limited to magazine articles."

"On how to multiply your orgasms."

"And that you probably wouldn't know a good book from a good . . . uh . . . ."

"Fill in the blank," Parker concluded with a beatific smile.

She had listened without interrupting or altering her expression. Now she came around slowly to face Parker, and he could fully appreciate all the metaphors he'd read about sparks shooting from someone's eyes.

Maris's eyes were bluish gray, like the rain clouds that rolled in from the west on summer afternoons and benevolently blocked the hot sun. They were basically benign, their turbulence only temporary. But even if short-lived, the turbulence was occasionally fierce. Her eyes had darkened to the hue of a storm cloud about to spawn a lightning bolt.

"I'm sure you're pissed." He shrugged, an unrepentant gesture. "I did everything I could, said everything I could think of to say, to discourage you from coming down here. But you came anyway. Last night when I . . ." He glanced at Mike and immediately decided not to mention kissing her. "When I tried convincing you to leave, you chose to stay."

His explanation fell short of earning her forgiveness. "You are an unmitigated son of a bitch, aren't you?"

"Pretty much, yeah," he said agreeably.

"You tried to trap me."

"Guilty."

"If I had gushed over how good your writing was, you would have known I was insincere."

"Or a lousy editor."

"But I knew better," Mike interjected. "I've read books that you edited, Maris. I told Parker, made a fifty-dollar bet with him, that his low opinion of you was unfounded and just plain wrong."

Maris heard all this, of course, but she hadn't even glanced in Mike's direction. Her anger was fixed on Parker. He smiled the sly grin of a gator that had just devoured a nest of ducklings, a grin that he knew would only make her more angry. "Sorry you came? Want to call the boat to take you back now?"

She tossed back her damp hair. "What caused Todd's father's death?"

Parker's heart gave a little flutter of gladness and relief. His wicked grin had been a lying indicator of the anxiety he'd been harboring.

"Was his death sudden or did it follow a lingering illness?" she asked.

"Does this mean you're still interested?"

"Did Todd take his death hard or was he glad to see the end of him? Was his father his idol? Or did the death release him from years of emotional abuse?"

She pushed an armchair close to him and snatched the pages from his hands as she sat down. "Do you understand what I'm getting at?"

"The characters need to be fleshed out."

"Precisely. Where do they come from? What were their

families like? Rich, poor, middle class? Did they have similar upbringings or were their childhoods vastly different? We know they want to be writers, but you haven't told us why. Simply for the love of books? Or is writing a catharsis for Roark, a way for him to vent his anger? Is it a panacea for Todd's unhappiness?"

"Panacea?"

"Are you listening?"

"I'll look it up later."

"You know what it means," she snapped.

He smiled again. "Yes. I do." From the corner of his eye, he noticed Mike leaving the room and pulling the door closed behind him.

Maris was still in high gear. "Life in the fraternity house—"

"There's more of that in the next chapter."

"There's a next chapter?"

"I worked on it this morning."

"Great. I liked that part. Very much. It's vivid. As I read, I could smell the gym socks." She shuddered delicately. "And the bit with the toothbrush . . ."

"Yeah?"

"It's almost too outrageous to be fiction. Personal experience?"

"What else needs work?" he asked.

"Ah. I get it. Personal questions are disallowed."

"If you washed out your undies last night, what did you sleep in?"

She sucked in a quick breath, opened her mouth to speak, then thought better of it. Her teeth clicked softly when she closed her mouth.

Tilting his head, he squinted his eyes as though to bring her into sharper focus. "Nothing, right?"

She lowered her eyes to her lap. Or maybe to his lap. He was tempted to say, *Yeah, it works, but if you're curious, why not touch it and find out?* But he didn't because she just might summon that boat to the mainland after all.

"You've made your point," she said gruffly. "No personal questions."

Picking up the manuscript pages again, she thumbed through them to refresh her memory on the notes she had jotted in the margins. "I'd like to see you expand, well, just about all of it." She glanced up at him to gauge his reaction, and when he declined to respond, she sat back with a sigh. "You expected this, didn't you? You knew what I was going to say."

He nodded. "I skimmed the surface, just as you said."

"To test my competence."

"Hmm."

"You auditioned me."

"Something like that."

Her smile was self-deprecating. She was being a good sport and letting him off more lightly than he deserved. Actually he would prefer that she rant and rave, lambast him with foul language, haul off and let him have it right in the kisser. What he had to do would be easier to do if she were as much of a bitch as he was a bastard. They were unequally matched opponents. She was out of her league and didn't even know it.

He said, "You had every right to tell Mike and me to go fuck ourselves."

"My father would never have tolerated that kind of language from me."

"So you *are* a daddy's girl?"

"Big time. Because he's such a good daddy. He's a gentleman and a scholar. He would like you."

He laughed harshly. "Not if he's a gentleman, he wouldn't."

"You're wrong. He would admire your audacity. He'd probably even call it 'balls.'"

Parker smiled. "A man after my own heart."

"He read your prologue and liked it. He encouraged me to pursue this project."

He gestured toward the manuscript pages. "So pursue it."

Consulting her notes again, she resumed. "Take your time, Parker. There's no page limit. Leave the trimming and editing to me. That's my job. You don't need to reveal all the background information in the first few chapters. It can be scattered throughout, but learn what the lives of these characters were like prior to the time they met."

"I already know." He tapped his temple. "Up here."

"Excellent. But the reader can't read your mind."

"I understand."

"That's it, for now."

She evened up the edges of the sheets, then laid them in her lap. "I'm glad I passed that silly test of yours," she said candidly. "I've missed being involved in this stage of the process. I didn't realize how much I'd missed it until I began making these notes last night. I love molding the story, brainstorming with the writer, especially a talented writer."

He pointed to himself. "And that would be me?"

"That would be you. Definitely."

Her gaze, so candid and earnest, made him uncomfortable. He looked out toward the ocean so he wouldn't have to see her sincerity, wouldn't have to feel . . . so he wouldn't have to feel, period.

Maybe he was the one playing out of his league.

Leaning toward him, she nudged his knee and lowered her voice to a near whisper. "I don't suppose you've changed your mind about letting me know which character—"

"Beat it, will ya?" He spun his chair away from her and pushed it toward his worktable. "I've got a bitch of an editor and she's piled a shitload of work on me."

That Tuesday morning two days before Thanksgiving dawned cloudy and cold. As though on cue, as though roasted turkey and pumpkin pie would be incompatible with mild weather, a cold front lowered the temperature just in time for the holiday.

Roark's alarm clock was set for seven-thirty. By seven-forty-five, he was shaved, showered, and dressed. By ten minutes to eight, he was downstairs in the residence dining hall, drinking coffee, glancing through his manuscript, and wondering how much abuse Professor Hadley was going to inflict on this creative effort into which he had poured his heart and soul.

The quality of his Thanksgiving holiday depended upon the outcome of the conference. He would either spend the long weekend relaxed and comfortable in the knowledge that his work had met with his professor's approval or foundering in the lake of misery called self-doubt.

Either way, he didn't have much longer to wait. The verdict would be read soon. Whether Hadley's remarks were good, bad, or ugly, hearing them would be a relief. This anticipation was hell.

"Sweet roll, Roark?"

He glanced up to see the house mom standing beside his chair. "Sure, Mom, thanks."

Soon after pledging, Roark had ordained the fraternity house mother the most long-suffering woman alive. Mrs. Brenda Thompson had given up a peaceful widowhood to voluntarily move into a three-story house with eighty-two men who behaved like miscreants sent away to a nine-month summer camp.

They respected nothing, neither persons nor property. Nothing was sacred—not God or country, one's hometown, one's pet, one's sister, or one's mother. It was open season on anything an individual held near and dear. Everything was subject to ribald ridicule.

They had the decorum of swine. As male *Homo sapiens* tend to do when gathered in groups of two or more, these eighty-two had regressed to the level of cavemen not nearly as refined as Neanderthals. Everything their mothers had forbidden them to do at home, they did in the fraternity house. Zealously and with relish, they celebrated rude behavior.

Mrs. Thompson, a soft-spoken and dignified lady, tolerated their language, which was foul, and their personal habits, which were fouler. Her maternal nature invited their confidences and earned their affection. But, unlike a parent, she exercised no discipline over them.

She turned a blind eye to the drinking, cussing, and fornicating, in which they participated with wild abandon. Without a complaint from her they could play their sound systems as loudly as they wished. They could sleep on their sheets for a semester or longer before laundering them. When they shaved the fraternity letters into the fur of a cat belonging to a girl who had jilted one of their members, Mom's only comment was on how nicely they had lined up the letters.

In her presence, particularly on Wednesday evenings during their one formal meal of the week, where jackets and ties and some semblance of civilization was required, they apologized for their expletives, belches, and farts with an obligatory and questionably sincere, "Excuse me, Mom." With a patient little smile, she always pardoned the offender, even though a similar offense would be forthcoming seconds later.

In her they had the Dream Mom.

Roark suspected that she favored him over some of the others, although he couldn't imagine why she did. He'd been as crude and badly behaved as any. After a toga party his sophomore year, he had passed out under the baby grand piano in the downstairs parlor and woke himself up choking on Jack Daniel's-flavored vomit.

Mrs. Thompson appeared in a long flannel robe and slippers, patting his shoulder and asking him if he was all right. "I'm fine," he mumbled, although clearly he wasn't.

Without censure and with the dignity of a nun, she removed the blanket that someone had tossed over an inflatable doll, the anatomically obscene, unofficial house mascot, and carried it back to Roark. She covered him with it where he lay, miserably cold, sick as a dog, and stinking to high heaven.

From that night forward, Mom seemed to have a special fondness for him. Maybe because when he had sobered up, he thanked her for the kindness and apologized for disturbing her sleep. Maybe because he'd had the rug beneath the piano cleaned at his own expense. No one else in the house had noticed—either that he had soiled the rug or that he'd had it cleaned. But Mrs. Thompson had noticed. He supposed these nods toward common decency demonstrated to her that he was redeemable, that he had at least some breeding.

"You're up earlier than usual, aren't you?" she asked now as she placed a jelly doughnut on a paper plate beside his coffee mug.

Ordinarily she didn't serve the boys food. They served themselves from a cafeteria-style line, taking what they wanted from the fare a surly cook put out for them in the manner of a farmer filling the feed trough for his herd.

"I'm meeting with my senior advisor this morning," he explained. In deference to her, he remembered to use a napkin instead of licking the doughnut's sugar glaze off his fingers.

She motioned to his manuscript. "Is that the book you're writing for your capstone?"

"Yes, ma'am. What I've got so far."

"I'm sure it'll be very good."

"Thanks, Mom. I hope so."

She wished him good luck with his meeting, then went over to say good morning to another boy who had just straggled in. He was the most handsome member in the house and attracted girls like moths to flame. His brothers wanted to hate him for his unearned good fortune, but he was too nice a guy to hate. Rather than exploit his movie-star looks, he downplayed them, seemed almost embarrassed by them. He glanced over at Roark and raised his cleft chin in greeting. "What's up, Shakespeare?"

"What's up, RB?"

Everyone had a nickname, and the accepted house greeting was, "What's up?" To which no one ever replied. That's just what they said.

Roark's nickname—to everyone except Todd—was Shakespeare. His fraternity brothers knew he liked to write, and William Shakespeare was the one writer that most of them could possibly call to mind if a gun were held to their heads. He had never tried to explain that Shakespeare wrote plays in blank verse, while he wrote stories in prose. Some concepts were just too complex to grasp, especially for individuals like the fraternity brother who, upon being asked by his English lit teacher to identify the bard by his portrait, had responded, "How the fuck you expect me to know all the presidents?"

Roark was flattered by the nickname, but this morning it seemed particularly presumptuous. Checking his wristwatch, he saw that he had fifteen minutes to reach Hadley's office. More than enough time. Nevertheless, he drained his coffee, stuffed his manuscript back into its worn folder, put the folder into his backpack, and left the dining hall.

Not until he got outside did he realize the drastic change in the weather that had occurred overnight. The wind chill put the temperature down around the freezing point, not cold enough to freeze the pond in the center of campus, but enough to make him wish he had grabbed a heavier coat before setting out.

The Language Arts Building, like most on campus, was basically Georgian in design. Older and statelier than the newer halls, it had a wide portico with six white columns. The aged red brick on the north wall was completely covered in Boston ivy that had turned from green to orange in a matter of days.

As soon as Roark was in sight of the building, he picked up his pace, more for warmth than for fear of being late. Despite his conservative upbringing, which had included church on Sundays, he was ambiguous about the existence, nature, and disposition of a Supreme Being. He wasn't certain that an entity with the omniscience attributed to God would give a flip about Roark Slade's daily trials. But today wasn't the day to reject any possible advantage, so he offered up an obscure little prayer as he crossed the portico and entered the building.

He was assailed by the burning-dust smell of old furnaces. Apparently they'd been cranked up to full capacity this morning, because the building was uncomfortably warm. He shrugged off his backpack and jacket as he jogged up the stairs to the second floor.

He was greeted by several students with whom he shared his major. One, a rail-thin hippy with pink-tinted John Lennon glasses and stringy hair, loped up to him. "Yo, Slade."

Only girls called him Roark. Except for Todd, he wasn't sure there was a male on campus who even knew his first name.

"Coffee later? We're getting together a study group for finals. Ten o'clock in the Union."

"I don't know if I'll be free. I'm on my way to see Hadley."

"You mean like now?"

"As we speak."

"Fuck, man, that sucks. Good luck."

"Thanks. Later."

"Later."

Roark continued down the hallway. The jelly doughnut hadn't been such a good idea. It felt like a bowling ball in his stomach. The coffee had left a sour taste in his mouth, and he admonished himself for not having a breath mint. When he arrived at office number 207 he paused to draw a deep breath. The door was standing slightly ajar. He wiped his damp palm on the leg of his jeans and knocked softly.

"Come in."

Professor Hadley was seated behind his desk. His feet, laced into a pair of brown suede Hush Puppies, were propped on the open top drawer. A stack of reading matter was in his lap, which was only one of myriad surfaces in the room that was stacked with reading matter. An inestimable number of trees had sacrificed their lives to provide the paper that filled Hadley's office. Per square inch, it was probably the largest consumer of paper globally.

"Good morning, Professor."

"Mr. Slade."

Was it just his imagination, or did Hadley's greeting sound peremptory?

The advisor's manner could never be described as friendly. Unlike some instructors, he didn't get chummy with his students. In fact, it was customary for him to treat them with barely concealed contempt. Even a respectable grade on a writing assignment didn't inoculate one against his scorn.

His teaching style was to make a student feel like an ignoramus. Only after the student had been knocked off the pedestal of his self-esteem, and the pedestal itself reduced to rubble, did Hadley drive home his point and teach him something. He seemed to believe that abject humility sharpened one's ability to learn.

As he stepped into the cramped office, Roark reassured himself that the curtness was a habit with Hadley and that he shouldn't take it personally.

"No, don't close the door," Hadley told him.

"Oh. Sorry." Roark reached back to catch the door, which he had been about to close.

"You should be."

"Sir?"

"Is there something wrong with your hearing, Mr. Slade?"

"My hearing? No, sir."

"Then you heard me correctly when I said that you should be sorry. You are now . . ." He glanced at something beyond Roark's left shoulder. "Fifty-six and one-half minutes late."

Roark turned. On the wall behind him was a clock. White face. Stark black numerals. A dash marking each of the sixty minutes. The short hand was already on the nine. The minute hand was three dashes away from the twelve.

The old man's lost it, Roark thought. *Something's pickled his brain. Paper fumes, maybe. Is there such a thing?*

He cleared his throat. "Excuse me, sir, but I'm right on time. Our meeting was scheduled for nine."

"Eight."

"Originally, yes. But don't you remember calling and changing it to nine? You left a message with my roommate."

"I assure you that my memory is in perfect working order, Mr. Slade. I made no such call." Hadley glared up at him from beneath dense eyebrows. "Our meeting was at eight."

He was an old man.

Not until recently had Daniel Matherly thought of himself as aged. He had refused to acknowledge his elderly status far past the reasonable time to do so. Unsolicited literature mailed to him by the AARP was discarded unopened, and he declined to take advantage of senior citizen discounts.

Lately, however, the reflection in his mirror was tough to dispute, and his joints made an even better argument that he was definitely a . . . graduating senior.

Today, as he sat behind his desk in his home study, Daniel was amused by his own thoughts. If reflecting on one's life wasn't proof of advancing age, what was? His preoccupation with his degenerating body was a firm indication that it was degenerating. Who else but the very old dwelled on such things?

Young people didn't have the time. They didn't ponder death because they were too busy living. Getting an education. Pursuing their chosen profession. Entering or exiting marriages. Rearing children. They couldn't be bothered with thoughts of death. "Mortality" was just a word that they kept shelved to think about in the distant future. Occasionally they might glance at it and grow uneasy, but their attention was hastily diverted to matters related to living, not dying.

But the distant future inexorably drew closer until the day arrived when one could no longer save the topic of his own mortality for later contemplation, when one must take it from the shelf and examine it closely. Daniel wasn't morbidly fixated on the inevitable, but he knew that the time had come for him to address it and consider all its implications.

The faithful Maxine thought that he slumbered peacefully every night, but he didn't. When he told Maris that he slept like a baby, she had no reason to doubt him. As a young man, he had never required more than four or five hours of sleep per night. Those required hours had decreased in proportion to his aging. Now, if he was lucky, on any given night he would sleep for two or three hours.

The others he spent lying in bed reading his beloved books—classics he had devoured as a boy, bestsellers that other houses had been lucky enough to publish and profit from, books he himself had edited and published.

When he wasn't reading, he reflected on his life—his proud moments and, in fairness, those he wasn't proud of. He thought frequently about the prep school friend who had died of leukemia. If he'd been born several decades later, he probably would have been treated and cured to live a long and fulfilling life. To this day, Daniel missed him and longed for the years of friendship they had been denied.

He remembered the pain of losing his first love to another man. Looking back, he acknowledged that the young lady's choice had been right for both of them, but at the time, he had believed he would die of a broken heart. He never saw her after her wedding day. He heard that she and her husband had moved to California. He wondered if her life there had been happy. He wondered if she was still living.

His first wife had been a lovely woman, and he'd been devastated when she died. But then he'd met Rosemary, Maris's mother, and she had been, without question, the love of his life. Beautiful, charming, gracious, artistic, intelligent, a perfect companion and ardent lover. She had been supportive of a husband who put in long hours at the office and was too often distracted by the pressures of managing a business. He had appreciated her patience and devotion to him and their marriage but was certain he had failed to let her know the extent of his appreciation.

In hindsight, he regretted all the times his responsibilities at Matherly Press had kept him from Rosemary. He wished he had those days back. His choices would be different. He would rearrange his priorities, appropriate more time and energy to his family.

Or, in all honesty, he would probably make the same bad choices, commit the same mistakes all over again.

Thankfully, his regrets were few and minor, although there were a couple of major ones. Once he had fired an editor out of pique, over a silly difference of opinion. Slyly, he had leaked the secret that the man was homosexual, this at a time when it wasn't accepted or even tolerated. He hinted that the man's personal life had begun affecting his work—which was an outright lie. The man was an excellent editor and his work ethic was impeccable.

Despite his qualifications, no one would hire him because of Daniel's rumor. He became a pariah in the industry he loved and ultimately moved away from the city. Daniel's spite had ruined the man's promising career and had cost publishing a talented contributor. He would carry the guilt over that to his grave.

Several years following Rosemary's death, he had engaged in an affair he wasn't proud of. It had been difficult for a middle-age bachelor to conduct a romance while living with a teenage daughter. It required finesse and a constant juggling of schedules. The woman had been jealous of his relationship with Maris. She became demanding, continually forcing him to choose between her and Maris. Daniel finally let his head overrule his desire. He realized that he could never love anyone who didn't love and accept his daughter wholly, completely, and without reservation. He ended the affair.

Through decades he had managed to maintain his reputation as an excellent publisher. He seemed to have been blessed with a sixth sense for which manuscripts to grab and which to decline. During his tenure, he had increased the company's worth a hundredfold. He had earned more money than he could possibly spend, more than Maris could spend in her lifetime, and probably more than her children could spend.

Money was a nice by-product of his success, but it wasn't what motivated him. His drive came from wanting to preserve what his ancestors had worked so painstakingly to create. Before he turned thirty, he had inherited the stewardship of the family business. It had fallen to him to protect and improve it for the next generation.

Which was Maris, his crowning achievement. She was a thousand times more precious to him than Matherly Press, and he was more dedicated to protecting her than he was to protecting his publishing house from the wolves that got bigger and hungrier each year.

He couldn't shelter her completely, of course. No parent could spare his child life's knocks, and even if he could, it would be unfair. Maris had to live her own life, and integral to living were mishaps and mistakes.

He only hoped that her disappointments wouldn't be too severe, that her triumphs and joys would outnumber them, and that when she reached his age, if she was fortunate to live that long, she would look back on her life with at least the same degree of satisfaction as he had been graced to do.

He wasn't afraid of death. To no one's knowledge, save Maxine's, he'd had several recent discussions with a priest. Rosemary had been a devout and practicing Catholic. He'd never converted, but he had absorbed some of her faith through osmosis. He firmly believed that they would enjoy the afterlife together.

He didn't fear dying.

He did fear dying a fool.

That was the worry that had robbed him of sleep last night. Deeply troubled, he'd been unable to read the nighttime hours away. Morning had brought no relief from this pervasive uneasiness.

He couldn't shake the feeling that he was missing something, that a revealing word or deed or demeanor that he would have detected when he was younger and sharper—five years ago, even one year ago—was escaping him.

Was this paranoia valid? Or a symptom of encroaching dementia?

Before his grandfather's death, Daniel remembered him ranting about his nurse's thievery. One day he accused her of being a German spy on a mission to assassinate U.S. war veterans. With the conviction of the mentally unhinged, he had claimed that the housekeeper was pregnant with his child. Nothing could convince him that the sixty-seven-year-old Englishwoman couldn't possibly be with child.

Was that where he was headed? Was this obscure and unnamed disquiet the harbinger of full-blown senility?

Or—and this is what he chose to believe—was it an indication that he had lost none of his faculties, that he was as astute as ever, and that the intuitiveness that had successfully guided him through fifty years of publishing was still reliable?

Until they proved to be untrustworthy, he chose to trust his instincts. They were telling him that something wasn't right. He sensed it as a stag senses the presence of a stalking hunter from a mile away.

Perhaps he was just overly troubled by Maris's unhappiness. She wasn't as good as she believed at concealing her feelings from him. He'd picked up signals of marital disharmony. The cause and severity of that disharmony he didn't yet know. But if it was disharmonious enough to visibly disturb Maris, it disturbed him.

And then there was Noah. He wanted to trust the man both as a protégé and as a son-in-law, but only if Noah deserved his trust.

Grunting with the effort, Daniel brought his leather desk chair upright and opened a desk drawer. He withdrew his day planner and unzipped it, then removed a business card from one of the smaller compartments.

"William Sutherland," the card read. No company name or address. Only that name and a telephone number engraved in crisp navy blue block letters.

Daniel thoughtfully fingered the card, as he often had since obtaining it several weeks ago. He hadn't called the number. He hadn't yet spoken to Mr. Sutherland personally, but after this morning's ruminations, he felt that the time was right to do so.

It was a sneaky and underhanded thing to do. Merely thinking about it made him feel deceitful. No one ever need know, of course. Unless—God forbid—something came of it. Probably nothing would. Probably he was overreacting. But it wasn't within his makeup to be careless. There was too much at stake to let twinges of guilt overshadow prudence. Given a choice between conscience and caution, there was no choice. The adage applied: Better to be safe than sorry.

As he reached for the telephone, he resolved to be more watchful, alert to nuances in speech and expressions, more attuned to what was going on around him. He didn't want to be the last to know . . . anything.

He didn't fear dying. But he did fear dying a fool.

"You should stay away from it. It's ready to fall down," Mike told Maris as he took a swipe at the mantel with a piece of fine sandpaper.

"If it's that dilapidated, is it safe for Parker to go there alone?"

"Of course not. But try telling him that."

"Mike . . ."

Sensing her hesitation, he turned toward her.

"Never mind," she said. "It wouldn't be fair to either you or Parker for me to ask."

"About . . . ?"

"His disability."

"No, it wouldn't be fair."

She nodded, shook off the solemn mood, and asked, "How do I get there?"

"It could be dangerous."

"I promise to run if it starts to fall down."

"I wasn't talking about the building. I meant you could be in danger from Parker. He doesn't like to be disturbed."

"I'll take my chances. Is it close enough to walk?"

"Do you walk a lot in New York?"

"Every day, if the weather's good."

"Then it's close enough to walk."

After giving directions, he cautioned her once again. "He won't like it when you show up."

"Probably not," she replied, laughing lightly.

She had spent all day indoors, reading until her eyes felt strained. It was good to get outside, although by no stretch of the imagination could this be referred to as "fresh air." The heat was impossible, the humidity worse. The sunlight was glaring and relentless, but even shade offered little relief from the sweltering heat.

Still, the island was exotically beautiful, and the climate was essential to it. The live oak trees had an ancient, almost mystical dignity that was enhanced by the curly Spanish moss draping their limbs. The dense air smelled of salt water and fish, not altogether unpleasant when mingled with the intoxicating perfumes of the flowering plants that bloomed in profusion.

Maris passed a house that was set well back from the road. Children were playing in the yard. The boy and girl were young enough to dance around the lawn sprinkler without self-consciousness. They squealed in glee as they took turns leaping over the oscillating spray.

At another house, she spotted a large dog lying in the shade of a pickup truck. She crossed the road and watched him warily as she moved past, but she needn't have worried. He raised his head, looked at her with disinterest, stood, stretched, made three tight circles in the dirt, then resumed his original spot and closed his eyes.

She met no cars on the road. Her only company were the cicadas that buzzed loudly but lazily under cover of the thick foliage.

The abandoned cotton gin was located right were Mike had said it would be, although if his directions hadn't been so precise she might have missed it. The forest had reclaimed the structure. From some angles, it would have been totally camouflaged by the greenery that enfolded it.

To reach it from the road, one had to take a crushed-shell path. It wasn't much of a path, however. Maris regarded it dubiously. It was no more than a yard wide, at most. Tall weeds grew on either side of it. Looking down at her bare ankles, she seriously considered passing up the gin in favor of the island's other points of interest that Mike had recommended.

"'Fraidy-cat," she muttered.

She looked around for a stick, and when she found one that was suitable, she started up the path, reaching far out in front of her to beat at the tall weeds. She wanted to alert any varmints, reptilian or otherwise, to her presence and give them an opportunity to relocate before she saw them.

Thankfully, she made it up the path without encountering any local fauna. She dropped her stick, dusted off her hands, and took a good look at the hulking building. It was, as Mike had described, a structure on the brink of collapse.

The wood was gray and weathered. The tin roof had been corroded by rust. Large patches of the exterior and part of the roof were covered by an impenetrable carpet of vines. One species bloomed bright purple flowers that seemed incompatible with the overall feeling of dilapidation and abandonment.

With misgiving, Maris approached the wide door that was standing open. The interior was even larger than indicated by the exterior. It was cavernous and dark inside, with only an occasional stripe of sunlight shining through a separation in the vertical wooden slats that formed the walls or a miniature spotlight cast on the dirt floor by a hole in the roof.

The rear half of the lower story was covered by a loft. The ceiling of the overhang was built of massive wood beams. A large wheel about ten feet in diameter was situated just beneath this ceiling and was connected to the dirt floor by a wood column as big around as a barrel. Maris had never seen anything like it.

She blinked to adjust her eyes to the gloom. "Hello?" Receiving no answer, she stepped inside and took a few hesitant steps forward. "Parker?" After a moment, she repeated, "Hello?"

"Here."

She jumped and flattened her hand against her heart, coming about quickly. He was in a corner behind her, invisible except for one ray of sunlight coming through the roof and reflecting off the chrome of his chair.

Recovering, she asked crossly, "Didn't you hear me?"

"Are you serious? All that thrashing? You'd never make it as an Indian brave."

"Then why didn't you say something?"

"How'd you get here?"

"Walked. How'd you get here?"

"How do I get everywhere?"

"You can roll your chair along that path?"

"I manage."

He remained where he was, but she could feel him looking at her and realized that she must appear only a silhouette against the square of light behind her. She advanced farther inside but only a few steps.

"Where'd you get the clothes?"

She glanced down at her casual skirt, shirt, and sandals as though she'd never seen them before. It was an outfit she usually took to their country house for a summer weekend of cookouts and antique shopping. She'd packed it herself in New York just two days ago, but it seemed much longer ago than that and much farther away.

"Mike arranged for my suitcase to be picked up at the hotel and sent over. He went to the dock and met the boat."

"He's gone dotty."

"Pardon?"

"He's got a crush on you."

"He's just being nice."

"We've had this conversation already."

They had. She didn't want to repeat it. The last time, it had ended . . . She didn't want to think about how it had ended.

A silence ensued. Her eyes had adjusted to the dimness, but she could still barely see him where he remained in the deep shadows of the corner. To fill the awkward silence, she said, "This is a picturesque building."

"Which you accidentally happened upon?"

"Mike gave me directions."

"Mike talks too much."

"Not that much. He gives away none of your secrets."

"Until a few minutes ago this building was my secret. I come here to be alone."

She ignored the implication that he didn't welcome her company and took a look around. The dirt floor was littered with animal droppings and trash. At one time, someone had built a fire. Traces of ash and charred wood were still scattered about. A staircase attached to one wall led up to the second level, but many of the steps were missing, and those that remained appeared incapable of supporting anything heavier than a beetle.

All in all, it was a spooky old place, especially the rear portion with its low overhang and antiquated industrial apparatus that looked to her like something an evil giant might use to physically torture an enemy giant. She couldn't imagine why Parker chose to spend time here.

"What's its history?"

"Do you know anything about cotton?"

Cheekily she quoted a popular TV commercial. "'It's the fabric of our lives.'"

To her surprise, Parker laughed. A real laugh, not that scornful sound that usually served as his laughs. Taking advantage of this rarity, she added, "It's also useful when it comes to removing nail polish."

His laughter subsided, making the resulting silence even more noticeable. Then he said gruffly, "Come here."

Parker waited out her hesitation. He didn't repeat the request, figuring she would call his implied dare, and she did. After a moment or two of consideration, she carefully picked her way across the distance separating them.

Her hair had been gathered into a makeshift ponytail that subtracted at least five years from her appearance. Her white shirt was tied in a knot at her waist. Her khaki skirt was short enough to show a couple inches of thigh. Smooth, shapely thighs that invited libidinous speculation.

"When this gin was first built," he said, "three sides of it were left open. The machinery was animal-powered."

"Animal-powered?"

"Follow me."

He wheeled toward the back of the building. As she followed him beneath the overhang, she reflexively ducked her head, causing him to smile. She had cleared the low, spider-infested ceiling, but not by much.

"I've never had that problem myself," he said. He then pointed to the faint ring in the hard-packed earth. "If you look closely, you can see a circular depression there in the dirt. That's the path worn by the mules that turned the drive wheel that powered the gin stand."

"Up there?"

"Right. When cotton was king, it was brought here by the wagonload. Long-strand sea island cotton. High grade. Silky in texture and more easily separated from its seeds than other varieties."

"Therefore very desirable."

He nodded. "And the island's sandy soil was ideal for growing it. It was unloaded onto a platform outside and carried up to the second floor, where the gin separated the fiber from the seeds.

"The lint was then blown out, collected, and carried to an outdoor screw press, which was also mule-powered. Once it was pressed into bales, they were bagged and hauled cross-island to the dock for transport to the cotton exchanges on the mainland."

"It sounds very labor-intensive."

"You're right. From the time a cotton seed was planted in early spring until the last bale of the crop was shipped out, the process took a year."

"Was this the only gin on the island?"

"Right again. One planter, one gin, one family. The family that built my house. They had a monopoly that made them rich until the whole market collapsed. They tried to switch to oyster canning, which was being done on other sea islands, but they didn't know anything about it, went completely broke within a year, and cleared out."

"So this structure more or less chronicles the island's history."

"Nineteenth century history for sure," he said. "It's documented that in 1878 a little girl, a child of a worker, walked behind one of the mules turning the screw press outside. The ornery animal kicked her in the head. She died two days later. Her father put down the mule, execution-style. The details of what he did to the carcass are gruesome. A duel between feuding brothers is also recorded. They shot and killed each other in 1855.

"Then there's a romantic myth about the love affair between a white overseer and a beautiful slave woman. It's told that their affair was looked upon with such vicious disfavor that they were cast off the island in a small boat. It's said they were bound for Charleston, but folks watching their departure through spyglasses reported that they saw them capsize and perish, which many thought was a befitting punishment.

"However, years later, a colony of mulattos was discovered living peacefully on another sea island previously thought to be uninhabited. These people were believed to be the descendants of the mixed couple and the survivors of a shipwrecked slave ship. They were an incredibly handsome clan. Some had skin the color of café au lait and eyes as green as jade.

"A visiting French nobleman, who was deep-sea fishing in the area, sought refuge from a storm on their island. While he was there, one of the nubile young ladies caught his eye and captured his heart. They married and he took all her family back to France with him. Where they lived happ'ly ever after."

Maris drew in a long, slow breath. "You tell good stories, Parker."

"It's a fable. Probably untrue."

"It's still a good story."

"So you're a romantic?"

"Unabashed." She smiled, then said, "You know a lot about the gin. Was your family in the cotton business?"

"I think my great-granddaddy picked it by hand during the Depression. But so did just about every able-bodied person in the South. Women, children, blacks, whites, all struggling to survive. Hunger doesn't discriminate."

"What did your father do?"

"Physician. Family practice. The gamut. From delivering babies to lancing boils."

"Is he retired?"

He shook his head. "He couldn't break a forty-year habit, and he couldn't heal himself when lung cancer caught up with him. He died long before he should have."

"And your mother?"

"Outlived him twelve years. She died several years ago. And before you ask, I'm an only child."

"So am I."

"I know."

After registering momentary surprise that he knew that, she said, "Oh. The article."

"Yeah."

Several strands of hair had come loose from her ponytail and were lying against her nape. The wheat-colored strands appeared slightly damp and curled from the humidity. He caught himself staring at them.

He looked away to clear his vision. "Yeah, that article was chock-full of information about you, your father, and your husband. What's he like?"

"Very robust. Especially for a man of seventy-eight."

"I meant your husband. Is he also very robust?"

"We agreed not to ask any personal questions."

"That's personal? What don't you want me to know about your husband?"

"Nothing. It's not that."

"Then what?"

"I followed you here to talk about *Envy.*"

"Want to sit down?"

Apparently confused by his sudden shift of topic, she shook her head. "There's nowhere to sit." She glanced at the beams overhead. "Besides, it's creepy under here."

He swept his arm toward the front part of the building and she preceded him from beneath the overhang. Her attention was drawn to a circle of bricks in the dirt floor. They were stacked two deep, forming an enclosure roughly five feet in diameter. "What's that?"

"Careful," Parker warned as he quickly rolled his chair to her side. "That's an abandoned well."

"Why in here?"

"One of the more innovative patriarchs of the cotton dynasty decided to convert the gin to steam power. He began digging this well for the water supply, but died of diphtheria before the project was completed. His heir abandoned the idea as impractical. Rightly, I believe. It wasn't economically feasible for the amount of their production."

She peered over the rim of bricks into the darkness of the hole. "How deep is it?"

"Deep enough."

"For what?"

After holding her gaze for a moment, he backed up, then wheeled past her. He hitched his chin toward an upended crate. "That'll do for a perch if you're not too particular."

After testing the crate's sturdiness, she gingerly sat down on the rough wood.

"Be careful of splinters," he warned. "Although my picking them out of the backs of your thighs is a bewitching thought."

She shot him a withering look. "I'll take care not to fidget."

"I'm sure I would enjoy extracting the splinters, but I'm equally sure your very robust husband wouldn't approve."

"Was that thunder?"

"Changing the subject, Maris?"

"Yes."

Grinning, he glanced over his shoulder toward the open door. It had grown noticeably darker outside as well as in. "Afternoon thunderstorms frequently boil up during the summer. Sometimes they pass over in an hour or less, sometimes they linger through the night. You never can tell." Overhead the first raindrops struck the roof with fat-sounding slaps.

She inhaled deeply. "You can smell the rain."

"Smells good, doesn't it?"

"Sounds wonderful, too."

"Um-huh."

The rain didn't cool the air much, but it had a definite effect on the atmosphere. It became closer, denser. He was aware of it. And so was Maris. She probably couldn't characterize this sudden change any better than he could, but it was distinctly felt.

Her eyes moved away from watching the rain through the open door and found his. They stared at each other through the deepening gloom. Oddly, it wasn't an uncomfortable exchange. If he'd been forced to use an applicable adverb to describe the way in which they were looking at one another, he would choose "expectantly," a modifier that combined curiosity with caution, wonderment with undertones of wariness.

He felt her gaze like a tug on his chest drawing him closer, and he was looking at her with the same level of intensity. Given the electricity arcing between them, he was curious to know what she would say.

She played it safe by commenting on *Envy*. "That was a rotten trick that Todd played on Roark."

"Rigging it so he missed his appointment with Hadley."

"You set me up perfectly. I didn't see it coming."

"That's good."

"Now what is Roark going to do about it?"

"What do you think he should do?"

"Beat the hell out of Todd."

He whistled at her vehemence.

"Well, isn't that what a guy would do?"

"Probably," he replied. "Fury would be his initial reaction, and he would seek a physical outlet. But let's talk about it. Remember, Todd was only paying Roark back for the toothbrush stunt."

"But that was a prank," she exclaimed. "Gross and disgusting, granted. But college boys do stuff like that to each other, don't they?"

"Did you know college boys who did stuff like that?"

"I attended a girls' school."

"Right, right, I read that," he said, as though just reminded of that part of her bio, which he knew as well as if he'd written it himself. "So it's safe to assume that you have no experience of college boys and how they act."

"No, it's safe to assume that my experience is limited to how they act on dates with girls, which is different from how they interact with each other."

"Is that how you met your husband? On a date during college?"

"Much later than that."

"How much later?"

"When he came to work at Matherly Press."

"Smart move on his part. He married the boss's daughter."

That irked her. So much so that Parker knew he wasn't the first to connect those two dots. It had crossed her mind, too. Perhaps too often for comfort. Her expression turned professional and peeved.

"Can we get back to your book, please?"

"Sure. Sorry for the digression."

While taking a moment to collect her thoughts, she pulled her lower lip through her teeth a couple of times and absently fiddled with a button on her blouse. Parker wondered when those two insignificant, subconsciously feminine gestures had become so goddamn sexy.

"A prank is one thing," she said. "But Todd's joke had a meanness about it that was unmistakable. It wasn't harmless. It couldn't be undone as easily as buying a new toothbrush. He was tinkering with Roark's future. This practical joke could damage Roark's grade, compromise his capstone, affect his writing ambitions, and possibly even crush them. He can't let it pass and do nothing."

"True. Roark won't fold. He won't easily forgive the experience, but it'll sure as hell motivate him."

"Yes, yes," she said excitedly. "This will fuel his determination to succeed."

"To reach a level of success that Todd will—"

"Envy," she said, finishing the thought for him.

He grinned. "Per your suggestion, I'll let him blow off steam, land a few punches, which Todd will concede he deserved."

"So they remain friends?"

"It wouldn't be a book if they didn't. If their friendship fell apart here, the story would be over."

"Not necessarily. It could be just as powerful if they became bitter enemies at this point."

"Wait and see, Maris."

"What?"

"Give me time."

Her eyes widened marginally. "You've got it plotted already, don't you?"

"For the most part," he confessed with a negligent shrug. "There are some details still to hammer out."

She tried, but failed, to looked piqued. "You've been stringing me along."

"To get you excited."

"I'm excited." Her animation proved it. "May I make another suggestion?"

"I don't promise to take it."

"Agreed."

"Then fire away."

"Could we see Roark falling in love?"

"With the girl who went back to her boyfriend?"

"Yes. You told the reader that he fell in love, but we didn't get to see it. We didn't experience it along with him. You don't even give this girl a name. I think it could be very poignant, as well as useful toward developing his character. How he handles the disappointment. That kind of thing. And what if . . ."

"Go on," he said when she hesitated.

"What if Todd were somehow involved in their breakup?"

Frowning, he thoughtfully scratched his cheek, reminding him that he hadn't shaved that morning. "Wouldn't that be too much antagonism too soon? In those first few chapters, I'm trying to establish that these two guys are truly friends. Eventually the friendship is overtaken and then ultimately destroyed by their competitiveness. But if Todd interferes with Roark's love life, then screws him over with Hadley, that immediately makes him out the villain and Roark the hero."

"Isn't that the way it's supposed to be? I think of them that way."

"You do?"

"You're surprised?"

"The story isn't over yet. By the time you get to the ending, you might change your mind."

Her eyes probed his, as though trying to see the denouement behind them. "I really don't have a choice, do I?"

"No."

"Okay. In the meantime, what do you think of my suggestion about Roark's love life?"

"I repeat, Maris, give me time."

She leaned forward eagerly. "You've already changed it, haven't you? There's more, isn't there? Same girl?"

"Why don't you have your navel pierced?"

"I beg your pardon?"

"If you're going to wear hip-riding skirts and shirts that tie at the waist, why don't you have—"

"I heard you."

"Then why?"

"Because I don't want to."

"Too bad."

"The thought of it gives me the willies."

"A small loop. A tiny diamond stud. It'd be sexy. Er. *Sexier.*" His eyes moved up from her midsection to her face. "Those glimpses of your belly button are already a major turn-on."

She squared her shoulders. "Parker, if we're going to have a professional relationship, you cannot talk to me like that."

"I can talk to you any damn way I please."

She gave a stubborn shake of her head. "Not if you want to work with me, you can't."

"You're free to go."

But she stayed seated on the crate, as he'd known she would. As he'd hoped she would.

Thunder rumbled and rain pelted the roof, but the racket only emphasized the strained silence between them. Parker rolled his chair closer to her until his knees were only inches from hers. "What did you tell your husband?"

"About what?"

"Being here. I assume you called him."

"I did. I left word that things were going well."

"Left word?"

"With his secretary."

"He doesn't have a cell phone? See, he strikes me as the kind of guy who would have one of those damn things practically glued to his ear."

"He was having lunch with the editor of our electronic publishing division. I didn't want to interrupt them. I'll call him later."

"As you're going to bed?"

"Possibly. What difference does it make?"

"I was just wondering if you'll be wearing a nightie tonight. Or do you always sleep sans raiment like you did last night?"

"Parker—"

"What'll you talk about?"

"None of your damn business."

"That good, huh? Or that bad?"

She drew a deep breath and said tightly, "I'll tell him that I've discovered an extremely talented writer who—"

"Please, I'm blushing."

"Who is also the crudest, rudest, most obnoxious man I've ever met."

He grinned. "Well, that would be the truth." Then his smile gradually faded. Giving the wheels of his chair a small push, he rolled another inch or two nearer to her. "I bet you won't tell him I kissed you," he said in low voice. "I bet you omit that part."

She stood up hastily, knocking the crate over backward. She tried going around him, but he moved equally fast and used his chair to block her path. "Get out of my way, Parker. I'm going back to the house now."

"It's raining."

"I won't melt."

"Melt down, maybe. You're angry. Or afraid."

"I'm not afraid of you."

"Then sit back down." When she failed to move, he motioned toward the door. "Fine. Go. Get drenched. Which will mean making explanations to Mike. It'll get messy, but if that's what you want . . ."

She glanced outside at the downpour, then reluctantly upturned the crate and resumed her seat on it, primly and looking pissed.

"Tell me how you met your husband, Maris."

"Why?"

"I want to know."

"What for?"

"Call it creative curiosity."

"Call it nosiness."

"You're right. Euphemisms are a crutch. I'm nosy."

Gauging her expression, he expected her to clam up and refuse to continue their conversation, but she folded her arms across her middle—no doubt to hide her navel—and said, "Noah came to work at Matherly Press. But long before that, I knew him by reputation as the brains behind a rival publishing house. When he joined us, I was thrilled at the opportunity to be working with him. Over time, however, I realized that my feelings ran much deeper than admiration for a colleague. I was in love with him.

"At first my father was concerned about my entering into an

office romance. He was also worried that Noah is ten years older than I. He encouraged me to date other men and even dabbled in some blatant matchmaking with sons and nephews of his friends and associates. But Noah was the one I wanted. Luckily he felt the same. We married." She bobbed her head for punctuation. "There. Satisfied?"

"How long have you been married?"

"Almost two years."

"Children?"

"No."

"How come?"

She glared at him and he held up a hand in conciliation. "You're right, that's too personal. If you're sterile—"

"I'm not."

"So it's him?"

She was about to come off the crate again, but he patted the air between them. "Okay, okay, the topic of children is taboo. I won't go there." He paused as though realigning his thoughts. "So you were seeing Noah every day at work and fell head over heels in no time."

"Actually I had had a mad crush on him even before I met him."

"How's that?"

"I had read his book."

The Vanquished.

"You know it? Oh, of course, the article again. It referenced Noah's novel."

"Yes, but I was already familiar with it," he said. "I'd read it when it came out."

"So did I. About fifty times."

"Are you kidding?"

"No. I love it. The main character, Sawyer Bennington, became the man in my romantic fantasies."

"You have fantasies?"

"Doesn't everyone? It's nothing to be ashamed of."

"Maybe not for you. But I've had some fantasies that were pretty shameful. Want to hear them?"

"You're irrepressible."

"That's exactly how my preschool teacher described me to my mom."

"When . . . ?"

"When for three days straight she caught me in the boys' restroom test-driving my new favorite toy."

"I won't even ask."

"You'd be better off not to. Anyway, what were we talking about?"

"Sawyer Bennington."

"Right. Your hero and the object of your romantic fantasies. Which strikes me as strange."

"Why?"

"Wasn't he a criminal of some sort?"

"A thief and a murderer."

"Generally considered criminal."

"But his crimes were justified because of what was done to his wife and child. When he discovered their bodies, I cried buckets. I still cry every time I read it." Her expression turned dreamy and wistful.

"Sawyer is such a hard man. With everybody except Charlotte. They loved so passionately, and it was the kind of love that even death couldn't destroy. When they hanged him for his crimes, he was thinking about . . ."

Her voice trailed off. Embarrassed, she gave a slight shrug. "Forgive me, Parker. I guess you can tell how much I love that novel."

"You talk about the characters as though they're real."

"Noah did such a fantastic job of drawing them that sometimes I forget they're fiction. I actually start missing them. When I do, I open my copy to any page and read a few paragraphs, and it's like I've visited them."

"Didn't they make a movie?"

"It was junk that didn't do the book justice. But to be fair to the movie makers, I don't think any movie could have. Some critics touted *The Vanquished* as the best historical novel since *Gone with the Wind*."

"Strong praise."

"But, in my opinion, warranted."

"So what'd he follow it with?"

"He didn't." Her exuberance waned considerably. "Noah got very involved with publishing *The Vanquished* and decided that his calling was in that arena, not writing. And, I suppose, when your debut novel receives such critical and popular acclaim, the thought of following it with something equally good is daunting. Even terrifying. He never wrote again. Not until recently."

Parker's gaze sharpened. "He's writing again?"

"He's set up an office specifically for that purpose. I'm very pleased."

But she didn't look very pleased, or even moderately pleased. A shallow but distinct vertical line had formed between her eyebrows. Parker doubted she realized how revealing her facial expressions were or she would school them better.

After a quiet moment, he asked, "What other fictional characters have played key roles in your fantasies?"

"Several," she admitted with a light laugh. "But none to the extent of Sawyer Bennington."

Parker leaned forward in his chair and spoke only loud enough to be heard above the pounding rain. "Maris? Is it remotely possible that you fell in love with the character and not the author?"

Her expression turned angry, but the anger came and went with the speed of a lightning flash. She smiled with chagrin. "Considering the way I've carried on about Sawyer, I suppose that's a fair question. I've had authors tell me that readers frequently superimpose them onto a character they've created, and that when readers meet them at book signings, they're disappointed to find that they're ordinary people. They don't live up to the larger-than-life image the reader had formed of them."

"Good discourse, but it didn't answer any question."

Her irritation returned. "Don't be ridiculous. I fell in love with my husband. His talent first and then the man himself. I'm still in love with him."

He stared at her for a long moment. "What was he thinking?"

"Who, Noah?"

He shook his head. "The hero of the book. Sawyer. You said when they hanged him he was thinking . . ."

"Oh. He was thinking about the first time he saw Charlotte." She hesitated, but Parker motioned for her to continue.

"Noah wrote that passage so vividly, with such detail, that I could see the orchard, smell the ripening fruit, feel the heat. Sawyer had been traveling for days, remember? He comes upon Charlotte's family's farm, where he hopes to get water for himself and his horse.

"No one is around, the place seems deserted. But as he makes his way toward the water trough, he spots Charlotte sleeping on a pallet of quilts in the shade of a peach tree. A baby is sleeping beside her. Sawyer assumes the child is hers." Maris smiled and added softly, "He's glad to learn later that the child is her baby brother."

Parker was entranced by the cadence of her voice. He felt himself being pulled into the scene.

"Charlotte is the most beautiful woman Sawyer has ever seen. Her long hair was unbound. Descriptions of it, her complexion, her lips, go on for paragraphs. Because of the heat, she had raised her dress as high as her knees, and she's barefoot. Sawyer is a lusty young man. Seeing her bare calf and foot inflames him. She might just as well have been naked. He's fascinated by the breathing motion of her bosom. And yet, there's a reverent aspect to his admiration of her, as though she were as untouchable as the Madonna.

"He should have been a gentleman and politely withdrawn

the moment he saw her. Instead, he stays and gazes at her until he hears a wagon approaching, announcing the return of her family, who had gone into town for supplies.

"Charlotte never knew that Sawyer had watched her sleeping that day. He never told her, which I think was particularly dear of him. It was too special a memory to share even with her. It was so special that he called it forward on the day of his execution. He was reliving it when the trapdoor of the gallows dropped open beneath him. Because it was the most pivotal day of his life, he died reliving his first sight of Charlotte."

Parker had listened. Motionless. Intent on every word. For several moments after she stopped speaking, they just looked at one another. Neither was capable of dispelling the mood, or willing to.

When he finally spoke, his voice was abnormally husky. "You should have been the writer, Maris."

"Me? No," she said, shaking her head and laughing softly. "I envy the gift. I can recognize it in those who've been blessed with it, but I'm a facilitator, not a creator."

He pondered that for a time, then said, "Do you know what made that scene so erotic?"

She tilted her head inquisitively.

"It was his having that much access to a woman, his having cerebral intimacy with her, without her knowledge."

"Yes."

"His eyes and mind had touched what his hands and lips wanted to. He hadn't seen much, but he felt guilty for looking at all."

"The forbidden."

He nodded and said in an even lower voice, "The strongest sexual stimulant of all. What isn't good for us. What we can't have. What we want so badly we can taste but can't touch."

Maris drew in a shaky little breath and exhaled it slowly. For the first time becoming aware of the loose strands of hair on her neck, she raised her hand to them, but repair seemed beyond her. She lowered her hand back to her lap, but not before it made a brief stop at that button she had fiddled with before. This time, she merely brushed it with her fingertips as though to reassure herself that it was still there. But Parker's gaze fastened on it and remained.

Suddenly she stood up in the narrow space separating them. "I'm going back now. The rain has stopped."

That wasn't altogether true. It had stopped coming down so hard, but it was still raining lightly. Parker didn't argue, however. He let her pass.

Almost.

Before she could take a full step, he reached out and stopped her with his hands. They clasped her just below her waist, the heels of them pressing her hipbones, his fingers curved back toward her hips. He was eye level with that alluring strip of bare skin between blouse and skirt. Slowly, his eyes moved up.

She was looking down at him, startled and apprehensive. Her arms were raised, her hands in front of her shoulders as though she were unsure where to place them, what to do with them.

"We know why I kissed you last night, Maris."

"To frighten me off."

He frowned. "That doesn't even merit an argument. I kissed you because you braved Terry's and showed up everybody in the place, including me. I kissed you because just looking at you made me ache. I kissed you because I'm a rotten son of a bitch and your mouth looked so goddamn kissable. Simply put, I kissed you because I wanted to. It's something I admit and you damn well know. But there is one question that's driving me fucking crazy."

His eyes focused harder on hers and, by doing so, penetrated. "Why did you kiss me back?"

Maris's call came at an inopportune time, but Noah figured he had better take it to avoid her becoming suspicious. Even though he had a meeting scheduled in ten minutes, he asked his assistant to put her call through. "Darling! I'm so glad to hear from you."

"It's nice to finally talk to you, too," she said. "It's been so long, your voice sounds strange."

"Strange?"

"My ears have become attuned to a southern drawl."

"God help you."

"Even worse, I've actually slipped and said 'y'all' a few times, and I've acquired a taste for grits. The secret is lots of salt and pepper and drenching them in butter."

"Keep packing down a diet like that and you'll return to me fat."

"Don't be surprised if I do. What the southerners don't cook in butter, they cook in bacon grease, and it's all delicious. Have you ever had fried green tomatoes?"

"Like the movie title?"

"And the book. Both named after the real thing. Dredged in

cornmeal, fried in bacon grease, they're scrumptious. Mike taught me how to make them."

"The author extraordinaire also cooks?"

"Mike's not the author. He's . . . well, Mike does just about everything around here except the writing."

Noah checked the sterling Tiffany clock on his desk and wondered when he could gracefully break this off. "Is the book coming along? How's it working out with the author?"

"He's talented, Noah. He's also opinionated, difficult at times, and impossible at others. But he's a challenge I can't resist."

"So the trip has been productive?"

"Yes. And unless there's something that requires me to come home, I'm going to stay here through the weekend and spoon-feed him constructive criticism and encouragement. There's no reason for me to rush back, is there?"

"Besides my missing you, no."

"Your missing me is no small thing."

"I wouldn't selfishly have you return strictly on my account. I can tell by the enthusiasm in your voice that you're enjoying being a hands-on editor again."

"Very much. Are you writing?"

"When I can. I've been busy going over second-quarter reports, but I've managed to put in a couple hours writing each evening." After a short pause, he asked, "You aren't going to start nagging me about my output, are you?"

"I wouldn't call it nagging."

"Just remember it's a part-time job, Maris. It can't take precedence over my responsibilities here."

"I understand. It's just that I'm eager to read something new by my favorite author."

"Don't hold your breath. It might take a while and the process can't be rushed."

"Has your idea gelled?"

"It's getting there," he replied evasively.

"Whatever you write will be well worth the wait."

"If you've got that much time for leisure reading, we're not keeping you busy enough."

"No worry there," she said with a laugh. "I've got my hands full with this project, in addition to the other manuscripts coming due in the next few months. I'll be editing in my sleep."

He liked the sound of that. If she was distracted by work, he'd be freer to devote more time to finalizing his deal with WorldView. He was feeling the pressure of the deadline unexpectedly set by Morris Blume. While it was uncomfortably compressing, he welcomed having a definite goal, a finish line toward which to make a final push.

He wasn't panicked, but he definitely experienced an adrenaline rush every time he thought about it. He was confident he would meet the deadline. If for any reason he didn't, he was equally confident that he could persuade Blume to extend it. The CEO coveted Matherly Press too much to relinquish it over a matter of days.

Meanwhile, this was a perfect time for Maris to be out of town. Her absence made it more convenient for him to manipulate Daniel. The old man had to be carefully finessed. Subtlety was key. Hit Daniel over the head with something, and he would fight it to his dying breath. Stroke him lightly, and his mind could be changed. Perhaps not as easily as most, but Noah didn't doubt his ability to eventually whittle down all of his father-in-law's objections to a merger.

Maris's absence also allowed him more time with Nadia. She could be a harpy if she was unhappy, and she was unhappiest when deprived of the time and attention she felt she deserved.

"I can't wait for you to read this book, Noah," Maris said, drawing him back into their conversation.

What had she been talking about for the last few minutes? Lost in his own thoughts, he hadn't retained a word of what she'd said. He couldn't see that his inattention mattered much.

"The author hasn't shared with me the whole plot," she went on, "but I think it's going to be good."

"If you think it's going to be good, then it will be. Listen, darling, I hate to cut short our conversation, but I'm due down the hall in two minutes."

"So what else is new?" She posed the question tongue-in-cheek and without rancor. Their exchanges during work hours were typically brief.

"I have a meeting with Howard, and you know what a stickler he is about punctuality." Howard Bancroft was Matherly Press's chief counsel and head of the legal department. "If I'm a nanosecond late, he'll stay miffed for days."

"What's the meeting about?"

"I can't recall off the top of my head. Something to do with one of our foreign licensees, I believe."

"I hate to get you on Howard's bad side," she said, "but there is something else I wanted to talk about."

He had to work at keeping the impatience out of his voice. "Then I'll take the time. What's on your mind?"

"Is Dad all right?"

"Seems to be. I saw him last evening and talked to him again this morning."

"He came into the office?"

"No, he called to ask if I could muddle through without him today. I urged him to take off not only today but the remainder of the week. You're not here, so we haven't any scheduled meetings that I can't handle alone. It's an ideal time for him to take it easy."

"He'll get bored."

"Actually he's got a fairly heavy schedule. He said he planned to spend the morning at his desk at home to handle some personal chores, then he was having a late lunch with an old crony. They were meeting at the Four Seasons."

"Lunch with an old crony," she repeated absently. "I hope he doesn't drink too much wine."

"He's certainly earned the right to have a few glasses of wine at lunch if he wants them, Maris."

"I know, but I worry about him negotiating the stairs at home. With that weakness in his joints—"

"He needs full command of his equilibrium. I see your point."

"When someone his age falls and breaks a hip, they sometimes never completely recover. He couldn't abide being bedridden."

"I'll ask Maxine to keep a closer eye on him."

"No! That would start World War Three," she exclaimed. "He'll get mad at her for babying him, and then he'll get mad at me for asking her to."

"Another good point," he said. "How about . . ."

"What?"

"Well, I was going to suggest that I talk to him about it. Caution him confidentially. Man to man."

"Yes," she said, sounding relieved. "I like that plan much better."

"Then I'll go over this evening and have a chat with him."

"Thank you, Noah."

"You're welcome. Anything else?"

"Why?"

"Howard's waiting on me."

"Oh, I'm sorry, I forgot. I shouldn't have kept you."

"Nonsense. This was important." He wanted to end the call quickly, but he didn't want to leave her worrying over Daniel. Concern might bring her rushing back. "Maris, don't worry about Daniel," he said tenderly. "He's a tough old bird, stronger than we give him credit for. There's really no cause for alarm. If anything, over the past few days he's seemed more like his old self. Full of piss and vinegar."

"I'm sure you're right. It's just that when I'm not with him, my imagination gets away from me and I start worrying."

"Unnecessarily, I assure you. Now, forgive me, but I really must run."

"Apologize to Howard for me. Tell him it's all my fault that you're late."

"Don't worry. I will." He chuckled. " 'Bye, now."

"Noah," she added just before he disconnected, "I love you."

For a moment, he was taken aback. Then, in the absent-minded way of a devoted but preoccupied husband, he replied, "I love you, too, darling."

Professions of love meant nothing to him. They were sequences of words without any relevance. He'd told many a woman that he loved her, but only when trying to woo her into bed. He'd vocally expressed his love for Maris when they were courting because it was expected. He'd vowed his love for her in order to win her father's blessing on their marriage, and he'd played the expressive newlywed husband to the hilt. But in the last several months his avowals had become increasingly infrequent.

By contrast, Maris had an affectionate nature. She was touchy-feely to an irritating degree. She declared her love at least once a day, and while he'd become accustomed to hearing it, he still felt no connection to the sentiment.

But this most recent profession of love gave him pause. It wasn't the words themselves that had been curious, but the manner in which she'd spoken them. It had sounded to him almost as though she were trying to reestablish, either in his mind or her own, that she loved him. Had the surprise anniversary party failed to reassure her of his devotion? Did she still suspect him of infidelity?

As he breezed past Bancroft's assistant with barely a nod and entered the counsel's private office, the exchange with Maris lingered on his mind. It had raised questions that required further thought. Her "I love you" had been declared with an undercurrent of desperation. He must determine what, if anything, that signified.

One thing was certain: She would not be proclaiming her

love for him if she knew the contents of the folder he carried into the lawyer's office with him.

"Hello, Howard. Sorry I'm late." He banged ahead to prevent Bancroft from remarking on his tardiness. "I was on the telephone with Maris, informing her that she would be receiving this document either tomorrow or the day after at the latest. She's in the boonies, on the outskirts of nowhere, but she assured me that the parcel carriers deliver."

Without invitation he sat down on an upholstered love seat and spread his arms along the back of it, a study in nonchalance. Looking through the windows behind the attorney's desk, he remarked, "You know, Howard, I don't know what you did to rate this office. It's got an incredible view."

His cavalier attitude was calculated to distract Bancroft from the business at hand. But he knew from experience that the little Jew was no pushover. His wizened appearance added a decade to his age. He stood five feet five inches tall in elevated shoes. He had a bald, pointed head with a distinct knob on the crown. He favored wide suspenders and wore them with tweed trousers regardless of the season. On his nose were perched small round reading glasses. Howard Bancroft looked like a gnome. Or exactly what he was—a shrewd legal mind.

"Is the document ready?" Noah asked, even though the referenced document was lying in plain view on the lawyer's desk.

"It's ready," Bancroft replied.

"Thank you for preparing it so expediently."

Noah leaned forward and reached for the document, but Bancroft laid his heavily veined and spotted hand on it. "Not so fast, Noah. I'm unwilling to let you have this today."

"Why's that?"

"I followed your directives and drew up the document as you requested, but . . . May I be candid?"

"That would save time."

"I was reluctant to write the document as you specified. Its content is troubling."

The lawyer removed his glasses and began polishing them with a large white handkerchief he'd taken from his pants pocket. Shaking it out, it looked to Noah as though he were waving a flag of surrender, which he might just as well do. Howard Bancroft could not win this fight.

"Oh? How is it troubling?" Noah gave his voice just enough edge to caution the attorney that Noah's reasons for requesting the document were not open for discussion. They weren't even to be questioned. Bancroft, however, did not take the hint.

"You're certain that Maris approves of this?"

"I made the request on her behalf, Howard."

"Why does she feel that such a document is necessary?"

"You know as I do, as Maris does, that publishing isn't the gentleman's cottage industry it was a century ago. It's gone cutthroat like everything else. If you stand still in this marketplace, you'd just as well be backing up. If you're merely maintaining the status quo, your competitors will pass you by, and before you can blink, you're in last place. We don't want Matherly Press to be choking on the heel dust of the others, do we?"

"That's a stirring speech, Noah. I suggest you deliver it at the next sales conference to rally the troops. However, I fail to see how the valid points you made relate to either my question or this document."

"That document," Noah said, pointing to it where it still lay on the desk, "is our safety net. Publishing is changing constantly and swiftly. Matherly Press must be prepared for any contingency. We must be able to operate with fluidity, so that if an opportunity arises, it can be immediately seized."

"Without Daniel's consent."

Noah assumed a sad expression. "Ah, Howard, that's the hitch. It breaks Maris's heart, as it does mine, that Daniel is getting on in years. That's a sad fact we've been forced to accept. If he should take a sudden downward turn, say a stroke that renders him incapable of making business decisions, this power of attorney guarantees a smooth transition and protects the company from being pitched into chaos."

"I wrote the provisos, Noah. I know their purpose. I also know that similar documents are already in place and have been for years. Daniel's personal lawyer, Mr. Stern, drew them up when Maris turned twenty-one. I've got copies in my files, so I know that these documents include a living will and, as you say, cover every contingency. Should the unforeseen happen, Maris has been granted full power of attorney to make all Daniel's decisions for him, personally and professionally."

"I'm aware of the previous documents. This one's different."

"Indeed it is. It supersedes the others. It also grants *you* power of attorney to make Daniel's decisions for him."

Noah took umbrage. "Are you suggesting that I'm insinuating myself—"

"No." Bancroft raised his hands, palms out. "Both Daniel and Maris have mentioned to me the need to amend their power of attorney documents to include you. But that responsibility should fall to Mr. Stern, not to me."

"You're more convenient."

"To whom?"

Noah glared at him. "What else do you find so *troubling,* Howard?"

The lawyer hesitated, as though knowing it was ill-advised to continue, but apparently his convictions won out over caution. "It feels sleight of hand. I get the impression that this is being done behind Daniel's back."

"He's authorized it. You said so yourself not thirty seconds ago."

Obviously frustrated, Bancroft ran a hand over his knobby head. "It also bothers me to release such an important document when it hasn't been signed and witnessed in my presence."

"I told Maris that I refuse to sign it until she has," Noah said. "I was adamant about that. She'll have her signature notarized in Georgia. When the document is returned, I'll sign it. As soon as she gets back, we'll meet with Daniel. Frankly, I think he'll be relieved that it's a fait accompli. No one likes to think of himself as vulnerable to incapacity or death. He'll be glad that we relieved him of this responsibility."

"I've never known Daniel Matherly to shrink from life's realities no matter how grim," Bancroft argued. "But, that aside, why not wait until Maris's return and do it all at one time? Explain to me the urgency."

Noah sighed as though getting a grip on his diminishing patience. "Her being away is one reason Maris wanted this done with dispatch. She's working with a reclusive fledgling author. Until his manuscript is finished, she'll be pulled away frequently, and she'll be out of town for extended and unspecified periods of time. Shit happens, Howard. Plane crashes. Car accidents. Sudden illness. In a worst-case scenario, she wants Matherly Press protected."

"Is that why the document becomes valid with your signature alone?"

Noah said tightly, "I told Maris, and I'm telling you, I will not sign it until her signature is in place."

Bancroft exchanged a long stare with him, then shook his head. "I'm sorry, Noah. I need Maris's verification that this is the document she wants, and even then I will advise her to rethink its provisos. They're unorthodox and inconsistent with prudence. I've worked for the Matherlys for a long time. They rely on me always to act in their best interest. Therefore, I'm sure you understand my precaution."

"Which is completely unnecessary, besides being a flagrant insult to me."

"Even so."

"All right. Call Maris." He gestured toward the telephone. It was a bluff, but he was gambling that Bancroft wouldn't call it. "Or better yet, Daniel's at home today. Ask him to come in and review this."

"I'd like to reacquaint myself with their original documents prior to a meeting with either of them. Until I've had an opportunity to do that, I don't wish to waste their time." Bancroft folded his hands on top of the document, a gesture that was a statement in itself. "Unless Daniel or Maris calls me and gives me authorization, I cannot release this document to you today."

Noah leveled a hard look on him. Then he grinned. And grinned wider. He had actually hoped the meeting would result in a standoff between him and Bancroft. He had hoped that the dwarf wouldn't capitulate too soon and spoil his fun. Everything till now had been a warm-up for this, the big finish. He was going to enjoy it to the fullest.

"Well, Howard," he said with soft menace, "it seems as though you suspect me of corporate subterfuge."

"I suspect you of no such thing," the lawyer returned blandly.

"That's good. I'm relieved to hear that. Because I would hate for you to suspect me of duplicity. I find that despicable, don't you? Duplicity. Betrayal. Disloyalty to one's family. One's race."

Noah held the lawyer's gaze as he picked up the folder that he'd brought in with him. Gently he set it on the desk and slid it toward Bancroft, who stared at it with the misgivings of one who must remove the lid from a basket, knowing that a cobra was coiled inside. After a full minute of palpable silence and dread, the attorney opened the cover and began to scan the printed material inside.

"Who would have thought it, Howard?" Noah said. "Your mother fucked Nazis."

Bancroft's narrow shoulders sagged forward.

"See, Howard, knowledge equates to power. I make it a point to learn all I can about the people around me, especially those who could be a hindrance. Investigating your background cost me a lot of money and took up valuable time, but I must say it yielded more than I bargained for.

"I paid your mother a visit in the nursing home where you had sequestered her. After a little arm-twisting, she confessed her shameful secret to me, and, for a nominal fee, an attendant wrote it all down word for word. Your mother signed it. Recognize her signature there on the last page? At that point she was so weak, she could barely hold the pen. Frankly, I wasn't surprised that she died just a few days later.

"You know the story well, Howard, but I was fascinated. She was twenty-three when she was dragged from her home in Poland. The rest of her family, her brothers, sister, parents, were backed against a wall and shot. She was lucky enough to be transported to a concentration camp.

"At that time, in the Old World, twenty-three was borderline spinsterhood. Your mother had prevented her younger sister from marrying an ardent suitor because she hadn't married first. Her inability to attract a man had created quite a rift in the family.

"But at the camp, she received a lot of attention from men. From the guards. See, Howard, your mother bartered her pussy for her life. Routinely. Over the next five years. She came to like the favors she was granted and flaunted them. She could have toiled alongside the other women prisoners, had her head shaved, subsisted on bread and water, lived in daily fear of her life. But no, she fucked her way into comfortable quarters. Ate well. Drank wine. Made merry with Nazis. She was the camp whore. And for that, she was despised.

"Now, is it any wonder she changed her name and created a fictitious history for herself when she emigrated to America?

"That story she told about the Jewish freedom fighter who had sacrificed his life for her and his unborn child was sweet, but it was completely untrue, as you yourself discovered when you were . . . what? Seven? Eight? Old enough to get the gist of the accusations hurled at her. You came home from school one day and asked your mother why everyone called you ugly names and spat on you. That's when she decided to relocate."

Howard Bancroft's hands were trembling so badly that when he removed his eyeglasses this time, he dropped them onto his desk. He covered his eyes and uttered a low moan.

"She couldn't be sure which of the camp guards was your father. She had spread her legs for so many, you see. But she suspected it was an officer who shot himself in the head hours before the Allied troops liberated the camp. You were born four months later. She was too far gone to abort you, I guess. Or maybe she had a soft spot for this particular officer. I've heard that even whores have feelings.

"Howard, Howard, what a nasty secret you've kept. I don't think the Jewish community would look too kindly on you if they knew that your mother happily serviced the men that marched them into the gas chambers, and that your father had ordered thousands of their people to be tortured and exterminated, do you?

"Considering the advocate you've been for Holocaust survivors, they might regard your crusade as hypocritical. Your friends in Israel—which are many, I understand—would revile you. Your blood is tainted with that of a traitorous whore and an Aryan murderer.

"Now, you might say to me, *You can't prove this.* But your reaction is proof enough, isn't it? Besides, I don't need to prove it. The rumor alone would effectively destroy your reputation as a good Jew. Even a hint of something this shameful would do irreparable damage.

"Your family would be shattered. Because even your wife and children believe the fabrication that you and your mother concocted. I shudder to think of the impact this would have on them. Imagine them having to explain to your grandchildren that Grandpa started as Nazi ejaculate. You would never be esteemed or trusted by anyone, ever again. Indeed, you would live in infamy as a liar and a traitor to your religion and your race, just as your mother was."

Howard Bancroft was weeping into his hands, his whole body shaking as uncontrollably as if he'd been inflicted with a palsy.

"No one need ever know, of course," Noah said, switching to an upbeat tone. He stood up and retrieved both his folder and the power of attorney document. "I can keep a secret. Cross my heart." He drew an invisible *X* on his chest.

"However, I'm sure you understand my precaution," he said, making a mockery of the lawyer's earlier statement. "A copy of your mother's confession is in my safe-deposit box. Another is with an attorney I retained solely for this purpose. He's an oily, unscrupulous, litigious individual with strong anti-Semitic leanings.

"Should anything untoward happen to me, he's under strict instructions to distribute your mother's signed statement to all the synagogues in and around the five boroughs. It would make for very interesting reading, don't you think? Especially the accounts of her sucking off the SS officers. Some were too fastidious to have intercourse with a Jewess, but apparently fellatio didn't count."

Noah crossed to the door. Although the lawyer had made no effort to move but continued to cry into his hands, Noah said, "No, no, Howard, don't bother seeing me out. Have a nice day."

CHAPTER 13

You're leaving tomorrow?"

"In the morning," Maris replied. Nervously her gaze moved around the solarium, never stopping directly on Parker. "Mike arranged for a boat to pick me up. I have a nine-thirty flight out of Savannah, connecting in Atlanta to La Guardia."

"Have a nice trip." His surly expression suggested he hoped she would have the trip from hell.

This was the first time she'd seen Parker today. This morning she had slipped into the kitchen for a quick breakfast of cold cereal, she'd skipped lunch altogether, and then had asked Mike to bring her a sandwich to the cottage for dinner. She used work as her excuse for the solitude. She wanted to reread the manuscript with total concentration and without distraction. Mike had accepted the explanation. At least he'd pretended to.

If Parker's scowl was any indication, she'd been smart to keep her distance all day. He looked ill-tempered, spoiling for a fight. The sooner she said what she had to say and left, the better.

"Before I leave," she began, "I thought we should have one

last discussion about the manuscript. I spent most of the day reevaluating it."

"Reevaluation. That's what we're calling it?"

"Calling what?"

"Your avoidance of me."

Okay. He wanted a fight. Why disappoint him? "Yes, I was avoiding you, Parker. Can you blame me? After—"

She broke off when Mike appeared with a service tray. "Fresh peach cobbler," he announced.

Parker's scowl deepened. "How come there's no ice cream?"

"Did you want it to melt before I could get it served? Jeez." Mike deposited the tray on the table, then stamped back into the kitchen, muttering about how grouchy everybody had been today. He returned with a carton of vanilla ice cream, which he scooped over the steaming portions of cobbler.

"I'm having mine in my room," he said, taking one of the bowls for himself. "There's a Bette Davis film festival on TV tonight. If *you* need anything, you can fetch it yourself," he said to Parker. "Maris, if you need something, just knock on my door. Upstairs. First door on your right."

"Thank you, Mike. I can't imagine that I'll need to disturb you. The cobbler looks delicious."

"Enjoy."

After Mike left them, Parker attacked his helping of cobbler and ice cream as though he were angry at it. When he finished, he dropped the spoon into the empty bowl with a loud clatter, returned it to the tray, then rolled his chair over to the computer desk. "Do you want to read what I've been working on, or what?"

"Of course I want to read it."

While the new pages were printing out, Maris ate her cobbler. Carrying the crockery bowl with her, she moved slowly along the crammed bookcase, surveying the titles in Parker's extensive collection. "You like mysteries."

His head came around. "If they're well written."

"You must think Mackensie Roone writes well."

"He's okay."

"Just okay? You have the entire Deck Cayton series."

"Ever read one?"

"A few, not all." She pulled one of the books from the shelf and thumbed through it. "I wish we were publishing them. They sell like hotcakes."

"Why do you think that is?"

"Why do you like them?"

He thought about it a moment. "They're fluff, but they're fun."

She nodded. "Millions of readers worldwide think so, too. The character of Deck Cayton appeals to both men and women, and why not? He's independently wealthy. Detective work is just his hobby. He lives on a fabulous houseboat, drives fast cars, flies his own jet. He's as comfortable in a tuxedo as he is in blue jeans."

"And even more comfortable out of them."

"You must've read the one about the murder in the nudist colony."

He grinned devilishly. "My personal favorite."

"Why am I not surprised?"

"Getting back to the character . . ."

Absently, she licked some dripping ice cream off her spoon. "Deck Cayton is well drawn. He's charming, witty, good-looking. He's—"

"A jerk."

"Sometimes he is. With a capital *J*. But he's been so engagingly written that a reader forgives his flaws. The author allows him to be human, and the readers appreciate and identify with that. And even though he's armed and dangerous and tough-talking, Deck has an underlying vulnerability."

"Because of his wife's death."

"Right. It's referred to, but I haven't read that particular book."

"First of the series," he explained. "Skiing accident. He challenged her to a downhill race, and she crashed into a tree. Autopsy revealed she was several weeks pregnant. They hadn't known. You should read it."

"I definitely will." She tapped the spoon against her front teeth. "Do you see how the author built in a reason for Deck's vulnerability? Readers can empathize with him because of that tragic and fatal accident."

"You're sounding like an editor."

She laughed. "Habit, I guess."

"You've given it a lot of thought."

"I analyze every bestseller. Especially the competition's. I need to know why Deck Cayton strikes such a positive chord. Part of my job is trying to predict what the buying public wants to read."

She polished off her cobbler. "But that doesn't make me any less a fan. Character motivation notwithstanding, Deck is your basic larger-than-life action hero who never fails to solve the mystery, nab the bad guy, bed the babe."

"And make her come."

Maris closed the book with a decisive snap and replaced it on the shelf among the others. He'd only said that to provoke her, and it had worked. But damned if she would let it show. "As I said, he appeals to men and women alike."

Her understatement made him grin, but he let it pass without comment. "Which was your favorite of the series?"

"*Loose Change.*"

He grimaced. "Seriously? In that book Deck came dangerously close to being a wimp."

"Because he showed more sensitivity toward the female character?"

Scornfully, Parker placed his hands over his heart. "He got in touch with his feminine side."

"But he soon reasserted himself as a real cad. By the end of the book, he was back to being the smooth operator that every man fantasizes being."

"Did he live up to your fantasy?"

"Deck Cayton?"

"Your husband. His book acted like a spark plug to your fantasy life. Did his performance in bed—*does* it—live up to your expectations?"

She faced him squarely. "Parker, that is an inappropriate question."

"That means it doesn't."

"That means it's none of your business. Your curiosity over my personal life is out of line. Which is precisely why I avoided being alone with you last night and all day today. What happened in the gin made me uncomfortable. I'm married."

"What happened in the gin? I don't remember anything happening in the gin that would compromise you as a married woman."

His feigned innocence infuriated her, but she wouldn't give him the satisfaction of showing it. She changed tactics and assumed an air of indifference as she returned her empty bowl to the tray on the table.

"You attached far too much significance to that kiss, Parker. You asked why I allowed it, and since you seem confused on that point, let me clarify. I allowed it because fighting you off would have been undignified and embarrassing for both of us. A glorified golf cart is no place to conduct a wrestling match to protect my virtue. And don't for a moment delude yourself into thinking I was afraid of you." She shot him an arch look. "I could've outrun you."

"Ouch! That one hurt, Maris. Now you're fighting dirty."

"Which is the only kind of fighting I think you understand."

"It's the only kind of fighting, period."

"In other words, what's the point of fighting if you don't fight to win?"

"Damn straight," he said tightly. "Win at all costs. No matter what it takes, no matter what you have to do. I learned—or rather was taught—that lesson. If you want to come out on top, you must be willing to go the distance."

Although his intensity on the topic intrigued her, there was a dangerous glint in his eyes that warned her against probing any further.

"I wanted to work with you on *Envy*. If one meaningless kiss bought me that opportunity, it was a small enough price to pay. Can't we put that childish episode behind us and concentrate on what brought me here in the first place? Your book and my desire to buy it."

"For how much?"

The subject of money had never been broached, and she was caught off guard by the introduction of it now. "I haven't thought about it."

"Well, do."

"It's premature."

"Maybe for you, not for me."

"I haven't seen a complete manuscript, Parker. I won't go to contract until I have."

"And I won't bust my balls finishing a book that you might ultimately reject."

"I'm sorry, that's the way the system works."

"Not my system."

The recently printed sheets were neatly stacked in his lap. She was itching to read them. But his jaw was squared, and he was just ornery enough to stick to his guns. "We could compromise."

"I'm listening," he said.

"I would be willing to offer you a moderate advance once I see a detailed outline."

"No sale. I don't want to do an outline."

"Why?"

"Because I enjoy the spontaneity of writing without one."

"You wouldn't have to adhere to it. If along the way a better idea occurs to you, I won't hold you to the outline. All I require is a general idea of where you're taking the story, a synopsis of the plot."

"That would spoil the surprises."

"I'm your editor. I don't need to be surprised."

"Of course you do. You're a reader first, an editor second. You're the first barometer of whether the book is good or it's crap. Plot twists are essential to its being good. Besides, I'd rather channel my energy into the story than to writing a stupid outline."

"I urge you to take the time, Parker. For your benefit as well as mine."

"I ain't doing it."

"You sound like Todd."

"Todd?"

She moved to the table where she had left her copy of the *Envy* manuscript. "Let's see . . . I think it's in chapter six. No, seven. It's a scene between him and Roark. He's telling Roark that Professor Hadley had suggested changes in his character's attitude toward his father, and Roark thinks the suggestion is a valid one."

She scanned the pages of text. "Here. Page ninety-two. Todd says, 'When our esteemed professor writes a book, he can do with his characters whatever he likes. You can do with yours what you want. But these are *my* characters. I created them. I know what makes them tick. I won't change them to suit Hadley. No. No, sir. I ain't doing it.'"

She looked over at him. He shrugged. "Okay. So I'll let Todd speak for me."

"God, you're stubborn."

They stared at one another until he finally asked, "Do you want to hear what I wrote today while you were busy avoiding me?"

Ignoring his sarcasm, she said, "Of course I want to—Did you say *hear* it?"

"I thought I would read it to you because it's very sloppy. I was writing fast. Didn't bother with capital letters, punctuation, stuff like that. Have a seat."

She sank into the deep cushions in one of the wicker arm-chairs, slipped off her sandals, and tucked her legs beneath her. He rolled his chair near hers, engaged the brake, and adjusted the shade of a floor lamp so that the light was directed down onto the pages. Except for that small pool of light, the room was dark.

"I took your advice, Maris, and enhanced the girl's role. She's interwoven into other scenes, but this one between her and Roark takes place on the night following his snafu with Hadley.

"The professor rescheduled their appointment for after the Thanksgiving holiday. Roark returns to the frat house, pulls Todd off his sleeping loft, and, as you suggested, commences to beat the hell out of him. Some frat brothers break up the fight. Roark inflicts no more damage than a busted lip and a bloody nose. Todd apologizes."

"He does?"

"He does. He says he thought it would be a good practical joke, but didn't think through the ramifications of screwing Roark with Hadley. Says he hadn't counted on Hadley being so severe when Roark turned up late. He had figured Roark would get the equivalent of a slap on his hand, and then Hadley would proceed with his consultation."

"Is Todd sincere?"

"We have no reason to believe otherwise, do we?"

"No. I suppose not."

"Okay, so Roark has accepted Todd's explanation and apol-ogy, but he's still mad as hell. Forlorn. In a crap mood. He calls up the girl and makes a date with her for that evening. He tells her that he really wants to see her, that he's had a shitty day, stuff like that."

"He's in need of some TLC."

"Exactly." Scanning as he went, Parker flipped through the top several pages, letting them drift one by one to the floor at the side of his chair. "You can read this transition on your own. Oh, I've named the girl Leslie."

"I like it."

"To paraphrase, Roark takes her to a Sonic Drive-in. They have chili Tater Tots and cherry limeades."

"Big spender."

"Hey, give him a break, okay? He's a kid on a budget. Besides, he happens to like chili Tater Tots and cherry limeades."

"Sorry. Go on."

"After they eat, Roark drives them out to the lake. He parks. He leaves the radio off. Somehow the silence seems appropriate. Let's see . . . yeah, here. 'The silence that enfolded him was as calming and comforting as a mother's breast. His day had been a chain of chaotic events, a jarring series of starts and stops. Between outbursts of anger, he'd suffered bone-crushing disappointment in his friend, in himself.'"

"Good."

"Thanks," he returned absently as he continued to scan the pages. "Throughout the evening Leslie has been unusually subdued, not her effervescent self. Roark figures that his dour mood must've been contagious, that it had rubbed off on her. Over the Tater Tots they'd carried on a desultory conversation about blah, blah, blah. You can read this for yourself."

He ran his finger down the page until he located the passage he sought. "Okay, listen."

"I'm listening."

"'A full moon hovered just above the horizon and was reflected in the water at such a severe angle that its wavering spotlight spanned the entire breadth of the lake. But it shed a chill light. On the far shore, towering pines and denuded hardwoods were unmoving in the windless night, stark and still, like India ink etchings against the sky that had turned wintry just that day.'"

"I like it."

"To encapsulate, their conversation has been forced, stilted. Leslie hadn't asked Roark where they were going when they left the Sonic. On the drive to the lake, she hadn't uttered a peep. . . . Jesus, did I write that?" He took a red pencil from his shirt pocket and made a slash through that line. "But by now her silence is beginning to wear on Roark's nerves. He wants to know what she's thinking."

He began to read again from the text. " 'Roark withheld asking until his chest felt tight enough to crack. "What are you so quiet for?" His tone of voice should have pissed her off. It would have pissed him off if somebody who had been as glum as an undertaker all evening had implicitly accused him of being the source of some unacknowledged complication.

" 'But when Leslie turned toward him, he saw only kindness in her expression. Instead of rebuke, understanding. And Roark was suddenly struck by how beautiful she was.

" 'Oh, the first time he saw her he'd thought she was pretty. Eye candy. He and the guys he'd been carousing with that night had picked her out of a crowd of coeds. Among themselves they had appraised her, lewdly remarking on the physical attributes that men lewdly remark upon. She had scored high.

" 'But tonight she was beautiful to him in a way that had nothing to do with the pleasant arrangement of her features or the proportions of her figure. She exuded a beauty that was deeper than her flawless complexion and rarer even than her extraordinarily blue eyes.

" 'She radiated a beauty that wasn't particularly appreciated. By contemporary society's standards, it didn't have much value. It wasn't sophisticated and cool, but homespun and warm. It made you feel loved and accepted despite your shortcomings, despite everything. Tonight Leslie was beautiful like you hoped your life partner would be.' "

When Parker stopped reading and glanced up at her, Maris managed only a slight nod and a motion for him to continue.

"Leslie asks him what had happened that day to put him in such a funk. Words to that effect." Parker sent that page sailing over the armrest of the wheelchair and found the spot on the following page where he wanted to resume reading.

"'Roark talked for ten solid minutes. The words gushed out in an uninterrupted stream, as though all day his subconscious had been choosing them and arranging them into an order that would give them the most impact and would most eloquently express the level of his despair.

"'But eventually his dejection turned to outrage. He articulated the fiery internal argument he'd been having with himself, the argument that justified his anger toward Todd. "Fuck his apology!" He closed his hand into a tight fist. "He can't undo the damage he's done that easily."

"'When he finished venting about Todd, he cursed the pompous professor for being such an unrelenting bastard, at the same time admitting to his fear of never reestablishing a rapport with Hadley and thereby guaranteeing a dismal grade on his capstone.

"'The words finally ebbed, then stopped altogether. Roark fell silent again and hunkered down into his jacket, not for the warmth it provided but from shame for sounding like such a goddamn crybaby.'"

Again, Parker raised his head and looked at Maris. "Well? Should I trash it or continue?"

"Continue. Please."

"I'll pick up with Leslie's response."

Returning to the manuscript, he read, "'She waited until the smoke of his wrath had cleared, when it became noticeable that the cold from outside was seeping into the car. Her breath formed plumes of vapor between them. She spoke quietly, as one would to a temperamental animal who was momentarily docile. "What happened today is a good thing, Roark."

"'He snorted, looked over at her. "Good? How in God's name is it good? Not that I believe in God."

"'He knew she wouldn't like the atheistic remark. She was a devout believer who took offense at jokes made over anything religious. Ordinarily she admonished him for making them and asked him to kindly keep his irreverent comments to himself. This time, she elected to overlook it.

"'"The reason you're taking this so hard is because your writing means so much to you."

"'It was a good point. He wanted to hear more. "And because it means so much to you, you'll succeed. If you were able to shrug off the misunderstanding with Professor Hadley or laugh about it, then I would advise you to rethink your choice of career. You could dismiss this incident only if you had no passion for writing.

"'"What happened illustrates the depth of your passion. Your despondency over this . . . what really amounts to a hiccup in the grand scheme of things . . . demonstrates the level of your desire to write and write well. It hit you where it hurts most, which affirms that you're doing what you were born to do." She smiled. "I didn't need it affirmed. But perhaps you did. And if you did, then this experience was worth all the anxiety it's caused."

"'She reached for his hand and pressed it between hers. "Think about it, Roark, and you'll realize that I'm right."'"

When Parker paused, Maris said, "She's a very intuitive young woman."

"You think?"

She nodded. Noticing the sheets still lying in his lap, she asked, "How does Parker respond?"

"The way most men respond to any emotionally charged situation."

"Which is?"

"Well, depending on if we're stimulated to feel bad or good, we either want to strike something or fuck something."

Maris cleared her throat. "I don't suppose Roark feels like striking something."

"Wasn't it you who suggested that I enhance their relationship?"

"It was."

"Okay, then. They kiss, and it gets predictably slippery. Roark opens her coat, cuddles up to her chest. She gives him access to some skin. 'Velvety, warm, fragrant woman skin,' it says here. I'll work on that." He made a notation.

"He caresses her breasts. For the first time since they began dating, he uses his mouth. He kisses her nipples, teaching her something about arousal and the pleasurable possibilities that are available to a man and woman who are willing to explore them."

Maris's heart bumped inside her chest.

"Her scent. Her breath. The texture of her against his tongue. Combined with the day's frustration. The foreplay just isn't hacking it. The guy's dying here. So he guides Leslie's hand inside his jeans and, to put it delicately, she gives him a hand job."

"That's putting it delicately?"

The huskiness of her voice brought his head up and he looked across at her. "Compared to some optional phrases, that's pretty delicate, yeah."

"Okay."

"Roark tells her he loves her."

"Does he mean it?"

"At that moment? With all his heart."

Parker's somber face caused her to laugh. "I'm sure. How does Leslie respond?"

"Ah," he said, frowning. "As it turns out, the hand job is her going-away present. She dumps him."

"Then and there?"

"It's right here in black and white."

"Hmm. Does she break up for the reasons stated in the first draft?"

"Yeah."

"Then she's being kind, isn't she? And smart. As much as it hurts her, she's doing what she realizes is best for both of them, especially Roark. She's thinking first of him and his career."

"Maybe. But I gotta tell you, Maris, fresh after you've climaxed, it's a real bummer if the woman up and walks out on you."

"I suppose."

"Oh, yeah," he said, nodding sagely. "Ask any guy."

"I'll take your word for it."

"In Roark's mind she's being a heartless bitch. He doesn't need her charity, and who the hell does she think she is? He's good and pissed." Maris was about to protest when Parker raised a finger to halt her. "At least initially." He picked up the remaining pages. "Shall I?"

"Please."

" 'The day had started off lousy and then it had gone to pure shit.

" 'He thought about getting drunk, but could see no good purpose in it. Today's disappointments would carry over into tomorrow, and then he would have to confront them with the handicap of a hangover.

" 'Besides, he hadn't earned an excuse to get drunk. That right belonged to a man only if he had a circumstance to celebrate . . . or to mourn. One was allowed to lament a disaster visited on him by random selection, such as an act of God or a whim of Fate. But regret over his own culpability earned a man no such privilege. Responsibility for one's sorry situation couldn't be that easily removed.

" 'As much as he wanted to lay blame on Leslie, on Hadley, on Todd, for today's miseries, Roark acknowledged that most of the blame, if not all of it, lay squarely with him.

" 'Leslie was wise beyond her years and experience. Moreover, she was honest to a painful degree. Their individual desires were too discordant, their dreams too disparate for them to have a future together. Their goals conflicted now. In the future they would clash resoundingly. When the inevitable separation came, they would be left scarred and embittered.

" 'The wisdom of her choice to return to her small-town aspirations and long-standing sweetheart didn't make it any easier to lose her now, but ending the relationship before it actually started would spare them future heartache. At least they had parted while all the memories were still sweet.

" 'Professor Hadley had been well within his right to be perturbed. He didn't want any stupid students under his tutelage. He had probably been as upset with Roark for being duped by his roommate as he had been by the tardiness. The professor's time was too limited, his instruction too valuable to squander on fools. Taking Todd's word for something as critical as that meeting had been nothing short of stupid.

" 'The challenge facing Roark now was to prove to Hadley that, all evidence pointing to the contrary, he was not an imbecile. He could learn from this experience. He must learn from it. If he didn't, he would be as foolish, as much a waste of time and effort, as Hadley believed him to be.

" 'Today had been the first cold day of the season. It was also the first day of Roark Slade's life as an adult. Without ceremony or sacrament, he had undergone a rite of passage. Whatever remnants of innocence he had awakened with this morning had been stripped from him. After today, trust was only a word, a remote ideal that would never have a practical application in his life. From today forward, any belief he entertained would be contaminated by skepticism.

" 'Roark wasn't aware of this transition until years later, when he leafed back through the pages of his personal history, searching for the defining moment when his life had ceased being charmed and became cursed. His search always ended on this day.

" 'For months following that Tuesday before Thanksgiving, Roark would think about Professor Hadley and what he could learn from that embarrassing experience. He would reflect on all that he had learned from Leslie about himself as a man and a writer. He would think on that quite a lot.

" 'But what he had learned about his best friend Todd, he avoided thinking about altogether.' "

When Parker finished reading the final page, he stared at the last sentence for a time, then let the sheet slip from his fingers and drift down to join the others. By now the floor around the wheelchair was littered with pages of manuscript.

Quietly, and without looking at Maris, he said, "That's it so far."

She slowly unfolded her legs and lowered her feet to the floor. She slid her palms up and down the tops of her thighs, then clasped her hands loosely, raised her shoulders around a deep breath, and released it gradually.

"All right, Parker. It goes against the company's policy as well as my own, but I'll give you a ten-thousand-dollar advance just to finish the manuscript. When it's completed, we'll negotiate the terms of a contract. If you decline our terms and sell the book elsewhere, the ten thousand must be repaid from the first proceeds you receive from the other publisher. If you accept, that initial ten thousand will be applied to the advance we ultimately agree upon. In the meantime, I suggest you get an agent."

"I suggest you get a grip on reality."

"That's a no?"

"Twenty-five thousand. Which barely covers my expenses. I've got to buy cartridges for my printer, paper."

"Mighty expensive paper," she said drolly. "Fifteen. That represents an act of good faith, considering that I don't even have an outline."

He mulled it over for several seconds. "Fifteen, no first-proceeds clause, and the fifteen is not applicable to the advance finally agreed upon. In other words, the fifteen's mine no matter what. If Matherly Press can't afford to gamble fifteen grand, you should padlock the doors tomorrow."

He was right, of course, and, except for saving face, she saw no point in arguing it further. The fierce deal-making could be reserved for the final contract negotiations.

"Deal. As soon as I return to New York, I'll have our legal department draw up a letter of agreement. For now, we have a gentlemen's agreement." She stuck out her hand.

He took her hand and used it to draw her closer to him. "By no stretch of the imagination are you a gentleman."

She leaned even farther forward, bringing her face very close to his and whispering, "Neither are you."

Laughing, he released her hand. "Got that right. Do you want to take the rest of this with you?" He indicated the pages scattered over the floor.

"Please. I'd like my father to read it."

"What about your husband?"

"Noah usually handles the business concerns and leaves the editorial to me, but since I've become so personally involved in this book, I'm sure he'll want to read it, too."

Parker wheeled his chair backward so she could kneel down and gather the manuscript pages. "I'd help, but—"

"No bother."

"—I like it this way. I've actually entertained fantasies of you on your knees in front of me."

"Groveling?"

"That, too."

She looked up at him but wished she hadn't. He wasn't smiling, wasn't teasing. The remark went beyond his typical innuendo.

"*Dirty* fantasies," he added. "In some states I could be arrested."

"Stop it, Parker."

"Okay, I will."

"Thank you."

"When you stop looking like that."

"Like what?"

"Thoroughly fuckable."

"That's not a word."

"Thoroughly? Is, too."

"I should have you charged with sexual harassment."

"I'd deny it."

"That's the only reason I don't." She continued to gather the pages with quick, angry motions. Then she noticed the scar.

He wasn't wearing socks, so his feet were bare inside a pair of docksiders that, sadly, looked new and unscuffed. The scar crossed the vamp of his right foot and crawled up his ankle to disappear inside the leg of his trousers. The flesh was raised and buckled.

"It only gets worse from there. In fact, that one is damn near beautiful compared to some of the others."

She looked up at him. "I'm sorry, Parker."

"No need to apologize. It's human nature to be curious over something that grotesque. I'm accustomed to stares."

"No. I meant I'm sorry for whatever it was that happened to you. It must've been incredibly painful."

"At first." He affected an indifference she knew was false.

"But after a few years I learned to live with it. Eventually the pain dwindled to a familiar ache. Except in cold weather. Then it can hurt like a son of a bitch."

"Is that why you moved to St. Anne? To escape harsh winters?"

"One of the reasons." He wheeled his chair around. "I'm going to get more cobbler. Want some?"

With all the sheets now in hand, she came to her feet. "No, thanks. I need to get to bed. I left an early wake-up call with Mike."

"Right."

In a matter of seconds, his attitude had turned frosty. She'd seen his scars, internal ones as well as those on his legs, and he couldn't tolerate that. He equated the scars to weakness, a limitation to his masculinity. Which was ridiculous.

Because, with the exception of those scarred legs, Parker defined maleness. He was broad through his shoulders and chest. As she had noticed the night they met, his arms were heavily muscled. Even his legs, what she could make out of them beneath his trousers, were muscular. In a private conversation with Mike, she had asked why Parker didn't use a motorized chair. He'd said that Parker wanted to stay as fit as possible and wheeling himself around helped keep his muscles toned.

He wasn't as classically handsome as Noah. There was a distinct asymmetry to Parker's features, but the irregularities made his face arresting and interesting. The square jaw, stern visage, and a head of hair over which he exercised limited control, all contributed to an attractiveness that was altogether manly.

A manliness from which the safest distance for a married woman was full retreat.

"I'll be in touch soon, Parker."

"I'm not going anywhere," he said flippantly.

"Write your heart out."

"Yeah. Good-bye, Maris." He wheeled himself into the kitchen, never looking back. He might just as well have sprinted away from her. The door swished shut behind him.

Left standing alone in the empty, dim room, Maris felt awkward and a bit deflated. She didn't know what she had expected, but Parker's desertion seemed anticlimactic. She had what she'd come for—an agreement with him to finish *Envy*. One more handshake to seal that agreement wouldn't have killed him, would it? He hadn't mentioned being around to see her off in the morning. She certainly hadn't expected a protracted and syrupy good-bye; nevertheless, she felt a bit crestfallen.

Honestly? She was sad to be leaving. When she should be eager to return to her turf, where the accents and the cuisine and the night sounds were familiar, she realized she dreaded tomorrow's departure.

The island had captivated her with its lavish landscape and its musical insects whose concert lulled her to sleep every night. At first she'd found the humidity cloying and almost unbearable, but she had actually come to like the feel of it against her skin. With its moss-laden trees that were almost as ancient as the surf, the island was otherworldly, entrancing, and seductive.

And so was Parker Evans. But she shoved that thought aside.

She noticed that the manuscript pages had actually grown damp within her tight grip. Relaxing her fist, she shook her head with chagrin. There was no mystery as to the source of these sensual thoughts. They had taken root in her mind when Parker read that damned passage about slippery kisses and nipples and the pleasurable possibilities available to a man and woman willing to explore them.

She had planned to return to the guest cottage and read these pages for herself, but she changed her mind. They could wait to be read when she was back in New York, under fluorescent lights, in familiar surroundings, behind the safe barricade of her own desk and heavy workload. They could be read when their author wasn't in the next room entertaining fantasies about her that he could be arrested for.

Before she left the solarium, she borrowed a Mackensie Roone novel from Parker's library. She had a feeling that falling asleep was going to be difficult. The mystery would be a pleasant diversion. Deck Cayton could keep her company.

When Parker entered the gin the following morning, he startled a raccoon. "It's almost daybreak, pal. Better haul ass." The animal scuttled out between broken boards in the wall.

He liked coming to the cotton gin before the sun came up, when it was still reasonably cool and there was a light breeze coming off the ocean. He liked watching the first light find its way through the cracks in the walls. He fancied the building having a soul, awakening at sunrise in the vain hope that the new day would bring life and vitality back to it.

He fancied it because he could identify with it.

He knew what it was like for people to shut you down, lock you up, and go away sadly shaking their heads and saying that you weren't going to be worth much to anybody ever again.

Countless mornings he had awakened like that. Before he had time to remember his circumstances, he would experience a flicker of anticipation for what the day would bring. Then pain would bring him fully awake, and with consciousness came the cruel realization that the day would bring nothing except the same desolation and hopelessness as had the day before, and the one before that.

Thank God he had clawed his way free of that self-defeating miasma.

By an act of will, he had given his days purpose. He had set himself a goal. Although it had cost him excruciating physical pain and many times had beaten his persistence almost into surrender, he had clung to it. Now he was mere weeks away from achieving that goal.

A bird sailed into the building from the open doorway, startling Parker out of his reverie. The brown, spotted thing—Mike was the bird-watcher who could probably identify this one from thirty yards—perched on the edge of the loft and, tilting its feathered head, regarded Parker curiously.

"Bet you're wondering what I'm doing here."

He wondered what the hell he was doing talking to the animals this morning, but it didn't worry him overmuch. He had once screamed invectives at a whole battalion of imaginary rats that were scaling his motionless legs, crawling over his groin and belly and up his chest to attack his neck and face with their long, sharp teeth. So he wasn't too concerned now about rationally addressing something as harmless, and real, as a common bird.

He came here to the emptiness of this ruin to rethink his plot and look for holes in it. He came here to check on his preparedness and to ask himself repeatedly what he could have possibly overlooked. He came to anticipate how sweet it was going to be to have his revenge, to see an end to it, to bring it to closure after fourteen years.

Sometimes he came here simply to escape Mike. Two opinionated bachelors sharing a house had the potential of becoming one opinionated bachelor too many. When tempers sparked, it was always Parker's fault. Compared to him, Mike had the disposition and patience of a saint.

He couldn't do without Mike and couldn't bear to think about the day when he would be forced to. Mike wouldn't 'fess up to his actual age, but Parker knew he must be past seventy. Thank God he appeared to be in good health and had the energy of a man half his age.

He was really fond of—no, he *loved* that old man.

But there were days when even the long-suffering Mike Strother grated on him, when he needed complete solitude, when one room didn't provide him enough space in which to battle his demons.

This morning he'd come here to think specifically about Maris. Within these weathered walls, he had hatched the plan to get her to St. Anne Island, under his roof, and under his influence.

He hadn't planned on her getting under his skin.

He couldn't go feeling sorry for her, though. If he was to treat Noah Reed to a taste of hell on earth, utilizing Noah's wife was necessary. She would get caught in the crossfire that was sure to come, but that was too damn bad. She would get no better than she deserved for marrying the cocksucker. She looked and talked smart, but she couldn't be very bright.

"I mean, come on, marrying a guy because she fell in love with a character in a book? How stupid can you get?" he asked the sparrow.

No, he couldn't let himself get mushy over Maris Matherly-Reed. So what if she made him laugh? And gave good dialogue? And looked up at him with woeful, watercolor eyes and felt compassion for his scars? He didn't want her pity. He didn't need it. And she damn well wouldn't be pitying him if she knew what was in store for—

"You son of a bitch!"

Parker spun his chair around barely in time to duck the hardcover book hurled at his head.

C H A P T E R 15

Parker batted the book away a nanosecond before it could connect with his temple. It landed in the dirt beside his chair, sending up a puff of dust. He recognized the cover. It was the first volume of the Deck Cayton series.

Maris was standing just inside the open doorway. The first time she came to the deserted cotton gin, she'd been apprehensive and hesitant to enter. This morning her aura was glowing as red hot as a new star. If the threshold on which she was standing had been the gateway to hell, Parker doubted she would have been intimidated.

Given that he could see the outline of her legs—all the way to the top—through her skirt, her fury was ineffectual. At the very least, it was compromised. His eyes were drawn to that vaguely defined delta, but he concentrated on keeping them in a neutral zone above her waist. God knew he didn't need to provoke her any more than she was already provoked.

Unflappably, he asked, "You didn't like the book?"

"Fuck you."

"I guess not."

With her hands clenched into fists that she held stiffly at her sides, she walked toward him, quoting as she came, "'At least they had parted while all the memories were still sweet.'" She came to a stop within a yard of his chair and he noted that she was wearing eyeglasses. "You're either a plagiarist or a consummate liar, and either way you're a son of a bitch."

"So you said. I got it the first time."

"Which is it? Just so I'll know. One's as despicable as the other."

"I believe you quoted from chapter seventeen, page two hundred forty-three. Deck is at his late wife's grave." He feigned puzzlement. "I'm not sure if one can plagiarize oneself. Can one?"

She was too angry to speak.

"Deck is grief-stricken but grateful that he'd had her in his life for even a short time," he continued. "It was rather good, I thought."

"Good enough to use again. In *Envy*. After Leslie broke up with Roark."

At what hour of the day had she discovered the telltale passage? he wondered. Had it been late last night as she lay in the guest cottage bed, or had she been reading over her morning coffee? The circumstances really didn't matter. She knew his secret, and she was pissed.

"Why did you lie to me, Parker?"

"I never lied about it," he countered calmly. "You never asked me if I was Mackensie Roone. You never asked me if I wrote a mystery series featuring Deck Cayton. Even when we were talking about him last night, you never once said—"

"Don't be obtuse, Parker! You lied by omission. Otherwise, you would have volunteered that vital piece of information."

"Vital? Hardly. It wasn't even important. It wasn't relevant. If you'd've asked, I would have—"

"Invented some bullshit story. Like this has been from the very beginning."

"If I hadn't wanted to be found out, I wouldn't have deliberately used that sentence in *Envy* and then recommended that you read the first Deck Cayton book."

"Which was another of your games to test how sharp I am," she shouted.

Her hair was tousled and her cheeks were pink, as though she'd run all the way here from the house. Truth be told, she looked adorably disheveled and smelled of the vanilla in freshly baked tea cakes. But she wouldn't welcome the compliments.

"I've never seen you wearing glasses. Do you ordinarily wear contacts?"

Impatiently she raked her hair back. "What I want to know is why."

She had lowered the timbre of her voice, although it appeared to have been an effort. Her chest was rising and falling rapidly as though the volume and vituperation trapped inside were creating inner turbulence.

"Why did you play this ridiculous game with me, Parker? Or Mackensie or whatever the hell your name is."

"Parker Mackensie Evans. Mackensie was my mother's maiden name. When I was deciding on a pseudonym, it seemed a logical choice. Tickled my mom no end for me to use it. It has a nice ring. It's androgynous. It's—"

"Answer me"

"—safe."

"From what?"

"Discovery." He tossed out the word like a gauntlet. For long moments, it seemed to lie there between them on the dirt floor alongside the book. Finally he said, "When I sold the Deck Cayton series, I wished to remain anonymous. I still do."

"The series has been enormously popular. Why hide behind a pseudonym?"

He folded his arms across his chest and gave her a pointed look. "Why do you suppose, Maris?"

Her lips parted as though to speak, but then realization dawned, and her lips closed. She looked away, embarrassed.

"Right. Deck Cayton is every man's fantasy. Every woman's, too, according to you. He's agile and quick, he can chase the bad guys and carry a woman to his bed. Why would I want to dispel his dashing image by showing up at personal appearances in a wheelchair?"

"No author photographs on the book jackets," she mused out loud. "No book signings or personal appearances. I often questioned your publisher's marketing strategy and wondered why it didn't include you. They were protecting you."

"Wrong. I was protecting me. Even my publisher doesn't know who Mackensie Roone is. My editor doesn't know my real name or whether Mackensie Roone is male or female. No one knows anything about Mackensie Roone's true identity. My agent tells me the speculation has run the gamut from—"

"Of course," Maris interrupted on a soft cry. "Mackensie Roone has an agent! I know her. You didn't go through her when you submitted *Envy*. Why?"

"She doesn't know about it."

"Why?"

"Because I haven't told her. She'll get her percentage of anything *Envy* earns because I'll bring her in to negotiate the final contract. But until that time, I chose to go this one alone."

"Why?"

"Is there an echo in here?"

"Before I kill you, I want to understand this, Parker."

Despite the first half of that statement, she appeared more befuddled than angry now, although he sensed he was being granted only a temporary reprieve. If he knew her at all, and he felt he was coming to, once she had time to think about all this at length, she was going to get as mad as hell all over again.

"Explain yourself, Parker. Why the secrecy?"

"I wanted to write a different book. Totally different from the snappy dialogue and fast-paced action in the Deck Cayton books. Don't get me wrong, they're not easy to write." He grinned ruefully. "Frankly, it surprises the hell out of me how popular they've become.

"But because they're so popular, and Deck is so well-known to the fans—I mean, to some, he's like a member of the family who's merely away from home between books—they expect a lot from me. They want the same, but different. They want each book to take Deck into a new and exciting adventure, but they'd turn vicious if I deviated too far from the formula.

"It's hard to deliver every time out of the chute. Each successive book has outsold the previous one, and I'm glad. But that also raises the stakes and the standard, and makes each book harder to top."

"That's a refrain I've heard from other successful novelists," Maris remarked. "They say it's difficult to top themselves. Noah has said that about *The Vanquished*."

Parker didn't want to talk about Noah and his goddamned success story.

"I've come clean with you, Maris, now be truthful with me. If my agent had called you up one day and said, 'Guess what I've got? Lying on my desk as we speak is a new novel by the author of the Deck Cayton series. Something entirely different from the mysteries. Very hush-hush. And he wants *you* to see it first.' You'd have creamed, right?"

She blinked at the offensive expression, but she didn't shy away from his eyes as they bore into hers.

"I wanted you to cream over *Envy*, Maris. But without knowing anything about me or my past successes."

She looked away, readjusted her eyeglasses, absently brushed a gnat off her arm. When she looked at him again, she said, "All right, yes. I wouldn't have used your crude terminology, but I would've been excited by such a call. Why would that have been such a terrible thing?"

"Because I wanted an unbiased opinion of the writing."

"Which entitled you to make a fool of me."

"No, dammit! That wasn't . . ." He felt his own ire rising, and he suspected it was because her argument had merit. He began again. "I sent the prologue to you unsolicited because that was the only way to guarantee an impartial reading. I wanted you

214 | SANDRA BROWN

to approach it without preconceptions. I wanted it to stand on its own, not on my reputation as a bestselling author. I wanted it to be good."

"It would have been just as good without the charade, Parker. My reaction to it would have been the same."

"But I would never have known for sure, would I?" He gave her time to respond, but she didn't. She couldn't. He was right, and she knew it. "I tricked you, yes. But I needed to prove to myself that there was more in me than a scotch-drinking, skirt-chasing hunk with a big gun and a bigger dick."

"Deck Cayton has more substance than that."

"Thanks. I think so. I wasn't sure you did."

She bent down and picked up the book.

"Are you going to bang me over the head with that?"

"Maybe." Her anger hadn't dissipated. It was still there, simmering. She just had it under control. "But even as mad as I am," she said, "I can't abuse a book. It goes against my nature even to dog-ear a page."

"I'm that way, too."

She returned his peacemaking smile with a glare. "Don't you dare try to charm me, Parker." She passed the book down to him and dusted her hands. "What you did was—"

"Terrifying."

"That wasn't the word I was going to use."

"But it's the correct one. When I put that prologue in the mail, I was scared shitless."

"Of what? Rejection?"

"Big time. You could have sent me a curt letter. Said no thanks. Said I stunk. Said I should give up writing and try stringing beads or basket weaving instead. I'd have probably bought a package of razor blades and locked myself in the bathroom."

"That isn't funny."

"You're right, it isn't."

"Besides, you're too egotistical for suicide."

How little she knew. There had been times during those darkest days when his soul had been as twisted as his legs and his emotions were as raw as the flesh that defied healing, when, had he been able to move, he would have taken the path of least resistance and ended it there.

But while he was in that pit of despair, he had been imbued with a will to live. Determination had been breathed into him by some omnipotent power or cosmic authority greater than his paltry human spirit.

Not an angel, though. Not an angel as angels are typically portrayed. There was nothing benevolent, God-blessed, or holy about his plans for Noah Reed.

He reached for Maris's hand and squeezed it hard. "Don't underestimate how important this is to me."

She didn't squeeze back but searched his eyes. "Why did you send *Envy* to me, Parker? I know your editor for the Mackensie Roone books. He's very capable."

"He is," he agreed solemnly.

"My question stands. There are hundreds of editors in a dozen major publishing houses. What set me apart? Why'd you choose me?"

"The article in the magazine." He hoped she wouldn't detect that he was lying. The answer seemed plausible enough to him, but she was looking at him with an intensity that was unnerving. "The things you were quoted as saying convinced me you were the editor for *Envy.*

"I liked what you said about commerce versus quality, and how the balance in publishing is in danger of shifting in favor of the former. I'm not writing this book for the money. I've got more money than I'll ever need. Deck Cayton has seen to that.

"I'm writing *Envy* for me. If it finds an audience, I'll be pleased. If it doesn't, you still saw something worthwhile in it, and to me that's damn good confirmation of my talent."

"It'll find an audience." She pulled her hand free of his. "I'll see to that. I have too much invested in it not to."

"A measly fifteen grand?"

"I wasn't referring to the advance."

His silly smile collapsed and he matched her gravity. "I know."

"I was referring to . . ."

He thought he saw the start of tears, but it might have been a tricky reflection off the lenses of her glasses. "I know what you were talking about, Maris."

They exchanged a long and meaningful look. He was consumed with the desire to touch her. "I don't want you to leave."

He hadn't known he was going to say that until he heard his own gruff voice filling the heavy silence. He hadn't made a conscious decision to speak the words, but he meant them. And he meant them for reasons that had absolutely nothing to do with his revenge on Noah Reed.

"Write your book, Parker."

"Stay."

"I'll be in touch." She backed up several steps before turning and walking away from him.

"Maris!"

But she didn't stop or even slow down, and she didn't look back, not even when he called her name again.

This visit is long overdue. I'm glad you were free." Nadia Schuller sent a smile across the table to her luncheon guest.

As the setting for this intimate get-together, Nadia had chosen a small, cozy restaurant on Park Avenue. Its menu was unaffected; the decor was country French. Nadia thought the lace panels in the windows were a bit precious for Manhattan, but they contributed to the restaurant's friendly ambience.

And that was the note she was trying to strike with this lunch—friendliness.

Which was somewhat of a challenge when you were screwing your guest's husband.

"Thank you for the invitation." Maris offered a strained little smile and opened her menu, a not so subtle hint that she was ready to get lunch under way and over with as quickly as etiquette permitted.

A waiter in a long white apron approached their table. "What would you like to drink, Maris?" Nadia asked.

"Iced tea, please."

"I'm having white wine. Would you rather have that?" She made it sound as though she were granting Maris permission to have an alcoholic beverage if she preferred.

Addressing the waiter this time, Maris repeated, "Iced tea, please. Lots of ice and a fresh wedge of lemon." Turning back to Nadia, she said, "I formed the habit when I was in the South."

"They drink it year-'round down there, don't they? That and moonshine." Nadia ordered her wine and the waiter withdrew. "I heard all about your trip to Dixie."

"Oh?"

"From your secretary. When I called to invite you to lunch."

"I thought perhaps Noah had told you."

"No, I haven't seen Noah in, hmm . . . actually, I think it was the night I saw the two of you at the awards banquet."

They made small talk until the waiter returned with their drink order, then listened to his recitation of the chef's specials. Nadia requested a few minutes for them to think over their selections. This delay in the proceedings seemed to perturb Maris, but Nadia wasn't going to be brushed off like a piece of lint.

She didn't like Maris in the least, and she was absolutely certain that her dislike was reciprocated. Both were successful businesswomen, but their approach to their careers, to men, to life in general, couldn't be more dissimilar.

Maris Matherly-Reed had enjoyed all the advantages that Nadia had been denied. Maris had been born into a wealthy and well-respected family and had cut her perfectly straight teeth on a silver spoon.

She had attended exclusive private schools and was a frequent guest at the tony parties held in the tony estates in the Hamptons. Her photograph often appeared in the society columns. She had traveled extensively.

Maris had culture out the ass—an ass that hadn't required painful, expensive liposuction to get it slim and taut. Shapely as it was, however, you couldn't melt an ice cube on it.

Nadia, née Nadine, had been born poor. Her family's poverty was forgivable. It was their ignorance and uncouthness she had found intolerable. As early as preadolescence, she determined not to remain in Brooklyn and marry some boorish loser of a husband with whom she would fight over how they were going to house and feed their ever-increasing brood.

She was destined for far better things.

She lost her virginity at thirteen to her first employer, the manager of a novelty store where she clerked in the afternoons after school. He caught her stealing nail polish and lipstick from the store's stock and had given her a choice between his sweaty coupling or arrest and juvenile court.

Besides the discomfort of being screwed on top of shipping crates in a dank stockroom by someone with clumsy, damp hands and garlic breath, it hadn't been that bad a trade-off.

That was only the first of many times Nadia bartered sex to get something she wanted or to avoid something she didn't. She perceived high school as a sentence she must serve, but amused herself by stealing her classmates' boyfriends.

She didn't give a fig about the broken hearts she caused. It didn't worry her that she didn't have a single girlfriend. As long as there were boys lusting after her, vying for her attention, giving her presents, and taking her places in exchange for doing what she would have enjoyed doing anyway, why should she care?

When her grades fell short of meeting graduation requirements, her rudimentary math teacher agreed to favorably adjust her score in exchange for a blow job. Her world history teacher, a pathetically homely woman, had been tearfully grateful when Nadia professed a secret affection for her. In the span of one rainy evening in the teacher's apartment that smelled of cat-litter boxes, Nadia's grade escalated from a D to a B+.

Once she had her diploma, she eschewed higher education. She had no patience for scholastics. Instead, she plowed straight into the workforce, moving from job to job at six-month intervals, until she was hired as a copy editor for a local neighborhood weekly newspaper.

This was the first job that had appealed to her and that she felt was worthy of her. Within weeks of being hired, she resolved that this was the field in which she would re-create herself—beginning with changing her name—and become famous.

Eventually she talked the managing editor into letting her write an occasional article. The negotiation took place in the backseat of his car in the shadow of the row house where he lived with his wife and four children. Nadia had straddled his lap and, working him into a state of near delirium, got his gasping promise to give her idea a trial run.

The Nadia Schuller pieces were gossipy, chatty, anecdotal stories about the lives and loves of people who lived in the neighborhood. It soon became the most popular feature of the newspaper. Nadia was on her way.

Now, twelve years and countless lovers later, she sat across from Maris Matherly-Reed, behaving in a civilized manner but harboring an enormous amount of antipathy for a woman who bested her without even trying. Were Maris to hate her more, Nadia would hate Maris less. What she couldn't tolerate was Maris's seeming indifference toward her. As though she merited no notice at all.

For instance, when they met at the entrance to the restaurant, Nadia had remarked on the light tan Maris had acquired while she was in Georgia and rather cattily reminded her how damaging sun exposure was to the complexion.

Maris's cool comeback had been, "Next time I go, I'll be sure to take a hat."

They placed their entrée orders with the waiter. As Nadia passed Maris a basket of bread, she remarked, "Tragic news about Howard Bancroft."

That elicited a reaction. Maris declined the bread basket with a small shake of her head and her eyes turned sad. "Very tragic. I didn't learn of it until I returned late yesterday afternoon."

"How many years had he been at the helm of your legal department?"

"Since before I was born. We were all shocked."

"Has anyone speculated on why he killed himself?"

"Nadia, I—"

"Oh, this isn't for 'Book Chat.' The facts were in the news-paper account, and it painted a grisly scene. I got the official, sanitized press release from your PR department. It said little about his manner of death and was more about his contribution to Matherly Press."

Howard Bancroft had been discovered in his car, parked half a block from his house on Long Island, with his brains blown to smithereens and a pistol in his hand.

"The people at Matherly Press are a closely knit group. No one picked up warning signals?"

"No," Maris replied. "In fact, Noah had a meeting with him just that afternoon. He said Howard was being typically Howard." She shook her head with remorse. "He was such a well-loved man, especially in the Jewish community. I can't imagine what drove him to commit such a desperate act."

Their main courses arrived. As they ate, they switched to a brighter topic—the books Matherly Press had scheduled for its fall lineup. "I predict that it's going to be a very successful hol-iday season for us," Maris told her. "Our best ever."

"May I quote that in my column?"

"You may."

Nadia opened her ever-present notebook and asked Maris to enumerate the titles and authors she was especially excited about. After jotting them down, she laid aside her pen and took a dainty bite of grilled sea bass. "Tell me about this project you're working on in Georgia."

"I can't."

Nadia stopped eating. "Why not?"

"It's not open to discussion."

"How positively fabulous. I love projects swathed in mystery."

"This one is and must remain that way. And even my telling you that is off the record. Don't use it."

Nadia took a sip of wine, gazing at Maris over the rim of the glass. "You've just increased my curiosity about a thousand times over."

"You'll have to remain curious."

"The author—"

"Chooses to remain anonymous. That's also off the record. Even my staff doesn't know the writer's identity, so it will do you no good to try and trick or wheedle information from anyone at Matherly Press."

"No one knows who he is?"

"I never said it was a he."

"Right, right, you didn't. Does that mean it's a she?"

"It means I'm not telling."

"Give me something," Nadia cajoled. "Friend to friend."

"You're not my friend."

Nadia was taken aback by Maris's tone. Suddenly, with that terse statement, they were no longer talking about the unnamed writer in Georgia.

She kept her smile in place, saying, "That's true, Maris. We haven't been. We've been too busy with our respective careers to get to know one another and cultivate a friendship, but I'd like to change that. I'd like—"

"We will never be friends, Nadia."

Again, Nadia was taken off guard by Maris's candor. "Why do you say that?"

"Because you want to sleep with my husband."

In spite of herself, Nadia was impressed. Miss Goody-Two-Shoes wasn't so goody after all. She had more grit than the girls' school polish suggested. Dropping all pretense, she met Maris's level gaze. "You can't wonder why. Noah is an attractive man."

"An attractive *married* man."

"A distinction that has never stopped me."

"That's what I hear."

Rather than being insulted, Nadia laughed. "Good. I love being the topic of scandalous conversation."

She took another sip of wine, then ran her index finger around the rim of the glass as she continued to study Maris with a new appreciation. She admired directness but never would have believed the former debutante capable of it to this degree.

But she wondered how cool Maris would remain if she confessed to her affair with Noah. What if she gave wifey a blow-by-blow—pun intended—account of what they had done in bed last night? She would bet that for all Maris's composure, that would rattle her right down to her Manolo Blahniks.

While that would be fun, it wouldn't be wise. There was too much at stake. Curbing the temptation to flaunt the affair, she asked, "Have you spoken to Noah about this?"

"Yes."

"And what did he say?"

"That his interest in you is strictly business-related. That your column is so influential, he can't risk offending you. That's why he goes along with your obvious machinations."

Nadia shrugged. "There you have it. I've established myself by using people as sources of information. In turn, they use me for free publicity and promotion. Noah understands the way it works."

She had managed to dance around the topic without either lying or telling the whole truth, and she hoped Maris would leave it at that. The WorldView deal needed no further complications.

Taking advantage of Maris's silence, she said, "I'm glad we cleared the air. Would you like a bite of sea bass?"

"No, thank you."

"It's delicious, but I've had my fill."

Actually, she was still hungry, but she pushed her plate away. One area of thigh tissue absorbed fat like a goddamn sponge despite the procedure she had undergone. She fanatically counted every calorie. Exercise was the only religion she believed in or practiced, and she worshiped strenuously every day.

Noah teased her about her rigid fitness regimen, saying she even brought it to bed with her. In fact, she counted sex as an aerobic exercise. She knew precisely how many calories were burned with each act of coitus.

Noah knew her well. He could be the sole man on the planet to whom she might be faithful. She didn't love him, any more than he loved her. Neither of them bought into the myth of romantic love. He had readily admitted that his marriage hadn't been inspired by amorous passion, but rather his burning desire to become part of the Matherly dynasty via the only Matherly available to him.

He had developed a mentor-protégé relationship with Daniel, but even that wasn't enough to satisfy his ambition. Becoming the old man's son-in-law was the next best thing to a blood kinship. Marrying Maris would cement his future, so he had made it happen.

Nadia admired that kind of single-minded scheming and the guts it took to carry out a bold plan. To her, ruthlessness was an aphrodisiac like no other. She spotted it in Noah the first time she met him. Recognizing in him a self-serving ambition that was equal to her own, she had wanted him, and she hadn't played coy.

Their first business lunch date had carried over into an afternoon spent in bed at the Pierre. To her delight, Noah approached sex with the same self-gratifying appetite and animalistic detachment as she. By the time he left her lying tangled up in the damp sheets, she was raw and sore and exhilarated.

They were also compatible out of bed. They understood one another. Their individual drives to achieve were harmonious but competitive enough to spark arguments and add zest. They were good for each other. They complemented each other. As a team, they would be unconquerable. That was why Nadia wanted to become Mrs. Noah Reed.

Well, that was *one* reason why.

The other was harder for her to acknowledge: There was just enough of Nadine remaining in her to want to be married before she died. She didn't want to grow old alone. Somewhere between power lunches and sundown specials, a single woman became a spinster.

Through her twenties and thirties, she had scorned the very idea of matrimony. To anybody who would listen she claimed no interest whatsoever in monogamy and the marriage bed. What a fucking—literally—bore.

But the truth was that, for all the men who had shared her bed, who had sighed and cried and groaned and crowed between her thighs, not one, not a single one, had ever asked her to be his wife.

And, to be brutally honest, Noah hadn't actually proposed, either. He wasn't the hearts-and-flowers-and-bended-knee type. She had more diamond rings than she had fingers and toes. How their plans for matrimony had come about was that she had told him she wanted to marry him. And Nadia never took no for an answer.

Now her future husband's present wife was finishing a cappuccino that she hadn't wanted. Usually Nadia could sweet-talk or browbeat someone out of a tidbit of information that she could expand into an item for her column, but Maris had remained stubbornly mute about her secret project. She seemed disinclined to talk on any level about the nature of the book or about the writer.

Not that Nadia gave a flip about Maris's silly secret project. The purpose of this lunch had been to keep Maris derailed, unaware, and blissfully ignorant of what Nadia and Noah were doing with WorldView behind her back.

But Maris had tipped her hand. Noah should be warned that she might not be as malleable and naive as she looked. Nadia hoped her suspicion of an affair had been quelled, because the last thing they needed in these important final weeks was a jealous wife breathing down their necks.

"Anything else, Maris?" she offered graciously. "Another cappuccino?"

"No, thank you. I should get back to the office. I'm playing catch-up after being away, as I knew I would be."

"Then why'd you come?" The question was out before Nadia realized she was going to ask it. But having done so, she owned up to being curious. Why had Maris accepted her invitation?

"For a long time now, we've detested the sight of one another. But we always played polite," Maris said. "I hate phoniness, especially in myself." She looked inward for a second, then added, "Or maybe I'm just disgusted with lies and liars. In any case, I thought it was time to tell you to your face that I'm on to you."

Nadia took it all in, then smiled wryly. "Fair enough." As they made their way to the entrance, she said, "You'll still feed me industry news items, won't you?"

"News. Not gossip."

"When you're ready to reveal this mysterious author and book, will you give me the scoop?"

"The author is very publicity-shy. I doubt—"

"Nadia, what a nice surprise."

Nadia turned at the greeting and found herself looking into the colorless countenance of Morris Blume, the last person on earth she would choose to bump into when Maris Matherly-Reed was standing beside her. She didn't find the surprise nice at all.

"How are you, Morris?" She extended her hand to him but kept her tone aloof and uninviting. "I recommend the sea bass."

"And I recommend the martinis," he said, raising his frosted glass. "In fact, I coached the bartender here on how to make one just right."

"Stirred or shaken?"

"Shaken."

Maris had moved to the coat check to retrieve her raincoat,

so Nadia felt free to engage in a mild flirtation. It wouldn't be smart to be too aloof. Her dinner with him at the Rainbow Room had been enjoyable. If she gave him the brush-off now, he would wonder why.

"Gin or vodka?"

"Vodka. Straight up and extra dirty."

One of her artfully waxed eyebrows arched. "I like the sound of that."

"Here." He lifted the pick from his glass and extended it toward her mouth.

Keeping her eyes on his, she touched the tip of her tongue to the olive, then closed her lips around it and sucked it into her mouth. "Hmm. My favorite thing."

"Join me in one?"

"I'm afraid I can't, Morris. Rain check?"

"I'll call."

She flashed him her most promising smile. It had been mastered after years of practice and was now practically habitual. She told him to enjoy his lunch and turned away to rejoin Maris.

To her consternation, the smile worked too well. Blume trailed her, making an introduction to Maris unavoidable. She executed it with as much casualness as she could affect.

As the two shook hands, Blume said, "I've long been an admirer of your publishing house."

"And a suitor," Maris remarked.

He grinned disarmingly. "So you've read the numerous letters I've written to your esteemed father?"

"Along with his replies."

"Do you agree with him?"

"Wholeheartedly. While we're flattered that an entity like WorldView is interested in merging with us, we like ourselves the way we are."

"So your husband told me during our last meeting."

Noah was reviewing the company's most recent shipping invoices when his wife stormed into his office and slammed the door behind her, stunning his secretary.

She tossed her handbag and damp raincoat into the nearest chair and strode to the edge of his desk. She'd been testy and despondent since her return from Georgia last evening, but she had never looked better. Today she was dressed in a suit tailored for office wear, but it was a form-fitting one he'd always admired. Time spent on the beach had put some color in her cheeks and stripped it from her hair. Sun-bleached strands framed her face, giving her a youthful, healthy appearance.

Her expression, however, wasn't sunny.

"Hello, Maris. How was your lunch?"

"I was just introduced to WorldView's whiz kid, Morris Blume. He told me to give you his regards."

Goddamn Nadia! he thought. Why hadn't she called to warn him of this? Then he remembered: He had given Cindy strict instructions to hold his calls until after he'd had time to review the financial statements stacked on his desk—ironically because of WorldView. He'd been going over the charts and columns entry by entry, becoming intimately familiar with them, seeking potential trouble spots which might cause Blume and company concern. Should they pose any questions, Noah wanted to have an explanation ready.

Remaining as unflappable as possible, he said, "How nice of Mr. Blume to remember me."

"Apparently it wasn't that much of a stretch for him, Noah, given you two had a recent meeting." She braced herself on his desk with stiff arms and leaned toward him, her eyes flashing. "What meeting is he talking about, Noah? And why wasn't I informed of it? *What* meeting?"

He stood up and came around the desk. "Maris, kindly calm down."

"Don't tell me to calm down."

"All right, then, I'm asking you to. Please."

He reached out to take her by the shoulders, but she backed away and slung off his extended hands.

"Would you like a glass of water?"

"I would like an explanation," she said, enunciating each word. "You know how Dad and I feel about conglomerates like WorldView."

"I share your opinion." He hiked his hip over the corner of his desk and placidly folded his hands on his thigh, although he would have liked to wrap them around her slender neck. "That's why I agreed to the meeting with WorldView."

She shook her head in disbelief, as though up until that time she had been clinging to the hope that Blume was lying. "You met with those jackals? You actually did? Behind my back and without my knowledge?"

Noah sighed and gave her a pained look. "Yes, I met with them. But before you go into orbit, can you be reasonable and give me an opportunity to explain?" He took her fuming silence for permission to continue.

"Blume's flunkies had been hounding me for months. They called until I stopped taking or returning their calls. With no regard for that blatant hint, they began faxing me until I got tired of throwing the damn things away.

"They made nuisances of themselves until I determined that the most expedient way to handle the situation was to attend a meeting and tell Blume to his baby's-ass face that we were not interested in anything he had to offer by way of a merger. Period. End of discussion. I don't think I could have made our position any clearer. I didn't tell you about it because you were extremely busy and didn't need any additional stress."

"I'm always busy."

"The meeting was inconsequential."

"I hardly think so."

"And, frankly," he said, "I anticipated that you would react emotionally rather than rationally. I predicted that you would fly off the handle and lose all perspective. I hoped to avoid a scene such as this."

"This isn't a *scene*, Noah. This is a private conversation between husband and wife, between business partners. Two relationships that should come with an implied trust."

"Exactly," he said, raising his voice to match the level of hers. "Which is why I'm amazed, both as your husband and your business partner, by your apparent lack of trust in me."

"Chalk it up to my reacting emotionally, flying off the handle, and going into orbit!"

"Which are fair analogies, Maris. You came barging in here and practically accused me of treason against Matherly Press."

"At the very least you consorted with the enemy!"

A knock on the door brought them around. Daniel was standing on the threshold, leaning heavily on his cane. "I'm exercising one privilege of old age, which is to intrude when uninvited."

Noah shot his cuffs. "Of course you're welcome, Daniel. Maris has just returned from lunch. We were having a discussion about—"

"I heard. From all the way down the hall." Daniel came in

and closed the door. "Maris is upset about the meeting you had with WorldView."

She reacted with a start. "You knew about it?"

"Noah told me of his decision to meet with them. I thought it was a sound idea and was glad he was going instead of me. I don't think I could have stomached it."

"Why wasn't I informed?"

She addressed the question to both of them, but Noah answered. "You were leaving for Georgia. Daniel and I could see how excited you were about this project and were afraid that if you knew about WorldView you'd change your plans. There was no reason to bother you with it."

"I'm not a child." She glowered at him, then at Daniel.

"We made a mistake in judgment," Daniel conceded. "It wasn't our intention to slight you."

"I don't feel slighted, I feel babied. I don't need protection, Dad. Or coddling. Or special favors. When it comes to business, I'm not a daughter or a wife, I'm an officer of this corporation.

"I should have been consulted on something this major, I don't care how busy I was or what my travel plans were. You were remiss and just plain wrong to exclude me from those discussions. I'm also mad as hell at both of you for letting me be made a fool of in front of Morris Blume and Nadia Schuller."

"I apologize," Daniel said.

"So do I," Noah echoed. "I'm terribly sorry that you were embarrassed today at lunch. I take full responsibility for that."

She didn't verbally accept their apologies, but Daniel took her silence as a tacit pardon. "Are we still on for dinner tonight? Maxine's making pot roast."

"We'll see you at seven," Noah confirmed. Daniel split an uneasy glance between them and then left them alone.

Maris went to the window and turned her back to the room. Noah remained where he was, still perched on the corner of his desk. Several minutes passed before she spoke. "I'm sorry I lost my temper."

"It hasn't been that long ago that I told you how beautiful you are when you're angry."

She came around quickly and angrily. "Don't patronize me, Noah."

"Don't be so goddamn sensitive," he snapped.

"I resent belittling, sexist remarks like that."

"That's a sexist remark? Can't I pay you a compliment without your reading something into it?"

"Not when we're fighting."

It was upsetting, and a little alarming, that his charm seemed to have lost some of its effectiveness. "What's with you, Maris? Since you got back yesterday, you've been as prickly as a porcupine. If working on this project," he said, slinging out his hand as though to shake off a contagion, "is going to cause a chronic case of PMS—"

"And that's not sexist?"

"—then I recommend you—"

"This has nothing to do with that!"

"Then what?"

"Nadia."

"Nadia?"

"Did she know about your meeting with Blume?"

He covered his discomfiture with a short laugh. "What? You think I called up our local gossip columnist and leaked the story?"

Folding her arms across her middle, Maris turned back to the window. "You're lying."

He came off the desk. "I beg your pardon?"

"She knew, Noah. Nadia's the most conniving woman I've ever met, and ordinarily she makes no secret of it. In fact, she takes pride in it. But when Blume mentioned his meeting with you, she blanched, looking as though she'd just been exposed. Then she couldn't hustle me away from him and out of there fast enough. As we said good-bye, she oozed goodwill, but nervously." She came around slowly. "She knew."

The look she gave him was so damned superior, it enraged him. He felt blood rushing to his head. He imagined capillaries bursting behind his eyeballs. Fury pulsated through him. Only by an act of will could he keep his voice from revealing it.

"Why would I tell Nadia, Maris? There was nothing to tell. If Nadia knew, she heard it from Blume. I've seen them with their heads together on more than one occasion. They probably stroke each other for inside information."

"Yes, that's how it works," she whispered as though to herself. When she refocused on him, she asked, "If Blume told her, why didn't she write about it in her column?"

"That's simple. WorldView owns a chain of newspapers that carry her column. She couldn't risk inflaming them by blabbing that David had thumbed his nose at Goliath, which is exactly what my meeting with them amounted to. If I'd known it was going to cause this much hullabaloo, I'd have continued avoiding them. I swear to God, I thought that meeting would be the end of their persistence."

"She confessed."

His heart knocked against his chest. It was difficult to keep his features impassive. "What? Who? Confessed what?"

"I told Nadia that I was on to her. That I could see through her and knew that she had designs on you."

"Designs?" he repeated with amusement. "What quaint phraseology."

"I didn't use it to be cute, Noah," she said testily. "Today I had lunch with a woman who told me to my face that she wants to sleep with you."

He rolled his eyes toward the ceiling. "Maris. For God's sake. Nadia wants to sleep with every man. She's made it her life's quest. She's one giant, raging hormone. She's come on to me, sure. Do you think I'm that easily flattered? She also comes on to waiters and doormen and probably to her garbage collector."

"A lot of men find her attractive."

"She is. But I didn't have an affair with her when I was single, and I sure as hell wouldn't jeopardize my marriage to you by having one with her now." He sighed and shook his head ruefully. "Is that what all this has been about? You let Nadia upset you?"

"No. I was more upset over the WorldView thing than I was about Nadia. If you want Nadia, then you deserve her."

He forced himself to smile. "I'm glad you gave me an opportunity to explain both misunderstandings. These things shouldn't fester. It's bad for our marriage."

He gave her a few moments to ruminate on that, then smiled the tentative smile of a scolded puppy. "If that's the end of the interrogation, I'd like to hug my interrogator."

Since she didn't raise any barriers, either real or suggested, he joined her where she stood and placed his arms around her. He pressed his face into her hair. "I was angry when I made that ludicrous statement about chronic PMS, but it has a basis of truth, doesn't it? You're not yourself." He stroked her back. "Was that little island so horrible?"

"I wondered if you were ever going to express any interest in my trip."

"That's unfair, Maris. Since your return, you haven't exactly invited conversation. You've been sullen and standoffish. In fact, I've considered approaching you with a chair and whip." Undaunted by her failure to laugh, he kissed her temple. "How was your trip? What's the island like?"

"Not horrible at all. Different."

"From what?"

He felt her shrug. "It's hard to explain. Just different."

"And the author, was he as difficult to work with as you expected?"

"More difficult than I expected."

"We've got an impressive slate of books to publish next year from our authors under contract. Why bother with this recluse?"

"Because he writes well. Very well."

"But is he worth the difficulty he puts you through?"

"I won't give up on this book, Noah."

"I'm only thinking of you. If working with him makes you edgy and—"

"It doesn't."

Luckily she couldn't see his expression or she would have realized how close she came to being slapped senseless for interrupting him. He took a moment to tamp down his anger before asking in a deceptively pleasant voice, "What is this literary marvel's name?"

"I'm sworn to secrecy."

"Isn't he carrying the anonymity to a ludicrous degree?"

"There's a reason. He's disabled."

"How so?"

"I really can't talk about it, Noah. I can't betray his trust."

"Are you sure your opinion of the writing hasn't been swayed by his disability?"

"I loved the writing before I knew about his circumstances, which don't affect his talent. He'd be talented in any form. In spite of all the difficulty working with him imposes, I'm enjoying the work. It's going to be good for me. I'm getting to flex some editorial muscle. Over the last few years, I've become fat and lazy."

"A little lazy, maybe, but not fat."

He slid his hands over her butt, a caress he knew she liked and that usually evoked an agreeable response. This time it was less effective. "I was speaking metaphorically, Noah."

"I realize that. Still . . ." He bent his head and kissed her, first on the cheek, then her mouth. He wanted to be assured that her outburst wasn't an indicator of something more serious, specifically that she doubted his loyalty to Matherly Press.

She returned the kiss. Not with the fervor he sought, perhaps, but when he pulled back she smiled up at him, assuaging his concern.

"If these financials didn't need my attention," he growled, "I'd be tempted to lock the door and take you right here."

"Why don't you say 'damn the financials' and do just that? I could be taken."

He kissed her again, then purposefully set her away from him. "Sorely tempting, darling. But duties call."

"I understand."

"Tonight? After dinner with Daniel?"

"You have a date." She kissed him quickly, then retrieved her raincoat and handbag. "I may stay late and try to clear my desk, so I probably won't change before dinner."

"Then we'll leave straight from here and ride over together. I'll have a car waiting downstairs at six-forty-five."

"See you then."

He blew her a kiss as she went out, then returned to his desk, confident that he had dodged a bullet. As always, Maris had been pacified with a little attention and affection. But her upset over the WorldView meeting was no small matter.

When he considered how close he'd come to being caught today, he wished to watch Morris Blume slowly and agonizingly bleed to death. Telling Maris about that meeting had obviously been Blume's way of reminding him that the deadline was fast approaching. Blume had seized an unplanned opportunity to make a power play, to remind him that WorldView was ultimately in charge of this transaction.

It had been a close call. It had cost him some valuable time. In the long run, however, the incident had caused no permanent damage. Thank God he'd had the foresight to inform Daniel of that meeting with just this contingency in mind. In the event that he or Maris had gotten wind of it—and the industry grapevine was notorious—he had taken the old man into his confidence, thereby throwing him off track.

The Matherlys weren't fools. But they were nowhere close to being as clever as he. He left absolutely nothing to chance. He planned meticulously. His schemes were long-range and therefore took a steely patience and perseverance that lesser individuals lacked.

He relied on his instincts and his intelligence, but also on the best possible resource, the one that was virtually unfailing and always in full supply—human nature. Mind control was easy if you knew a person's likes, dislikes, secrets, weaknesses, fears.

He possessed a gift for getting people to go right where he wanted them to go and to do exactly what he wanted them to do. He was talented that way. He had an uncanny knack for manipulating people, for persuading them to make a decision they mistakenly thought was their own and to act on it. He had done it before. Most recently with Howard Bancroft. But he had honed this particular skill long before he had ever heard of Howard Bancroft.

His desk phone rang. Before he could even speak, Cindy apologized for the interruption. "I'm sorry, Mr. Reed, but Ms. Schuller has called five times and insists on being put through."

"Fine." Noah depressed the blinking button. "Hello, Nadia," he said breezily. "I understand you had quite an exciting lunch."

"Envy" Ch. 12
Key West, Florida, 1986

Todd Grayson's first impression of Key West was a crushing disappointment.

Making the move had been nearly all he'd talked about for months. He'd thought of little else and had practically exed off the days of his calendar like a child counting down toward Christmas. He'd resented anything that interfered with his daydreaming and planning, including his final semester's studies. His heart, mind, and soul had been focused singly on getting to his Floridian mecca.

But now, having arrived, having fulfilled a long-held dream, his first sight of it left him less than spiritually enraptured.

He likened the place to an old whore. It looked used, seedy, a little unhealthy, and a lot tired. Continuing the metaphor in his mind as though he were writing it down, Key West appeared to be more a common streetwalker who advertised her wares on a corner, rather than an exotic courtesan who enticed with whispered promises. Once the tacky and rather pathetic attempts at glamour were stripped away, the town had little to offer and nothing to recommend her. She was cheap and common, and the only promise at which she hinted was one of dissipation.

His and Roark's plan had been to depart for Florida the afternoon of their college graduation. They had everything packed and ready, their only chore before hitting the road being to return the caps and gowns in which they'd marched to "Pomp and Circumstance" and received their degrees.

They planned to caravan in their respective automobiles and had agreed to stop just before their arrival and toss a coin to determine which of them got to lead the way to Duval Street.

But fate intervened. Their well-laid plans were changed for them. A family obligation prevented Todd from leaving that day. Roark offered to postpone leaving, too, but after a rushed consultation, they agreed that he should go ahead and start looking for housing.

"I'll be the scout. By the time you get there, I'll have camp set up," Roark had said as they exchanged their dejected good-byes. Roark's Toyota was packed to the gills. Every square inch of interior space had been utilized to transport all that he owned in the world from the fraternity house where he had lived for the past three years to the next phase of his life.

"This sucks," Todd muttered.

"Big time. But hey, it's only a minor setback."

"Easy for you to say. It's not your setback. While I'm languishing, you'll be down there writing your ass off."

"Hardly, man. I'll be busy scoping out things, finding us a place to live. Getting the telephone hooked up. That kinda shit. I won't get any serious writing done."

Todd knew that wasn't true. Roark always wrote—drunk or sober, tired or wired, sick or well. He wrote when he was happy and when he was sad. He wrote just as much when he was in a good mood as he did when he was pissed over something. He wrote when it was flowing easily and when the phrases simply would not come. He wrote no matter what. Any

which way you looked at it, despite all his arguments to the
contrary, this was giving him a head start, and Todd resented
it like hell.

As Roark wedged himself into the driver's seat of his
packed Toyota, he tried again to lift Todd's spirits. "I know
this seems like a big deal now, but one day we'll barely
remember it. You'll see."

As agreed, he had called Todd immediately upon his arrival
in Key West. A few days later he phoned again to report that
he had rented them an apartment. Todd barraged him with
questions about it, but his answers were evasive, his descriptions vague. After hanging up, Todd realized that all he really
knew about their new place of residence was that it fit into
their budget.

It was six weeks before Todd was able to set out for his relocation to the tip of the continent. The morning of his departure,
as he left his childhood home for what would be the last time,
he wasted no time on sentiment and never looked back.
Instead, he equated it to a release from prison.

He drove almost twenty hours that first day and crossed the
state line into Florida before pulling off at a roadside park and
napping in the driver's seat of his car. He arrived in Key West
at midafternoon the second day. Although not all his
expectations were met upon his arrival, some were.

The air, for instance. It was warm and balmy. No more
running to an early class on a bitterly cold and windy morning
ever again, thank you very much. The sun was hot. Palms and
banana trees grew in abundance. Jimmy Buffett music was pervasive, as though it were secreted through the pores of the city.

As he navigated the tourist-clogged streets, following the
rudimentary directions Roark had given him, his initial disappointment began to recede and was replaced by flurries of excitement. His mood was buoyed by the sights and sounds and
smells.

But this flicker of encouragement didn't last. It was snuffed
out when he located his newly leased domicile. Dismayed, he

checked the address twice, hoping to God he'd made a wrong turn.

Surely this was one of Roark's practical jokes.

Tall oleander bushes formed a unkempt hedge between the street and the shallow, weedy lawn in front of the building. He expected Roark to leap from between the blooming shrubs, grinning like a jackass and braying, "Man you oughta see your expression. Looks like you've been hit in the face with a sack of buzzard shit."

They would have a good laugh, then Roark would guide him to their actual address. Later they'd go out for a beer and relive the moment, and that would be the first of a thousand times they would retell the story, as they retold all their good stories when they wanted or needed a laugh.

Except the one about the incident with Professor Hadley. That was one story that neither retold. They never talked about it at all.

Todd parked his car at the crumbling curb and got out. He was reluctant even to step between the oleanders—which looked like shrubs on steroids—and follow the cracked sidewalk up to the door of the three-story building. The cinder-block exterior had been painted a flaming flamingo pink, as though the lurid hue would conceal the low-grade building material. Instead, the color accented the lack of quality.

A crack as wide as Todd's index finger ran through the wall of blocks from eaves to foundation. A wild fern was growing out of it at one spot. Hurricane shutters, the color of pea soup, were missing slats and seemed to be clinging to the building only out of fear of falling into the stagnant water that had collected around the foundation. As wide as a moat, it was a flourishing mosquito hatchery.

The frame of the aluminum screen door probably had once been rectangular, but it had been dented and bent so many times that it was grossly misshapen. A large part of the mesh had been peeled away, making it totally ineffectual against flying insects—or chameleons, Todd discovered when he opened

the door and stepped into a dank vestibule with a concrete
floor. Two of the green lizards were lounging on the interior
wall. One scampered away when Todd entered. The other
puffed out his red throat as though in protest of the intrusion.

Six mailboxes, which would usually be found on the outside
of a building, had been secured to the wall. Once his eyes had
adjusted to the dimness, Todd read, to his distress, his and
Roark's name on one of the boxes.

There were six apartments in all, two on each floor. Theirs
was on the third. Stepping over a puddle of unidentifiable fluid,
he started upstairs. When he reached the second-floor landing,
he could hear *The Price Is Right* coming from a TV within one
of the apartments. Otherwise the building was quiet.

By the time he reached the third floor, he was sweating. He
cursed the same balminess he'd been extolling only minutes
before as he'd driven through the streets with the car windows
rolled down, ogling the bare-shouldered, bare-legged girls
strolling the sidewalks.

Surely the individual apartments were air-conditioned, he
thought as he tried the door knob on 3A. It was locked. He
knocked—three times in all before Roark answered. His
suntanned face broke into a wide grin. "Hey, you made it! An
hour early."

"No air-conditioning? Are you fucking kidding me?"

The heat inside the apartment was, if anything, more
stifling than the unventilated vestibule and staircase. And
that was only one of the many amenities the apartment
lacked. As Todd surveyed it, his misgivings were realized.
And then some.

It was a rat hole, and that was putting it kindly. Actually, it
would need to undergo a major renovation to reach the classification of a rat hole. No self-respecting rat would be caught
dead here.

An oscillating fan was blowing hot air around the matching
beanbag chairs that served as living room furniture. It was also
circulating the stench of leftover pizza that had congealed

inside its box on the small table that, along with a two-burner hot plate and a sink, comprised the kitchen.

"I was in the shower." Indeed, Roark had answered the door sopping wet. His only nod toward modesty was a hand towel clutched around his hips.

"I thought maybe you'd gone homo," Todd said querulously.

"Come on, you gotta see this." Roark turned and headed toward an open door that led into another room.

Todd was so angry he could barely suck the stifling oxygen into his lungs. His deposit money had been squandered. If Roark had signed a lease on this place, then he could eat it for all Todd cared. He would flatly refuse to be responsible. Obviously his friend had suffered a mental lapse, or had lost their pooled money along the way, or had gotten it stolen, or something.

No rational person, no one who wasn't absolutely destitute and desperate, would voluntarily take shelter in this building. Being homeless had more stability than this, because unless the sky fell, a homeless person wouldn't have to fear being crushed to death by a loose plaster ceiling.

"Roark, damn you!" Todd struck out after him, shouting his name. "Roark! What the fuck?"

The door led into a small cubicle of a room with twin beds. One was groaning under the weight of Roark's belongings, most of which were still packed. Articles of clothing had been pulled from the crates and were spilling out over the tops of them like entrails.

On the other, Roark had been sleeping. And working, apparently. A computer terminal and keyboard were on the bed itself, the tower and printer were on the floor beside it.

"A computer?" Todd exclaimed. "You got a *pc*? When?" They had wanted word processors the way most collegiates covet TransAms. Roark had said nothing to him about buying a computer. "Is that what you spent our money on?"

"My uncle gave it to me for graduation," Roark called in a stage whisper. "Now will you shut up about that and get in here? Hurry."

Todd turned toward the opening where a door should have been. Instead, the detached door had been propped against the adjacent wall. Todd had a fleeting thought that it might have been placed there to provide the wall with additional support.

Through the opening was a bathroom. What differentiated this one from the communal bathroom in the fraternity house was that the one in the frat house had been cleaner and more sanitary—tobacco spit cups, shower fungi, and unattended fixtures notwithstanding.

But even more appalling than the condition of the sink and toilet was the sight of his friend, who had dropped the towel and reentered the shower. He was standing beneath the spray and staring out an open window.

"What uncle? Why didn't you tell me your uncle had given you a pc for graduation?"

Roark glanced over his shoulder. "Are you coming, or what?"

"I'm not getting into that filthy shower with you. I'm waiting for you to tell me what the—"

"Just shut up and come here. Quick. Before they go inside."

Roark's excitement was contagious and compelling. In spite of everything else, Todd was intrigued. He slipped off his sneakers and stepped into the shower fully clothed. Pushing Roark away from the window, he peered through the rusty screen.

On the second-floor roof of the neighboring building, three naked girls were sunbathing. Naked meaning completely nude. Not just topless, but mother nekkid. All they had on was a glistening layer of suntan oil. In fact, while he stood there stupefied, one of the girls was languidly spreading the oil over her torso.

"That one's name is Amber," Roark whispered.

Amber was rubbing her breasts now, smearing the oil over nipples as large and red as strawberries. Todd gulped. "You know them?"

"Hell, yeah. To speak to and call by name. Our buildings share a parking lot. They dance at a strip joint."

Which explained why they were visions of the most carnal variety. This was no trio of ordinary-looking women. They were spectacular. Their tits probably weren't the ones they'd been born with, but who the hell cared?

"The one with the shaved crotch is Starlight," Roark informed him. "For her grand finale it glitters with this sparkly stuff."

"Her pussy glitters?"

"Swear to God. They aim the spotlight right at it."

"Damn."

"The brunette is Mary Catherine."

"Doesn't sound like a stripper's name."

"She strips out of a nun's habit. Then she takes this rosary and—"

"Don't tell me. Let me be surprised." The brunette was lying facedown on her towel. Todd kissed the air. "Look at that ass."

"I have," Roark said with a chuckle. "Like a valentine, isn't it? Frankly I'm partial to her. She's the friendliest, too."

"They do this every day?"

"Except on Sundays. Saturday nights they do three shows, so they usually sleep all day Sunday."

Amber capped the bottle of suntan oil, then lay down on her beach towel, spreading her thighs wide enough to make certain the sun could reach the insides of them.

"Oh, man," Todd groaned.

Laughing, Roark stepped from the shower and retrieved his towel. "I think you need a few minutes of privacy."

"It won't take a few minutes, buddy."

Roark was dressed in a pair of shorts, sitting cross-legged on his bed, his keyboard bridging his knees, when Todd appeared in the doorway and propped himself weakly against the jamb. Roark looked over at him and grinned. "Well, what do you think of the apartment?"

"Fucking fantastic, man. I can't think of anyplace I'd rather live."

Mike Strother laid the manuscript pages aside. He sipped from his glass of lemonade made with lemons he had squeezed himself. He was taking a day off from working on the mantel. Yesterday he had applied a coat of varnish and was giving it an extra day to dry because of the humidity. That was the explanation he'd given Parker anyway.

Throughout the morning, Mike had worked outdoors. Parker had seen him on his hands and knees turning the soil in the flower beds with a trowel. Later, he'd swept the veranda and washed the front windows. But the afternoon heat had driven him inside in time to prepare Parker's lunch, which he was only now getting around to eating.

He had been writing—actually rewriting—since dawn and was now anxious to hear Mike's reaction to this latest draft.

Parker valued Mike's critiques of his work, even when they were negative. Although he sometimes felt like telling the older man to go to hell and to take his lousy opinion with him, he invariably reread the disputed passages with a different perspective, only to realize that Mike's observations were well founded. Even if he didn't agree with them, he took Mike's insights into consideration during his rewrites.

Mike was never quick to comment, whether his review was good or bad. But when he was piqued at Parker for one reason or another, he deliberately withheld his remarks until Parker asked for them. Today, he was taking even more time than usual, and Parker knew he was doing so just to be vexing.

But Parker was feeling rather ornery himself. He stubbornly waited as Mike thumbed through the pages a second time, rereading several passages, making noncommittal harrumphing sounds like a physician listening to a hypochondriac's litany of complaints, and tugging thoughtfully on his lower lip.

This continued for at least ten minutes more. Parker was the first to crack. "Could you please translate those grunts into a semblance of verbiage?"

Mike looked across at him as though he had forgotten he was there, which Parker knew to be a ruse. "You use the word 'fuck' and its derivatives a lot."

"That's it? That took ten minutes of contemplation? That's the substance of your critique?"

"I couldn't help but notice."

"Guys their age use that kind of language. Particularly in the company of other guys. In fact, they try and top each other, see who can be the most vulgar, talk the dirtiest."

"I didn't."

"You're an aberration."

Mike scowled but let the insult pass. "You also use the word 'homo.' Very offensive."

"Granted. But in '88, we hadn't yet coined the term 'politically correct.' And, again, I'm staying true to my characters. Randy, heterosexual males having a private conversation aren't going to be sensitive and deferential when referring to gay men."

"Or to the female anatomy, it seems."

"Particularly to the female anatomy," Parker said, ignoring the implied reproof. "They wouldn't use the polite or clinical word for an act or a body part when there's an off-color alternative. Now that your fussiness over the coarse language has been addressed, what did you think—"

"You didn't go to the cotton gin today, did you?"

"What's that got to do with the manuscript?" Parker asked impatiently.

"*Does* it have something to do with the manuscript?"

"You're being awfully contrary this afternoon. Did you forget to take your stool softener last night?"

"You're changing the subject, Parker."

"Or is that lemonade spiked with Jack Daniel's?"

"More to the point, you're *avoiding* the subject."

"Me? I thought the subject was my manuscript. You brought up—"

"Maris."

"The gin."

"The two are linked," Mike said. "After months of preoccupation with that place, you haven't been back to it since she left."

"So?"

"So the fact that you haven't gone back to the gin has nothing to do with what happened there between you and Maris the morning she left?"

"No. I mean yes. I mean . . . Shit. Whatever the hell you just said." Parker hunched his shoulders cantankerously. "Besides, nothing happened."

"Going there wouldn't bring back memories either pleasant or disturbing? It wouldn't remind you of her? Wouldn't make you recall something that she said or something that you said that you'd rather forget?"

"You know what?" Parker tilted his head back and eyed Mike down the length of his nose. "You should have been a woman."

"Let's see. During this one conversation you've managed to accuse me of being a freak, then a closet drunk with bowel problems, and now you're insulting my masculinity."

"You're as nosy as an old woman who has nothing else to do except butt into other people's business."

"Maris is my business, too, Parker."

His sharp tone changed the character of the conversation and signaled that the banter was over. Parker turned away and stared out over the ocean. It was calm this afternoon, a mirror casting a brassy reflection of the sun off its surface.

As they did each day at about this time, a small flock of pelicans flew in formation just above the treetops toward their nighttime roost. Parker wondered if it was constraining or comforting to be part of such a closely knit group. He had been a loner for so many years, he couldn't remember what it was like to be a member of a family, or a fraternity, or any community of individuals.

Mackensie Roone was beloved by readers all over the world. He resided on their nightstands and in their briefcases. He accompanied them to the beach, to the toilet, and on modes of mass transit. He was taken into their bathtubs and beds. He shared a rare intimacy with them.

But Parker Evans was known only by a few and loved by no one. That had been his choice, of course, and a necessary one. Recently, however, he had begun to realize the tremendous price he had paid for his years of reclusion. Over time, he had become accustomed to being alone. But lately he'd begun feeling lonely. There was a difference. That difference became evident the moment you realized that you no longer liked being alone as well as you liked being with someone else. That's when aloneness turned to loneliness.

Staving off the threatening despair, he quietly apologized to Mike for involving him in his scheme. "I know you feel responsible to some extent, and I admire you for having a conscience about it."

"I played along with that ridiculous test we put her through because you asked me to. Was that necessary?"

"Probably not," Parker admitted in a quiet voice.

"I could have told her you were Mackensie Roone. I could have pretended that it slipped out. You would have been angry at me, but you would have gotten over it. Instead, I went along with the whole charade, and I'm ashamed of myself for it."

"Don't be, Mike. You're blameless. This is all my doing. From start to finish, beginning to end—whatever the end may be— I'm the guilty party here, not you."

"That doesn't exactly absolve me for my voluntary participation."

With a rueful shrug, Parker said, "No, but that's the best I can do."

They lapsed into a weighty silence. Eventually Mike picked up his reading glasses, unknowingly reminding Parker of Maris and the eyeglasses she had been wearing the last time he saw her. Which might have been the last time he would ever see her, he reminded himself.

"These young men seem to have reconciled completely," Mike remarked as he thumbed through the pages again. "I don't sense any residual hostility between them."

"Following the incident with Hadley, Roark carried on as though it had never happened," Parker explained. "He made a conscious decision not to let it affect their friendship."

"Noble of him. Nevertheless, it's still—"

"There," Parker interrupted, completing the other man's thought. "Like an unsightly birthmark that mars an otherwise beautiful baby's face. Neither wants to acknowledge the blemish on their friendship. Both look past it, hoping that it will gradually fade and ultimately disappear completely, as some birthmarks do, so that, eventually, no one can remember the baby having had it."

"Good analogy."

"It is, isn't it? I may use it." He jotted himself a note.

"You didn't specify or explain the family obligation that prevented Todd from leaving with Roark."

"It's discussed in the next scene. Roark extends condolences to Todd for his mother's death. She didn't want to worry him during those last few crucial months leading up to his college graduation, so she didn't tell him that she'd been diagnosed with a rampant cancer. She attended the commencement exercise, but it was an effort for her. The therapy she'd been receiving had weakened her, but unfortunately had had no effect on the malignancy. So rather than leaving for Florida, Todd accompanied her home. He stayed with her until she died."

"Quite a sacrifice, especially when you consider what moving to Key West represented to him."

Parker smiled sardonically. "Save the kudos. I have him saying . . . Wait, let me read it to you." He shuffled through the sheets of handwritten notes scattered across his worktable until he found the one he was looking for.

"Todd thanks Roark for his expression of sympathy, so on and so forth, then he says, '"Actually, her death was very convenient."' Roark reacts with appropriate shock. Then Todd adds, '"I'm only being honest."

"'"Cruelly honest," says Roark.

"'Todd shrugs indifferently. "Maybe, but at least I'm not a hypocrite. Am I sorry she's dead? No. Her dying left me completely untethered and unencumbered. Free. I've got no one to think about except myself now. No one to account to. Nothing to cater to except my writing."'"

Mike assimilated that. "So the white gloves are coming off in the next segment."

"If by that you mean that Todd's true character will be revealed, no. Not entirely. We do, however, begin to detect chinks in the facade."

"The same way Noah Reed's true character was revealed to you once you moved to Key West. Bit by bit."

Parker felt his facial muscles stiffen as they did whenever Noah was called to the forefront of his mind. "It takes Roark only a few chapters to see his so-called friend for what he really is. It took me a couple of years. And by then it was too late."

He stared hard at his legs for several moments, then, forcing those ugly memories aside, he referred once again to his handwritten notes. "Professor Hadley is also resurrected in the next scene."

Mike poured himself another glass of lemonade, then sat back in his chair and assumed a listening aspect.

"Actually, it's Todd who introduces the subject," Parker explained. "He comments on how wonderful it is that they managed to turn that situation around. He says if he hadn't pulled that trick on Roark, their present relationship with the professor might not be as solid as it is. He says Roark should be thanking him for what he did."

"Roark isn't ready to go so far as to thank him, but he concedes that it worked to their advantage in the long run." Parker took a breath. "This conversation is to inform the reader that Professor Hadley had seen such promise in these talented young men, he's offered to continue critiquing their work even though they're no longer his students."

"Very generous of him."

Parker frowned. "He's not completely selfless. I have a chapter planned, written from his point of view, where the reader learns that he would coach these two young writers simply because he recognizes their talent and wants to see it honed and refined, and then, hopefully, published and shared with an appreciative audience."

"I sense a 'however' coming."

"*However,* wouldn't it be a star in his crown if he discovered the next generation's defining novelists?"

"In other words, he's an opportunistic old bastard."

Parker laughed. "Everyone is opportunistic, Mike. Everyone. Without exception. Only the degree of one's opportunism separates him from others. How far is one willing to go to get what he wants?

"Some fall by the wayside early. They give up, or take another course, or simply decide that what they're after isn't worth the risks or the costs involved in getting it. But others . . ."

He paused and focused on a spot in near space. "To get what

they want, others are willing to go to any lengths. *Any* lengths. They'll go beyond what's lawful, or decent, or moral so long as they come out ahead."

Mike seemed about to remark on that bit of philosophizing, when he changed his mind and asked a question that Parker guessed was less incendiary. "Do you want to assign that much importance to a secondary character?"

"Hadley, you mean? He's important to the plot."

"He is?"

"Integral. I have to set that up."

Mike nodded, seemingly distracted by another thought. Half a minute passed. Finally Parker asked him what was on his mind. "The pacing? The dialogue? Too much narrative about the Key West apartment, or not enough?"

"The brunette stripper on the roof—"

"Mary Catherine."

"Is the girl—"

"In the prologue who accompanies them on the boat. Remember, one of the boys removes her bikini top and waves it above his head before they're even out of the harbor. So it's important that I establish in the reader's mind that she's a friendly, playful sort. There's more about her in an upcoming scene."

"She's a nice girl, Parker."

"The stripper with the heart-shaped ass?"

Mike gave him a sour look.

Parker cursed beneath his breath. Mike was determined to talk about Maris, and when Mike got something into his head to talk about, he would continue dredging it up until it was talked about.

Parker returned his notes to the worktable, knowing that he might just as well get this conversation out of the way so he could get on with the rest of his afternoon. "First of all, Maris is a woman, not a girl. And whoever said she wasn't nice? Not me. Did you ever hear me say she wasn't nice? She says 'please' and 'thank you,' keeps her napkin in her lap, and covers her mouth when she yawns."

Mike fixed an admonishing glare on him. "Admit it. She's not what you expected."

"No. She's taller by a couple inches." He was on the receiving end of another baleful look. He spread his arms wide. "What do you want me to say? That she's not the snob I thought she'd be? Okay, she's not."

"You expected a spoiled rich girl."

"A total bitch."

"An aggressive and abrasive—"

"Ball-buster."

"Who would blow in here, disrupting the peace and trying to intimidate us with her New York sophistication and superiority. Instead, Maris was . . . well, you know better than I what she was like." As an afterthought, the old man said, "All the same, she did make an impact, didn't she?"

Yes, she had. Just a much softer, more feminine impact than Parker had expected. He glanced at the vase on the coffee table. Maris had gathered sprigs of honeysuckle during a morning stroll and had asked if he would object to her putting them in water. "Just to brighten the room up a bit," she'd said.

Mike, infatuated with her to the point of idiocy, had turned the kitchen upside down until he found a suitable container. For days, the wild bouquet had filled the solarium with a heady fragrance. Now it was an eyesore. The blossoms were shriveled, the water swampy and smelly. But Parker hadn't asked Mike to remove it, and Mike hadn't taken it upon himself to empty the vase. It was a reminder of her they weren't quite ready to relinquish.

The shells she had collected on the beach were still spread out on the end table where she'd proudly displayed them. When she carried them in, her feet had been bare and dusted with sand. They'd left footprints on the tile floor, which she had insisted on sweeping up herself.

His dying houseplant was rallying because she had moved it to a better spot and had watered it just enough, not too much.

Two fashion magazines that she'd browsed through while he worked on his novel were still lying in the chair she'd last occupied.

It was that throw pillow there, the one with the fringe around it, that she had hugged to her breasts while she listened to him reading a passage from his manuscript.

Everywhere he looked, there was evidence of her.

"She's an intelligent woman," Mike said. "She proved that. Smart but sensitive."

Mike was speaking in a hushed voice, as though he felt her spirit in the room and didn't want to frighten it away. Which annoyed Parker more than if he'd scraped his fingernails down a chalkboard. They were acting like saps. He as much as Mike. A pair of sentimental fools.

And anyway, who said his room had needed to be brightened up a bit? He had liked it just fine the way it was before Maris Matherly-Reed had ever darkened the door.

"Don't get misty, Mike," he said, a shade more harshly than he had intended. "She plays sensitive because she wants a book from me."

"A book. Not income. I don't think she cares if *Envy* makes her company a red cent. She loves your writing."

Parker shrugged indifferently, but secretly he agreed. In spite of the haggling, Maris seemed much more interested in the storytelling aspects of his book than in its earning potential.

"She can also laugh at herself. I like that in a person." Then, looking at Parker askance, Mike added, "I guess there's no need mentioning that she's beautiful."

"Then why'd you mention it?"

"So you noticed?"

"What, you think I'm blind as well as lame? Yeah, she's good to look at." He made a gesture that said, *So what?* "Her looks were no surprise. We saw her picture in that magazine article."

"The photo didn't do her justice."

"I expected her to be attractive. Noah never dated an ugly girl," Parker muttered. "Not that I knew about."

When Mike declined to comment one way or another, Parker went on. "You know what? I'm glad she's attractive. Real glad. It'll make what I'm going to do all the more enjoyable."

"What are you going to do?"

"You know I never talk over a plot until I've written at least some of it down. Guess you'll have to use your imagination."

"You're going to use Maris."

"Fuckin'-A. And if you don't approve of my language, cover your ears." He wiped a bead of sweat from his forehead. The air conditioner was working, so why did it feel so damn hot in here? "Now, can we please end this discussion? I've got work to do."

Mike calmly finished his glass of lemonade, then rifled through the manuscript pages again. At last he stood, crossed to Parker, and passed the sheets to him. "It's coming along."

"Don't go overboard with the praise," Parker said drolly. "I might get a swelled head."

On his way out, Mike said, "You may want to rethink your motivation."

"My characters' motivation is perfectly clear."

Mike didn't even deign to turn around and address Parker face-to-face when he said, "I wasn't referring to your characters."

CHAPTER 19

This is my favorite room." Maris basked in the familiar comfort of her father's home study, where they were having cocktails.

At the last minute Noah had needed to consult with the contracts manager over a disputed clause, so he had urged her to go to Daniel's house ahead of him. She hadn't minded his being detained. Since her return from Georgia, she hadn't spent any time alone with her father.

"I'm rather partial to this room myself," Daniel said. "I spend a lot of time in here, but I like it even more when you're sharing it with me."

She laughed. "You didn't always feel that way. I remember times when I'd come in here hoping to coax you away from the work that you'd brought home with you. I made a pest of myself." They smiled at the shared recollections, but Daniel's expression turned somber.

"I wish I had those times to relive, Maris. If I did, I'd spend more time skating in the park or playing Monopoly with you. I regret passing up those opportunities."

"I wasn't deprived much, Dad. In fact, I wasn't deprived of anything. Most of all you."

"You're being far too generous, but I thank you for saying that."

Maris sensed a melancholia in him tonight. He'd been very glad to see her, but his jocularity didn't quite ring true. His comic bickering with Maxine seemed forced. His smiles were good counterfeits of the real thing, but they were noticeably strained.

"Dad, aren't you feeling well? Is something wrong?"

He cited Howard Bancroft's funeral. "It's tomorrow morning."

She nodded sympathetically. "Howard wasn't just your corporate lawyer, he was a good and trusted friend."

"I'm going to miss him. He'll be missed all over this city. For the life of me, I can't understand what drove him to do such a terrible thing."

He was grieving his loss, naturally, but Maris wasn't entirely sure that Bancroft's suicide was the only thing weighing heavily on Daniel's mind. She reasoned that his mood might be in response to her own. She wasn't exactly a barrel of laughs tonight, either. She could attribute her moodiness to two things. Well, actually two *people*. Noah and Parker.

Noah's explanation for his meeting with WorldView had been plausible. Daniel had even verified it. Nevertheless, it rankled that they had kept her unaware of something so vitally important to the future of Matherly Press. She had never been *that* busy.

Had she been anyone else, her high ranking in the company would have demanded she be kept apprised. Their personal relationships should not have been a factor. As senior vice president of the corporation, she had deserved to be informed of Blume's poaching. As a wife, she deserved her husband's respect.

That's what had really infuriated her—Noah's nonchalant dismissal of her anger.

He'd treated her like a child who could be easily mollified with a candy stick, or a pet whose trust could be earned with a pat on the head. His peacemaking platitudes had been textbook standards. Marriage 101, lesson three: How to Fight Constructively.

The way in which he'd placated her had been more belittling than his original offense. Didn't he know her any better than to think she could be so easily defused and dismissed?

"Maris?"

She raised her head and smiled at Daniel with chagrin. "Did I drift?"

"No farther than a million miles."

"I'm sorry. I've got a lot on my mind."

"Would you freshen my drink, please?" When she hesitated, he waved his hand irritably. "I know, I know. You think I'm drinking too much. By the way, I saw through that man-to-man advice Noah gave me. It came straight from you."

"I worry about you navigating the stairs after you've had a few, that's all. You're a little unsteady to start."

"If I get drunk tonight, you can carry me up the stairs piggyback, how's that?" Chastening him with a look, she crossed the room to get his glass and carried it with her to the bar. "While you're at it, why don't you have another?" he suggested. "I think you could use it."

She poured him another scotch and refilled her wineglass with Chardonnay. "Why?"

"Why do I think you need alcoholic reinforcement this evening? Because you look like your puppy has run away from home."

True. She was feeling a huge sense of loss. She'd been reluctant to pinpoint the source of it and assign it a name, but in her heart of hearts, she knew its name: Parker Evans.

She resettled in her chair, and as Daniel methodically refilled the bowl of his pipe, she let her gaze wander around the room. She took in her father's extensive collection of coveted leather-bound first editions. They were meticulously lined up on the shelves of a massive cabinet with gleaming glass doors.

She couldn't help but compare this neat and costly library to

Parker's haphazardly crammed bookshelves. She contrasted the expensive furnishings and appointments of this room to the wicker chairs and chintz cushions in Parker's solarium. This room had an imported marble fireplace that had been salvaged from an Italian palace. The wood mantel in Parker's house had been carved by a slave named Phineas.

And she realized that, as much as she loved this house, this room, and the fond memories of childhood they evoked, she was homesick for St. Anne Island, and Parker's house with its creaky hardwood floors, and the cozy guest cottage with its claw-footed bathtub.

She was homesick for Mike's clattering in the kitchen and the click of the keys as Parker typed in his rapid, two-fingered, hunt-and-peck method. She missed the oddly harmonious racket of the cicadas, and the distant swish of the surf breaking on the beach, and the scent of honeysuckle, and the feel of the salt air, so heavy it was like raiment against her skin, and . . . Parker.

She missed Parker.

"Are you thinking about him?" Daniel asked softly, interrupting her thoughts. "Is he what has made you sad?"

"Made me sad? Hardly," she said, giving her head a firm shake. "Has he made me angry? Yes. Would I like to throttle him? Definitely. He's provoking on every level, starting with how he approaches his profession. Only rarely does he take a suggestion or criticism without first putting up an argument, which invariably turns fierce.

"He stays hidden away in that house, on that island. Lovely as the house and island are, he uses them as a refuge. He should be out among people. A writer usually seizes every opportunity to promote his work. But not him. Oh, no. He adopts this lofty attitude and pretends to be above all that, but I know better. The reason he remains a recluse is because of his disability.

"Oh, have I told you that, Dad? He's wheelchair-bound. I

didn't learn that until I got there. At first I was shocked because when talking to him over the telephone, I got no indication that he was in any way impaired, except when it came to manners. It took me totally by surprise. But after a while . . . I don't know, Dad, it's strange. When I look at him now, I don't even see the wheelchair."

She paused to reflect on that, realizing how profoundly true the statement was. She no longer saw Parker's chair or his disability, and she wondered at what point that had happened.

"I suppose it's the potency of his personality that makes his disability seem not just inconsequential, but invisible. He's got an extraordinary command of the language. Even his bawdy— make that crude—vocabulary is impressive.

"He has a sly sense of humor. Wicked, sometimes. He can be awfully grouchy, too, but then I suppose he's entitled to be. Anyone in his circumstances would be resentful. I mean, he's young, in his prime, so his bitterness over being confined to a wheelchair is understandable and forgivable.

"He's self-conscious of his scars, but he shouldn't be. People, especially women, would find him attractive no matter what his legs look like. He's not . . . not handsome, exactly, but . . . he's got an . . . an animal magnetism, I guess you'd call it. You sense an energy radiating from him even when he's sitting still.

"When he speaks to you, you're drawn right into his eyes. The intensity with which he holds your attention makes up for his incapacity. But don't get the impression that he's feeble. He's not. In fact he's quite strong. His hands are . . ."

His hands. When they had kept her head in place for his kiss. When they had trapped her hips and held her still beside his chair. Those times they had felt incredibly strong and commanding. Yet at other times, like when he had plucked a leaf from her hair, his touch had been light and deft, even playful.

When she'd held a seashell in her palm for him to admire, he had traced the delicate whorls with his fingertip gingerly, as though afraid to apply too much pressure and risk crushing it.

A woman would never have to flinch from his touch.

"He's the most complex individual I've ever met," she said huskily. "Extremely talented." She conjured up Parker's face and heard herself saying, "Also angry. Very angry. You can sense it in his writing. But even when he's relaxed and joking with Mike, his anger is detectable.

"His smiles have a disturbing element. There's a cruelty to them, and that's unfortunate because I don't believe he could be cruel at all if not for the anger. It's always there, just beneath the surface.

"There's a passage in his novel where he describes Roark's anger toward Todd. He compares it to a serpent gliding through still, dark water, never surfacing, never revealing itself, but constantly there, silent, sinister, and deadly, waiting to poison them both.

"Probably he's just angry over being trapped in a wheelchair. But I sense there's something . . . something I don't know, something I've missed, like there's one more secret yet to come to light."

She laughed softly. "I can't imagine what it might be. He's sprung so many surprises on me. Not all of them good." She took a sip of wine and raised her shoulders in a helpless shrug. "That's the best way I know to answer your question."

Daniel studied her thoughtfully for a long moment as he continued to pack tobacco into his pipe. He rarely lighted it. He just liked the ritualistic activity. It gave him something to do while assembling his thoughts.

When he finally spoke, it was to quietly say, "Actually, Maris, my question referred to Noah."

Embarrassed, she flushed hotly. For five solid minutes she had rattled on about Parker. "Oh . . . oh, well," she stammered, "yes, he . . . I wouldn't say Noah made me *sad*, but I was upset over his meeting with WorldView. I was even more upset that he chose not to tell me about it."

Daniel set the pipe aside and picked up his tumbler. As he

contemplated the amber contents, he asked, "Did Noah tell you that he had a meeting with Howard the afternoon he killed himself?"

The manner in which he had posed the question caused her throat to constrict. This wasn't a casual inquiry. "He mentioned it."

"It took place only a couple of hours before Howard ended his life."

Maris lost all appetite for the wine. Setting the crystal stem on the end table, she wiped condensation, or perspiration, off her palms. "What was the nature of their meeting?"

"According to Noah, Howard needed him to sign off on the final draft of a contract between us and one of our foreign licensees. Noah approved the amended language and that was the extent of it."

That's what Noah had told her, too. "Do you . . ." She cleared her throat and began again. "Do you doubt that?"

"I have no reason to. Although . . ." Maris waited in breathless suspension for him to continue. "Howard's secretary told me that his meeting with Noah was his last for the day, and that when he left the office, he wasn't himself."

"Specifically?"

"He seemed distressed. I think her exact words were 'extremely upset.'" Daniel took a sip of whisky. "Of course, one event probably has nothing to do with the other. Howard could have been upset over any number of things, something in his personal life, something that didn't relate to Matherly Press or Noah."

But her father didn't believe that. If he did, they wouldn't be having this conversation. "Dad, do you think—"

"Good. I see you started without me." Noah pushed open the double doors and breezed in. "Darling, I apologize again for making you come over alone." He bent down and kissed Maris, then smacked his lips as though tasting them. "Good wine."

"It is. Very." She got up and moved to the wet bar, trying to hide from the men and herself that her knees were wobbly. "I'll pour you some."

"Thanks, but I'd rather have what Daniel is having. Rocks only. It's been that kind of day."

Noah crossed the room to shake hands with his father-in-law, then rejoined Maris on the love seat and placed his arm around her as she handed him a highball glass. "Cheers." After taking a sip of his drink, he said, "Maxine sent me in with the message that dinner is in ten minutes."

"I hope her pot roast isn't as dry as it was last time," Daniel grumbled.

"Her pot roast is never dry," Maris said, wondering how they could be discussing something as trivial as pot roast when only moments ago the topic had been a man's inexplicable suicide.

"Dry or not, I'm going to wreak havoc on it," Noah said. "I'm starving."

Of course, one event probably has nothing to do with the other.

She clung to her father's statement, desperate to believe it. This was Noah they were talking about. Her husband. The man she had fallen in love with, and the man she still loved. Noah. The man she slept beside every night. The man with whom she wanted to have children.

She placed her hand on his thigh, and he, without even a pause in his conversation with Daniel, covered her hand with his own and pressed it affectionately. It was an absentminded, husbandly, and reassuring gesture.

Dinner was delicious and the pot roast lived up to Maxine's standards of excellence. But by the time the lemon tarts were served, Daniel was yawning. As soon as Maxine removed the dessert dishes, he asked to be excused.

"Stay and enjoy another cup of coffee," he told his guests as he stood up. "But I should retire. I'll be up early to attend

Howard's funeral. Can't say I'm looking forward to it."

"I need to say good night, too, Dad. Today was long and strenuous."

As they left the dining room, Maris held back and detained Noah. Laying her hands on his lapels, she went up on tiptoe to kissed him tenderly on the lips. "I think I'll go home ahead of you."

He placed his hands at her waist and drew her closer. "I thought you and I had plans for later this evening."

"We do. But I'm about to ask a favor. Would you please stay and help Dad get to bed? I know it's not your place—"

"I don't mind at all."

"He's prickly on the subject of his instability, and it's already come up once tonight. But if you invent an excuse to walk upstairs with him, it won't appear that you're escorting him. I would appreciate it."

"Consider it done, sweetheart. I'll follow your lead."

At the door, she pretended to remember that she wanted to retrieve an old address book from her third-floor bedroom. "I'll have to look for it. I'm not sure where I left it."

Noah offered to get it for her and suggested that she go ahead of him while he searched. She wasn't sure Daniel believed their playacting, but he went along with it.

When they said their good nights, Daniel hugged her tightly. Then he set her away from him and peered closely into her eyes as though trying to decipher the troubling thoughts behind them. "I want to hear more about this new book and the complex man who's writing it."

The reminder of how she'd gone on and on about Parker brought color to her cheeks again. "I always value your input, Dad. I'll have a copy of the manuscript sent over by courier tomorrow. We'll get together later in the week to discuss it."

He squeezed her hand with a confidentiality and caring that made her want to crawl up into his lap as she had when she was little, seeking comfort and assurance that everything was going to be fine, that all her concerns were needless, and that there was no basis for her undefined disquiet.

But, of course, she couldn't. She'd outgrown his lap, and her confidences were a woman's, not a child's. They couldn't be shared with her father.

Daniel moved aside and Noah stepped up to hug her. "Daniel's looking a little down in the mouth tonight," he whispered. "Once he's tucked in, I think I'll offer to have a bedtime brandy with him."

"Do. But make it a short one. I'll be waiting."

Maris didn't go straight home. She had never intended to. Using her father as a pawn to delay Noah made her feel guilty, but only a little. She would never have deceived them if she weren't desperate to rid herself of nagging doubts that had taken a tenacious hold on her.

She took a taxi downtown to the apartment in Chelsea. By the time she reached the door of the apartment, her heart was beating hard, and not because of the steep staircase. She was anxious about what she might find inside.

She unlocked the door with the key she'd had in her possession since the night of her surprise party and, remembering where the light switch was, flipped it on. The air-conditioning unit was humming softly, but otherwise the apartment was silent. She noted that the cushions on the sofa looked freshly plumped.

Moving into the kitchen, she looked into a spotless dry sink. There were no dishes in the dishwasher, not even a drinking glass. The wastebasket beneath the sink was empty, its plastic liner as pristine as when it had been placed there.

Maid service? Noah hadn't mentioned retaining anyone to clean this apartment, but that didn't mean he hadn't.

Back in the living room she moved toward the room designated as Noah's office. Hand on the doorknob, she paused and said a prayer, although she couldn't specifically say what she was praying for. She pushed open the door.

In a single glance she took it all in, then slumped dejectedly against the doorjamb. The room looked exactly as they'd left it that night. Nothing had been disturbed or changed. There were no paper balls in the trash can, no reference books with pages marked, no notes stuck to the computer screen or scrawled on ruled legal tablets.

She knew what a writer's work area was supposed to look like. Parker's would have cost an obsessive-compulsive years of therapy. It was strewn with coffee-stained notes, and red pencils whose leads were worn down to nubs, and tablets filled with thoughts and diagrams and doodles, and file envelopes with curled, fraying edges, and unstable pyramids of reference material, and paper clips bent out of shape during periods of torturous concentration.

Yet if one thing were touched or moved on Parker's desk, he would bark at the offender. He knew exactly where everything was, and he wanted it left the way he had it. Mike was forbidden to clean in the area, as though the disarray contributed to Parker's creativity.

Noah's writing space was immaculate. Although, upon closer inspection, Maris saw that his computer keyboard sported a fine layer of dust. The keys had never been touched.

Her heart wasn't beating fast now. In fact it felt like a stone inside her chest as she turned off the lights and left the apartment. She conscientiously locked the door behind her, although she didn't know why she bothered. There was absolutely nothing of value to her inside.

She exited the building and descended the front steps, lost in thought, her motions listless. She was weighted down with dread for the inevitable confrontation with Noah. When he returned from her father's house, he would be expecting his docile wife to be waiting for him at home, eager and ready to make love to him.

That's what she had deliberately led him to expect.

She had led him to believe that she was as moldable as warm clay, gullible, blindly accepting, and he had been easily deceived, because up until recently that's exactly what she'd been.

He would arrive home thinking that their argument about WorldView was a forgotten episode, that she didn't question the nature of his meeting with Howard Bancroft, that she had no reason to doubt him when he told her he had resumed writing.

Meek and mild and malleable Maris. Stupid Maris. That's what he thought of her.

But he thought wrong.

As she reached street level, she noticed a passenger alighting from a taxi half a block away. She hadn't expected the good fortune of finding a cab so soon and raised her hand to signal the driver.

As soon as he received his fare, he drove the short distance to where Maris stood at the curb. But she was no longer looking at the taxi. Instead she was watching the man who had alighted from it as he jogged up the steps of another brownstone, entering it with an air of familiarity, as though he belonged.

Gradually Maris lowered her arm, until then not realizing that it was still raised. She motioned the taxi driver to go on. Walking briskly, she quickly covered the distance to the other apartment building.

It was as quaint as the one she'd just left. There was no doorman or other form of security to prevent her from entering the vestibule. She checked the mailboxes. All except one were labeled with a name. Either the apartment was vacant . . . or the tenant in 2A received mail at another location.

Again, she climbed stairs. But it was with amazing calm that she approached the door of apartment 2A. She rapped smartly and looked directly into the peephole, knowing that it was probably being looked through from the other side.

Nadia Schuller opened the door, and the two of them stood face-to-face. She was dressed for romance, wearing only a silk wrapper, which appeared to have been hastily tied at her waist as she made her way to answer the door. She didn't even have the decency to look alarmed or shamefaced. Her expression was one of smug amusement as she stepped back and opened the door wider.

Maris's gaze slid past her to Noah, who was coming from a connecting room, presumably a kitchen, with a drink in each hand. He was in shirtsleeves, having wasted no time in removing his jacket and tie.

Upon seeing her, he stopped dead in his tracks. "Maris."

Nadia said, "I hope this doesn't turn into one of those dreadful farces à la a Ronald Reagan movie."

Maris ignored her. Nadia was insignificant. The only thing she signified was Noah's bad taste in mistresses. She didn't waste any contempt on Nadia. Instead she directed it all toward the man she had married less than two years ago.

"Don't bother apologizing or explaining, even if that's what you had in mind to do, Noah. You're a liar and an adulterer, and I want you out of my life. Out. Immediately. I'll have Maxine come over and pack up your things because I can't bear the thought of touching them myself. You can arrange with the doorman a time to pick them up when I'm not there. I don't want to see you again, Noah. Ever."

Then she turned and jogged down the stairs, across the small lobby, down the steps, and onto the sidewalk. She wasn't crying. In fact, her eyes were dry. She didn't feel angry, or sad, or miserable. In fact, she felt surprisingly unshackled and lighthearted. She had no sense of leaving something, but rather of going toward something.

She didn't get far.

Noah gripped her arm from behind and roughly jerked her around. He grinned down at her, but it was a cold and frightening grin. "Well, well, Maris. Clever you."

"Let go of me!" She struggled to pull her arm free from his grasp, but he didn't yield. In fact, his fingers closed more tightly around her biceps. "I said for you to let—"

"Shut up," he hissed, shaking her so hard that she bit her tongue and cried out in pain. "I heard what you had to say, Maris. Every single word. Brave speech. I was impressed.

"But now let *me* tell *you* how it's going to be. Our marriage has been and will remain on my terms. You don't order me out of your life. You don't order me to leave. I leave you only when I'm goddamn good and ready. I hope you understand that, Maris. Your life will be so much easier if you do."

"You're hurting me, Noah."

He laughed at that. "I haven't begun to hurt you yet." To underscore his point, he squeezed her arm tightly, cruelly, his fingers mashing muscle against bone. Although tears of pain sprang to her eyes, she didn't recoil.

"In the meantime, I'll fuck Nadia, I'll fuck whoever I want to, and I don't care if you watch. But you'll stay the obedient little wife, understand? Or I'll make your life, and the lives of everyone dear to you, a living hell, Maris. I can, you know. I will." His eyes glinted with an evil light as he leaned even closer and whispered, "I *will*. I promise you."

Then he released her so suddenly she staggered and fell against the iron fence that enclosed trash receptacles, painfully banging her shoulder.

As he turned away from her and started back toward the brownstone he shared with Nadia, he called cheerfully, "Don't wait up."

Too stunned to move, Maris watched him go and continued to stare at the empty doorway long after he had disappeared inside. She wasn't so afraid as dumbfounded. Incredulity kept her rooted to the concrete. Although her arm was throbbing and she could taste blood in her mouth, she couldn't believe what had just happened. Noah? Threatening her? Physically threatening her with an icy calm that glazed his threats with certainty and made them terrifying?

She shivered then, violently and uncontrollably, her blood running cold with the sudden but unarguable realization that she was married to a total stranger. The man she thought she knew didn't exist. Noah had assumed a role, that's all. He had mimicked a character in a book because he knew she'd been infatuated with that character. He had played the part well, never stepping out of character. Not once. Until tonight.

She was jolted by the fact that just now, for the first time, she had been introduced to the real Noah Reed.

"Roark?"

He rubbed sleep from his eyes as he juggled the telephone receiver in the general direction of his ear. "Yeah?"

"Were you sleeping?"

It was four-thirty in the morning. He hadn't gotten to bed until after three. The nightclub where he and Todd worked didn't close until two. One of his responsibilities was to close out the registers, and he couldn't do that until the last customer left. After writing all day, then putting in an eight-hour shift, he hadn't merely been sleeping, he'd been comatose.

"Who is this?"

"Mary Catherine. I hate to bother you."

He swung his legs over the side of the bed. His bare foot knocked over an empty drink can and it noisily rolled across the concrete floor toward Todd's bed. He growled a protest into his pillow.

"What's up?" Roark asked in a whisper.

"Can you come over?"

"Uh . . . now?"

The strip joint was only a few doors down from the nightclub for which he tended bar and Todd parked cars. Occasionally, during their breaks, they could catch their neighbors' acts. He and Todd had come to know the girls well enough to be admitted gratis. A bouncer let them in through a rear entrance. They watched from backstage. Sometimes they went together, sometimes separately, and they were rarely able to stay longer than fifteen or twenty minutes at a time, but those few minutes relieved the drudgery of their lives.

Their limited budgets had reduced dating to a bare minimum. Thankfully, the trio of exotic dancers had been "neighborly" to them in more ways than giving free peep shows.

One day Roark had volunteered to take Starlight's car to a garage for an oil change and tune-up. What the mechanic did for the car's engine was nothing compared to what Starlight did to Roark's. As thank-yous went, Starlight beat Hallmark all to hell.

But this telephone call didn't have the tone of a come-on, and, much to his regret, Mary Catherine had never shown any romantic interest in him. She'd treated him in a brotherly fashion, while she flirted shamelessly with Todd and had graced him with several sleepovers.

"Could you, Roark? Please? I'm here by myself and, well . . . I need a favor."

His heart thumped with optimism. "Sure. Be right there."

"Don't mention it to Todd, okay?"

That dampened his enthusiasm somewhat, because he would enjoy ribbing Todd about getting a middle-of-the-night call from one of his regular lays. Where women were concerned Todd was a cocksure bastard.

He pulled on a pair of shorts and a T-shirt, pushed his feet into a pair of sandals, and let himself out without waking Todd. He hurdled the foul-smelling moat surrounding the apartment building and followed the now-familiar and well-worn path to the girls' building. He took the stairs two at a time, arriving at their door slightly out of breath. Mary Catherine opened the door before he could even knock.

"I was watching for you through the window."

He stepped inside, trying not to give away how crestfallen he was by her appearance.

She didn't even resemble the stunner she was when she peeled away the vestiges of her nun's habit and stood in the spotlight gloriously naked, or even when she lay spread-eagled on the roof basting in suntan oil.

Her face was free of stage makeup. Her eyes and nose were red, as though she'd been crying. Her long, curly hair had been gathered into a scraggly ponytail. Most disappointing of all, she wasn't dressed for seduction. She was wearing an unflattering, oversized Dolphins jersey and a baggy pair of plaid boxer shorts.

"I got you up, didn't I?"

"I was writing," he lied.

"Your lights were out."

"I was plotting inside my head."

"Oh." She twisted the hem of the jersey in her fist. "I hate to ask you to do this, Roark, but . . ."

"Is something wrong?"

"I miscarried tonight."

He gaped stupidly and speechlessly.

"A baby." She flipped out her hand. "Well, I guess it wasn't really a baby yet, just, you know . . . Anyway, I need some things, and I'm not feeling too good, so I wondered if you'd run down to the twenty-four-hour market for me."

He swallowed what felt like a bowling ball, then reflexively wet his lips. "Uh, sure. Be glad to."

"I'd really appreciate it."

"No problem, but are you okay? Should you call a doctor or something? Want me to take you to the hospital? Have, uh, things checked out?"

"No, I'm okay." Taking a deep but shaky breath, she said, "This isn't the first time."

He dragged his hand down over his mouth and chin. "You didn't do anything crazy, did you? You didn't cause it? On purpose, I mean."

She shook her head and smiled weakly. "No. Nothing that dramatic. It just happened, Roark. An accident of nature. The first time, yeah, I went to a clinic and had it sucked out. But this time it came out on its own. I started feeling bad at work. Cramps, you know."

He nodded sympathetically, although she could have been talking about ice sculpting, for all he knew about it. In fact he probably knew more about ice sculpting.

"I was invited out with the other girls to a private party. But it had all the makings of an all-nighter, so I begged off, came home, went straight to bed. Woke up about an hour ago in a . . . a mess." She raised her shoulders. "No more baby."

He saw tears shining in her eyes, but she quickly turned away and reached for a small slip of paper and several folded bills. "I made a detailed list. Name brands and sizes. Figured you wouldn't know what to get if I didn't."

"You're right about that," he said, trying to sound goofily cheerful and failing miserably.

"This should cover it."

He took the list and money from her. "Anything else?"

"I think it's all on there. I'll leave the door unlocked so you can just come in when you get back." He nodded and turned to go, but she touched his arm and brought him back around. "Thanks, Roark. Really. Thanks."

He patted the small hand resting on his arm. "Go lie down. I'll be back soon as I can."

When he returned, she was stretched out on the sofa, one arm across her eyes, the other hand resting on her abdomen. She lowered her arm and smiled wanly at him as he approached on tiptoe. "Find everything?"

"I think so."

"Did I send enough money?"

"Don't worry about it. Why aren't you in bed?"

"Well, as I said, it's kind of a mess."

At the end of a short hallway one of the bedroom doors was standing ajar. He set the sack of purchases on the floor beside the sofa. "Here's your stuff." Then he started down the hall toward the bedroom.

"Roark, no," she protested weakly as she sat up.

"Take care of yourself, Mary Catherine. I'll take care of this."

He did, but it wasn't pleasant.

For one thing, it was much more difficult to remain detached than he had imagined it would be. He couldn't get it out of his mind that the "mess" represented a human life, which had started out exactly as every human life did. For reasons that would never be known, it had decided to give it up, cash in early, let go. It was said that miscarriages were blessings in disguise, that it was the natural way for a uterus to discard an imperfection. Nevertheless, knowing that a life had ended tonight was depressing as hell.

Also she must have been fairly far along, because there was more bloody substance than he'd expected. As efficiently as possible, he stripped the linens, including the mattress pad, and crammed them into a plastic trash bag he found in a kitchen pantry. He sealed it tightly, then carried it out to the Dumpster behind the building.

On his way back through the apartment, he heard the shower running in the bathroom. He found fresh linens in a hall closet and remade the bed. He was finishing up when she came into the bedroom, looking scrubbed and wearing another ensemble of loose T-shirt and baggy boxers.

He swept his arm wide to indicate the bed. "Climb in." She did, sighing with relief as she lay down. "Everything all right?"

"Sure."

"Did you take some of the Tylenol?"

"Three. Figured they couldn't hurt."

"How about some tea?"

"You've done enough."

"How about some tea?"

She looked up at him. "You'd really make me tea?"

"Do you have a kettle?"

"I don't think so."

"A microwave?"

"Of course."

Five minutes later, he was back with a steaming cup of tea, packets of sweetener, and a spoon. "I didn't know if you took sugar or not."

"Two, please." As he stirred the sweetener into her tea, he glanced over at the TV. The sound was muted, but she was staring into the screen. "I love this movie," she told him. "I bought the video and must've watched it a thousand times. Audrey Hepburn and Cary Grant."

"A winning combo. Careful, it's hot," he said, passing her the mug. She made room for him beside her on the bed, and he sat down, leaning back against the wall. "What's it about?"

"She's gorgeous and in trouble. He's handsome and comes to her rescue. She's scared. He's suave. They fall in love in the end."

They watched the video in silence until it played out, then she clicked off the TV and he took the empty cup from her. "Thanks, Roark, that helped. Nobody's ever made me tea before."

"My mom always made me tea when I was sick."

"Was she nice to you?"

"Real nice. I was lucky."

"Yeah, you were. My old lady kicked me out when I was fifteen."

"How come?"

"She caught her boyfriend waving his weenie at me."

"Why didn't she kick him out?"

She laughed as though that were funny, although Roark hadn't meant it to be. "You're a nice guy, Roark." When he grimaced, she added, "I meant it as a compliment."

"Well, thanks. Must say, though, I'd rather be thought of as dashing and dangerous."

Her smile faded. Her eyes lost their sparkle and seemed to look inward into something that caused her unhappiness. "No, that's Todd."

Roark didn't how to respond to that and reasoned that it was best to say nothing. He slapped his thighs and moved to get up. "Well, I should be—"

"Wait, Roark. You've been so sweet. I mean, really fuckin' great. I hate women who're clingy and needy, but I don't want to be alone tonight. Would you stay? Just until I fall asleep?"

"Okay. Sure."

"Lie down."

Awkwardly, Roark stretched out beside her on the bed. She snuggled against him and rested her head on his shoulder. He placed an arm around her. "Maybe tomorrow you should call a doctor," he suggested.

"Yeah. He'll likely want to do a D and C. Yuk."

Roark's thought exactly. He had a vague idea of what was involved in the procedure, and he preferred keeping the idea vague. "You weren't on the pill?"

"No. They make me fat," she explained. "And he forgot to bring condoms. At least he told me he forgot them. Guess I was stupid not to insist."

"Damn straight. Pregnancy's not the worst that can happen."

"I know, but he's the type who'd be careful about disease and stuff."

"So this guy wasn't random? I mean, he's somebody you know well?"

"Roark, don't ask, okay?"

"Okay."

"Let's talk about something else."

But they didn't talk. Not for a while. They didn't even move, except for his fingers sifting through strands of her hair, which was fanned out over the pillow, drying from her shower.

"My name's not really Mary Catherine," she confessed softly.

"No?"

"It's Sheila."

"That's pretty."

"I just use Mary Catherine for the nun bit."

"I figured."

"I thought you might. You're smart. Me, I quit school when I left home, middle of tenth grade. I'm an idiot."

"I don't think so."

"I know so. Anyway, when the customers get tired of the nun act, I'll work up something else, and I'll probably change my name to fit the new act. I'm playing with an idea. What to hear it?"

"Love to."

"I thought I could maybe be a mermaid? You know, I'd have this tail that was all pearly and shimmery. I'd wear a long, flowing wig that came down to my ass. Maybe even to my knees."

"You'd be a knockout. You could call yourself Lorelei."

"Lorelei?"

"Like the siren. In mythology." She stared back at him with misapprehension. "She had a beautiful singing voice," he explained. "She used it to lure sailors into the rocks where they would shipwreck."

"No shit? I gotta remember that."

"I can write it down for you so you won't forget."

She propped herself up on her elbow and regarded him with patent admiration. "See? You're so fuckin' smart."

He laughed, and she laughed, and then they looked at one another seriously for a long moment, and then she said, "You can play with them if you want to."

Immediately his eyes dropped to her chest. She raised the hem of her T-shirt up over her breasts. The objects of his affection and fantasies, what he had admired from afar, were inches from his eyes, his fingertips, his lips. She was giving them to him. A gift.

But when he extended his hand, it was to lower her T-shirt back into place.

"What's the matter?" she asked. "I can't screw tonight, but I could blow you."

"That's not necessary."

"You think I'd be doing it just for you? Think again." She slid her hand down to his crotch and took his penis in her hand. "I've been wondering what you packed. Starlight's a lying bitch, but I can tell she was telling the truth about you." She squeezed him, and he caught his breath. Blood rushed to the pressure point made by each of her fingers.

But he moved her hand away from him. "I'd be taking advantage of the situation."

"So?"

"I wouldn't feel right about it, Sheila."

"Jesus, most guys would kill for an offer like this. Are you for real?"

"I'm real, all right. I'll be cursing myself in the morning."

"Well, you can jerk off in the shower while you watch us sunbathe." She giggled at his astonishment. "We're not *that* ignorant, Roark. Why else would y'all take so many showers? And at the same time we're sunbathing?"

She smiled and lay back down, snuggling against him again. "Truth is, I couldn't have given you my best tonight. I really do feel like shit, you know?"

"Go to sleep, Sheila. When you wake up, this'll seem like a bad dream."

"You're sweet."

"So are you."

He stroked her back, and caressed her hair, and continued to hold her even after she had fallen asleep. When he returned to his apartment the following morning, Todd was already up and pecking away at his keyboard. "Where've you been?"

"Walking on the beach."

Todd squinted at him suspiciously.

"Alone."

"Who is she?"

"Alone," Roark repeated testily.

"Huh." Todd went back to his typing, saying only one thing more. "Coffee's made, but I used the last of the milk."

Noah decided to give Maris a week to simmer down.

He concluded that a woman who catches her husband in adultery deserves a seven-day grace period in which to lick her wounds. It was more than an adequate amount of time for an ego to be restored. If the God of Genesis could create the cosmos in that length of time, surely a wife could come to terms with her husband's infidelity.

He also set the deadline to coincide with the one that Morris Blume had imposed on him. When next they met, Noah needed to report that everything was going smoothly and proceeding according to schedule. It would be nice and tidy if he patched things up with Maris before making that claim.

He was of value to Blume only as long as he was a member of the Matherly family. His pending deal with WorldView would be jeopardized by an estrangement from Maris and Daniel. Even a minor tiff with them might cause Blume to balk. Before that important meeting, he must reconcile with Maris.

If within a week's time she hadn't approached him, he planned to go to her hat in hand and beg her forgiveness. He would rather choke than be penitent, but the ultimate reward would be well worth a few minutes of contrition. In the meantime, he had a suite at the Plaza. He would give her space, give her plenty of time to stew . . . and to contemplate the consequences of ordering him from her life.

Like hell, Maris, my dear. He hoped he had made himself clear on that point.

Unfortunately, he was forced to see Maris the morning following their nasty scene outside Nadia's apartment. Avoiding Howard Bancroft's funeral was not an option. When he arrived, he saw Daniel standing alone on the steps of the synagogue and knew immediately that his father-in-law was unaware of what had transpired the night before. Daniel greeted him as though nothing untoward had happened.

As they somberly shook hands, Daniel asked him where Maris was.

"On her way, I'm sure. I had to leave ahead of her so I could make a quick stop at the office." The old man bought the lie. In any case, he let Noah lead him inside to get out of the drizzle that had begun to fall.

Maris arrived a few minutes later. She looked pale and wan in an unflattering black dress. It wasn't her best color. He'd never liked her in black. She spotted him standing with Daniel in the vestibule, wearing paper yarmulkes, waiting for her.

After a slight hesitation, she moved through the crowd toward them. She was too respectful of the situation to cause a scene. He had counted on her discretion, just as he had counted on her not telling Daniel about his extramarital affair with Nadia. Besides being proud to a fault, Maris was boringly predictable.

She hugged Daniel tenderly. "How are you this morning, Dad?"

"Sad for all of us, but especially for Howard's family. Shall we go in?"

They filed down the long aisle. Maris maneuvered it so that when they entered the pew Daniel was between them. She was the epitome of decorum, yet Noah knew she must be gnashing her teeth even to be in his presence. Imagining what an endurance test this was for her, he could barely contain his amusement.

Following the service, she consoled Daniel and, for his benefit, invented an excuse for having to take a separate taxi back to Midtown. Noah didn't see her for the remainder of the day.

Nor did he seek her out for the next several days. During scheduled business meetings, she pretended that everything was normal. They had never been overtly affectionate at work, except occasionally behind the closed door of either his or her private office. Around staff members, they had always conducted themselves in a professional manner. Consequently, no one at Matherly Press noticed the chill between them.

He went to their apartment when he knew she wouldn't be there to collect a few changes of clothing. He wasn't surprised to find that everything was exactly as he had left it. Maris had not sent for Maxine to pack up his belongings. She would never have entrusted the secret of their separation to her father's loyal housekeeper. The bad news would have gone straight from Maxine to Daniel, and Maris wanted to prevent Daniel from hearing of it. She would want to spare the old man from worrying about their marital problems and the damaging effect such problems would have on the publishing house.

Daniel, none the wiser, continued to take Noah's calls, and Noah continued to pay him brief visits in the late afternoons to discuss the events of the day. His relationship with his father-in-law remained solid. Maris was suffering in silence and alone, and she had only herself to blame. She should never have taken that haughty stance with him. She should have thought twice before issuing ultimatums that served only to make her look and sound ridiculous.

He relished the thought of her pacing, regretting her thoughtless outburst, and having absolutely no one in whom to confide. Each time he envisioned her wallowing in her lonely, self-inflicted torment, he smiled.

After a few days, however, Noah began to tire of the situation. He considered approaching Maris and putting an end to the silliness. But he stubbornly resolved to let her brood for the full seven days before approaching her.

She would weep and call him names and beg to know how he could have hurt her so terribly when she had done absolutely nothing to deserve it. He would give her the opportunity to vent. Once she had, she would grant him forgiveness. No doubt of that.

She would forgive him for the old man's sake. Maris could always be counted on to spare Daniel any kind of unhappiness. She would forgive him also because women love to forgive and then to make the forgiven miserable every day thereafter for the rest of his postforgiven life. That wasn't going to be his future, of course, but he figured that's what Maris had planned for him. In light of his deal with WorldView, he would do nothing at this point to enlighten her. That would come later.

In the meantime, the temporary separation wasn't without its perks. While Maris wasn't speaking to him, he didn't have to listen to her harping.

Nadia was another matter entirely. She continually nagged him to divorce Maris. Her persistence had become tiresome and had created a tension between them that came to a head, ironically enough, on the final day of his self-imposed deadline.

They had scheduled a luncheon meeting in an outrageously expensive, trendy uptown restaurant. One of Matherly Press's bestselling authors was joining them to be interviewed by Nadia for "Book Chat." The writer hadn't yet arrived when they ordered prelunch cocktails.

To other diners, which included a large number of publishing industry personnel, it appeared they were having a civil conversation about current market trends or perhaps the sci-fi phenomenon that had rocked the book world by securing the top spot on every bestseller list, when, in fact, they were arguing about their immediate future.

"She knows about us, so why wait? File for divorce now and get it over with."

"I can't leave the family until the deal with WorldView is cemented," he argued.

"What does one have to do with the other?"

"That is an incredibly stupid question, Nadia."

The insulting remark froze Nadia's smile into place. Had they been anyplace else, her temper might have erupted on the scale of Vesuvius. As it was, she took a languid sip of her martini, smoothed the starched linen napkin in her lap, and adjusted the triple strand of pearls around her neck—which he noticed was suffused with angry color. "Be careful, Noah," she said quietly. "You do not want me angry at you."

Like her, he kept his smile in place, but his voice had an edge. "Are you threatening me?"

"Being the cold, heartless bastard you are, I think you recognize a threat when you hear one."

"Isn't it because I'm a cold, heartless bastard that you can't resist me?"

Seeing that the awaited writer had arrived and was being escorted to their table by the maître d', Nadia flashed him a brilliant smile and spoke for his ears alone. "Do yourself a favor, Noah, and remember that I could give you lessons on how to be heartless."

Following the tedious lunch, he escorted her out of the restaurant and onto the sidewalk. A chauffeured car was waiting for them, but Nadia politely declined his invitation of a lift back to her office.

He took her hand in what he hoped looked like a friendly handshake between two professionals, but he addressed her with a confidential pitch he knew she would understand.

"If it seems like I'm dragging my feet on this divorce issue, it's because I don't want to make an error that could cost us this deal. I want it for us, Nadia. But in order to get it, we must be willing to make a few sacrifices. I can't dissolve my marriage to Maris now. It's out of the question. You understand that, don't you?"

To his immense relief, she smiled up at him and looked appropriately contrite. "Of course I understand. I'm just impatient to be with you."

"No more than I. In fact," he said, moving a half step nearer to her, "I want to be inside you right now."

She closed her eyes and swayed slightly toward him, then glanced around to make certain no one had noticed or could overhear. "Naughty you. You've made me wet."

"Then six o'clock can't come soon enough."

He squeezed her hand quickly, then climbed into the backseat of the waiting car, smiling to himself. The secret to keeping Nadia content was to keep her agitated between her legs. That was the mainspring of her self-worth. Her self-image revolved around it. If she was happy there, she was happy.

He disliked her constant nagging, but his argument with her had been stimulating and had geared him up for his showdown with Maris. *Call it a rehearsal,* he thought as he stepped off the elevator and pushed through the glass doors leading into the executive offices of Matherly Press.

He went into Maris's office straightaway, but she wasn't there. On his way out, he bumped into her assistant. "Can I help you, Mr. Reed?"

"I'm looking for Maris."

Her eyes were magnified by the thick lenses of her glasses as she looked at him quizzically. "She's not coming in today, Mr. Reed. Remember, she's going back to Georgia."

Going back to Georgia? Since when? *Shit!* This didn't fit into his timetable at all.

It required all his acting skills not to give his ignorance away to the secretary. "Right, right. I know she's leaving today, but she said she was stopping here briefly before going to the airport."

"She did? That's not what she told me."

"Hmm, I guess she changed her mind." He forced a smile and hoped it looked more natural than it felt. "I'll catch her on her cell phone."

He called no less than a dozen times but kept getting Maris's voice mail. It was obvious that she did not want to be reached. He cursed her throughout the remainder of the workday. If she had suddenly appeared, he could well have killed her with his bare hands.

This was the worst possible time for her to play the betrayed wife and run away. Hadn't he made it plain to her that he wasn't going to stand for any crap from her, and that if he told her to roll over and play dead that's what she was to do? Her pouting could ruin this whole thing.

On second thought, fuck her.

He had the document that Howard Bancroft had drawn up for him. Unless he was given no other choice, he would rather not use it. From a legal standpoint, that document could make things sticky, and he would rather avoid any legal stickiness. But it was there in his safe-deposit box, an insurance policy, an emergency measure to be used if it became necessary.

Feeling confident and unconquerable again, he arrived at Nadia's Chelsea apartment shortly after six o'clock. He was in the mood for a cold drink and a cool shower, topped off by hot, aggressive sex.

He was whistling as he jogged up the staircase. But when he let himself into the apartment, his whistling abruptly died.

A beefy young man dressed in a tight-fitting black T-shirt and black slacks was emerging from the bedroom, strapping on his wristwatch. He then shouldered his gym bag and casually eased past Noah on his way out the door. His only acknowledgment of Noah was a negligent nod.

For minutes after the young man left, Noah remained on the threshold in a slow burn. A burn so hot that he was a combustion chamber, well decked out in Hugo Boss. He shot his monogrammed cuffs, smoothed down his hair, wiped the perspiration from his upper lip. These were conscious gestures, activities for his hands so he wouldn't use them to rip, bash, or otherwise destroy something, animate or otherwise, he wasn't particular at the moment.

When he was finally under moderate control, he moved toward the bedroom and gave the door a gentle push. It swung back on silent hinges. Nadia was sprawled naked on the wide bed amid rumpled silk sheets. Her hair was damp and tangled. Her skin merely damp.

Seeing him, she stirred and smiled drowsily. "Noah, darling, is it six o'clock already? I lost all track of time."

The blood vessels in his temples were pounding to the point of pain, but his voice remained calm. "Who was that man?"

"Oh, you met Frankie? He's a personal trainer at my health club."

"What was he doing here?"

She levered herself up onto one elbow and looked at him with malice, mitigated only slightly by a sly smile. "That is an incredibly stupid question, Noah."

Daniel Matherly finished reading the last page of the manuscript. As he lined up the edges and stacked the pages, he said, "That's all you've got so far?"

Maris nodded. "I haven't received anything from him since I returned. I've called several times to give him a pep talk, but I've spoken only to Mike, his aide. According to him, P . . . the author isn't writing much these days."

"I wonder why."

"He's sulking."

"His muse has flown."

"Nothing that mystical. He's being his stubborn and mule-headed self. Like any mule, he requires prodding." She hesitated before adding, "So I'm going back."

"Really? When?"

"I'm on my way to the airport now."

"I see."

"I only stopped by to check on you, tell you good-bye, and to hear your opinion of what you've read so far."

She had postponed her departure for a week. After catching Noah in Nadia Schuller's apartment, it was a foregone conclusion that she would return to Georgia and see Parker again.

Her husband's affair had given her a green light to examine her ambiguous and conflicting feelings for Parker. But in order to be fair to him, and to herself, she had delayed going until she had thought it through from every angle. She didn't want her return to be a knee-jerk reaction to a rapid series of shocking developments in her life. She didn't want it to be the reaction of an angry and vindictive wife. Rather, she wanted it to be an action taken after days of careful consideration.

For the past seven days, she had thought of little else.

She had been terribly angry at Parker the morning she left, but the truth of the matter was she hadn't wanted to leave. She could admit that now. And every moment since her leaving, she had wanted to be with him again.

Initially, guilt had burned inside her like a live coal. She was married. She had made a commitment at the wedding altar, and she had regarded it a lifetime pledge. All her marriage vows she had taken seriously.

But apparently she had been the only one standing at the altar that day who had. Noah had broken his vows. For all she knew, Nadia wasn't the first woman with whom he had cheated. He had certainly had no shortage of girlfriends prior to his marriage. It was possible he had never changed his pattern of behavior from that of a bachelor to that of a married man. He had willfully chosen to be unfaithful to her. She would just as willfully choose to end the marriage. By taking a lover, he had squandered the right and the privilege to be her husband.

But even if she hadn't caught him with Nadia, she would be

leaving him. That night on the sidewalk in Chelsea, Noah had revealed an aspect of himself that appalled, repelled, and frightened her. She would not live another day with a man who hinted at violence so effectively that she believed him capable of it. Their marriage was over. Noah Reed was her past.

What she needed to determine was if Parker Evans was her future.

She could no longer ignore or deny her attraction to him. It wasn't strictly his intellect and talent that appealed to her, as she had tried to delude herself into believing. She was attracted to him, the man. Countless times she had fantasized kissing him again, having his hands on her, having her mouth on him.

She didn't even know if he was capable of making love in the conventional sense, but it didn't matter. She wanted to touch him and to be touched. She wanted to be intimate with him on whatever level and by whatever means it could be achieved.

While married she never would have acted on that desire. During her courtship and marriage, she had never looked at another man or thought of one in a sexual context, which had made her spontaneous attraction to Parker all the more disturbing.

During her return flight to New York, she had convinced herself that the island was responsible for the romantic yearnings she had experienced there and that once she was back in familiar territory, they would stop. By the time the plane touched down at La Guardia, she had persuaded herself that the rift between her and Noah was curable, that the temporary lull in their marriage had left her open to fanciful daydreams that would vanish the moment their dozing passion was reawakened.

She had talked herself into believing that with a little ingenuity on her part she could revive their love life and feel again the exhilaration and excitement she had when she left the church on Noah's arm as his bride.

What a naive strategy that had been!

It made her angry now that she had been willing to assume all the responsibility for their marriage being out of sorts. How could she have been so gullible? Did everyone except her know about Noah's affair? The people with whom they both worked every day—had they known? Was she a comically tragic figure, the last-to-know wife? The staff must have thought, *Poor Maris,* as she toiled away at book publishing while her husband periodically slipped out for an illicit rendezvous with his mistress.

Noah had his adversaries among the staff, but he also had his allies, people he had pirated from the publisher with which he'd been formerly affiliated. Divorcing him would be easy compared to disassociating him from Matherly Press.

Which brought her to the next hurdle she must face: informing Daniel of their split.

She would postpone it for as long as possible. It would come as a double blow for him. He would be losing not only his son-in-law, but his protégé. Maris was confident that her father was strong enough to handle it, as he had handled all the other setbacks and disappointments in his life, but she saw no point in upsetting him prematurely. However, until the time came when it was necessary for him to know, it was going to be a challenge to keep up the pretense that everything was normal.

He was watching her now with his unsettling intuitiveness. It was hard not to squirm under the direct gaze. "So what do you think, Dad?"

"About the book? I think it's very good. Speaking as a publisher, I would prod the author to complete it."

"Then I guess I'm off." She stood up and began pulling on her raincoat.

"What does Noah think?"

"He hasn't read it yet."

"I wasn't referring to the manuscript, Maris. What does he think of your going away to spend more time with this writer?"

"I don't need his permission." Seeing that he was taken

aback by the sharpness of her tone, she amended it. "I'm sorry, Dad. I didn't mean to snap at you."

"Apology accepted. I don't presume to interfere with your personal life. It's just that . . ."

"Don't stop there. You've come this far."

He reached for her hand. "It's just that I remember well when you fell in love with a book, and then with the author."

She gave him a faint smile. "Is that what you're thinking? That I've got a schoolgirl's crush on this writer?"

"It wouldn't be for the first time."

"I'm older and wiser now." She stopped herself from saying, *I've learned my lesson.* "This book, this author, have nothing to do with Noah and our marriage. Nothing whatsoever."

That was the truth. Her marriage was over whether or not she ever saw Parker Evans again. Had she never heard of Parker or *Envy,* her marriage would have ended. It would have ended because her husband was false and their marriage a sham.

"So Noah's agreeable to your going?"

Noah's feelings on the matter seemed very important to her father. But they wouldn't be if he knew the whole story. She was tempted to roll up her sleeves and show him the bruises on her arms that even a week's time hadn't faded. She could tell him how she'd spat blood for an hour after biting her tongue. What if she repeated Noah's harsh threats, using the same sinister inflection that had been almost more alarming than the words themselves? Her father would be as shocked as she had been. He would be ready to find Noah and mete out punishment with his own hand.

That's why she wouldn't expose Noah to him now. She would save it for a day when she had things more sorted out in her own mind, when she wasn't on her way out of town, when she had a workable plan for Matherly Press as well as her personal life. Until she had answers already in place in her own mind, she wouldn't detail the problems to her father.

Instead, she looked him straight in the eye and, for the first time in her life, lied to him. "Yes. He's agreeable."

He took her face between his hands and kissed her on both cheeks. "What time is your flight?"

"I've barely got time to make it." Plagued by guilt for lying to him, she embraced him tightly. She squeezed her eyes closed and wasn't surprised to feel tears in them. "You're my best friend, Dad. I love you very much."

"And I love you, Maris." He set her away from him so he could look into her face. "More than you could ever know."

Parker answered the door. For several moments he looked at her blankly. Finally he said, "Did you forget something?"

"Very cute."

"Thank you."

"Are you going to ask me in?"

He hesitated as though thinking it over, then pushed his chair backward into the foyer, giving her room to step inside. "Where's Mike?"

"He went to the mainland for groceries, toilet paper, stuff like that."

"And left you here alone?"

"I'm not helpless," he said in what amounted to a snarl. "I lived by myself before Mike came onboard. Besides, I'm not alone."

He was with a woman.

Maris realized now that all the signs were there. Mike was away. Parker's shirt was unbuttoned, and his hair was more disheveled than usual. "I'm sorry. I . . . I should have called before I came."

"Yeah, you should have," he said crossly. "But since you've made the trip, you might just as well come on in. We're in here."

He wheeled his chair around and rolled it into the dining room. Reluctantly Maris followed, wishing there were a way she could turn and run without looking like a coward. Short of that, she wished she didn't have to meet his lady friend looking so bedraggled.

She wasn't up to an introduction to anyone, but especially not to a woman that Parker had invited over for some afternoon delight. The skirt of her linen suit was badly wrinkled. There was a run in her stocking. The raincoat, which she had needed in New York, was as out of place here as a snorkel mask in the Sahara.

She stood her suitcase in the foyer and folded her coat over it, then combed her fingers through her hair, which had been wind-damaged during the boat ride over from the mainland. There was no time for further repair. Fortifying herself with a deep breath, she stepped through the arched opening between the hallway and dining room.

Her primping had been unnecessary. Except for Parker, the room was empty. She looked at him inquisitively. "Up there," he said, motioning with his chin.

"I've noticed it swaying before," she told him, looking overhead at the chandelier. "It catches the current from the air-conditioning vent."

"Reasonable explanation. But wrong. It's the hanging ghost."

She expelled a short laugh. Finding him alone after all had left her feeling a little giddy. "Hanging ghost?"

He proceeded to tell her a tale about a planter who'd fallen on hard times. "His desperate attempts to recoup the family fortune were ill-conceived and only plunged them deeper into financial ruin. He hanged himself right here in the dining room." Upon reflection, he added, "I trust no one was having dinner at the time."

"You really believe that his ghost is . . ." She motioned toward the swaying fixture. "Up there?"

"Hell, yes."

"It doesn't bother you to have a ghost residing in your house?"

"He lived here for almost a century before Mike and I moved in." He shrugged. "He doesn't seem to mind us, so we ignore him. Ordinarily. Today, he's kept me company. Pretty damned good conversationalist."

Maris peered at Parker suspiciously, then her eyes strayed to the open decanter on the sideboard. Coming back to him, she said, "You're drunk."

"Not yet."

"But well on your way."

"Working on it." He rolled his chair over to the sideboard. "Care to join me?"

"Sure."

His head came around quickly, his surprise over her answer turning into a wicked grin of approval. "Sin suits you, Mrs. Matherly-Reed. You should engage in it more often." He took a clean glass from a silver tray and began to pour from the decanter. "Say when."

"When."

After pouring the two drinks, he wedged both glasses between his thighs and rolled his chair back to her. "Help yourself."

It was a blatant dare. Keeping her eyes locked with his, she reached between his legs for one of the glasses. "Take your time," he drawled.

She pulled the glass from between his thighs and clinked it against the one remaining. "Cheers."

He grinned again. "That might put some needed color in your cheeks, but you're gonna have to drink more than that if you want to catch up with me." After saluting her with his glass, he tossed his drink back like a shot.

She sipped the straight bourbon more cautiously. "Is this what you do now instead of write? You drink?"

"You must've been talking to Mike."

"When you refused to take my calls."

"He's a tattletale."

"Some things I can see for myself."

"You're a clever girl, all right."

"Why have you stopped working on *Envy,* and why are you getting drunk in the middle of the afternoon?"

"What better time? Besides, all the great writers were drunks. Didn't you know? I'll bet Homer went to the ancient Greek's equivalent of AA. From Edgar Allan Poe, to Fitzgerald, to—"

"Parker, why are you doing this?"

"Why'd you come back?" he snapped in return.

"I asked you first."

"Because I don't have any of the narcotics I used to take, and I'd have a hard time hanging myself from the chandelier."

"That's not funny."

"It wasn't meant to be."

"You've mentioned suicide twice. It's offensive and tasteless. Particularly since a good friend of mind blew his brains out last week."

The exchange ended there. Parker averted his head, and for a time neither of them spoke. Maris sipped her bourbon until she'd drunk it all, then returned the empty glass to the sideboard.

Finally Parker said, "Mike finished the mantel."

"I noticed. It's beautiful." She crossed to the fireplace and ran her fingertips over the wood's satin finish. "He did an excellent job."

"Be sure and tell him."

"I will."

"Who was your friend?"

She turned back to him. "Our corporate lawyer. I'd known him all my life. He was like an uncle to me."

"I'm sorry."

"For him it was over before he felt any pain. For the people who cared about him, it wasn't that easy. They'll feel the pain of it for a long time."

"Problems?"

"Not that anyone knew of."

"Then why'd he do it?"

"That remains a mystery." Speaking to the mantel, she said almost as an afterthought, "Noah had a meeting with him that afternoon."

"He detected nothing wrong?"

"No, nothing."

"What was their meeting about?"

"Normal business. Why?"

"Just wondering."

She faced him again. "Why?"

Rather than answer, he asked if she wanted another drink.

"No, thank you. My toes are already tingling."

He glanced down at her shoes. "You're dressed for New York. Why don't you change, then you can read the segment I've been working on since you left."

She smiled in surprise. "So you have been writing?"

"Mike only *thinks* he knows everything."

"This couldn't have worked out more perfectly. We can speak freely." Noah was pretending a nonchalance he didn't feel. To further convince his visitor of his insouciance, he idly twirled the skewered olive in his martini glass. "Maris went out of town again."

"Is this typical of her?"

Morris Blume had arrived at the Reeds' West Side co-op, wearing his condescending attitude like a fashion accessory. Noah had insisted that they meet informally and alone, without Blume's flunkies. They were like hummingbirds around a tropical blossom, hovering when they weren't actually fluttering.

Noah had given his doorman an exorbitant tip to admit

Blume and to ensure his memory loss about it later. He'd been hospitably waiting for Blume when Blume stepped out of the elevator. Blume had practically marched into the apartment, surveying it as a drill sergeant would a barracks, his colorless eyes seeming to be searching for flaws. Apparently it passed inspection. "Very nice."

Noah had attributed the tasteful decor to Maris. "She has an eye for such things. Drink?"

Now they were seated on facing sofas, Tiffany martini glasses in hand, and Maris's name had entered the conversation again. "She goes away frequently, doesn't she?" Blume asked.

"Not until recently when she began working on a project with an author who lives on an island off the coast of Georgia."

"You're sure of this?"

Since Noah felt his control over his wife and his mistress had slipped lately, Blume's insinuation smarted. "Sure about what?" he asked testily. "My wife's whereabouts?"

Blume stretched his colorless lips into his distinctive facsimile of a smile. "I knew a man whose wife was allegedly interviewing interior decorators to redo their recently purchased winery in Sonoma. Turns out she was consulting with a notorious divorce lawyer in LA who did his best work in bed. The wife wound up with the lawyer, the winery, and just about everything else. Once the fleecing was over, the man considered himself lucky to come away with his dick still attached. There's a lesson to be learned there."

The implied criticism rankled, but Noah chuckled. "This writer is shriveled and disabled, wheelchair-bound. Passion hasn't drawn Maris to Georgia."

"The draw could be something more damaging than a love affair."

Noah pulled the olive off the skewer with his teeth and chewed around his lazy grin. "If you're suggesting that Maris is up to some corporate subterfuge, you truly don't know her. She doesn't think as we do, Morris. She's a bookworm. A romantic,

a dreamer. Head in the clouds. Trust me, she won't be spring-
ing any nasty surprises on us."

"I assume she'll be surprised when Matherly Press becomes
part of WorldView."

"We'll know soon."

"I like the confident ring of that."

Still smiling slyly, Noah set his glass on the coffee table and
reached for his briefcase. With a flourish, he clicked open the
latches. "Delivered on time, as promised."

He passed Blume the document prepared by Howard Bancroft. After finding Nadia naked in bed and reeking of another
man's sweat, following closely Maris's inconvenient and unexpected disappearance, he had determined that his next action
must be bold and definitive.

He was tired of playing cautiously, tired of other people—
women, for God's sake!—dictating what he did and when he did
it. He must move quickly and aggressively. It was time to take
care of Noah, and only Noah, and let the rest of them go fuck
themselves. Or their meatheaded personal trainers. Jesus.

Blume scanned the document, rapidly flipping through the
pages. He was familiar enough with legal jargon to catch the
gist of it. Noah waited to be congratulated.

But when Blume finished glancing over the last page, he returned the document to the coffee table. "Very nice. Now all
that's needed is their signatures."

Noah's inflated chest emptied like a punctured balloon. "Not
necessary, Morris. Didn't you read—"

"That it's valid with your signature alone?" He chuckled as
he stood up and buttoned the top button of his perfectly tailored gray suit jacket. "A problematic clause, Noah. Very. I'm
already dodging antitrust laws and myriad other trade regulations." He waved his pale hand in a dismissive gesture.
"They're nothing more than time-consuming nuisances. But
only if everything else is in perfect order, and I mean all the *i*'s
dotted and *t*'s crossed.

"I couldn't swing a deal of this magnitude with a legal trapdoor like this waiting to open up beneath me. I wouldn't even want to try. This document, as it is now, would flag the feds. Even if it didn't, the Matherlys could raise a hue and cry, and then we'd all be screwed. I don't know about you, but when I get screwed, I like it to feel good."

He winked and Noah wanted to kill him.

"Now, if you'll excuse me, I have a dinner date."

He turned and headed for the door. Noah blinked the pulsing red lights out of his vision and followed. "Not to worry, Morris. I'll get the signatures."

Blume said, "I never worry."

He opened the door, then paused and turned back to Noah. "One of their signatures would probably be sufficient. Either your father-in-law's or your wife's." He mulled it over for several seconds, then nodded. "Yes. I'd feel protected with only one in addition to yours."

"You keep the antitrust thugs off our backs," Noah said stiffly. "Leave the Matherlys to me."

"Gladly. Between the two, I'd rather take on the federal government." His grin made him look like a leering skull recently exhumed. "Call me when you have that signature. Only when you have it, all right? My time is extremely valuable, and this has taken far too long already."

Then he was gone.

An hour later, Noah entered Daniel's home study. Seared by Blume's parting shot, he had deliberated for only a few minutes before deciding which Matherly to approach.

He hadn't spoken to Maris in more than a week. She was still pissed over Nadia. The power-of-attorney document was hardly an olive branch to hold out to her. Besides, she had recently revealed a stubborn streak he hadn't known she had.

Daniel was the weaker of them. He had earned his spurs

years ago, but age had dulled them. He was no longer the for-
midable force he'd been. Tired and in declining health, he
wasn't as obstinate as he once was. If he put up any resistance
at all, Noah was confident of his ability to wear him down.

Maxine answered the door and told him that Daniel was in
his study. "He went in there immediately after dinner. Said he
was going to read for a while before bedtime."

Sure enough, when Noah went in, an open book was resting
on Daniel's lap. But his head was bowed low over his chest, and
for a second Noah feared the old bastard had died. That's the
way his luck had been running lately. "Daniel?"

He raised his head. "Hello, Noah. I was just reading."

"Do you always snore when you read?"

"Tell me I wasn't drooling, too."

"Not that I saw."

"Good. Have a seat. Drink?"

"No, thanks."

On the way over, an unpleasant thought had crossed Noah's
mind. What if Maris had told her father about his affair with
Nadia? Maybe she had confided in Daniel before running off to
Georgia. To crown a totally shitty day, all he needed was for his
father-in-law to accuse him of adultery and order him from his
house. But the old man was behaving normally.

Noah sat down on the love seat. "I'm sorry to disturb you.
But Maris will call later, and I'll be required to give her a full
report, right down to what you ate for dinner."

"Grilled sole, brown rice, and steamed vegetables."

"A menu she'll approve. She also put me in charge of keeping
you company while she's away."

Daniel snorted. "I don't need a baby-sitter."

"I agree. But please go along with me or I'll catch hell when
she returns." He set his elbows on his knees and leaned forward.
"What say we go to the country tomorrow for the weekend? Get
in some fishing. Relaxation. I could use it, God knows."

"I rarely go up there anymore."

"Before she left, I ran the idea past Maris, and it met with wholehearted approval. I think she feels guilty for not taking you to the farm more often. If we go, it will alleviate her guilt and give her peace of mind knowing that you're enjoying yourself."

Daniel pondered it for a moment. Noah said no more. He couldn't push too hard or the old man would become suspicious. He'd made his pitch; it was time to shut up and let Daniel make his decision.

"What time tomorrow?"

Noah's tension eased and he smiled. "I have a breakfast meeting that would be difficult to reschedule. We could leave right after."

"That doesn't give Maxine much time to—"

"Actually, Daniel, I was thinking that we could go alone. Really bach it." He glanced over his shoulder as though to assure himself that the housekeeper wasn't eavesdropping. Lowering his voice, he said, "If Maxine goes, she'll fuss over you like a mother hen. You'll be accounting to her for every drink, every fat gram. Forget puffing your pipe."

"She nags worse than a wife, and everything I do will be reported straight to Maris."

"Sometimes we men must take a stand."

"Hear, hear."

"So, are we all set?"

"I am if you are."

"Great!" He stood and crossed the room to shake Daniel's hand. "I'll be over in the morning around ten. Pack light. I'll call the grocer up there and have him deliver food and drink to the house, so it'll be well stocked when we arrive." As he moved toward the door, he spoke over his shoulder. "I'll even volunteer to break the news to Maxine that she's not invited."

CHAPTER 22

While Maris studied his manuscript, Parker studied her.

She had taken a full hour in the guest cottage and had returned wearing a loose, casual skirt that came almost to her ankles, along with the sleeveless shirt that tied at her waist and allowed an occasional glimpse of bare midriff. She had kicked off her sandals when she settled into the easy chair and tucked her feet beneath her.

Her hair had been shampooed. A fresh application of lip gloss had left her mouth with a peachy shine. And whether it was the whisky she'd drunk or cosmetics, there was more color in her cheeks than when she arrived. She looked and smelled delectable.

He supposed he should be grateful that she found his manuscript so absorbing that she was unaware of his scrutiny. She was focused solely on the pages lying in her lap, and he was irrationally jealous of his own work for the amount of her attention it was receiving.

Before her unheralded arrival this afternoon, he'd been well on his way to getting good and trashed. He hadn't been able to write worth a crap all day, although from a meteorological standpoint it was a perfect day for it. Cloudy, gloomy, and gray, it was the kind of day when he usually immersed himself in his story and came up for air only when forced to by hunger, thirst, or needing to relieve himself.

But his mind had been a blank. Well . . . not a blank. He just wasn't able to write down what was on his mind, because all that was on his mind was Maris. As it had been since she left, he could think of little else today.

Maris presiding over a meeting.

Maris smiling at Noah.

Maris hailing a taxi.

Maris kissing Noah.

Maris working at her desk.

Maris sleeping beside Noah.

Maris shopping on Fifth Avenue.

Maris opening her thighs to Noah.

The revolving mental images had been enough to drive him crazy. Had been enough to drive him to drink, anyway.

He wondered now if he'd had a premonition of her arrival. Yeah, maybe he had. Because he'd been in the dining room, a room he visited only rarely. He'd been feeling sorry for himself, quaffing Wild Turkey as fast as he could pour it, and glumly staring out the window at nothing.

When he heard a motorized vehicle turning into the lane off the main road, he had assumed it was Mike returning. He remembered hoping that Mike hadn't forgotten to get a bag of bite-sized Milky Way bars.

When he saw Maris behind the wheel of the approaching golf cart, his heart had sputtered and knocked like an ailing engine.

Subconsciously, had he been watching for her, pining like a grass widow searching the horizon for sight of her sailor's ship? He hated to think of himself as some wretched, pathetic figure waiting for Maris to grace him with her presence. God, had he sunk that low?

But he realized now that that's exactly what he'd been doing since she'd turned her back on him and stalked out of the cotton gin. Since that morning, he'd been steeping in his misery, stewing in his jealous sweat, sucking on whisky bottles, and nursing his fantasies.

Torturous fantasies of her with Noah.

Delicious ones of her with him.

At night he had erotic dreams in which she clutched him and chanted his name in breathless, urgent, orgasmic whispers. During the daylight hours, he occupied himself with visions of her caressing him, of her fingertips skimming his chest and belly, of her mouth silkily sliding—

"Was it Todd's?"

He jerked upright as though his wheelchair had goosed him. "Huh?" He cleared his throat and shook off the sexual reverie. "Pardon?"

"The baby that Mary Catherine miscarried. Was it Todd's?"

"What do you think?"

"It's suggested. Do we ever know?"

He shook his head. "I think it's better to leave it with just a suggestion. Let the reader come to his own conclusion."

"I agree." She thumbed through the pages again, stopping occasionally to reread a passage. "He's a remarkable character. Roark, I mean. He's so . . . well, heroic. As Mary Catherine says, he's nice."

Parker grimaced. "He's not *too* nice, is he? I don't want him coming across as a saint. Or worse, a puss."

"He doesn't." She smiled reassurance, but he continued to frown doubtfully. "Trust me, Parker. I'd tell you if he were nice to the point of being dull."

"Women readers aren't turned on by nice heroes any more than male readers lust after heroines who are too virtuous. There should be at least a hint, maybe even a promise, of corruptibility."

"You don't have to worry about Roark in that regard. Women readers will love him, for this scene alone if for no other. He's very male. His responses are instinctually masculine. He looks at everything in a sexual context first, before expanding his viewpoint to include other factors, like morality.

"At the same time, he's sensitive to Mary Catherine's needs. He declined her invitation to have sex, demonstrating that he knows where the lines of decency are drawn. Without hitting the reader over the head with his goodness, you imply that he has a strong conscience and moral fiber. He upholds a code of honor, a . . ." She glanced up and caught him silently laughing at her. "What?"

"You really get worked up over this stuff, don't you?"

"That's my job."

"I understand your need to get excited over it. But at the end of the day, it's still only a book, Maris."

"Not to me it isn't." She spoke softly and a bit shyly. "When I really love a book, the characters become real to me. I think it stems from losing my mother at such an early age. I needed people around me, so the princes and princesses I read about became my adopted brothers and sisters.

"I lived in palaces and on pirate ships. I climbed mountain peaks and hacked my way through dark jungles. Captain Nemo's submarine became as familiar to me as my own bedroom. The characters in my books took me along on their adventures. I laughed and cried with them. I was involved in their lives. I was privy to all their secrets. I knew their hopes and dreams as well as their fears. They became like family."

She straightened a bent corner of one of the manuscript pages and gave a small, self-conscious, self-deprecating shrug. "I suppose that passion for fiction carried over into adulthood."

For several ponderous moments, she kept her head down. Eventually she looked across at him. He leaned toward her and spoke very softly. "If you can get that turned on by a book, I'd like to know what else you have a passion for."

She knew exactly what he was thinking. Their minds were moving along the same track. He could see it in the way her eyes turned smoky and hear it in the catch of her breath.

"The *f* word turns me on," she whispered.

"The *f* word?"

"Food."

He threw back his head and laughed. It rumbled up out of his chest and felt so good it startled him. For the first time in years, his laughter was spontaneous. It wasn't tinged with bitterness and cynicism.

She fired a fake pistol at him. "Gotcha."

"I concede. You're hungry?"

"Famished."

"Mike will never forgive me for being such a rotten host. I suppose I can put together some sort of meal, but you have to help."

"Lead on."

They moved into the kitchen and, working side by side, assembled BLTs. "Avocado?" he asked, as he set the microwave to cook the bacon strips.

"Yum."

"You have to peel it. Mike says I can't do it without bruising it."

"One thing I like about you, Parker—"

"Only one?"

"—is that you own up to your shortcomings."

"Well, there are so few of them, I can afford to be humble." She threw a Frito at him.

They ate the chips out of the bag and pickles straight from the jar. "Different from what you're used to, isn't it?" he asked around a mouthful.

"Obviously you have me confused with a pampered, spoiled brat."

"No," he replied honestly. "You work too hard to fit that description."

"Thank you."

"You're dedicated."

"Yes, I am."

"You get the job done."

"I try."

"So is that why you came back? Am I a job you left unfinished?"

"I came back to deliver the letter of agreement along with your signing check for fifteen thousand."

"You never heard of Federal Express?"

"I wasn't sure a carrier would deliver to St. Anne."

He gave her a look that said he knew better, and she got busy picking at the crust on her bread. "Okay, we're being honest. I wanted to make sure you were writing, Parker, and if you weren't, to prod you along. My dad advised it."

"Oh, so you came back because your *daddy* thought it was a good idea."

"Not exactly."

"Then why, Maris? Exactly."

She looked over at him, opened her mouth to speak, reconsidered, and began again. "We had quarreled before I left. I wanted to clear the air between us. Otherwise our working relationship would—"

He bleated a sound like the buzzer on a TV game show. "To you this might look like the backwoods, but believe it or not, we've got telephones, e-mails, faxes, various methods of communication."

"But you wouldn't take my calls or answer my e-mails and faxes."

"Eventually I would have."

"I wasn't sure."

"Yes, you were." He ended the parley there by holding up his hand and stopping her next argument. "You hopped that jet plane because you wanted to see me again. Admit it, Maris."

Her chin went up defiantly, and he thought she might deny it. But she surprised him again. "All right, yes. I did. I wanted to see you."

Folding his arms on the tabletop, he leaned toward her. "Why? Not because of my natural charm. We established early on that I have none." He stroked his chin. "So I'm wondering, did you and your hubby have a spat? Afterward, you thought, *I'll show him. I'll trot myself down to Hicksville and have a fling with a gimp.* Is that why you came back?"

He figured she would storm from the room, retrieve her things from the guest cottage, then hightail it to her golf cart and leave him in a wake of epithets. But, again, he guessed wrong. She remained where she was and addressed him in a remarkably calm voice.

"Tell me, Parker, why do you insist on being cruel? Does being mean to people make you feel stronger and more manly? Do you use meanness to cancel out the wheelchair? Or do you deliberately piss people off in order to keep them at arm's length? Do you hurt them before they have a chance to hurt you? If that's the case, then I'm truly sorry for you. Indeed, for the first time since I met you, I pity you."

When she did leave the table, her pace and posture were dignified. Her back was straight, her head high, and as Parker watched her disappear through the kitchen door, he felt like the lowest life-form on earth.

He had accused her of using him to get to Noah, when precisely the opposite was at play. He was using her to get to Noah.

Afraid she would leave before he could apologize, he backed his chair out of the kitchen and quickly rolled it down the central hallway and through the front door. He was relieved to find her on the veranda, leaning into one of the support columns, staring out at the giant live oaks that stood sentinel on both sides of the front path.

"Maris."

"I'll leave in the morning."

"I don't want you to go."

She laughed softly but without humor. "You don't know what you want, Parker. To write. Not to write. To be famous. To be a recluse. To have me here. To send me away. You don't even know whether or not you want to go on living.

"Whatever the case, I shouldn't have come back. My reasons for returning were muddled at best, even to me. I should have stayed in New York where I belong and left you alone to luxuriate in your anger and bitterness and to keep boozy company with a ghost. You can get back to your pathetic pastimes tomorrow after I leave."

He rolled his chair directly behind her and placed his hands on either side of her waist where it flared into hips. "Don't leave."

Leaning forward, he pressed his forehead into the small of her back. He rolled it to the left and right of that shallow depression while his fingers flexed, tightening his grasp on her.

"I don't give a damn why you came back, Maris. I swear I don't. Even if you are here just to make your husband angry, I don't care. You're here, and I want you to be."

He moved his hands around to her front, where he rested them for a time on the knot of her shirt before slipping them beneath it and touching her skin. Massaging gently, he gradually drew her backward.

She spoke his name plaintively, part statement, part query, part sigh of resignation.

He continued to draw her backward until her knees bent and he settled her onto his lap. He turned her, draping her legs over an armrest of his chair so that he was cradling her like an infant.

She looked up at him with concern. "Is this all right?"

He sifted her hair through his fingers. He stroked her cheek with his thumb, then dragged it across her lower lip. "This is perfect."

CHAPTER 23

It required all his willpower not to kiss her then. He knew she expected it, which was one reason he didn't. The other was because he was still feeling guilty over suggesting that her motives weren't pure. As though his were.

"Want to go for a ride?" he asked.

"A ride?"

"Down to the beach."

"I can walk."

"You can ride."

He disengaged the brake and navigated the wheelchair down the ramp off the veranda onto a paved path that led through the woods. "This is convenient," she remarked.

"I had the paths laid during the reconstruction of the house."

"Mike said you never even considered using a motorized chair, that you like doing things the hard way."

"Self-propulsion is good exercise. Mike feeds me well. I don't want to go to flab."

"What is that wonderful smell?"

"Magnolia."

"There aren't any fireflies out tonight."

"The *lightning bugs* think it's going to rain."

"Is it?"

"We'll see, won't we?"

The paved path went as far as the sand dunes, where it connected to an elevated path constructed of weathered wood planks. Sea oats brushed against Maris's legs as they went over the dunes. Beyond them, the path expanded into a platform exactly eight feet square. Parker stopped and set the brake on the wheelchair.

The deserted beach spread out before them. From this stretch of it, the mainland couldn't be seen. It looked as primordial as it had been when it was formed. The moon was obscured by the dense cloud cover, but it shed enough light to see the surf as it broke. It left a silvery residue that sparkled briefly before dissolving into the sand. The breeze was as soft as the breath of a sleeping baby, and the only sound was the redundant swish of the tide.

"This is an amazing place." Maris spoke in a reverential whisper usually reserved for church. "Dense forest growing right up to the beach."

"And no high-rise hotels to spoil the view." Rather than appreciating the view, he was rubbing a strand of Maris's hair between his fingers, studying the texture, enjoying the feel of it.

She turned her head to look at him. "What kind of narcotics?"

"Ah. I should've known you'd catch that slip of the tongue."

"I did. And it's been on my mind ever since. What kind of narcotics did you take?" Her expression wasn't censorious, simply interested. Sympathetic, maybe.

He let go of her hair and lowered his hand. "Pharmaceuticals. Painkillers. Great big quantities of them. Heaping handfuls."

"Because of your legs?"

"It was a long recovery."

"From what, Parker?"

"My own stupidity." After a short pause for emphasis, he

continued. "I underwent several operations, first to reconstruct the bones and replace the missing pieces with plastic or metal. Then the muscles and tendons had to be reattached. After that, the skin. . . .

"Hell, Maris, you don't want to hear all that, and I really don't want to talk about it. Bottom line, I was in the hospital for over a year, then in . . . other facilities. I went through years of physical therapy. It was a bitch. Like hell must be, only worse. That's when I got hooked on prescription painkillers. When the doctors refused to prescribe any more, I bought the pills off the street from independent vendors."

"Drug dealers."

"With whom I became bosom buddies." She didn't appear to be shocked, but she might be if he told her the depths to which he had sunk in order to maintain his stash. So he summed it up. "I was a mess."

"But you pulled yourself out of it."

"No, I got grabbed by the balls and yanked out of it."

"Mike."

"Mike," he repeated, shaking his head over the miracle of it. "For reasons I will never understand, he befriended me. He appeared one day out of nowhere. Through the blurred vision of a drugged-out stupor, I saw him standing there amid the squalor, looking at me as though trying to decide if I was worth the effort it was going to take to save me from myself."

"Maybe he was sent to you."

"A guardian angel? Fairy godfather? At least he wasn't the Grim Reaper. Although in the weeks just following his *rescue*, I sometimes wished I was dead. Before I knew what was happening, he seized my stash and slapped me into detox."

"That couldn't have been pleasant."

"You don't want to know. Believe me. When I got out, he enrolled me in more therapy, physical *and* emotional. Cleaned me up, installed me in an apartment outfitted for the physically challenged, asked what I intended to do with the rest of my life.

When I told him I had an itch to write, he set me up with a computer."

"He started you writing."

"He put it in the form of a dare."

"Which gave you a reason to go on living."

"No, by then I had decided I must go on living." *I had a damn good reason to,* he thought darkly.

"Can I ask a very personal question, Parker?"

"You can. You might regret it."

"Is Roark you?"

He'd known she would get around to it sooner or later. She was too smart not to have pieced it together. A writer writing about a writer. Naturally she would see the parallel and ask. The answer he had ready wasn't a lie, just not the whole truth. "Not entirely."

"Loosely based upon?"

"Fair to say."

She nodded solemnly but pried no further. "Did you start writing the mystery series right away?"

"No, I tried several genres. Devised and discarded a dozen plots a week for almost two years. Several thousand acres of trees went into my trash can before the Deck Cayton character clicked. He was the first thing that held my interest, that took my mind off my physical limitations.

"When I had what I thought was a publishable story, I retained an agent and told her she could submit the manuscript if she swore on her life and the lives of her children never to reveal my identity to anyone."

"And Mackensie Roone came to be." She touched his cheek. "It was a rebirth for which we can all be grateful. I'm just sorry for the suffering you had to endure to get there."

"In the long run, it's going to be worth it."

The moment the sentence was out, he realized he'd spoken it in the present tense. He feared Maris might notice and question him about his ultimate goal, but she had turned her head away from him and was gazing out across the surface of the water. The lights of a tanker winked on the horizon.

Raindrops began to fall, creating wet dimples in the sand. They fell on the wood platform in light spatters. Parker heard them even before he felt the sprinkles on his skin. They felt as warm and soft as tears.

"Parker?"

"Hmm?"

"Remember that first day I came to the cotton gin, you suggested that Noah had married the boss's daughter to further his career?"

"That yanked your chain."

"Yes. But only because you hit the nail on the head. Deep down I knew it." She turned and looked into his face. "I caught him this week with another woman." The simple statement was followed by a pause that gave him time to respond. He kept his expression neutral. "I won't bore you with the sordid details."

"How sordid?"

"Sufficiently sordid."

"Enough to send you scrambling back here? Payback time?"

"No. I swear that's not why I'm here. Noah's affair provided me with justification for coming back. But the truth is, I didn't want to leave in the first place."

"Then why did you go?"

"It was a matter of conscience."

"Over what? Nothing happened."

"Something happened to me," she exclaimed softly, pressing her fist against her chest. "I wanted to stay with you, and that was reason enough for me to leave. Being around you wasn't healthy for my marriage. What I was feeling for you frightened me. For my peace of mind, I needed to reestablish myself as a happily married woman. Ironically, I'd been back in New York only one day when I discovered that Noah had broken our marriage vows."

"He's a fool."

She gave him a smile for the indirect compliment, but it turned rueful. "So am I. I'm a fool for not acknowledging sooner that our marriage wasn't what I wanted it to be. Nor was Noah the man I wanted him to be. He wasn't the hero of his book."

"And now you think of Roark as a hero."

Shaking her head, she said, "I'm not confusing fact with fiction, Parker. I've outgrown that. You're real. I can touch you." She reached for his hand, studying it as she traced the veins on the back of it with her fingertip. "My marriage, such as it was, is over. Behind me. I don't want to talk about Noah anymore."

"Fine by me."

He gathered a handful of her hair, then wound it around his fist and drew her closer until their faces were inches apart. He hesitated for several heartbeats, then settled his lips against hers, tested the angle, readjusted. He was moderately controlled until he heard a small whimper from her. He backed off, looked down into her eyes, and recognized a desire that equaled his own.

Control was abandoned. He covered her face with wild, random, artless kisses and she was doing the same to him. Then mouths melded and tongues touched, and they kissed with carnal greed.

Eventually Parker pulled back and caught his breath, then proceeded with more temperance. His tongue stroked her lower lip; he raked it gently between his teeth. He laid light kisses at the corners of her lips before pressing his tongue into her mouth. He angled his head first to one side, then the other, but he never broke contact. Even when he withdrew, his lips remained against hers, making sipping motions as gentle as the rainfall.

Her lips barely moving against his, she whispered, "The night we met, when you kissed me . . ."

"Hmm?"

"I didn't want you to stop."

"I know."

"You *know*?"

"Don't you think I felt it, too, Maris?"

In reply, she threaded her fingers up through his hair and played sexy with her tongue. As they kissed, he unbuttoned the row of buttons, untied the knot at her waist, and pulled open her shirt.

Her breasts were proportionately small, beautifully round, and, now, sprinkled with rainwater. Heavier drops beaded on her skin. Some formed rivulets that trickled over the smooth curves, intersecting and crisscrossing in erotic patterns.

"Parker? You know it's raining."

"Yeah." He cupped her breast and reshaped it with his hand. His thumb whisked a raindrop off the tip. He leaned down and rubbed his lips across it. "As you told me once, you won't melt."

Then he took her nipple into his mouth.

"I might," she sighed.

Making his dream a reality, she folded her arms around his head and clutched him to her, repeating his name on ragged breaths.

His hand waded through what seemed like unfurled bolts of fabric until he found skin. He slid his hand between her thighs, all the way up, to her center. He touched her through her underpants. "Okay?"

She made a sound that he took for a yes. Her sex was pliant and very wet. He eased his fingers into her.

"Ohgod, Parker."

His fingers stroked her from within while his thumb drew circles on the outside. Soon she was thrusting her hips up against his hand.

"Just let it happen, Maris."

She relaxed and, although her breathing was still shallow and quick, she stopped working at trying to climax. He continued to nuzzle her breasts. Her nipples became small and hard against his flicking tongue. The stroking of his fingers intensified and the circles drawn by his thumb shrank to center on one spot.

Then he felt it, that unique tension that claimed her. Involuntary. Imperative. Impossible to bridle. Uncontainable. Her back arched. Her head fell back and she covered her eyes with her forearm. Her exposed neck begged to be kissed. He bent over it and pressed his lips against the hollow of her throat while sweet sounds vibrated from it. He remained there until the last of the aftershocks had rippled through her and she went limp.

He withdrew his hand from beneath her skirt and smoothed it back into place. He then gathered her close, securing her against his chest by resting his chin on the top of her head.

Weakly she laid her hand on his chest. "You buttoned your shirt."

"For supper. One of my mom's rules."

She undid the buttons and rubbed her cheek against his chest hair, then laid her head against his heart. "Better."

The rain continued to fall on them, soaking their hair and clothes, but neither noticed or cared. He stroked her back, his fingers stopping at each individual vertebra. "He hasn't fucked you worth a damn, has he?"

He felt her stiffen, and for a moment he feared that he'd gone too far, said too much, offended her with his blunt language. But it was an initial reaction that passed quickly. She relaxed against him again and said softly, "I thought so. Until a few minutes ago."

"You were hungry for it."

"I didn't know that until you touched me. My sex life was another self-delusion."

She must have felt his smile, because she raised her head and looked at him. "You must be feeling pretty good about yourself."

His grin was unrepentantly cocky, but it turned into a soft smile. "I feel good." He kissed her lips softly, growling against them, "But you feel better."

They kissed long and deeply. He was reluctant to end it but eventually did. "We'd better get back to the house before Mike organizes a search party."

He reached for the brake lever to release it, but she stopped him. "What about you? This?" She rocked her hips against his erection. "Don't you want me to . . . do something?"

Wincing, he clasped her firmly around the waist and gasped, "Yeah, I want you to stop moving like that."

"Oh. Sorry."

He gave her a crooked smile and curved his hand around the back of her neck. "When we make love, I want to be concentrating on the pleasure of it and not worrying about how I'm going to come without dumping us out of this chair."

"It's that earthshaking?"

"It will be, yes."

"But I had all the fun."

"Shows how little you know."

She smiled and he kissed her quickly, then turned them around and headed for home. "By the way, since I need two hands to drive this damn thing, you'd better button up your shirt or Mike'll get an eyeful."

The following morning Daniel got up early. He showered and dressed quickly, then packed a few changes of clothing to take to the country before going downstairs. Maxine had been most unhappy to hear about his planned weekend without her and had made her displeasure known. So he was very meek this morning when he asked her if it would be too much trouble for him to have his breakfast in the courtyard.

"No trouble at all, Mr. Matherly. It'll take me just a few minutes to get the tray ready."

"Perfect. I can use the time to make a couple of calls."

He went into his study and placed the first call to a number he now had memorized. He said little during the five-minute call. The majority of the time was spent listening.

Mr. William Sutherland finally said everything he had to say and asked, "Do you want me to proceed, Mr. Matherly?"

"By all means."

Daniel placed the second call of the morning to Becker-Howe. He wasn't surprised that even at this time of day, when most New Yorkers were queuing up at Starbucks and crowding subways to get to their offices at a reasonable hour, his call was answered by Mr. Oliver Howe himself.

Howe, rather pompously, had always boasted that he put in a fourteen-hour workday, except on holidays when he worked only eight. Apparently his schedule was as arduous as it had always been, despite his advanced age.

Howe's publishing career had been launched at approximately the same time as Daniel's and in a similar fashion. Howe was bequeathed his company from his grandfather within months of his graduation from his university. He and Daniel had remained friendly rivals through the years, and eventually their acquaintance had evolved into a grudging friendship. They held one another in the highest esteem.

"Ollie, it's Daniel Matherly."

As expected, his old colleague was delighted to hear from him. After exchanging pleasantries, Oliver Howe said, "I can't play golf anymore, Danny Boy. Goddamn rheumatism won't let me."

"That's not why I'm calling, Ollie. This is business-related."

"I thought you had retired."

"That's the rumor, but you of all people should know better. The fact is, I've run across an exciting proposition that I thought might interest you."

Daniel emerged from his study a few minutes later without the benefit of his cane. He felt invigorated. He was even rubbing his palms together as he approached Maxine. "Would you please go out and buy some bread at that Kosher bakery I like?"

"They don't have bread in Massachusetts? Mr. Reed said he was going to have the house stocked with food."

"I know, but I'm hungry for . . . you know the kind. With the seeds on it."

"I know the kind. That bakery is across town. I'll go after you've had breakfast."

"Noah will be picking me up after breakfast. Better go now. I can serve myself breakfast."

She eyed him suspiciously, and with good cause. His sudden yen for a particular bread was a ruse to get her out of the house. He had a guest coming for breakfast and he didn't want anyone to know about it.

Maxine continued to argue, but eventually she huffed out the service entrance, muttering to herself. She'd only been gone a few minutes when Daniel answered the front doorbell and invited his guest inside.

"My housekeeper is out on an errand," he explained as he led the way to the courtyard. Maxine always set the table for three on the chance that Maris or Noah or both would drop by. Even though Maris was out of town and Noah was due to arrive later, Daniel was relieved to see that she hadn't broken with habit. He indicated a chair at the round wrought-iron table. "Please sit. Coffee?"

"Yes, thank you."

Daniel poured. As he passed the cream and sugar, he said, "Thank you for coming on such short notice."

"It wasn't so much an invitation as an edict, Mr. Matherly."

"Then why did you come?"

"Curiosity."

Daniel acknowledged the candor with an appreciative nod. "So you were surprised to hear from me?"

"Shocked, actually."

"I'm glad that we can speak frankly with one another, because I know your time is valuable and I'm on a tight schedule myself this morning. My son-in-law is picking me up at ten o'clock and driving me to our house in the country. He invited me to spend some quality time alone with him while my daughter is away." He lifted a napkin-lined silver basket toward his guest. "Muffin?"

"No, thanks."

"For bran muffins, they're not bad. My housekeeper makes them herself."

"No, thank you."

He returned the basket to the tabletop. "Where was I?"

"Mr. Matherly, I know that you're not in your dotage, so please don't insult my intelligence by pretending to be. You didn't invite me here to sample your housekeeper's bran muffins."

Daniel dropped the pose. Planting his elbows on the table, he clasped his hands together and looked at his guest from beneath his white eyebrows, now drawn into a steep V above the bridge of his nose.

"I would stake my fortune on the probability that when Noah and I arrive at our country place, he will have in his possession a document of some sort that empowers him to conduct business for my publishing house." He spoke with the brusque efficacy that had always been at his command and on which he had built his reputation for hard and sometimes ruthless dealing.

"Over the course of the weekend, I will be pressed into signing this document." He raised his hand to stop his guest from speaking. "No. Say nothing. You would do well only to listen."

Following a long, thoughtful, somewhat mistrustful hesitation, Daniel was motioned to continue.

Todd hadn't counted on it taking this long.

He was impatient to attain wealth and achieve fame—in that order.

After the mortgage on his parents' house was paid off, the profit he'd made on its sale had been a pittance. Each parent had carried a meager life insurance policy, but his mother had used his father's to bury him, and Todd had used hers to lay her to rest. Once all their their affairs were settled, the leftovers that comprised his legacy were hardly worth counting. He barely had enough to finance his relocation to Florida and had arrived in Key West virtually penniless.

The cost of living was far higher than he and Roark had estimated, even though they were living in veritable squalor and eating cheaply. He earned good tips parking cars, but the cash was quickly consumed by rent, gas, food, and other necessities.

And his monthly installments on a pc. He, unlike his roommate, wasn't fortunate enough to have a great-uncle he had seen only twice in his entire life but who had felt a familial obligation to give his grandnephew an expensive college graduation gift. Roark's advantage had rankled. Todd had wasted no time in leveling the playing field and acquiring a computer on a lease-purchase plan.

He was bummed over his chronic shortage of legal tender. He was even more bummed over his chronic shortage of creativity.

Fame, even more than wealth, seemed so elusive as to be out of the question. Writing fiction was hard work. He had dozed through countless boring lectures on the subject, but he was fairly certain that none of his creative writing instructors had emphasized how labor-intensive it was. That had never been a starred point in his classroom notes. That question had never been asked on an exam. True or false, writing is damn hard work.

At least once a week, he and Roark went to Hemingway's home. The Spanish Colonial estate was their shrine, and they went as pilgrims to pay homage. Todd had always been an admirer, of course. But he was only now beginning to appreciate Hemingway's greatness.

Talent was something you were born with. Either you had it or you didn't. But talent by itself was useless. Hours of tedious effort were required to awaken and exercise that talent, to write that riveting "one true sentence" that seemed so damn simple when read.

That simplicity was deceptive. It didn't happen by accident. Nor was it a skill easily acquired. Writing was demanding, solitary, backbreaking work. A writer mined the tunnels of his brain, using words for his pickaxe. A week's effort might yield only one nugget that was worth keeping, and you could weep with pathetic gratitude over that.

Todd admired those who wrote and wrote well. But his admiration was tinged with resentment. Hemingway and his ilk were stingy with their talent and skill. One would think that after having spent so much time studying their work, poring over every phrase, analyzing it word by goddamn word, the ability to write like that would rub off, that the brilliance would be contagious. Didn't desire count for something? But there were days when he couldn't find even a grain of genius in his own work.

Nor could anyone else, it seemed.

He balled up the written critique he had received from Professor Hadley and hurled it toward the corner of the room.

Roark walked in just as the paper ball landed on the floor several inches short of the trash can. "Hadley was a hard-ass?"

"Hadley is an ass*hole*."

"Don't I know it. He raked me over the coals, too."

"Seriously?"

"Then left me there to smolder. So, what I thought is, tonight being our night off, we should get drunk."

"Love to," Todd said moodily. "Can't afford it."

"Neither can I. But being a bartender isn't without its perks." With that, Roark brought his hand from behind his back and waggled a bottle of cheap scotch.

"You stole it?"

"This piss won't be missed."

"You're a poet."

"And didn't know it. Let's go."

Todd rolled off his bunk. "You don't have to ask me twice."

On the beach, they passed the bottle back and forth between them, toasting the sunset, then the twilight, finally the night sky. They continued to toast the heavens until individual stars began to blur and bob and the universe became a little fuzzy around the edges.

"Starlight, star bright, first star . . . et cetera. Make a wish, Roark."

"I wish you'd pass me the whisky."

Todd handed him the bottle. Roark drank, handed it back, then stretched out on the sand and stacked his hands beneath his head. He began to laugh.

"What?" Todd asked as he used his butt to grind a more comfortable depression into the sand.

"Wishes," Roark replied. "Reminds me of a genie joke."

"There are hundreds. Which one?"

"This guy finds a magic lamp, rubs it, genie pops out, grants him three wishes. The guy wishes for a Ferrari, and *poof!* Next morning there's a shiny new Ferrari parked in his driveway. He rubs the lamp again, genie pops out, says he's got two more wishes. The guy wishes for ten million dollars and *poof!* Next morning ten million dollars is neatly stacked on his nightstand. He rubs the lamp again, genie pops out, says he's got one last wish. The guy wishes for a penis that would reach the ground, and *poof!* Next morning he wakes up and his legs are three inches long."

When their laughter subsided, Roark added, "Moral of the story, be careful what you wish for."

Todd grumbled, "I wish Hadley's dick would shrivel to nothing and then drop off. If he's even got one. Which I doubt."

"Which manuscript did you send him?"

"The Vanquished."

"You've been working your ass off on that book. What'd he say?"

Todd took another swig from the bottle. "The plot stretches plausibility. My dialogue sucks."

"Hadley said 'sucks'?"

"Words to that effect."

"Hmm."

"What?"

"He said my dialogue was crisp and well paced, but my plot is predictable and needs punch." He looked over at Todd. "Maybe we should collaborate."

"Shit, no. No sharing. I've put in a two-year apprenticeship without any remuneration."

"You sold a short story," Roark reminded him.

"One lousy short story to a local magazine for twenty-five bucks. It'll be read in the crapper if at all." He pitched a seashell back into the surf. "I'm living in an apartment where the roaches are carnivorous and the tenants downstairs are armed and dangerous."

"But you can't beat the view. You can, however, beat your meat while taking in the view."

"There is that," Todd replied solemnly. "I've never jerked off so much in my life."

"The palm of your hand isn't sprouting hair, is it?"

"Here's to nude sunbathing among exotic dancers."

He raised the bottle in salute, but Roark took it from him and helped himself to another swallow.

"I'm broke all the friggin' time," Todd continued morosely. "My car's got over a hundred and sixty thousand miles on it."

"Meanwhile, you're parking Porsches and BMWs."

"A job you could train a chimpanzee to do."

"A chimp is cuter. Would probably get better tips."

Todd glared at Roark. "Are you gonna let me finish this or what?"

"Sorry. Didn't mean to interrupt your pity party." Roark passed the bottle back to him. "Have another drink."

"Thank you." Todd drank and belched a loud, gurgling burp. "When all this hardship pays off, I want the glory to go to me, myself, and I. No offense."

"None taken. I don't want to collaborate with you, either. I was joking."

"Oh." Todd flopped down onto his back in the sand. "So what did Hadley really say in his notes to you?"

"I told you."

"Was it the truth?"

"Why would I lie?"

"To make me feel better."

Roark snorted. "I'm not that charitable."

"Right, right, you're a son of a bitch. So maybe you would lie for another reason."

Roark sat up. "Something on your mind, Todd? If so, why don't you just say it?"

"You always downplay Hadley's critiques."

"I'm not gonna wear a hair shirt over one man's opinion,

which is all his critiques are. I don't let myself get depressed over them the way you do."

"Maybe."

"Maybe what?"

"Maybe that explains why you downplay them. On the other hand, you might be trying to throw me off track."

Roark shook his head in bafflement. "What the fuck are you talking about?"

"Forget it."

"Like hell I will. First you accused me of lying and then you provided me with a shitty motivation for it. I take exception to both."

"And I take exception to your thinking you're a better writer than me."

"Than I," Roark corrected.

"Fuck you!" Todd surged to his feet, but the earth tilted drastically and threw him off balance. He landed back in the sand.

Roark grabbed him by the shoulders and brought him around. "Why would I deliberately mislead you about Hadley's critiques?"

Todd flung his hands up and threw Roark's off. "To get the jump on me. You can't stand the idea of me getting—of *my* getting—published before you."

"Oh, like you'd be thrilled if I sold a manuscript ahead of you."

"I'd rather have my guts ripped out up through my throat."

For several moments the narrow distance between them was volatile, teeming with molecules of hostility ready to spark. Todd made his hands into fists in anticipation of an attack.

To his surprise, Roark started to laugh. "You'd rather have your guts ripped out up through your throat?"

Todd tried not to smile, but he lost the battle and soon he was laughing, too. "In the heat of the moment, not to mention my inebriation, that's all I could think of to say."

"I don't recommend it for your book."

"Point taken."

They stared at the oceanscape for several minutes, then Roark said, "I'm done for the night. Think we can make it to the car?"

Todd took satisfaction in Roark's being the first to cave. "Fuck, man, I don't know. I'm wasted."

Roark threw his arm across Todd's shoulders and helped him to his feet. They made it to the parking lot, although it took a while because they stumbled often and stopped frequently. Their drunken efforts made them weak-kneed with hilarity. Neither was in any condition to drive, but Roark got behind the wheel because he was slightly less drunk than Todd.

It was past noon the following day, as they medicated their hangovers with burgers and fries, that Todd resumed the conversation. "You know, a little rivalry could be good for us."

Roark groaned. "Don't start that again. I don't consider you a rival, Todd."

"Bullshit. Of course you do."

"How could rivalry possibly be good for us?"

"It makes us work harder. Admit it, when you see me writing, there's no way you can shirk off. If I'm at my keyboard, you can't sit down and watch a ball game on TV. I'm the same. If you're writing, I feel guilty if I'm not writing, too. If you put in seven hours a day, I've got to put in at least that much. That competitive edge is what drives us."

"I'm driven by nothing except a desire to write good fiction."

Todd waved his hands in the air. "Saint Roark. Glory and hallelujah."

"You're pissing me off."

"Okay, okay, I'll drop it." He took a bite of his cheeseburger. "Anyway, the point's moot. I'll be offered megabucks for *The Vanquished* before you even complete your book. Then we'll see who's green with envy."

"That is *not* going to happen."

Todd laughed. "Oh, man, I wish you could see the malicious glint in your eye. You just won my argument for me."

Is there any coffee?"

"Isn't there always?"

Parker shot Mike a dark glance as he rolled his chair across the kitchen and poured himself a fresh mug from the coffeemaker. "Usually you come and ask if I'd like a refill, check and see if I need anything."

"I didn't want to take a chance on having my head bit off. You made it plain at breakfast that Maris and I should make ourselves scarce today, and that's what we're doing."

"I'm working on a difficult passage. I didn't want any distractions or interruptions."

He was on his way back through the connecting door when he heard Mike mutter, "You could've asked us nicely."

Parker stopped and reversed direction. "Did you say something?"

Mike threw down the dish towel he'd been using and did an about face. "I said her blouse was buttoned wrong last night when you finally saw fit to bring her in out of the rain and let me know where you were."

"Wow! You covered several transgressions in one sentence,

Mike. Shall we break it down and discuss it iniquity by iniquity? Or should I just acknowledge that you're riled in general and get back to my work?"

"I came home after a day on the mainland to find the house wide open, lights on, nobody home. I thought you'd been abducted."

"Did it occur to you that I could have been taken up in the Rapture and that you'd been left behind? Bet that really would've pissed you off."

"You and the Rapture are irreconcilable themes. I would never pair you with a thought about it. And I soon ruled out the possibility of kidnapping. Who'd be crazy enough to want you?"

"Man! You *are* ticked."

"I have a right to be. I wouldn't have even known Maris had come back if I hadn't noticed two sets of dishes in the sink and went out to check the guest house."

"You're a regular Sherlock Holmes."

"You could have left a note telling me you were going down to the beach."

"I could have. But I was afraid your maternal instincts would kick in and you'd follow us down there to make sure we kiddies were all right."

"And not up to any mischief."

Parker dropped all vestiges of humor, saying tightly, "That's right, Mike. I didn't want you to catch us playing naughty. I wouldn't care, but Maris might."

"Which brings me to the next point."

"I don't want to hear it."

"You've cooked up a plot of vengeance and you're going to act it out to the bitter end, aren't you?"

"We've been over this."

"Aren't you?"

"Damn right I am!" Parker shouted.

His raised voice didn't deter Mike, however. "What's the final chapter going to be?"

"What, give away the ending? Tell you and spoil the surprise? I don't think so."

Mike glared at him. "It's not going to be a happy ending."

"I'm not after rave reviews."

"Only revenge."

"Which always makes for good motivation, ergo a good plot. Now, are you finished?"

"Not quite. What about Maris?"

"She's definitely a plot device."

"You're using her, aren't you? In spite of who she is."

"*Because* of who she is."

Mike must have sensed Parker's unshakable resolve. Or maybe his imperious tone reminded the older man that he had overstepped his bounds. Or maybe he simply wore out. Whatever the cause, Mike's anger dissolved. His angry posture settled back into its elderly sag. "Parker, I implore you to give this up. Let go of it. Tell Maris everything. For your good as well as hers. Tell her."

"Tell me what?"

At the sound of her voice, the two men turned quickly. Evidently she had walked into a spirited exchange, and it felt like a quarrel. "Tell me what?" she repeated.

"I've written some new pages," Parker said. "They're printing out now."

"I'll get them." Mike gave Parker a look that was rife with meaning. But whatever the meaning was, Maris couldn't decipher it. He went into the solarium, leaving them alone.

"He just made a fresh pot of coffee," Parker remarked.

"Thanks, but I've passed my limit. If I drink any more this morning, I'll be swinging from the chandelier along with your ghost friend."

"I'd pay to see that." His smile was forced and the attempted humor fell flat.

Maris couldn't account for the mood in the house, mainly because she couldn't define the mood. It had started last night when she and Parker returned from the beach. Mike, who had arrived in their absence, had been on the veranda watching for them, standing with his hands on his hips and looking perturbed. He'd admonished them for getting soaked to the skin. He said he expected that kind of nutty, irresponsible behavior from Parker, but Parker had no right to subject Maris to his zaniness.

He had then hustled Parker into his bedroom at the back of the house. Maris knew which room it was, but she'd never been invited to see it, not even when Mike had conducted her on a guided tour of the house, including his suite and the unfinished rooms on the second floor.

Feeling slightly downcast over the abrupt conclusion to the romantic evening, she had returned to the guest cottage. She sensed that it wasn't their getting caught in the rain or even their unexplained absence from the house that had upset Mike. He was more than slightly annoyed, more concerned than the situation had warranted.

She couldn't figure out what they had done or hadn't done to provoke him.

If it were anyone else, she would guess that the personal valet was jealous of the newcomer. It stood to reason that someone in Mike's position would resent an intruder into the comfortable life he had made for his charge. Their days had a rhythm that he wouldn't want disturbed.

Understandably the interloper would be regarded as a threat. His first instinct would be to protect his position and importance. He would also want to shield the individual he cared for against any potential harm.

But Mike hadn't behaved jealously toward her. He didn't treat her as a danger who might damage Parker. On the contrary, he seemed genuinely pleased that she had entered their lives. He'd shown her every kindness, and, in even the most insignificant disputes, he took her side over Parker's more often than not.

Nevertheless, she couldn't help but feel that Mike had a general idea of what they'd been doing down at the beach and that he disapproved. Whatever else had factored in, this was the basis of his indignation. When she returned to the guest cottage, she'd discovered that she hadn't buttoned her shirt correctly, that in her haste, she'd skipped a button. A dead giveaway to hanky-panky.

Still, she was more mystified than embarrassed. She and Parker were well beyond the age of accountability, and it should have been clear to Mike that whatever had transpired on the beach had been consensual. Could it be a moral issue with him? Not knowing the present state of her marriage, did Mike think Parker was romancing another man's wife?

In any case, their return to the house had quelled any plans either she or Parker had for continuing what had been started on the beach. She prudently remained in the guest cottage until this morning, and although she'd lain awake for a long time half expecting Parker to come to her, he hadn't. This morning at breakfast, he'd been testy and irritable. More so than usual. And he'd acted as though their time on the beach together had never happened.

All this was weighing heavily on her mind. She was trying desperately to stave off a bad case of the blues. Despite the tender lovemaking last night, her relationship with Parker was still unspecified and tenuous. At any moment, she feared a geocentric shift of emotions that would plunge her headlong into despair.

She'd been made a fool of by one man. She didn't want to repeat that particular mistake. Ever. But certainly not within the same week.

Following that first lame attempt at conversation about caffeine, neither she nor Parker had said a word. Their eye contact had been haphazard and fleeting. Parker seemed to be making a concerted effort to avoid it altogether.

Feeling awkward, she asked if he was happy with what he'd written that morning.

"It's all right, I guess," he mumbled into his coffee mug, keeping his head down.

This was silly. They were grown-ups, not adolescents. Up till now, he had seized every opportunity to slip a blatant sexual innuendo into their conversation. He certainly hadn't been shy about demonstrating his attraction to her, starting with the night they met. His sudden bashfulness made no sense.

"Did Mike lecture you?"

He looked over at her. "About the foreplay?"

"I . . . I was going to say about seducing a married woman."

"Is that what I did?"

"Not without a lot of encouragement."

"Then does it count as a bona fide seduction?"

"Parker, are we going to play a game of semantics, or are you going to answer my question?"

"Mike is concerned for you."

"Why?"

"He thinks I'm rotten to the core."

"He thinks the sun rises and sets in you."

"He's afraid I'll hurt you."

Looking at him intently, she asked, "Will you?"

"Yes."

Startled by his blunt reply, she sat down at the kitchen table without breaking the eye contact they had finally established. "At least you're honest."

"Brutally so. It puts most people off."

"Noted. But I'm not most people."

The hard line of his lips softened. Something sparked in his eyes, which had been so remote only seconds ago. They moved over her, alighting for a time on her mouth, her breasts, her lap. Those spots that had experienced his intimate touch began to tingle with sensual recollection.

When his gaze reconnected with hers, he said gruffly, "Noted."

They lapsed into a long stare that went unbroken until Mike reentered the kitchen, bringing with him several pages of text. "The print was getting dim, so I had to replace the cartridge." He handed the pages of manuscript to Maris.

"I need to get back to it," Parker said, wheeling his chair toward the solarium. "Don't talk about me while I'm gone."

"We've got better things to talk about," Mike retorted.

Parker slammed the door shut behind him.

Maris laughed. "You two are like quarreling siblings. Or an old married couple."

"God forbid."

"Were you ever married, Mike?"

"A confirmed bachelor. How does crab au gratin sound for dinner?"

"Delicious. Was Parker?"

"Married? No."

"Women?"

He removed a package of frozen crabmeat from the freezer and set it on the countertop before turning to her. "What do you think?"

She lowered her eyes and traced the wood grain in the tabletop with her fingertip. "Of course there have been women."

"More than a few, fewer than many. Nothing lasting. Never serious."

She nodded. He went back to assembling the ingredients for his recipe.

"Parker shared with me how you rescued him from the pit, so to speak."

When he turned back to her, she saw that this revelation had surprised him. But he recovered and said, "He gives me more credit than I deserve. All I did was tell him things he already knew."

"Like?"

"I told him that he was on a sure path of self-destruction. However, I pointed out to him what a slow path he'd taken. I asked why he was dilly-dallying. I told him that if he truly wanted to be dead, he could have found a way to take himself out."

"Good psychology."

He shrugged modestly. "The main thing is, it worked." He indicated the manuscript pages she had carried in with her from the guest house. "Do you like the latest installment?"

"I've been rereading the chapter about Mary Catherine's miscarriage. Todd is beginning to reveal himself as the villain."

"Interesting," Mike murmured. "That you think of him as the villain."

"Aren't I supposed to?"

"I believe that's Parker's intention, yes."

"Do you read everything he writes?"

"Only what he asks me to."

"Which is?"

He grinned at her as he reached into the cabinet for a casserole dish. "Everything he writes."

"I'm sure he values your opinion."

Mike scoffed at that. "He thinks the only opinion that counts is his."

"It's more the feedback than the opinion that he wants. I've learned by working with writers that they like having a sounding board. Even if the sounding board never talks back, they need someone to listen to them as they process thoughts and ideas. You perform a valuable service to Parker—beyond the obvious."

He didn't carry the conversation toward the "obvious" services he performed for Parker. Instead he asked if any of her associates at Matherly Press had read the manuscript.

"To honor Parker's request for anonymity, I'm keeping it under wraps. I did share it with my father, though. He's as positive about it as I am."

"Nobody else?"

"No."

Several times she had urged Noah to read it. Each time he

had shown little interest, but in a rushed and absentminded way had promised that he would get to it as soon as his schedule permitted. Now she knew why his schedule was so tight. Much of his time had been allocated to his mistress.

Switching gears, she said, "Speaking of Dad . . ." It was unlikely that her cell phone had rung without her hearing it, but she took it from her skirt pocket and checked the lighted readout. No missed calls. "I should go call him again. I haven't been able to get an answer at his house this morning, and that's unusual."

She wasn't worried yet, just a little curious as to why Maxine was out so long. Ordinarily she had supplies delivered so she wouldn't have to leave the house and Daniel unattended for extended periods of time. Her errands were usually quickly dispatched.

Daniel hadn't gone to the office today; Maris had checked.

So apparently he and Maxine were out somewhere together. Maybe they'd gone for a walk in Central Park, or to a museum, or to a movie. Daniel enjoyed all those things, and Maxine sometimes accompanied him, welcoming the break from her routine.

But Maris had been trying to reach them for hours. She had left voice-mail messages for them to call her as soon as they returned. Either they hadn't checked for messages or they had been out for a very long time, and one was as uncustomary as the other.

"You're welcome to use our phone," Mike told her.

"Thanks, but I'll use my cell." Before leaving she asked Mike if there was anything she could do to help him with dinner. "I'm a working woman, but not a total stranger to the kitchen."

"I'll let you pour the wine when the time comes."

She had known he would refuse her offer, as Maxine always did, but she wanted to offer anyway. "Then will you excuse me?" Collecting the new pages of manuscript, she headed for the back door. "I'm eager to curl up with the next chapter."

Noah answered his ringing cell phone. "Hello?"

"Where are you?"

"Nadia?"

"Yes, Noah, Nadia," she replied waspishly.

He took a cautionary glance over his shoulder to make certain that Daniel hadn't yet made his way downstairs. Afternoon sunlight was pouring in through the open slats of the window shutters, casting long stripes of light and shadow across the hardwood floor and lending the pale saffron walls a mellow glow.

The Matherlys' country house was a bit fussy and cluttered to suit his taste. He favored contemporary. Right angles and sleek surfaces. But for what it was, the restored Colonial had been nicely done. Several years ago it had been featured in *Architectural Digest*—the country retreat of a book-publishing icon.

Here in the living room the easy chairs were wide and deep, and each had a requisite footstool. The intricate brass fireplace screen was an original to the house. Rosemary Matherly's collection of china plates from all over the world was displayed behind the glass doors of a tall cabinet.

Scattered about on end tables and in shelves were photographs of Daniel with notable authors and luminaries from
other fields of endeavor ranging from the entertainment industry, to sports, to politics, including two presidents. Pictures
of Maris chronicled her childhood, adolescence, and emer-
gence into young womanhood.

There were several photos of Noah and Maris together. One
taken at their wedding reception showed the laughing bride
hand-feeding him a bite of wedding cake. He took perverse
pleasure in looking at it now as he talked to his most recent
mistress.

"I've been calling you all day," she said.

"And I've been avoiding you. When I see one of your numbers
on the caller ID, I let it ring."

"I figured that. So this time I'm calling from a friend's
phone."

"Male or female?"

"That depends on whether or not you're speaking to me."

"You've got a selective memory, Nadia. Obviously you've forgotten why I'm not speaking to you."

"Of course I haven't forgotten. But I woke up this morning
deciding to forgive you, so—"

"You decided to forgive *me*? I didn't boink my personal
trainer."

"I've seen your personal trainer, Noah. No one would want to
boink him."

She was at it again. Mocking him. Being condescending. Just
as she'd been when he found her swaddled in damp sheets and
postcoitus bliss. Hearing the ridicule in her voice now resurrected the rage he'd felt then. The emotion that had roiled inside him hadn't been inspired by jealousy. He couldn't care less
who she fucked or how often. Being mocked by her—that's
what had rankled.

Rather than reacting with embarrassment, or remorse, or
shame, or fear—which was the reaction he really craved to see

from her—she had smiled at him insolently. How dare the bitch.

He'd been angry enough to kill her. He'd even entertained vivid mental flashes of placing his hands around her slender neck and squeezing until her eyes bulged, squeezing until her heart stopped.

He'd had the presence of mind not to act on the murderous impulse, but it had been strong enough for him to get a glimpse of his soul's dark side. Like the dark side of the moon, it was out of sight, but always there.

Several times during his life, it had been necessary to step over the boundary between light and darkness. But those brief forays into that dark region had left him shaken, feeling that he'd been lucky to return. He didn't venture into it unless he was given no other choice.

But recently he'd taken two prolonged glimpses into its shadows. First with Maris outside Nadia's apartment following her discovery of their affair. Then again with Nadia. In both instances, he'd wanted badly to hurt the offender. Silence her. Injure her beyond recovery. Kill her.

He was intrigued now, beguiled by the extent of his dark side. He hadn't known it was so expansive and dense. The urge to explore it to its farthest reaches was almost irresistible.

Never guessing the malicious nature of his thoughts, Nadia still believed they were arguing over her fling with the weight lifter.

"The point is that you acted like a complete ass at lunch that day, Noah. I felt it appropriate to remind you that nobody calls Nadia Schuller 'incredibly stupid' and gets away with it. You got in your shot, and I got in mine. Now can we please move beyond this?"

He was tempted to call her the obscene name that so aptly applied and then hang up. That's what he wanted to do. But it wouldn't be smart to alienate her now. The deal with World-View hung in the balance. Breaking with Nadia might jinx it.

Morris Blume seemed to like her. She'd been instrumental in bringing them together. Why not continue to take advantage of her usefulness? Ultimately she would get what she had coming, but not until the WorldView deal was secured. His reward for eating a small portion of crow now would be ten million dollars. In fact, for ten million dollars and control of Matherly Press, he was willing to do much worse.

"Noah, please. Please tell me where you are."

Her voice had turned soft and conciliatory. She was even making it easy on him. It was a win-win situation, and he couldn't ask for better.

Smiling to himself, he said, "I'm alone in the country house with my father-in-law."

"Daniel Matherly?"

He chuckled. "He's the only father-in-law I've got."

"Why would you subject yourself to that?"

"Actually I invited him. We've got business to discuss."

"Ah, WorldView. You're planning a coup de grâce."

"Precisely." He explained that Maris was out of town again and that Maxine had been left in the city. "It's just me and the old man. Fishing. Male bonding."

"Then a little arm-twisting."

"I doubt it'll come to that."

"He's not going to give in easily, Noah."

"Not easily, but he'll eventually be persuaded. I'm sure of it."

"Need a cheerleader for your side? I could drive up. You could tuck me into a corner somewhere. Is the country house roomy enough to accommodate you, me, and your father-in-law?"

"Interesting proposition. I'm tempted to sneak you in, but it wouldn't be prudent. Once the old man is into his cups, he tends to wander. What if he ventured into the wrong bedroom and saw something straight out of the *Kama Sutra*?"

"Which page?"

"You're incorrigible."

"Absolutely. I have no shame whatsoever. That's why I'm willing to risk being caught. If the old man stumbles in on us, who knows? It might do his heart good." She lowered her voice seductively. "The best sex is making-up sex, you know. I could bring along a box of chocolates. The gooey kind. The ones with the soft, creamy centers that you love to lick out."

"Good phone sex, Nadia. I'm aroused," he said truthfully.

"Give me two hours."

"I wish I could see you right now. But you know that you can't come here."

"Oh, I know it's out of the question. I have an enormous stake in this merger, too, and wouldn't do anything to jeopardize it. It's just that I miss you. Guess I'll have to be satisfied with my trusty vibrator."

"Do you have enough batteries?"

"I'm never without."

"Oops, I hear Daniel coming. Must go. I'll see you when I get back to the city."

"Later, darling."

He clicked off, then added, "Love you, too, sweetheart," to a dead phone. He turned just in time to see Daniel entering the living room. "Oh, damn! That was Maris. She wouldn't let me call you to the phone, afraid she'd be interrupting a nap. Want me to get her back? She said they were about to sit down to dinner, but I can probably catch—"

"No, no. How is she?"

"Working hard on the manuscript. Says it's awfully hot. The weather, not the manuscript," he added with a grin. "Misses us terribly, otherwise fine."

"Then don't bother her." Daniel settled into one of the easy chairs and propped his cane beside it. "I worked up quite a thirst during my nap."

Noah laughed easily as he crossed to the table that served as a bar. "Thirsty work, naps. Double scotch?"

"On the rocks, please."

"I called the deli in town. They'll soon be delivering double-thick Reuben sandwiches, potato salad made with real mayo, chocolate cake and vanilla ice cream for dessert."

"God, I love the bachelor life," Daniel said as he accepted the drink from his son-in-law. "What a good idea this was."

Maris was glad she had changed for dinner because for the first time since her arrival, it was being served in the formal dining room, the hanging ghost notwithstanding.

She was wearing a gray silk dress she had bought early in the season at Bergdorf's, thinking it would be perfect for dinner out in the country. She reasoned that the lightweight fabric, slip-style bodice, and flared skirt were also perfect for dinner at home in an antebellum plantation house. She had accessorized it with a choker of pale coral beads.

Mike had laid a beautiful table. Fragrant magnolia blossoms had been arranged in a crystal bowl in the center of the table, flanked by silver candlesticks with white tapers. He'd used china, silver, and crystal stemware that represented good taste and a sizable investment.

"This is lovely, Mike," she remarked as he held the lyre-back chair for her.

"Don't be too impressed," Parker said from his place at the head of the table. "It's all rented for the evening."

"Yes, from Terry's Bar and Grill," Mike said drolly. "Besides smoking baby back ribs, he does a huge formal party rental business."

She laughed. "Wherever it came from, I like it."

"It all belonged to Parker's mother," Mike informed her as he poured the wine, forgetting that he'd delegated that job to her.

She looked toward Parker for confirmation. "The tableware was handed down through generations of Mom's family. It was bequeathed to either the first daughter or daughter-in-law. My mother had neither, so it came to me by default. It's been in storage since she died. This is the first time it's been used." He slid a glance toward Mike. "Can't imagine what the special occasion is."

Maris raised her wineglass. "To the completion of *Envy*."

"I'll drink to that." Mike raised his glass.

"It's not finished yet," Parker reminded them, but he raised his glass all the same.

The crystal stems sounded like chimes when they clinked them together. The Pinot Grigio was cold and crisp, a perfect complement to the meal Mike had prepared.

Parker might have disavowed that this was a special occasion, but she noticed that he had changed for dinner, too. She wondered if Mike had mandated the extra grooming or if it had been voluntary. Although his only nod toward styling his hair was to rake his fingers through it, the tousled look suited him. He had recently shaved; she could smell the sandalwood soap. He was wearing his customary casual pants, but his shirt was tucked in. The sleeves were rolled back to just below his elbows, revealing his strong forearms.

The candlelight blurred the lines that years of pain had etched into his face. It softened the hardness that resentment had stamped on his features and allayed the bitterness that compromised his smiles.

He also seemed to be relaxed and enjoying himself. While they ate, he regaled them with wild stories about Terry, of Bar and Grill fame, who was reputed to be everything from a modern-day pirate to a drug runner to a white slave trader.

"I don't know or care which rumor is true or if any of them are. He grills one hell of a burger."

Maris shuddered at the memory of the tavern. "I can't recommend the place. Totally unsavory clientele."

"Hey!" Parker said, looking affronted.

She gracefully turned the conversation back to the book. "The tension mounts."

"I presume you mean between Roark and Todd."

"It's becoming palpable," she said. "What I read today leads me to believe that it's soon to come to a head."

"I'm giving nothing away."

"A hint? Please?"

He looked at Mike. "Think I should divulge a few plot twists?"

The older man considered it for several seconds. "She *is* your editor."

"That's right, I is," Maris declared. They laughed, then she leaned toward Parker to make her appeal. "What if you're about to make a fatal mistake, editorially speaking? If you talk me through the next few scenes, I could steer you clear of any potential pitfalls and save you a lot of rewrites."

Parker's eyes narrowed suspiciously. "You know what that sounds like? A veiled threat."

"Not at all." She flashed him a saccharine smile. "It's outright extortion."

He placed his palm over the mouth of his wineglass, and his strong fingers absently traced the pattern cut into the crystal. His eyes remained on her. She looked back at him with challenge.

Mike pushed back his chair and stood up. "Who's ready for strawberry sorbet? I made it myself from fresh berries."

Without disengaging her eyes from Parker's, she asked, "Need any help?"

"No, thank you." Mike went into the kitchen through the connecting door and it swung closed behind him.

Maris was slightly short of breath. Her tummy felt weightless despite the meal she'd just eaten. Two glasses of wine were hardly enough to make her feel this light-headed. So she attributed her sudden case of the flutters to the way Parker was looking at her—like she was the tastiest item at the table that evening.

"Well? What's it to be, Mr. Parker?"

"Tell you what." His eyes, which had strayed to the vicinity of her breasts, moved slowly up to her face. "We'll play a game of high-card draw."

She arched her brow inquisitively.

"Remember the scene in *Grass Widow*," he continued, "where Cayton and the reluctant witness to the murder played that game?"

"Vaguely," she lied. Actually she remembered it vividly. When the book was published, that scene had created a buzz. "Erotically charged," was how *Publishers Weekly* had described it. "The reluctant witness was a woman, right?"

"Frenchy. Fragile, fair, and flighty. So nicknamed because—"

"That part I remember."

He grinned a fox's grin. The one he grinned right after isolating the plumpest hen in the flock. Maris knew she'd been had, but she didn't care. In fact, she was struggling to contain the idiotic smile her lips were aching to smile.

Pulling a serious face, she said, "My memory is a little dim on the rules of this game."

"Easy. They used a standard deck of cards. They each draw a card. High card wins."

"Wins what?"

"If Cayton won, Frenchy had to give him a clue to the murderer's identity."

"What if she drew the high card?"

"Cayton granted her a sexual favor."

"*He* granted *her* a sexual favor."

"Right."

She tapped her pursed lips with her fingertip as though stymied by the illogic. "It seems to me that—and correct me if I'm wrong—that Cayton would win either way."

"Well, see, he made up the rules, and he's no dummy."

"But Frenchy—"

"A crotch-throb by any standards. Long red hair. Legs that go on forever. Pale freckles on her tits. An ass that . . . Well, you know the type. But, unfortunately, she's not the brightest bulb in the chandelier."

Maris gave the swaying chandelier overhead a glance before continuing. "So the outcome of this game was that Cayton got the information *and* the crotch-throb."

"Was that a brilliant idea or what?"

"And you expect me to be no brighter than Frenchy? You expect me to play by these rules?"

"I guess that depends."

"On how badly I want to hear those plot twists?"

"Or on how badly you want those sexual favors."

CHAPTER 26

Daniel was holding in his hand the final handiwork of Howard Bancroft's legal career. Noah had waited until after dinner to produce it. They were relaxing in the cozy living room, now lighted only by the soft glow of table lamps.

Daniel had just finished reading the power-of-attorney document. He peered at Noah over his reading glasses. "So, there was an ulterior motive behind this weekend of togetherness."

Noah expelled a puff of cigar smoke. "Not at all, Daniel. I could have presented this to you in the city. At any time."

"But you chose to give it to me here. Why?"

"Because here in the country your mind is uncluttered. We can talk uninterrupted, away from the distractions of the office, without Maxine fussing over you at home. We can speak frankly, one man to another, son-in-law to father-in-law."

He could see that the old man was still dubious. He had expected him to be. In fact, he had expected a fiery outburst. Daniel's reaction was much milder than Noah had been braced for.

But the old man was stubborn and unpredictable. His mood could fluctuate drastically within seconds. There might yet be an eruption of temper, and it might come at any moment. Noah watched warily as Daniel worked his way out of his easy chair and propped himself on his cane.

Noah leaned forward solicitously. "Do you need something, Daniel? More port? Let me get it for you."

"I'll get it myself, thank you," Daniel said brusquely.

He did so, leaving Noah in a state of carefully concealed agitation. His feet were propped on the ottoman in front of his chair. His posture was a slouch. He appeared to have nothing weightier on his mind than the smoke rings he blew toward the ceiling.

Daniel returned to his chair and declined to speak until he had taken a few sips of his port. "If this is a family meeting, why have you chosen to conduct it when one family member is noticeably absent?"

Noah took his time answering. He studied the smoldering tip of his cigar as though carefully choosing, then analyzing, what he was about to say. "This is an extremely delicate matter, Daniel."

"Which is my point."

"Mine also. It's not an issue to spring on Maris over the telephone." He took a sip of his single-malt scotch. As he returned the tumbler to the end table, he noticed the wedding reception photograph of them. He touched the silver frame wistfully and smiled fondly. "Maris thinks first with her heart, then with her head." His gaze moving back to Daniel, he added, "You know that. You've lived with her longer than I have."

"She's not a child."

"True. She's a woman, and her instincts and reactions are purely feminine. They're endearing. They make her the lovely person she is. But they don't always serve her well professionally. Remember how emotionally she reacted last week when she learned of my meeting with WorldView? I predict her reaction to this document would be even more irrational."

For several moments he stared at the document that now lay

on the coffee table between them. "If I know my wife, she would panic. She would think that we're shielding her from something ugly. She would leap to an erroneous conclusion. You have terminal cancer. You need a heart transplant. You . . . well, you get my drift. God knows what she would imagine, and we would have a hell of a time dispelling her worst fears."

He shook his head and laughed softly. "Last week she accused us of leaving her out of the loop and needlessly protecting her from an unpleasant situation. If—"

"If I sign that document without discussing it with her first, she'll be furious with us."

"No doubt. I guess it comes down to choosing when we want to have a scene like the one we had last week. Before or after the document is in place. If it's before, her response time will be protracted. She'll put you through a battery of physical exams before she's satisfied that you're not at death's door.

"If it's after the document is signed," he continued, "her reaction time will be abbreviated. Which, personally, I think is our best option. We all have better things to do with our time and energy." He paused to take a few puffs on his cigar. "I'm thinking of Maris, too, Daniel. I'm trying to spare her from having to make a difficult decision. She cannot bring herself to accept some of life's inescapable certainties."

"Like my mortality."

Noah nodded solemnly. "Or even the possibility of reduced capacity. She is in complete denial on the subject. You've always been her hero. She would look upon this document as a betrayal of that image. She might even feel that by executing a power-of-attorney document like this, we're tempting fate. That as soon as she signs it, you'll be stricken with a debilitating malady."

He paused strategically and pretended to consider his wife's behavior. "In all honesty, I doubt Maris would sign it at all unless you had signed it first. That would ease her mind. Relieve her conscience and her sense of responsibility."

Daniel picked up the document with one hand and tugged thoughtfully on his lower lip with the other. "I'm not a moron, Noah."

Noah's breath caught in his throat.

"I see the validity of such a document."

He expelled that anxious breath slowly and tried to sound perfectly composed as he said, "Apparently so did Howard. He authored it."

"Which puzzles me. Howard knew that a similar document is already in place, along with my will and other personal documents. Mr. Stern drew them up years ago, but Howard had copies in his files."

"As Howard explained it to me, those documents were outdated."

And now came the tricky part. Up to this point, he had counted on it being an exercise in persuasion. His arguments were sound, and, as Daniel had noted, not without validity. Now, however, he must do some fancy footwork and one misstep could trip him up.

With calculated casualness, he rolled the ash off the tip of his cigar into a pewter ashtray. "I think Howard realized how obsolete that previous power-of-attorney document was. He brought it to my attention first, instead of bringing it up with Maris, for the reasons we've cited tonight. He didn't want to upset her."

"Why didn't he bring it to my attention?"

"For the same reason, Daniel." He averted his gaze as though it pained him to say what he was compelled to say. "Howard was worried what your reaction would be. He didn't want you to think that he thought you were no longer capable of making these kinds of decisions for yourself."

"We were better friends than that," Daniel snapped. "For God's sake, we'd been confiding candidly in each other for decades. I had joked with him about the foibles of growing old."

"This goes beyond complaining about a few aches and pains.

Howard was sensitive to the delicate nature of this document."
Noah raised his hand when he saw that Daniel was about to interrupt. "I'm only telling you what he told me. He was afraid
you would take umbrage."

"That I'd shoot the messenger?"

Noah shrugged as though to say, *Something like that.* "It's such
a personal, private matter, Howard thought it might be better
if someone in the family were to bring it to your attention."

Daniel harrumphed and took a sip of port. He flipped
through the document again. He paused to reread a particular
clause, and even before he said anything, Noah knew which
clause had snagged his attention.

"Until Maris signs this—"

"I would have full power of attorney. I know. I spotted that
flaw, too."

"Why would Howard construct the document this way, when
he knew it would go expressly against my wishes? Not that I
mistrust you, Noah, but Maris is Matherly Press, and vice
versa. There will never be a decision made or acted upon without her involvement and approval."

"Of course. Howard knew that. As do I. As does everyone.
When I pointed the loophole out to him, he was mortified and
acknowledged that it was an oversight."

Noah chuckled. "I think his Old World heritage sneaked in
while he wasn't looking. He was thinking of Maris as a daughter and wife, not as a senior executive of a multimillion-dollar
company. He had enormous affection for her, as you know, and
probably still regarded her as the sweet little girl in pigtails he
used to bounce on his knee. Anyhow, I insisted that he add the
codicil on the last page, which stipulates that the document is
invalid until signed by all of us."

He hoped that Daniel wouldn't notice that the last page
could be detached without it appearing that the document had
been tampered with or altered. That had been a last-minute
brainstorm, one he should have thought of sooner. He'd hired

the unscrupulous lawyer with whom he'd threatened Bancroft to write the codicil. The legalese sounded legitimate, although it lacked the classy touch of the rest of the document. He hoped Daniel wouldn't notice that, either.

Noah took one final draw on his cigar, then ground out the lighted tip and left it lying in the ashtray. He slapped his thighs lightly as he stood up, officially closing his sales pitch. "Speaking for myself, I'm bushed. Obviously you need to sleep on this. We can talk about it later. Have you thought about what you'd like for breakfast? There's enough food—"

"I don't need to sleep on it," Daniel said abruptly. "Let me sign the damn thing and get it over with. I'm tired of talking about it."

Noah hesitated. "Don't decide anything this weekend, Daniel. Take the document back to the city. Have Mr. Stern review it."

"And by doing so question the judgment of my late friend? No. Howard's suicide has already generated nasty speculation. I won't have people saying that his competence had slipped. Where's a damn pen?"

"Signing won't make it legal. It has to be notarized." That had been another potential problem with an obvious solution—the lawyer downtown, whose breath was stronger than his principles. After this was all settled, Noah would have to deal with him or risk being blackmailed. But that was a problem for another day.

"We'll make it official once we get to the city," Daniel grumbled. "But I want this matter concluded tonight. For my own peace of mind. Otherwise I won't be able to relax, or think about breakfast, or anything else. Tomorrow, I want nothing on my mind more problematic than baiting a hook. So give me a goddamn pen."

Noah's acting performance was superb, if he did say so himself. He reluctantly produced a pen and passed it over to Daniel. But before releasing it, he gazed deeply into Daniel's eyes. "You've had a lot to drink," he said, oozing concern. "Nothing will be lost by waiting until—"

Daniel yanked the pen from his son-in-law's hand and scrawled his signature on the appropriate line.

The dinner party on St. Anne Island was moved out onto the veranda when a yellow jacket invaded the dining room.

The buzzing menace appeared out of nowhere and alighted on the rim of Maris's as-yet-unused coffee cup. She sent up a faint squeal—ill-timed because it immediately followed Parker's statement about sexual favors.

Remembering the instruction of a summer camp counselor many years before as to what one should do when stinging insects threatened, she froze in place.

Parker, seeing the real cause of her squeal, yelled, "Mike! Bug spray! Now!"

Mike charged out of the kitchen armed with a can of Black Flag. He aimed it with deadly accuracy, and the yellow jacket died an agonizing death, witnessed by the three who fanned chemical fumes away from their faces.

Parker ventured that the pest had been hiding in the flowers in the centerpiece. Mike insisted that if the magnolia blooms had had a yellow jacket in them when he brought them inside, he would have discovered it long before now.

Before a full-blown argument could ensue, Maris tactfully submitted that the insect could have gotten into the house any number of ways, and then suggested that they take their desserts onto the veranda, which should be comfortably cool if Mike were to turn on the ceiling fans that had been thoughtfully installed during the house's refurbishing.

He served their pink sorbets in frosted compotes garnished with sprigs of mint. Maris insisted on pouring the coffee in the gracious manner that Maxine had taught her and accomplished serving them without one rattle of cup against saucer.

Parker frowned down into the bone china cup. "This thimble doesn't hold enough coffee to taste. What's wrong with an ordinary mug?"

Neither she nor Mike paid any attention to his grumbling. She rocked contentedly in the porch swing, listening to the night sounds that had been so foreign to her when she arrived and had now become so familiar.

"Penny for them," Parker said.

"I was wondering if I'll ever become reaccustomed to the sounds of traffic on Manhattan's streets. I've gotten used to cicadas and bullfrogs."

Mike gathered their empty dessert dishes onto a tray, then carried it into the house.

As soon as Mike was out of earshot, Parker asked, "Planning on leaving us anytime soon?"

The overhead fans blew gently on his hair. The light spilling through the front windows was cast onto only one side of his face, leaving the other side in shadow. Maris couldn't make out his eyes at all, and what she could see of his expression was inscrutable.

"I'll have to leave eventually," she replied softly. "When your first draft of *Envy* is finished and you no longer need me around."

"Two different things entirely, Maris."

His stirring voice caused her tummy to go weightless again.

The front door squeaked with a homey, comforting sound as Mike rejoined them and refilled their coffee cups, giving Parker a mug this time. When he sat down in the wicker rocking chair, it creaked dangerously and they all laughed.

"Hope that relic holds up," Parker remarked.

"Are you referring to me or the chair?" Mike asked good-naturedly.

"I don't dare sit in it," Maris said, patting her stomach. "Too much dinner."

"It was a good meal, Mike," Parker said. "Thanks."

"You're welcome." He idly stirred a sugar cube into his coffee. "What we need to round out the evening is a good story."

"Hmm. If only we knew a good storyteller." Being deliberately coy, Maris looked at Parker from beneath her eyelashes.

He grimaced and groaned, but he was pleased by their curiosity. Clasping his hands, he turned them palms out and stretched them above his head until his knuckles popped. "Okay, okay, I can't fight both of you. Where'd you leave off?"

"They'd gone to the beach and killed a bottle of whisky," Maris said, the scene still fresh in her mind.

"I still don't understand why their language must be so vulgar."

Parker frowned at Mike's comment and motioned for Maris to continue.

"Todd accused Roark of being less than straightforward about the critiques he had received from the professor."

"Have you read the part where Roark got pissed?" Parker asked.

"Yes, and his anger was justified. He's never given Todd any reason to mistrust him."

"Conversely, he's been burned by Todd on numerous occasions," Mike noted.

"Most recently with Mary Catherine. I think I need to add another scene with her," Parker said, almost to himself. "Maybe she tells Roark that the child she miscarried was Todd's."

"I thought you'd decided to let the reader draw his own conclusion."

"I had. But I might change my mind. This would strengthen the animosity building between Roark and Todd. What if . . ." he thought it over for a moment before continuing. "What if Todd drops Mary Catherine flat? Avoids her. Even complains to Roark that she's a pest, a clinging vine, something like that.

"Meanwhile, she pours her heart out to Roark. She admits that it was Todd's baby she lost, and that she has fallen in love with him, and so forth. Roark likes her as a friend, and he was there that night to clean up Todd's mess, literally, so he's really bothered by the way Todd treats her."

"Does Todd ever know about the baby?" Maris asked.

"No, I don't think so. Mary Catherine doesn't want him to know, and Roark won't betray her confidence by telling him."

"I told you this guy had honor."

"Not so fast," Parker said quietly. "Didn't it strike you that he protested too much when Todd accused him of being less than honest about Hadley's critiques?"

Slowly, she nodded. "Now that I think about it . . . Have they been more favorable than he let on?"

Parker withdrew several sheets of folded paper from the breast pocket of his shirt. "I dashed this off just before I quit for the day."

She reached for the pages, but Mike suggested that Parker read them out loud.

"Want me to?" Parker asked, addressing Maris.

"By all means. Please."

Parker unfolded the sheets of manuscript and held them up to catch the light.

"'Dear Mr. Slade,' he read, 'according to your last letter, you wish me to send future pieces of correspondence to your recently acquired post office box instead of to the street address. As it makes no difference to me, I can only assume that the request arises out of an unspecified desire to convenience yourself.'"

Parker cringed. "Good God. Verbose old bastard, isn't he?"

"Well, he does teach creative writing," Maris said. "One would expect him to be effusive."

"Effusive is one thing, but that is obnoxious."

Parker gave his outspoken valet a dirty look. "Thank you, Mike, for that unsolicited and tactless observation."

"You criticized it first."

"I'm allowed. I'm the author."

Maris smothered a laugh. "You might consider trimming some of the fat, Parker. Just a little."

"Okay. No problem. On the other hand, just for the sake of argument, Hadley's verbosity is consistent with his character.

Remember that he hails from an old and distinguished southern family. They had more stiff-necked pride than money and lived well beyond their means. Confederate sabers on display in the parlor. A matriarch whose 'headache medicine' was Tennessee sour mash. A batty maiden aunt—read 'deflowered, then jilted'—who lived in the attic, smelled of gardenia, and wouldn't eat uncooked fruit."

"I remember reading those colorful details," Maris said.

"My grandparents had friends like Hadley's family is described," Parker told her. "I remember their speech being flowery and overblown."

Maris looked toward Mike for confirmation. "I rely on your superior knowledge of southern culture and heritage. Is it too much?"

"As usual, he's exaggerating," the older man replied. "But there's definitely an element of truth there. If you scratch the surface of just about every multigenerational southern family, you'll find at least one cleric, one loony, one outlaw, and enough liquor to float an armada."

Laughing, she turned back to Parker. "Go on with the letter."

He located the spot where he'd felt off.

"'Once a relationship has been built on a particular foundation, it's extremely difficult to destroy that foundation and reconstruct it with different specifications, without also destroying the original relationship.'"

"You've lost me," Mike said. "What's he talking about?"

"I agreed to trim the fat, okay?" Parker said, annoyed by the interruption. He ran his finger down several lines of text. "In summary, he's saying that they began as professor and student. He says it's hard to break the habit of assuming a professorial role with Roark, hard not to lecture or teach, and instead to address his comments to him as a peer." He looked over at Mike. "Got that?"

"Thank you."

"Okay, here . . . 'Not that I am your peer, Mr. Slade. Your

writing has surpassed my ability to critique it. It deserves an appraisal more distinguished than mine, although you could not solicit one that would be more appreciative of your talent.'

"He goes on for several paragraphs, confessing that he had entertained writing aspirations of his own before being forced to acknowledge that he wasn't gifted with the talent. He says his role is to teach, instruct, inspire, yaddah-yaddah."

He flipped to the second page.

"'Rarely does one with my limited ability have the opportunity to work with someone as talented as you. I consider it a privilege to witness the development of a great American novelist, for that's what I believe you will ultimately become.'"

Parker raised his index finger, letting them know that he was getting to the crux of the passage. "'Your writing far surpasses that of any other student, past or present, including your friend Todd Grayson. He has written an engaging story with several interesting characters, specifically his protagonist. However, his writing lacks the emotional depth, the *heart,* with which yours resonates. I have no doubt that he will publish. He can produce a mechanically correct manuscript, incorporating all the textbook elements of fiction.

"'That does not necessarily mean that he writes well.

"'I can teach students the basics of writing, acquaint them with the rules of fiction, familiarize them with the writers who have mastered these techniques, but only God dispenses talent. That indefinable and elusive quality cannot be taught or otherwise acquired no matter how earnestly one desires and seeks it. I learned this sad truth from my own experience. Were talent attainable, I would be writing my own novels.

"'Thank the god to whom you pray, Mr. Slade, for you were blessed with that magic. You were christened with a rare and wonderful ability. Your friend was not. I fear that eventually this lopsided appropriation of talent will cause a breach between you.

"'During my tenure, I have observed thousands of young

men and women. Because of this vast exposure to people from diverse backgrounds, I consider myself a superior judge of character. At the very least, I'm an astute observer of it.

"'Some human characteristics are common to us all. Manifestation of these characteristics is dependent upon circumstance. Everyone has temporary displays of fear, happiness, frustration, and so on.

"'Other traits are unique to certain individuals. They define the person and his character. Among these traits are admirable examples like humility, charity, bravery.

"'Unfortunately these have dark counterparts like jealousy, greed, and envy. Persons governed by one of these traits typically cloak it with charm, and most are very successful at it, because along with the trait invariably comes the cunning to conceal it.

"'Nevertheless, the trait lives and matures inside them as insidiously as an eel inside a cave, waiting, even anticipating, the times when it can strike anything or anyone that threatens.

"'I do not wish to speak ill of your friend. I would like to think that my barometer for integrity has failed me completely, and that I am terribly wrong about the qualities that motivate him.

"'But I remember Mr. Grayson's machinations which caused you to be late for an important meeting with me. Plainly put, it was a dirty trick with malicious overtones. Frankly, I'm surprised that the friendship survived it. It's a credit to you that it did. I don't think Mr. Grayson has it within himself to forgive to that extent, which is yet another notable disparity between your characters.

"'I wouldn't presume to choose your friends for you. I wouldn't want the responsibility even if you were to grant it to me. But I'll conclude by using an expression I've heard around campus. It's a contemporary idiom which does the English language a grave disservice, but which, in this distance, seems appropriate: Heads-up.

"'I look forward to reading the next draft of your manuscript. In your cover letters, you never fail to apologize for taking up my time, and to thank me for the careful consideration I give your work. Mr. Slade, be clear on this: it is a privilege, not an imposition. Sincerely yours, Professor Hadley.'"

Parker refolded the pages and returned them to his shirt pocket. No one spoke for a moment. Maris had been lulled by his words and the cadence with which he'd read them. She shook off the mild daze and gave the swing a gentle push.

"So Todd's gut instincts were right. Roark's reviews from Hadley *were* better than the ones he received."

Parker nodded. "And Roark was dishonest about it."

"I don't think that matters."

He looked across at her, and the intensity of his stare compelled her to continue the thought.

"Todd wouldn't have taken it well if Roark had said, 'You guessed right. Hadley thinks you're a hack with limited talent, while he believes I have the potential of being the next Steinbeck.'"

Mike agreed. "If Roark had told him the truth out there on the beach, Todd would have ended their relationship then and there. Your story would be over. The end."

Parker grunted a nonresponse.

Reading from the manuscript seemed to have darkened his mood, although Maris couldn't figure why. The content had obviously captivated her and Mike. The letter had been a clever way to move his story along without relying strictly on narrative. Since she and Mike had approved it, she couldn't account for his sullenness. "What's bothering you, Parker?"

"Roark's supposed to be the good guy, right? He's the lamb in the goat/lamb comparison."

"That's one way of looking at it, I suppose."

"It doesn't bother you that he deceived his friend?"

"His motivation wasn't deception. It was kindness. He was trying to spare Todd from what Hadley referred to as the 'sad truth,' because he knew it would be devastating. Todd simply wasn't as talented as Roark. Roark might have sensed from the beginning that Todd lacked—"

She snapped her fingers. "No, he *knew* it. Didn't he? Of course he knew that he was better. He had to know it. Or else why did he get a post office box to prevent his mail from coming to their apartment? He was afraid that Todd would intercept one of his glowing critiques from Hadley."

"Nothing escapes you," he said, his mood seeming to lift. "Now forget that you know it."

"Why?"

"Because it becomes crucial in the next chapter or so."

"The mention of the post office box was a foreshadowing?"

He smiled enigmatically.

"Todd intercepts one of the letters, right?" she guessed. "Maybe even this letter, because this is the one that could be the most damaging to the friendship. It spells out the differences in their talent and their characters. Todd . . . uh, let's see, he borrows a pair of jeans or something, maybe without asking Roark, and he finds the letter in a pocket."

"Thanks. I hadn't figured out yet how he was going to get his hands on it. That's pretty good."

She beamed. "Todd reads this letter. He can't believe what he's reading. His secret fear is realized. Roark is superior to him. That's why he had tried to sabotage Roark with Professor Hadley. It hadn't worked. Indeed, it backfired. Hadley saw through him. Furthermore, Roark has won Hadley's praise. A double whammy for Todd. He reacts by . . . doing what?"

"You tell me."

She concentrated hard, unconsciously gnawing on a corner of her lip. "I was going to say that he would be crushed, but, on second thought, that would be out of character." She shook her head. "No, he's too egotistical to let a university professor destroy his ambition. I think he would be furious. Livid." She formed claws with her hands and held them at the sides of her head. "Explosively, volcanically enraged."

"How does he channel that rage, Maris?"

"He confronts Roark with the letter."

"No, he doesn't."

"Parker," Mike cut in softly.

"He's not honest enough to take that approach. He—"

"Parker," Mike repeated.

"He waits. He—"

"Parker."

"He—"

"Parker!"

"*Goddammit, Mike!* What?"

He rounded on the older man, but Mike didn't flinch from his hard look. In fact, he returned it. The air was electrically charged, as it had been in the kitchen this morning. In both instances, thoughts were telegraphed that Maris couldn't interpret.

Parker was the first to relent. He closed his eyes and massaged his forehead. "I'm sorry, Mike. Forgive me. I was following a train of thought."

"It's okay. I know you hate distractions when you're on a roll."

"Dinner was great."

"So you said."

"Oh. Yeah. Right. Well, thanks again."

"You're welcome. I'm glad you enjoyed it." Mike stood and picked up the silver serving tray that held the empty carafe and coffee cups. "Before the mosquitoes carry me off, I think I'll go in."

"Good idea. Good night."

"Good night, Mike," Maris echoed.

At the door Mike turned and addressed Parker. "Do you want me to wait up and help—"

"No, no. I'll be fine tonight. Go to bed."

The older man hesitated, glanced at Maris, then nodded and went inside.

Once they were alone, Maris raised her hands in a helpless shrug. "Explain to me what just happened."

"When?"

"Just now. Between you and Mike."

"Nothing."

"Parker," she cried softly.

He blinked innocently. "Nothing."

She stared him down, but he didn't relent. Vexed over being totally shut out, she got up from the swing. "Fine. Play word games. But play them without me. Good night."

"Don't go away mad."

"Then don't talk down to me. I hate being patronized."

He dragged his hands down his face. "And you should. I'm sorry." He sucked in a breath of the sultry air and turned his head away to stare out at the row of live oaks.

"It's this . . . this *thing* between Mike and me. Sometimes he sees a darkness creeping over me. A mean ugliness. Like I was when he found me. It scares him, I guess. He's afraid I'll drop back into that abyss. He yanks me out of it before I can sink too far."

Turning back, he fixed his eyes on her. "Something like that."

"Thank you."

They simply looked at one another for several moments, then he smiled crookedly. "It's been a roller-coaster evening."

"Yes, it has. But I wouldn't trade a minute of it."

He reached out, encircled her wrist with his fingers, and gave it a tug. She moved nearer, but not close enough to suit him. He curved an arm around her waist and pulled her closer. Hooking the other hand around the back of her neck, he drew her down for a kiss. She placed her hands on his hard cheeks. Their mouths melded and tongues plundered in a delirium of longing.

When at last they pulled apart, he pressed his face into the softness of her middle. "I've been craving this all day."

"There were times when I thought you'd forgotten about last night."

He gave a soft, harsh laugh. "Not fucking hardly."

His head nudged her breasts through the silk cloth of her dress. His humid breath filtered through it to her skin. He cupped her bottom in his hands, buried his face deeper into her.

Threading her fingers through his hair, she sighed, "Ah, Parker, please."

"Yes. Anything. Just ask."

"I . . . um . . ."

"What?"

"I can't do this."

"You can. You have. You did. Last night. Remember?" One hand found bare skin beneath her skirt, warmth between her thighs.

Her knees went weak, but she pushed his hand down and stepped out of his reach. "I can't. We can't."

He gulped a breath and blinked her into focus. "Why not?"

She licked her lips, tasted him. "I'm worried about my father."

"Your father?" He seemed to grope for a definition of the word. "Your father? You're afraid that he wouldn't approve? That he'd come after me with a shotgun? What?"

She smiled and shook her head. "No, nothing like that. I've been trying to reach him all day."

She gave him a quick summary of her attempts. "Finally, just before dinner, I tracked our housekeeper Maxine to her sister's house. She stays with her when she takes a day off. Which is rarely.

"Anyhow, she told me that Dad had gone to our country house in western Massachusetts for the weekend. He and Noah. They insisted she stay behind. They wanted to go by themselves."

"So? They're big boys. What does their leaving New York for the weekend have to do with us necking here on the veranda?"

"Nothing. Directly."

"Then I don't get it."

"Maxine watches Dad like a hawk. Or a mother hen. I wouldn't be worried if she were with him. I don't like the idea of his being alone."

"He's not."

No, he was alone with Noah.

What she didn't tell Parker was that Noah had assured Maxine that Maris was aware of their weekend plans, that she had sanctioned them. The loyal employee had been distraught to learn that Maris had not been consulted. "Why did Mr. Reed mislead me?"

Why indeed?

Maxine had then told her that Daniel had entertained a guest for breakfast.

"Who?"

"I don't know." She explained about the errand he'd sent her on. "I think Mr. Matherly dreamed up a reason to get me out of the house. When I got back, he was washing dishes."

"Washing dishes?"

"He didn't want me to know that two place settings had been used. When I questioned him about it, he got defensive and said that they were his dishes and that if he wanted to use a dozen place settings at breakfast, he could. It was all nonsense, Maris. He apologized for it later. The important thing is that someone definitely came to the house while I was out, and he didn't want anyone to know about it."

"Did he seem upset?"

"No. In fact, he seemed very upbeat and eager to be off when Mr. Reed arrived to pick him up."

"Then I'm sure we're worrying over nothing."

Maris hoped her assurances sounded sincere to the anxious housekeeper. To her own ears they rang hollow, even as she repeated them to Parker now. "I'm relieved to know where he is, and I'm sure he's all right. But I'll feel better once I talk to him."

"Did you try contacting him at the country house?"

"The line has been busy for hours. And even though I didn't want to speak to Noah, I also tried his cell phone. It was busy, too, so I left a voice-mail message and the phone number here. I hope you don't mind."

"So long as you didn't give my name."

"Of course not. But the point is moot. Nobody's called. I need to check my cell, see if there's a message on it."

"Sorta weird."

"What?"

"That your dad would agree to spending a weekend with your estranged husband."

"Dad doesn't know we're separated." He registered the expected surprise. "I guess I should have told him right away, but the time never seemed right. I wanted to choose a time when it would have the least impact."

"Do you think Noah plans to spring the unhappy news on him this weekend?"

"That was my first thought," she said tightly. "Or possibly to ask Dad to intervene on his behalf. He's got his position at Matherly Press to protect. If that's the reason he married me, that'll be his reason for wanting to prevent a divorce."

"Would your father intervene on Noah's behalf?"

"Absolutely not. He knows I've been unhappy. He just doesn't know the extent of my unhappiness." Lowering her voice, she said, "Until I came to St. Anne Island and met you, *I* didn't know how unhappy I'd been."

He groaned. "Don't look at me like that, Maris."

"Like what?"

"Misty-eyed. In fact, you'd better git before I decide not to be so gracious and understanding about this. We wasted another perfectly good hard-on. I'm oh for two."

"You're vulgar. Just as Mike said." Laughing, she smoothed her hand over his ravaged hair. "It was a lovely evening."

"It was getting lovelier," he groused.

"I'm sorry." She bent down and laid a soft kiss on his lips. "Sleep well."

"Oh, yeah, like a baby. A horny little baby."

"If it's any consolation, Parker . . ."

"What?"

"I can. I have. I did. Last night. And I do remember."

There were no messages on Maris's phone.

She tried Noah's cell, but a recording informed her that the number she had called was unavailable. Terribly worried now, she dialed the house telephone.

Daniel answered on the second ring.

She slumped with relief, but her greeting sounded like a reprimand. "Dad, where have you been?"

"Most recently I've been to the bathroom. Did I forget to ask permission?"

"I'm sorry. I didn't mean to jump down your throat. It's just that I've been trying to reach you all day. I didn't know you'd gone to the country until I talked to Maxine. Since then, I've called repeatedly."

"This is the first time the telephone has rung. I noticed just before coming upstairs to bed that the receiver on the telephone in the kitchen was askew. Apparently Noah didn't hang it up properly when he called in a food delivery."

More likely he had left it off the hook deliberately, knowing she would want to talk to her father. He knew she would be crazy with worry when she couldn't reach him. Was this Noah's mean form of punishment for her leaving him? It was amazing how clearly she could see his true nature now. What had kept her blind to it for so many years? *A book*, she thought, scornful of her own naïveté.

Well, she was no longer naive. She wanted him gone, expunged from their lives. She couldn't stand his being a member of their family for another day. Why wait to tell her father about the dissolution of her marriage?

Fortunately, she came to her senses before she could act on the impulse.

First of all, that would necessitate a lengthy discussion, and it was as late in Massachusetts as it was on St. Anne Island. Second, that was a conversation that should be conducted face-to-face, especially since it involved their business interests as well as their personal lives.

Setting her enmity for Noah aside for the time being, she asked Daniel if he was all right.

"Why wouldn't I be?"

"Since I hadn't talked to you, I had imagined all sorts of things."

"None of them good, I'll bet. The way I used to worry if you were ten minutes late coming home."

"Have our roles reversed, Dad?"

"Not at all. I still worry about you if you're ten minutes late. But rest assured that I've had a very pleasant day."

Starting with a mystery guest for breakfast. She wanted to ask him about that but couldn't without giving away that Maxine had tattled on him. She hoped he would volunteer the information. "What did you do that made your day so pleasant?"

"Nothing much, and that was the beauty of it."

"Was the house in order when you arrived?"

"Spic and span."

"Where did you go for dinner? Harry's or another of your favorite spots?"

"We ate in. I thought Noah would have told you."

"When?"

"When you called this afternoon. I came downstairs just as he was hanging up."

She opened her mouth but closed it without saying anything. Noah had lied to him. Apparently Daniel had caught the tail end of a telephone conversation, and Noah had pretended it was she. Damn him!

"Maybe he did mention it and I forgot."

"Not surprising," he said, seeming to have missed the anger in her voice. "You've got a lot on your mind. How's the book coming?"

"Great, actually. The story is really percolating now. It's amazing to watch how the writer's mind works. I've never been this involved with the creative process, and it's fascinating."

"I can tell that you're enjoying it."

"Immensely."

"And the author? Still the curmudgeon?"

"Either he's mellowing or I'm becoming accustomed to him. I don't know which."

"Probably a little of both."

"Probably."

Maris sensed him hesitating. Then he said, "I'm glad you heeded your instincts and went back to work with him."

"So am I, Dad. It was the right decision. I'm positive of that."

"You're happy there? With the work? With everything?"

"Yes. Very," she said quietly.

"Good. You deserve to be, Maris."

To anyone listening, the conversation sounded innocent enough. But given the one they'd had directly before her departure from New York, she knew that her father was conveying more than he was saying.

He knew she'd been unhappy with Noah and their marriage. It wouldn't surprise her if he knew about Noah's infidelity. Daniel Matherly was known for his ability to ferret out secrets. During her last visit with him, she had hardly kept secret her feelings for Parker. Without naming him, she had talked about him nonstop with the uncontainable excitement of someone falling in love.

This roundabout conversation was her dad's way of letting her know that he sanctioned it.

She swallowed a knot of emotion. "I needed to hear your voice, Dad."

"It's good to hear yours, too."

"I'm sorry I disturbed you so late."

"You could never disturb me, but in any case, I wasn't asleep."

"I'll call you again tomorrow. No, wait."

Considering the lies Noah had told today, the thought of him being with her father like the faithful son-in-law for the remainder of the weekend turned her stomach. He probably had in mind to get chummy, to get on Daniel's good side. Maybe he planned to make a tearful confession and plead his case with Daniel before Maris told him about their separation.

Not if she could help it.

"Dad, I'd like to send Maxine up there tomorrow. She's been dying to go to the country and see the summer flowers in bloom. Would you mind?"

"Flowers . . ." He harrumphed skeptically, letting her know the excuse was transparent. "I've had only one day's peace away from her. But," he sighed, "if it would make you feel better . . ."

"It would make me feel better. I'll call her first thing in the morning." It relieved her to know that Maxine would drop everything and go at a moment's notice. She could be there well before noon. "Call me when she arrives, so I'll know she made the drive safely."

"All right, sweetheart. I'll call you tomorrow. And Maris?"

"Yes."

"Make the most of your time there. Don't deny yourself the happiness being there gives you. Don't worry about anything. Are you listening to your old dad? Everything is going to work out well. Will you trust me on that, sweetheart?"

"I always have." She leaned her cheek into the small telephone, wishing it were his spotted, wrinkled hand. "Good night, Dad. I love you."

"I love you, too."

Parker's bed was a monstrosity. It was narrow by king-sized standards, but what it lacked in width, it made up for in height. The headboard was tall and carved, the wood aged to a saddle-brown patina that reflected the glow from his reading lamp on the nightstand.

The bed was standing on an area rug that looked like an authentic Aubusson. The overhead fan was like those Maris had seen before only in movies. A brass pole was suspended horizontally six feet below the tall ceiling. At each end of the pole was an axle that idly turned a set of papyrus blades.

There were no draperies on the three tall windows, only louvered shutters, which were painted white to tastefully contrast with the caramel-colored walls and dark hardwood floor. One wall accommodated a massive chifforobe that was crowned with carvings that matched those on the apex of the headboard. Apparently it held all his clothing because there was no closet built into the room.

The TV and VCR, housed in a cabinet on the wall opposite the bed, were the room's only nods toward modernity—other than the wheelchair parked in front of the nightstand. There was no other apparatus one would assume to find in the bedroom of a disabled person, but she wasn't too surprised. She'd seen him lift himself into and out of the Gator.

Parker was bare-chested, propped against the headboard reading, when Maris slipped through the door. He slowly lowered the book to his lap. "Hello. Are you lost?"

She laughed nervously, a bit breathlessly. "Nice try, but I think I was expected."

"I hoped. I even said my prayers."

"Then it's all right if I come in?"

"Are you joking?"

"I thought maybe . . . will Mike—"

"Not if you lock the door."

Since coming into the room, she'd kept her hands behind her. Feeling for the doorknob at the small of her back, she depressed the lock button to guarantee their privacy. Keeping her hands behind her back, she approached the bed.

The polished floor planks felt cool against the bare soles of her feet. Her short nightgown was no weightier than air against her skin, and judging from the intensity with which Parker was watching her as she moved toward him, he had noticed that it wasn't very substantial.

She brought her hands from behind her back. "I brought you presents. Two, to be exact."

The first was a standard drinking glass that belonged to the wet bar in the guest house. She extended it to him. He took the glass from her and held it up, looked at it for a few seconds, then laughed when he saw the winking phosphorescent lights inside. "Lightning bugs."

"I caught them myself," she said proudly. "I saw them through the guest house window while I was dressing for dinner and chased out after them."

She'd sealed them inside the glass by stretching a piece of plastic wrap over the top, then puncturing it to ensure the fireflies a longer life.

When he looked up at her, his eyes shone with feeling. "It's a great present. Thank you."

"You're welcome. Shall I?" She took them back and set them on the nightstand.

"What's the other?" He indicated the book she was now hugging to her chest. "Are you going to read me a bedtime story?"

"Sort of."

"I wondered why you were wearing your glasses."

"I took my contacts out." Nodding toward the empty side of his bed, she asked, "May I?"

"Be my guest."

She rounded the end of the bed and crawled onto it, then folded her legs beneath her and sat back on her heels, facing him. "You're already reading a bedtime story."

He closed the book lying in his lap and set it on the nightstand. "I'd rather hear yours." She turned the book toward him so he could see the title stamped in gold into the green cloth cover. *"Grass Widow,"* he read, smiling.

"A novel by my favorite author."

"What, him?"

"There's no call for false modesty."

"But you've got high standards, Ms. Matherly. You're a hard sell. What do you like about this novel?"

His use of her maiden name didn't escape her, but she didn't interrupt their game by acknowledging it. She opened the book. "Well, in particular, I like the scene where Deck Cayton, the handsome, sexy, roguish, but engaging hero, uses a card game to obtain information from the bimbo."

"Frenchy."

"Whatever. It's a provocative and involving scene."

"The fans certainly thought so. Critics, too."

She pursed her lips and frowned. "However—"

"Uh-oh. Here it comes."

"The scene has raised a few points."

"Typical editor," he said under his breath. "For every compliment there's a criticism."

"Look, Mr. Evans, if you don't value my points—"

"No, no. I do value them, those raised points of yours." His eyes dropped to her breasts. "I'll take them like a man." He placed one hand behind his head and gave her a smug grin. "That was a metaphor."

"I got it," she said dryly. "Shall I proceed?"

"Please. Give me a for-instance."

"Uh . . ." She dragged her eyes away from the furry hollow of his armpit. "For instance, the language is very descriptive."

"Isn't it supposed to be?"

"Yes, but in this passage it's—"

"Explicit?"

"To the extreme."

"Why's that bad?"

"I didn't say it was bad. My problem is with its accuracy."

"Accuracy."

"Right. I'm not sure that the, uh, mating positions you've described are anatomically possible. For human beings, I mean."

He snuffled a laugh, then stroked his chin somberly. "I see. Could you be more specific?"

"There are several examples. So what I thought," she said, pausing to clear her throat, as she opened to the marked page, "is that we could act it out and see if these . . . configurations . . . are doable."

"That's what you thought?" he drawled sexily.

"Yes, that's what I thought."

He remained very still for several moments, gazing at her. Then slowly he removed his hand from behind his head. "As I recall, our handsome, sexy, roguish, but engaging hero begins by placing his hand on Frenchy's thigh. It's a comforting gesture. Nothing more. He wants to reassure her that he poses no threat."

He placed his hand on her thigh just above her bent knee and squeezed it lightly. Through the baby-blue silk of her nightgown, she felt the heat and strength of all five fingers individually.

"Debatable," she murmured. "The part about him posing no threat, but we'll give him the benefit of the doubt."

"In exchange for that gesture of kindness, and despite the fact that Deck had drawn the low card, Frenchy tells him that at the time of the murder, she had heard a noise coming from the alley."

"Which caused her to look out her bedroom window. That's when she saw . . ." Needlessly Maris referred to the printed page. "The man in the red baseball cap running from the neighboring building."

"A valuable piece of information," Parker said. "Especially since Frenchy can describe the cap right down to the logo embroidered on it. Our hero thanks her with a kiss."

Parker removed her eyeglasses and framed her face between his hands. His thumbs stroked her cheekbones while his eyes touched on every feature. He followed their path with his lips. When he reached her mouth, he kissed it softly, sensually.

Maris struggled to keep her response down to a low moan of arousal.

When he pulled back, he whispered, "She tastes incredible."

"It doesn't say that."

"It doesn't? It should. He's compelled to go back for more."

"Frenchy doesn't resist."

He kept the kisses gentle. They teased and tantalized and left her wanting. It was several minutes before they separated, and by then Maris felt drugged. A delicious lassitude had afflicted her limbs. Even so, she had enough presence of mind to continue the game.

Needlessly, she reached for her glasses and fumbled trying to get them on correctly. "Never mind." She dropped them alongside the book. "I know what comes next. Frenchy, that lucky girl, draws the high card again."

"Cayton's pretty damn lucky himself. He gets to grant her a sexual favor."

"But he's uncomfortable with their position, so he pulls her astride his lap."

Parker curved his hands around her waist. She came up on her knees and straddled him. "If I'm remembering correctly, Cayton kisses her ears, her throat, her . . ."

But Parker was way ahead of her. He had, after all, written the scene and knew the sequence. The straps of her nightgown had been lowered before she was completely settled on him. Her breasts lay cupped in his hands, his thumbs brushing her nipples. And now he was taking one into his mouth and sucking it lustily, pressing it hard between his tongue and the roof of his mouth.

Shamelessly she folded her arms around his head, holding it fast. Whimpering wordless sounds, she kissed the crown of his head, his temple, anyplace that she could reach without dislodging him, because she didn't want him to stop.

Her sex softened and swelled, opening like a piece of fruit that had been ripened beyond its ability to contain itself. Parker reached between her thighs and when he touched her, she shuddered involuntarily. Her body closed wetly around his fingers.

"Go ahead," he urged. "You know what you want to do."

His name staggered out on an uneven breath.

"Go ahead, Maris."

She began to move, rocking her hips against his hand, forcing his fingers deeper into her, responding to his subtle stroking until she was in the throes of an orgasm.

Or so she thought.

Until he slid beneath her and simultaneously lifted her up higher, supporting her hips with his strong hands and drawing her to his mouth. She gave a harsh, dry gasp of pure shock, but it was soon expelled as a low, keening sigh of incredible pleasure.

She flattened her palms against the headboard, and when that became insufficient support, she leaned into it, resting her cheek against the cool wood while giving herself over to the mastery of his tongue.

His flexing fingers embedded themselves in her flesh. His hair was soft against her lower belly, the stubble on his cheeks pleasantly scratchy against her inner thighs.

She became lost in the sensations. Utterly lost. Her mind and body were governed by sensual impulses to the exclusion of all else. She surrendered herself to the primal rhythms pulsing through her.

Numerous times she strained toward orgasm, but he would quieten her efforts with the softest of kisses and the sweetest of words before wickedly coaxing her to the brink again. When he did let her come, it was shattering. The last tether on consciousness was clipped and she soared, lost touch, spun in delirium.

Coherence returned gradually. Languorously. A feather drifting down.

Her skin was damp, her chest flushed, her nipples taut and red. Her heart was pounding and each beat echoed inside her head. She rested against the headboard until her breathing had slowed. When she finally opened her eyes, she realized they were wet with tears.

She lowered herself to sprawl on Parker's torso like a shipwreck victim washed ashore. Her nightgown was wadded around her waist. Her hair clung to her cheeks and neck in damp strands. Parker smoothed his hands down her back, over her hips. They settled on her ass. He squeezed it gently and made her smile.

His heart was beating hard and strong directly into her ear. Each time she inhaled, her nose was tickled by chest hair. She had an up-close view of his nipple, which was flat until she touched it, then it beaded up hard against her fingertip and she felt his quick intake of breath. Between their bellies, she could feel his erection.

"Give me a moment," she said weakly.

Laughter rumbled in his chest. "I'm not going anywhere."

Several minutes passed. She soaked up the intimacy, realizing how bloody fabulous it was to be a woman in such intimate contact with a man. No, not a man. She'd had a man. She loved being intimate with *this* man. Until now, she hadn't known there could be such a vast difference between two members of the same sex, of the same species.

"You deviated from the book," she whispered.

"Did I? My memory's a little foggy."

"There was nothing like that in the book. Nothing that even comes close. In any book."

She raised her head and looked at him, inched up and softly kissed his lips, then slipped her tongue into his mouth and rubbed the tip of his. As the kiss intensified, she seductively ground her pelvis against his erection.

He broke from their kiss and angled his head back until it was buried in his pillow. His skin appeared to be stretched tightly over the bones of his face. His hands were gripping her hips hard in an effort to keep her still.

"What?" she asked innocently.

"That's not in the book, either."

"Oh, sorry. Let's see what comes next." Without changing their position, she awkwardly reached for her glasses and slipped them on, then opened the book and pretended to read silently. "Oh, yes, I remember now. He takes her hand and guides it to . . ."

"His cock."

"That's what it says."

Coming off him slowly, she resumed her original place beside him. She straightened her nightgown and was about to replace the straps on her shoulders, when Parker gave his head a negative shake. Maris pulled the gown off over her head. For a few seconds she held it against her chest, then tossed it toward the foot of the bed. Parker took a deep breath, his nostrils flaring slightly.

He ran his hand over her breasts, down her rib cage and belly, and combed his fingertips through her damp pubic hair before returning to her breast. He lightly pinched the nipple between his fingers and watched it harden.

She laid her hand on his stomach. The hair grew laterally toward a silky strip that took a downward turn at his navel. Her eyes tracked it; her hand followed it beneath the sheet.

But Parker reached down and stopped it. "This is where the fantasy ends, Maris."

Her gaze swung up to his. His expression was set and hard. He wasn't kidding. In a matter of moments, he had physically withdrawn and taken a giant step backward emotionally. "I don't understand."

"This isn't fiction."

"I'm glad it's not."

"This is reality."

"I know."

"You don't have a clue," he said harshly. "You pull that sheet back and you'll get a jolt of reality you never bargained for."

She took a quick glance at his legs beneath the covering of the sheet. Smiling softly, she shook her head. "Do you think I care about your scars?"

"I think you will, yeah."

"You're wrong." She gazed into his face, and, near tears, said, "Parker, you can't possibly comprehend what you've done for me. No, listen, please," she said when he was about to interrupt. "I may only have the courage to say this once."

She removed her glasses, rubbed her eyes, moistened her lips, smiled ruefully. "I've never played sex games like this before. I've only read about this kind of play. I thought it only occurred in books. What you said the other night on the beach, while crude, was correct. With Noah, I never felt free to express myself sexually. What happened between us just now? Would have been unthinkable to me a few weeks ago.

"That was totally out of character with the woman who entered Terry's Bar and Grill looking for you. I didn't know until now what I've been missing. I've been craving that kind of passion. Sensual meltdown. Absolute and unapologetic sexual abandon. You gave me that. But it's incomplete. It won't mean anything unless we share it. Let me share it," she finished huskily. "Please."

He continued to stare at her, but his expression was no

longer tense and set. In fact, he looked more vulnerable than she would have believed possible. "I'm not pretty, Maris."

"You're beautiful."

Tentatively, she leaned toward him. He didn't stop her. She began at his neck and kissed her way down. Her lips whisked across his skin, her tongue licked it softly. Her mouth wetly covered his nipple and he hissed a profanity and sank his fingers into her hair.

She pressed another openmouthed kiss just below his navel as she pushed the sheet down below his hips. He groaned her name when she encircled his penis with her hand. It throbbed with life and vitality. She stroked it slowly, varying the tension of her fingers as she worked her way up. She rubbed her thumb across the tip, smearing a pearly bead of semen that had leaked from it.

"Isn't this how Frenchy got her nickname?" she asked in a voice unintentionally smoky.

"Maris . . ." Her name vaporized on his lips when she bent over him.

She reveled in the musky taste and scent. She loved feeling the quickening in his belly, hearing his hoarse exclamations of arousal, experiencing the feel of him inside her mouth.

His grip on her hair tightened, not enough to hurt, only enough to let her know it was time to switch positions. She bridged him with her thighs and remained poised above him while he took his penis in his own hand and rubbed the smooth head against her, baiting her desire until she had to have him inside her. Then she sank down, sheathing him slowly, her body stretching to take all of him.

He took several rapid breaths and as he exhaled, he whispered, "Wait."

So she remained still. He slid his hands up and down her thighs. His thumbs met in the mesh of their public hair and stroked her V until her head fell back against her shoulders and she moaned his name.

Only then did he angle his hips up, encouraging her to ride him. She did, changing tempos and angles, holding still when he indicated that's what he wished her to do to protract the pleasure. During those pauses, she used the walls of her body to milk him; his eyes would darken, he would swear lavishly, then he would nudge her into motion again.

Leaning down, she guided his head to her breast. He rubbed his rough cheek against it, then his closed lips, before caressing her nipple with his tongue. Lightly and rapidly. Until she called his name and pressed her hips deeply into his belly, securing him inside her.

He pulled her down onto his chest and they came together. As he pulsed inside her, he splayed one hand over her bottom, and cupped the back of her head with the other, and, holding her possessively with both, kissed her mouth. They couldn't get close enough, deep enough, into each other far enough to satisfy the passion.

When it finally waned, she stretched out on top of him. She could feel the rugged terrain of his scarred legs beneath hers. But she couldn't, wouldn't, think about that now. She had scars, too. Less visible than his, but there nonetheless. Later, there would be time and opportunity to ask questions and to listen and to sympathize, and then to return their previous unhappiness to the past where it belonged.

Right now she wanted nothing to intrude on the present. She wanted to bask in the knowledge that she had pleased Parker well. She hated Noah Reed for all the times he had rejected her overtures, making her feel awkward and undesired, and then if he did respond for making her feel somehow insufficient.

But she didn't waste this precious time thinking about him, either. The thought of him was fleeting, like a twinge in one's side, that's painful only for an instant before it disappears.

Instead she concentrated on the wonderful pressure of Parker still nestling inside her. She kept her thighs tightly closed, her belly pressed firmly against his to maximize the closeness.

Moving only her lips, she kissed his throat. "The end?"

Several moments elapsed before he replied. "Not quite, Maris."

But she had already fallen asleep.

CHAPTER | 29

Daniel stood at the kitchen window, eating a sandwich and staring out at the rainy night. Periodically lightning illuminated the countryside, but it was a friendly storm, unthreatening and nonviolent, a summer thundershower that would dissipate quickly and leave the skies clear by dawn.

His telephone conversation with Maris had thrust his mind into overdrive. It was churning a mile a minute. He wished his body, like his brain, would experience occasional energizing jump starts like this. If it did, he'd be able to bicycle back to New York and then run a marathon. Mentally, he felt that athletic and robust.

After the call, he'd tried for an hour to fall asleep. Finally surrendering to his insomnia he had come downstairs. Midnight snacks were verboten at home, especially when they added up to more fat grams than he was allotted for a week. But Maxine wasn't guarding the refrigerator tonight, and what she didn't know wouldn't hurt her. She would be here soon enough, bossing and monitoring him as if he were a child.

Thank God, he thought with a chuckle. He didn't know what

he would have done without Maxine caring for him and Maris all these years.

He polished off the sandwich. The leftover Reuben had been satisfying—to say nothing of the warmth that two fingers of brandy had spread through him. Rather than making him feel languid and sleepy, however, the alcohol had invigorated him. He was restless and ready to act.

He'd always been a man of action, seldom placing problems on the back burner and letting them simmer. He favored confronting them immediately. Standing still wasn't his style. He preferred channeling his energy positively and productively rather than squandering it on self-doubt and hand-wringing indecision.

But this situation warranted more consideration than most. He was uncertain about the order in which to take the actions necessary to rectify it. He had his strategy in place, but it required careful orchestration and perfect timing. That's what had his mind working double-time tonight.

This situation didn't have a nucleus on which he could focus his problem-solving ability. It didn't lend itself to a swift and fatal attack. It was mercurial, constantly changing. It was a multilayered and complex conundrum involving both family and business, individuals and money, power and emotions. A complicated mix. Especially when one of the persons involved was his daughter.

He was glad Maris was in Georgia, away from New York. Things were about to get ugly. Bluntly, the shit was about to hit the fan. The more distance between it and Maris, the better. Inevitably she would catch some of the media fallout, but he hoped to buffer her as much as possible, and the geography would help. Sorting through the personal aspects of this mess was going to be painful enough for her. Doing so in the public eye would be hell.

Although, he thought, smiling, *she won't be without consolation.*

It had been evident to him for months that she was unhappy

with her husband and their marriage. It had become equally evident that the book-in-progress alone hadn't drawn her back to the sea island, exotic and lush as it might be.

Her duties and responsibilities at Matherly Press were enough to keep an overachiever like her stretched thin. Normally her daily grind would prevent her from becoming personally involved with one author and one book, even if she were so inclined to invest that much of herself, which she never had been before.

It didn't take a rocket scientist to conclude that the allure wasn't strictly the book, but the author Parker Evans, a.k.a. Mackensie Roone.

Oh, yes. He had discovered the name of Maris's elusive author, as well as his successful pen name. Years earlier, when the Deck Cayton mystery series had started appearing routinely on the bestseller lists, he had tried to flatter, coax, blackmail, and threaten the author's real name out of his agent, in the hope of luring the writer to Matherly Press.

She, however, would not be intimidated, even by the venerable Daniel Matherly. "If I told you, Daniel, I'd have to kill you." She had steadfastly protected her client's identity against disclosure, and Daniel had grudgingly admired her for it.

But he knew it now.

For several weeks, he'd had a private investigator on retainer. Hoping that his misgivings about Noah were proved wrong, he had hired the investigator to probe into his son-in-law's past, including his life prior to the publication of *The Vanquished*.

The whole idea of a covert investigation had been distasteful to him. His approach had always been bold and forthright, and he despised the furtiveness associated with a private investigator. He had envisioned having to consort with a sleazy B-movie type with a stained necktie and a leering yellow grin.

But when William Sutherland arrived for their discreet appointment, he contradicted the stereotype. Sutherland was the founder of an elite and expensive agency, a retired Secret Service agent wearing a well-tailored dark suit. He had a firm handshake, an authoritative bearing, and a distinguished service record.

Within five minutes of that first handshake, Daniel was outlining his requests. The last thing Daniel had expected to learn from Sutherland's initial report was novelist Mackensie Roone's true identity. That's not what he'd been looking for. Unexpectedly, one of publishing's best-kept secrets had landed in his lap in a sealed manila folder.

But the staggering revelation was yet to come: Parker Evans and Noah Reed had a history.

They had been roommates at a university in Tennessee, and then after graduation they had lived together in Key West. There, they'd had some sort of falling out, the particulars of which were still unknown. Sutherland was presently investigating further, and Daniel was certain that soon all the facts would be disclosed.

In the meantime, he had pieced together the facts he knew, and they would have made an engrossing novel. Maris was presently residing in a plantation house on a remote island belonging to Parker Evans, her estranged husband's former friend with whom he'd parted antagonistically. The synopsis alone brimmed with the ingredients of a juicy novel—friendship, love, hate, deception, revenge. Envy? Possibly.

The only thing lacking in this scenario was a motive for the main character, Parker Evans.

He had lured Maris with his book for a specific purpose. He hadn't selected her at random. What had motivated him to become involved with Maris, even professionally, when he must know that she was Noah's wife?

Daniel wondered if she was aware of their connection. Considering Noah's unfaithfulness, she would feel justified to play tit for tat with his former fraternity brother. But a childish retaliation wasn't like her.

Daniel doubted she knew. If she knew, she would have been reluctant to fall in love with Parker Evans. And she was in love. That became clearer by the day.

Daniel wanted to celebrate her newfound happiness, but he would be wary of the budding romance until he knew why Parker Evans had engineered this chain of events. He had been tempted to confront the man, either in person or through Sutherland, and demand to know just what kind of story he was plotting. But he couldn't do that without tipping his hand to both Maris and Noah, and he wasn't quite prepared to do that. Close, but not quite.

So he'd been forced to bide his time while Sutherland delved deeper.

It was possible that Evans's motivation would come to light in another form—his manuscript. Having read the latest installment that Maris had shared with him, Daniel was convinced the writer was chronicling his rocky friendship with Noah. Depending on how long it took him to commit the story to paper, it might be told through the pages of his personal record before Sutherland could wade through the official one.

During the wait, Daniel's primary concern was Maris. He'd known about Parker Evans before she returned to St. Anne. He could have stopped her. He didn't. For one thing, it was clear to him that she yearned to go. He was also comforted by the fact that Parker Evans was spoken well of by the people who lived on St. Anne, who ordinarily resented the intrusion of outsiders, as Sutherland had discovered when he sent a man down there to ask questions.

Daniel had gambled that Maris, and her heart, would be safe with the writer. If his friendship with Noah had ended over a matter of honor, then Daniel must assume that Parker Evans was an honorable man.

Indisputably Noah Reed was not. Regardless of what else transpired, Noah's affiliation with the Matherlys was about to come to an end. He thought he had smiled and cajoled himself into Daniel's good graces with this male-bonding-weekend malarkey. Daniel had gone along for his own curiosity and amusement, secretly appalled by the extent of Noah's deceit.

Unbeknownst to the self-assured and insufferably smug Mr. Reed, his head was on the chopping block and the axe was about to fall.

In a symbolic gesture, Daniel dusted bread crumbs off his hands and put his plate and empty brandy snifter in the sink. Contrary to his weather predictions, the storm had intensified. Flashes of lightning were closer, the thunder louder. One clap of thunder shook the house, causing Rosemary's china plates to jingle in their cabinet.

Dear Rosemary. Twenty years she'd been gone, and he still missed her. This house made him particularly homesick for her. They'd spent such happy times here.

Switching off the kitchen light, he made his way through the dark house. As he climbed the staircase, he favored his arthritic joints by leaning heavily upon the balustrade. Damn, he hated getting old!

No sooner had the thought flashed through his mind than a voice came out of the darkness at the top of the stairs. "You forgot your cane."

"Jesus!" Daniel raised his hand to his lurching heart. In a brief glare of blue-white lightning, he saw Noah on the landing. "You startled me."

"It's careless of you not to use your cane, Daniel."

"I'm all right." He continued up the stairs, having to put both feet on each tread before progressing to the next one. "Did the storm wake you?"

"I never went to sleep."

Noah's remote tone of voice gave Daniel pause, but he smiled up at his son-in-law with affected congeniality. "I was having trouble sleeping myself, so I took advantage of being away from Sergeant Maxine to eat a snack."

By now he was only two steps below the landing, but Noah appeared to have taken root there. He made no attempt either to assist Daniel or to step aside. Indeed, he seemed to be blocking his path.

He disliked having Noah looming over him, but he tried to act casually as he indicated the sheets of paper Noah was holding at his side. "Reviewing the document I signed earlier?"

Let him, Daniel thought. *Let him memorize it, for all the good it will do him.* The document wasn't worth spit except in Noah's devious and disillusioned mind.

"No," Noah replied calmly. "This is the report on me from your private investigator, Mr. William Sutherland."

More than being shocked or alarmed, Daniel was angry that his privacy had been invaded. His lips narrowed into the firm thin line that anyone who had been subject to his stern disapproval would recognize. "That was locked in a drawer in my desk at home."

"Yes, I know. It took some rifling, but eventually I found it. Interesting reading."

"I thought so, too," Daniel said stiffly.

"Did you really think I wouldn't know I was being investigated?" Noah asked, laughing lightly. "Your bloodhound is good, Daniel. The best that money can buy, I'm sure. Secret Service training and all that. But he asked questions of one friend too many."

"According to the report, you don't have any friends."

"Call my doubles tennis partner an acquaintance, then. Smart fellow. Smart enough to see through Sutherland's lame reason for the inquiries." His smile, which had been in place up to this point, vanished. "I'm curious to know only when the surveillance began."

There was no reason now to play dumb or to equivocate. "I'd been deliberating it for months. It commenced shortly after your premature anniversary party."

"Why then?"

"Because that was the night I became convinced that you are a seasoned deceiver and liar."

Noah kept every urbane feature schooled, except one eyebrow. He raised it in query. "Really?"

"I don't know if you've been deceiving us all along or if you've been walking the straight and narrow until only the last several months when Morris Blume approached you about selling my publishing company out from under me. I prefer to think the latter, because that would make me less of a fool for being taken in by you. But I fear that one could not acquire and perfect your skills for duplicity in such a short period of time. They've been cultivated, honed—"

"You're becoming redundant, Daniel. You've already said I was a *seasoned* liar."

"Quite right. The night of the party at the Chelsea apartment, I caught you in several lies. And while some could be explained as necessary for surprising Maris, others bothered me. It was also unlike you to think so far ahead and plan a celebration, when ordinarily you rely on your secretary to buy Maris's gifts for every special occasion. So I began observing you carefully, looking beyond the obvious, beyond the man you show to the world. That's when I began seeing you for who you really are."

"How clever of you, Daniel."

"No. If I'd been clever I wouldn't have been duped at the start. You're very good at the masquerade, Noah. Exceptional. You've also proved your mettle as a businessman and publisher. I had admired your abilities long before you came to Matherly Press. Like Maris, I was impressed by *The Vanquished,* and wrongly assumed that only a person with integrity could author a book of matching integrity."

Noah folded his arms across his chest and smiled as he enunciated, "It's fiction, Daniel. It wasn't by accident that I wrote *The Vanquished* from that humble, hillbilly-righteous point of view. I created characters with high-minded ideals, not because I adhere to them, or even believe in them, but because I know that's what sells books. The average Joe and Judy want to believe that valorous people do exist, that evil can be overcome by good, that virtue is a reward unto itself. They get off on that kind of bullshit.

"*The Vanquished* was bloated with the sentimental, southern sappiness that my parents spoon-fed me. I was forced to stomach it when I was growing up. So I used it. I poured it all into that novel so I could close the cover on it and leave it there forever.

"The dewy-eyed heroine," he continued scornfully. "The flawed but valiant hero. Their blood-stirring, star-crossed love story. Every word of it was tripe disguised by pretty prose. It didn't mean shit to me, except for the royalties it earned and the reviews that brought me to the attention of publishers and ultimately paved the way into your office."

"Why ultimately to me?"

"Because, Daniel, you were the only supremely successful publisher with a marriageable daughter, who, to my good fortune, had gone on record claiming that *The Vanquished* was her favorite book."

Even knowing Noah's true nature, Daniel was stunned by this declaration. "You freely confess to being that callous? Is that how you honestly feel about your profession, about people, and life in general?"

"And then some."

Daniel shook his head sadly. "Such a sad waste of talent."

"Come on, Daniel. Let's not weep over my hypocrisy. We publish a gritty police series that's written by a flaming fag. He takes breaks from writing about his tough, heterosexual hero to get fucked up the ass by his young assistant. One of our religious book authors has been convicted of tax evasion and insurance fraud.

"Hypocrisy? On your Christmas party list are several hopeless alcoholics, a brother-and-sister writing team whose oh-so-close relationship would scandalize the mothers who read their books aloud to their children. We publish one cocaine addict for whom you've footed the bill of a rehab clinic at least twice that I know of.

"All of them write very good books, and we publish them. I don't see you getting squeamish over their addictions and aberrations when the profits come rolling in. Those profits pay for your weekly massages, and this house, and chauffeured limousines, and all the other niceties you pompously enjoy up there in your ivory tower."

"You've made your point," Daniel conceded angrily. "I've never denied keeping an eye on the bottom line. I pride myself on having been a good businessman. I've fought countless corporate battles against unscrupulous foes and outlasted economic crises that naysayers predicted could not be withstood.

"And yes, there have been times when, for the good of Matherly Press, I've had to be disingenuous. I've resorted to guile when I felt it was necessary." His eyes pierced through the darkness separating them. "That's why I was able to detect it in you, Noah. And once I got a whiff of it, it became obvious to me that you reek of it."

Noah crossed his legs at the ankles and leaned indolently against the newel post. He looked over the sheets in his hand, although he couldn't have actually been reading them. Except for flashes of lightning, it was too dark to read. "I'll admit that some of this is less than flattering."

Daniel wondered how much he knew. Was this only the initial report? He couldn't remember what had been committed to paper and what the investigator had told him over the telephone that morning, promising that he would receive a written update as soon as it was available.

Noah said, "If you believe this, I'm a wretched human being. I actually admire your ability to keep a civil tongue when speaking to me."

"It hasn't been easy."

"No, I suppose not. I assume you're most upset over my traitorous alliance with WorldView?"

Daniel chose not to disabuse him. Better to let him continue entertaining his misconceptions. "I can forgive that before I can forgive your mistreatment of Maris."

"She knows, by the way," he said placidly, dropping the sheets and letting them scatter. "About the affair with Nadia."

"I know."

He was obviously taken aback. "She told you?"

"No, but her unhappiness with you and your marriage has been apparent for some time."

"She's been happy enough," he said with a blasé flick of his hand. "She loves her work more than ever, now that she's working with this new author. He's handicapped, and that really appeals to her. It's important to her to feel needed."

So he didn't know about Parker Evans! Daniel happily clung to that secret knowledge.

"Maybe I didn't cater to the nurturing aspect of Maris's personality," Noah continued with a nonchalance that Daniel found nauseating. "I'm self-sufficient to a fault. That caused a few minor tiffs. But your precious daughter wasn't too dissatisfied with her life. Not until she caught me with Nadia."

"Her happiness came from within herself. She was happy in spite of you, Noah, not because of you. You even sabotaged her chance of being truly happy."

Noah snapped his fingers. "You're referring to the vasectomy."

"Yes," Daniel said bitterly. That had been one of the most disheartening discoveries to come from Sutherland's report. "The secret vasectomy. As I recall, you cited business obligations as your reason for not accompanying us to Greece."

"Maris had in mind for us to screw our way through the Mediterranean and return pregnant. I invented a plausible excuse for wiggling out of the trip and used the time you were away to have the procedure that ensured I wouldn't have to worry about birth control again."

"I was puzzled when I first read about the vasectomy,"

Daniel admitted. "Wouldn't a child have secured your ties to us and the Matherly fortune? And therein lay the answer." He looked Noah full in the face. "You didn't want a child competing with you for a share."

Noah uncrossed his ankles. "That's the first thing you've said during this conversation that's incorrect, Daniel."

"You deny it?"

"Not at all," he said blandly. "You're wrong in that I'd ever settle for a measly *share.*"

Daniel snorted with contempt. "Don't count your chickens yet, Noah. That document I signed tonight is worthless."

"You think so?" he asked smoothly.

"I was only playing along, seeing how far you would go. What I really find galling is that you attached Howard Bancroft's name to that document. He would never have drawn up a—"

"Oh, but he would," Noah said, interrupting. "He did. Rather than let it be circulated that his father was a Nazi officer who was personally responsible for exterminating thousands of his kindred."

Daniel received that news like a punch to the gut. "You used that to coerce him?"

"So," Noah said with a slow smile, "you knew about his whoring mother?"

"Howard was my friend." Daniel practically strained the words through his clenched teeth. "He confided in me years ago. I admired him for making his life into what it was instead of letting what he couldn't change defeat him."

"Well, it did, didn't it? In the long run, he couldn't live with the tragic truth."

"A truth you threatened to spread," Daniel said, seeing the clear picture now.

Noah shrugged and smiled beatifically. "See, that's the difference between you and me, Daniel. Come to think of it, between me and just about everybody. You go after what you want, but you fall short of total commitment. Your conscience has drawn an invisible line, and you never step across it. You're shackled by principles and ethics. And while that moral demarcation is admired, it's terribly restricting.

"I, on the other hand, suffer no such impediment. I am willing to do whatever it takes to get what I want. I stop at nothing, and I let nothing stand in my way. My credo is: Find a man's weakness, and you own him. To achieve the goal I've set for myself, I'll go to any lengths."

"Even to talking a man, a good man, into committing suicide."

"I didn't talk Howard into anything. He thought that up all by himself. Although I'll admit that he did me a huge favor when he stuck that pistol in his mouth. What do you suppose he was thinking about when he pulled the trigger? Heaven? Hell? His mother with her legs spread? What?"

Daniel's beloved friend Howard had suffered untold heartache over his terrible secret. All his life he had tried to atone for it with good deeds, kindness, and tolerance. At last, he had come to terms with it.

Then this travesty of a human being had tortured him with it. Worse yet, he could stand there and smile about it.

Daniel realized he was looking into the face of a pure, unrepentant depravity. Noah's indifference to the evil he had done enraged him. Tears of godly wrath blurred his vision. Heat blasted through his veins as though the temperature of his blood had reached the boiling point in a matter of heartbeats.

"You are despicable," he growled, and charged up the last two steps.

Parker was the first thing Maris saw when she opened her eyes, and nothing could have pleased her more. He was sitting in his wheelchair beside the bed watching her while she slept. Even before stirring, she smiled into her pillow and asked drowsily, "How'd you manage to get up and into your chair without waking me?"

"Practice."

She sighed and stretched luxuriously, then sat up and drew the sheet as high as her collarbone. "What time is it?"

"Time for you to clear out. Unless you want Mike to catch you flagrante delicto."

He was wearing only a pair of boxer shorts. His shoulders and arms, as she knew, were well formed, the muscles taut and defined. His belly was flat, and beneath it, his sex was appreciably full, even while relaxed.

Beyond his lap were his legs. Last night she had made a point to show no interest in them because of his self-consciousness. Apparently, their lovemaking had convinced him that his apprehension was unnecessary. He wouldn't be sitting here now with his legs exposed, making no attempt to cover them, if he didn't want her to see them.

So she looked.

And it was impossible to conceal her reaction. She stopped just short of gasping out loud, but the sudden catch in her breath couldn't have been missed, especially since he was watching her so closely.

His features were rigidly set. His eyes were shuttered. His voice sliced like a razor. "I warned you that it wasn't pretty."

"Oh, my darling, you were terribly, horribly hurt."

She slid from the bed to kneel in front of him. *Shark attack* was the first thing that came to mind. She'd seen pictures of victims who'd barely escaped with their lives, having huge chunks of their flesh mangled or ripped away. Parker's scars could be compared only to something that vicious.

The worst of them was a hollow as large as her fist where a section of his quadriceps had been gouged out. From there a scar cut a gully half an inch wide down the entire length of his right thigh and curved around toward the back of his knee. On his lower legs was a network of crisscrossing scars, some raised and bumpy, while others looked like flat, shiny ribbons of plastic that had been stretched between puckered skin. His calves were disproportionately small and flaccid. He was missing the smallest two toes on his right foot.

Overwhelmed with compassion for the agony he must have suffered, she timorously traced one of the raised scars with her fingertip. "Do they still hurt?"

"Sometimes."

She looked up at him sorrowfully, then leaned forward and kissed one of the worst of the scars that snaked up his shin. Reaching down, he stroked her cheek. She lifted his hand to her mouth and kissed the palm.

He said, "Now that your morbid curiosity has been satisfied, can we get in one fast fuck before breakfast?"

She yanked her head back. "What?"

"I think you heard me."

As shocked as if he'd struck her, she stood up, reached for her nightgown, and held it against her, a flimsy shield. "What's the matter?"

"Nothing except an early morning woodie that needs your attention."

She shook her head in befuddlement. The coarse language wasn't that startling. But he wasn't being naughty for naughtiness' sake. No flirtatious wink accompanied his words. He was being purposefully, hurtfully crude. "Why are you acting like this?"

"This is what I'm like, Maris."

"No, you're not."

He gave a dismissive shrug. "Okay, whatever." He pushed his chair backward, then turned it away from her and headed across the room toward the chifforobe. "I've got something for you."

"Parker?" she called in exasperation.

"What?"

"Why are you acting this way? I don't understand. What happened between last night and this morning?"

"You don't remember? Well, let's see. Between last night and this morning, I'd say your orgasms outnumbered mine about two to one, but after your fifth or sixth, I honestly lost count. Of course, with women it's sometimes hard to tell when one leaves off and another starts, or if they're even for real. But if you fake it, honey, you fake it convincingly."

He'd opened the door to the chifforobe and removed a box from one of the interior drawers. Now he spun around and faced her, grinning cruelly as he looked her up and down. "And I'll say this for you, Mrs. Matherly-Reed. You're tight. As a goddamn fist. And wet as a mouth. Very nice. I wonder why your husband went out for it."

Tears of mortification filled her eyes. Angrily she swiped one away as it slid down her cheek. Hastily, she pulled on her nightgown, the only article of clothing available. "I don't know what's the matter with you, but I won't continue this. I can't match you for vulgarity."

"Sure you can. You've got an expansive vocabulary. Maybe not one as colorful as mine, but if you put your mind to it, I'll bet you come up with something suitable to say. Maybe on your plane ride back to New York. I assume you're leaving."

Not even deigning to answer, she headed for the door.

"Wait!" He rolled his chair over to her. "*Envy*. The final draft."

He practically thrust the box into her hands, so she had no choice but to take it. She looked at it, then at him. "It's finished?"

"Has been. All along. From the beginning. What you've been reading in installments is the polishing draft."

She gaped at him. Words failed her.

"I never submit a partial manuscript, Maris. No one sees my book until it's finished. I wouldn't have sent a prologue unless I had a book behind it."

"Why, Parker? Why?"

Deliberately mistaking her meaning, he shrugged. "Personal policy. That's just the way I work."

Maris felt as though the spot on which she stood were eroding rapidly and that at any second it would disappear out from under her altogether. But she wasn't going to sink without a fight.

"That's just the way you work?" she repeated, raising her voice to a shout. "What the hell was all this for, Parker? Or is that even your name? How many do you have? What in hell has this been about? Why the lies, the games?"

"They seemed like fun at the time. We both got laid. Several times last night you moaned, 'Yes, yes, harder, faster, Parker.' X-rated things, too. Sounded to me like you were having fun."

For several beats, she just stared at him, wondering at what point he had become this sarcastic stranger. Then she hurled the box as far as she could throw it. It upended in midair, the lid came off, and some four hundred manuscript pages scattered in that many directions across the polished hardwood floor and Aubusson rug.

Maris stalked to the door and jerked it open.

Mike was standing on the other side of it, one hand raised,

about to knock. The other was holding a cordless telephone. "Maris." There was no surprise in his voice. He had expected her to be with Parker. Her emotional state, however, seemed to alarm him.

Looking beyond her shoulder, he took in the situation at a glance. The look he gave Parker went beyond reproof; it was that of a hanging judge about to hand down the sentence. Stiffly, he extended the telephone toward Maris. "For you. I hated to disturb you, but the gentleman said it was an emergency."

She took the telephone from him with a shaking hand and stepped out into the hallway. Mike went into the bedroom and closed the door behind him. Maris leaned against the wall and took several seconds to compose herself. She breathed deeply, sniffed her nose hard, blinked away tears.

Then, clearing her throat, she said, "Hello?"

"Maris?"

"Noah?" His voice was strangely muffled and subdued. She barely recognized it.

"It's imperative that you return to New York immediately. I took the liberty of making your travel arrangements. A ticket is waiting for you at the Savannah airport. Your flight departs at eleven-ten, so you haven't got much time."

Her dread was so absolute, it felt as though her heart had been replaced with an anvil. She was suddenly very cold. She closed her eyes, but tears leaked through. It would have been useless to try and hold them back. "It's Dad, isn't it?"

"I'm afraid so, yes."

"Is it bad? A stroke?"

"He . . . God, this is tough. Telling you like this. You shouldn't have to hear this news over the telephone, Maris, but . . . he's dead."

She cried out. Her knees buckled and she sank to the floor.

*   *   *

Parker was at his worktable in the solarium, but he wasn't working. Instead he was staring out at the ocean. He broke his stare only occasionally, and that was when he compressed his bowed head between his hands in abject despair and self-loathing.

He'd heard Mike when he returned from the mainland, but he didn't seek him out, and Mike didn't come to him. He'd gone straight upstairs and had been moving around in his room ever since. It sounded as though he were pacing.

Parker had been replaying in his head his last conversation with Maris. If you could call it a conversation. His stomach knotted when he recalled the horrible things he'd said to her. Her stricken expression haunted him.

She might be consoled to know that he was as miserable as she, but he doubted it. The only way she might be consoled was if he were drawn and quartered and the pieces thrown to a herd of ravenous wild pigs. Starting with his mouth. His foul, abusive, nasty mouth.

The afternoon dragged on interminably. It was hot and muggy outside and that oppression had eked into the house to contribute to his feelings of suffocation. Or was the weather to blame? Maybe he was being smothered by remorse.

"I stayed with Maris until they boarded her flight."

Parker hadn't heard Mike come into the solarium. He sat bolt upright and glanced over his shoulder toward the door. Mike was standing as stiff as a girder in his seersucker suit.

"It took off on time," he added.

As soon as Maris could pack her things, she and Mike had departed for the mainland. She left without a word to Parker, but he hadn't expected her to tell him good-bye. He didn't deserve it. He didn't deserve a *kiss my ass*, or a *go to hell*, or even a *screw you*. Her leaving without even acknowledging him had been more eloquent than any epithet. Eloquent, classy, and dignified. Typical of her.

Hiding behind the drapery, he had watched her departure

through the dining room window. She had looked very small beneath her wide-brimmed straw hat. She'd also worn sunglasses to conceal her weeping eyes from prying strangers. The tan she had acquired on the beach seemed to have faded with the news of her father's death. She had looked pale and vulnerable, fragile enough to break from the air pressure alone.

Yet there was a brave dignity about her that suggested an enviable inner strength.

Mike had stowed her bags in the trailer of the Gator, then assisted her into the seat. Parker saw her lips move as she thanked him. Then he watched until the utility vehicle disappeared from sight through the tunnel of trees. He would probably never see her again. He had expected that.

What he hadn't expected was that it would hurt so goddamn much.

He had believed himself to be beyond the grasp of pain. After what he had endured, he had imagined himself immune to it. He wasn't. He had decided to anesthetize himself with several belts of bourbon, but the first one had made him so sick, he'd thrown it up. He didn't think there was an analgesic that would be effective against this particular kind of pain.

Now his back was still to Mike. He kept his stinging eyes on the surf. "Maris was worried about her father last night. Maybe she had a premonition."

"I wouldn't be surprised. They were very close."

After Noah's call, she had been in a state of complete emotional collapse, but she'd had the wherewithal to tell Mike that her father had fallen down the stairs of their country house. She'd been told that he had died instantly of a broken neck. It had happened during the middle of the night.

The noise had awakened Noah. He had rushed to Daniel's aid, but when he couldn't get a response out of him, he called 911. The rural emergency service had reached the house in a matter of minutes, but it didn't matter—Daniel Matherly was dead.

Noah had refused to accept the paramedics' word for it. The ambulance ran hot to the small community hospital. Doctors there pronounced Daniel dead, making it official and indisputable. Noah had seen no point in calling Maris until daylight.

"She probably feels guilty for not being there," Parker said.

"She said as much on the way to the mainland."

"How was she when she left?"

"How do you think she was, Parker?"

He frowned at Mike's snide comeback, but he didn't challenge it. He had asked a stupid question with an obvious answer. "She probably felt like she'd been run through a thrasher."

"You certainly did your part."

Unlike its predecessor, that cutting remark demanded to be addressed. Parker came around. "Are you suggesting that I've been a bad boy?"

"You know it without my saying so."

"What are you going to do, Mike? Park me in the corner? Ground me for a month? Restrict my TV time? Rap my knuckles with a ruler?"

"Actually, I was thinking that you're the one who should be run through a thrasher."

Parker agreed that that was the least he deserved, but, while it was okay for him to think it, he resented hearing it from someone else. "Getting Maris into bed was part of the plot. You probably guessed that."

"I guessed it. That doesn't mean I liked it."

"Nobody asked you to like it."

"Did *you*?"

"Did I what?"

"Like it."

A scathing retort was on the tip of his tongue, but he foundered under Mike's incisive stare. Turning his head away, he mumbled, "Irrelevant."

"I don't think so. I think it's not only relevant but key to how you progress from here."

Parker went back to his keyboard. "Excuse me. I'm trying to write."

"Fine. Turn your back on me. Stare into that blank screen. Count the ticks of the cursor till hell freezes over, for all I care. Delude yourself into believing that you're writing. We both know you're not."

Parker came back around, angry now. "Obviously you've reached a conclusion that you're just dying to share. So spit it out. Get it out of your system. God knows I won't have a minute's peace until you do."

The older man refused to take umbrage. "I'm not going to fight with you, Parker," he said evenly. "But yes, I will tell you something you need to hear." Ignoring Parker's roll of the eyes, he went on. "You resurrected yourself when, for all practical purposes, your life was over. I was there to help. I needled you and badgered you along. But you did it. It was a heroic effort. You're to be commended for overcoming incredible obstacles. You beat overwhelming odds. Beyond putting your life back on track, you have thrived."

"Yea, me."

The caustic interruption went ignored and Mike doggedly continued. "Your body has healed, but not your soul. The damage done to it was a thousand times worse than the injuries to your legs. Your soul is more twisted than they ever were. Pins and plates hold your bones together, and new skin patches the places where there was no skin left, but your soul hasn't been mended. It's still raw and bleeding, and you snarl at anyone who extends a hand to help you heal it."

"That's what I've been trying to tell you for years, Mike," he said sweetly. "I'm a lost cause."

"You're not a lost cause, you're a coward," Mike shouted angrily. "It takes far less courage to cling to the past than it does to face the future."

"Very good, Mike. I should write that down. What was it again? 'It takes far less—'"

"Sarcasm? Good. If I'm pissing you off, at least I know I have your attention." Mike's lined features softened and turned earnest. "Parker, consign Noah Reed to God. Or to the devil. Let them haggle over who's to be his judge and what his punishment is to be.

"Then go to Maris. If you can get her to talk to you, lay open your heart. Explain everything. Start at the beginning and tell her all of it. Tell her Noah's part. Confess yours. She may forgive you. She may not. But either way, you'll be rid of it. For the first time in fourteen long years, you'll be free of everything that happened in Key West. You will have saved yourself. Again. And in the only way that really matters."

Parker's heart was pounding hard and loudly against his eardrums, but he kept his expression passive. "Good sermon, Mike. Honestly. Very moving. But I'm going to stick to plan A."

"And throw away a chance to be happy with a woman you love?"

"Love?" he scoffed. "Who said that?"

"You did. Every time you looked at her."

"Have you been sneak-reading romance novels again? They're not good for your blood pressure."

"Okay, be funny. Deny you're in love with her. You're only wasting your breath. Maris hit you like those drugs you used to take. The night she came here, you got high on her, and after that you couldn't get enough. She's—"

"She's Noah's *wife*."

Parker felt his control snap like the string on a tennis racket that had been whacked one too many times.

"She is Noah's 'dearly beloved, we are gathered here' bride. That's the important thing. That's the *only* thing," he yelled, slicing the air with his hand. "Nothing else matters. Not how I feel about her, or how she feels about me, or even how they feel about each other.

"She is Noah Reed's wife, and I had her. But good. She was finger-fucked, and tongue-fucked, and mind-fucked. By *me!*"

He pounded his chest with his fist, his eyes shimmering with tears spawned by the white-hot rage that consumed him whenever he thought of Noah's treachery. And now by the agony of his own guilt.

Mike's features surrendered to gravity and settled into an aged mask of profound disappointment. "Perhaps you're right, Parker. Perhaps you are a lost cause. Your cruelty to her goes beyond reprehensible. All you care about is this revenge plot of yours."

"That's right. Now you're catching on."

"What's the next chapter?"

"Well, since Maris threw the manuscript at me, I don't think I can count on her to get it to Noah. So I guess I'll have to send it to him myself, registered and receipt requested, along with a cover letter saying that *Envy* is being simultaneously submitted to every publishing house in New York. If that doesn't give his short-and-curlies a smart tug, then perhaps a postscript about his wife's talent for giving head will."

Mike shook his head with disgust. "And then what, Parker?"

"The gripping climax, of course."

Mike subjected him to a long, hard stare, then turned and picked up two suitcases, which had been left in the kitchen and up till now out of Parker's sight. "Going somewhere?"

"Away from you. I won't be a party to this."

Mike was walking out on him? That shook him up more than he let on. "You helped get her here, don't forget. You played along."

"For which I am now very ashamed. In any case, let this serve as notice that my participation is over."

"Fine. Go. Have a nice trip."

"Will you be all right?"

"Not your problem anymore, is it?"

He spun his chair around and faced his blank computer screen. A few moments later, he heard Mike leaving through the back door. And he was truly alone.

Afterward, Maris could barely remember her return trip to
New York. She had operated in a dreamlike state, except without the subconscious surety that it was unreal and that she
would wake up soon. Parker's inexplicable behavior and her father's death had been a double-barreled assault. To protect itself, her mind had put conscious thought and reasoning powers
on autopilot and allowed her to function only by rote.

Discreetly Mike Strother had alerted the flight attendant to
her bereavement, so she had been treated deferentially, basically left alone. She passed the flight staring vacantly out the
window, unaware and uncaring of what was going on around her.

Noah was at LaGuardia to meet her. She wasn't happy to see
him, but he relieved her of the arrival hassle at a major airport.
Her baggage was reclaimed with dispatch. He had a car and
driver waiting.

As the limo wended its way through heavy traffic into Manhattan, he somberly filled in the details that he hadn't told her
over the telephone. Daniel's body was still in Massachusetts,
where the autopsy would be conducted. There could have been
a contributing health factor that caused him to fall, Noah ex-

plained. Pulmonary embolism. Cardiac arrest. An aneurysm that hadn't shown up during his last physical.

"Most probably," he told her, "Noah simply lost his balance on the dark staircase."

Daniel's cane had been found in his bedroom. It was believed that he was ascending the stairs. Without his cane for additional support, he had tripped.

"He'd also had more than a few drinks," Noah added reluctantly. "You know, Maris, we had feared something like this would happen."

He informed her that following the autopsy the body would be transferred to New York. He'd made preliminary funeral arrangements but was awaiting her approval before finalizing them. Knowing she would be particular about the casket, he had held off making a selection until her return.

She commented on how expeditiously he had handled everything.

"I wanted to spare you as much unpleasantness as possible."

He was solicitous, soft-spoken, obsequious.

She couldn't bear to be near him.

She deplored even having to breathe the same air as he and instructed the chauffeur to take her to her father's house. Accepting a friend's offer to help in any way she could, Maris sent her to her apartment with a list of clothing and articles she wanted brought to her. If she could help it, she would never return to the residence she had shared with Noah.

She moved back into her old bedroom in Daniel's house. For the next three days, when she and Maxine weren't receiving people who came to pay their respects and offer condolences, they comforted one another. The housekeeper was disconsolate. She blamed herself for letting Daniel go to the country house without her, as though her presence could have prevented the accident. Maris tried to assuage her feelings of partial responsibility, all the while empathizing with them. She suffered similarly.

Her father had died while she'd been making love to Parker. Each time her thoughts drifted in that direction, which was frequently, she halted them abruptly. She refused to wear a mantle of guilt for that. Daniel had urged her to return to Georgia. She had been there with his blessing. The last thing he had said to her was that she deserved her happiness and that he loved her. His death had nothing to do with her sharing Parker's bed.

Nevertheless, the connection between the two had been made, and she would never think of one without recalling the other.

She learned that a death in the family was a time-consuming event, especially if the deceased was a person of Daniel Matherly's standing. He was the last patriarch of the publishing dynasty; he was one of New York's own. His obituary made the front page of the *New York Times*. Local media covered his funeral.

Maris endured the day-long affair with a steely determination not to crack under pressure. Dressed head to toe in black, she was photographed entering the cathedral, exiting the cathedral, standing at the grave site with her head bowed in prayer, receiving the mayor's condolences.

The silent expressions of grief were the ones she appreciated most—a small squeeze of her hand, eye contact that conveyed sympathy and understanding. Most people said too much. Well-meaning folk told her to take comfort in the fact that Daniel had lived a long and productive life. That he hadn't suffered before he died. That we should all be so lucky to go that quickly. That at least he hadn't withered and died slowly. That a sudden death is a blessing.

Statements to that effect sorely tested her composure.

However, no one surprised or offended her more than Nadia Schuller. Noah was speaking to a group of publishing colleagues when Nadia sidled up to Maris immediately following the grave-site observance and gripped her hand. "I'm sorry, Maris. Terribly, terribly sorry."

Maris was struck not only by Nadia's audacity in attending the service, but also by her convincing portrayal of shocked bereavement. Maris pulled back her hand, thanked Nadia coldly, and tried to turn away. But Nadia wouldn't be shaken off. "We need to talk. Soon."

"If you want a quote for your column, call our publicity department."

"Please, Maris," Nadia said, leaning closer. "This is important. Call me." She pressed a business card into Maris's hand, then turned and walked quickly away. She had the decency not to lock eyes with Noah before she left.

He was the worst part of Maris's endurance test.

She tried not to visibly flinch each time he came near her. Yet he seemed determined to be near her. At the reception following the funeral, he was never far from her side, often placing his arm around her shoulders, pressing her hand, demonstrating to their friends and associates a loving affection that was grossly false. The act would have been hilarious if it weren't so obscene.

Dusk had fallen before the house cleared of guests. Maxine refused to retire to her room as Maris suggested and instead began supervising the caterers' cleanup. That's when Maris approached Noah. "I want to talk to you."

"Certainly, darling."

His ingratiating manner set her teeth on edge. He was thoroughly repugnant. It seemed that the two years she had shared a home, a bed with him had happened to another woman in another time. She couldn't fathom doing so now.

Her only saving grace, her only reasonable excuse, was that he was an excellent role player. He was an adroit liar. She and Daniel had fallen for an act he had perfected.

"You can drop the pretense, Noah. No one's around except Maxine, and she already knows that I've left you."

She led him into her father's study. The room smelled of him and of his pipe tobacco. It smelled of his brandy and the books he had loved. The room evoked such poignant memories for her, it was claustrophobic and comforting at the same time.

She sat down in the large tufted leather chair behind Daniel's desk. It was the closest she could come to being hugged by him. She had spent the past four nights curled up in this chair, weeping over her loss between brief and restless naps in which she dreamed of Parker moving ever farther away from her as she screamed his name. No matter how desperately she tried to touch him, he was always beyond her reach. She would wake herself up sobbing over the dual loss.

Noah pinched up the creases of his dark suit trousers and lowered himself into an easy chair. "I had hoped your second visit south had mellowed you, Maris. You're as prickly as you were before you left."

"Dad's death didn't change anything between us. Nor did it change your character. You're a liar and an adulterer." She paused a beat before adding, "And possibly those are the least of your sins."

His eyes sharpened. "What does that mean?"

She opened the lap drawer of Daniel's desk and took out a business card. "I came across this in Dad's day planner while I was looking up addresses for acknowledgment cards. It's an innocuous card with a scarcity of information on it. Only a name and telephone number. Curious, I called. Imagine my surprise."

He stared at her, saying nothing, then indolently raised his shoulders in silent inquiry.

"I spoke personally to the man Dad had retained to investigate you," she told him. "Mr. Sutherland conveyed his sympathy over Dad's passing. Then I asked him how his business card had found its way into Dad's day planner. He was very discreet, extremely professional, and finally apologetic.

"Ethically, he couldn't discuss another client's business, even a late client's. However, he said, if I had access to Dad's files, he was sure I'd find his report among them. If I wished to continue the investigation that wasn't yet complete, he would welcome me as a client and offered to apply the advance Dad had paid him to my account."

She spread her arms across the top of the desk. "I've searched for the mentioned report, Noah. It's not here. Not in any of Dad's files here, or at the office, not in the personal safe upstairs in his bedroom closet, or in his safe-deposit box at the bank.

"Coincidentally, you spent time in here the morning before you left for the country. While Dad was upstairs packing some last-minute items, you told Maxine that you had calls to make and came in here, ostensibly to use the telephone. You closed the door behind you. She thought it odd at the time, since you typically use your cell phone, but she thought no more about it. Not until I asked her if you'd been snooping around in Dad's personal things that day."

He shook his head and laughed softly. "Maris, I have no idea what you're talking about. I might have come in here that morning. Frankly, I don't remember if I did or not. But since when is this room off limits to me? From the time we began dating, I've been in this room hundreds of times. When I make private calls I usually close the door. Everybody does. If this is about Nadia—"

"It isn't," she said tersely. "I don't give a damn about Nadia or anyone else you sleep with."

He gave her a look that said he seriously doubted that. She wanted to strike him, to pound the conceit out of his expression. "I also spoke to the authorities in Massachusetts."

"My, my, you've been a busy girl."

"I questioned their ruling that Dad's death was accidental." She hadn't struck him physically, as she would have liked to. All the same, her statement rid him of a measure of arrogance. His smile grew a little stiff, as though it had congealed. His spine straightened. "Honoring my request, they've agreed to reinvestigate. This time they'll be looking for evidence."

That brought him to his feet. "Evidence of what?"

"We have an appointment with Chief of Police Randall tomorrow to discuss their findings," she informed him coldly. "I suggest you be there."

The burg's police department had a staff of six—one chief, four patrolmen, and a clerk who also served as dispatcher and official town gossip. The department handled minor emergencies such as broken-down snowplows and lost pets, parking tickets when tourists passing through stayed too long in an antique shop, and an occasional DUI.

By big-city standards, the gossip wasn't all that scandalous. It might revolve around who had recently gone to New York City for a face-lift, who was selling their country house to a movie star who futilely wished to remain anonymous, and who had checked their daughter-gone-wild into drug rehab after a tempestuous family intervention. Residents could safely leave their homes and cars unlocked because thefts were rare.

The last homicide in the county had occurred during Lyndon Johnson's administration. It had been an open-and-shut case. The culprit had confessed to the killing when police arrived at the scene.

The department's lack of experience as crime solvers worked in Maris's disfavor. But it worked to her advantage in that a murder investigation stimulated more enthusiasm than tacking up notices of a lost kitty or setting up bleachers for the Fourth of July concert and fireworks display.

The officers had approached the investigation of Daniel's death with a zealous desire to sniff out the ruthless killer of an esteemed citizen, even if he was a weekender.

She and Noah drove up in separate cars. The exterior of the ivy-covered building looked more like a yarn-and-woolens boutique than a police station. Maris arrived a few minutes ahead of Noah. As soon as he got there, they were ushered into the chief's office. Both declined an offer of coffee and sweet rolls from the local bakery.

Chief Randall, a ruddy-faced man with a bad, blond comb-over, sensing her desire to cut to the chase, kept the pleasantries to a minimum and settled behind his desk. He seemed more disappointed than relieved to report the outcome of his department's investigation.

"I'm afraid I haven't got all that much more to tell you that wasn't in the initial report, Mrs. Matherly-Reed. My people went over the house with a fine-toothed comb. Didn't find a thing that suggested foul play."

Out of the corner of her eye, she saw Noah complacently fold his hands in his lap.

"The officers think, and I concur, that your father simply fell down the stairs. There were some bloodstains on the floor where he was found, but they're explained by the gash on his scalp. It split open when his head struck the floor."

She swallowed, then asked, "What about the autopsy report?"

He opened the case file and slipped on a pair of reading glasses that were too narrow for his wide face. The stems were stretched and caused the glasses to perch crookedly on his nose. "The contents of his stomach verify that he ate only minutes before he died, which is what Mr. Reed had assumed." He peered at Noah over the eyeglasses.

Noah gave a solemn nod. "When I went into the kitchen to call 911, there were dirty dishes in the sink. I had cleaned up after dinner, so I surmised that Daniel had gone downstairs for something to eat. On his way back up, he fell."

"Is it possible that the scene was staged, Chief Randall?"

"Staged?"

"Perhaps the dishes were placed in the sink to make everyone think Dad had used them."

"Oh, he used them," Chief Randall assured her. "His fingerprints were on them. Nobody else's."

"The dishes could have been used upstairs. He often ate off a bed tray. How do we know he was downstairs?"

"Crumbs."

"Excuse me?"

"Bread crumbs on his robe, his slippers, and on the floor near the sink. My best guess is that he stood and looked out the kitchen window while he ate his sandwich."

Patting his comb-over as though to make sure it was still in place, he referred to the file again. "His blood alcohol level was above the legal driving limit but not by much."

"Any trace of a controlled substance?"

"Only the medications he was taking. We checked out the prescriptions with his physician in New York. Dating from when they were last refilled, the correct amount of dosages remained. There was no sign that a struggle had taken place anywhere in the house."

"You found his cane in his bedroom?"

"Leaning against the nightstand, and yes, we checked it for prints," he said before she could ask. "His were the only ones on it. No evidence of a break-in by an intruder. Not a mark on your father's body except for the cut on his head, which the ME said was consistent with the fall. He also places the time of death within minutes of when Mr. Reed's 911 call was received. That's all documented."

He removed his glasses and rested his clasped hands on top of the binder containing the report. He cleared his throat and looked at her sympathetically. "When a tragic accident like this occurs and someone dies, their loved ones look for reasons. A scapegoat. Something or someone to blame. I know it's hard for you to accept, but it appears that your father ran into some difficulty as he was making his way upstairs. He lost his balance and suffered a fatal fall. I'm sorry, Mrs. Matherly-Reed."

Maris was neither heartened nor disappointed. The findings were exactly what she had expected them to be. She gathered her handbag and stood. Reaching across the desk, she shook hands with the police chief. "I appreciate your time and effort."

"That's what I'm here for. I've put your house on our regular drive-by route. We'll keep a check on it for you."

"That's very thoughtful of you. Thank you."

Once outside, Maris made a beeline for her car. Noah caught up with her before she could get in.

He gripped her upper arm, pulled her around, and pushed his face close to hers. "Satisfied?"

"Completely." Looking at him evenly, she said, "I'm convinced beyond a shadow of doubt that you were the 'difficulty' Dad encountered on his way up the staircase."

His narrow lips stretched into a smile that raised the hair on the back of her neck. "There's absolutely nothing to substantiate these nasty suspicions of yours."

"Let go of my arm, Noah, or I'm going to start screaming bloody murder. That nice chief of police would dearly love to rush to my rescue."

Seeing the wisdom of letting go, he did.

"Chief Randall might be interested to know that my father had retained Mr. William Sutherland to investigate you."

"Which is circumstantial. So where does that get you?"

"Nowhere. You made certain there was no evidence of wrongdoing. But you underestimate my ability to recognize a good plot."

"This isn't a novel."

"Unfortunately. But if it were, I would suspect you of being the villain. Part of my job is to isolate a character's motivation, right? His goal must be clear or the story has no legs on which to stand. Well, Noah, you goal is glaringly apparent. Why did you shuttle Dad off to the country house while I was conveniently out of town, especially since we were separated? Why, when you enjoy being waited on, did you insist that Maxine remain in the city?

"You lied about Nadia. You lied about taking up writing again. What else have you lied about? WorldView? Surely. On that I would bet everything I hold dear. When Morris Blume inadvertently mentioned that secret meeting to me, you finessed your way through an explanation. You had covered your rear by informing Dad of it, on the outside chance that one of us would get wind of it. But I wasn't convinced of your innocence then, and I'm even more certain of your guilt now.

"I think Dad was on to you. Why else would he retain Mr. Sutherland? I think he knew you were dirty-dealing. Maybe he even had proof. When he confronted you with it, you killed him.

"I hope you haven't committed murder in the hope of securing a deal with WorldView. Because if you have, you're going to be sorely disappointed. Understand this, Noah. Matherly Press will remain autonomous, just as it always has been."

"Be very careful, Maris." His voice was low, but it vibrated with menace. He reached up and took a strand of her hair, winding it tightly around his index finger. To anyone passing by who happened to glance at them, it would look like an affectionate gesture. But he pulled the strand of hair taut enough to hurt.

"It's *you* who needs to understand *this*," he said. "Nobody is going to prevent me from having everything I want."

She had been right to fear him the night before she left for Georgia. The latent violence she had sensed in him then hadn't been imagined. She had glimpsed an evil component of Noah that was no longer content to lie dormant.

But, oddly, she was no longer afraid of him. He had lost the power to intimidate or frighten her. She laughed softly. "What are you going to do, Noah? Push me down a staircase, too?"

"Daniel alone was responsible for his death. He lost his temper, reacted recklessly, temporarily forgot his physical limitations, and suffered the consequences. If you want to place blame, place it on him. But," he continued silkily, "I'll admit that his death was very convenient."

She recoiled and, because he still had hold of her hair, the sudden movement caused a painful yank on her scalp. It was sharp enough to bring tears to her eyes. But she hardly noticed. Because the yank on her memory had been even sharper.

Actually, her death was very convenient.

She'd read that line a dozen or more times. It was a key piece of dialogue, so she had dwelled on it. She had played with ideas on how the statement could be improved or enhanced, but after trying several changes she had concluded that it didn't need improving or enhancing. It was perfect as it was. Its cold candor was deliberate. It made the statement all the more shocking. Parker had used that simple sentence to provide a revealing sneak peek into the dark soul of the character. Realization slammed into her.

"You're Todd."

Noah's chin went back. "What? Who?"

Thoughts were snapping and popping in her mind like a sail in a high wind, but one thought isolated itself and became jarringly clear: This could not be a coincidence.

With more ferocity than she believed herself capable of, she said, "For the last time, Noah, let go of me."

"Of course, darling." He uncoiled her hair from around his finger. "You're free to go. Now that we understand one another."

She slid into the driver's seat and started the motor. Before pulling the door closed, she said, "You have no idea how well I understand you."

"Envy" Ch. 22
Key West, Florida, 1988

It was one of those days when the words simply would not come.

Roark pressed his skull between his hands, squeezing it like a melon, trying to force the words out through his pores. To no avail. He came up dry. So far today, he had contributed exactly two and one-half sentences to his manuscript. Nineteen words total. For the past three hours, his cursor had been stuck in the same spot, winking at him.

"Mocking little bastard," he whispered to it now.

Deliberately he typed, *The grass is green. The sky is blue.* "See, you son of a bitch? I can write a sentence when I want to."

It made little difference that yesterday, his day off from the club, had been a productive one. He had put in sixteen hard hours of writing, going without food or drink and taking bathroom breaks only when absolutely forced. He had over twenty pages to show for his labors. But the euphoria had lasted only until he awakened this morning to discover that evil spirits had sneaked in during the night while he slept and robbed him of yesterday's talent. What other explanation could there be for its overnight disappearance?

His frustration was such that he considered shutting down for the day, taking in a movie, or going to the beach, or getting in some fishing. But that kind of retreat was easily habit-forming. It was too convenient to surrender to a momentary block. It might become a permanent block, and that was the dreadful possibility that kept him shackled to his chair, staring into a blank screen while being taunted by a blinking cursor that didn't go any-goddamn-where.

"Roark!"

The door slammed three floors below and Todd's running footsteps echoed in the stairwell. Lately, he had been working through the restaurant's lunch hours to earn extra money. Roark welcomed the time Todd was out, when he was left alone in the apartment to write without the distraction that even having another warm body nearby could create.

He turned around in time to see Todd barge through their door. "What's up? Is the building on fire? I wish."

"I sold it."

"Your car?" That was the first thing that popped into Roark's head. Todd was constantly bitching about his car.

"My book! I sold my book!" His cheeks were flushed, his eyes were feverishly bright, his smile was toothpaste-commercial caliber.

Roark just looked at him, dumbfounded.

"Did you hear what I said?" Todd's voice scaled upward to an abnormally shrill pitch. "I sold my manuscript."

Unsteadily Roark came to his feet. "I . . . th-that's great. I didn't even know you . . . When did you submit it?"

Todd somehow managed to look abashed while maintaining his wide grin. "I didn't tell you. I sent it on a whim about two months ago. I didn't want to make a big deal of it because I was afraid— Jesus, I was *positive*—I'd get another rejection letter. Then today, just now, less than an hour ago, I got this call at work."

"The publisher had your work number?"

"Well, yeah. In my cover letter, I listed every conceivable way they could contact me. Just in case, you know? Anyway, the manager of the club, that fag we hate, prances over and tells me someone wants me on the phone in his office. He says that personal calls aren't allowed and to please limit the conversation to three minutes. Like we were busy," he snorted.

"I hadn't parked a car in half an hour. I figured it was you or one of the babes calling." To Todd, their neighbors had collectively become "the babes." "Overflowing toilet or something, you know? But instead, *instead,* this guy identifies himself as an editor, says he's read my manuscript, says it blew him away. Those words. 'It blew me away.' Says he wants to publish it. I nearly shit right there, man.

"Then, for a heartbeat or two, I thought you or somebody, maybe the fag we hate, was jacking with me, you know, playing a trick. But no, this editor goes on and on about my story, calls the characters by name. Says he's willing to offer in the neighborhood of high five figures, but I'm sure that was only his starting point. As much as he raved over the book, there's got to be wiggle room to up the ante."

Suddenly he puffed out his cheeks, then emptied them like a bellows. "Listen to me, will ya?" he chortled. "Holy shit! It hasn't even sunk in yet. I'm standing here talking about negotiating an advance, but I haven't even grasped it yet. I've sold a book!"

Roark, forcing himself to move, forcing elation into his expression, crossed the room and gave Todd a mighty hug, thumping him on the back, lifting him off the floor, congratulating him in the spirit of a good fraternity brother and colleague. "Congratulations, man. You've worked hard for this. You deserve it."

"Thanks, Roark."

Todd pushed him back, looked him square in the eye, and stuck out his hand. They shook hands, but the solemnity was short-lived. Within seconds Todd was whooping like an air-raid siren and bouncing around the apartment with the jerky, disjointed hyperactivity of a rhesus on speed.

"I don't know what to do first," he said, laughing.

"Call Hadley," Roark suggested.

"Hadley can go fuck himself. He didn't show any confidence in me. Why should I share my good news with him? I know," he said, vigorously rubbing his hands together. "A celebration. Blowout party. You and me. On me."

Roark, feeling less like celebrating than he ever had in his life, was already shaking his head. "You don't have to—"

"I know I don't have to. I want to. Tonight. I'll make all the arrangements."

"I've got to work."

"Screw work."

"Easy for you to say. You've sold a book. For high five figures with wiggle room."

The statements jerked a knot in the rhesus's tail. Todd stopped bouncing and turned toward Roark. He treated him to several moments of hard scrutiny. "Oh. Now I get it. You're pissed because I sold before you did."

"No, I'm not."

"Well, that's good," Todd said sarcastically. "Because if you were pissed, you might be acting like a jackass instead of my best friend on the happiest day of my life."

True. He was acting like a jackass. Rank jealousy had turned him into a prick, and he was running headlong toward ruining the happiest day of his best friend's life.

Not that it would be any different if the situation were reversed. Todd would behave just as badly, probably worse. He would sulk and mouth about life's injustices. He would be resentful and caustic, and then he'd turn cruel.

But since when was Todd Grayson his standard for good behavior? He liked to think he was a finer person and better friend than Todd. He liked to think he had a stronger character and more integrity.

He plastered on a fake grin. "What the hell, I'll call in sick. Let that fag we hate fire me. What time's the party start?"

* * *

Todd said to give him time to make a few arrangements, and Roark said fine because he needed to close out his work for the day anyway. As soon as Todd flew out to run his errands, Roark surrendered to his dejection. It set in with a vengeance.

He stared into his computer screen, wondering why he had been cursed with a burning desire to do something creative but shortchanged the ability and opportunity to do it. Why would God play a dirty trick like that? Entice you with a dream, provide you with enough talent to make it appear reachable, then keep the dream just this side of being realized?

Like a mantra, he repeated to himself how happy he was over Todd's success. And he was. He *was.* But he also resented it. He resented the sneakiness with which Todd had submitted his manuscript. They hadn't made a pact to inform each other whenever they submitted work, but it had certainly been their habit. Todd hadn't actually violated a sacred agreement, but that's what it felt like.

Uncharitably, Roark wanted to attribute Todd's success to luck, fluky timing, a slow book market, even to an editor with lousy taste, all the while acknowledging that such thoughts were unfair. Todd had worked hard. He was a talented writer. He was dedicated to the craft. He deserved to be published.

But Roark earnestly felt that he deserved it more.

Todd returned within an hour bringing a bottle of champagne for each of them and insisting that they drink them before moving to phase two of the celebration.

Phase two included Mary Catherine. One Sunday afternoon shortly after her miscarriage, Roark had taken her out for ice cream. Seeing the promenade of young couples with babies had caused her to get weepy. She confided that Todd had fathered the embryo she lost.

"Son of a bitch must've had a sixth sense about it. He's avoided me ever since."

Months went by. The two were civil to one another but cool.

Eventually they reestablished themselves as friends but only friends. To Roark's knowledge they hadn't slept together again. He assumed by tacit agreement.

Today, the rift and the cause for it were distant memories. Wearing three postage-stamp-sized patches of electric-blue fabric that passed for a bikini, Mary Catherine arrived ready to party. She got there just in time to help them polish off the champagne.

"Foul!" she cried petulantly. "I only got two swallows."

"There's more where that came from, sweetheart." Todd rubbed her ass and smacked his lips, first with appreciation, then regret. He turned her around and gave her a gentle push toward Roark. "She's all yours tonight, pal. Don't say I never gave you anything."

"Consolation prize?" The good-natured question had only a trace of an edge.

"Can you imagine a better one?"

Mary Catherine looped her arms around Roark's neck, mashed her breasts against his chest, and massaged his crotch with hers. "Fine by me. I've had a lech for you for a long time." She poked her tongue into his mouth.

Courtesy of the champagne, he had a lively buzz going. She tasted good. She felt damn good. He liked her. He had sustained a blow to his ego, and Todd was trying to make it up to him. He'd be an asshole to decline his friend's gesture of condolence.

He applied himself to kissing her.

"Hey," Todd said after a few moments. "Am I gonna have to turn the water hose on you two?"

Laughing, they clomped downstairs and piled into Todd's much-maligned car. He drove them to a marina where he had chartered a boat from an old salt named Hatch Walker. They'd leased boats from him before. His rates were the cheapest in Key West, and he got only mildly abusive if you stretched your contract time and came in late.

Walker wasn't long on charm anytime, but today he was particularly querulous. He was wary of turning one of his boats over to three people who had obviously been drinking. Roark was just drunk enough on champagne—and wildly aroused because on the drive to the marina, Mary Catherine had given him a private lap dance in the passenger seat—not to care about the old man's opinion of them or the amount of their alcohol intake.

As soon as the rental agreement was signed, Todd jumped aboard and climbed the steps to the pilot's chair. Roark staggered aboard, then turned to lend a hand to Mary Catherine, who managed to stumble against him as she stepped onto the deck. "Oopsy-daisy," she giggled as she squirmed against him. She gave old Hatch a gay little wave as he untied the ropes from the cleats and tossed them onto the deck.

"Crazy kids," he muttered.

"I don't think he likes us," Mary Catherine whined.

"What I think is, you have on too many clothes."

Roark reached around to untie her top. She shrieked and slapped at his hands, but the protests were all for show. Roark came away with her bikini top and waved it like a banner above his head as Todd slowly guided the boat out of the marina. As soon as the craft cleared the channel, he gave it full throttle and it shot into the Atlantic.

Todd had proclaimed this would be a celebration none of them would ever forget and obviously he meant it. Roark was surprised by his friend's extravagance. The coolers he had brought onboard were stocked with brand-name liquors. The food came from a deli that had the self-confidence to call itself Delectables.

"This is a mean shrimp salad." Roark licked spiced mayonnaise from the corner of his lips.

"Let me do that." Mary Catherine straddled his lap and sponged away the mayo with her tongue. She had taken her role as consolation prize to heart, devoting herself entirely to entertaining him and granting his every wish. That or converting him into a hedonist. Either way, he wasn't fighting it.

The shared secret of the miscarriage had forged a special bond between them. When they were alone he called her Sheila. She'd given up on the mermaid idea as impractical because "the tail would probably be itchy." But she was considering a chambermaid routine and had asked him to come up with a catchy name for her.

Although they flirted frequently and outrageously, the friendship had remained platonic. She'd made subtle overtures, but Roark had pretended not to notice them because he hadn't wanted to mess up a good friendship.

But as she sucked at his lips, he asked himself what would be so terrible about altering their friendship to include sex. Be friends with Sheila, but don't have sex with Mary Catherine. Who wrote the rule that you couldn't be both friend and lover?

Why not make happy with the iron hard-on he was sporting, compliments of her incredible proportions and her agile tongue and her hands, which were keeping themselves busy inside his swim trunks?

Maybe Todd had paid for her services today. So what? She was a good kid, trying to make a decent living using the assets she'd been given.

It was also possible that she was coming on to him only to make Todd jealous. He wouldn't let that bother him, either. In fact, he wasn't going to let anything bother him tonight.

Fuck writing. Fuck getting published. Fuck words that wouldn't come.

Fuck Mary Catherine. That topped his things-to-do list. Definitely. He was sick to death of being such a damn Boy Scout. Nose to the grindstone all the time. For what? For freaking *nothing*, that's what.

He was going to eat this rich food until he puked on it. He was going to get slobbery drunk. He was going to let Mary Catherine perform on him every debauched act in her extensive repertoire. He was going to have a good time tonight if it killed him.

Roark woke up with Mary Catherine draped across him. After a bout of rowdy copulation in the small berth, they had both passed out. Thirsty and needing badly to pee, he wiggled out from under her. She moaned a garbled objection and reached out to hold him back, but it was a halfhearted effort.

He successfully extricated himself and retrieved his trunks from the floor. It required some challenging concentration and a few fumbling attempts, but he finally managed to get his feet into the legs.

He was still pulling on the trunks as he stumbled up the steps to the deck. Todd had a bottle of Bacardi cradled in his arm and was staring at the constellations. Hearing Roark, he turned and smiled. "You survived?"

He stretched out the elastic waistband of his trunks and peered into them. "All parts present and accounted for, sir."

Todd chuckled. "Judging from the racket, there were times I thought I might have to come down there and rescue you."

"There were times when *I* thought you might have to." He relieved himself over the side of the craft.

Todd asked, "Did she do that thing with her thumb?"

Roark tucked himself back into his trunks, turned, smiled, but said nothing.

"Oh. I forgot. Sir Roark never shares the juicy details. A real gallant."

Roark was about to bow at the waist but figured that in his present condition that might be a tricky move, so he settled for a clumsy salute.

Todd motioned toward one of the ice chests. "Help yourself to a fresh bottle."

"Thanks, but I'm still too wasted to stand."

"And jealous."

Roark used one arm to brace himself against the exterior wall of the cabin. "Huh?"

"You're jealous."

Roark shrugged. "Maybe." He gave a weak grin. "Okay, a little."

"More than a little, Roark. More than a little." Todd raised the rum bottle to his eye like a telescope and peered down the length of it at Roark. "Admit it, you thought you'd be the first to sell."

Roark's stomach was queasy. The horizon was seesawing. He was also uncomfortable with the direction the conversation had taken. "Todd, I couldn't be happier."

"Oh, yeah, you could. If you'd sold your book today, you'd be a hell of a lot happier. So would Hadley. I think he probably jacks off over your manuscripts. Your work makes him positively giddy, doesn't it? What was that he said about it being an honor and privilege to review your work?" He took a swig of rum. "Something like that."

"You read his letter to me?"

"Clever of you to get that post office box, but careless of you to leave his letter in the pocket of your jeans. I was short the cash to pay for a pizza delivery and saw your jeans lying in the floor where you'd stepped out of them. Raided the pockets looking for money, and . . . pulled out a plum."

"You shouldn't have read my mail."

"You shouldn't have lied to me about Hadley's enthusiasm for your work and his lack of it for mine."

"What do you care what Hadley thinks of your work?"

"I don't. Last laugh is on him and you. I've sold. You haven't."

"So fine. Let's just drop it."

"No. I don't believe I will."

Todd stood up slowly. He was steadier on his feet than he should have been, leaving Roark to question if he had drunk as much as he had pretended to. He moved along the deck with a predatory, malevolent tread.

"What's eating you, Todd? You won. Hadley was wrong."

"Maybe about my writing. Not about the other."

"Other?"

"My character. Remember how flawed I am? Driven by greed and jealousy and envy. Those undesirable character traits about which Hadley waxed poetic."

Roark's stomach heaved and he swallowed a throatful of sour bile. "That's all bullshit. I didn't pay any attention to it."

"Well, I did."

He didn't see it coming. Moving sinuously only a second before, Todd now lunged at him and took a vicious swing at his head with the liquor bottle. Roark caught it on the temple, and if it had been a sledgehammer, it couldn't have hurt any worse. He roared in pain and outrage.

But he had enough wits to see the bottle arcing once again above his head. He dodged it just in time to spare himself another concussion. Instead it shattered against the wall of the cabin, showering them with broken glass and rum.

Todd attacked with a fury then, throwing blows one right after the other aimed at Roark's face and head. Most of them connected, crunching cartilage and splitting skin. Dazed but fueled by anger, Roark struck back. He landed a fist against Todd's mouth and felt the scrape of teeth against his knuckles. It hurt, but it hurt Todd more. His mouth gushed blood.

The drawing of blood was a primal and powerful exhilaration. At any other time Roark would have been astonished over how much satisfaction he derived from making Todd bleed. Propelled by jealousy, he wanted to see more of Todd's blood on his hands. He wanted to punish him for succeeding first and making him feel like a failure.

But his hot rage was tepid compared to Todd's. Todd's bloodlust had escalated into savagery. With feral growls, he came at Roark, clawing and pounding.

Roark's temper was soon spent. He was ready to back off, cool down, and call a truce.

Todd was beyond that. He didn't let up, not even when Roark stopped being aggressive and only deflected blows in order to protect himself.

"Goddammit, enough!"

"Never enough." Todd's clenched teeth were smeared with blood. Bubbles of it foamed over his lips. "Never enough."

And he launched a fresh attack.

"Wha'sgoin'on?" Mary Catherine appeared in the open doorway of the cabin, naked except for a golden ankle bracelet. Ignored, she drunkenly staggered onto the deck and stepped on a piece of broken glass. "Ow! What the fuck is going on?"

"Shut up!"

Todd rounded on her and struck a blow that caught her at waist level. Favoring her bleeding foot, she was already off balance. His blow sent her reeling backward. The chrome side railing caught her in the back of her knees. Arms windmilling, she went overboard with a scream that died as soon as she hit the water.

Roark stared at the empty space she'd left at the boat's railing and sobered instantly. "She's too drunk to swim!"

He executed a shallow dive into the water. The salt water seared the open wounds on his face and he came up gasping. He was fighting nausea from too much liquor and what he knew must be a concussion where he'd been hit with the bottle.

But all this hardly registered. Treading water, he blinked his eyes as clear as he could get them and frantically searched the surface of the dark water for a sign of Mary Catherine.

"Do you see her?" he yelled up at Todd, who was standing on the deck looking down at him, blood dripping from his chin onto his smooth chest. "Todd? Christ, did you hear me? Do you see her?"

"No."

"Turn on the lights."

Todd just stood there staring into the water, apparently shocked into immobility.

"Shit."

Heart pounding, head bursting, Roark jackknifed beneath the surface. Although it stung like crazy, he kept his eyes open. But it didn't matter. He might just as well have been swimming through a bottle of ink. He couldn't even see his own hands as he waved them about, searching blindly, hoping to make contact with a limb, skin, hair.

He stayed under until he couldn't stand the burning in his lungs an instant longer. Breaking the surface, he took a huge gulp of air. He was surprised to see how far he had swum away from the boat. At least Todd had shaken off his stupor and turned on the underwater lights. They cast an eerie green glow around the craft, but they didn't penetrate nearly far enough.

Although his arms and legs felt like lead and his brain seemed to have relinquished control of them, Roark began swimming toward the boat. Todd was doing something on the port side. Hope surged inside Roark's chest. He shouted, "Did you find her? Is she over there?"

Todd returned to the starboard side. "No luck?"

Luck? This wasn't a fishing trip. What was the matter with him? "Call the Coast Guard. I can't find her. Oh, Jesus." He sobbed when the full impact of the situation hit him. She might be dead already. Mary Catherine—Sheila—might have drowned because of his inability to save her.

"Call the Coast Guard," he repeated before diving beneath the surface again.

Knowing it was futile, he pushed himself through the seawater, eyes open but seeing nothing, hands groping but feeling nothing. Still, he was unwilling to give up. If there was the slimmest chance that she was hanging on, clinging to life, desperate for help . . .

Again and again he went down, coming up only long enough to take a breath before going down again, diving so deep it made his ears hurt.

He struggled to the surface one last time, fearing that he wouldn't make it, afraid that he had made one foray too many. At last he tasted air. Greedily he sucked it into his lungs. He couldn't survive another submersion. He was too tired even to swim the distance between him and the boat. Weakly he treaded water, barely able to keep himself afloat.

"Todd," he called hoarsely. "Todd."

Todd appeared at the rail. Roark's eyes had been scoured by the salt water. His vision was cloudy. "I can't find her. I can't look anymore. Throw me the preserver."

Todd left to get the preserver, and Roark wondered vaguely why he hadn't had it ready.

Exhausted, he longed to close his burning eyes but was afraid that if he did he would slip beneath the surface and drown before he could garner the energy to save himself. But his eyes must have closed on their own. He must have been only a heartbeat away from losing consciousness, because he was startled awake when the boat's motor roared to life.

Todd shouldn't be starting the motor. He should be throwing him a life preserver. If the Coast Guard had been given the co-ordinates of their location, they should stay in that spot until help arrived. It was damn stupid to start up an outboard with Mary Catherine and him in the water this close to the boat.

These thoughts flashed through his mind in a nanosecond, not in individual words, but as fully formed and intact conclusions. "Todd, what are you doing?"

He kicked his legs and feebly moved his arms in a parody of swim strokes, but it was like trying to push Jell-O through quicksand. But there was no need to try and swim after all. Look. Todd was bringing the boat to him.

Only thing, he was running it too hot and too fast for safety. "Hey!"

It was a nightmare's yell, when you open your mouth and try to scream but you can't utter a sound and that intensifies the horror of the nightmare. He tried to wave his arms, but they weighed a thousand pounds apiece. He couldn't even lift them out of the water.

"Todd," he croaked. "Turn to port! I'm here! Can't you see me?"

He could see him. He was looking straight at him through the plastic windshield that protected the cockpit. Control panel lights were making a Halloween mask of his bruised and swelling face. His eyes glowed red. Torches of hell.

Roark screamed one last time before fear sent him plunging beneath the surface. In seconds he was engulfed in churning, strangling waters. Then the terror gripped him. Undiluted ter-ror. The kind that few men ever have the misfortune of experiencing. Terror so absolute that death seems a blessing.

Terror championed only by pain. Excruciating and immeasurable.

Pain that splinters the body but slays the soul.

Nadia arrived at the martini bar wearing a snug black dress with a deceptively demure neckline and a cocktail hat, one of those saucy numbers with a veil that covered half her face. A black feathered handbag hung from her shoulder on a slender gold chain. Very fetching. Very femme fatale.

Heads turned as she made her way through the bar. It was packed with Manhattan's in crowd and wannabes. People spoke to her as she passed by. She waved to a party of three seated at a corner table.

When she reached Noah's table, he was inflated with pride that the most exquisite woman in the room was joining him. He embraced her warmly but circumspectly. Pecking a friendly kiss on her cheek, he whispered, "I could fuck you right here."

"Ever the romantic." She slid into the banquette beside him.

"Martini?"

"By all means."

He placed their order with the waiter who had rushed to the table within seconds of Nadia's arrival, then turned to her with a smile. "You're known here."

"I'm known everywhere."

He laughed at her conceit. "I've missed your sharp come-backs. It's been far too long since I've seen you."

"That silly quarrel."

"Ancient history now." He inhaled deeply. "Ahh. Your provocative scent."

"Chanel."

He shook his head and grinned slyly. "Sex. Too bad you can't bottle it. You'd make a fortune." His adoring gaze moved over her face. "You look sensational. I like the veil."

"Thank you."

"It lends you a mysterious air that's incredibly sexy." Beneath the table, he pressed her thigh with his.

"You're coming on awfully strong tonight. You haven't been getting any, have you?"

"I've been otherwise occupied."

"Yes, you have." She seemed to become fascinated with the layered arrangement of the feathers on her handbag. She ran her finger over the smooth, iridescent plumes. "You've been busy laying your father-in-law to rest."

"What a lot of folderol."

"I thought the eulogies were rather moving."

"It was the kind of send-off Daniel Matherly merited, I suppose. I'm just glad it's over. Now the rest of us can stop applauding his life and resume living our own."

"Ordinarily you enjoy being in the limelight. I thought the role of loyal and bereaved son-in-law would have appealed to you."

He laid his hand over his heart. "I did my best." Their martinis arrived. They clinked glasses, sipped. "Actually, it wasn't all that bad, except for having to keep Maris's hysteria at bay."

"Wasn't it natural for her to be upset?"

"Her behavior went beyond normal grief." She gave up her study of the feathers and looked at him. "My wife got the hare-brained notion that I was responsible for her father's fall." He peered past the veil into Nadia's eyes. "Can you imagine that?"

She raised the martini glass to her lips. "Yes. I can."

The steadiness of her gaze was a bit unnerving. He deliberately mistook her meaning. "Maris has always been excitable and reactionary, but this time she carried it to the extreme."

"At the funeral, she seemed the picture of composure."

"True. But once it was over, she lost all reason. She coerced the local police in Massachusetts to reinvestigate the fatal accident."

"And?"

"Naturally they found nothing to substantiate her suspicions."

"How lucky for you."

"Luck had nothing to do with it, Nadia."

"I'm sure that's true." She stared out over the crowd, speaking almost to herself. "If you had pushed the old gentleman down the staircase, you would be shrewd enough not to get caught."

"I didn't. But you're right. I would be shrewd enough not to get caught. And that's why you like me so well."

She turned back to him. "True. I would never become involved with a loser. I wouldn't hitch my wagon to a falling star. Only to one that's ascending."

"We're so much alike it's frightening." Leaning closer to her, he added confidentially, "At least it should be frightening to everyone else." Complacently he took another sip of his martini. "Anyhow, Daniel's dead and buried. That's the good news."

"For God's sake, Noah." She glanced around as though fearing that he'd been overheard. "What's the bad?"

"Not bad, darling. Better. His death was the final nail in the coffin of my marriage. It is now beyond repair."

She raised her glass to toast him. "Congratulations or condolences?"

"Definitely the former. Because I have even better news than that."

"I can hardly wait."

"Are you sure you want me to tell you here and now? It may bring on an orgasm."

"Have you ever known me to turn down an opportunity like that?"

His smile widened. "Before his accidental fall, I persuaded Daniel to sign an important power-of-attorney document. It enables me to sell Matherly Press to WorldView, and Maris can't do a damn thing about it."

Nadia's eyes went wide with bewilderment. "But Matherly Press isn't yours to sell."

"Nadia! There you are!" Morris Blume suddenly materialized on the other side of the table.

Noah hadn't noticed his approach, and he didn't welcome the intrusion. His plan for this evening had been to wine, dine, and romance Nadia back into his good graces. Before proceeding with WorldView, he wanted her well entrenched in his cheering section. He needed good press, and no one could provide that better than Nadia.

Of all the damn luck, running into Morris Blume. World-View's CEO looked as colorless as ever in a gray suit, gray shirt, silver tie. To Noah, even his teeth and gums looked unhealthily gray as he smiled down at them.

"I didn't see you at first and thought there'd been a mix-up on the time," he was saying to Nadia.

"Your timing couldn't be more perfect."

She scooted from behind the table and, to Noah's dismay, walked into Blume's embrace. They locked lips. When the kiss ended, she affectionately patted his necktie back into place.

Blume appraised her from hat to heels. "You look positively gorgeous."

"I'm glad you think so. I bought the ensemble with you in mind."

"Sensational."

His compliment caused her to simper in a coquettish way

that was totally unlike Nadia. Blume was stroking her waist with suggestive familiarity. Her pelvis was tilted against his, a specialty of Nadia's that made a man think of nothing except his dick and planting it inside her.

For all the attention they were paying him, Noah might just as well have been one of the pop art paintings on the wall. His whole body throbbed with anger. And something else, something rare to him—humiliation. People had noticed that Nadia was now snuggling with Blume. He'd lost the most popular girl at the party to a bloodless, bald geek.

"Ready for a drink, darling?" she asked him.

"You read my mind. You always do."

Nadia signaled the waiter, who scurried over and took Blume's order. She didn't return to sit beside Noah on the banquette, but took the chair Blume was holding for her. They now faced him across the table.

She sat as close to Blume as possible without actually sharing the same chair. Her breast was making itself cozy beneath his arm. Blume's hand was on her thigh—high on her thigh. Proprietary.

Noah was certain that these public displays of affection were for his benefit. Nadia was being deliberately seductive. She was gloating. It made him want to reach across the table and slap the shit out of her.

She had set him up. She had planned this little scenario. He had called her on his drive back from Massachusetts—following that pathetic attempt of Maris's to incriminate him—and had invited her to join him this evening. "We're free to be seen together now," he had told her.

Nadia had been her sexy self, every word suggestive, every breath an erotic promise. She had named the time and place as though she couldn't wait to see him. Instead, he'd walked into a goddamn female trap.

Okay. If she wanted to flaunt her new boyfriend in front of him, fine. It didn't change anything—except that her sex life would take a severe downward plunge. Judging by Blume's pallid coloring, getting blood to his penis would be a chore.

After thanking the waiter for his drink, Blume turned to Noah. "My secretary told me that you called today requesting a meeting."

"That's right. In light of my recent family tragedy—"

"My condolences, by the way."

"Thank you." He brushed an invisible speck off the cuff of his shirt. "Daniel's death imposed a temporary postponement of our schedule. Now we're able to pick up where we left off. You're going to be very pleased by the developments that have taken place since we last spoke. What's your schedule like tomorrow?"

"I really don't see the need for a meeting now."

"Now" was a troubling adverb. "Now" indicated that circumstances had undergone a change. Noah avoided looking at Nadia and kept his features carefully schooled. "Why is that?"

"Noah and I were getting to this when you joined us, Morris," Nadia said. "Apparently there's been some confusion." She gave Noah a pained look. "I'm terribly embarrassed."

"Well, since I seem to be the only one in the dark here, perhaps you'll enlighten me."

She glanced toward Blume as though asking his advice, but he merely shrugged. Pulling her lower lip through her teeth, she turned back to Noah. "I thought someone would have told you by now. Out of respect for Daniel, I've been sitting on this story for a week."

Noah was growing uncomfortably warm inside his clothes. One martini couldn't account for the sweat trickling down his ribs. He felt like a man about to hear the result of a biopsy on testicular tissue. "What story?"

Taking center stage, Nadia readjusted herself even closer to Blume. "Out of the blue, Daniel Matherly invited me to his house for breakfast. It was the same morning you left for the country. Who could have guessed that your retreat would end so tragically? I wish I'd had the foresight then to urge him not to go." She looked squarely at Noah and let that sink in.

"Anyhow," she said, shaking her head slightly as though to get back on track, "he gave me a scoop, but asked me to sit on it for a few days, at least until Maris returned from Georgia."

Blume was gazing at Nadia as though he might begin sucking on her neck at any moment. She was absently stroking the back of his hand still resting on her thigh. Noah forced himself to smile. "You still haven't told me the nature of this exclusive story."

"Daniel appointed Maris as chairman and CEO of Matherly Press. I thought perhaps Daniel would tell you while you were away together in the country. No? Well . . . he probably thought it only fair that Maris be informed first."

Eyeing him closely, she ran her fingers up and down the stem of her martini glass. "You had led me to believe that Daniel Matherly was borderline senile. Having talked with him at length, I found the opposite to be the case. He was in total command of his faculties. He knew exactly what he was doing."

Every capillary in Noah's body had expanded. Behind his eyeballs, his eardrums, behind every square inch of skin, he could feel the increased pressure of his pulse. Somehow he managed to smile. "Daniel didn't think too highly of you, Nadia. I think he played a cruel practical joke on you."

"The possibility crossed my mind. He was known to be cagey. So I had the story corroborated by a Mr. Stern, the Matherlys' attorney. He verified it. Maris's appointment is irrevocable and incontestable. Her authority can be revoked only if she chooses to resign."

Noah pried loose his tongue from the roof of his mouth where it had become stuck. "I'm curious as to why you didn't mention this to me earlier, Nadia. For instance when we spoke earlier today." *Or the night I talked to you by phone from the country,* he thought. The bitch had known then. She had been amusing herself with him.

"It wasn't my place."

"But now it is?"

"I'm sparing you having to read it in my column. The story runs tomorrow." She gave him a sympathetic smile. "Honestly, Noah, I thought that by now you would have been officially informed. I suppose that since your marriage is over, you're no longer in the inner circle. You're only hired help."

"Would you like another drink, Noah?"

"No, thank you, Morris. I'm late for another appointment." If he didn't get out of here, away from Nadia, he was either going to kill her or explode. He'd rather not do either in front of witnesses.

"Oh, please stay," Nadia said in a cajoling voice. "We've got so much to celebrate. One of Morris's fondest desires has been fulfilled. WorldView has acquired Becker-Howe. You know Oliver Howe, I'm sure, because he and Daniel were old friends. In fact, it was Daniel who put Morris in contact with him. Daniel knew that WorldView was shopping for a publishing house and that, unlike him, Ollie Howe would welcome their interest."

"I had my heart set on Matherly Press," Blume said. "But since Maris will be at the helm—"

"I felt it only fair to tell him," Nadia interjected.

"And Maris has made absolutely clear her intention never to sell it, so I decided to acquire another company."

Noah was clenching his jaw so tightly it ached. "How nice for you."

"I paid too much for it, but what the hell?" he chuckled. "It's a profitable outfit. We'll easily earn back our investment. Becker-Howe is only slightly smaller than Matherly Press. But not for long." He winked at Noah. "I'll be your competitor now. Watch out."

And the horse you rode in on, you bloodless son of a bitch, Noah thought. He made a show of checking his wristwatch. "I really hate to break up the party, but I must get on my way."

"Wait! That's not the only good news." Nadia thrust her left hand across the table. "You failed to notice—or were too polite to mention—that I'm wearing an obscenely enormous diamond ring. Morris and I are getting married next Sunday at the Plaza." She beamed at Morris, then turned back to Noah. "Three o'clock. We'll be crushed if you're not there."

*D*amn *Michael Strother.*

Cursing his friend—former friend, it appeared—was the only fresh thought in Parker's mind. Angrily he switched off his computer, concluding another unproductive session of writing. He had sat all day, hands poised above the keyboard, waiting for a burst of inspiration that never came. It was a condition that was recurring with alarming frequency.

He had been working on the next Mackensie Roone book. Deck Cayton had turned into a real dullard with nothing clever to say. He was no longer roguish or engaging. The villain wasn't innately evil; he was a caricature. And the girl . . . Parker didn't like the girl, either. She was shallow and stupid.

He hadn't heard from Mike since he had announced his resignation and left the house. He hadn't composed a readable sentence since then, either. The old man must have put a hex on him, something he'd learned from the Gullahs who lived on the southern tip of St. Anne. Mike had been fascinated by their language and customs, which had been passed from generation to generation dating back to their African ancestry. Parker dismissed spells and potions and such as hogwash. But maybe there was something to them after all.

When Mike was there, Parker had constantly sought solitude and silence in which to write. But it was amazing how much he missed having the old man puttering around. He found himself subconsciously listening for Mike's footsteps or the clang of pots and pans in the kitchen, the closing of a door, the whirr of the vacuum cleaner somewhere in the house. The sounds would be welcome distractions now. Comforts. Because he felt terribly alone.

Years back, while he lay in hospital wards with strangers in neighboring beds, being attended by capable but impersonal nurses, he had felt utterly friendless. Completely alone. That's when Hatred became his companion. His imaginary friend. His security blanket.

Through the years that followed, there were times when Hatred was an exhausting sidekick. Particularly after he'd succeeded with the mystery series, he grew tired of it constantly hanging around, never going home. It grew to be a nuisance. He wished to be rid of it.

Sometimes he kicked it around, hoping that it would leave of its own accord, but it never did. It stayed, and he could never bring himself to abandon it. Instead, he had fed it daily, keeping it loyal to him, until his relationship with it became codependent. It needed him to survive. He needed it for motivation.

Now Mike was gone, and he was left again with only Hatred, his trusty but parasitical ally.

He was feeling awfully sorry for himself, but the irony didn't escape him. His misery was self-imposed. "Poor you. But look at it this way, Parker," he whispered to himself. "The end is in sight."

The last die had been cast when he sent the *Envy* manuscript to Noah. It was too late now for second-guessing. One way or another it would soon be over and he'd have closure. Everything he had done, said, or written in the past fourteen years had been with this goal in mind. It all funneled down to here and now.

Whatever the outcome, whether in his favor or not, it hadn't come cheaply. He had achieved worldwide acclaim, yet no one knew his name. He had sacrificed fame in exchange for anonymity. He had money but nothing to spend it on. He owned a beautiful house, but it wasn't a home. He shared the empty rooms with only a hanging man's ghost. His need for vengeance had cost him his one true friend. Ultimately it had cost him Maris.

He missed her with a physical ache. If he were a woman or a child, he would cry himself to sleep each night. He moved through the house touching things he had seen her touch, inhaling deeply in the hope of catching a whiff of her fragrance. He was pathetic, as daffy as Professor Hadley's jilted aunt who lived in the attic with only bittersweet memories and her fear of fresh fruit.

Maris had been essential to his plot, but he hadn't expected her to become essential to him. In the brief time she had been in his life, she had become the most important element of it.

Second most important, he corrected.

If she were the most important, he would leave Noah to the devil as Mike had advised and spend the rest of his life loving her and letting himself be loved. At night when he couldn't sleep, he'd get downright sappy. He envisioned them on the beach, tossing a stick to a golden retriever and supervising a couple of sturdy, laughing kids building a sand castle. A greeting-card tableau. A Kodak commercial.

Too often for his mental health, he relived making love to her. God, it had been sweet. But perhaps the sweetest part had been holding her. Just that. Holding her close. Feeling her heartbeat beneath his hand, her breath against his skin. Allowing himself to forget for a few moments that he had only this one night with her and that, come morning, he would hurt her terribly and irreparably.

Maris was the one plot element that might have caused him to change his outline and end the thing differently.

But he couldn't have even if he'd wanted to. Because the revenge he sought wasn't only for himself. It was for Mary Catherine. He might not deserve restitution, but Sheila damn sure did. By most moral measuring sticks, she would come up short. But he knew better. That spectacular body had been home to a kind and generous spirit. In many respects, she was innocent.

And Noah had killed her.

As surely as he had killed Daniel Matherly.

Parker hoped that Maris and the authorities were thoroughly investigating Matherly's death, because Noah's account of it smelled to high heaven. It stank of Noah. It was doubtful they'd find anything that implicated him. He would make certain they didn't. He would have made the old man's death look like a tragic accident, and his explanation for how it had come about would be perfectly plausible. He was gifted that way.

Overt aggression wasn't his style. He was smarter and more subtle than that. Oh, he could hold his own in a fistfight. Parker still had the scar above his eyebrow to prove it. But Noah's real power wasn't physical. It was cerebral. His strength was his cunning. He maneuvered insidiously. You didn't see him coming until it was too late. Which made him the most dangerous kind of animal on the planet.

But he had a major flaw: his intolerance for anyone getting the best of him.

When Noah read the *Envy* manuscript, he would come south on the next flight. He'd be unable to resist. The book would be a red flag waved in his face, and it simply wasn't in Noah Reed to ignore it.

During these intervening years, if Noah thought of Parker at all, he had probably imagined him as he'd last seen him—a vanquished enemy, a threat he had eliminated.

If for no other reason, he would come to St. Anne out of curiosity. He'd come to see how old Parker had fared. He would come to see for himself what his wife had found so interesting about his former roommate.

Noah would come.

And when he got here, Parker would be waiting.

Eight o'clock classes were just about to convene when Maris parked her rental car in a lot reserved for campus visitors. It was the summer session, so there weren't as many students rushing into the classroom buildings as there would be when the fall semester began after Labor Day.

Although she had never been here before, she didn't need to be oriented or to ask for directions. The university campus wasn't similar to the one described in *Envy*. It *was* the one described in *Envy*.

And it was a long way from the police station in rural Massachusetts where she had been less than twenty-four hours ago.

With Noah's words replaying inside her head, *his death was convenient,* she'd driven back to New York with a sense of urgency. Using her cell phone, she had reserved her airline ticket to Nashville as she sped down the parkway, breaking every speed limit between Chief Randall's police department and the Matherly Press offices in Midtown Manhattan.

She had planned to be in the office only long enough to consult briefly with her assistant and check her mail, before returning to Daniel's house to pack, then to dash to the airport in time for the late evening flight.

It didn't quite go according to plan.

Her appearance in the office had galvanized her assistant. "Thank God you're here. I've been trying to reach you on your cell."

"My battery ran out about an hour ago."

"Don't move." The secretary placed a call. "Tell Mr. Stern she just came in." She depressed the hold button. "He told me it was mandatory that he speak with you today, Maris."

"Concerning what? Did he say?"

"No, but he's been calling since early morning. He assumed you'd be coming in."

"I had an errand out of town." She hadn't had time for a lengthy conversation with the attorney and had said so.

Her assistant apologized. "He made me swear to notify him the moment I spoke to you. He'll be on line two."

Maris went into her office and sat down behind her desk. And it was fortunate that she'd been seated, because the news Stern had imparted was staggering.

"Mr. Matherly had in mind to announce his decision when you returned from Georgia. I think he wanted it to be a ceremonious occasion. Unhappily, he didn't have that opportunity, but, as it turns out, his timing for putting this into place was extraordinary." He paused, then said, "I hope you're pleased."

She was deeply touched to know that her father had placed so much confidence in her. "Enormously."

Stern had continued to go over the details with her, but the important thing she heard was that her father had entrusted her with the business that had been his life's work. She wouldn't take the responsibility lightly. But very proudly.

Stern had coughed delicately, then said, "It's at your discretion whether or not to keep Mr. Reed on staff. Mr. Matherly intimated to me that having him there even in a menial position might be awkward for you considering your pending divorce."

So he had known. Of course he had known. His timing hadn't been as extraordinary as Mr. Stern believed. Probably Daniel had been planning this for some time, realizing that upon the dissolution of her marriage, an ugly battle for control would have been waged. Daniel had seen to it that such a battle would never take place.

"Frankly, your father no longer trusted Mr. Reed to perform in the best interest of the publishing house," the lawyer had told her. "But, as I said, his continuance with the company is up to you."

They had talked a few minutes longer. Maris wrapped it up by saying, "Thank you, Mr. Stern. Thank you very much."

"No thanks necessary. I hope you'll want me to continue in my present capacity."

"That goes without saying."

"I'm honored." He paused, then asked, "Tell me, Ms. Matherly, how does it feel to be one of the most powerful women in New York?"

She laughed. "Right now? I feel very rushed to make a flight."

Following that conversation and a swift delegation of duties to her assistant, she opted to leave her car in the parking garage near the office building and take a cab to Daniel's house.

Where another shock had awaited her.

As she was jogging up the steps of the brownstone, a limousine had pulled to the curb. Nadia Schuller alighted before the chauffeur had time to come around and open the door for her.

"Hello, Maris."

She was dressed in a black dress and cocktail hat that on anyone else would have looked ridiculous. Nadia had the panache to wear it.

"I understand why you don't want to talk to me. I know you think of me as something to be scraped off the sole of your shoe. But I need one minute of your time."

"I don't have one minute. I'm in a hurry."

"Please. I fortified myself with two martinis before I came."

Maris debated it for several seconds, then reluctantly agreed to hear her out.

She had listened with dismay as Nadia told her about her breakfast meeting with Daniel. "I was told he'd had a mystery guest. You would have been the last person I would have guessed."

"Me, too. I was floored when he called and extended the invitation. I got the feeling that he was sneaking me in while his housekeeper was out. But the real shocker came when he told me about this bogus document Noah was going to press him to sign. He then offered me an exclusive on your promotion. Congratulations."

"Thank you."

"The story about the transfer of power will run in my column tomorrow. Mr. Matherly asked me to hold it for a week. I agreed. Of course, when I did, I had no idea that . . . that he wouldn't be here to read it."

Maris had been further surprised to see tears in Nadia's eyes that even her veil couldn't conceal. "Your father was a gentleman, Maris. Even toward me." She covered her mouth with her hand for several seconds before continuing. "I wish I had warned him not to go."

"With Noah?"

She nodded. "Maybe even more than you, I know how treacherous Noah can be. I never thought he would go so far as to commit murder. But when I heard the circumstances of Mr. Matherly's death, I wondered."

"So did I."

"Noah said as much."

Maris then told her about hers and Noah's meeting with the Massachusetts police. "If he did push Dad down those stairs, he got away with it."

"That morning, as I told your father good-bye, I should have said something. Should have warned him." Her eyes pleaded with Maris for absolution.

"I had a chance to warn him, too, Nadia. I didn't, either."

"I guess all of us underestimated Noah."

"I guess."

"By the way, he and I are history."

"I don't care."

Nadia nodded, one woman understanding another's scorn because it was deserved. "Just before coming here, I had the pleasure of telling him about the shift of power from your father to you. I don't think he took it well. Be careful, Maris."

"I'm not afraid of him."

Nadia looked at her closely and with admiration. "No. I don't believe you are." She ducked her head for a second, then looked bravely into Maris's face again. "I never feel guilty over anything. This was a rare exception. Thank you for listening."

Maris nodded and had turned toward the steps. But before reaching the stoop, she turned back. Morris Blume had stepped out of the limo and was holding the door for Nadia. He nodded politely to Maris, but it was Nadia whom she addressed.

"Why do you suppose Dad invited you to breakfast and gave you this story?"

"I asked myself that a thousand times. I finally reached a conclusion. Speculation, of course."

"I'd like to hear it."

"He knew Noah had cheated on you, but Mr. Matherly was too old to defend your honor by beating him up. So he wanted to use my column to kick him in the teeth. He knew Noah would be publicly humiliated when the article appeared and it was there in black and white for all the world to see that publishing's boy wonder had been stripped of his stripes." Smiling over the irony, she added, "And no doubt your father saw the poetic justice in baiting Noah's illicit lover with a story she couldn't resist."

"No doubt," Maris said with a fond smile. It was her aged father they'd all underestimated.

"Maris, if it means anything to you . . ."

"Yes?"

"I think he had fun doing it. He was in great spirits that morning."

"Thank you for telling me that. It means a great deal."

She was in the townhouse less than half an hour and had arrived at the departure gate as they were boarding the flight to Nashville. She had checked into an inexpensive chain motel near the airport and collapsed into bed without even undressing. This morning she had eaten a lumberjack's breakfast, then driven two hours to reach the university.

Now, as she strolled along the paved paths of the campus reviewing yesterday's startling events, she could hardly believe she was here. She had strong feelings of déjà vu, which wasn't surprising. She had been here before, through the pages of Parker's book. Although he had assigned a fictitious name to the university, his descriptions had been dead-on.

She walked straight to the fraternity house, knowing precisely where it was located. It was exactly as Parker had described. The three-story brick building with the gabled windows and the Bradford pear trees lining the front walkway had been abandoned for the summer, but she could imagine how lively it would be when it reopened for occupation in the fall.

From the fraternity house, she followed the path that Roark had taken that blustery November morning two days before Thanksgiving holiday. Parker's vivid narrative led her to the classroom building where Professor Hadley had his office. She ascended the stairs where Roark had been greeted by a classmate and invited to join a study group.

The second-floor corridor stretched out in front of her— long, dim, deserted, and silent. She passed only one office with an open door. A woman was working at a computer terminal, but she didn't notice as Maris walked past.

She continued all the way down the hallway to the office numbered 207. The door was standing slightly ajar, as it had been that morning Roark approached it with his capstone manuscript inside his backpack. Her heart was thumping as hard as his as she gave the door a gentle push and it swung open.

A man was seated at a desk, his back to her. "Professor Hadley?"

He turned around. "Hello, Maris."

She sagged against the doorjamb and snuffled a laugh of self-deprecation. "Mike."

"Have a seat."

He picked up a stack of books and magazines off the only other available chair and set it on the floor, alongside several other similar towers of reading material. Maris lowered herself into the chair, but her eyes never left him.

He smiled at her. "I knew you'd eventually figure it out. What was the breakthrough?"

"I guessed days ago that Roark was Parker. At least aspects of him. Yesterday Noah said something that was almost a direct quote from the book. About how convenient my father's death was to him."

"As his mother's death was. It enabled him to move to Florida without further delay."

"I should have realized sooner that you were Hadley."

"Frankly, I'm glad you didn't. Parker's descriptions weren't always flattering. I'd have been insulted if you'd seen me in them."

Her eyes roved the cluttered office. "Parker described your office to a tee. What's your position here at the university?"

"Professor emeritus."

"That's an honor."

He harrumphed. "It's an empty title that doesn't mean a thing except that you're too damn old to do what you used to do. I get to keep the office till I die. In exchange, once each semester I give a lecture on Faulkner to a couple hundred bored young people who attend only because they're required to. I'm flattered if one of them stays awake for the duration of my lecture. Beyond that, I have no responsibilities whatsoever."

Quietly she said, "I'll bet Parker stayed awake for all your lectures."

"He was exceptional. In his book, he hasn't exaggerated how I felt about 'Roark' and his budding talent. If anything, he's minimized it."

"Is it true that you rescued him from drug addiction?"

"As I've said many times, he rescued himself. He'd become reliant on painkillers. Considering what he suffered, I can't say I blamed him. But it had reached a point where he was taking the pills more to dull his emotional pain than anything else.

"All I did was sound the alarm inside his head. He's the one who went through the hell of withdrawal and then whipped himself back into shape." He smiled. "I guess it's fair to say that I handed him the whip."

"Still, he's indebted to you."

"As I am to him. I've been privileged to work with an amazingly talented writer."

"Too bad he's not as fine a human being as he is a writer."

Mike studied her for a moment, then reached across his desk and pulled forward a manuscript that was bound with a wide rubber band. He passed it to her. She looked down at the cover sheet and her lips curled with bitterness. "I've read it."

"Most of it," he corrected. "Not all. There's some you haven't read. Read it before you judge Parker too harshly." He stood up and made his way to the door. "I'm going for coffee. Can I bring you back something?"

One of Noah's strongest personality traits was his ability to deny that anything was wrong. Refusing to acknowledge a setback was the same as there being no setback to acknowledge.

The morning following his disastrous martini date with Nadia, he took a taxi to Matherly Press, pretending, indeed believing, that he would manipulate his way through this problem and actually come out better in the long run. On the Richter scale of complications, this was a blip.

He was glad that Matherly Press would remain autonomous. WorldView had bought itself a white elephant. Becker-Howe had been hanging on by its fingernails for years, and everybody in the industry knew it. Ollie Howe was more stiff-necked than Daniel. He was unyielding to the rapid changes taking place and baffled by the concept of electronic publishing.

Noah would personally see to it that the merger was an abysmal failure and that Morris Blume became an industry laughingstock, first for fancying himself a publisher, and second for marrying a whore. Every man he shook hands with was likely to have had a piece of his wife.

As for Nadia's exclusive story, he would deny it.

Daniel wasn't around to corroborate it. Nadia was probably lying about Stern's corroboration. Noah would claim she had written it out of spite. He would admit that he and Nadia had engaged in a temporary and ill-advised affair, one he now deeply regretted. The sudden death of his father-in-law had made him see the error of his ways and returned him to his wife and the sanctity of their marriage. When he broke off with Nadia, she retaliated by fabricating this story about him and his family.

By the time all the hubbub died down, no one would remember the details of the original story. The facts would have been confused in the multiple retells. No one would know what or whom to believe. He could walk away from the whole mess virtually unscathed and looking valorous for owning up to an extramarital affair for which he would publicly ask his wife's forgiveness.

His wife. Maris was the hitch in this plan.

He was counting on her to ignore Nadia's story. She wouldn't give Nadia the satisfaction of denying or confirming it. But it went beyond that. What was he to do if in fact Daniel had given Maris control of Matherly Press? Say the attorney, Stern, had knowledge of a transference of power and the documentation to prove it. What then?

All right. He would go along. He would say that Daniel had informed him of it while they were in the country. Yes! They'd discussed it at length, and Noah had agreed that Maris should have the title and the authority that it conveyed. But Daniel had asked him to be her helpmate. To serve as her advisor. To guard her back against marauders and steer her around pitfalls.

Yes, that was very good. And who could contradict him?

Perhaps he should confess that he had flirted with the idea of merging Matherly Press with a media giant and had met with Blume to discuss it. But now that Daniel was gone, he looked forward to working side by side with Maris to preserve and even strengthen Matherly Press.

Excellent.

Now, what to do about their personal relationship? Tricky to resolve, but not impossible. She was so easily pacified. Maybe he would take a special interest in this book she was so excited about. He would offer to become personally involved in its publication and devote himself to making it a huge success. She'd like that.

Or maybe he'd suggest that they try harder to produce an heir to continue the dynasty. Physically impossible, of course, but she could be happy in her ignorance until he devised something else to keep her preoccupied and malleable.

There were several options from which to choose. He was confident one would be a workable solution for their present rift.

Finally, there was the problem of the private investigator. He might dig deep enough to uncover that nasty business in Florida. But what if he did? It was an unhappy story, nothing more. He had never been incriminated. Resurrecting the incident might generate some unfavorable speculation about him, but he would dismiss any rumors as vicious gossip.

Having worked out these solutions, it was with a jaunty and optimistic air that he stepped off the elevator and walked briskly down the hallway toward his office. Even his assistant was standing at attention at her desk, wringing her hands as though anxious to please him. "Coffee, please, Cindy."

"Mr. Reed, he—"

He sailed past her and entered his office, where he came to a standstill so abruptly he might as well have walked into a glass wall. "Stern?"

Appearancewise, this attorney and Howard Bancroft were practically interchangeable. The same bald, pointed head bobbed as the man said curtly, "Mr. Reed."

"What the fuck are you doing in my office, behind my desk?"

Overlooking the obscenity, Stern gestured toward the two men with him. "These gentlemen work as paralegals for my law firm. They have agreed to help you box up your personal items. A project I will closely monitor. You have one hour to complete the task, at which time I will relieve you of your keys to this office and your security pass into the building. I will then escort you out through the Fifty-first Street exit.

"When stipulating to me the terms of your immediate dismissal, Ms. Matherly was very specific about that. She did not want to cause you any embarrassment by conducting you outside through the main entrance. In my opinion, that was most gracious of her and more consideration than you deserve." With a quick motion of his hand, he activated the paralegals. He checked his wristwatch. "The clock is ticking. I think we should begin."

Cindy squeezed in through the door behind him. "Excuse me, Mr. Reed? The deliveryman won't release this package until you personally sign the return receipt."

She was the most convenient outlet for his rage. He rounded on her, eyes blazing.

She recoiled but thrust the package at him and managed to say, "It's from a Mr. Parker Evans."

Maris had just completed her read-through when Mike returned. She was sitting motionless, the manuscript pages lying in her lap. She had stared at the last line until the letters blurred.

Pain that splinters the body but slays the soul.

Because she was dazed by that line and those that had come before it, Mike's return didn't register until he nudged her shoulder. "I remembered that you enjoy tea sometimes. I hope that's all right."

Nodding dumbly, she took the warm Styrofoam cup from him. He sat down in his desk chair. When he ripped open a packet of artificial sweetener, the sound seemed abnormally loud in the small room. "One or two?" he asked.

"One's fine."

She removed the tight plastic lid from her cup. Mike dumped the contents of the packet into the fragrant, steaming tea, then passed her a plastic stir stick. She stirred much longer than required to dissolve the sweetener. When she tasted the tea, it burned her tongue.

"This isn't the ending, is it?" she asked.

Mike frowned into his coffee. "He hasn't shown the last chapter even to me. I'm not sure he's written it. It may be too painful for him to write."

"More painful than this? God," she cried softly. "It's incredible. I can't believe it happened."

Mike looked at her meaningfully. What she'd said was rhetoric, because actually she believed every word of Parker's account. Noah had done this to his friends. She knew he had. She knew he was capable of it.

"What happened afterward, Mike?"

"Todd—"

"Noah. This isn't fiction."

"Noah returned to the marina."

"As related in the prologue. He faked hysteria. Claimed that Parker had gone crazy onboard the boat. Abused the girl. Attacked him. They fought. The girl went overboard and so did Parker. Noah tried to save them."

"He must've gone into the water so his clothes would be wet and it would appear he'd searched for them."

"He blamed Parker's violent outburst on envy."

"A lie, of course. But a damn good one. Believable. The Coast Guard organized a search-and-rescue effort."

"Mary Catherine?"

"Her body was never recovered. It was officially ruled death by drowning."

"What about Parker?"

Mike sipped his coffee before answering, a delay tactic she saw through.

"Parker was found that night by sheer accident. A fisherman

spotted him. The coordinates Todd had given the Coast Guard were 'approximate.'"

"Meaning off by miles."

"Miles. After being in the water for hours, it was a miracle that Parker was still alive. Shock probably saved his life. He had kept his arms moving so he wouldn't sink and drown, but God knows how he was able to move at all. His legs had been chewed to pieces by the blades of the outboard motor. When the fishermen first saw him, they mistook him for an animal carcass that had been used for chum. There was so much blood around him, you see."

With a shaky hand, Maris set aside her tea, untasted after that first sip.

"For over a week, his condition was listed as critical," Mike continued. "Somehow, he lived. Eventually his legs were pieced back together bit by bit."

"He told me he underwent several operations. What was Noah doing all this time? Surely he was afraid that Parker would give his version of the story and convince the authorities of the truth."

"I've given you a much-abbreviated summary," Mike explained. "The reconstruction of Parker's legs took years. In those first few days, the trauma doctors worked frantically just to keep him alive. Eventually he was taken off the critical list, but he spent weeks in an ICU fighting off infection. There weren't drugs strong enough to keep him unconscious except for brief periods. The rest of the time he spent screaming, begging them to kill him. He's admitted that much to me."

Maris covered her trembling lips with her hand, which was cold and clammy. Tears stung her eyes.

"He'd suffered tremendous blood loss. Perhaps that's why they didn't amputate his legs immediately. They were afraid he'd bleed out on the operating table. Or they wanted his condition to stabilize before they attempted a surgery that traumatic. I'm surmising. I don't know. I learned all this long after the fact. No one notified me of the incident. I found out later, by happenstance.

"When he was strong enough to begin the reconstructive process, he fought like hell if any of the consulting physicians so much as mentioned amputation. Even partial. Honestly, I don't know why they heeded his wishes. Maybe because he was a young man. Maybe . . . I don't know," he repeated with a shrug. "Divine intervention? Providence? Maybe the doctors simply admired the power of his will and decided to honor it. Anyway, they didn't take his legs. They elected to rebuild them the best they could."

"I've seen his scars."

"The visible ones. The ones you can't see are even deeper."

"Caused by Noah's betrayal."

"During those weeks that Parker was fighting for his life, Noah was putting on quite a dog-and-pony show for the authorities. Mary Catherine wasn't there to dispute his version of what had happened. It came down to his word against Parker's. He painted Parker as a jealous, envious hothead who had gotten drunk and snapped, turned violent. He attacked Noah. When Mary Catherine tried to break them apart, Parker lashed out and knocked her over the railing. His momentum caused him to fall overboard, too.

"By the time the doctors granted the investigators permission to question him, Parker had already been cast in the defensive role. Confronted with these false accusations, Parker, by his own account, played right into Noah's hands. He reacted like a jealous, envious hothead with violent tendencies. His ranted denials made him appear guilty rather than innocent. From his hospital bed, he threatened to kill his lying friend."

Mike smiled. "I imagine that he put his command of the English language, as well as his gutter vernacular, to good use. I can imagine him pulling against arm restraints and practically foaming at the mouth."

"That probably isn't exaggerating by much."

"In any case he came across as a raving maniac, dangerous to himself and others. Noah was believed. Parker wasn't. He was charged with involuntary manslaughter for Mary Catherine's drowning. When he was well enough to leave the hospital, he was taken to court for his arraignment. He pled no contest."

"Why?" Maris exclaimed. "He wasn't guilty."

"But he felt responsible."

She shook her head. "Noah was."

"I agree with you. But Parker blamed himself for being unable to save her. Noah didn't attend Parker's sentencing, but he sent a videotaped deposition. He was humble, sorrowful, soft-spoken when he wasn't openly weeping. He said he regretted having to tell the horrible truth about that day. A dual tragedy had occurred, he said. Mary Catherine's drowning. And the death of his friendship with Parker Evans. He thought he knew him, but in a matter of hours his best friend had become his enemy.

"He said that he and Parker had been closer than any two brothers. But when Noah succeeded ahead of him, it did something to Parker. Twisted him. Noah looked earnestly into the camera and sobbed. 'I don't understand what happened to Parker that day. He turned devious, lecherous, and murderous.' I think I'm quoting correctly."

Maris took a deep breath and expelled it slowly. "So Noah went to New York in a blaze of glory because of *The Vanquished*."

"And Parker went to prison."

"*Prison?* Prison." She lowered her head and ground her palm against her forehead. "He told me once that he had spent years in rehab hospitals and 'other facilities.' I would never have imagined he was referring to prison."

"Because of the mitigating circumstances of his case and his physical condition, he was sent to a minimum-security prison and allowed to continue with his treatment program and physical therapy. He was released after serving twenty-two months of an eight-year sentence.

"He might have been better off if the state had kept him longer. On his own, he didn't fare very well." He looked at her from beneath his eyebrows. "I believe you know that he'd sunk pretty low by the time I heard what had happened to my star pupil and went looking for him."

She picked up the manuscript pages in her lap and straightened them. "I regret that I ever met Noah Reed. I loved him, Mike. Or thought I did. I was married to him. Wanted to have his children. How could I not have seen what he is?"

"You weren't looking. You didn't know to look."

"But I should have read the signs. I knew this is where he'd attended university, but he never talked about his life before coming to New York. Not even a casual reference. He didn't have any keepsakes or photographs, except one of his mother and father with him as a boy. He was never in touch with old friends. He never reminisced. He said he preferred living the present to visiting the past, and I stupidly accepted that explanation without question. Why did it never occur to me that he was hiding something?"

"Don't be too hard on yourself, Maris. Noah is like two different men occupying one body. You weren't the only one he hoodwinked."

"Was it a plot device for *Envy*, or did you actually write Parker a letter, cautioning him not to turn his back on Noah?"

"I wrote a letter very similar to the one Parker read aloud to us. Almost word for word, in fact."

"So *you* saw through Noah, and he was only your student. I was his wife. Not a strong recommendation for my perception skills."

"Parker lived with him, too, remember. For nearly six years. Here at the university, then in Florida. Occasionally he saw traces of selfishness and self-absorption, but not until he was in the water that night did he realize that Noah is evil."

"I believe that. Recently I've had glimpses of that evil alter ego." Looking down at the pages still lying in her lap, she ran her fingers across the top sheet in something like a caress. "Parker's not evil like Noah. But he's cruel." Raising her head and looking across at Mike, she said, "Why did he do this, Mike?"

"Revenge."

"Why did he involve me?"

"I apologize for my part, Maris. I was uncomfortable with it from the start. I certainly didn't like it once I came to know you." He eased back in his chair and focused on a corner of the ceiling as he arranged his thoughts. "You see, in that damning video deposition, Noah accused Parker of lechery with Mary Catherine."

"So he made the accusation a reality. With me."

"Something like that. Parker's success with the Mackensie Roone books should have been enough for him. But it wasn't. The best revenge he could devise was to write his and Noah's story and write it well enough to captivate you, a respected editor."

"Who also happened to be Noah's wife."

"I think the idea sparked when he read that Noah had married you."

"I was the element that made the plot work."

Mike nodded somberly. "Every good plot has one component that links all the others. The common thread that seams the pieces together."

"What's the ending to be?"

"He wouldn't tell me."

"Maybe he doesn't have an ending. Maybe deceiving me, bedding me, and being able to laugh up his sleeve at Noah over it is vengeance enough for him."

Mike responded to the bitterness she couldn't conceal. "I'm not justifying what he's done, Maris. But I can understand it. Parker feels everything passionately or not at all. It's the only level of experience that makes sense to him. Otherwise, why bother? How could he be less passionate about vengeance?

"He wanted Noah to experience at least twinges of the pain

he had suffered because of him. He wanted Noah to know what it felt like to be deceived and betrayed to the *n*th degree. So Parker tricked you into coming to him. You both betrayed Noah by sleeping—"

"Oh, my God!" She reached out and gripped Mike's sleeve. "I've just figured out his plot."

"His—"

"*Plot*. His ending." She wet her lips, spoke hurriedly. "Earlier, you quoted Noah from his videotaped deposition. He claimed that Parker had turned devious, lecherous, and . . ."

"Murderous," Mike finished, slapping his forehead. "Goddamn me for being so old and stupid. As many plots as I've analyzed, I should have realized where he was going. That's why he hasn't shared the last chapter with me."

Maris rattled off her racing thoughts. "Parker's done everything Noah accused him of. Except—" She looked at Mike with alarm. "He couldn't," she said huskily. "He wouldn't. I know he wouldn't."

"I don't believe so, either."

But neither sounded convinced. "He's not capable of it," she stressed. "I wouldn't have been attracted to him, wouldn't have—"

"Loved him?"

"For God's sake, Mike, I fell in love with the main character of *The Vanquished*. And transferred that love to the author. Look where that got me. I no longer trust my emotions. I believed that Parker at least cared for me. If I hadn't believed that, I wouldn't have slept with him. But maybe I'm wrong again. Maybe . . ."

She pressed her fist against her heart, recalling how cruel Parker had been that awful morning. Considering all the pain and resentment, bitterness and anger that had been simmering inside him for the past fourteen years, perhaps he was capable of murder.

To his mind, Noah had stolen the life he'd had planned for

himself. Tit for tat. An eye for an eye. Noah's life for the one Noah had taken from him. Noah's life in exchange for Mary Catherine's.

Now, *that* she could easily believe. Parker might not kill for revenge, but he might for justice. He had liked that girl. He had regarded her as his friend and felt compassion for her. He would feel justified seeking vengeance for her death.

She surged to her feet. "We've got to stop him."

But at the door, she drew herself up short. She had panicked unnecessarily. Clasping her hands, she bowed her head over them as though in prayer. "Thank God." Turning back around, she said to Mike, "We're not too late. Noah doesn't know that the writer I've been working with is Parker. He hasn't read *Envy*."

Mike dragged his hands down his face, groaning, "Oh, no."

Noah, fresh off a chartered boat from the mainland, entered Terry's Bar and Grill with a condescending attitude that immediately catapulted him to the top of the endangered species list.

The locals disliked nonislanders in general, but they particularly disliked any who looked down their noses at them. They despised Noah Reed on sight. In fact, he might not have been allowed to tie up his boat at the dock if Parker hadn't spread word around that he was expecting a citified visitor from up north. If anybody spotted such a person, he was to be directed to Terry's, where Parker would be waiting.

Noah approached the bar and addressed Terry with a rude, "Hey!"

Terry, who happened to be uncapping a longneck at the time, sent the bottle of beer sliding down the bar toward one of his regulars, ignoring Noah.

"Didn't you hear me?"

Terry shifted a gnawed matchstick from one corner of his mouth to the other. "I heard ya. People wanna talk to me, they talk to me proper, else they're likely to disappear. Now get the fuck outta my place."

"I think you've already worn out your welcome, Noah." At the sound of his voice, Noah spun around. Parker grinned up at him. "Record time, too."

Noah gave Parker and his wheelchair a long, slow once-over. "She told me you were a cripple."

Terry produced a baseball bat from beneath the bar. One of the regulars reached for the sheathed knife attached to his belt. Others merely glowered.

"She told me you were a prick," Parker returned, keeping his smile in place. "But then I already knew that."

Noah laughed. "Right back to our usual banter, aren't we? I didn't realize how much I'd missed it."

"Funny. I haven't missed it at all. Want a beer?"

Noah glanced at Terry. "I think I'll pass."

Parker motioned with his head for Noah to follow him outside. "I'll settle up with you later, Terry."

"No problem."

Every eye in the bar was on them as they left through the screen door and went out into the sweltering heat.

"You've got nerve, Noah. I'll give you that."

Noah scoffed. "Coming to see you?"

"No. Going into Terry's bar wearing those loafers." He looked down at Noah's Gucci shoes with the gold trademark on the vamp. "Very fancy."

Noah ignored the dig and slipped off his jacket. "Lovely climate," he said sarcastically.

"Sorta reminiscent of Key West."

Noah never faltered, but he didn't take the bait, either. Parker led him to the Gator. "Climb in."

"How quaint." He settled into the bright yellow seat. "You don't see many of these on Park Avenue."

Using his arms, Parker raised himself into the driver's seat, then reached down for his wheelchair, folded it, and placed it in the trailer. As he clicked on the ignition, he said, "Noah, you've grown into a regular Yankee snob."

"You've just grown old."

"Pain and suffering will do that to you."

For the next five minutes, they rode in silence. Noah showed a marked lack of interest in the island. He kept his eyes on the narrow road ahead, never once commenting on the scenery or even looking at it. Parker, on the other hand, returned the waves of people they happened to pass along the way.

After one lady called out a greeting from her front porch, Noah turned to him. "What are you, the local celebrity?"

"Only cripple on the island."

"I see."

"And the only professional writer they know."

"You haven't sold this book of yours yet."

"No, but the Mackensie Roone books sell like rubbers in a whorehouse."

Finally. He'd finally gotten an honest reaction out of Noah. He laughed at his stunned expression. "You didn't know? Well . . . surprise!"

With an aplomb that Parker remembered, Noah recovered quickly. "So that's how you afford the lovely home and loyal valet that my wife mentioned."

Parker was quick to catch Noah's possessive reference to Maris, but he didn't address it. "I'm trying to make the house a home. It still needs a lot of work. And my loyal valet up and quit on me this week."

"How come?"

"He thinks I'm a rotten person and said he wanted no part of me."

"You call that loyal?"

"Oh, he'll be back."

"You're sure of this?"

"Fairly sure, yes."

The sun had sunk below the tree line by the time they reached the derelict cotton gin. The gathering dusk made it

appear even more forlorn than it did in full daylight. Its en-
shrouding vines seemed to be hugging it tighter, as though to
protect it from the onset of darkness.

Noah assessed the dilapidated building. "I can see what you
mean by the place still needing a lot of work."

Parker reached into the trailer for his wheelchair and swung
it to the ground. "It's not the homestead, but it's an interesting
building. As long as you're here, you might just as well get a
taste of local history."

He wheeled his chair into the gin, leaving Noah no choice except to follow. Inside, waning sunlight squeezed through the
cracks in the walls. The holes in the ceiling projected miniature disks of light onto the floor. They looked like scattered
coins. Otherwise, the interior was gloomy with deep shadows.
The air was so heavy and still it almost required conscious
thought to inhale it.

Like a tour guide with a rehearsed spiel, Parker pointed out
certain aspects of the gin and related some of its history and
fact-based legends, as he had related them to Maris, including
the failed plan to convert to steam power.

Noah tired of the monologue and interrupted Parker in mid-
sentence. "I read your book."

Parker slowly brought his wheelchair around to face him.
"Of course you did, Noah. You wouldn't be here if you hadn't.
When did you receive it?"

"This morning."

"Quick response. Every anxious writer's dream."

"I only had to read the first few pages to realize where the
plot was going. It's very good writing, by the way."

"Thanks."

"I chartered a private jet to ensure the shortest trip possible.
On the flight, I scanned the remainder of the manuscript."

"But you already know the story."

"I know it'll never see print."

Parker shrugged goofily. "Just goes to show how wrong a

person can be. Here I was thinking that maybe, after all these years, you'd be ready to relieve your conscience."

"Cut the bullshit, Parker." Noah's voice cracked across the stillness like a whip. "I assume this *Envy* is the manuscript that Maris has been raving about?"

"The very one. She's read every word. Several times. Likes the story. Loves the concept, the dynamic of the competitive friends. Says the characters are vividly drawn. Thinks Roark is a prince and Todd is . . . well, not a prince."

"She's easily impressed by melodrama."

"Wrong. She's a good editor."

"A schoolgirl playing dress-up."

"She's a classy lady."

"Jesus." Noah snickered. "You've fucked her, haven't you?"

Parker clenched his jaw and refused to answer, which caused Noah to laugh.

"Ah, Parker, Parker. Your hair is graying and your face has more lines than a road map. But some things haven't changed. You're still the chivalrous lover who never kisses and tells."

He shook his head with amusement. "You always did have a soft spot for the ladies. Of course, I know why you had a burning desire to get Maris in bed. You wanted to cuckold me. You went to a hell of a lot of trouble to do it, so I hope you weren't too disappointed. She's not exactly a firecracker in the sack, is she?"

He looked pointedly at Parker's lap. "Or maybe you're pitifully grateful for any kind of sexual activity. Even Maris's stilted efforts." Thoughtfully, he scratched the side of his nose. "She does have that luxuriant bush, though. If you left the lights on, I'm sure you noticed."

Parker wished very badly to kill him then. He wanted to watch him die, slowly and in agony and feeling the flames of hell licking at his ankles.

Seemingly oblivious to the murderous impulses he was fostering, Noah continued nonchalantly. "Not that I'm complaining about Maris, you understand. She's certainly proved herself useful."

"In the furtherance of your career."

"That's right." He took a step closer. "And you must know, Parker, that I won't let anything or anyone rob me of all that I've achieved. This book of yours will never be published."

"Actually, Noah, I didn't write it for publication. I wrote it for myself."

"As a cathartic autobiography?"

"No."

"As a ticket to fuck my wife?"

"No."

"You're stretching my patience, Parker."

"I wrote it to get you here, on my turf, so that I could be watching your face when you die, just like you were watching me from the pilot's wheel of the boat that night."

Noah snorted. "What? You're going to run me down with your wheelchair?"

Parker merely smiled and withdrew a small transistor from his shirt pocket.

"Oh, I see, you're going to beat me to death with a remote control."

"I own this building," Parker said conversationally. "I like it. Good atmosphere. But some folks think it's a hazard to kids who might wander in here. That abandoned well and all." He hitched his thumb in that direction. "So I've decided to do my fellow islanders a favor and destroy it."

He depressed one of the rubberized buttons on the transistor. Out of the shadows in a far corner came a loud pop followed by a spark. Startled, Noah spun around and watched as a flame leaped up against the weathered wood.

Parker gave his chair a hard push toward him. Noah, sensing the motion, turned and lunged at him. Noah's daily workouts in the gym had kept him trim. His reflexes were good. He landed a couple of good punches.

But Parker's arm and chest muscles were exceptionally well developed from years of having to rely on them. He staved off many of Noah's slugs and had enough upper body strength to keep himself in his chair. His real advantage, however, was in knowing how Noah fought. Noah fought dirty. Noah fought to win. And he didn't care how he won.

When Noah began pushing him backward toward the open well, Parker wasn't surprised. His efforts became defensive. He took reckless swings that Noah easily dodged. Sensing that Parker was weakening, Noah fought even harder. Parker's frantic struggling only increased Noah's determination to defeat him. He came on more ferociously, blindly, the predator moving in for the kill.

Then, at precisely the right instant, Parker jammed down the brake lever of his wheelchair. It bit into the rubber wheel and brought the chair to a jarring stop. Noah hadn't expected it. Inertia propelled him forward. His Gucci shoes caught the low rim of the well, tripping him. He groped at air. Then he stepped into nothingness.

His startled cry was a hellish echo of Mary Catherine's scream as she fell backward over the railing of the boat.

Parker's breathing was harsh and loud. He wiped his bloody nose on his shirtsleeve.

"You son of a bitch!" Noah shouted up at him.

"So the fall didn't kill you?"

"Motherfucker!"

"You're a sore loser, Noah. The cripple outsmarted you. Isn't that what you had in mind for me? To push me down that well? Why do you think I kept referring to it? Foreshadowing, Noah. Any writer worth a damn should have recognized it for what it was."

"Get me out of here."

"Ah, don't be such a crybaby, Noah. It's not nearly as deep as the Atlantic. To the best of my knowledge there are no saltwater carnivores in there. Don't know about snakes, though," he added in an intentional afterthought.

"What are you going to do, flood it with water and let me drown?"

"Give me some credit. All you'd have to do is keep treading water till it got to the top."

"Then what's the point?"

Parker set off another of the charges. "There are twelve more like that, Noah. But long before I've set all of them off, you'll already be choking. Smoke inhalation doesn't have quite the drama of ocean water flooding your lungs, or being eaten by a shark, but it's pretty damn effective, wouldn't you say?"

"Ooh, you're scaring me, Parker. You expect me to believe that you would let me die down here?"

"Why wouldn't you believe it? I'm a killer. You said so yourself. Remember? Come on, flex the old memory muscles. I'm sure you'll remember. After all, you must've rehearsed that blubbering speech a thousand times. The tears were a convincing touch, I must say. Even I came close to believing you. We were David and Jonathan until that day on the boat. Then I turned devious, lecherous, and murderous. Does that jiggle your memory?"

"I was . . . I was . . ."

"You were sentencing me to prison. Since I did the time, I think it's only fair that I commit the crime."

Noah was silent for a moment, then said, "I think my ankle's broken."

"You're breaking my heart."

"Listen, Parker, I'm in pain down here."

"Don't even go there, Noah."

"Okay, what I did . . . it was wrong. I got scared. Froze up. Ran away. Once I realized what I'd done, there was no way out for me but to do what I did. I can understand your carrying a grudge. But you've made your point."

"Like you could have made yours by leaving me in the ocean to die. Wasn't that enough? Did you have to let Mary Catherine die, too?"

"You won't get away with this," Noah said in a new tone of voice.

"Oh, I think I will. You did."

"People will see the smoke, call the fire department."

"It's on the other side of the island. You'll suffocate before they get here."

"And you'll be blamed."

"I don't think so. Everyone inside Terry's heard your cruel remark. They know your wife's been living under my roof for a couple weeks. They'll figure you came down here from Yankee-land to bust my ass. But to them I'm the poor crippled man who lives down the lane. Now, who do you think they're going to believe? Who do you think they'll *choose* to believe?

"All I have to do is tell them the truth. We had words. You attacked me, and I've got the bloody nose to prove it. You lost your balance and fell into the well. Unfortunately, I had already set off the charges and couldn't stop the inevitable. I tried to save you, but it was no use. I'm a cripple, remember?"

He peered over the rim and smiled down at Noah, whose face was a pale oval looking up at him from the bottom of the dry well. "It's as plausible as the story you told the Coast Guard, don't you think?"

"Parker. Parker. Listen to me."

"Excuse me just a moment." He depressed a button and another charge sparked. By now flames were eating the wood on the outside walls in two places, working their way up toward the loft.

"Stop this, Parker." Noah cried.

"No."

"For God's sake!"

"For God's sake? Don't you mean for your sake, Noah? I think even God would understand and forgive anything I did to you. I thought of shooting you and getting it over with. I'd've pled self-defense and would have gotten away with it.

"But then I thought about the hours I flailed about in that fucking ocean before I was rescued. I thought about the hours I spent in excruciating pain in rehab hospitals. Somehow shooting seemed much too good for you. I had to wait fourteen years for this. If you met death quickly, it wouldn't be nearly as gratifying. I considered cutting off your balls and letting you bleed out, like I nearly did. But that would have been messy and I couldn't think of a reasonable defense.

"Then one day I was in here plotting a Deck Cayton novel, and I happened to catch myself staring at this well, and just like that," he said, snapping his fingers, "the idea came to me. I got a mental image of you struggling for air, your eyes streaming tears, your nose running snot. I got so aroused, I nearly came inside my shorts.

"By the way, the equipment works just fine, thank you. And Maris might have been married to you, but she was never your *wife*. You don't know her. You never even came close to knowing her.

"Now, where was I? Oh, yeah, I got an ol' boy who lives on the island to set these charges for me. Simple. Like automatic fireplace starters. I sent out notices that I was going to burn the place down. A controlled fire, you see. Like they once used to burn the sugarcane fields right here on the island. Not much flame. Lots of smoke."

By now the smell of it was strong.

"Parker, you've got to get us out of here."

Parker laughed. "I won't have trouble getting out. I've got wheels. You, by contrast, are screwed."

Noah tried another tack. "Okay, you want me to beg. I'm begging. Get me out of here."

Parker coughed on smoke. "Sorry, Noah. Even if I wanted to, it's too late. I've got to save myself. I'll be depriving myself the pleasure of watching you die, but—"

"Parker! Don't do this." Noah sobbed. "Please. Don't let me die. What can I say?"

Parker stared down at him, his features turning hard, all traces of humor vanishing. "Say you're sorry."

Noah stopped sobbing but remained stubbornly silent.

"Did you even know Mary Catherine's real name?"

"What difference does it make?"

"It was Sheila. You should've at least known the name of the girl who miscarried your baby."

"It wasn't a baby. It was a female trick. A trap."

"So you did know," Parker murmured. "I wondered."

"Ancient history, Parker."

"Wrong. It's very timely. If you want to get out of here alive, Noah, admit that you knocked Mary Catherine overboard and did nothing, fucking *nothing*, to try and save her."

Noah hesitated. Parker placed his hand on the wheels of his chair and started to turn it around. "See ya."

"Wait! All right! What happened to Mary Catherine—"

"Sheila."

"Sheila. What happened to Sheila was my fault."

"And me. You deliberately ran that boat over me."

"Yes."

"Say it."

"I deliberately ran that boat over you."

"Why?"

"I . . . I was trying to kill you and make it look like an accident. I wanted you out of the way."

"Of your career."

"That's right."

"Was that also why you killed Daniel Matherly?"

"Damn you!"

"You did kill him, didn't you?" Parker shouted down at him. "Admit it or you suffocate, you son of a bitch. If you don't drown in your own nervous piss first."

"I . . . I . . ."

"How'd you arrange that fall, Noah?"

"I provoked him. About this old friend of his. He got angry, came at me. I deflected—"

"You pushed him."

"All right."

"Say it!"

Desperate now, Noah relented. "I pushed him. I didn't have to, but I did. Just to make sure."

Parker coughed on smoke. It was stinging his eyes. "You are an abomination, Noah. A miserable human being. A murderer." He shook his head regretfully. "But you're not worth killing."

Parker wheeled his chair backward. Panicked, Noah shouted his name from the bottom of the well. He was out of sight only for the amount of time it took him to retrieve the rope he had stashed earlier in preparation for this moment. He dangled it above the well where Noah could see it. "Are you sure you want me to save you? You'll go to prison, you know."

"Throw it down." He was reaching up in an imploring gesture.

"I know exactly how you feel," Parker told him. "I knew my legs were shot to hell. I'd have done anything to stop the pain. Anything except die. I thought I wanted to. But when those fishermen reached for me, I grabbed hold for all I was worth."

He threaded the rope down to Noah, who grasped it frantically. "Make a few loops around your chest and tie it tightly," Parker instructed.

"Okay," Noah called when he was done. "Pull me up."

Parker backed away, pulling the rope taut. "Ready? If you can get some footholds, walk the wall."

"I can't. My ankle."

"Okay, but easy does it. Don't—"

He was about to say "yank." But it was too late.

CHAPTER 36

In his panic to be rescued, Noah had pulled sharply on the rope. Parker wasn't braced for it. He was jerked forward out of the wheelchair, landing on the packed dirt floor. "Goddammit!"

"What? What's happening? Parker?"

For several seconds, Parker lay there with his forehead resting on the floor. He took several deep breaths. Then, using his forearms to pull him along, he inched his way over to the rim of the well and peered down into it.

"You pulled me out of my chair."

"Well, get back in it."

"I'm open to suggestions on how I should go about it."

"Well, do something."

Noah's voice was now ragged with desperation. Even at the bottom of the well, he must have been able to hear the crackle of old wood burning. The smoke grew thicker by the second.

"Parker, you've got to get me out of here!"

"Can't help you, buddy. I'm a cripple, remember?" He shook his head ruefully. "I'll admit this isn't the way I had the ending plotted. I never intended for you to die. I wanted to give you a taste of what it's like to face your mortality. To experience that all-encompassing terror. I wanted to scare you into confessing your sins. I wanted you to grovel and beg me for your life. And you did. It was supposed to end there."

He laughed. "I realize that you're panicked, Noah, and that your mind is preoccupied with surviving. But I hope you're thinking clearly enough to grasp the irony of this situation.

"Think about it. I'm your only hope of salvation. But I'm powerless to save you because of the injuries you inflicted on me. That's rich, isn't it? It's a shame that neither of us will have the opportunity to use it in a book. It's the kind of built-in irony that Professor Mike Strother loved."

At the mention of their mentor's name, the distance between them seemed to shrink. Their eyes made a connection that was almost audible. Parker spoke softly. "You have one more sin to confess, don't you, Noah?"

"I had to be first, Parker. I had to be."

"Professor Strother hadn't heard from either of us for more than a year. All his correspondence had been returned unopened, addressees unknown, no forwarding addresses. He was puzzled and slightly offended by our sudden and inexplicable disappearance.

"He didn't realize you'd sold *The Vanquished* until he saw it in his local bookstore. He recognized the title and your name immediately, of course. He purchased a copy. He was curious to read how you had finalized your manuscript. He wanted to see if you had incorporated any of his suggestions. Naturally, he was proud that one of his students had written the novel that was all the rage, the topic of conversation at cocktail parties and beauty shops and office commissaries, the book that was on every bestseller list."

"Parker—"

"Now imagine Professor Strother's surprise when he settled into his reading chair, adjusted his lamp, opened his copy of *The Vanquished* by Noah Reed. And read the first page of my book. *My* book, Noah!"

"It was that letter," Noah shouted back at him. "Strother always favoring you. Always thinking you were the one with the most talent. He thought your manuscript was so fucking fine. I thought I'd test it, get a second opinion. One day while you were out, I went into your computer and printed out a copy. I put my title on it and submitted it under my name."

"And when it sold, you had to get rid of me. Immediately. That day."

"That was the plan."

"Bet you shit when I turned up alive."

"It gave me pause, but I didn't panic. I hurriedly put your book into my computer, and mine into yours. You couldn't have proven your claims to the authorities because by then I had painted you as unstable and violent."

"Strother always gave you credit for clever plotting."

"Our dear professor was another concern, but I figured that if he ever came forward and tried to expose me, I'd . . ."

"You'd think of a way to worm your way out."

"I always have."

"Until now."

"At least I'll die knowing that you're right behind me. You might even beat me into hell."

"You think so?"

"You can't crawl along on your belly fast enough to get out of here now, Parker."

"No, but I can walk fast enough." Then, as Noah watched with mounting disbelief, Parker struggled to his knees and then stood up.

"You cocksucking son of a—"

"It's a Mackensie Roone trademark, Noah," Parker said, smiling down at him. "Save one final plot twist for the very very end."

"I'll kill you, Parker. I'll see you in hell! I'll—"

"You all right, Mr. Evans?" Deputy Sheriff Dwight Harris rushed through the door, accompanied by two other deputies.

"Exhausted," Parker told him. "Otherwise okay." He depressed a button on the remote control and the flames immediately died.

"Fire truck's outside. We were getting worried." Just then the spray from the fire hose struck the exterior wall with a hard *whomp*.

"I was getting a little worried myself," Parker said. "Those smoke machines are killers."

Deputy Harris glanced at the scorched walls. "Those smudge pots did some damage to your building."

"It's survived worse. Besides, it was worth it."

"So you got it?"

"Every incriminating word." Parker pulled out his shirttail and removed a cassette tape recorder clipped to the waistband of his pants. He disconnected it from the microphone wire and passed it to the sheriff. He winced only slightly when he ripped off the tiny microphone taped to his chest. "Thanks for setting this up, Deputy Harris."

"No thanks necessary. I appreciate your calling me. It'll probably be the only elaborate sting of my career." The two shook hands.

Noah had continued to shout obscenities, but the deputy hadn't acknowledged him until now. "I'm anxious to meet your guest here, Mr. Evans. Let's haul him up outta there," Harris said, motioning to the other two deputies, who were standing by with ropes.

"How you doin' down there, Mr. Reed? The police chief up in Mass'chusitts sure is anxious to hear what you had to say about your daddy-in-law's fall. My department's talking to the folks down in Florida, too."

Parker turned away, symbolically leaving Noah to the devil as Mike had urged him to.

He was taken aback, but not really shocked, to see his old friend standing just beyond the gin's wide door. Mike always seemed to be there when he'd most needed him.

Maris was standing with him.

Deputy Harris noticed his hesitation and sidled up behind him. "They were tearing up the road in a golf cart. Intercepted them before they could barge in here and ruin the whole thing. Had a hell of a time keeping them out. They were worried about you."

"Afraid Noah would kill me?"

"No, sir. Afraid *you* would kill *him*."

Parker smiled. "Wonder where they got that idea."

"The old man said something about your plot. Said Ms. Matherly pieced it together, figured it out."

"That doesn't surprise me."

Shuffling across the dirt floor in a stiff-legged, awkward gait, his legacy of Noah's treachery, he slowly made his way outside. Mike seemed to know he needed to make this walk alone and didn't rush to assist him. He was within touching distance before Mike asked if he wanted his wheelchair.

"Thanks, Mike."

Mike went to fetch his chair. Maris continued to stand stone still, staring at him.

"You thought I was paralyzed?"

She nodded.

"I figured. Thought it best to let you go on thinking that. For this to work, I needed Noah to think that, too." He decided he might just as well tell her the worst of it flat out. "I ride whenever I can. This is about the best I can do. Will ever do."

A tear rolled down her cheek. "It doesn't matter. It never did."

"The sweetest gift I ever received in my life was that glass of fireflies." Parker was stroking her back in the aftermath of lovemaking.

"Lightning bugs."

He chuckled. "You're learning. With help you might become a bona fide belle."

"That was a sweet night all-'round. The sweetest. Until tonight."

"Maris, that next morning—"

"Shh. I understand now why you had to be so wretched."

"You do?"

"You had to get rid of me before you could bring Noah here."

He tipped her chin up so he could see her face. "But you know I used you to get to him."

"Your original plan was probably to have him catch us like this."

He glanced down the length of their entwined bodies. "Yeah."

"But that changed when you fell in love with me. You couldn't bring yourself to subject me to an ugly scene like that. So you hurt me in order to protect me. You made certain I would leave."

He stroked her cheek. "You're so smart you amaze me."

"So I'm right?"

"As rain. Especially about me falling in love with you."

"You did?"

"I am. Present tense." He lifted her face toward his and kissed her in a way that left no room for doubt.

"There is one thing I can't figure out," she said when the kiss finally ended. "I know we promised not to talk about this tonight, but I'd like to have one point clarified."

They had agreed that they wouldn't rehash everything tonight. They faced months, possibly years, of legal entanglements before Parker was exonerated and Noah was tried and punished for his crimes. She had a publishing house to run, and he had books to write. They didn't yet know how they were going to divide their time between New York and St. Anne Island. She would grieve her father's death for a long while yet, and Parker was deliberating whether or not to reveal Mackensie Roone to his legion of fans. They had much to work out but were committed to making it work.

However, they had agreed that tomorrow didn't start until sunrise and that they deserved tonight to strictly enjoy one another.

"I don't want to invite Noah into bed with us," he said.

"I understand. And agree. But this isn't really about him."

"Okay. One point and then I want to do some more of what we were doing."

"I promise," she said, smiling. "Mike discovered that *The Vanquished* was actually your book with Noah's title on it."

"Right."

"And he tried to contact you for an explanation."

"It took him almost a year to track me down. By then the paperback edition had already come out."

"Why didn't Mike expose Noah then?"

"Because I threatened his life if he did."

"Why?"

"I was in piss-poor condition, Maris. An ex-con who looked like a beggar and was living like one. I was wheelchair-bound. Only after years of physical therapy am I able to walk at all. If you can even call that walking. When Mike found me, I was weak, wasted. Addicted to pills." He shook his head stubbornly. "I refused to confront Noah in such a reduced state when he was the book world's crowned prince."

"Enjoying the success that rightfully belonged to you."

"I chose to wait until I was strong and confident."

"And successful."

"That, too. I wanted to challenge him as an equal, when I had the credentials to back up my claim that he'd stolen my book. I knew it might take years, but I was willing to wait."

"I'm surprised you got Mike to agree."

"He didn't agree. He just gave in."

"Or?"

"Or I swore that I would never write another word as long as I lived."

"Ahh. That would have cinched it."

Now that he had answered her question, she eased herself on top of him and opened her thighs. With a grunt of satisfaction, he pressed himself inside her, began to stroke with the barest upward motion of his hips.

"Hmm. You are incredibly talented, Mr. Evans."

"Yeah, and I can write a fairly decent book, too."

Sitting up, she reached behind her, between his legs, and stroked the underside of his penis at its base. He strained a curse between his teeth. "You've got talents of your own, Ms. Matherly. Where'd you learn that trick?"

"I read it in one of your books."

"Damn, I'm good."

She continued to caress him until he pulled her down onto his chest and hugged her tightly around the waist while he pushed into her as high as possible. His raw, choppy breaths were muffled against her breasts.

Finally he relaxed, his head falling back onto the pillow. She smoothed his hair back from his damp forehead. "Felt good?"

"It still does." Cradling her face between his hands, he kissed her, whispering into her mouth, "We're being awfully messy here."

"I don't mind it. I'd like a baby."

"I can live with that."

"Or two."

"Even better."

"Parker?"

"Hmm?"

"Make me come."

She was ready. It took only a few strokes of his fingertip.

Later, they lay facing each other, their heads sharing the pillow. He was tracing her fragile collarbone when she said, "I recognized you the first time you kissed me. The night we met."

His finger fell still in the hollow just beneath her shoulder. He raised his eyes to hers. "What?"

"That's why that kiss alarmed me. Because I knew you. And not just knew you, but knew you well. Intimately. I had spent so many nights with you, poring over every word. Your book was like a personal love letter. Like you wrote it to me. Just for me.

"When you kissed me, it was so familiar, it was as though you had kissed me like that a thousand times." Adoringly, she touched every feature of his face. "I have loved you for so long, Parker. For years. From the day I first read *The Vanquished.*"

He swallowed hard. "When you talked about it with such passion . . . You got it, Maris," he said with glad emphasis. "You got exactly what I had wanted to get across with those characters and that story. God, listening to you talk about it, my heart nearly burst. Can you imagine how hard it was for me not to tell you that I was the author? That it was me, not Noah, you'd fallen in love with?"

"Why didn't you tell me?"

"I couldn't. Not then. Not yet. Besides, I was afraid I wouldn't live up to your expectations."

She ran her fingers through his hair. "You surpassed them, Parker. You created my fantasies. Now you're fulfilling them."

They kissed long and deeply and when they finally pulled apart, she asked him what his original title had been.

And he told her.

And she told him that she liked it much better.

municipalities in the cities of Calcutta, Delhi and Ahmedabad during the field survey also corroborated this. According to a tentative estimate given by the officials of the Ahmedabad Municipal Corporation, 25 per cent of the population within the municipal area consumes 90 per cent of the water supplied while the remaining 75 per cent have to make do with only 10 per cent of the water. In Calcutta and Bombay too, the supply in slum areas through public stand posts is much less than in other areas. In Calcutta, per capita water supply in slums is 20 gallons per day whereas in non-slum areas it is 60 gallons. In Bombay the corresponding figures are 90 lpcd and 130 lpcd, respectively. All these figures substantiate the conclusion based on the NSS data that the distribution of water in urban areas is extremely inequitable and biased against the poor.

The number of persons per stand post in slum areas is much above the maximum recommended under different slum improvement programmes (the EIUS norm is one tap for 150 people) in all large cities, as noted in Chapter 4. A survey conducted by the Town and Country Planning Organisation (TCPO 1984) showed that the number of slum dwellers per stand post was 170 in Rajkot, 200 in Ahmedabad, 421 in Kolhapur, 454 in Miraj and 692 in Godhra. The significant finding of the TCPO study, covering thirty urban centres belonging to different size classes, was that a substantial segment of the slum population in many of these cities was doing without the public water supply. The study cited the example of Kolhapur where a major slum cluster of 3,502 persons depended on just two wells. Our field survey in Delhi revealed that about 200 families were served by one stand post in the selected slums.

Accessibility to a water source does not necessarily mean that it is available near the premises. In many localities, the public stand post is situated at a considerable distance from the hutments. The NIUA (1988) survey showed that as many as 31 per cent of the sample households had to walk between 50 and 100 feet to collect water and many among the poor—the women and children—had to cover the distance not once but several times a day to collect the daily requirement. During the field survey in Ahmedabad, it was observed that in the eastern part of the city—which has been recently included in the municipal corporation—the poor had to walk more than half a kilometre to get one bucket of water from the roadside taps where the water supply is very erratic and is available only for a short period of time. In Delhi, 37.3 per cent of the population surveyed identified the water source being away from their houses as the major difficulty in getting water. Another important factor affecting the access of the poor to water is low water pressure and short duration of supply in public stand posts. They have to wait in long queues for their turn and in Delhi more than 80 per cent of the people complained of this.

Access to Sanitation Facilities

The basic information on the access of people in different consumption brackets to sanitation facilities analysed in this section has been taken from the 38th round of the NSS, as mentioned earlier.

Table 6.13 shows the percentages of households with access to different types of latrines and without any latrine facility over the expenditure categories. It is noted that the percentage without any latrine is very high in the lower expenditure groups and the figure goes down with the increase in the expenditure level. Accessibility to a toilet facility is, thus, positively related with per capita monthly expenditure. In the case of tap water as well, a similar relationship is noted but the disparity in distribution and the gap between the lower and upper fractiles in the latrine facility is significantly higher than in the former. It is striking that in the lower fractiles (except the bottom fractile where the total number of households is very small) only about 35 per cent of the population has latrine facilities, the figure becoming as high as 80 per cent in the top two fractiles.

The distribution of population with latrines of different types in this Table shows that poorer people are more dependent on service latrines than on septic tanks and only minimally on flush latrines. Correspondingly, people in the higher expenditure categories have more septic tanks and flush latrines. It is important that around 50 per cent of the population in the higher consumption fractiles has flush latrines that are generally connected to the sewerage system. These are managed and maintained by local authorities and for which, in some cases, only a nominal user charge is levied, as has

Table 6.13: *Percentage Distribution of Households over Types of Latrines by Per Capita Expenditure Classes in 1983*

Monthly Per Capita Expenditure Class (Rs.)	No Latrine Facility	Latrine Type			
		Service	Septic Tank	Flush System	All Households
1	2	3	4	5	6
0–30	39.86	21.03	58.23	20.73	100.00
30–40	67.04	39.29	43.99	16.72	100.00
40–50	66.00	44.92	43.43	11.65	100.00
50–60	62.17	63.37	19.90	16.73	100.00
60–70	59.54	54.97	22.28	17.75	100.00
70–85	56.63	53.93	27.28	18.79	100.00
85–100	52.17	45.96	31.20	22.83	100.00
100–125	44.49	42.85	32.84	24.30	100.00
125–150	36.98	34.52	36.85	28.62	100.00
150–200	32.27	30.08	37.50	32.41	100.00
200–250	26.57	24.18	39.15	36.67	100.00
250–300	22.21	19.32	38.72	41.96	100.00
Above 300	16.27	14.22	34.06	51.73	100.00
All Classes	36.82	30.71	35.10	34.19	100.00

Source: Based on NSSO (1987).

been noted earlier (see Chapter 3). One can, thus, argue that a heavily subsidised system of toilet and sanitation facilities is available to relatively well-off sections of the population.

The figures in Table 6.14 show that among those who have latrine facility, the incidence of shared latrines is extremely high at lower levels of consumption. There is a steady decline in the percentage of households dependent on shared latrines as we move from lower to higher consumption fractiles. People with higher consumption, thus, not only have the privilege of latrine facilities but also have them for their exclusive use. The pattern for the poor households is just the opposite, as mentioned earlier. Less than 40 per cent of the households with a monthly per capita expenditure of Rs. 85 or less have a toilet facility, and about 70 per cent of those with a toilet facility share it with others. Only in the top three fractiles are the percentages of households dependent on shared latrines less than the national average of 58 per cent.

Table 6.14: *Percentage Distribution of Households over Latrine Facilities by Per Capita Expenditure Classes in 1983*

Monthly Per Capita Expenditure Class (Rs.)	Households with Latrines	
	Shared	Exclusive
1	2	3
0–30	88.03	11.93
30–40	78.37	21.63
40–50	67.53	32.47
50–60	60.56	39.44
60–70	62.33	37.67
70–85	59.21	40.79
85–100	62.51	37.49
100–125	60.71	39.29
125–150	59.33	40.67
150–200	58.84	41.16
200–250	55.60	44.40
250–300	55.91	44.09
Above 300	51.53	48.47
All Classes	57.60	42.40

Source: Based on NSSO (1987).

In Table 6.15, the figures for the bottom 40 per cent (roughly) of households with a per capita expenditure up to Rs. 125 have been combined. The Table presents the access of these households to latrine facilities in different states and union territories. It may be seen that the average figure for households without a latrine facility for all expenditure groups is only 36.82 per cent. The corresponding figure for the bottom 40 per cent of households is substantially higher at 51.82 per cent.

It is noted that accessibility of the poor to sanitation facilities as opposed to water supply is worse in most of the states and union territories. In states such as Andhra Pradesh, Bihar, Karnataka, Madhya Pradesh, Orissa, Rajasthan and Tamil Nadu, the percentage of households without a latrine facility is much higher than the all-India average. In the eastern states of Nagaland, Manipur, Mizoram and even West Bengal, the corresponding figures for households without latrines are even lower.

In the discussion on inter-state variations in the access of the poor to water supply in the preceding section, it was observed that

Housing & Basic Amenities Available to the Urban Poor • 251

Table 6.15: *Percentage of Households with Latrine Facilities among Households with Per Capita Consumption Expenditure up to Rs. 125 in 1983*

States/Union Territories	No Latrine Facility	Households with Latrines	
		Shared	Exclusive
1	2	3	4
Andhra Pradesh	66.37	77.85	22.15
Assam	33.90	42.54	57.46
Bihar	65.97	71.67	28.33
Gujarat	43.72	54.44	45.56
Haryana	47.51	24.29	75.71
Himachal Pradesh	51.50	24.44	75.56
Jammu & Kashmir	26.63	67.00	33.00
Karnataka	61.60	60.81	39.19
Kerala	45.51	19.58	80.42
Madhya Pradesh	60.59	59.37	40.63
Maharashtra	48.58	80.03	19.97
Manipur	4.85	69.59	30.40
Nagaland	10.07	37.75	62.25
Orissa	79.75	42.52	57.48
Punjab	39.48	49.77	50.23
Rajasthan	60.33	57.15	42.85
Sikkim	32.10	63.22	36.78
Tamil Nadu	65.39	65.99	34.01
Uttar Pradesh	34.52	54.23	45.77
West Bengal	21.79	65.11	34.89
Andaman & Nicobar	52.72	73.10	26.90
Chandigarh	34.16	28.13	71.87
Delhi	47.61	50.22	49.78
Goa, Daman & Diu	81.43	24.88	75.12
Mizoram	16.99	38.42	61.58
Pondicherry	89.44	21.40	78.60
All-India	51.82	61.41	38.59

Source: Based on NSSO (1987).

the access of the poor is directly related to the level of development and the average level of water supply facilities in the state. A similar pattern, however, does not emerge in the case of sanitation facilities. The absence of latrine facilities for the poor cannot be attributed to the backwardness of the state or its overall low level of sanitation facilities. It is seen that a very high proportion of the poor households (belonging to the bottom 40 per cent) in relatively developed states like Tamil Nadu, Maharashtra and Gujarat are denied latrine facilities.

Among the households with some sort of latrine facility, over 60 per cent share it with others (Table 6.15). The states and union territories where the percentages of population sharing the facility are higher than the national average are Andhra Pradesh, Bihar, Jammu and Kashmir, Maharashtra, Tamil Nadu, West Bengal, Andaman and Nicobar Islands, Manipur and Sikkim. In Maharashtra, the figure is as high as 80 per cent and in Andhra Pradesh, Bihar, Andaman and Nicobar, it is more than 70 per cent. In Assam, Haryana, Orissa, Himachal Pradesh, Goa, Daman and Diu, Pondicherry and Mizoram, large segments among the poor have exclusive latrines, although overall population coverage with this facility is very low. Chandigarh and Nagaland appear to be exceptional cases where a large percentage of the poor have latrines and that too for their exclusive use. This is because Chandigarh and Nagaland have new and well-planned cities where the percentage of workers in private enterprises, particularly in the unorganised units, is very low.

The foregoing analysis of the availability of toilet and sanitation facilities in urban India clearly brings out the fact that the poor have a much lower share of them than the non-poor. It is indeed very alarming that more than one-third of the urban households do not have any latrine facility. Among those who do, a high percentage depend on service latrines which are unhygienic and often pose a threat to the micro environment. The provision of latrine facilities becomes more of an individual rather than a government effort as one goes from higher to lower income or consumption levels, as was noted in the case of water supply as well. Sharing of latrines is quite common among poor households as over 60 per cent among them have shared latrines. The figure is as high as 80 per cent in some states. The rich, on the other hand, have individual flush latrines that are efficient, convenient and highly subsidised by the state or local governments.

The above analysis corroborates the view of the National Commission on Urbanisation (1988) that, 'if the water supply system is unequal in favour of the rich, the sewerage system is more unjust and even more biased in favour of the rich.' Several studies at the town and state levels based on field surveys strengthen some of our results. The study conducted by the TCPO revealed that sewerage

facilities existed in only eighteen of the thirty towns/cities surveyed and here too only a small proportion of the well-to-do
population was covered. The study of Rajkot by the Operations
Research Group (ORG 1989) showed that 48 per cent of the
households did not have private latrines, 28 per cent used open
spaces for defecation and 20 per cent used public latrines. It was
noted during the field survey in Delhi, and subsequently confirmed
by the municipal authorities, that of the 44 resettlement colonies in
the city only nine were connected to the sewerage system. In
others, either the sewer lines were partly laid or were not laid at
all. The conditions in *jhuggi jhompri* clusters in Delhi are much
worse. Nearly 37 per cent of the households surveyed did not have
access to any type of latrine or sanitation facility. Another 26 per
cent used community toilets, while only 2.4 per cent had individual
toilets.

The public authorities in different cities have tried to provide
toilets with low cost technology which requires less water and no
sewerage system. But these are, more often than not, very
poorly maintained and the number of persons per toilet seat is
several times the stipulated maximum. As in the case of water
supply, the distance of the facility from one's residence is the
major problem. In Delhi, nearly 36 per cent of the households
surveyed complained of this. Long queues, dirty toilets and water
shortage (in the toilets) were the three major factors identified by
the slum dwellers for their not using the public system. Similar
situations exist in other large cities like Calcutta, Bombay, Madras
and Ahmedabad as well.

Access to the Health Care System

Data on the access of people in different consumption fractiles to
medical facilities were collected by the NSSO as a part of its 42nd
round during the period July 1986 to June 1987 (see NSSO 1989).
The households covered in the survey have generally been placed
in ten fractiles based on their per capita consumption expenditure. It
may be noted that the sample for Schedule 25.7, which provides
information on medical services, is a truncated one since a part of
the population (not reporting any ailment) has been excluded, as

discussed in the previous chapter. However, the limits of per capita expenditure obtained for the total population have been used here for classification. The percentage share of each fractile in the total households would, therefore, be 10 per cent if it is assumed that the structure of the truncated sample is not very different from that of the total sample.

Among the patients opting for hospitalisation, nearly 60 per cent go to public hospitals and PHCs, and only 30 per cent to private hospitals. The nursing homes and hospitals run by voluntary agencies together claim the remaining 10 per cent. In view of this, a detailed analysis of the availability of types of medical facilities has been attempted for the public and private hospitals only.

It may be seen that the share of people belonging to the bottom two fractiles in free ward facilities in public hospitals is higher than their share in the population (see Table 6.16). The corresponding share of the top two fractiles, on the other hand, is less than their population share. This reveals some progressivity in the distribution of free medical facilities as the poor claim a share marginally higher than the average. This is, however, not true for paying general wards where the share of the bottom three fractiles is much lower than their share in the population while for the top three fractiles the opposite is true. It must be noted that the paying general wards offer facilities at nominal charges and in most cases government expenditure per patient is much higher than in the free wards.

It is surprising that the share of the bottom two fractiles in the free wards in private hospitals is much less than their population share, while for households in the 60 to 80 fractile it is significantly higher. This implies that the poor, for some reason, are not in a position to have access to the free facilities in private hospitals. Perhaps there are other factors responsible for this. People in the middle consumption brackets are, however, doing much better in this respect. The share of the bottom two fractiles in the paying general ward in the private hospital is significantly higher than for the free ward. This suggests that when the poor seek hospitalisation in private hospitals, they are obliged to go in for the paying general wards and sometimes even the paying special wards.

Comparing the special paying ward facilities in public and private hospitals, it is noted that the top three fractiles claim a significantly

Table 6.16: Percentage Distribution of Hospitalised Cases over Per Capita Consumption Fractiles, Social Groups and Educational Categories in 1986-87

	Public Hospitals			Private Hospitals			All Hospitals				
	Free Ward	Paying General Ward	Paying Special Ward	Free Ward	Paying General Ward	Paying Special Ward	Free Ward	Paying General Ward	Paying Special Ward	All Hospitalisation Cases	Popu-lation
1	2	3	4	5	6	7	8	9	10	11	12
A. Consumption (Expenditure) Fractile											
0-10	13.46	7.78	4.33	5.52	10.88	4.12	13.12	10.02	4.31	10.99	13.05
10-20	14.67	5.19	3.72	7.88	8.64	8.69	14.18	7.50	6.09	11.00	11.62
20-40	23.53	22.07	8.04	18.57	22.18	23.21	23.21	22.82	10.38	21.42	24.37
40-60	21.25	18.91	26.32	17.69	22.14	15.39	20.96	20.13	17.25	20.21	20.27
60-80	20.22	25.28	35.80	35.24	25.64	29.08	20.97	26.47	33.28	24.32	17.04
80-90	4.32	8.39	10.40	11.78	5.13	4.47	4.47	6.59	15.91	6.80	7.32
90-100	2.55	12.38	11.39	3.32	5.39	12.19	2.79	6.47	12.81	5.26	6.01
All	100.00	100.00	100.00	100.00	100.00	100.00	100.00	100.00	100.00	100.00	100.00
B. Social Groups											
1. Scheduled Tribe	1.76	2.12	0.21	0.67	2.18	1.07	1.89	1.84	0.79	1.73	2.64
2. Scheduled Caste	19.42	11.98	2.64	15.45	12.27	3.21	19.04	12.68	2.69	14.90	12.32
3. Others	78.51	85.87	97.15	83.71	85.31	96.04	78.75	85.29	96.23	83.10	85.03
All	100.00	100.00	100.00	100.00	100.00	100.00	100.00	100.00	100.00	100.00	100.00
C. Educational Categories											
1. Illiterate	13.84	5.40	0.34	4.15	7.88	2.92	13.19	6.88	2.01	9.72	38.13
2. Literate but Below Primary	7.13	2.18	1.46	11.12	4.80	5.78	7.46	3.88	4.17	5.89	8.17
3. Primary but Below Secondary	38.58	32.67	25.21	25.77	35.33	15.75	37.44	33.91	17.90	33.78	31.09
4. Secondary and Above	40.32	59.75	72.99	58.59	51.99	75.55	41.73	55.38	75.92	50.51	22.61

Source: Based on NSSO (1989).

higher share in public rather than in private hospitals (Table 6.16). This is against the general belief that the poor always go to public hospitals and the rich prefer private ones. It is well-known that the component of subsidy in the public hospitals, even in the special paying wards, is substantial and is cornered largely by the well-to-do as a result of their higher paying capacity or better connections.

The use of paying special wards in private hospitals by the poor is limited to cases of emergency. This becomes necessary owing to the non-availability of specialised testing and treatment facilities in the public hospitals to the urban poor, even in critical cases, forcing them to go to private hospitals on payment far beyond their affordability. This could also be because of deliberate mis-reporting of consumption expenditure by certain people using expensive medical facilities or sampling errors.

When we consider the total number of hospitalisation cases (free as well as paying) in the public sector, the bias in favour of the poor, as noted in the case of free ward facilities, becomes much less. The percentage among the poor who are successful in getting beds in public hospitals is about the same as for the general population. There is, thus, no evidence to suggest that the government hospitals are being patronised largely by the poor. The slightly higher share of the bottom 20 per cent of the population in the free wards of public hospitals may be attributed to the withdrawal of the rich from these hospitals because of their indifferent quality.

Among the social groups, the Scheduled Tribes are definitely underprivileged as their share in all types of medical facilities is less than their population share. For the Scheduled Caste population, however, the share is significantly higher for free ward facilities, both in public and private hospitals. This indicates that the Scheduled Castes are well integrated with the urban society (which is not the case with the Scheduled Tribes) and are therefore able to get a fair share of the subsidised medical facilities.

Illiteracy emerges as a major factor explaining non-access to medical facilities. Illiterates have a very low share in all types of hospital facilities. Their share even in free wards or general paying wards, in public as well as private hospitals, is significantly below their population share. However, people with an educational level of secondary school and above claim a very large share in free and paid medical facilities, which reflects better awareness, connections and paying capacity.

The shares of different fractiles in free hospitalisation cases show a bias in favour of the poor (Table 6.17). However, the bottom four fractiles claim a small share under the employer's medical benefit scheme largely because most of the people in these categories work in informal activities and are not covered under the scheme. The top two fractiles also claim a share much smaller than their share in the population. It is the middle class, belonging to the 60 to 80 fractile, which corners a large share of benefits under the scheme.

Table 6.17: *Percentage Distribution of Hospitalised Cases over Per Capita Consumption Fractiles, Payment Categories and Average Payment in 1986-87*

Consumption (Expenditure) Fractiles	Payment Categories		Average Payment (Rs. 0.00)	
	No Payment	Claiming from Employer's Medical Scheme	Government	Private
1	2	3	4	5
0–10	17.37	5.07	309.64	602.33
10–20	14.74	6.78	136.50	661.58
20–30	16.83	7.47	295.66	753.05
30–40	10.46	7.59	695.69	864.78
40–50	11.52	13.86	217.55	1177.10
50–60	6.75	10.23	360.30	1207.39
60–70	7.93	14.99	211.72	1020.23
70–80	8.86	20.53	486.03	1499.08
80–90	3.15	8.68	444.49	1800.46
90–100	2.39	4.80	945.05	2564.13
All	100.00	100.00	385.02	1206.01

Source: Based on NSSO (1989).

The average payment for hospitalisation in public hospitals is about 40 per cent of the private hospitals, which indicates that treatment in the former works out to be cheaper than in the latter. However, the average payment in public hospitals for the bottom three fractiles does not work out to be very much less than the average for all categories. The corresponding figure for these fractiles in private hospitals is, however, about half of the all-urban average. One can therefore argue that while the private hospitals are able to charge different rates from people in different income brackets by varying the size of the room, occupancy, duration of stay, quality of services, etc., such flexibility does not exist in public hospitals.

Government hospitals emerge as an important facility providing out-patient treatment as well, its share being 22.6 per cent of all cases which compares favourably with the figure of 16.2 for private hospitals. Private doctors, however, are the single most important source for providing out-patient treatment, their share being 51.8 per cent. Public hospitals exhibit a sensitivity in favour of the poor which is absent in the case of private hospitals (see Table 6.18). Private doctors, on the other hand, cater to the needs of people in all levels of consumption (and income), their share being similar across the fractiles. This reflects that private doctors are important

Table 6.18: *Percentage Distribution of Treatment (other than Hospitalisation) over Per Capita Consumption Fractiles and Sources of Treatment in 1986–87*

Consumption Expenditure (Fractiles)	Public Hospital	Private Hospital	Private Doctor	All	Population
1	2	3	4	5	6
0–10	13.55	10.03	10.21	12.19	13.02
10–20	14.99	7.57	10.12	9.39	11.62
20–30	16.21	15.37	12.38	10.99	12.54
30–40	8.55	7.88	8.69	11.80	11.82
40–50	11.25	11.10	11.23	7.03	9.55
50–60	7.38	10.68	8.03	10.82	10.72
60–70	8.24	10.54	12.02	10.41	8.65
70–80	11.21	13.15	15.96	9.37	8.39
80–90	5.00	8.02	5.81	11.70	7.32
90–100	3.62	5.66	5.55	6.30	6.01
All	100.00	100.00	100.00	100.00	100.00
Per Cent Cases Treated	(22.60)	(16.18)	(51.83)	(100.00)	–

Source: Based on NSSO (1989).
Note: Figures in brackets are percentage shares of each source of treatment to all treatments. The figures for these do not add up to 100 as some other types of treatment are excluded in the Table.

in providing medical facilities to the poor as well. This fact emerged in the slum survey of Delhi as well where approximately 92 per cent of people reported going to private physicians. Major ailments were relatively few while minor ailments occurred frequently. This has a bearing on the preference for private doctors: 60 per cent of the households reported proximity as the most important reason for availing of the services of private doctors whereas 15 per cent said it was because they were given immediate attention. This implies (see Table 6.19) that hospitals and dispensaries are not in a position to meet the needs of the poor by providing easy accessibility and immediate attention. The grievances with regard to government hospitals are presented in Table 6.20. About 90 per cent of the households considered the unsympathetic attitude of the doctors and other staff, long waiting time and distance from home as the major factors inhibiting their use of public hospitals.

Table 6.19: Percentage Distribution of Households by Reasons for Using Private Doctors/Dispensaries in Delhi

Reasons	Priority						Total
	1	2	3				
	1	2	3	4	5		
Doctor is close by	65.52	18.45	16.11	33.00			
Immediate attention	16.16	44.65	25.58	29.04			
Quality of treatment is good	6.36	18.45	36.84	20.62			
Sympathetic attitude	4.20	12.04	12.32	9.50			
No long queues	7.76	6.41	9.15	7.76			

Source: Primary data from the Survey of Slums conducted for this study during December 1989 and January 1990.

Interestingly, the exhorbitant charges of private doctors was not mentioned as a hindrance in availing of their services. This may be because the immediate and personalised attention of the private doctors compensates for their•higher charges. What the slum dwellers want is quick and easy access to a doctor, proper attention and quick relief through medication so that the loss of wages earned on a daily basis is minimal.

Table 6.21 shows that those in the bottom fractiles have a slightly higher share than their population in out-patient treatment

Table 6.20: *Percentage Distribution of Households by Grievances about Government Hospitals in Delhi*

Grievances	Ist	IInd	IIIrd	Total
1	2	3	4	5
Long waiting time	31.51	30.08	25.29	29.18
Unsympathetic attitude	36.88	24.78	21.04	27.79
Distance from home	24.87	14.30	18.92	19.51
Non-availability of free medicine	4.74	22.56	29.23	16.56
Unsuitable time	2.00	8.26	10.52	6.96

Source: Slum Survey of Delhi, December 1989.

Table 6.21: *Percentage Distribution of Out-patient Treatment over Per Capita Consumption Fractiles, Payment Categories and Average Payment in 1986–87*

Consumption (Expenditure) Fractiles	Payment Categories		Average Payment (Rs.)	
	No Payment	Claiming from Employer's Medical Scheme	Government	Private
1	2	3	4	5
0–10	14.11	7.58	42.26	50.35
10–20	14.85	5.15	39.82	53.05
20–30	15.19	7.92	59.43	53.43
30–40	7.49	8.50	142.77	75.13
40–50	12.08	10.15	29.44	52.90
50–60	7.92	11.16	57.59	65.27
60–70	8.41	11.45	180.38	75.05
70–80	10.61	20.84	55.70	139.71
80–90	5.61	9.43	95.31	132.90
90–100	3.73	8.82	84.95	142.39
All	100.00	100.00	74.17	80.49

Source: Based on NSSO (1989).

without payment. Claiming benefits under the employer's medical scheme appears to be the privilege of the 60 to 80 fractile, as noted in the case of hospitalisation. The top two fractiles also have a much higher share in the benefits of this medical scheme than their population share as given in Table 6.16. The slum survey of Delhi clearly brought out the fact that as people in the lower consumption fractiles are engaged largely in the informal sector or are self-employed in petty activities, they are not covered under any employer's medical scheme. It is not surprising that there is not much variation in average payment, both in the case of government and private hospitals across fractiles. The flexibility in charging (by varying the quality of services), as noted in the case of hospitalisation facilities, is absent here. This implies that the medical system, both in the public and the private sector, does not significantly differentiate between people in different income categories based on their paying capacity and thereby fails to cater to the urban poor.

In order to assess the dependence of people in different fractiles on different systems of medicine, indices of specialisation (Sij) have been computed as in case of drinking water facilities earlier in this chapter. Here these are obtained by dividing the percentage share of each fractile in the total number of cases under a specific system by the share of that fractile in the total population, as shown below:

$$Sij = \dfrac{\dfrac{\text{Persons in the } ith \text{ fractile using the } jth \text{ system}}{\text{All persons using the } jth \text{ system}}}{\dfrac{\text{Persons in the } ith \text{ fractile using any system}}{\text{All persons using any system}}}$$

The index for hospitalisation under the allopathic system works out to be near unity for all fractiles implying that it is used by people irrespective of their consumption (or income) level (Table 6.22). The values, however, are more than unity for ayurvedic and unani systems for the bottom fractiles which may be viewed with some concern. Although judgement regarding the relative superiority of a system of medicine is not warranted here, the way these two systems of medicine are practised currently in the country leaves much scope for informal treatment and sub-standard facilities. The remedy would either be to increase the coverage of the poor under the allopathic system or improve the quality of ayurvedic and unani hospitals. The latter would be more difficult to implement than the former. The category 'others' (Table 6.22) shows a very

Table 6.22: *Specialisation Index for Different Systems of Medicine by Per Capita Consumption Fractiles for Hospitalisation Cases in 1986–87*

Consumption (Expenditure) Fractiles	Allopathy	Homoeo-pathy	Ayurvedic	Unani	Others
1	2	3	4	5	6
0–10	1.00	0.82	1.42	0.00	0.98
10–20	1.00	0.75	1.36	1.24	1.95
20–30	1.00	0.96	1.78	1.83	0.50
30–40	1.00	0.66	1.43	0.11	1.11
40–50	1.00	2.09	1.43	0.11	1.11
50–60	1.00	1.28	0.18	1.59	0.75
60–70	1.00	0.37	0.72	0.58	0.80
70–80	1.00	0.69	0.64	2.77	0.78
80–90	1.00	1.44	0.64	0.25	1.18
90–100	0.99	1.09	0.77	0.00	2.41

Source: Based on NSSO (1989).

high specialisation index of 2.41 for the top-most fractile, indicating that a section among the rich goes to yoga centres and other therapeutic hospitals which are becoming popular.

The pattern for out-patient treatment is similar to that of hospitalisation when the systems of medicine are taken into consideration (Table 6.23). The values of the specialisation index are near unity for allopathic treatment in all the fractiles. It is not possible to claim that only the poor opt for ayurvedic and unani treatment since some of the upper fractiles also show higher values. The bottom fractile has a specialisation index of 2.70 for 'other systems' which is obviously because the poorest among the poor often resort to informal treatment based on tradition and superstition.

Another aspect of access to medical facilities can be analysed by considering the persons receiving treatment as a percentage of those with ailments across various consumption fractiles. The percentage goes up systematically from 84.7 for the bottom fractile to 91.8 per cent for the 60 to 80 fractile, the figure stabilising thereafter (Table 6.24). The trend is similar for males and females (not shown in the Table). Education emerges as an important factor in access to medical facilities. Disaggregative NSS data for rural and urban areas show that while among the illiterate males, only 84.8 per cent cases receive treatment, the figure is 91.7 for those with

Table 6.23: *Specialisation Index for Different Systems of Medicine by Per Capita Consumption (Expenditure) Fractile for Out-patient Treatment*

Consumption (Expenditure) Fractiles	Allopathy	Homoeo-pathy	Ayurvedic	Unani	Others
1	2	3	4	5	6
0–10	0.98	1.20	1.09	0.94	2.70
10–20	1.02	1.44	1.06	1.88	0.53
20–30	1.00	1.00	1.01	0.69	1.00
30–40	1.00	1.03	1.00	1.17	0.87
40–50	1.01	0.90	1.09	0.45	0.87
50–60	0.99	0.96	1.42	1.52	1.34
60–70	1.01	0.83	0.94	0.68	1.40
70–80	1.02	1.12	0.69	0.95	0.27
80–90	0.96	1.72	1.18	1.27	0.31
90–100	1.01	1.06	0.46	0.86	0.00

Source: Based on NSSO (1989).

primary (but below secondary) education. The corresponding fig-ures for females are 75.5 per cent and 89.2 per cent. It may further be noted that the rural-urban difference in the rate of receiving treatment is marginal for people with secondary and higher levels of education, although this is significant for persons with lower levels of education.

Table 6.24, which shows the percentage of treatment to ailment over consumption fractiles for different states, confirms that the higher the level of consumption, the higher the coverage, although the inter-fractile variation is not very significant. The variation across states too is not great once one excludes Andhra Pradesh where only 73 per cent of ailments are treated against the all-India average of 89 per cent. It is, thus, obvious that access to any kind of medical facility is not a major problem for the urban poor. The real problem relates to the nature of the facility, its quality and the amount to be paid while availing of it.

The specialisation index for non-treatment (Table 6.25) shows that the major reason inhibiting the access of the poor to medical facilities is lack of finance since the values for the bottom three fractiles are very high. This is true for the Scheduled Castes and Scheduled Tribes, as also for the illiterate population. Lack of faith in the available system of medicine and long waiting time also emerge as

Table 6.24: *Percentage of Persons with Ailments Treated as Out-patients to All Persons with Ailments (Excluding Hospitalisation Cases) in 1986-87*

States	0–10	10–20	20–40	40–60	60–80	80–90	90–100	All
1	2	3	4	5	6	7	8	9
Andhra Pradesh	60.2	72.2	75.4	77.0	71.4	76.2	73.7	73.0
Assam	68.0	85.5	85.9	94.9	90.2	95.7	93.6	87.2
Bihar	83.5	90.7	94.8	89.9	94.8	94.3	93.9	91.5
Gujarat	87.3	98.9	95.4	89.5	96.4	97.5	95.6	94.6
Haryana	82.6	93.3	88.6	89.6	91.2	97.2	10.0	90.9
Himachal Pradesh	–	–	–	–	–	–	–	–
Jammu & Kashmir	10.0	96.8	94.9	10.0	98.6	10.0	10.0	98.1
Karnataka	97.1	98.8	95.3	92.7	93.6	94.9	94.9	95.2
Kerala	97.4	85.3	88.7	92.1	89.2	99.7	84.1	90.1
Madhya Pradesh	82.2	83.2	84.1	90.5	92.7	89.9	91.7	87.0
Maharashtra	91.7	95.7	91.1	95.1	98.2	96.3	98.6	95.2
Orissa	87.5	92.3	75.9	94.1	94.8	95.8	89.5	88.6
Punjab	99.0	89.9	94.8	97.9	98.1	97.2	99.4	96.5
Rajasthan	86.8	87.9	93.1	90.1	93.3	97.8	81.9	90.5
Tamil Nadu	78.10	90.7	88.9	87.2	90.6	92.8	84.6	88.4
Tripura	97.2	10.0	84.0	95.5	93.5	87.4	10.0	93.7
Uttar Pradesh	88.6	86.4	85.9	89.2	90.6	37.6	92.8	88.1
West Bengal	75.7	87.3	90.6	89.0	90.7	90.7	90.9	88.1
All-India	84.7	87.8	88.5	89.2	91.8	90.9	89.3	89.1

Source: Based on NSSO (1989).

Table 6.25: *Specialisation Index for Reasons of Non-Treatment by Consumption Fractiles, Social Groups and Educational Categories in 1986–87*

Consumption (Expenditure) Fractiles	Reasons for Non-treatment			
	No Medical Facilities	Lack of Faith in the System	Long Waiting	Financial Reasons
1	2	3	4	5
0–10	1.07	1.29	1.21	1.73
10–20	–	0.81	1.98	1.65
20–30	2.28	0.27	0.90	1.77
30–40	0.38	0.31	0.74	0.57
40–50	–	0.73	0.40	0.62
50–60	–	0.34	0.19	0.65
60–70	–	0.37	0.42	0.63
70–80	3.99	3.10	1.17	0.24
80–90	–	3.71	5.32	0.28
90–100	1.20	–	–	0.01
Social Groups				
1. Scheduled Tribes	13.07	2.65	0.10	1.24
2. Scheduled Castes	0.09	2.24	1.24	1.20
3. Others	0.85	0.67	0.97	0.95
Educational Categories				
1. Illiterate	2.13	1.18	1.08	1.85
2. Literate but below primary	–	1.63	1.65	1.30
3. Primary but below secondary	0.16	1.40	1.09	0.95
4. Secondary and above	1.20	0.55	0.79	0.58

Source: Based on NSSO (1989).

important factors inhibiting the access of the poor. This conclusion is further supported by the findings of the micro-level study of Delhi where 82 per cent of the households reported long waiting time and the consequent loss of wage-hours as one of the three factors responsible for non-use of public hospitals, as shown in Table 6.20. However, those in the higher consumption fractiles also reported these as important explanations for non-treatment (Table 6.25).

It may be noted that there are aberrations to the general pattern

Table 6.26: *Percentage Share of Bottom 40 Per cent Households in the Total Hospitalisation Cases over Sources of Treatment in Selected States*

States	Public Hospital	Primary Health Centre	Private Hospital	Nursing Home	Charitable Hospital	All	Population
1	2	3	4	5	6	7	8
Andhra Pradesh	45.72	N.A.	33.67	26.28	55.42	38.73	44.20
Assam	48.95	60.02	63.76	11.18	100.00	42.77	51.62
Bihar	59.88	30.68	19.04	42.73	18.49	42.57	47.87
Gujarat	48.79	N.A.	35.65	44.32	28.81	58.79	48.22
Haryana	41.20	N.A.	34.62	63.73	44.06	40.80	53.96
Himachal Pradesh	78.58	100.00	86.28	N.A.	N.A.	80.86	58.22
Jammu & Kashmir	48.80	66.35	59.58	N.A.	N.A.	49.48	48.78
Karnataka	44.46	N.A.	29.79	21.01	13.74	35.68	47.08
Kerala	61.95	100.00	53.94	56.09	100.00	59.05	51.78
Madhya Pradesh	48.22	34.95	34.95	18.69	37.61	44.40	47.08
Maharashtra	43.77	29.79	29.79	4.07	32.14	35.61	48.54
Orissa	53.94	42.26	66.36	–	32.66	53.94	49.38
Punjab	56.55	100.00	34.34	47.02	98.47	47.65	50.64
Rajasthan	50.18	90.56	27.40	47.12	12.48	48.01	57.08
Tamil Nadu	55.84	11.44	30.65	7.67	28.78	43.51	46.10
Tripura	72.97	48.58	N.A.	N.A.	N.A.	71.55	45.58
Uttar Pradesh	54.61	27.58	47.42	44.48	39.56	51.80	51.82
West Bengal	52.96	97.84	36.87	18.75	16.64	46.43	48.01
All-India	48.22	49.11	36.52	31.56	44.68	43.41	48.66

Source: Based on NSSO (1989).

Table 6.27: *Percentage Share of Bottom 40 Per cent Households in Total Cases of Out-patient Treatment over Sources of Treatment in Selected States*

States	Public Hospital	Primary Health Centre	Public Dispensary	Private Hospital	Nursing Home	Charitable Dispensary	ESI/AMA	Private Doctors	All	Population
1	2	3	4	5	6	7	8	9	10	11
Andhra Pradesh	46.58	96.44	48.76	27.73	23.89	100.00	22.23	4.56	35.52	44.20
Assam	60.55	85.48	92.81	19.57	96.11	–	–	27.36	42.89	51.62
Bihar	58.26	35.08	39.65	23.73	56.80	–	–	56.75	49.38	47.87
Gujarat	35.63	19.48	90.30	51.94	–	51.39	32.80	37.21	44.63	48.22
Haryana	26.31	–	–	23.36	26.01	–	27.80	44.22	37.57	53.96
Himachal Pradesh	46.83	42.36	–	30.69	–	–	–	57.78	50.74	58.22
Jammu & Kashmir	49.64	61.92	80.05	35.30	–	44.99	53.07	44.30	49.01	48.78
Karnataka	56.29	53.72	18.99	30.84	25.78	11.80	25.63	44.68	43.42	47.08
Kerala	68.87	69.55	94.84	55.75	43.52	100.00	8.35	49.54	59.04	51.78
Madhya Pradesh	48.89	70.51	87.92	35.77	48.82	61.59	72.41	39.68	43.45	47.08
Maharashtra	50.53	25.08	25.27	28.76	8.03	34.26	22.56	32.82	34.82	48.54
Orissa	60.27	5.94	32.52	64.04	–	80.25	22.03	42.04	50.08	49.38
Punjab	43.92	20.44	54.40	42.85	39.01	79.67	81.11	37.95	39.26	50.64
Rajasthan	52.33	51.50	44.59	60.02	16.32	100.00	100.00	57.48	55.09	57.08
Tamil Nadu	55.46	24.21	9.62	35.26	21.67	92.44	20.90	40.87	42.44	46.10
Tripura	66.83	91.93	31.53	–	–	–	–	61.72	64.40	45.58
Uttar Pradesh	61.72	62.10	14.87	56.22	31.50	66.94	22.19	57.64	57.55	51.82
West Bengal	49.13	86.53	79.91	8.13	–	76.80	44.76	38.92	40.93	48.01
All-India	53.30	52.11	37.33	40.85	26.74	61.39	22.37	41.40	43.74	48.66

Source: Based on NSSO (1989).

discussed in the present section (and in earlier sections) as the values in certain fractiles do not conform to the pattern. These, however, can be attributed to sampling errors or random factors. Nonetheless, recognition of the values that go against the pattern should weaken our confidence in the general results discussed above.

Inter-state variations in the shares of those in the bottom four fractiles (covering roughly the bottom 40 per cent of the households) in medical facilities (see Tables 6.26 and 6.27) are not very high. The hill states of Himachal Pradesh and Tripura and the coastal state of Kerala show very high availability of hospitalisation facilities to the poor as compared to the national average. The other states that report relatively higher values are the less developed states of Bihar, Orissa and Uttar Pradesh and the developed states of Punjab, Tamil Nadu and West Bengal. The states that report low values are Haryana, Maharashtra and Karnataka. For out-patient treatment the pattern is similar (Table 6.27), except that Himachal Pradesh reports only the average level of the facility although Tripura and Kerala maintain their advantage. Further, Maharashtra comes near the national average or slightly above it while the position of Haryana goes down further. It is difficult to explain this pattern of access in terms of the levels of economic development or the (average) level of medical facilities in the states since the corresponding correlation works out to be statistically insignificant.

Access to the Public Distribution System

Data for the 42nd round of the NSS on the utilisation of the public distribution system (PDS) have been collected using a moving reference period of thirty days preceding the date of enquiry. Persons reporting purchase of a commodity provided through the PDS have been put in three categories: (a) those purchasing it only from the PDS, (b) those buying from the PDS as well as from other sources, and (c) those buying entirely from other sources. People in these three categories, for any particular commodity, therefore, would not add up to the total sample size because there are persons who do not buy that commodity from any source. These would be people who produce the commodity or get it free (in rural areas), and those who do not have any preference for it. Table 6.28 shows the percentage of persons who buy their total or partial requirements of rice, wheat, other cereals and sugar from the PDS to all persons reporting the purchase of that commodity from any source. Similarly, Table 6.29 gives the percentage of persons who purchase their total supply of these commodities from the PDS alone. If the figures in Table 6.29 are subtracted from the corresponding figures in Table 6.28 for any commodity, one would arrive at the percentage of persons who buy that commodity both from the PDS and other sources.

Table 6.28: *Percentage of Persons Dependent Fully or Partially on the PDS to All Persons over Consumption Fractiles for Select Items in 1986–87*

Fractile Groups	Rice	Wheat	Other Cereals	Sugar
1	2	3	4	5
0–10	47.67	32.86	5.16	72.45
10–20	42.87	36.52	6.43	73.35
20–40	36.42	39.00	5.37	76.36
40–60	39.20	39.89	4.93	76.65
60–80	35.04	35.94	3.97	76.12
80–90	31.53	33.05	3.93	78.73
90–100	25.96	28.32	1.03	74.55
All	39.03	36.70	4.76	75.63

Source: Based on NSSO (1990b).

Note: The category 'Other Cereals' is the same as that used by the NSS and does not include *jowar* and *bajra*.

It may be seen from Table 6.28 that the percentage of persons who buy sugar wholly or partially from the PDS is higher than that for rice, wheat or other cereals, the figures being 76, 39, 37 and 5 per cent, respectively. Obviously a large number of persons buy sugar from ration shops as the difference between the PDS and the market price is quite significant for sugar than for any other item. Also, the possibility of variation in the quality of sugar is likely to be less than for cereals. Thus, one can clearly see that a section

Table 6.29: *Percentage of Persons Dependent Fully on the PDS to All Persons over Consumption Fractiles for Select Items in 1986–87*

Fractile Groups	Rice	Wheat	Other Cereals	Sugar
1	2	3	4	5
0–10	10.72	26.37	3.68	43.89
10–20	9.86	31.00	5.33	36.92
20–40	11.23	30.64	4.02	31.72
40–60	13.24	31.33	2.70	26.22
60–80	10.91	28.29	2.93	22.91
80–90	10.53	28.12	3.53	19.06
90–100	8.27	23.87	1.03	14.89
0–40	10.77	29.39	4.20	36.03
All	11.13	29.48	3.44	29.18

Source: Based on NSSO (1990b).
Note: The category 'Other Cereals' is the same as that used by the NSS and does not include *jowar* and *bajra*.

among the relatively better-off purchases only sugar and not cereals from the PDS.

The variation in the percentage of persons buying sugar from the PDS, partially or fully, is not very high across the fractiles (Table 6.28). Nevertheless, the pattern is important. While in the bottom two fractiles the percentage of persons buying sugar is 72 and 73 per cent, for the top two fractiles the figures are 80 and 75 per cent. It is thus clear that as far as sugar is concerned, the dependence of the rich on the PDS is as much as that of the poor, if not more.

The percentage of persons buying sugar only from the PDS is 43.9 in the lowest fractile, the figure being 14.9 per cent for the highest fractile (Table 6.29). This is primarily because many among the poor manage within their ration quota by curtailing their sugar requirement while the rich buy from the market in addition to the amount available from the PDS. In the slums of Delhi, our survey showed that 65.3 per cent of the households obtained their entire supply of sugar from the PDS.

The percentage of persons buying rice and wheat partially or fully from the PDS varies significantly over the fractiles, the pattern being different from that for sugar. It is interesting that the average percentage of persons buying rice is about the same as for wheat. However, inter-fractile variations are high for rice but not so for wheat. In the bottom fractile, 48 per cent buy rice from the PDS while the corresponding figure for wheat is only 33. For the top-most fractile the figures are 26 and 28 per cent for the two cereals, respectively. The high dependence of people in the bottom fractile for rice from the PDS can be explained by the policies of certain state governments like Assam, Tripura, Andhra Pradesh, Tamil Nadu, Karnataka and Kerala: the policy of strengthening their public distribution system for rice by adding their own supply and providing it at a cheaper rate to the poor than to other sections of the population. If the southern states (that report high variation in the percentage of people covered, fully or partially, by the PDS for rice across the fractiles) are excluded, the percentage of persons buying rice from the PDS in the bottom fractile will come down from 47 to a value near the average. This would also reduce the inter-fractile variations in rice and the pattern would become similar to that of wheat.

It is important that 89 per cent of the people buying rice and 74 per cent of those buying wheat are dependent partially or fully on the open market. In large metropolitan cities where the PDS is somewhat better organised, the figures are probably not that high. In the case of Delhi, for example, only 65 per cent of the population buys these items from the market. It may be seen that the figures for the bottom-most fractile are slightly higher than the national averages. This lack of sensitivity of the PDS in favour of the poor reflects a significant deficiency in the system throughout the country. It may be noted from Table 6.29 that the percentages of persons buying rice only from the PDS do not vary across the fractiles, except in the case of the top fractile. The same is true for wheat as well. One may also note that the figure for the bottom fractile for wheat is less than the national (urban) average. This reflects lack of progressivity in favour of the poor, which alone can justify the large subsidies that are being handed over to the consumers through this system. A major failure of the PDS is this lack of progressivity in the distribution of cereals which goes against the general impression that the rich buy only sugar from the PDS.

The percentage of persons partially dependent on the PDS for rice is four times that for wheat, the figures being 28 and 7 per cent respectively (the figures can be obtained by subtracting the values in Table 6.29 from the corresponding values in Table 6.28). There is significant variation in the figures for rice, ranging from 37 per cent for the bottom fractile to 18 per cent for the top fractile, primarily because of the provision of rice to the poor at highly subsidised rates in the southern states, as discussed earlier. The quantity available, however, is not enough and compels households in these states to buy from the open market as well. For wheat the inter-fractile variation is less. It may therefore be argued that while in the case of wheat, the thrust of the policy should be to increase the coverage of persons, for rice it should be both to increase the coverage and quantity supplied.

The higher percentage of persons totally dependent on the PDS for wheat may not be taken to reflect a satisfactory situation relating to the amount of supply. The high value (relative to rice) is partially due to the higher figures in rice-eating states where people buy wheat from the PDS only to supplement their cereal consumption and therefore do not have to buy it (wheat) from the market. It is important that in the bottom fractile a larger percentage of persons rely totally on the market for the purchase of wheat, namely, 67 per cent as opposed to 52 per cent for rice. One can argue that among those buying wheat and rice only from the market, a large majority do not possess a ration card. When the only option left to a poor person is to buy cereals from the open market, he or she chooses wheat instead of rice, the former being less expensive. For the same reason, some people buy wheat from the open market when the supply of rice from the PDS is inadequate. However, substitution of wheat for rice is unlikely because of the relative prices.

The importance of the PDS in terms of quantity supplied is evident from Table 6.30. The PDS supplies 47 per cent of the total demand of sugar. The figure works out to be high basically due to the higher value for the lower fractiles where supply restricts demand. People in the lower fractiles adjust their requirements according to the availability through the PDS, as mentioned earlier. The lower share of PDS sugar for higher consumption groups is due to higher demand and the fact that the PDS entitlement is often uniform (per member in the card-holding household) across the consumption fractiles.[1]

The percentage share of PDS purchase to total purchase falling marginally over the fractiles (Table 6.30) for rice reflects a desirable

Table 6.30: *Percentage of Quantity Purchased from the PDS to Total Amount Purchased over Consumption Fractiles for Select Items in 1986–87*

Fractile Groups	Rice	Wheat	Other Cereals	Sugar
1	2	3	4	5
0–10	21.52	12.34	1.93	58.40
10–20	21.04	16.60	3.40	54.52
20–40	18.45	18.12	3.40	51.30
40–60	19.60	23.50	4.15	45.92
60–80	18.24	20.00	4.50	42.85
80–90	16.70	22.11	4.75	40.71
90–100	14.65	19.50	1.30	36.26
All	19.02	19.33	3.59	46.78
Estimated Quantity of Total Purchase (in thousand kg)	7,68,462	5,24,129	36,642	1,54,994

Source: Based on NSSO (1990b).

progressivity. The values, however, are not very different except for the top two fractiles. A perverse pattern is, however, perceptible in the case of wheat, the share of the PDS being higher in higher consumption fractiles. The national average works out to be more than one and a half times the share of the bottom fractile. This clearly suggests that the richer section of the population obtain a higher share of its wheat requirement from the PDS than the poor. It is interesting that using the same data and similar tabulation schemes for rice and wheat, Mahendra Dev and Satyanarayana (1991) have come to the conclusion that there is no bias in the PDS in favour of the rich.

The figures in Table 6.31 can be obtained by first computing the percentage of PDS to market purchases from the figures in Table 6.30 and then multiplying the latter by the price-relative P_1/P_2, where P_1 and P_2 are the PDS and open market prices, respectively. The values in Table 6.31 being less than the corresponding figures in Table 6.30 suggests that P_1/P_2 is less than unity, since the PDS price is lower than that in the market. The decline, however, is not uniform across the fractiles. The values go down much more for the lower fractiles in the case of rice while the opposite is true for wheat. This implies that the price-relative (PDS to open market price) is more

Table 6.31: *Value of Purchase from the PDS as Percentage of Total Purchase over Consumption Fractiles for Select Items in 1986–87*

Fractile Groups		Rice	Wheat	Other Cereals	Sugar
1		2	3	4	5
0–10		15.44	11.95	1.65	48.64
10–20		15.45	16.04	3.11	44.97
20–40		13.43	16.89	2.96	41.68
40–60		14.01	20.88	3.42	36.80
60–80		12.94	17.66	3.00	33.81
80–90		11.46	18.71	3.18	31.75
90–100		9.63	15.11	0.66	28.14
All		13.53	17.41	2.81	37.40
Estimated Value of Total Purchase (in thousand Rs.)		28,31,371	12,34,778	1,07,568	8,48,203

Source: Based on NSSO (1990b).

favourable to the poor for rice than for wheat. This is primarily because the poor are charged a lower price for rice in several states which is, generally, not the case for wheat.

It may be mentioned that among the consumers of other cereals in the bottom-most fractile, 95 per cent buy all their requirements from the market. This is because 'other cereals' are not covered under the PDS in several states. This may also be attributed to the open market price not being significantly higher than the PDS price in this case.

Table 6.32 gives the percentage of persons in the 0 to 40 fractiles using only the PDS for rice, wheat and sugar in different states, while Table 6.33 shows the corresponding figures for persons using the PDS as well as other sources. It is clear that the all-India figures for the 0 to 40 fractile are not very different from the averages for all fractiles, given in Tables 6.28 and 6.29. This further corroborates the fact that the PDS lacks a bias in favour of the poor in the distribution of cereals. It is important that in the states of Jammu and Kashmir, Gujarat, West Bengal and Maharashtra, the access of the poor to the PDS for cereals is reasonably satisfactory. In the rice-eating states of south India and in the north-eastern states of Assam and Tripura, the percentage in the 0

Table 6.32: Percentage of Persons belonging to the Bottom 40 Per cent Expenditure Category Depending Solely on the PDS for Select Items in 1986–87

States	Items	Rice	Wheat	Sugar
		2	3	4
	1			
Andhra Pradesh		6.78	52.73	51.12
Assam		0.94	5.28	7.88
Bihar		0.32	3.64	48.40
Gujarat		28.33	24.50	15.77
Haryana		10.40	0.00	4.03
Himachal Pradesh		21.22	9.95	8.10
Jammu & Kashmir		30.36	25.62	58.26
Karnataka		6.74	59.84	43.71
Kerala		4.22	95.01	22.30
Madhya Pradesh		17.44	5.67	81.23
Maharashtra		24.67	24.61	11.67
Orissa		–	18.88	47.97
Punjab		2.40	–	1.46
Rajasthan		3.08	6.44	22.04
Tamil Nadu		2.28	75.98	50.63
Tripura		4.72	–	80.70
Uttar Pradesh		6.83	0.99	51.07
West Bengal		11.49	68.41	38.40
All-India		10.77	29.39	36.02

Source: Based on NSSO (1990b).

to 40 fractile who get their total supply of rice from the PDS is very low (Table 6.32). However, the percentage of people buying it partially from the PDS is very high (Table 6.33) in these states, which in a way compensates for the former. In wheat-eating states like Bihar, Uttar Pradesh, Madhya Pradesh, Punjab and Rajasthan, interestingly, the percentage of people who buy wheat only from the PDS is very low—much less than the national average. Un-fortunately, however, there is no compensation in terms of a larger percentage of people buying it partially from the PDS—the figure once again being less than the national average. One would, therefore, argue that while in the case of rice-eating states the major problem is inadequate supply, in wheat-eating states it is inadequate coverage as well, as has been suggested in the foregoing discussion.

Table 6.33: *Percentage of Persons belonging to the Bottom 40 Per cent Expenditure Category Depending Partially on the PDS in 1986–87*

States	Items		
	Rice	*Wheat*	*Sugar*
1	2	3	4
Andhra Pradesh	58.20	26.84	27.41
Assam	51.18	28.62	83.39
Bihar	0.95	2.62	14.80
Gujarat	27.52	14.14	73.38
Haryana	4.21	0.00	72.66
Himachal Pradesh	16.90	3.42	58.90
Jammu & Kashmir	51.65	55.87	29.51
Karnataka	56.41	7.54	30.61
Kerala	88.11	3.55	71.64
Madhya Pradesh	9.67	3.32	11.33
Maharashtra	23.97	17.75	63.18
Orissa	–	1.66	19.88
Punjab	2.39	–	60.85
Rajasthan	0.46	1.71	29.73
Tamil Nadu	57.32	5.48	26.12
Tripura	58.79	5.16	11.81
Uttar Pradesh	1.83	2.43	1.39
West Bengal	35.49	4.40	48.15
All-India	32.15	7.05	38.63

Source: Based on NSSO (1990b).

Why is it that less than 40 per cent of those who buy wheat or rice do so from the PDS (totally or partially) when the figure is as high as 76 per cent for sugar? It may be seen from Table 6.34 that 17 per cent of the people buy rice from the market because they do not possess a ration card. The corresponding figure for the purchase of wheat is 11 per cent. There is thus a need to increase the coverage of people both with respect to rice and wheat. Non-availability of credit facility is not regarded as important as only 1 per cent of the population considers this to be a reason for their not using the PDS. The major complaint of rice-eaters is, however, the inadequate supply through the PDS. Over 23 per cent of the people complain of inadequate supply of rice, against the corresponding figure of 5 per cent for wheat (Table 6.34). Therefore, it is important to increase the quantity of rice supplied to the card

Table 6.34: Persons not Wholly Dependent on the PDS over Reasons for No Purchase or Partial Purchase of Select Items in 1986-87

	Rice	Wheat	Sugar
	2	3	4
Not entitled (no ration card)	16.76	11.18	18.26
Not available in ration shop	19.35	21.13	8.03
Quality not satisfactory	19.55	15.85	3.77
Not available in sufficient quantity	22.88	4.68	53.52
Not available in small quantities	0.57	0.21	1.49
Credit purchase not possible	0.88	0.86	1.19
Not required	14.95	39.96	6.30
Others	4.92	5.05	5.02

Source: Based on NSSO (1990b).

holders, particularly to those below the poverty line, as they show the highest incidence of partial purchase from the PDS.

Interestingly, our slum survey in Delhi also showed that over 80 per cent of the households considered an unsatisfactory distribution system and actual supply less than the entitlement as major reasons for buying cereals from the open market. Absence of credit facility under the PDS was not very important as only 4 per cent of those surveyed complained on this count.

Yet another problem surfaced during the unstructured interviews. Many among the rice-eaters have been issued cards meant for wheat-eaters, with a very small entitlement of rice. People keep using these cards because they are ignorant of the procedures as well as the difficulties involved in changing the cards. There is, thus, a larger deficit in the supply of rice than in wheat, a fact which was brought out in the analysis of national-level NSS data as well. The Delhi survey further revealed that those not covered under the PDS were anxious to get ration cards for the purchase of subsidised cereals as also for some sort of security against eviction. About 80 per cent of the slum dwellers without ration cards had applied for them. Those who had not applied either did not know the procedure or had no permanent address (mostly the new migrants). Many among them also complained about the extremely cumbersome procedure involved in securing a ration card.

Two points emerge quite significantly from the field survey of Delhi that strengthen the conclusions drawn from the analysis of secondary data. First, the coverage of the population under the PDS must increase by simplifying the procedure and properly identifying the resident population in slum colonies to provide them with ration cards. Second, the cards which entitle a person to wheat should be converted into cards meant for the purchase of rice, which would necessitate a substantial increase in the supply of rice through the PDS.

Note

1. It is surprising that Mahendra Dev and Suryanarayana (1991) interpret this in terms of a bias in the PDS in favour of the poor.

References

Ahmedabad Municipal Corporation. (1976). *Report on Census of Slums in Ahmedabad*. Planning Cell, AMC, Ahmedabad.

Madras Metropolitan Development Authority. (1986). *Survey of Slums in Madras Metropolitan Area*. Economist Group, MMDA, Madras.

Mahendra Dev, S. and **M.M. Suryanarayana.** (1991). 'Is PDS Urban Biased and Pro-Rich—An Evaluation', *Economic and Political Weekly*, 26(41).

National Commission on Urbanisation. (1988). *Report Vol. II*. National Commission on Urbanisation, New Delhi.

National Institute of Urban Affairs. (1988). *Upgrading Municipal Services—Norms and Financial Implications*. NIUA, New Delhi.

National Sample Survey Organisation. (1987). *Tables with Notes on Particulars of Dwelling Units*, 38th Round, Number 339. Government of India, New Delhi.

———. (1989). *Morbidity and Utilisation of Medical Services*, 42nd Round, Number 364. Government of India, New Delhi.

———. (1990a). 'A Profile of Households and Population by Economic Class and Social Group and Availability of Drinking Water, Electricity and Disinfection of Dwelling', 42nd Round, *Sarvekshana*, 13(4).

———. (1990b). 'Utilisation of Public Distribution System', 42nd Round, *Sarvekshana*, 13(4).

Operations Research Group. (1989). *Delivery and Financing of Urban Services*. Operations Research Group, Baroda.

Town and Country Planning Organisation. (1984). *Level and Cost of Selected Municipal Services—An Empirical Study*. Town and Country Planning Organisation, New Delhi.

Conclusions and Recommendations

Structural adjustment within the framework of a liberal politico-economic order has become an integral part of our policy today. Whether India emerges successful through this process, or is plunged into a debt trap, or remains in a perpetual state of flux, is a matter of speculation. What is of prime importance, however, is to see how the country proposes to protect its socially and economically deprived sections of population against some of the problems of structural adjustment. Economic liberalisation, therefore, does not mean a state of *laissez faire*. On the other hand, it requires greater vigil and intervention in a few critical sectors of the economy.

Interventions would be important in the provision of basic amenities like housing, drinking water, sanitation and sewerage facilities, and health care, as also in the distribution of essential commodities through the PDS. The conclusions and recommendations emerging out of the analysis of the government's role in these sectors and the future perspectives have been presented in the following pages.

Housing

The high income elasticity of demand for housing implies that it has virtually become a luxury commodity for those in upper income brackets. It would, therefore, be important not to treat housing per se as a priority sector or subsidise it without considering the distributional aspects. Our analysis shows that the subsidies that have gone into this sector have ultimately reached the middle and upper income sections. The government should, therefore, gradually curtail its involvement in these programmes and concentrate only on those benefiting the urban poor directly.

The organisations within the housing sector, barring perhaps the slum clearance boards and the slum wings of municipal corporations, do not show much sensitivity in favour of the urban poor; in fact, owing to the financial and administrative stipulations, most of their programmes tend to exclude the poor. The government has not been able to provide minimum housing facilities to the poor through its current formal housing schemes. Even the most generous scheme—EWS-II, funded by HUDCO, under which minimum-sized houses of 20 sq.m. are provided on a hire-purchase basis—requires the payment of instalments amounting to 20 per cent or more of the total expenditure of households below the poverty line. This is definitely beyond their affordability. These agencies must, therefore, reduce their costs by redesigning their housing schemes and make them affordable to the poor. This can be achieved through the construction of one-room tenements with common space and shared water supply and toilet facilities. These should, as far as possible, be taken up within the existing slums so that there is no dislocation of people from their places of work. Given the high price of land, two- or three-storeyed structures would often work out to be economical. The major thrust of the public housing agencies should, therefore, be on these programmes. A few such programmes can also be taken up in locations at the city's periphery or beyond it. This would then have to be tied up with programmes for employment generation, provision of raw materials and marketing of finished products, which can be organised through community participation and backed by voluntary agencies.

The poor mostly live in *katcha* and self-occupied houses that are illegally constructed or acquired. Thus, a large section of the poor needs only a piece of serviced land with legal status. Two strategies can, therefore, be proposed for housing them. The first would be the construction of one-room tenements on a massive scale, primarily through public agencies, as discussed earlier. The second would be to give them serviced land, but only in situations where the first strategy does not prove feasible. The meagre government resources available for this sector should be largely reserved for these two strategies.

Public authorities should be given the responsibility of identifying vacant lands at convenient locations within the cities and acquiring them through legal means for housing the poor. The authorities should undertake land ownership surveys for this purpose and identify vacant lands suitable for the programme. In most metropolitan cities, there are large tracts of land, owned by public and private agencies, lying vacant within the municipal limits. Local bodies should be empowered to acquire these, for which substantial modifications in and strengthening of the existing legislative system along with simplification of procedures is necessary.

Land values tend to go up when the land titles are given to the urban poor under slum improvement programmes. The same is true in the case of built-up accommodations given to individuals. Land, thus, becomes a marketable commodity which, in the event of a social exigency or pressures from the market, is passed on to people in upper income classes. The poor, thus, get pushed out of the programmes and massive subsidies reach the richer sections of the population. It is thus essential to give houses or land to associations formed by the local communities, preferably on a leasehold basis, and restrict transfer of property through legal and community control. These associations can further be entrusted with the responsibility of maintaining community facilities within the locality.

A large segment of the population living in *chawls* and *bustees* belongs to the non-poor category. About 75 per cent of those living in *pucca chawls* and *bustees* are above the poverty line. Proper identification of *chawls* and *bustees* inhabited by the poor must, therefore, be undertaken for the implementation of slum improvement and upgradation programmes.

Quite apart from the regular *bustees* and squatter settlements, a sizeable floating population can be found in most of the large cities, especially in the central areas, around the railway stations, bus terminals and near public places such as hospitals. Their main requirements are a protected place to sleep, bedding, covering during the winter, and water supply and sanitation facilities. Medium-sized night shelters, accommodating fifty to 100 people, should be constructed in areas where there is such a demand. These could be two- to three-storeyed buildings, keeping in mind the high value of land in these localities. Use of personal bedding and covering should also be permitted for those living in these shelters for longer periods. A large number of these night shelters should be built in different parts of the city and the facilities should be made available at nominal charges.

Water Supply

Water is another basic need in urban areas. Here, the public water supply system is heavily subsidised through government grants, advanced from time to time to meet capital as well as current expenditures. The system, however, does not show a significant bias in favour of households in the lower consumption fractiles. About 66 per cent of the people below the poverty line are covered by piped water supply which is significantly below the figure for the total population i.e., 72 per cent. The disparity comes out much more sharply when the per capita consumption of water by people in different consumption fractiles, estimated through micro-level surveys, is considered. These surveys indicate that the majority of the poor do not get the minimum quantity of water necessary for their daily use. This is primarily because the existing organisational structure, pricing policy, etc., have not been designed to provide this minimum quantity of water to all sections of the population, despite the claims made on that account. In only a few states have slum clearance boards taken up water supply projects in low income areas. The responsibility of distributing water to different localities and maintaining the system, however, lies primarily with the local bodies, where the vested interests of the middle and upper classes predominate. It is, therefore, advisable to create special slum wings within the municipal bodies in cities that have large slum populations, and entrust them with the specific responsibility of providing water (and sanitation) facilities to them. State governments should provide special assistance to these wings, based on an assessment of their requirements and performance.

The localities inhabited by the poor are mostly served by public stand posts (PSPs), handpumps and tubewells. Water in these localities is generally available at low pressure and for a short duration. The number of persons dependent on a stand post or a handpump/tubewell is also very high. It is, therefore, important to increase the number of PSPs and handpumps/tubewells. How the PSPs are to be located can be worked out using information regarding the distance currently travelled to obtain water, complaints regarding long waiting time, etc. At the same time, water pressure and duration of water supply in the PSPs can be increased to ensure adequate supply to the poor households.

There is no significant progressivity in the pricing of water in most of the states and cities, as a result of which a large portion of this subsidised facility is used by the higher income groups. This results in wastage and non-priority use of water. All domestic connections should be metered and the cost of the meters should preferably be charged to the beneficiaries. A low rate for a stipulated minimum consumption should be maintained, beyond which the rates should increase progressively. Further, there is a need to standardise the rate structure across the states and cities. All these measures would go a long way in ensuring judicious consumption of water by people in higher income brackets and the surplus quantity thus generated could be diverted to the slum localities. The local community should be involved in the day-to-day maintenance and minor repair of stand posts and handpumps. There is little evidence to suggest that there is a tremendous wastage of water through these sources, except in a few localities. A small amount can be charged from the beneficiary households in the slums which would help in further reducing wastage.

Provision of water through tankers can only be a temporary solution for the urban poor. Currently, both the rich and the poor benefit through this facility arranged by the local authorities, mostly in situations of exigency. The permanent provision of potable water must be made through PSPs or tubewells in areas (within or outside the municipal limits) which do not have a permanent water source.

Sanitation

Like other basic amenities, the sanitation and sewerage system organised by the local governments has not benefited the poor as much as the other sections of the urban population. The percentage of households without latrines is very high among the poor—60 per cent. The majority of poor households with toilet facilities use community latrines. In view of the cost of providing exclusive latrines, it is recommended that a large number of community toilets be constructed at appropriate locations for use by slum and pavement dwellers.

The responsibility for maintaining toilet facilities should be entrusted to organisations set up by the local community, under the overall supervision of the slum wing of the municipality/corporation. A small sum should be charged from the households to meet at least a part of the current expenditure. Agencies like Sulabh International can also be involved in the construction and maintenance of the facilities. They should be asked to charge discriminatory rates. The profits earned through the facilities located at market places, bus or train terminals can compensate for the losses incurred in slum colonies. Furthermore, local bodies may have to provide a grant on a long-term basis to these agencies to help maintain the sanitation complexes in these colonies.

Municipal bodies must impose sewerage charges in areas covered by an expensive sewerage system which is not available to most of the urban population. Sewerage surcharge as a percentage of water charges can be levied on people residing in these areas, which should cover at least the current expenditure on the system.

Health Care

A majority of the urban poor live in congested and unhygienic conditions plagued by malnutrition and other health hazards. This underlines the importance of medical facilities and their accessibility to the economically underprivileged in urban areas.

The urban health care delivery system by its very design is biased in favour of public sector employees, workers in the organised sector and people in high income classes. Large public and private organisations have developed their own systems for exclusive use by their employees and their dependents and these are generally better than the services available to the common people. Within the organised sector as well, there is a gradation of services—the employees of public undertakings and those in certain government jobs (the army, for instance) have access to better facilities along with the provision for reimbursement of expenses for treatment in private hospitals. The facilities available to the general population are of a low quality that have further deteriorated with the better-off sections opting to not use them. The urban poor have to compete with the general population for these limited facilities.

Substantial restructuring in the organisation of the public health care delivery system and improvement in its quality are necessary to make it more sensitive to the needs of the poor. If the rich and poor are dependent on the same public medical system, it could ensure improvement in its quality.

About 48 per cent of the urban poor go to private doctors and another 12 per cent to private hospitals for out-patient treatment. They are discouraged from using public hospitals because of long distances to be travelled, long waiting hours and the indifferent attitude of the medical staff. To increase the access of the poor to health facilities, small health care units should be set up within easy reach of the slum population and mobile medical facilities should be organised for them. A large section of the poor currently opts for treatment outside the allopathic system. They use ayurvedic, unani and informal facilities that are usually of indifferent quality. Provision of medical facilities at doorsteps through a decentralised structure, as proposed, would help bring this section under the formal health care system.

The urban poor have a slightly higher share than the average population in the facility for free ward hospitalisation in the public sector. This can be attributed in part to non-use by the better-off sections of the population because of indifferent quality. The share of the poor in the paying general ward or paying special ward facilities is, however, much smaller. It must be noted that for these facilities the per capita subsidy works out to be much more than in the free ward. It is, thus, evident that the high quality and specialised medical services in the public sector are being cornered by middle and upper income households. These services must be made avail-able to the poor either by strengthening and augmenting the facilities at the grass-roots level or by designing an appropriate referral system.

There is very little progressivity in the payments to be made for the use of in- or out-patient services in public hospitals, much less than in private hospitals. People in the upper consumption fractiles must be made to pay for medicines and for the cost of maintenance of the facilities. However, for the poor these should be available at the existing nominal rates as a large section among them reports lack of money as a major reason for non-treatment of ailments.

In private hospitals, the poor have little access to the free wards and are often obliged to use the paying facilities. The free ward facilities, on the other hand, are used by a section of the non-poor on the strength of their social status or connections with the management and the staff. Most of the private hospitals and nursing homes receive subsidised land and various other facilities including grants from the government and in return are obliged to provide certain free services to the poor. It would, therefore, be necessary to impose stipulations and norms for the allotment of free ward facilities to the deserving sections of the population and administer them properly.

The Public Distribution System

Stabilising the price level of essential consumption goods is a major challenge and responsibility of the government in the process of structural adjustment. It would be difficult to keep their prices low in relation to those of capital goods or consumer durables, as also in relation to the incomes of the poor, through fiscal measures alone. Strengthening the PDS and orienting it to the needs and affordability of the poor seems to be the only option.

The existing system in different states, however, does not show much progressivity in the coverage of population across the consumption fractiles. The percentage of population buying sugar and wheat partially or wholly from the PDS in the upper fractiles is higher than or equal to the average figure for other categories. The corresponding figure for rice is, however, higher in the lower fractiles than at the higher end, but here too the progressivity is only marginal. It may further be noted that about 15 per cent of the households, comprising largely the urban poor, report non-entitlement as the reason for their not buying cereals from the PDS. It is therefore necessary to increase coverage through yearly drives to identify those households below the poverty line without ration cards. A large majority of the poor without ration cards are new migrants. A system of issuing temporary ration cards (which was in existence in a few cities) must be introduced in all large cities. These migrants should be able to register with the local authorities by indicating their place of temporary residence (a night shelter, for instance) or of work. The night shelters should start community kitchens to provide meals at cheap rates and for this they should be given cereals through the PDS.

It is surprising that although 74 per cent of the households in the bottom three consumption fractiles buy sugar from the PDS, the corresponding figures for rice and wheat are 40 and 36 only. Evidently a large number of persons who have ration cards and buy sugar from the PDS do not get cereals because of non-availability or other difficulties. It is also a matter of concern that the poor buy less than 20 per cent of their cereal requirements from the PDS. This is a reflection of the inadequacy and leakages in the system. It would, therefore, be important to strengthen it by increasing the supply and through proper monitoring.

In view of the greater demand for rice (relative to supply) among the poor, it is suggested that the quantity of rice supplied through the PDS be increased by 20 per cent. It is unfortunate that the percentage of wheat purchased from the PDS to total purchases by people in the bottom two fractiles is significantly lower than the average for all categories. In the case of rice, there is only a marginal variation in the share of purchases from the PDS across the fractiles. The major criticism of the PDS would, therefore, be the lack of sensitivity in favour of the poor.

The massive subsidy being pumped into the system can only be justified if a large part of it reaches the poor. The distribution system under the PDS must, therefore, be drastically altered to ensure that at least 60 per cent of the purchase of cereals by the poor is through PDS. This would not, however, require a quantum jump in the total supply as a substantial part going to the upper consumption fractiles can easily be diverted to the lower fractiles.

Index

Accelerated Slum Improvement Scheme (Madras), 158, 181n., 182n.

Acharya and Trikha (1978), 34

actual and imputed rent per unit area, 238

affordability, 19, 20, 34, 47, 62, 95, 118, 125, 141, 150, 162, 165, 256, 280, 286; financial, 18, the problem of, 23–25, 78

Aga Khan Fund for Economic Development, Geneva, 60

Agriculture, Ministry of, 171

Agriculture Price Commission, 183n.

Ahmad (1982), 34

Ahmedabad, 68; number of slum dwellers per stand post in, 247; per capita water supply in, 247; public toilet in, 253; slums in, 228, 231, 234, 235; UCD projects in, 143, 172

Ahmedabad Municipal Corporation (1976), 231, 234, 235

All-India Debt and Investment Survey, 40

All-India Food Conferences, 95

All-India Institute of Medical Sciences (AIIMS), 82

Andaman and Nicobar Islands, 87, 188, 208, 252

Andhra Pradesh, 72, 73; housing in, 188, 189, 204; medical facilities in, 86, 216, 263; performance in water supply in, 203, 204; public distribution system in, 103, 175, 222, 225, 271; rents in, 240; sanitation and toilet facilities in, 208, 213, 250, 252; UCD projects in, 142, 143

Andhra Pradesh Health and Medical Housing Infrastructure Development Corporation, 52

Andhra Pradesh Slum Improvement (Acquisition of Land) Act (1956), 181n.

Andhra Pradesh State Housing Corporation (APSHC), 52, 144

anganwadis, 171

Apex Cooperative Housing Finance Society, 58–59, 63, 64

Armed Forces Medical Services, 83

Arunachal Pradesh, 86; public distribution system in, 222; Public Works Department, 51; sanitation facilities in, 208

Asian Development Bank (ADB), 23 (1983), 42n.

Assam, 87; housing in, 188, 189; medical facilities in, 215, 217, 220; water facilities in, 204, 245; public distribution system in, 220, 222, 225, 226, 271, 274; sanitation and toilet facilities in, 208, 209, 252

asset categories in urban areas, pattern of debt, 41

average per capita floor area, 233, 241

Bangalore, income distribution of the population, 33; Metropolitan Water Supply Board, 68; water consumption in, 246

Bapat (1988), 183n.

Bardhan (1970), 42n.; (1973), 42n.

Baroda, UCD projects in, 142

Basic Services Programme, 135, 137, 138

Bharat Heavy Electricals Limited (BHEL), 53, 87

Bhatia (1990), 99

Bhavnagar, UCD projects in, 142

Bhilai, water supply and drainage system in, 68

Bihar, 84; housing in, 188, 189, 194; hospitalisation facilities in, 268; medical facilities in, 216; water facilities in, 203, 204; public distribution system in, 102, 103, 222, 224, 226, 275; toilet and sanitation facilities in, 250, 252

Bihar State Housing Cooperative Federation Limited, 58

Bima Niwas Yojna, 60

Birla Institute of Scientific Research (BISR), New Delhi, 46

Bombay, 68, 72; water supply and sanitation facilities in, 149, 247; public toilets in, 253; study on poverty in, 34

Bombay Metropolitan Regional Development Authority (BMRDA), 146, 161; (1861), 34

Bombay Urban Development Project (BUDP), 146, 156, 160, 161, 183n.

Borsi (1990), 159, 162

box surface drain (BSD), 209

Bureau of Economics and Statistics (Andhra Pradesh), data collected by, 32

Calcutta, 72; the Bustee Improvement Programme in, 139; Slum Improvement Programme in, 34, 157, 228, 247, 253; statutory rationing in, 175; UCD projects in, 142, 145, 146

Calcutta Improvement Trust (CIT), 68, 69

Calcutta Metropolitan Area (CMA), 68

Calcutta Metropolitan Development Authority (CMDA), 52, 68, 69, 77, 145

Calcutta Metropolitan Planning Organisation (CMPO), 157

Calcutta Metropolitan Water and Sanitation Authority (CMWSA), 68, 69

Calcutta Municipal Corporation (CMC), 69, 77

Calcutta Urban Development Project, 158

Calcutta Urban Development Project—III (CUDP-III), 69, 182n.

Can-Fin Homes Limited, 60, 61

Canara Bank, 60, 61

Can Bank Financial Services, 60

capital assets, 68; responsibility of maintaining, 70-71; investment in, 70-71

category of houses (all-India), percentage distribution of households over, 186

Census of India 1981, 185, 187, 189; state-level town directories of, 198

Central Government Health Services (CGHS), 82; polyclinics, 83

Central Public Health and Environmental Engineering Organisation (CPHEEO), 67, 198, 201; (1983), 47

Central Public Works Department (CPWD), 54

Central Social Welfare Board, 171

Central Statistical Organisation (CSO), 17, 18, 25, 28; implicit consumer price index, 26, 27, 29, 35

Certificate of Deposit Scheme, 61

Chandigarh, 87; housing in, 189, 228, 240; sanitation and toilet facilities in, 209, 252

City Industrial Development Corporation (CIDCO), 51

Civil Supplies, Department of, 97

Civil Supplies and Cooperation, Ministry of, 97

Commission on Agricultural Costs and Prices, 102

community participation, 141, 142, 163

conservancy tax, 74, 76

Consumer Price Index (1970-71 to 1983-84), 27

Consumer Price Index for Industrial Workers (CPIIW), 26, 27, 28

Consumer Price Index for Non-Manual Employees (CPINM), 26, 27

Consumer Price Index for Total Urban Population (CPITU), 27

consumption expenditure, adjusting for different classes, 25, 28–31, cut-off levels of, 18; different fractiles of, 19

consumption expenditure on food, 31–35

Consumption Pattern of the Middle Income Urban Population (CPIMU), 27, 28, 32

cooperative housing schemes, 56

cooperative housing societies, types of, 53–54

coverage with sanitation facilities, the state-level analysis of, 208

credit facility, non-availability/absence of, 276, 277

Cumulative Interest Scheme, 61

Dadra and Nagar Haveli, 87

Daman and Diu, 87, 189, 252

Dandekar Committee, 97

Dandekar and Rath (1971), 25, 26

Delhi, 68; hospitals and dispensaries in, 86; housing in, 117, 189, 194, 240; water supply in, 247, 248; public distribution system in, 176, 270, 271, 277; sanitation facilities in, 208, 209, 253; slums in, 228, 229; the slum survey of, 233, 234, 235, 236, 259, 261, 277; study in, 34

Delhi Administration, 107n.

Delhi Cantonment, 107n.

Delhi Cooperative Housing Society Act, 106n.

Delhi Cooperative Housing Finance Society Limited, 59

Delhi Development Authority (DDA), 51, 77, 90, 117, 179n.

Delhi Water Supply and Sewage Disposal Undertaking (DWS and SDU), 107n.

Dharavi Redevelopment Scheme, 145, 146

Dharia, Mohan, 97, 98

Diabetes Control Programme, 168

distribution network, deficiencies in, 19

Dock Labour Housing, 106n., 116

drainage, low-cost schemes in, 147; tax, 74, 76

drinking water, 21, 67, 70, 135, 182n., 243, 261; intervention in the provision for, 279; the specialisation index for the major sources of, 243, 244

drinking water, agencies and sources of, percentage distribution of, 201–03, 205, 242

Durgapur, statutory rationing in, 175

dwelling unit, legal status of, 230

economic infrastructure, 146; development of, 147

economic liberalisation, 99, 171, 279

EWS (Economically Weaker Sections) schemes, 64, 65, 118, 119, 123, 124, 134, 142, 144, 145, 151, 156, 157, 160, 180n., 280

education, as a factor in access to medical facilities, 262; public expenditure in, 228

Employees' State Insurance Act (1948), 86

Employees' State Insurance (ESI) hospitals, 85

employment generation, 280

Engineers India Limited, reimbursement system of, 90

Environmental Improvement of Urban Slums (EIUS), 67, 137, 139–40, 158, 159, 164, 165, 166, 247

essential commodities, distribution of, 279

Essential Commodities Act, 96

Essential Commodities and Articles on Mass Consumption, Committee on, 97

Essential Supplies Programme, 98

Expanded Programme on Immunisation (EPI), 169; *see also* Universal Immunisation Programme

Factories Act (1948), 86

fair price shops/fair price system, 97, 104–105; indicators of, 221
Family Planning Programme, 170
family planning sector, total allocation to, 183n.
Federation of Consumer Corporation Limited (Bihar), 103
Federation of Indian Chambers of Commerce and Industries (FICCI), 98; Bihar, 103
finished products, marketing of, 280
floor area per capita, 234, 240; the cost of, 230
Food and Agriculture, Ministry of (1966), 97; (1968), 97
Food and Civil Supplies, Ministry of, 171, (1987), 104
Food Corporation Act (1964), 101
Food Corporation of India (FCI), 97, 101, 102, 103, 104, 177
foodgrains, distribution of, 19, 21, 228
Foodgrains Enquiry Committee (1957), 96
Foodgrains Policy Committee (1943), 95, 96
Foodgrains Procurement Committee (1950), 96
Ford Foundation, 23
Formal Housing Schemes, Financing of, 14–15

G.B. Pant Hospital, 85
General Insurance Corporation (GIC), 55, 60, 63, 66, 71
Goa, 87; houseless households in, 189; public distribution system in, 174; slums in, 228; sanitation and toilet facilities in, 209, 252
Godhra, number of slum dwellers per stand post in, 247
Goitre Control Programme, 168, 169
Gross, 23
Gujarat, 60, 70, 73; housing in, 52, 104, 156, 194, 240; land revenue in, 72; low-cost water supply and sanitation projects in, 149, 245; medical facilities in, 86, 217, 220; public distribution system in, 102,

103, 174, 176, 222, 223, 226, 274; sanitation and toilet facilities in, 208, 209, 213, 252; UCD projects in, 142
Gujarat Cooperative Society Act, 106n.
Gujarat Housing Board, 123, 180n.
Gujarat Rural Housing Finance Corporation Limited, 60
Gujarat State Cooperative Housing Finance Limited, 59
Guwahati, UCD projects in, 142

Habitat Housing Scheme, 181n.
Haryana, medical facilities in, 216, 268; public distribution system in, 103, 222, 224; housing in, 189, 194, 240; sanitation and toilet facilities in, 208, 213, 252, tap water in, 246
Haryana Housing Board, 180n.
health and nutrition, 141, 171
health care, 19, 21, 37, 147, 284–86; intervention in the provision for, 279; programmes for, 167–73; public expenditure in, 228
health care facilities, private and public undertakings, 87–88; the provision of 81–84
health care services, at the state level, 84–86; the availability of, 229; contribution of local bodies in, 86–87; levels of, 80–81; referral system in, 91
health care system, 215, 216, 217, 219, 229; access to, 252–68
health delivery system, 169, 216, 284; and the poor, 91–95;
health facilities for states, indices of, 215
health services, for central government employees, 82–83; departmental hospitals for employees, 83–84; general public, 81–82; low-cost, 142
Himachal Pradesh, hospitalisation facilities in, 268; medical facilities in, 217; public distribution system in, 103, 220, 223; tap water in, 246; toilet and sanitation facilities in, 252

hire-purchase system, 113, 117–24, 157, 160, 280; HUDCO-loans for public housing agencies, 122; schemes under, 56, 57, 120–21
Home Improvement Loan (HIL), 160
Home Loan Account (HLA), 57, 132, 133
hospitalisation, 254, 257; state-wise indicators of, 257; the index for, 261
House Rent Allowance, 113, 133–34
house-type, percentage distribution of households, 188, 192–97, 232, 234–37; latrine types, percentage distribution of households, 208, 209, 249, 250
households using, private doctors/ dispensaries, 259
housing, 25, 38, 40, 50–54, 91, 94, 134, 135, 279–81; access to, 229–42; agencies at the state level, 51–52; central government agencies, 50–51; city-level agencies, 52–53; construction agencies, 54; HUDCO-sponsored schemes for, 40; intervention in the provision for, 279; investment in, 18; primary cooperative societies, 53–54; quality of, 185–98; the type of structure, 230
housing and other non-food items, expenditure on, 35–40
Housing and Urban Development Corporation (HUDCO), 40, 55–57, 59, 60, 61, 64, 65, 66, 69, 71, 118, 119, 123, 124, 125, 135, 150, 151, 157, 158, 159, 160, 161, 164, 165, 180n.; EWS-II Scheme, 129, 144, 280; loan, 144, 149
Housing Loan System, 113, 125–29; Schemes under, 126–28
Housing Development Finance Corporation (HDFC), 55, 59, 60, 61, 62, 63, 64, 124, 125; Certificate of Deposit Scheme, 129; Cumulative Interest Scheme, 129; Home Savings Plan, 61, 129, 132, 133; Loan-Linked Deposits Scheme, 61, 129
housing finance, 54–62

Housing Promotion and Finance Corporation Limited, 60
Howrah Improvement Trust (HIT), 69
Howrah Municipal Corporation, 69
Human Resources Development, Ministry of, 170, 171
Hyderabad, 181n.; UCD projects in, 142, 143, 145, 162, 163, 172

Indian Council of Medical Research, 42n
Indian Institute of Management, Ahmedabad, 46
Indore, Sites and Services Schemes in, 156; UCD projects in, 172
Industrial Development Corporations, state-level, 52
Industrial Housing Scheme, 106n.
informal sector household, 23, 24
Infrastructure Leasing and Financial Services Limited, 61
Integrated Child Development Services (ICDS), 142, 170, 171, 172
Integrated Development of Small and Medium Towns (IDSMT), 67, 137, 138, 142, 146–48, 151, 157, 164, 166, 167
Integrated Subsidised Housing Scheme (ISHS), 116
International Finance Corporation, Washington, 60
International Water Supply and Sanitation Decade, 148, 181; Programme, 198, 202, 203, 206, 208

Jagannath and Haldar (1988), 34
Jahangirpur, the slum locality of, 229
Jain (1991), 27
Jaipur, Public Health Engineering Department, 69
Jaipur Development Authority, Kalpataru and Kuber schemes, 124
Jama Masjid, the slum locality of, 229
Jammu, slums in, 228
Jammu and Kashmir, 87; fair price shops at, 105; medical facilities in, 215, 217, 220; housing in, 194, 240;

public distribution system in, 175, 222, 223, 274; sanitation and toilet facilities in, 208, 209, 252; tap water in, 203, 246

Jammu and Kashmir Housing Board, 180n.

Jamnagar, UCD projects in, 142

Jamshedpur, water supply and drainage system in, 68

Jawaharlal Institute of Post-Graduate Medical Education and Research (JIPMER), Pondicherry, 82

Kabra and Ittyerah (1986), 174, 178

Kanhert (1986), 42n.

Kanpur, Sites and Services Schemes in, 156; state-level water boards in, 69

Kanpur Urban Development Projects (KUDP), 182n.

Kansal (1988), 18

Karnataka, 73; hospitalistion facilities in, 268; housing in, 189, 194, 240; medical facilities in, 217; public distribution system in, 175, 222, 225, 271; sanitation and toilet facilities in, 208, 209, 213, 250; towns of, 246; Water Supply and Swerage Boards, 68

Kerala, 87; hospitalisation facilities in, 268; water supply and sanitation in 68, 149, 204, 209, 213, 245; medical facilities in, 215, 219, 220, 268; housing in, 194; public distribution system in, 103, 174, 176, 222, 271

Kerala School Teachers, and Non-teaching Staff Welfare Corporation Limited, 52

Kerala State Development Corporation for Christian Converts from Scheduled Castes and Recommended Communities Limited, 52

Kerala State Development Corporation for Scheduled Castes and Tribes, 52

KfW (Germany), 56

Kolhapur, number of slum dwellers per stand post in, 247

Krishnamurthy (1988), 161

Lakshadweep, 87, 222

Lall (1986), 24

latrine facilities in states and union territories, percentage distribution of, 210–11

latrine types, 248–49

lease-cum-sale agreement, 160, 162, 163

Lele (1971), 183n.; (1986), 23

Life Insurance Corporation (LIC), 51, 55, 56, 58, 60, 63, 66, 69, 70, 71, 72, 106n., 107n., 129

Loan Linked Deposit Scheme, 61, 129

Local Authorities Loans Act (1914), 73, 108n.

local government, 70; resources of, 71–74

Local Self-Government, Department of, 67

lower income group 118, 119, 123, 124, 134, 156, 180n.

Lucknow, state-level water boards, 69

Madhya Pradesh, 84; entry tax in, 72; housing in, 188, 189, 194; water supply in, 204; medical facilities in, 217; public distribution system in, 103, 174, 222, 223, 224, 226, 275; sanitation and toilet facilities in, 208, 213, 250

Madhya Pradesh Housing Corporation for the Employees of the Police Department, 52

Madhya Pradesh State Cooperative Housing Federation Limited, 58

Madras, 72, 183n.; Metropolitan Water Supply Boards, 68; public toilets in, 253; slum surveys in, 231, 235; UCD projects in, 142, 145

Madras Metropolitan Development Authority (MMDA), 145; the income distribution study undertaken by, 33, 231

Madras Urban Development Project, Phase I (MUDP-I), 156, 157, 159, 162; Phase II, 156, 157, 159, 162, 179

Maharashtra, 73; medical facilities in, 86, 216, 217, 220, 268; municipality in, 74; housing in, 189, 194, 240; public distribution system in, 102, 103, 107n., 176, 223, 226, 274; sanitation and toilet facilities in, 208, 209, 252; tap water in, 246; Water Supply and Sewerage Boards, 68

Maharashtra Cooperative Society Act, 104n.

Maharashtra Housing and Area Development Authority (MHADA), 51, 146, 180n.

Maharashtra Housing Corporation for the Employees of the Police Department, 52

Maharashtra State Cooperative Housing Finance Limited, 58

Mahatma Gandhi Institute, Sewagram (Wardha), 82

Mahendra Dev and Satyanarayana (1991) 273

Malaria Eradication Programme, 168, 169, 170

Malpezzi, 23

management system, secondary information on, 19

Manipur housing in, 188, 240; medical facilities in, 215, 220; public distribution system in, 103, 222; sanitation and toilet facilities in, 209, 250, 252

Manipur Planning and Development Authority, 51

Mark II handpumps, 141

Maternal and Child Health Programme, 170

Mayo, 23; and Gross (1985), 42n.

medical facilities, 49, 185, 259, 263, 284; access to, 262; availability and utilisation of, 214–20; inter-state variations in, 268; mobile 285; types of, 254, 256

medicine, specialisation index for, 243, 262

Meghalaya, 87, medical facilities in, 217, 220; households living in one-room houses in, 194; public distribution system in, 222; sanitation facilities in, 209

Mental Health Programme, 168, 169

middle income group (MIG), 119, 123, 124, 156, 180n

Mineral and Metal Trading Corporation (MMTC), reimbursement system, 90

Minhas (1970), 42n.; (1988), 37; (1991), 27; and others (1987a and 1987b), 18, 27, 29

Minimum Needs Programme (MNP), 98, 139, 140

Miraj, number of slum dwellers per stand post in, 247

Misra and Sharma (1979), 77

Mizoram, 93; Local Administration Department, 51; public distribution system in, 222; sanitation and toilet facilities in, 209, 250, 252

Modinagar, water supply and drainage systems, 68

motor vehicle tax, 72

municipal corporations/bodies, the slum wings of, 280, 282, 284

Municipal Corporation of Delhi (MCD), 107n.

Municipal Finance Commissions, 73; West Bengal, 108n.

Nagaland, 87; housing in, 186, 240; public distribution system in, 222; sanitation and toilet facilities in, 208, 209, 250, 252; Works and Housing Department, 51

Nagpur, slums in, 228; state-level water boards in, 69

Nand Nagri, the slum locality of, 229

Narora Congress Camp, 98

National Accounts Statistics (NAS), 29, 37

National Building Construction Company (NBCC), 54

National Building Organisation (NBO), 187; (1984), 47

National Centre for Human Settlements and Environments (NCHSE) (1987), survey conducted by, 33
National Commission on Agriculture, 97
National Commission on Urbanisation (NCU), the assessment of, 163; recommendation of, 146; Report of (1988), 47, 48, 76, 246, 252
National Council of Applied Economic Research (NCAER), 31, 32
National Guinea Worm Eradication Programme, 168, 169, 170
Nationa. Health Policy (1982), 170
National Housing Bank (NHB), 24, 40, 55, 57–58, 60, 66, 129, 132, 133, 180n.; Home Loan Account, 57, 116, 132, 133
National Institute of Communicable Diseases, 168, 170
National Institute of Urban Affairs (NIUA), 47, 246, 247; study conducted by, 32, 33, 42n.
National Leprosy Eradication Board, 169
National Leprosy Eradication Commission (NLEC), 169
National Leprosy Eradication Programme, 168, 169
national policy on children, 170
National Sample Survey, data of, 18, 19, 21, 24, 25, 28, 29, 30, 32, 33, 34, 35, 37, 38, 40, 185, 187, 189, 198, 201, 209, 215, 216, 217, 228, 229, 242, 246, 247, 248, 262, 268, 277
National Sample Survey Organisation (NSSO), 185, 230, 234, 235, 242, 253
National Thermal Power Construction (NTPC), 87; reimbursement system, 90
nationalised commercial banks, 59–60, 63
New Delhi Municipal Committee (NDMC), 107n.
New Residents Welfare Trust, 145

Ninth Finance Commission, 138, 146
non-food items in urban areas, expenditure on, 36
Notified Area Committee (Rourkela), 53
Nutrition Expert Group, 31

open surface drain (OSD), 209, 213
Operations Research Group (ORG, 1980), 33, (1989), 253
Orissa, 73; housing in, 188, 189, 194; medical facilities in, 217, 220, 268; water supply in, 204, 245; public distribution system in, 175, 222, 224, 226; rents in, 240; sanitation and toilet facilities in, 214, 250, 252
out-patient medical treatment, indicators of, 219
out-patient, percentage of, 264
out-patient treatment, 258, 259, 262, 268, 285
Overseas Development Administration (ODA), UK, 56, 143, 144
Own Your Home Scheme, 60

pavement dwellers, 23, 65, 77; night shelters for, 106n., 116, 117
PDS, persons dependent on, 226, 269, 270, 277
Planning Commission, 17, 25, 26, 28, 32, 33, 35, 47, 140; methodology on poverty estimates, 26; (1980), 135; (1983), 72, 106n., 108n.; (1985), 98, 224; (1985b), 103
Pondicherry, 87; housing in, 188, 189, 194; public distribution system in, 222; sanitation and toilet facilities in, 209, 252
Post-Graduate Institute of Medical Education and Research (PGIMER), Chandigarh, 82
poverty line (critical minimum consumption expenditure), determining, 25–26, 42n.; updating, 18, 25, 26–28, 29
poverty population, 17, 18, 30, 31, 32

Prakasa Rao and Tewari (1979), 33
Primary Health Centre (PHC), 217, 219
Prime Minister's Fund, 138
private and public undertakings, health care facilities, 87–88
private housing finance institutions, 60–62
Programme Evaluation Organisation, 224
property or house tax, 74
public distribution system, 49, 95–106, 279, 286–87; access to, 268–78; administrative and functional structure of, 100; and the poor, 105–106, 177–79; areas of decision-making at various levels, 100–101; the availability of, 229; central level, 101–102; dependence on and utilisation of, 185; district level, 103–104; evolution of, 95–99; fair price shops, 104–105; operational aspects of, 173–79; organisational structure, 99; periodicity of purchase/sale, 176, 178–79; state-level, 102–103; use of, 220–26
Public Health Engineering Department (PHED), 67, 69
public stand post (PSD), 77, 78, 142, 182n., 246, 247, 282, 283
Public Works Department (PWD), 51, 52, 67, 68, 148
Pune, state-level water boards, 69; Pune Municipal Corporation, slum settlement project of, 183n.
Punjab, Estate Department, 51; housing corporations for the employees of the police department, 52; housing in, 189, 194, 240; medical facilities in, 268; public distribution system in, 102, 103, 174, 175, 222, 224, 275; sanitation and toilet facilities in, 209, 213, 214, 252; water supply in, 203, 204; Water Supply and Sewerage Boards, 68
Punjab National Bank, 60

Quilon, UCD Projects in, 142

Radhakrishna and others (1988), 32
Raghubir Nagar, the slum locality of, 229
Rajasthan, housing in, 189, 194, 240; medical facilities in, 217; the municipality in, 74; water supply in, 203, 204; public distribution system in, 103, 176, 222, 224, 226, 275; sanitation and toilet facilities in, 208, 209, 250
Rajivnagar, the slum locality of, 229
Rajkot, number of slum dwellers per stand post in, 247; Operations Research Group (ORG) of, 253; UCD projects in, 142
ration cards, the method of issuing, 174–76, 177, 286
rationing system, 96, 97; the differentiated system of, 175; modified, 175
reasons for non-treatment, specialisation index for, 265
referral system, 285
reimbursement system, 89–91
Rental Control Act, 240
rental housing scheme, 106n., 113, 116–17, 118
Reserve Bank of India (RBI), 58, 59, 73, 91, 96, 125, 181n.; (1987), 65
retail lending, 60
Revised Family Welfare Strategy, 170
Revised Grant Structure (RGS), 108n.
Rourkela, water supply and drainage system of, 68
Rudra (1974), 42n.
rural-urban price differential, 25, 26

Sail-ul-Atab (Kalkaji), the slum locality of, 229
sanitation facilities/programme, 19, 21, 37, 49, 67, 68, 69, 70, 74, 79, 91, 92, 94, 135, 139, 167, 206–14, 229, 280, 281, 282, 283–84; access to, 248–53; intervention in provision for, 279; low-cost, 47, 137, 138, 141, 142, 147, 148–49, 165, 166, 171, 182.
savings-linked loan schemes, 59, 113, 116, 129–33

scavenging tax, 74, 76
Scheduled Castes, 256, 263
Scheduled Tribes, 256, 263
Seemapuri and Trilokpuri, the re-settlement colonies of, 229
selective credit control, 96
Self-financing Scheme/System, 56, 57, 113, 114, 124
service latrines, the percentage of, 208
sewerage, 19, 21, 67, 68, 69, 70, 71, 74, 166, 167, 182n.; low-cost schemes in, 147; the user charge for, 76
sewerage facilities, 91, 92, 94, 134, 206–14, 253; intervention in the provision for, 279; investment in, 18
sewerage system, 47, 48, 49, 209, 213, 206–14, 283, 284; the provision of, 148
Shadipur Depot, the slum locality of, 229
shared latrines, incidence of, 249
shelter, 19, 21, 34, 35, 37, 50, 64, 142, 145, 147, 149, 161, 163, 281; the quality of, 230; upgradation, 160
Shelter and Basic Services, Pro-grammes for, 134–73, 150–57
Shelter-cum-Services Programmes, 135, 137, 138; details of, 152–53
Sikkim, 87; the average imputed rental values in, 194; medical facilities in, 217; public distribution system in, 220, 222; toilet and sanitation facilities in, 252
Sinha (1990), 159, 182n.
Sites and Services (S & S) schemes, 129, 135, 137, 147, 149, 150–57, 159, 182.; HUDCO-financed, 51
Slingsby (1989), 156
Slum Clearance Boards, 62, 77, 117, 135, 136, 161, 164, 166, 180n., 280, 282; Gujarat, 51; Karnataka, 51; Madhya Pradesh, 51; Tamil Nadu, 51
Slum Clearance Scheme (SCS), 106n., 116, 117

slum development programmes, types of, 158
slum dwellers, 23, 65, 144, 177, 208, 247, 253, 259, 277; six services to, 139–40; social and economic condi-tions of, 158, 171
slum improvement, 142, 143, 144
Slum Improvement Board, 148
Slum Improvement Programmes (SIP), 157, 158–59, 181n., 281
Slum Improvement Schemes, 134, 139, 156
slum reconstruction, 158, 162
slum upgradation, 149, 158; pro-gramme, 159–63, 281; schemes, 150
Slum Upgradation and Environmental Improvement Scheme, 161
Slum Upgradation-cum-Improvement, Programme, 157–63; schemes, 137
Small and Medium Town Develop-ment, 141, 171
Society for Development Studies (SDS), 23, 24
solid waste disposal, 67
Special Area Development Authority (Korba), 53
Special Schemes (Basic Services Pro-grammes), 137
specialisation, indices for (Sij), 261, 262
squatter settlement, 50, 139, 235, 236, 281
Srivastava (1968), 96
states and union territories, the aver-age per capita floor area for, 194
State Bank of India (SBI), 61; a sub-sidiary of, 60
state civil supplies corporations, 102; Andhra Pradesh, 103
state civil supplies department, 105
state cooperative federations, 103
state electiricity boards, 52
State Essential Commodities Corpor-ation, Andhra Pradesh, 103
State Food and Civil Supplies, Bihar, 103
state health delivery system, types of, 85–86

state-level housing boards, 117, 135
state-level housing finance agencies, 55
state-level town directories, 198
state special hospital, 85–86
State Trading Corporation, 102; reimbursement system, 90
State Transport Corporation, 52
state's 'gap-filling grant', 108n.
STD & AIDS Control Programme, 168
Steel Authority of India (SAIL), Bhilai, 53, 87; reimbursement system, 90
structural adjustment, 99, 279; the process of, 286
Struyk and Turner (1986), 42n.
Subsidised Industrial Housing Scheme (SIHS), 116
Sulabh International, 165, 284
sulabh sauchalayas, 148
support services through voluntary agencies, 88–89
Surat, UCD projects in, 142
Swedish International Development Agency (SIDA), 169

Taleyarkhan (1964), 179n.
Tamil Nadu, 84; the Directorate of Municipal Administration, 68; entertainment tax in, 72; fair price shops at, 105; housing in, 188; 189, 194; medical facilities in, 86, 217, 268; water supply and sanitation projects in, 149; public distribution system in, 103, 175, 222, 225, 271; rents in, 240; sanitation and toilet facilities in, 209, 250, 252; S & S Schemes in, 156
Tamil Nadu Handloom Weavers' Cooperative Society Limited, 52
Tamil Nadu Housing Board (TNHB), 107n., 145, 180n.
Tamil Nadu Slum Clearance Board (TNSCB), 145, 158, 180n.
Tamil Nadu Urban Development Project (TUDP), 156, 160, 161, 183n.
Tata Institute of Social Studies, 34

Technology Mission, 169
Tendulkar (1991), 27
Tigri JJ Colony, the slum locality of, 229
Timarpur, the slum locality of, 229
Town and Country Planning Department, 148
Town and Country Planning Organisation (TCPO), 67, 142; the study conducted by, 252; (1984), 247
traffic and transportation system. improvement in, 147
transport, 19, 25, 37; local, 21
Tripura, 87; hospitalisation facilities in, 268; housing in, 189; out-patient treatment in, 268; public distribution system in, 103, 176, 222, 271, 274; sanitation facilities in, 208
Tuberculosis Control, Programme for, 168, 169
Twenty Point Programme, 101, 139; New, 98

Unit Trust of India (UTI), 56, 60, 61
United Nations (1978), 42n.
United Nations Development Programme (UNDP), 148
UNICEF, 141, 143, 169, 171, 172
United States, decline in food aid from, 101; India received foodgrains from, 96
United States Agency for International Development (USAID), 23, 50, 70
Universal Immunisation Programme, 168, 169; *see also* Expanded Programme on Immunisation
urban amenities, the production and distribution of, 19
Urban Basic Services (UBS), 67, 171, 172, 173
Urban Community Development (UCD), 137, 138, 141, 142–45, 164, 171, 172
Urban Development, Department, 67, Ministry of, 50, 57, 67, 107n., 138, 198; Task Forces on, 47, 48, 108n., 134

urban households, asset structure of, 41

Urban Land Ceiling Act, 64

urban poor, assets and liabilities of, 40–43; bankability of, 40–43; the income and saving potential of, 23

urban poverty, estimate, 29; methodology for estimating, 25

user charge, 70, 74, 78, 79; methods of determining, 75–76

Uttar Pradesh, 84; housing in, 189, 194; medical facilities in, 86, 268; water supply in, 203, 204, 245; public distribution system in, 103, 222, 224, 226, 275; sanitation facilities in, 208; Water Supply and Sewerage Boards, 68

Uttar Pradesh Construction Corporation, 54

Vaidya and Mukundan (1987), 33

Vallabhai Patel Chest Institute, Delhi, 82

Vassen (1989), 156

Verma (1985), 51

Vishakhapatnam, 181n.; Municipal Corporation of, 144; slums in, 228; UCD projects in, 142, 143, 162, 163, 172–73

voluntary agencies, 94, 95; support services through, 88–89

Warehousing Corporation, 102

water supply, 25, 37, 47, 48, 49, 67, 68, 69, 70, 71, 74, 91, 92, 94, 134, 135, 139, 141, 160, 166, 167, 182n., 228, 229, 250, 251, 252, 253, 280, 282–83; access to, 242–48; coverage, sources and agencies, 198–206;

domestic connections for, 78; investment in, 18; low-cost schemes in, 147; pricing systems, 75–76

water supply and sanitation facilities, 171, 229, 230; access of the poor to, 76–80; inter-state variations in, 185; municipal earnings and expenditure on, 76

Water Supply and Sanitation Decade, the Master Plan for, 167

water supply and sanitation facilities, the availability of, 229; inter-state variations of, 185; municipal expenditure and earning from, 76

Water Supply and Sewerage Boards, 68

water supply, pricing systems, flat rate, 75; increasing block rate schedule, 75–76; uniform rate structure, 75

water tax, 74; collecting, 70

ways-and-means loans, 63

West Bengal, housing in, 189, 194; medical facilities in, 86, 216, 217, 220, 268; water supply in, 203; public distribution system in, 103, 175, 176, 203, 222, 274; rents in, 240; sanitation and toilet facilities in, 209, 213, 250, 252

Women and Child Development, Department of, 170

World Bank, 23, 56, 58, 70, 71, 138, 149, 150, 151, 162, 164, 182n., and Sites and Services Schemes, 156–57; (1988), 161

World Development Report (1989), 106n.

World Health Organisation (WHO), 169